GEORGE CARR GLYN:
RAILWAYMAN AND BANKER

George Carr Glyn, Lord Wolverton
by Stephen Pearse (courtesy of Kendal Town Council).

George Carr Glyn

Railwayman and Banker

DAVID HODGKINS

Cover image: Looking down the lines to Hampstead Road Bridge with the gables of Euston Station and St Pancras New Church in the distance, by R.B Schnebbelie, 1837. (His view of the construction works shows sheaves for rope haulage on all four tracks, but they were only installed on the two left hand tracks.)

(© Camden Local Studies and Archives Centre)

First published in 2017 by Wolffe Press
wolffepress@icloud.com

ISBN 978-1-5272-0949-7

Designed and typeset by Carnegie Book Production
Printed and bound in the UK by Jellyfish Solutions

Contents

Acknowledgments

THE BIBLIOGRAPHY at the end of the book lists the many archives and libraries from which I have drawn material for this biographical study of George Carr Glyn, and I am grateful to their staff who have given generous assistance. I must however particularly thank Alison Turton and the staff at the Archives of the Royal Bank of Scotland in Edinburgh who made available to me Glyn's correspondence which they hold and many documents relating to the history of Glyn Mill's during George Carr's long involvement as a partner in the bank. The series of articles, largely by anonymous authors, on Glyn's Bank which appeared in the Three Banks Review from 1957 to 1981 contained extensive information drawn from these records. Without these sources any attempt at a biography would not have been possible. Their counterpart is the substantial body of records of the railway companies, particularly the London and Birmingham and the London and North Western held in The National Archives at Kew on which I have drawn extensively. I am also indebted to the London Library and the British Library.

I must thank Sir Richard Glyn, Bt, and his family at Ashton for granting me access to Gaunts House and St Kenelm's Church at Hinton Parva and to documents he holds.

I am grateful to the many earlier historians of banks and railways, including Roger Fulford, on whose work I have drawn and acknowledged in the footnotes. I am particularly grateful to the late Peter Braine whose work on Sir Richard Moon convinced me that there was a place for a biography of Glyn despite all that had been written on the London and North Western Railway and its predecessors in order to make an assessment of his personal contribution to railways and to the bank.

Finally I must thank Anna Goddard of Carnegie Book Production who enthusiastically entertained the idea of producing this biography and her team who prepared the material for publication, particularly Lucy Frontani who led the book through production and Rachel Clarke for her work on the typesetting, layout and maps. For any errors that remain the responsibility is mine.

Abbreviations of Names of Railway Companies

BDJR	Birmingham and Derby Junction Railway
BOJR	Birmingham and Oxford Junction Railway
BWDR	Birmingham, Wolverhampton and Dudley
CR	Caledonian Railway
CHR	Chester and Holyhead Railway
ECR	Eastern Counties Railway
EWIDBJR	East and West India Docks and Birmingham Junction Railway
GJR	Grand Junction Railway
GWR	Great Western Railway
KWR	Kendal and Windermere Railway
LBR	London and Birmingham Railway
LCR	Lancaster and Carlisle Railway
LGJR	London Grand Junction Railway
LMR	Liverpool and Manchester Railway
LNWR	London and North Western Railway
LSWR	London and South Western Railway
LWSSR	London, Worcester and South Staffordshire Railway
LYR	Lancashire and Yorkshire Railway
MBR	Manchester and Birmingham Railway
MCR	Midland Counties Railway
MSLR	Manchester, Sheffield and Lincolnshire Railway
NAHR	Newport, Abergavenny and Hereford Railway
NER	North Eastern Railway
NMR	North Midland Railway
NSR	North Staffordshire Railway

NWR	North Western Railway
ORR	Oxford and Rugby Railway
OWWR	Oxford Wolverhampton and Worcester Railway
SBR	Shrewsbury and Birmingham Railway
SCR	Shrewsbury and Chester Railway
SDLR	South Durham and Lancashire Railway
SDR	Stockton and Darlington Railway
TVR	Trent Valley Railway
WHR	Worcester and Hereford Railway
WMR	West Midland Railway
YNMR	York and North Midland Railway

Note

The title of the bank in which George Carr Glyn was a partner from 1819 until his death in 1873 changed a number of times in that period according to the composition of the partnership:

1819–22 Glyn, Mills, Hallifax, Glyn, Mills and Glyn
1822–26 Glyn, Mills, Hallifax, Glyn and Co.
1826–51 Glyn, Hallifax, Mills & Co.
1851–64 Glyn, Mills & Co.
1864–(1923) Glyn, Mills, Currie & Co.

For simplicity it is referred to in this book as Glyn's, and the Royal Bank of Scotland Archives are referred to as RBS Archives.

Plates

Maps

Preface

IN THE MID-NINETEENTH CENTURY George Carr Glyn was a key figure in the worlds of banking and railways but relatively little has been written about him. Roger Fulford's *Glyn's 1753–1953* contains by far the best and most detailed account of his life, but is inevitably limited in that it deals with 200 years of the history of the bank and only touches on his activities outside the bank. Glyn was not included in the *Dictionary of National Biography*, nor even less understandably in the *Dictionary of Business Biography*. This omission has to some extent been remedied by a relatively short entry in the *Oxford Dictionary of National Biography*.

By ancestry George Carr Glyn was a typical City figure. His father Richard Carr Glyn had become senior partner in Glyn, Mills, Mitton in 1789, served as Lord Mayor in 1798, was created a baronet in 1800 and eventually became senior alderman and so entitled to the distinction of being the Father of the City. His brother Richard Plumptre Glyn, who was ten years older, was already a partner in the bank when George Carr Glyn was made a partner in 1819 at the age of 22. The bank was then known as Glyn, Mills, Hallifax, Glyn, Mills & Glyn, the last two Glyns referring to the two brothers. George was to remain a partner in the bank until his death in 1873, by which time the bank had merged with Curries. From the early 1830s he was the leading partner in the bank though formally only became the senior partner in 1863 following the death of his brother, by then Sir Richard Plumptre Glyn. Bertram Currie said that in his youth George had the idea of becoming an alderman. His father, though himself senior alderman, had become increasingly dissatisfied with the ceremonials and customs of life in the City and is said to have advised his son 'the office is no longer fit for a man of your character and station.'[1] Whether this paternal

1 Quoted in Roger Fulford, *Glyn's, 1753–1853: Six Generations in Lombard Street*, 1953, 63–64.

advice had any direct effect on George is not clear, but he was never to hold office in the Corporation of London, though he became a deputy lieutenant. He developed the bank to become one of the two largest private banks in London. This did not mean that his career was confined to banking. He was to play a leading part in the promotion of St Katharine's Dock and in the development of the London and Birmingham Railway of which he became chairman. As the early railway historian, John Francis, put it, he was the early and efficient ally of the English railway system.[2] He went on to chair the largest railway company, the London and North Western, as well as to play a major part in the Grand Trunk Railway of Canada and to begin to develop Glyn's banking interests overseas. He was able to achieve these positions of power and influence by his role as banker to railway companies and other concerns – Glyn's became known as the railway bank, but he was always more than a banker, playing a significant role in the management of English railways during their formative period and having clearly articulated views on the principles of management at a time when others proceeded on a largely ad hoc basis. He was not a major political figure, though he was influential with the Government on banking matters, advising ministers on the state of the financial markets and acting as both witness and member of various committees of enquiry and royal commissions. He was an important spokesman for the City, particularly for City merchants. Perhaps because of this he was not a committed follower of either the Banking or Currency schools of thought, but a pragmatist ready to support discretionary and common sense policy to maintain confidence in the money market, though this led him on occasions firmly to oppose the currency school. Only in his 50s was he elected to Parliament, and in 1869 he was created a peer. His title, Baron Wolverton, was appropriately drawn from the town which was largely the creation of the railway company he had chaired and the development of which he had overseen.

[2] John Francis, *History of the English Railway*, 1851.

CHAPTER ONE

The Birth and Initial Years of the Family Bank

By the time George Carr Glyn became a partner, Glyn's was a long established private bank, though not one of the earliest City firms. It was opened on 5 January 1754 as Vere, Glyn and Hallifax.[1] The capital then amounted to £24,000, Vere and Glyn providing £10,000 each and Hallifax £4,000. Of the three initial partners only Joseph Vere was a banker. His father was a mercer of Paternoster Row, but Joseph had been apprenticed to Thomas Martin, who conducted his banking business at the sign of the Grasshopper in Lombard Street, and then was a partner successively in Glegg and Vere, and Vere and Asgill. Thomas Hallifax, the son of a Yorkshire clock maker, had abandoned his indentures as a grocer in Barnsley and came to London where he joined Martin's Bank and became their chief clerk.[2]

The third partner, Richard Glyn was baptised in 1711, the second son of Robert Glyn, an oilman and dry salter of Hatton Garden. His ancestors had come from North Wales and indeed both the Glyns of the City and the Glynnes of Hawarden, the family into which Gladstone married, had a common ancestor in William Glyn of Llandwrog, Caernarfonshire, who in the mid-16th century had sons who gave rise to both the Hawarden and banking dynasties. They claimed the family descended from Cilmin Troed Dhu, chief of the fourth tribe of North Wales who flourished in 843 and lived in Glynllyson. His grandfather Gwriad had been the last Celtic king

[1] The account of Glyn's bank in the eighteenth century relies extensively on Fulford and Alison Turton's article on *Sir Richard Glyn (1711–1773)* in the *Oxford DNB*.

[2] George Chandler, *Four Centuries of Banking, as illustrated by the bankers, customers, and staff associated with the constituent banks of Martins Bank Limited*, I, 1964, 134.

of the Isle of Man.[3] Roger Fulford in his bi-centenary history of Glyn's Bank says that as a youth George Carr Glyn kept a travel diary describing a pious peregrination made in a carriage with his father and mother to the seat of his forebears, the Glynnes of Hawarden.[4]

Educated at Westminster School Richard Glyn joined his father in his business as a wholesaler of the salt and chemicals used as preservatives and dyestuffs. In May 1733 he became a freeman of the Salters' Company and assumed control of the family business the following month, continuing after his father's death with Thomas Baskerfield as his partner. His standing in the City was such that he was master of the Salters' Company in 1751, alderman for the Dowgate Ward from 1750 to 1772 and sheriff, jointly with Charles Asgill, in 1752–53. Both he and Asgill were knighted on the occasion of their presenting to King George II a loyal address on his safe return from Hanover. While his trade in dye and chemicals was lucrative, particularly in supplying silk manufacturers, he also married well. In 1736 he married Susannah, daughter and sole heiress of George Lewen, who not only had the fine property of Ewell in Surrey as her dowry, but also the manor of Hinton Parva near Wimborne in Dorset which George Lewen had inherited from his uncle Sir William Lewen.[5] They had three sons but Susannah died in 1751. Among City aldermen Glyn was not alone in marrying into the gentry, unlike those of the Restoration period whose brides were generally from City families.[6] In 1754 he married Elizabeth, the heiress of Robert Carr, who came from Etal in Northumberland, where his brother Sir William Carr lived. Robert married Grace, daughter of Thomas Bigge of Byker, closely connected with the Bigge family, associated with Ridley, Bigge and Co. bankers at Newcastle from 1755.[7] He became one of the chief silk mercers of Ludgate Hill, 'a fashionable mercer who dealt in French silks,'[8] and an important business connection for the trade in dyestuffs. He lived at Hampton, Middlesex.

It was probably Glyn's connection with Asgill which led him to enter banking in 1753. He had no previous experience, but was able to introduce

[3] *Burke's Peerage and Baronetage*, 7th edition, 2003, II, 1574; *Illustrated London News*, 2 Jan. 1864; *Glyns and Gaunts, a Brief History*, 1. The present village of Llandrwog was built in the 1830s as the estate village of Glynilifon Park, the seat of Lord Newborough.

[4] Fulford, 117.

[5] John Hutchins, *History and Antiquities of the County of Dorse*t, 1868, 3, 137–138.

[6] Nicholas Rogers, Money, land and leverage: the big bourgoisie of Hanoverian London, *Social History*, 4, 1979, 445.

[7] Kenneth H. Vickers, *A History of Northumberland*, XI, 1922, 459–460; Allen B. Hinds, III, 1896, 580. Two generations later Thomas Christopher, the third son of Sir Richard Carr Glyn and George Carr Glyn's brother married another member of the Bigge family in 1817.

[8] Horace Walpole's description, quoted in Fulford, 5.

custom from the many rich silk merchants trading nearby. The bank combined the banking links of two of its partners with the mercantile connections of the other. It was not one of the banks which developed from a goldsmith's business and unlike the West End banks, such as Drummonds, Hoare, and Childs, which maintained the accounts of the aristocracy and lent on mortgage of land, City banks served business men, and a large proportion of Glyn's clients were in the silk or allied trades. The bank provided money for the financing of commerce, discounting bills and entering into connections with Scottish bankers, as well as the provincial silk districts of Coventry and Derby. Later in the century it acted more widely as agent to an increasing number of country bankers. However, like most other London banks who concentrated on deposit banking, Glyn's did not issue notes, though as the Bank of England had no branches, country banks from 1777 could issue notes at least £5 in value and often did so. The bank prospered as did many other City banks of which there were 29 in 1754, 52 in 1786 and 83 in 1810, despite some bankruptcies especially in the crash of 1772.[9] In 1760 Vere and Glyn reduced their capital to £6,000 each, but this was offset by the growing standing of the partners in the City. Vere died in 1766 and the bank was continued as Glyn and Hallifax.

Both partners were important City figures which helped establish the bank's reputation. Glyn was Lord Mayor in 1758–59, and created baronet in 1759. Hallifax was alderman in 1768, Lord Mayor in 1776 and later knighted. Glyn was defeated in his attempt to become MP for the City in 1754, but succeeded in 1758. However as a moderate Tory he became increasingly out of sympathy with the attempt by John Wilkes, Beckford and others to take the lead against the King. Defeated in the City in 1768 he won a seat at Coventry, a centre of the silk industry but an extremely corrupt and expensive constituency. Glyn voted in 1769 for the expulsion of Wilkes from the House of Commons. He was one of the founders of Equitable Life Insurance and President of Bridewell and Bethlem Hospitals, Vice President of the Honourable Artillery Company and Colonel of the Orange Regiment of the City Militia. He received an honorary degree from Oxford University in 1759 when the Earl of Northumberland was installed as chancellor, though Horace Walpole complained that he had only been invited because Sir William Calvert had been asked to the Duke of Newcastle's coronation so they dragged along the present Lord Mayor who was only a dry salter.[10] In 1770 Glyn bought Gaunts House at Hinton Parva, which had been built

[9] D.M. Joslin, London Private Bankers, 1720–85, *Economic History Review*, 7, 1954, 173.

[10] Walpole to George Montagu, 24 July 1759, Yale Edition of *Horace Walpole Correspondence with George Montagu*, ed. W.S. Lewis and R.S. Brown, 9, 1937, 241–242.

in Portland stone in about 1753, so consolidating his Dorset estate, but such a purchase was not typical of more than an important minority of City aldermen. Most went in for riverside villas or medium-sized mansions within close proximity of the capital.[11] The title of Gaunts is said to have derived from John of Gaunt who is thought to have had a hunting lodge there. Certainly he was closely associated with the area as he held the manor of Kingston Lacey and the chase of Wimbourneholt.[12]

An early example of Glyn's involvement with industry led to a major setback in 1772 on account of difficulties in Scotland where they had made loans to Garbett & Company which was closely associated with the Carron Iron Company at Falkirk and was dominated by Charles Gascoigne who had to flee the country to escape his creditors. Glyn's had also lent to Douglas Heron & Co, known as the Ayr Bank, and William Alexander in Edinburgh. The Ayr Bank was formed in 1769 with a capital of £96,000 and the Duke of Queensberry as its chairman, a major lowland land owner and agricultural improver and a strong supporter of Scottish economic development. He was Governor of the British Linen Company and Chairman of the Forth and Clyde Canal. The Ayr Bank was supported by other powerful landowners in southwest Scotland, including the Duke of Buccleugh and the Earl of Dumfries and by many southwestern business and professional people. The bank, whose management was almost completely lacking in banking experience, quickly overreached itself by opening branches, granting cash credits and issuing notes, greatly assisting the onset of a speculative frenzy in Scotland, as credit became available for unrealistic projects. It was said that the Ayr bank was responsible for two-thirds of the note issue in Central Scotland. It sold claims on London greater than the funds available to its London agents and then tried to keep the company afloat 'by the ruinous mode of raising money by a chain of bills on London'.[13] The bubble was pricked by the failure of Neale, James, Fordyce & Downe, a banking house in Edinburgh and London with extensive connections with the Ayr Bank, on 12 June 1772. Thirteen private bankers in Edinburgh failed and others like William Alexander had to suspend payment.[14] Glyn's were caught badly by this. It was believed that they had accepted and discounted £100,000 Scottish bills. Glyn's had to suspend payment on 22 June when a creditor issued a commission of bankruptcy against them. Payment only resumed on

[11] Rogers, 448–449.

[12] *John of Gaunt's Register, 1379–1383*, ed. Eleanor C. Lodge and Robert Somerville, 1937, f. 1011.

[13] Sir William Forbes, *Memoirs of a Banking-House*, 1860, 39–41.

[14] S.G. Checkland, *Scottish Banking, A History, 1695–1973*, 1975, 124–134 for the Ayr Bank.

8 August though apparently delayed by the long absence of the petitioner from London. Advances to Glyn's from private parties and a substantial loan from the Bank of England to William Alexander of Edinburgh which enabled the latter to repay part of their debt to Glyn's, meant that in general the bank emerged relatively unscathed in reputation, with the debts being paid off in eighteen months without any support from the Bank of England. There were two more lasting effects. The financial business with Garbett and Co and the Carron Company was not finally unravelled until 1819. Second William Mills became a partner in the Bank. He is supposed to have advanced £10,000 in the crisis on condition that he became a partner and that his nephew Charles should also come into the Bank. Mills was prominent in the Orient trade, as was his father in law, Sir John Salter.

Sir Richard Glyn died on New Year's Day 1773 of a slow fever, though the recent crisis in the bank led to rumours of suicide which his doctor had to combat by a public statement. He was succeeded at the Bank by the eldest son of his second marriage, Richard Carr Glyn, not quite eighteen at the time of his father's death. Like his father he was educated at Westminster. The only surviving son of his first marriage, George, inherited the baronetcy, the property at Ewell, and that part of the Hinton Parva property known as Ashton, but Gaunts went to Richard Carr, and had probably been purchased for that purpose. Because of his youth and the lack of experience in banking of the 60-year-old William Mills, Thomas Hallifax found himself the sole effective partner and so took Henry Mitton, one of the clerks, into partnership. Hallifax was an alderman from 1766, sheriff in 1768, Lord Mayor in 1776 and stood as MP for the City in 1772, but lost to Wilkes. He was elected at Aylesbury in 1784, having failed to gain election at Coventry in 1780. He died in 1789, a year after the firm moved in 1788 to new premises at 18 Birchin Lane. His son, Thomas Hallifax II became a partner in 1796 when he was 21, as did Henry Parry, like Mitton, a clerk.

Richard Carr Glyn then became senior partner. An alderman for the Bishopgate ward in 1790, as sheriff he was knighted in 1791, and he served as Lord Mayor in 1798 when he was made a baronet. He was elected MP for the St Ives Division of Cornwall in 1796. He spoke in support of the Seditious Meetings Bill and in favour of the Act of Union with Ireland but resigned his seat in 1802 as he found it difficult to combine Parliamentary work with the management of the Bank. Like his father he was president of the Bridewell and Bethlem Hospitals. He was also a fellow of the Society of Antiquities. When a committee was convened in 1805 to consider improvements to the Clearing House system, set up in 1770, he was one of six members. He married Mary, the only daughter of John Plumptre of Fredville near Dover. In 1809 he began to rebuild Gaunts at Hinton Parva, adding to the estate by acquiring Ashton so owning the whole of the parish of Hinton Parva. William Evans of Wimborne was employed to alter the house to a villa of five by five bays and to lay out a park of 200 acres. The Portland stone was covered in red brick so giving it its present appearance except that the Dutch style roof tops and other additions were made by George Devey in 1899.[15] In 1809 Richard Carr Glyn purchased the manor of Fontmell Magna from the Arundells of Wardour Castle. He also held about 70 acres of land in Harlesden, purchased by his grandfather Robert which like his Dorset estates descended to his eldest son Richard Plumptre, and then to Richard George, the eldest son of his second son Robert before being sold for housing.[16] Charles Mills, the nephew of William, had become a partner in 1776 when he was 21. He became a director of the East India Company and deputy chairman in 1801 but while a great asset to the bank he was probably a provider of business rather than a conductor of it. He was MP for Warwick from 1802 until his death in 1826, though an infrequent attender at the House.

Consequently Richard Carr Glyn was the active managing partner in this period. Under his direction the bank grew. In 1787 the year before Thomas Hallifax I died the bank had moved from 18 Birchin Lane to larger premises at No12 and the premises were further enlarged at the end of the 1790s and again in the first decade of the nineteenth century by the acquisition of adjacent houses. There were 7 staff in 1790 and 32 by 1810. Profits, £3,700 in 1765, had grown to £19,498 in 1810 and to £24,922 in 1820. Moreover the bank acquired a more prominent and central place in the banking system as it developed during the Revolutionary and Napoleonic Wars with the French. The war with France and the threat of invasion caused a drain of gold out of the Bank of England in early 1797, and the Bank was ordered to suspend convertibility, a step subsequently made statutory in the Restriction Act of that year. This led to the substitution of paper currency for gold, assisted by the lifting of the restrictions on the issue of small denomination bank-notes because of the lack of coins, and the increasing dependence of the Government on the private banks as well as the Bank of England for loans to finance the war. Relations between the

[15] Hutchins, 3, 138; *An Inventory of the Historical Monuments of the County of Dorset*, Royal Commission on Historical Monuments, 1975, 30; W. Shipp and J.C. Hudson, *The History and Antiquities of the County of Dorset*, 1868, 3, 246.

[16] *St Andrew's Parish Church, and Fontmell Magna with Bedchester, Parish and Village*, 2006 ed., 2; London Metropolitan Archives Acc/0158/001; *An account of the claims of freeholders and the awards of the Commissioners … in the parish of Willesden in the year 1816*, BL Cartographic Item, Add Ms 12456: TNA, PROB 11/1895, f 133, will of Sir Richard Carr Glyn.

Bank of England and the private banks grew closer especially as the Bank could not let other banks fail. Most private banks came to have accounts at the Bank. Glyn's opened their account on 21 January 1799 with a deposit of £30,000. One reason for opening such an account was that Bank of England notes circulated throughout the country while the notes of private bankers in London had only a metropolitan circulation. However the balance kept with the Bank of England was very small in the early years and in 1819–24 was under £750. The enlargement of taxation, particularly the introduction of income tax in 1799 meant that there was business to be gained from the tax gatherers. The Receiver of Taxes for the City and Westminster and parts of Middlesex kept his accounts with Glyn's and one of Glyn's clerks was appointed Deputy Receiver General.

Meanwhile there was a great expansion of country banks (i.e. private banks outside London). In 1750 there had been perhaps a dozen country banks in operation, but their numbers grew in periods of expansion to 280 in 1793, and to over 300 by the end of the century. By 1808–09 there were 755 country banks.[17] Many were started to meet the demands of industrial growth in wartime and the increased demand for discounting on London. The importance of the London bill and security markets meant that country banks had to have accounts with City banks. Glyn's in this period seem to have set out to attract and maintain their business as a London agency for country banks. In 1790 they held only four agencies. By 1800 they had 13, many less than Esdailes (39) and Robarts (26), but by 1815, Glyn's with 35 had established themselves as one of the main London holders of country bank agencies with Esdailes, Robarts, Barclays, Masterman and a few others.[18] Country banks would redeem on presentation notes issued by the country banker made payable in London and honour the bills and drafts drawn upon the capital. They would make transfers from the country bank's balance to London agents of other country banks. They would carry out stock transactions, including the purchase of securities and receipt of dividends and give advice and information to country banks on the conduct of business. When in 1797 Richard Carr Glyn gave evidence to the Parliamentary Committee of Secrecy on the Bank of England, he explained that Glyn's had connections with country banks in Scotland, Northumberland, the

[17] L.S. Pressnell, *Country Banking in the Industrial Revolution*, 1956, 4–11, though as Pressnell points out all that the various statistics do is to give a very approximate idea of the growth of country banking.

[18] Pressnell, 118–119. Iain S. Black's calculations from the London Post Office Directories for 1802 and 1820 differ in detail: The London Agency System in English Banking, 1780–1825, *London Journal*, 21, 1996, 116.

West of Yorkshire, Warwickshire, Cornwall, Dorset and Kent.[19] There were family links with most of those areas – Northumberland, through the Carr family, the West Riding through Hallifax and Mitton, and Warwickshire through the Mills. Sir Richard's parliamentary seat was in Cornwall, while his country house was in Dorset, and Kent was the home of the Plumptres. The bank's extensive contacts with Scotland have already been referred to. No doubt there were other reasons for the bank acting as agent to banks in these areas, but in the absence of detailed financial information much depended on trust and personal links were very important. Glyn's considered themselves as an agent to country bankers in money transactions. Country bank bills were drawn on Glyn's and country bank notes were made payable at Glyn's, the latter practice applying mainly to those banks in Warwickshire, Dorset and Kent as well as to Barnsley. Glyn's either charged commission on turnover, the rate varying according to whether they allowed interest or not, or by the maintenance of a minimum balance on the account which Glyn's could then use to advantage. These links enhanced the business of Glyn's and broadened the horizons of country banks, forming an important part of the unifying process between the local money markets and the centre.[20] Such was the success of Glyn's in this period that when the war began in 1793 9 clerks were employed; by the time it ended in 1815, 36 were employed. Most worked in Glyn's Bank itself but at least one undertook duties for the bank at the clearing house. Glyn's had a drawer there in which the clerks of other banks placed drafts on Glyn's which they wished to exchange for credit. Glyn's clerk periodically cleared the drawer and the contents were taken to Glyn's where the head clerk decided whether to pay or not. Those refused were sent back uncancelled. The final settlement was made between bank and bank in notes and cash offsetting balances by ledger, so minimising the actual transfer of Bank of England notes between member banks.

[19] Committee of secrecy appointed to examine outstanding demands on the Bank of England, House of Lords, 1797, xi.

[20] Michael Collins, *Money and Banking in the UK: a History*, 1988, 26.

CHAPTER TWO

The Young George Carr Glyn

ALTHOUGH Sir Richard Carr Glyn continued as the active senior partner in the 1820s, by then a new generation was making its presence felt. His fourth son George Carr Glyn was born on 27 March 1797. He was baptised at St James, Picadilly on 6 May: the family lived in nearby Arlington Street. Like his father and his four brothers he went to Westminster School. His cousin, Richard Carr Glyn, was already at the school but when George was admitted in October 1807, his three older brothers had already left. John Carr his younger brother joined him in 1810. Four cousins, the sons of Thomas Glyn, his father's brother, were at the school in George's time there, prompting George's friend and contemporary at the school, George Keppel, later sixth earl of Albemarle, to record in his memoirs 'there was a whole tribe of Glyns in my day' at Westminster.[1] When George was admitted he was ten and a half years of age. His eldest brother, Richard Plumptre, ten years older than George, had gone on to Christ Church, Oxford and then Brasenose and became a partner in the bank in 1808. By 1804 Robert, the second son, had left Westminster and was a writer in the East India Civil Service. He went to India and returned to England in 1823. In 1829 married Frederica Harford, daughter of Frederick Harford, the illegitimate son of Lord Baltimore, a marriage which was unwelcome to Sir Richard and other members of the Glyn family of his generation who remembered the scandalous life of Lord Baltimore.[2] Both Robert and Fredrica died in 1836. The third son, Thomas Christopher, had left Westminster in 1803 and like Richard Plumptre had gone on to

[1] G.F. Russell Barker and Alan H. Stenning, *The Westminster School Register from 1764 to 1883*, 1892, 92–93; George Thomas, Earl of Albemarle, *Fifty Years of My Life*, 1876, 1, 250.

[2] Fulford, 69. Frederick Calvert, 6th Baron Baltimore (1732–71) was a notorious libertine who was charged with rape, and though eventually acquitted, left the country in 1768 and died in Naples. Generally vilified as an example of aristocratic vice. (*ODNB*).

Christ Church. He later became a fellow of Merton and was called to the bar, becoming a Commissioner of Bankruptcy, but died in 1827, aged 37. John Carr, George's younger brother also went on to Christ Church before entering the church. He was to serve as rector of Hinton Parva[3] for over 60 years, a living of which the Glyns of Gaunts were the patrons, where he financed two local schools, founded the Girls Industrial Home in Poole and in the 1870s built at his own cost St John's Church, Wimborne. George's sister, Mary Elizabeth, married Edward Greathed of Uddens, about three miles from Gaunts.

When George went to Westminster William Carey was headmaster. Though a successful headmaster and later bishop, pleasant and affable and a favourite with parents and boys, he seems to have exercised insufficient supervision, so that the school was rather rough even by the standards of the time, perhaps because he believed in the hardening process. Augustus Short, later bishop of Adelaide, who entered the school in 1809 wrote 'the boys fought each other, they fought the masters, the masters fought them; they fought outsiders; in fact we were ready to fight everybody.'[4] Albemarle records that he was not to be found by his grandmother and Princess Charlotte when they came to take him out one Saturday because he was in the fighting green, 'the Great Cloisters' where he had not seen a better fought battle than that he was then watching between John Erskine and Paddy Brown.[5] Lord John Russell who was briefly at Westminster a few years before George Glyn regarded Westminster as a rough place. His father said that his stepmother had saved his life by taking him away from Westminster where the hard life was undermining his never very robust health.[6] Although the school was adjacent to the Abbey, the neighbourhood encouraged roughness. Tothill Fields between the Abbey and Millbank were only developed from 1832, and bull baiting continued until 1820. Lord John watched a fight in the 'Tuttle' Fields between young Belcher and another famous pugilist with his writing master when they should have been in class. How far the rough life suited George Glyn is not clear. The only clue we have is that Albemarle states that his old friend, George Glyn, funked his 'six-cutter' and prevailed upon a form fellow, William Wade, to take the blame and bear the punishment.[7]

[3] Also known as Stanbridge.

[4] Quoted in Lawrence E. Tanner, *Westminster School, A History*, 1934, 37.

[5] Albemarle, 1, 299. John Erskine later the Earl of Mar and Paddy Brown, later Sir John Benyon de Beauvoir.

[6] *Recollections of Lady Georgiana Peel compiled by her daughter Ethel Peel*, 1920, 8. (Lady Georgiana was Lord John's daughter.)

[7] Albemarle, 1, 250.

Another contemporary, Lord William Pitt Lennox described how as a fag he rose at 6 in summer and 7 in winter, fetched water from the pump in Dean's Yard, lit his master's fire, boiled his water and prepared his breakfast. School stated at 8 with an hour for breakfast which the fags prepared. The boys were in school from 10 to 12, and from 12 to 1 prepared for the afternoon's lessons with dinner in the Hall from 1 to 2. Evening school was from 2 to 5 on Mondays, Wednesdays and Fridays, and the fag then had to buy and prepare his master's meal. On Tuesdays and Thursdays boys might go to any relative who would receive them, as they could on Saturday afternoons until 8 on Monday mornings.[8] Edmund Goodenough, headmaster in the 1820s, found parents reluctant to send their sons to Westminster at an early age, (six was not uncommon), because they objected to them cleaning the shoes and candlesticks of their fagmaster, but he aroused considerable hostility when he insisted on abolishing these practices, and Westminster unlike Eton and Winchester was slow to reform and numbers dropped substantially.[9]

Although Glyn's coat of arms is one which is painted on the panelling of Up School, his memories of the school were not favourable. He did not send any of his sons to Westminster and when his eldest boy was at Rugby he commented 'the trio in that study has advantages which at Westminster would never have been conceived or thought of by us.'[10] His four older boys went to Rugby and the younger sons to Harrow.

In 1816 he accompanied his elder brother Robert, who was on leave from India where he was now a judge and magistrate, on what amounted to a Grand Tour though they went no further than Switzerland. Robert kept a dairy which records they left Dover on 22 April and completed their crossing of the Channel by abandoning the packet, King George, and continuing in a hired French fishing vessel with seven men rowing. Their itinerary was more conventional than their Channel crossing. They spent nearly two weeks in Paris when they visited Versailles, and then went on to Lyons where they engaged a small boat to take them down the Rhone in

8 Lord William Pitt Lennox, *Fifty Years Biographical Reminiscences*, 1863, 1, 112; Albemarle, 1, 254–255.

9 Tanner, 61.

10 Barclays Archives, 25/265, Langton Papers (LP) 340, Glyn to Joseph Langton, 28 Dec. 1837. Joseph Langton was manager of the Bank of Liverpool which opened on 16 May 1831, The Langton Papers consisting mostly of letters from Glyn to Langton were extensively drawn on by Michael Collins in The Langton Papers: Banking and the Bank of England Policy in the 1830s, *Economica*, 39, 1972, 47–59. The letters also contain references to other aspects of Glyn's life. The letters from Langton to Glyn have not survived.

what quickly became rough weather, forcing a halt to sleep in straw in the bottom of the boat. After three days in Geneva, they went on to Lausanne where their sister Mary Elizabeth was staying with her children and husband, Edward Greathed. At the beginning of July they began a tour of Switzerland, which took in Interlaken, Lucerne and Zurich as well as visits to notable waterfalls and glaciers. They returned to England in stages via the Rhineland, Belgium and Holland. The journal is very much Robert's account of the journey and although he explains at the beginning that he was accompanied by 'my fellow traveller George' there are no indications of George's reactions or the extent to which they visited different sites in particular places.[11]

How far the choice of career of the brothers was a clear preference on their part or the outcome of the view taken by their father as to their suitability as bankers is not known. George went directly into the bank where his eldest brother, Richard Plumptre, was already working. Sir Richard very much regarded the latter as his heir enjoining him in a letter to be opened after his death to purchase more land adjoining the estate at Gaunts or Fontmell or Melbury whenever an opportunity offered. He told his son that his son should be called Richard, but not Richard Carr. He did not expect him to be a banker, but his fortune would, he trusted, be ample and sufficient to give him consequence in life and in the County; he should be educated at Westminster School and Christ Church Oxford, and as to profession, the guards or the law and Parliament. In a postscript he was asked to take care of his brother George in the Banking House.[12] This letter demonstrates the inability of fathers to control the future of their families. Richard Plumptre followed his father's advice in that he made significant purchases of land in Fontmell Magna and Melbury, particularly in the 1840s, but he never married and his estate and title were inherited by Richard George, the son of Robert and Fredrica Harford. However although the line of succession did not work out as envisaged by Sir Richard, the letter also shows that the Glyns were alive to a problem which Martin Daunton identifies in his analysis of two other City bankers, the Hubbards and Gibbs – the need for dynastic security might mean the removal of money from the firm in order to preserve it from the risks of business. Similarly Lord Overstone had a deliberate aim to exchange the potentially larger, but less stable, income from his bank, Jones Loyd, for a steadier and more secure income from land and railways. By 1864 with the

[11] Robert Glyn's *Diary of Tour in France, Switzerland, etc* 1816, manuscript in the possession of Sir Richard Glyn, Bt, to whom I am grateful for an opportunity to consult it.

[12] Letter of 26 Jun. 1816, reproduced in Fulford, 68–70.

death of Richard Plumptre separate landowning and banking branches of the family had been created.[13]

Indeed George Carr Glyn seems to have been chosen by his father to join him and Richard Plumptre at the bank and since their father only died in 1838 his advice to Richard Plumptre about taking care of George was also superfluous as George was long before then very well established at the bank and in the City. However his father passed to him land in Fontmell Magna in 1825, a village with which he was to have close ties and to become the patron of the living.[14] He also had a share in other purchases of land made by his father and brother. By 1816 when only 19 George was writing from the bank to his father of the advantage of selling India Bonds and buying Consols. He became a partner in 1819, aged 22. The other five partners were then his father, Charles Mills and Thomas Hallifax of the older generation, and his contemporaries – his brother Richard Plumptre and Charles Mills' namesake and nephew, who had become a partner in 1813.[15] The Bank then became Glyn, Mills, Hallifax, Glyn, Mills & Glyn. In 1821 the Bank's premises were enlarged. Hitherto based in Birchin Lane and Change Alley, Glyn's purchased adjacent premises at 66 and 67 Lombard Street. The property was rebuilt as one, though the premises fronting onto Birchin Lane were relinquished in 1824.[16]

George became a partner when the banking system finally recovered from the consequences of the long period of wars with the French. The Resumption Act of 1819 enabled the Bank of England to restore convertibility which it did in 1821 following a period of deflation in which the Bank had built up its stock of gold, reduced the number of notes in circulation, and kept the discount rate at 5 per cent at a time of falling rates. This gave the discount houses, 'bill brokers' as they were then known, who had flourished in the war, further business as the private banks were slow to reduce their discount rate.[17]

The partnership agreement emphasised the family nature of the bank, the interest being divided according to the number of families rather than partners. Sir Richard and his family had a four-tenths interest, as did

[13] Martin Daunton, *State and Market in Victorian Britain: War, Welfare and Capitalism*, 2008, 186; R.C. Michie, Income, expenditure and investment of a Victorian millionaire: Lord Overstone, 1823–83, *Bulletin of the Institute of Historical Research*, 58, 1985, 59–77.

[14] Dorset Record Office, Q/S/M/1/15, Quarter Session Order Book, 1819–26.

[15] The younger Charles Mills was born in 1792 and educated at Harrow and Christ Church.

[16] Fulford, 165.

[17] W.T.C. King, *History of the London Discount Market*, 1936, 27–28.

Charles Mills and his family while Thomas Hallifax had a two-tenths interest. It was for the head of each family to apportion their tenth shares among the members of their family. The capital was £45,000 on which 4½ per cent was to be paid annually to the partners charged to the profit and loss account of the firm. For each tenth each partner should have £5,000 bank annuities in his name, making £75.000 in capital and reserve, 7.3 per cent of liabilities.[18] Comparable ratios are not available for this period, but it is much lower than figures given by Collins for the 1840s though his sample contains few London private banks. James Dick showed for a later period that the large London banks tended to operate on a smaller capital base than provincial firms.[19] It was not until 1885 that Glyn's published their annual accounts and balance sheet, but the bank's archives contain a yearly statement of assets and liabilities for all the years George Carr Glyn was a partner. In the year-end balance for 1820 the bank's assets amounted to £1,026,000. Bills discounted accounting for £686,000 with current accounts debtors balances amounting to £151,000, the major part in the country office with only £37,000 in the town, the two main divisions of the bank. There was also £181,000 in cash with only £130 at the Bank of England. Investments amounted to £7,624. The liabilities consisted mainly of the credits in the current accounts, £679,000 in the town office and £347,000 in the country. Profits were £24,922, a return of 33 per cent. Again comparable figures for other banks are not available, but the return for Barclays in the mid-1830s was 21 to 26 per cent.[20] The balance gradually rose to £1,484,000 at end-1824, an increase of nearly 50 per cent on 1820. The bills then discounted amounted to £1,118,000, and the credit balances in the town office current accounts also amounted to over £1,000,000.[21]

The relations between Glyn's and their country correspondents differed in detail in particular cases but the principles seem to have changed little over many years. In 1794 when Glyn's had only about eight country correspondents, Fryer, Andrews & Co of Wimborne were offered a choice.

[18] Royal Bank of Scotland (RBS) Archives, GM/997, copy of articles of co-partnership dated 1 October 1821, formalising the partnership which began on 25 Dec.1820. The ratio of capital to liabilities is much lower than the figures given by Collins for the 1840s, but the large London banks tended to operate on a smaller capital base than the provincial firms.

[19] Michael Collins, The Business of Banking: English Bank Balance Sheets, 1840–80, *Business History*, xxvi, 1984, 48–49.

[20] Margaret Ackrill and Leslie Hannah, *Barclays: The Business of Banking 1690–1996*, 2001, 413.

[21] RBS Archives, GM/718, Periodical Returns. The figures for profits are taken from Fulford, 59. I have been unable to trace the source in the RBS Archives.

First a commission of ⅛ per cent on drawings, and a charge of 5 per cent on overdrawing; second a commission of ¼ per cent on drawings and an allowance of 5 per cent on the credit balance, provided that did not exceed the amount of commission which was payable half-yearly, or third the latter arrangement modified by a reduction of commission to ⅛ per cent when drawings exceeded £100,000. In fact the Wimborne bank seems to have agreed on a lump sum. In 1795 Glyn's had agreed to undertake the work of Surtees, a Newcastle bank whose transactions were expected to amount to £800 to £900,000 a year for a deposit of £15,000, but on finding that the amount was likely to be nearly double that stated and that the Newcastle bank proposed to deal directly with a stockbroker Glyn's asked for an additional £5,000, which was sufficient to deter the move. This was an example of a country banker remunerating his London agent by means of a permanent deposit which received no interest, though in practice they were allowed interest on their balance, reduced by the charges for stock purchases. Deposits were probably sought when country bankers tended to run their accounts low.[22]

In the early 1820s it was still the practice to allow interest. Glyn's allowed 4 per cent in 1821 if commission were required from the country banker, but by 1832 Glyn was telling the Select Committee on the Bank of England charter that it was scarcely ever the custom to allow interest upon the money of the country bankers in the hands of the town agent. It was done to a large extent in time of war but not then. It was possible that the general decline in interest rates after 1815 encouraged country bankers to seek alternative outlets for their funds either locally or in bills or the growing discount market. Indeed Glyn added that Glyn's did not generally employ the funds deposited with them; rather they were employed in government securities or the country bank dealt directly with a bill broker giving him a credit with Glyns.[23] However the correspondence between Glyn and Joseph Langton, the manager of the Bank of Liverpool suggests more flexibility in paying interest. Initially a system of charging commission on transactions was in force and 2½ per cent was paid on floating cash balances, but in 1833 Glyn's accepted that the annual sum of £600, with an additional £200 for each million above two, should be paid in lieu of commission, though a pencilled note on Glyn's letter suggests that something more complicated was agreed. Certainly in August 1834 Glyn told Langton that he had a strong disinclination to commission 'as tending to cramp our friends in their operations

22 Pressnell, 86–87, 404–405, based on letters in the Glyn Mills letter book and the country ledger.

23 Pressnell, 414; Bank Charter Committee, Qs 2934–5.

through us and as inconvenient in other respects,' and emphasised this again in 1837. He then proposed to do the work for £800 per annum to which the Bank of Liverpool assented.[24] The commission in effect was a payment for agency services rendered by Glyn's for the country bank not just for financial transactions – meeting claims on the provincial bank when they fell due in London, paying cash for notes, drafts and bills drawn by, or on the country bank, buying securities and providing information on the financial markets generally or about particular clients. The commission could vary. In June 1836 Glyn reduced the rate of interest on the fluctuating cash balance from 2½ to 2 per cent and raised the remuneration from £800 to £1,000 considering the great increase of business during the previous two years.[25] In 1837 Glyn asked the Bank of Liverpool whether they employed Glyn's to receive the dividends of your friends in the English Funds. He had noticed few dividends considering their connection.[26]

The return to the gold standard in 1821 accompanied by a contraction of the note issue contributed to a fall in commodity prices and widespread unemployment, but as trade and employment recovered rates of interest remained low and the Bank did nothing to inhibit the expansion of the liabilities of country banks. There was a wave of speculation in 1824 and 1825, much of it in the South American trade and mining projects and also domestically, but these were a small minority of the 600 companies projected. Glyn's were bankers, jointly with Curtis & Co, to two South American mining companies, formed during the boom – the General South American Mining Association, to which Thomas Christopher Glyn was counsel, and Potosi La Paz and the Peruvian Mining Association, to the International Gas Company, British Commercial Life and the much smaller Scarlet Dye. All these survived at least to 1827, but Glyn's were also bankers to the London, Arundel Bay and Portsmouth Grand Ship Canal Co., and Egyptian Trading, both of which were abandoned as well as to four projected companies which came to nothing.[27]

In November 1825 a number of London bankers were called out of church on a Sunday by demands for gold from their country customers. On Sunday 4 December those Bank of England directors who were in London met at 8 am and though an immediate collapse of Sir Peter Pole & Co., the London agent of 44 country banks, was averted, it fell a week later unable

24 LP 1, 26, 71, 73 and 250, 15 Jul. 1831, 22 Mar. 1833, 8 and 30 Aug. 1834 and 9 Jan. 1837.

25 LP 181, 2 Jul. 1836.

26 LP 253, 11 Jan. 1837.

27 Henry English, *A Complete View of the Joint Stock Companies formed during the years 1824 and 1825,* 1827.

to meet demands from note-holders and depositors.[28] This precipitated a panic, only stopped by a sudden reversal of the Bank's restrictionist policy. In all six London banks and more than sixty country banks crashed. Glyn's emerged virtually unscathed from the panic of 1825 when many London banks were affected by an exceptional demand for gold from the country banks for which they were agents. Its liquid position and careful choice of country banks for whom it acted contributed to its success. Only two failed country banks had accounts with Glyn's, and they were quickly replaced by country banks whose London agents had failed.

The 1825 crash raised questions about the viability of country banks, the size of which was limited by the bar on joint stock banks. A contrast was drawn with Scotland which seemed 'almost immune to the virus'.[29] Scottish banks had relatively large partnerships, often operated more offices than English banks and had proved more stable during economic recessions. The Scottish example made a strong case for permitting the establishment of larger banks in England. Consequently in 1826 Parliament authorised the opening of joint stock banks for the issue of notes of at least £5 in denomination if such banks were outside a radius of 65 miles from London. At the same time the issue of notes for less than £5 was prohibited and their reissue had to end in April 1829. This put an increased emphasis on the supply of gold to country banks, which was one cause of difficulties between the country banks and the Bank of England. Another was that the 1826 Act permitted the establishment of Bank of England branches, according to Horsley Palmer a favourite measure of Lord Liverpool's because of the discredit of private bankers.[30] The Government's aim was to stabilise local money markets through the direct supply of Bank of England notes and discounting, so the Bank then tried to induce the provincial bankers to cease issuing banknotes by co-operating with them and offering concessions such as a preferential rate for discounting.[31]

The crisis of 1825 also brought about a major change in practice on the part of the London private banks. Hitherto they had generally pursued a policy of using their resources to the full, rediscounting at the Bank of England whenever the need for cash became pressing. The events of 1825 brought home to them that in acute crises the Bank had to bear the discount demands of the whole country. As Glyn put it to the Lords committee in 1848

[28] E.M. Forster, *Marianne Thornton, A Domestic Biography*, 1956, 110–112.

[29] Sir John Clapham, *The Bank of England, A History*, 1, 1944, 102.

[30] J.K. Horsefield, The Opinions of Horsley Palmer, *Economica*, 16, 1949, 151.

[31] Dieter Ziegler, *Central Bank, Peripheral Industry: The Bank of England and the Provinces, 1826–1913*, 1990, 12.

'in 1825 it is a notorious fact that the bankers of London, pressed upon by their country connections, discounted with the Bank of England. Since that period the private bankers never have discounted with the Bank of England'.[32] He explained to the 1832 Committee that London bankers held a portion of their current funds in Bank of England paper and a small portion in gold, but it was Glyn's custom and, he thought, of nearly every banking house to keep also a large deposit at the Bank of England. He denied that Glyn's held less in house because they had an account at the Bank. There was not a fixed proportion at the Bank. The aim was to have a certain proportion in the house. The proportion at the Bank would not normally be as much as half. It depended on a fluctuating daily deposit, and when asked if they were in touch with the Bank on a daily basis he answered 'Hourly, I may say'.[33] Moreover instead of employing their surplus funds in the purchase of Government securities, and discounting at the Bank, they, ceased to discount with the Bank and placed their funds on deposit with the bill brokers.[34]

The role of the discount houses was further enhanced when in 1830 the Bank began to allow discount houses to rediscount with the Bank itself so sending the flow of emergency funds through discount houses rather than the banks, and the Bank concentrated on systemic needs rather than whether particular banks deserved assistance. However although this had little impact immediately after the change of policy, the ease of rediscounting caused banks to discount bills of less and less quality and by the mid-1830s discount houses did not take account of the volume and quality of the liabilities created.

Glyn's relationship with the Bank was sufficiently good for the partners to assist the country banks for whom Glyn's acted as agents in times of difficulty. The Bank of England had established a branch at Newcastle-upon-Tyne in 1828, though the local chamber of commerce petitioned against it. Gold was then transmitted to the local district by delivering sovereigns to the country bank against money deposited with the Bank in London by their agent. The gold was increasingly necessary as new small denomination notes could no longer be issued. However the Bank soon insisted on several days notice before branches could issue gold as part of their policy of concentrating the

[32] Select Committee of the House of Lords on Commercial Distress, PP, 1847–8, viii, Q. 1916.

[33] Committee of Secrecy on Bank of England Charter, PP, 1831–2, vi, Qs 2870–80. From 1819 to 1824 Glyn's deposits at the Bank did not reach £1,000, but in 1825 were £29,170 and in 1826 £58,120 and up to 1832 fluctuated between £9,400 and £49,900. (at 31 Dec. each year, RBS Archives, GM/718, Periodical Returns)

[34] King, 64.

note issue of the country in their hands, a change which was resented by many country bankers, including Ridley, Bigge, Gibson & Co, at Newcastle for whom Glyn acted as London agents. Ridleys' complaint to the Bank of England in Newcastle was passed on to the Bank in London. The Bank wanted Ridleys to settle their balances in Newcastle and not take the old circuitous mode of settling them through London. The point having been made by the Manager of the Newcastle Branch of the Bank of England, the Governor was content to let the matter rest but said he would talk to Mr Glyn. The Bank's policy seems to have got tighter. They explicitly told Backhouse and Co., another Newcastle bank, that they could operate their account only if they relinquished their note issue, in which case there would be no difficulty in supplying them with gold for their colliery payments. In October 1831 the Bank applied this policy to Ridleys when they wished to draw gold from the Newcastle branch. The Governor saw George Glyn and explained to him that the bulk of the money had to be taken in bank notes. Ridleys did not think this good enough. They explained to Glyn that the sum was issued almost entirely for wages due to colliers, keelmen, glass manufacturers, lead miners and others. They earned 18s to 25s each weekly and it followed that they had to be paid in gold and silver. They explained that this gold and silver made a circuit and most of it would find its way back to the Newcastle branch and so by this route the Bank would ordinarily receive nearly sufficient to supply their demands. Ridleys asked that 'Mr Geo. Glyn, or any of your firm who is intimate with the Governor, to impress upon him the hope that they could obtain their supplies in the usual manner.' If not they asked that £5,000 be sent by the coaches from the White Horse, Fetter Lane on Thursday morning at 8 o'clock and they would receive it on Friday night. Glyn's were asked not to leave it at the coach office overnight and were told it had previously been packed in a strong fir box without any handles. Glyn again saw the Governor who agreed that the Newcastle branch was to make available gold on the old terms, blaming the fact that bankers had applied for gold to an extent which was only really needed in times of political excitement, something of an excuse as three days later there were serious riots over the Reform Bill. The Newcastle agent however took little notice of the governor's instruction and Glyn had to see the Governor again. When asked by the Committee on the Bank Charter Act whether the Bank during the previous year had refused to make gold available to country bankers, Glyn replied 'I believe that during a short period there was that refusal on the part of the Bank of England.'[35]

[35] This account is based on Anon, Glyn's and the Bank of England, *Three Banks Review*, 40, Dec. 1958, 21–32.

The 1820s as a whole were a period of growth for Glyn's, but after 1825 the increase was less marked. In 1830 the end year balance amounted to £1,748,000 with profits reaching £41,000. By 1833 £2,000,000 would be reached. Most of this increase was in the town balances; country balances were almost stationary, a third of the total in 1820, but less than a fifth in 1830. The ratio of current account debts to credit balances was back to about 10 per cent after a rise in the mid 1820s.[36] 49 country banks now used Glyn's as their London agent, compared with 32 in 1814. They were widely spread, but more concentrated in the South-east (12), the Midlands (9), Scotland (7), and Yorkshire (6).[37]

[36] RBS Archives, GM/718.

[37] The regional breakdown is based on the lists in Fulford, Appendix III, 246–255.

CHAPTER THREE

Family and Partners

On 17 March 1823 George Carr Glyn married Marianne, daughter of Pascoe Grenfell, at St James Church, Piccadilly. She was then 20 years of age and was one of the seven surviving daughters of Pascoe Grenfell and his second wife, Georgiana St Leger, daughter of the first Viscount Doneraile.

George and Marianne made their first home at 14 Stratton Street, off Piccadilly. At the end of the 1820s they moved to 11 Eaton Place possibly when that very broad street of graceful houses was built by Thomas Cubitt. In about 1840 they moved to 1, Upper Ecclestone Street, next to Belgrave Square, one of the last parts of Belgravia to be developed. Their neighbours initially included George Grote, the banker and writer, John Lewis Ricardo, MP for Stoke-on-Trent and later Chairman of the North Staffordshire Railway, and James Wilson, founder of the Economist, MP and Treasury minister. This remained their London home until George's death nearly 40 years later. The fact that Glyn's was a family bank is emphasised in a surviving letter from George to his father about some stock for a customer which needed to be transferred. It began 'My dear Father' and ended 'Marianne has not been quite well. Send love, your affectionate son.'[1] This may have been pregnancy sickness – their first child, George Grenfell was born on 24 February 1824.

Children followed at regular intervals over the next twenty years – St Leger Richard in 1825, Robert Riversdale in 1827, who died two years later, Henry Carr in 1829, Richard Riversdale, 1831, Pascoe Charles, 1833, Georgina Mary, 1834, and Sidney Carr, 1835. Glyn told Langton, manager of the Bank of Liverpool to whom he frequently wrote, in December 1837 that 'my seven children are all at home and I feel my patriarchal position

[1] RBS Archives, GM/1381/4, letter of 17 Nov. 1823.

and responsibility.' His responsibilities were soon added to by the arrival of further children: Ashley Carr, in 1839, Alice Carr in 1842, and lastly Edward in 1843, born when his eldest brother was nearly 20. None of the boys followed their father to Westminster. The four eldest boys went to Rugby during the headmastership of Thomas Arnold. The main reason for this choice seems to have been that their house master at Rugby was Rev Algernon Grenfell, 'a most excellent person', a master there from 1831 to 1845, who was a nephew of Glyn's father-in-law, Pascoe, though Glyn may have had dealings with Dr Arnold in the course of the building of the London and Birmingham Railway. Certainly Arnold, who had become headmaster in 1828, supported the railway and is supposed to have said when watching some of the earliest trains on one of the bridges 'I rejoice to see it and to think that feudality is gone forever; it is so great a blessing to think that any one evil is really extinct.'[2] When George Carr and Marianne first took George Grenfell to Rugby on 2 September 1837 he wrote that they were pleased with all they saw and specially so with Dr Arnold. Langton who had been a contemporary of George Carr's at Westminster,[3] had sent his sons to Rugby. George and Marianne left their son in the care of Langton's boys, who were in the same house. Glyn commented 'everything was cosy and pleasant here' and added that money was sufficiently wanted to check any wild schemes. After George's first term there he told Langton that, while it was premature to say much, he was exceedingly pleased and 'my boy likes it much.' He added that he hoped to place another son with Mr Grenfell in twelve months' time.[4] At the beginning of the next term he reported that George had been very unwell verging on a severe attack of jaundice which he attributed to eating too many sausages.[5] George went on to University College Oxford in 1842, Algernon Grenfell's old college. Meanwhile St Leger followed George to Rugby in 1839, Henry in 1842 and Richard in 1843. According to Henry Drummond Wolff, St Leger and Lawley[6] were really the showmen of the

[2] Wilfred L. Steel, *The History of the London & North Western Railway*, 1914, 66.

[3] According to M. Baker and M. Collins, Crisis Management: English Financial Markets in the 1830s, in *Monetary and Banking History, Essays in Honour of Forrest Capie*, 2011, 52. Langton is not recorded in the *Westminster School Register*, 1892, but the admissions records from 1788 to 1806 are deficient.

[4] Barclays Archives, 25/265, Langton Papers (LP) 323 and 340, 5 Sept. and 28 Dec. 1837.

[5] LP 341, 5 Jan. 1838.

[6] Frances Charles Lawley, 1825–1901, sportsman and journalist, also went on to Balliol, and then became as fellow of All Souls. Addicted to horse racing, he ruined his academic and embryonic political career by using inside knowledge to gamble in government stocks and went to US where he reported on the Civil War for *The Times*. Returned 1865 and pursued a career in journalism.

school and were generally admired when walking together for the brilliant way in which they were dressed.[7] St Leger went on to Balliol, graduating in 1847. Like several of their cousins Pascoe, Sidney, Ashley and Edward went to Harrow. A factor may have been Algernon Grenfell's death in 1845, but Glyn had become a governor of Harrow school in 1836, probably having had some dealings with the school on London and Birmingham Railway business. He remained a governor until 1871.

Three of Marianne's younger sisters were to marry well known Victorians. In 1834 Emily married Sydney Godolphin Osborne, a clergyman who was long a columnist for the *Times* writing under the initials SGO. He became Baron Godolphin in 1859 after his elder brother succeeded to the dukedom of Leeds. In 1839 Caroline married John Ashley Warre MP who was Liberal MP for Taunton from 1820–26, for Hastings from 1831–35, and for three years before his death in 1860, for Ripon. The unmarried Grenfell sisters, all educated privately, had been living at home, but when in 1838 their father died, they – Georgiana, Charlotte Maria, Henrietta, and Francis Eliza (Fanny) were 'installed with comfortable portions but little expectation of marriage' at Braziers Park, a Georgian Gothic House at Ipsden, Oxfordshire.[8] They were attracted to catholic spirituality but remained in the Church of England under Tractarian influences and considered forming or joining some kind of Anglican sisterhood similar to the Puseyite Park Village community established in 1845. Fanny, met Charles Kingsley, then an undergraduate at Cambridge, in the long vacation of 1839 when he stayed at the rectory in nearby Checkendon. He shared his religious difficulties with Fanny. In 1841 he and Fanny came to an understanding and he resolved to be a clergyman.

Kingsley was regarded by the sisters as a threat to their ascendancy over Fanny particularly that of Georgiana, the oldest, the mother superior of the little group. Fanny was much younger than Georgiana and Henrietta and her mother had died when she was four. They resented Fanny keeping her association with the much younger and socially unsuitable Kingsley secret.[9] Later Henrietta said that they thought of him 'as an oaf in manners, unorthodox in religion and too young for our sister Fanny.'[10] Her brother Pascoe St Leger and the Grenfell family were opposed to Kingsley – they

[7] H. Drummond Wolff, *Rambling Recollections*, 1908, 1, 22.

[8] The phrase is from Susan Chitty, *The Beast and the Monk, a Life of Charles Kingsley*, 1975, 54.

[9] Chitty, 54.

[10] Quoted in M.F. Thorp, *Charles Kingsley*, 1937, 35. Henrietta married Robert Merrtyins Bird in 1848, a former East India Company officer, then active in the Church Missionary Society.

sent Fanny abroad in 1841 with Lady Gainsborough whose family were staunch adherents of the evangelical movement, after Fanny had made clear that she would marry Kingsley or not at all, and she was abroad again in the winter of 1842–43. Marianne seems to have been sympathetic. Kingsley constantly dreamed of Fanny and wrote to his mother 'I dreamt last night that Fanny was with me at Mrs Glyn's as happy as a child and Mrs Glyn knowing all and pleased with all. Is it a good omen?'[11] He obtained a first in classics in 1842 and was ordained to a curacy at Eversley, Hampshire, which his father secured. When Fanny announced their engagement Mrs Glyn summoned her.[12] They married at Bath in January 1844 when Osborne officiated. By then her married sisters, Emily and Caroline had relented and were fully supporting Fanny. Caroline Warre lent them a farmhouse for their honeymoon and it was Osborne's influence which secured Kingsley a curacy at Pimperne in Dorset. He soon returned to Eversley as rector. When he took up this living he had to take out a loan of £300 from Glyn's bank and Fanny paid £1,000 towards the upkeep of the house.

Charlotte Maria met James Anthony Froude at Ilfracombe when visiting the Kingsleys who were on holiday there. Froude was then tutor to the Darbishire family in Manchester following his leaving Oxford in 1849, where he had been a fellow of Exeter, after the burning of his book the *Nemesis of Faith,* partly autobiographical, in which the hero thinks that the teachings of the church had ossified into meaningless dogmas out of touch with the modern age. High churchmen denounced it as heretical. Charlotte had become a Roman Catholic in 1847 but was persuaded by Froude to renounce Rome. They married in October 1849 at St Peter's, Belgrave Square. Osborne officiated. No doubt Marianne kept in touch with her sisters, but there is little to suggest that they or their husbands became part of Glyn's social circle though we know that Osborne when he was expecting to give evidence to the Royal Commission on Capital Punishment in 1860 had promised to stay at George Glyn's 'when I go up for it.'[13]

The Grenfell connection not only brought Glyn a happy marriage but also strong business links. His father-in-law Pascoe Grenfell was born in Cornwall, the son of a merchant and had been sent to Amsterdam to learn banking with the firm of Hope Brothers. He then entered into business with his father and uncle as merchants and dealers in tin and copper ores. He

[11] BL, Add Ms 41298, ff 18–20, Charles Kingsley to his mother, undated but as he refers to Fanny's expected return on 4 October, probably September 1841.

[12] Una Pope-Hennessy, *Canon Charles Kingsley, A Biography*, 1948, 35.

[13] Centre for Buckinghamshire Studies, D-GR/8/49–50, Sydney Godolphin to C.P. Grenfell.

subsequently became involved with Thomas Williams, 'the Copper King', first acting as his agent on a sales trip to France, and then running Williams' new office in London – the London Copper Office. In 1794 he went into partnership with Williams' son Owen to buy Cornish ores, primarily to supply Williams' works in Swansea which Owen and Pascoe took over on Williams' death in 1802. He also became a partner in Williams & Co. bankers at Chester.

Pascoe's first wife, Charlotte Granville had died in 1790 and in 1794 he bought Taplow House, near Maidenhead. He married Georgiana in 1798. As a diarist put it Georgiana happened to come to Pascoe's house at Taplow with an aunt and a match between her and Mr Grenfell was soon settled.[14] Dr Gretton, the rector of Hedsor, in 1806 spoke of the good society

> they have in the neighbourhood but in respect of consumptious living … the commercial men 'bear the Bill'. At Crauford Bruce's you dine off Plate and Champagne, Tokay, Hermitage, are proposed to you in succession as soon as you have begun to eat. Pascoe Grenfell still exceeds Bruce; his plate is gilt; he began his world without any fortune and is now supposed to be in receipt of £20,000 a year from his shares and concern in copper works, being a partner with the Williams's.[15]

On Thomas Williams' death Pascoe Grenfell succeeded him as MP for nearby Great Marlow, which he represented as a Grenvillite, until the dissolution of 1820. He was then elected for Penryn having secured the limited influence of the Tory, Lord Dunstanville. He topped the poll 'as a Cornishman' and sat for that borough until 1826.

A strong evangelical who spoke against the slave trade and was a friend of William Wilberforce, Grenfell did not stand for Penryn in 1826 because of the unpopularity of his pro-catholic emancipation opinions. He was recognised as an authority on finance. Though a shareholder in the Bank of England[16] he was one of the Bank's major critics. In 1816 when the Government agreed with the Bank to borrow £6,000,000 at four per cent for winding up expenditure after the Napoleonic Wars he said the Bank was lending the public six million of the public's own money. A move to disclose the amount of the Bank's profits was defeated heavily. He opposed

[14] Joseph Farington, *The Farington Diary*, ed. James Greig, 1922–28, II, 102.

[15] Farington, IV, 11–12. Crauford Bruce owned property in the area. His bank Bruce Simson failed in 1818.

[16] He first appeared on the Proprietors' List in 1804 when he had a holding of between £2,000 and £3,000, John Clapham, *The Bank of England*, 1944, II, 54, note 3.

a proposal to increase the Bank's capital by £3,000,000 and lend that sum to the Government. Grenfell told the Bank's Proprietors that considering the large profits made by the Bank from the suspension of cash payments and other sources, the public might wish to curb the Bank, perhaps to abolish its privileges and possibly set up another great banking company. This was rejected though Sir John Clapham has commented that the most loyal historian of the Bank might permit himself to sympathise with Grenfell, in view of the selfish attitude of the proprietors when the country was in depression and bad harvests meant rising wheat prices at a time when general prices were dropping sharply.[17]

In addition to his daughters, Pascoe Grenfell had four sons, two, George and Charles Pascoe by his first wife Charlotte Granville. Charles Pascoe Grenfell was for many years the senior partner in Pascoe Grenfell & Sons, formed in 1825 when Owen Williams withdrew from the partnership. He married Lady Georgiana Molyneux, eldest daughter of the second Earl of Sefton of Croxteth Hall across whose estates the Liverpool and Manchester Railway as projected in 1824 was to run. Sefton, an Irish peer who was regarded as an advanced liberal with a considerable influence in the House of Commons, was a leader of the opposition to the railway. He told Stephenson he would have a hundred men against them[18] and though the successful proposal of 1825 took a route designed to avoid his estates but at additional expense, he made clear that while his property would no longer be affected by the nuisance he had not abandoned the interests of other opponents and his opinion of railways had not changed. Nevertheless by 1831 he willingly consented to the Leeds and Liverpool Railway passing through his estate at Kirby.[19] Though Lady Georgiana died in 1826, Charles Pascoe Grenfell was often in Liverpool in this period and doubtless informed his brother-in-law, George Carr Glyn, of the progress of the LMR. He was to become chairman of the London and Brighton Railway from 1846–48 and stood unsuccessfully for Wigan in 1841 and was MP for Preston from 1847–52 and 1857–65. His journal shows he invested in other railways over this period, on occasions on a short term basis.[20] His main business link with his brother-in-law was through St Katharine's Dock rather than railways, and it was his half-brother Pascoe St Leger Grenfell who was a director of the

[17] Clapham, II, 54–57.

[18] W.O. Skeat, *George Stephenson – the Engineer and His Letters*, 1973, 77 (Stephenson to J. Pease,19 Oct. 1824)

[19] Robert E. Carlson, *The Liverpool and Manchester Railway Project*, 1969, 71–73, 147, 151 and 227.

[20] Journal of C.P. Grenfell, 1835–46, Centre for Buckinghamshire Studies, D-GR/9/5.

London and Birmingham Railway from its inception until it became part of the LNWR in 1846. Pascoe Grenfell had quarrelled with his eldest son George. In his will he instructed that all his estate be sold for the benefit of Charles Pascoe and so in 1839 Taplow House was sold to the Marquis of Thomond, but in 1852 Charles Pascoe purchased nearby Taplow Court from the Earl of Orkney where he died in 1867.[21]

When George Carr Glyn became a partner in Glyn's, in addition to his father and brother, members of the Mills and Hallifax family were partners. Charles Mills, the elder, died childless in 1826. His nephew Charles remained a partner until his death in 1872. He was a director of the East India Company from 1822 until 1858 when the company disbanded and then was a member of the East India Council and adviser to the Secretary of State on finance until 1868. Following his resignation he was created a baronet by Disraeli in recognition of 46 years in the home administration of India. In his capacity as a director he fairly distributed the valuable patronage which belonged to that office, though a good customer of the bank was not often refused. However when Willy Wodehouse, a nephew of Bertram Currie's, was offered a clerkship by Mills through the influence of his mother Lady Jane, he would not take it. Samuel Gurney persuaded Joshua Bates to take him as a clerk in Barings instead.[22]

With his brother Francis, who did not enter the bank, but later became chairman of Minerva Life insurance, Charles travelled in Europe. He is recorded under 'Fashionable Arrivals' as having returned from a tour and left for Barford, in Warwickshire where his uncle and aunt lived.[23] He

[21] D.R. Fisher, ed., *History of Parliament, The House of Commons, 1820–1832*, V, 2009, 409; J.J. Sheehan, *History and Topography of Buckinghamshire*, 1862, 852.

[22] Bertram W. Currie, *Recollections, Letters and Journals*, ed. C.C. Currie, 1905, I, 74 and 477. Joshua Bates was a partner in Barings.

[23] *Morning Post,* 10 Nov. 1824. It does however seem clear from Edith Clay's *William Gell in Italy, 1831–35,* 1976, 81, that the Charles Mills of the Villa Mills in Rome was not the banker, as supposed by Fulford, but Charles Andrew Mills (1760–1846), who lived there with Sir William Gell, who jointly owned it for some years. He was the son of Peter Matthew Mills, a sugar planter of St Kitts. Mills continued to live there until his death. Before he moved to Rome he frequented the circle surrounding Caroline, Princess of Wales. The duke of Buckingham wrote that the Villa was the property of a Mr Mills 'famous for having come over at the head of the Queen's witnesses during her trial and as having perjured himself more than most.' (*Private Diary of Richard, Duke of Buckingham and Chandos, KG,* 1862, i, 243–244). Fulford (85) does say that the Charles Mills, the friend of Disraeli, of Lady Blessington and her circle does seem to be a distinct personality from the Charles Mills (the banker) of later life. The latter does however seem to have been painted by D'Orsay in Rome.

joined White's as a young man in 1817 and lived a rather different social life from his partners the Glyns and Hallifax's. When in 1825 he was about to marry Emily Cox, daughter of the banker Richard Henry Cox, members of White's laid bets whether his wife would have a child within 10, 11 or 12 months from the day of his marriage. Mills himself won a bet that a certain gentleman known to the parties would be hanged by 21 December 1814.[24] He was thought to be the original of Canterton who briefly appears in Disraeli's Coningsby 'who used to be the fellow for history at Whites. He was always boring people with William the Conqueror, Julius Caesar and all that sort of thing.'[25] He and Emily lived at Little Hillingdon, Uxbridge, close to her parents at Hillingdon House. Greville admired the Cox family at Hillingdon and they caused him to think much and often of the theory of happiness, 'I am convinced that it is principally to be found in contented mediocrity.' Perhaps Emily's upbringing in the Cox household contributed to her pursuit of a different style of life after her marriage. In 1854–58 the Mills built Hillingdon Court in Vine Lane. P.C. Hardwick was the architect. The mansion had lavish interiors, and a large entrance hall with an elaborately carved staircase, flanked by reception rooms all sumptuously decorated in the French style of the late 18th century. Charles Mills was a collector of objets d'art and French furniture, who formed a splendid collection at Hillingdon. He built up an estate there of several thousand acres which considerably exceeded any similar property in Middlesex, having in 1858 purchased the manor of Hayes and so acquiring most of Hayes parish as well as parts of Norwood and Southall.[26]

The Mills town house was in Oxford Street at the top of Park Lane – Camelford House, built in 1771 by William Pitt's brother Thomas, first Baron Camelford, with a plain outside and a splendid interior with very fine plaster work. Lord Grenville and Princess Charlotte had resided there. Mills originally leased it from Lord Middleton in 1827.[27] Charles Mills' dinner parties were mentioned in the *Morning Post* and he is recorded as occupying Her Majesty's box at the Royal Opera House. His wife's balls were listed under the heading 'Fashionable Arrangements'. In May 1846 Mrs Charles

[24] The Betting Book from 1743 to 1878 in *The History of White's from 1743 to 1848,* Algernon Burkett, 1894, 187–191.

[25] Benjamin Disraeli, *Coningsby* (Everyman edition of 1911), 326. Canterton is listed as Mills in the Revised Key of 1845, 399–400.

[26] *Bankers Magazine*, 32, 1872, 872–873; *VCH, Middlesex*, 4, 26 and 29.

[27] Nottingham University Library, department of Manuscripts and Special Collections, Counterpart of unexpired lease for Camelford House for a payment of £19,000, 15 Aug. 1827.

Mills gave her first ball of the season when Camelford House was the scene of very brilliant hospitality, the guests included his Royal Highness Prince George of Cambridge, the Duchess of Beaufort and her daughters, and over thirty other members of the peerage. It is hard to see the names of more than one or two bankers in the extensive published guest list though more might be included in the 'etc etc' with which the list ends. In 1856 her ball was expected to be the most picturesque of the season – the style of costume being that of Louis XIV. Earlier that year the Mills were guests at the Royal Theatricals at Windsor Castle, and in June Mrs Mills was the only commoner to be listed among the Lady patronesses of the grand fancy dress ball on behalf of the Royal Academy of Music which the Queen honoured with her presence.[28] Perhaps the culmination of this association with the aristocracy was the marriage in 1857 of their eldest son, Charles Henry, to Louisa Isabella Lascelles, daughter of the third earl of Harewood. Mrs Mills is reputed to have said that the Lascelles family would find the marriage a bitter pill to swallow, to which her husband replied 'Then, my dear, we must gild it.'[29] Charlotte and Eleanor, Charles Henry's sisters, married the sons of Sir J.S.B. Johnstone, Bart and of Lord Faversham.[30]

Thomas Hallifax, who had been a partner since 1796, had few interests external to the bank. He did not enter City politics or seek a seat in the House of Commons. He was however a founder member of the Royal Yacht Club in 1815, graduating from Alfred, a cutter of 46 tons in 1815 to Sparrow Hawk of 84 tons in 1841.[31] He travelled particularly to France which he visited in 1814 as soon as Napoleon was defeated and sent to Elba. He lived at Blackheath and in Suffolk where he built Cavendish Hall in 1821–22. In 1823 he bought Chadacre Hall with its estate near Shimpling a few miles north east of Cavendish and in 1834 engaged Philip Hardwick to rebuild it.[32] He held the office of High Sheriff of Suffolk. He died in 1850 when he was the senior partner.

Glyn according to Bertram Currie his partner from 1864 was nearer to Hallifax than to Mills in his private life. He was a member of James Morrison's private circle which included fellow bankers like Samuel Gurney,

[28] *Morning Post*, 9 May 1831, 13 Sept. 1837, 5 Sept. 1839, 2 Apr. 1840, 8 May 1846, 30 Jun. 1851, 29 Jan. and 6 Jun. 1856. *Illustrated London News*, 3 May 1856. In the event in 1846 Mrs Mills's second ball of the season was cancelled.

[29] Fulford, 87.

[30] *Illustrated London News*, 26 Jan. 1850 and 22 Oct. 1859.

[31] Montague Guest and W.B. Bolton, *Memorials of the Royal Yacht Club*, 1815–1900, n.d., 484.

[32] James Bettley and Nikolaus Pevsner, *Buildings of England, Suffolk, West*, 2015, 179 and 483–484.

Abraham Robarts, John Smith and Timothy Wiggins.[33] He was a member of the Reform, Brook's and the City clubs. Currie was a contemporary of George Grenfell Glyn, George Carr Glyn's eldest son, and entered Currie's Bank in 1847 which amalgamated with Glyn's in 1864. He had wide interests outside the bank and rather despised his suburban neighbours in Surrey. He did not put Glyn in that category but said that his quickness and alertness of mind were remarkable, and if he had not been so engrossed in the details of business, and if his domestic life had been a little more intellectual and aesthetic, his natural talent for conversation and for society would have developed to a high pitch. But the puritanical and philistine element which prevailed in his days in the banking and mercantile world checked his flight and made his private life colourless and uninteresting.[34] This was a complete contrast to Thomas Baring whom Currie regarded as a merchant prince, and worthy successor of the Medici or the Fuggers[35] The social life of Glyn's sons was also something of a contrast.

[33] Richard Gatty, *Portrait of a Merchant Prince, James Morrison, 1789–1857*, 1977, 152. Morrison was a draper who amassed a large fortune, became an MP and took a close interest in improving railway legislation (see Chapter 9).

[34] Currie, I, 94–95.

[35] Ibid, I, 43.

CHAPTER FOUR

Early Interests outside the Bank – St Katharine's Dock

DAVID MORIER EVANS, writing in 1852, regarded the City as a world within itself, but was quite clear that the chief aim of the City man was to amass money.[1] Walter Bagehot's description of the private London banker in *Lombard Street* was published in 1873, the year of George Carr Glyn's death. By then Bagehot had doubts about the future of private banks, with the growth of joint stock banking, but what he said about private bankers was applicable to the whole period of Glyn's long career. Bagehot wrote –

> The name 'London Banker' had especially a charmed value. He was supposed to represent, and often did represent, a certain union of pecuniary sagacity and educated refinement which was scarcely to be found in any other part of society. In a time when the trading classes were much ruder than they now are, many private bankers possessed a variety of knowledge and a delicacy of attainment which would even now be very rare. Such a position is indeed singularly favourable. The calling is hereditary; the credit of the bank descends from father to son; this inherited wealth soon brings inherited refinement. Banking is a watchful but not a laborious trade. A banker even in large business can feel pretty sure that all his transactions are sound, and yet have much spare mind. A certain part of his time, and a considerable part of his thoughts, he can readily devote to other pursuits. And a London banker can also have the most intellectual society in the world if he chooses it. There has probably been very rarely ever been so happy

[1] D.M. Evans, *City Men and City Manners or the Physiology of London Business*, 1852, 1–2.

> a position as that of a London private banker; and never perhaps a happier.[2]

Perhaps this description was best exemplified by Thomas Baring of whom his partner, Joshua Bates, complained that he worked well at intervals, but claimed the right to be absent.

Glyn's interests outside the family bank, apart from insurance and other banking interests and his role as MP were concentrated in the worlds of docks and railways and it was the latter sector which led to his most distinguished achievement and also to the enhancement of his bank by its becoming the foremost banker to the railway companies.

Private banking however was essentially a term which described ownership rather than activity. The owners were partners with unlimited liability and were also in effect the managers. They engaged in all types of activity and Glyn's were nearer a merchant bank than most. Glyn devoted a considerable time to other pursuits as well as being the driving force behind the bank for the major part of his long career as a partner, certainly from the time his father died in 1838, and to an extent before that, until the merger with Curries in 1864. While he did not become involved in the governance of the City he played a part in various philanthropic ventures, e.g. in 1828 he was a steward at the twentieth annual dinner for the Refuge for the Destitute and on the committee for the relief of Spanish and Italian refugees.[3]

Glyn's first outside appointment came in July 1819 when he succeeded his father as a director of Globe Insurance.[4] In 1799 his father had been a founding director just as his grandfather had been with the Equitable in 1762. His father took 100 shares in the Globe and presented the Bill to the Commons. From the outset Glyn's were with Devaynes, Dawes and Co of Pall Mall, Treasurers and Bankers to the company.[5] The board contained many distinguished City figures, including eleven members of Parliament, two aldermen and six knights. The Globe was one of a number of insurance companies established in the first decade of the nineteenth century to challenge the domination of the older companies. Though the Globe succeeded in obtaining an Act of Parliament enabling the King to grant a

[2] Walter Bagehot, *Lombard Street: A Description of the Money Market*, 1873, 268–9.

[3] *The Times*, Apr. and 26 Nov. 1828.

[4] Liverpool Record Office, clerks engagement book no 1, list of directors.

[5] Liverpool Record Office, 22, Globe Minutes 1799, minutes of 29, 30 May and 11 Jun. 1799. The Globe's West End office was in Pall Mall. His father recorded in his will that he had already given 20 shares to George, possibly when he succeeded him as a director.

charter, they could not get official approval for their draft charter, so from 1803 they conducted their business as an unincorporated company under deed of settlement which described the firm's purpose, listed its rules and vested its assets in named trustees. As Barry Supple put it:

> When commercial law made it difficult to create orthodox companies in the eighteenth and early nineteenth centuries, unorthodox but highly effective legal devices were used to satisfy the corporate prerequisites of insurance growth.[6]

The founder and driving force was Sir Frederick Morton Eden, chairman until his early death in 1809. In his *On the Policy and Expediency of Granting Insurance Charters* he attacked the monopolies of the Royal Exchange and London in marine insurance. In 1806 he led a second, and equally unsuccessful attempt to obtain a charter to enable the Globe to transact marine business as well as life and fire, but the marine monopoly was only broken in 1824 when the Alliance Insurance Company, instigated by Nathan Rothschild and Moses Montefiore with the active support of Samuel Gurney and Francis Baring secured an Act of Parliament which effectively ended the Royal Exchange's monopoly of marine insurance stemming from its charter of 1719.[7]

The Globe, like the British Office founded in 1799, was met with hostility not so much because it offered competitive premium rates but because it altered the practice of insurance and simplified and extended policies. Griffin Stonestreet, the Assistant Secretary of the successful Phoenix Fire Office established in 1782, attacked it for trying to get a charter, but also its underwriting policy. He argued that different types of insurance business required the security of distinct financial reserves. The various categories of underwriting should be properly separated and then balanced with a wide spread of risk and sensible ceilings; wherever possible they should be separately funded rather than be based on a single capital fund as was the Globe's.[8]

The Globe and its contemporaries quickly had a marked effect on the market. The Globe offered fire and life insurance from the outset, though it never extended its business, nor altered its insurance practices to the extent that its original proposals anticipated.[9] The Globe directors argued that the

[6] Barry Supple, Insurance in British History in Oliver M. Westall, ed., *The Historian and the Business of Insurance*, 1984, 3.

[7] Barry Supple, *The Royal Exchange Assurance*, 1970, 198.

[8] George Griffin Stonestreet, *The Portentious Globe: An enquiry*, 1800.

[9] David Jenkins and Takau Yoneyama, eds, *History of Insurance*, 1, 2000, 196.

business of the office would, in a great measure, depend upon the selection of proper persons as country agents. They appointed 140 by September 1804 and 158 by Christmas 1805.[10] Eden estimated in 1806 that the impact of the Globe and the Imperial had reduced the premium rates for the newly opened West India Dock from 5s to 3s per £100 and that over the previous 20 years average fire premiums had fallen by at least 25 per cent under the influence of competition.[11] In 1816–20 the Globe had 5 per cent of the market of British fire offices, and in 1822 was the seventh largest with £18.4 million insured, but there was little growth thereafter. Two decades later its share was down to 3.5 per cent in a market increasingly dominated by the big four – the Sun, the Phoenix, REA and the Norwich. As early as 1825 Charles Babbage was critical of the Globe, as it had more directors than any other office, was still using the by then out-dated Northampton Mortality Tables and did not pay profits to the assured – it was one of only six companies which did not. He thought the additional security provided by the capital held by the Globe and similar companies was dearly purchased by the assured.[12] The sums assured by the Globe had only risen to £22.6 million by 1840 and were almost identical in 1850. In 1846–50 its market share was down to 2.8 per cent. In London the Globe maintained its position better than it did in the provinces, but again there was little growth and a decline after 1840. Similarly gross premium income for fire insurance averaged £33,227 from 1816 to 1820, a level not reached again until 1836–40 having dipped to £24,123 from 1826–30.[13] In the 1820s there were prices cuts and some insurance firms went out of business. The Globe reduced all premiums for fire insurance from 2s to 1s 6d, from 3s to 2 6d and from 5s to 4s 6d.[14] In 1829 an agreement by major London offices including the Globe and the Royal Exchange to maintain a rate of 3s at St Katharine's Dock collapsed when the Phoenix, the Sun and the Alliance reduced the rate to 2s.[15] Dock insurances remained a problem. The Royal Exchange was particularly concerned and after initially failing to get the other main offices to agree in 1842 acted unilaterally to raise rates but subsequently the Globe and others agreed to a further increase of the

[10] David Jenkins, The practice of Insurance against fire, 1750–1840, in Oliver M. Westall, *The Historian and the Business of Insurance*, 1984, 3.

[11] Supple, 1970, 122.

[12] Charles H. Babbage, *A comparative view of the various institutions for the assurance of lives,* reproduced in Jenkins and Yoneyama, 4, 2000, 257 and 290.

[13] Robin Pearson, *Insuring the Industrial Revolution: Fire Insurance in Great Britain, 1700–1850,* 2004, 182, 187–188, 190, (Tables 5.1, 5.2, 5.3 and 5.12).

[14] *Morning Post,* 23 Sept. 1825.

[15] Supple, 128 and 134.

London mercantile tariff and later an increase of the rates for Liverpool and Manchester mercantile risks and for cotton mills throughout England.[16] This led to the formation of the Fire Offices Committee of which the Globe was a member. The Globe's conservatism continued. Frederick Blayney in his comparison of insurance firms published in 1848 wrote:

> Whilst unyielding to the principle of dividing profits, the Globe hold out no inducement to those who desire to benefit by a participation therein nor are their rates of premium materially below those of many other contemporaneous offices which divide profits with the insured.[17]

In the same year Samuel Brown said that while in all Mutual Offices, the assured's policies have increased in value, in Proprietary companies, (he named the Equitable and the Globe) the surplus premiums had been applied to improve the shares of the proprietors. The Globe shares originally £1,000,000 were now worth £1,190,000, which he argued was a loss of £190,000 to the shareholders. He quoted figures for five Offices. The Globe had the largest capital but the smallest increase in value of its shares in cash and the contrast was much greater in percentage terms.[18] By 1852 the value of the Globe's shares had risen to £1,515,000 and it paid a dividend of six per cent.[19]

Eden had originally envisaged offering a savings bank and insurance to friendly societies but in practice the Globe's life business, like that of the Pelican and Royal Exchange, tended to concentrate on the aristocracy, who were lent large sums of money secured by the rental earned or the expectation of a future inheritance accompanied by a life insurance policy as the loans were impossible to recover if the debtor died before the loan was repaid.[20] The Globe sometimes had complex family situations with which to deal. In 1835 the Treasury Committee had to consider a proposal from the Hon George Talbot, brother of the Earl of Shrewsbury, and the likelihood of his succeeding to the earldom and estates. They decided to accept the proposal for a loan and insurance the loan at 8 per cent, as the terms had to include the risk that a male issue might intervene to defeat Talbot's claim to the earldom,

[16] Supple, 162–163.

[17] Frederick Blayney, *Life Assurance Societies considered as to their Comparative Merits*, 1848, reproduced in Jenkins and Yoneyama, 2000, 5, 249.

[18] Samuel Brown, *Defects in the Practice of Life Assurance and Suggestions for their Remedy*, 1848, reproduced in Jenkins and Yoneyama, 2000, 6, 47–48.

[19] Ibid, 84.

[20] Timothy Alborn, *Regulated Lives, Life Insurance and British Society, 1800–1914*, 2009, 145.

though the Earl had 'no son nor any child born for 20 years past'.[21] The sums involved were often large. Lord Huntingtower repaid £64,000 in 1834. In 1851 a reduction of the rate of interest was agreed on the £128,000 lent to Lord Dunstanville. The Treasury Committee turned down an application for a loan of £75,000 on the Hornby Castle estate in Lancashire in February 1852 and in April 1853, Lord Panmure who had succeeded his father in the previous year repaid £85,356 'being the final settlement of his arrangements with the company.'[22]

Glyn occasionally intervened in Parliament on insurance issues. In 1856 he supported the government in its proposed to bring British law in line with other countries where the 'average clause' was the law of the land, ie the insurer was only bound to pay the proportion of the loss that the amount of insurance bore to the value of the property. He thought the principle right, and the reduction of tax by the chancellor and the rates by the companies might also be desirable to make British companies competitive.[23] Glyn remained Treasurer of the Globe until it was taken over by the Liverpool and London, described in Chapter 18.

In January 1821 Glyn was appointed one of three trustees of the British Metropolitan Tontine, which for ten shillings a week per share subscribed for one year only which would in a few years produce an ample income to every shareholder and the last hundred surviving shareholders would be entitled to the capital which it was anticipated would be £500,000. The Lord Mayor and Sir William Rawlins were the other trustees and Glyn's were the bankers, so it looks very much as if the young George was the only trustee closely involved in the management of the Tontine.[24]

If George's first principal outside appointment, a seat on the Globe board, was virtually inherited, in the company boom of 1825 he was alive to new opportunities outside the existing sphere of the bank or family. He was one of the original directors of the Imperial Continental Gas Association, though Glyn's were not the bankers. The project was conceived by Major-General Sir William Congreve, a scientist and inventor responsible for the Congreve rockets. He was appointed Government Inspector of Gases and prepared reports on the new gas industry. He then interested a number of financiers in the Association intended to receive proposals for lighting any town or city on the continent. One of the presidents was Isaac Goldschmid, who

[21] London Metropolitan Archives, CLC B/192/MS 11658/2, Globe Treasury Committee, 15 Oct. 1835.

[22] Ibid, 6 Mar. 1834, MS 11658/4 14 Jul. 1851, 19 Feb. 1852 and 21 Apr. 1853.

[23] Parliamentary Debates (PD), 141, 1944–5, 4 May 1856.

[24] *Morning Post*, 16 Jan. 1821.

was on the board of the Globe, another was Matthew Attwood, the banker. Horsley Palmer and Poulett Thompson were on the board. It was criticised at an early stage for payments to directors though these included payments to Congreve, the chairman, for visits to the continent and for payments to agents in Europe. Glyn's association with the company was short lived as although he attended several early board meetings he retired before the annual general meeting in 1826.[25] Congreve died in 1828 before the company was profitable. Unlike many other companies established in the boom of 1825 in the longer term it was successful and had contracts in Ghent, Amsterdam, Berlin, and Vienna as well as in several French cities, though the capital remained overwhelmingly in English hands. From 1832 the Association regularly paid modest dividends and in the next ten years or so and raised more capital on three occasions. It later prospered and by 1900 its capital had grown to £7,524,000 when it was supplying ten major European cities and 29 small towns in France and Austria.[26]

George's involvement with the leading domestic gas company lasted much longer, though this arose when he seized an opportunity following a failure of another bank. The Gas Light and Coke Company, following a successful bill, had obtained a royal charter in 1812 with a capital of £1,000,000. In November 1828 its bankers, Frys and Chapman, suspended payment. The company tried to persuade the Bank of England to accept their account but the Bank refused as many of the dividend payments were for less than £5 and it was not their practice to make advances to account holders when requested to do so. Glyn wrote to Benjamin Newton, a director of the gas company to say, 'that it will give very great satisfaction to our house if the directors will allow us to offer them our services and any advance which they may require.' Discussions followed with Glyn and Charles Mills with the outcome that Glyn became Treasurer and Glyn's became the company's bankers, a role which continued until nationalisation, having lent the firm many millions without security.[27] Glyn himself was the Treasurer for 40 years until 1869 as advancing years gave warning that it was incumbent upon him to resign the post.[28]

25 London Metropolitan Archives (LMA), CLC/B/22 MS23327/1 and MS23341/1.

26 Ibid, 21 Jan. 1825; *The Times*, 9 Jan. 1826; *Imperial Continental Gas Association, 1824–1974*, 1974, 1–5; P.L. Cottrell, La Cooperation financiere, Franco-Anglaise, 1850–1880, in *La position internationale de la France: aspects économiques et financiers XIXe-XXe siècles*, ed. Maurice Lévy-Leboyer, 1977, 178, note 3.

27 Stirling Everard, *The History of the Gas Light and Coke Company, 1812–1849*, 1949, 109–110 (letter from Glyn dated 28 Nov. 1828).

28 Letter of 8 Nov. 1869, reproduced in Everard, 235–236.

The 1824–25 boom in company promotion did not bring George into the many railway projects that were initiated, except in one instance: he was one of the directors appointed at the initial meeting of the London and South Wales Railroad Committee at the City Tavern on 30 December 1824. Alderman Thompson was in the chair, and the directors included Thomas Wilson, MP for the City of London. Glyn's with Cocks and Biddulph, the West End bank, were bankers to the company, which was to have a capital of £1,000,000 but nothing came of the project.[29] Although his father-in-law, Pascoe Grenfell, was a deputy chairman of the abortive London Northern Railroad, neither George nor Glyn's Bank were involved – the bankers were Sir James Esdaile, Hammett and Grenfell, the Grenfell being Pascoe's son, Pascoe St Leger.[30]

However George was more closely and directly associated with a large and successful infrastructure project which pointed to his own future interest and that of the bank in the field of transport – St Katharine's Dock. Although there had been a considerable growth of docks in England throughout the eighteenth century the rapid increase came after 1785 stimulated by the upsurge in foreign trade. In the decade 1780–89 imports to the United Kingdom averaged £13.7 million a year, but by 1810–19 had risen to £31.6 million and were to rise still further in the 1820s to an average of £38.3 million. Exports in the 1780s were only £10.2 million, but by 1810–19 were averaging £35.0 million and £46.5 million in the 1820s.[31] There was a parallel growth in docks. In 1700 the first wet dock in the country had been constructed, nearly 10 acres in extent at Rotherhithe on the Thames in south east London. By 1787, there were 48 acres of dock and basin accommodation in England, and by the end of the century 78 acres. More rapid expansion followed and by 1815 the total stood at 340 acres. Most of this expansion was at four ports – London, Liverpool, Hull and Bristol. Over 180 acres of docks

[29] *The Times*, 31 Dec. 1824. William Thompson was a wealthy ironmaster, the proprietor of Pen Y Darran and Tredegar Works. For most of the period 1827–1854 he was a director of the Bank of England. Deputy chairman and then Chairman St Katharine's Dock 1848–54. Chairman of Lloyds. MP for various constituencies from 1820–54. Wilson acted as a spokesman for the City's shipping and mercantile interests, but refused to join the aldermanic body.

[30] Penny Watts-Russell, Travelling Steam, Pascoe Grenfell MP and the London Northern Railroad, *JRCHS*, 210, 2011, 34–46.

[31] These figures for imports and exports are expressed in official values which were largely related to constant prices in this period and so in effect were volume figures. They are taken from Peter Mathias, *The First Industrial Nation*, tables 14 and 15, 431 and 432, 1983 edition, 431–432 based on R.B. Mitchell and P. Deane, *Abstract of British Historical Statistics*, 1962, 279–281 and 203–205.

were constructed in London between 1800 and 1815, the West India Docks of 1806 and the Commercial Docks of 1815 being particularly extensive.[32] Some, like the West India Dock and the East India Dock, were mainly for goods traded to or from particular destinations for which they were granted monopolies. The London Docks had a similar monopoly in respect of certain products rather than geographical areas. Others like the Commercial Dock had no monopolies and aimed to attract trade particularly from Northern Europe, especially timber. The cost of dock space created in London in these 15 years was at least £15,400,000.[33] The end of the war meant there was little investment in docks between until the 1820s. The decline in the long term rate of interest after 1820 made investors seek more rewarding outlets for their funds. In the debate on the St Katharine's Dock Bill in 1824. William Haldimand, who was a leading shareholder pointed out that the interest on capital was so low that it forced money into new channels and reduced the rate of profit on old ones, Another factor was the decline in the price of goods. Bar iron was £13.5 per ton at the beginning of 1816, but only £8.8 in 1823 and the index of the price of the principal industrial products fell from an average of 190 in the years 1810–14 to 118 from 1820–24.[34]

However changes in the price of money and goods were not the only factors at work. To what extent the City of London was an active supporter of free trade in the nineteenth century has been a matter of debate between historians.[35] What is relevant here is that the drive for the removal of privileges in the London docks to reduce barriers to trade was supported by those who pressed for more general free trade. Thomas Tooke, a partner in the great Russian firm of Astell, Tooke and Thornton, attended a small dinner party at the house of S.C. Holland, a merchant from Liverpool and a partner in Barings since 1814. The intention was to further the cause of free trade but Tooke was struck by the poor grasp of economic principles on the part of many present and so was asked to draw up a petition. This was signed by almost 200 London merchants and presented to the House of Commons on 6 May 1820 by Alexander Baring who was to bring in the St Katharine's Dock Bill in 1825.[36] The petition asserted that the

[32] D. Swann, The Pace and Progress of Port Investment in England, *Yorkshire Bulletin of Economic and Social Research*, 12, 1960, 38–39.

[33] Walter M. Stern, The First London Dock Boom and the Growth of the West India Docks, *Economica*, 19, 1952, 71.

[34] A.D. Gayer, W.W. Rostow and A.J. Schwartz, *The Growth and Fluctuations of the British Economy, 1790–1850,* 1953, 1,152; Mathias, 421.

[35] A.C. Howe, Free Trade and the City of London, c 1820–1870, *History,* 77, 1992, 390.

[36] Then MP for Taunton. Created Baron Ashburton, 1835.

maxim of buying in the cheapest market and selling in the dearest, which regulated every merchant in his individual dealings, was strictly applicable for the whole of the nation. The signatories of the petition were perhaps not representative of the City as a whole but they included several who in April 1821 founded the Political Economy Club. G.W. Norman was at the heart of this group of radical intellectuals and city business men which did try to win over City figures to free trade. Norman noted that some city merchants so little appreciated the doctrine of free trade as to steadfastly resist its practical application, especially if it in any way appeared to touch the private interests of the signers.[37] Early members included C.G. de H. Larpent, a member of the East India merchants, Cockerell & Co., as well as Thomas Tooke, both directors of St Katharine's Dock and later of the London and Birmingham Railway. In 1829 John Horsley Palmer, also a director of the Dock Company, was elected to the Club.[38] Palmer, with George Carr Glyn's father, Sir Richard, and Larpent, Lubbock and Haldimand, three of the directors of St Katharine's Dock were among the signatories of the petition calling on the Lord Mayor to call a public meeting on the Corn Laws.[39] George himself had attended the meeting at the London Tavern in 1823 to adopt measures for the greater security of money advanced by merchants in the course of their financial transactions – the start of the successful campaign for the Factors Act of 1823.[40]

In the case of the docks a particular stimulus to the call for freer trade was that the privileges granted to existing dock companies were about to expire and their renewal was subject to the scrutiny of Parliament. Under the Act of 1799 all vessels arriving from the West Indies with cargoes of West Indian produce had to unload and land their cargoes within the West India Dock system. Outward bound vessels for the West Indies were required to load in the West India Docks. The purpose was to ensure that the proprietors would receive a satisfactory return on their capital. Similar privileges were granted to the London Dock by its Act of 1800.

In 1822 the West India Dock Company applied to Parliament for a renewal of their privileges, due to expire the following year, which was referred to the Commons Committee on Foreign Trade under the chairmanship of

[37] G.W. Norman, *Autobiography*, unpublished manuscript in Kent Archives Office, quoted in Howe, op cit, 392.

[38] David Kynaston, *The City of London, 1, A World of its Own, 1815–1890*, 1991, 44.

[39] *Morning Chronicle*, 5 Apr. 1825.

[40] Sean Thomas, The Origins of the Factors Acts, 1823 and 1825, *Journal of Legal History*, 32, 2011, 157–187.

Thomas Wallace, Vice-president of the Board of Trade from 1818 to 1823.[41] The West India Company argued that standard classification and treatment of goods was advantageous and security of the traders and the public revenue was brought about by the administration being in the hands of a company that could afford to do its work well. The docks had been profitable by 1803 and in subsequent years a dividend of 10 per cent had been declared. Moreover it would be unfair to curtail privileges when there was insufficient trade to fill warehouses when they had enjoyed them during the period of wartime prosperity. The London Dock whose own privileges were to expire in 1826 but which had never paid out more than 6 per cent, opposed the renewal of privileges in part because of their high capital expenditure, in part in the hope that they could divert some trade to themselves from the West India Dock.

The Committee on Foreign Trade reported on 3 June 1823. They took the view that the advantage to the public of open competition would not as a general principle be questioned. The grant of privilege was justified initially when it was necessary to hold out liberal compensation to those who invested their capital in a speculation which was doubtful of success despite the advantages it promised to the adventurous and the public. But it was for the parties soliciting exclusive privileges to show that so strong an especial case existed as to offer advantage sufficient to outweigh the beneficial principle of competition. In the case of the West India Dock the factors that led to the grant of privilege had long since vanished. The investment of capital had been fully compensated. The advantages were insufficient to warrant a continuation of privilege and should be replaced by open competition between docks in the Port of London.

Meanwhile the plan for St Katharine's Dock was getting under way. The site chosen was very close to the seat of commerce, being between the Tower of London and the newly constructed London Docks. How far this was the best site for new docks was vigorously debated at the time and later historians have also voiced strong doubts. A high price had to be paid for the site both in what would now be regarded as a loss of amenity and of housing, and in terms of money. Moreover it was an initiative by a committed group of private investors without any regard to any overall plan for the docks, though there was no body with any responsibility for such a plan.

Essentially the plan for the dock, drawn up by Thomas Telford in 1824, was superimposed on the existing street plan. The 23 acre site, though smaller than that required for the London Dock, included the old foundation

[41] He became Baron Wallace in 1828.

of St Katharine's Hospital with a landing place, a brewery, and some 1,100 houses. The hospital for the poor had been founded by Queen Matilda, wife of King Stephen, in the twelfth century on 13 acres of land belonging to the Canons of Augustine of the priory of Holy Trinity, Aldgate. Queen Philippa, wife of Edward III, had founded a chantry there. It subsequently became a royal peculiar removed from the civil jurisdiction of the City and the ecclesiastical jurisdiction of the Bishop of London and consequently had escaped confiscation at the time of the Dissolution of the Monasteries. It was maintained by an establishment of lay bothers and sisters. The sentimental interest of the public in St Katharine's Hospital was used by opponents of the new Dock. 'A Clergyman' argued in a tract that on every principle of propriety and decency the occupancy of the soil by St Katharine's church for seven centuries ought to operate as a barrier against secular intrusion and the dock company should be directed elsewhere. There were more generalised attacks on the project.[42] An anonymous member of the public wrote to Lords Liverpool and Eldon[43] claiming that the fatal doctrine might be established that a mercantile interest might be planted in the ruins of a sanctuary, and that the temples of the Deity might be violated for the purpose of erecting docks or dens.[44]

If the promoters can be criticised for demolishing an ancient church, the housing was of very poor quality. The St Katharine Dock promoters described it as a collection of hovels inhabited by the lowest sections of the community but more objective reports show that the inhabitants were small tradesmen, manufacturers and watermen as well as some wealthy residents. In any case the vocal opposition was largely removed by the trustees of the St Katharine Foundation coming to terms with the promoters of the new dock. The brothers exchanged their residences by the river for accommodation near the new Regent's Park, but the poor who lost their houses or hovels had no voice, and there was no obligation to find accommodation for the tenants of the houses whose landlords were compensated.[45]

It is not clear how or why Glyn's came to be associated with the project but from the start they were given the key banking role and George was chosen by his partners in the bank to represent them. His subscribers' notebook dated March 1824 contains an initial list of 67 names, overwhelmingly London, and mostly City, based.[46] The directors each got together a

[42] Sir Joseph G. Broadbank, *History of the Port of London*, 1921, 1, 153.

[43] The Prime Minister and Lord Chancellor.

[44] Museum of Docklands Archives, St Katharine's Dock, 95.

[45] Broadbent, 1, 154.

[46] RBS Archives, GM/176/3.

list generally totalling £50,000 of individual subscriptions. The largest individual subscriptions came from Pascoe Grenfell (£32,000), Baring Bros and Thomas Wilson (£30,000 each). George Carr Glyn's list included a personal subscription of £3,000, £4,000 from his father and £1,000 from his brother Thomas Christopher Glyn. Others in the Bank put up money – Charles Mills £3,000, his brother E. Wheeler Mills £2,000 and Thomas Hallifax £1.000, while William Crawshay and Thomas Fairlie each put up £5,000. William Crawshay was primarily a merchant in iron trading at George Yard, Upper Thames Street, who had inherited a share in the Cyfartha ironworks – Glyn's were the London agent for the Cyfartha Bank. He would have been well known to Pascoe Grenfell as Thomas Williams had briefly been in partnership with his father, Richard Crawshay, in the Union Ironworks in the Rhymney Valley, though William had refused to join. Pascoe Grenfell's list included, as well as his own subscription, his sons, Pascoe St Leger (£2,000) and Charles Pascoe (£1,000), Owen Williams (£9,000) and Sir Edmund Knowles Lacon, a Norfolk landowner and banker of Lacon, Youell & Co. in Yarmouth, for whom Glyn's were the London agents. Thomas Telford who was appointed engineer, did not subscribe personally but collected a list of four subscribers contributing £10,000 in total. The other prospective directors with lists were all influential figures. Palmer was then a member of a leading Indian House and by 1828 was the deputy Governor of the Bank of England and from 1830–33 was the Governor. Haldimand too was a director of the Bank, and MP for Ipswich.

Glyn's notebook of April 1824 has entries amounting to £900,000, compared with the cost estimated in February 1824 as £970,448 of which £278,000 was for purchase of the land, £270,000 for excavation, £372,000 for warehouses and £50,000 for surveys and legal management.

The MPs on the board, such as Haldimand, Thomas Wilson and Alexander Baring, as well as Pascoe Grenfell whose son was a director, facilitated the Bill's passage in Parliament. However because of shortage of time in the 1824 Session, opposition from other dock interests and criticism of the impact the dock would have on the parish of St Katharine's, the Bill did not succeed until 1825. The preamble to the Bill argued that docks in future should be established on the basis of free competition in trade and without any exclusive privileges and immunities. The London Dock Company denied in its petition that any additional docks were required.

On 25 February 1824 the House decided by 78 votes to 30 to grant leave to introduce the bill, but several owners and occupiers of land had submitted a petition in which they complained they had not had time to consider the matter. On 2 April a motion to delay the bill effectively to the next session was defeated by 74 votes to 55. There was however considerable opposition, and indeed a majority of those who spoke were against the Bill. Even the Chancellor of the Exchequer, F.J. Robinson,[47] was hesitant in the face of the views expressed. He explained that the Government had expressed acquiescence, and had no objection if it could be shown that benefit to the public would ensue. However they were not aware of all the circumstances: so many interests were involved. Grenfell replied that it was wrong to say that 10,000 persons were exposed to inconvenience, as had been alleged. The whole population of St Katharine's parish did not amount to 5,000 and of the 1,100 to 1,200 householders, 300 had expressed assent.[48] In Committee there was strong opposition from interested parties, so no further progress was made in the 1824 Session.

After this failure the committee of subscribers chaired by Thomas Tooke, of which Glyn was a member, reported to a general meeting held on 19 August 1824 when it was decided to go ahead. This committee supervised work on the Bill which was reintroduced at the beginning of the Session of 1825.

The directors then produced *Considerations*, at the end of which the cases in favour and against were summarised. In favour were the public, against them were ranged individual interests and advocates for exclusive privileges and compulsory regulations. In favour were the commercial, manufacturing and shipping interests, the importers of raw materials to the uses of British industry and the consumers of foreign commodities in the Metropolis and its vicinity and many of its outports; against were certain of the shareholders in the several docks of the Port of London, and some of the wharfingers and warehouse-keepers. For the Bill were friends of free trade competition, reasonable charges, and improved management. Against were the promoters of monopoly and such as benefit by exorbitant rates. The document ended with '*Publicum bonum privato preferendum est.*'

Grenfell and Alderman Thompson presented the petition for the Bill in 1825 which progressed quickly and smoothly through the Commons. In the Lord's the leading witness for the Bill was John Hall who had written *Considerations* and was to become secretary to the new company. He was a shipowner who was consul general for Hanover in the United Kingdom from 1816 to 1854.[49] He based the case for the new dock on the increase in traffic in the port of London – 13,949 ships in 1794 to 20,685 in 1822 and 23,618 in 1824. Although the building of docks had initially reduced the number of ships mooring in the river there were now more ships in the

47 Later Viscount Goderich and then Earl of Ripon.

48 PD, 11, 100 and 101, 2 Apr. 1824.

49 1779–1861, knighted 1831.

river than when dock building was first authorised. When the privileges of the East India Dock expired in 1827 the private Indiamen would want to move to docks nearer London and escape the high dock charges there. The London Dock quays were crowded.[50] Others supported him. Despite objections from the London and West India Dock companies the Lords approved the Bill. No monopolies were given to the company and the rates charged on shipping were limited to those in force at other docks protected by walls.

The Company's prospectus was quickly published on 30 June 1825. It emphasised the necessity of giving the public additional convenient wet docks and bonding accommodation near the seat of business in the Port of London. A reduction in the rates and charges was needed as it was alleged that trade had been lured away to Europe by lower charges. The new dock was to be surrounded by protective walls especially suitable for more valuable cargoes and the warehouses were to be close to the edge of the basin and quays to save on labour. It was envisaged that 1,400 merchant ships a year would be accommodated with the locks constructed as to provide access during any state of the tide.[51]

The Act stated that £1,352,750, the estimated cost of the new dock, should be the capital stock of the company. £1,089.000 had already been subscribed. Power was also given to raise a further £500,000 by capital stock or by borrowing or both. The capital was easily raised primarily from the directors and friends and families who had been listed in George Carr Glyn's notebook as prospective subscribers. Glyn himself was included in a shareholders list of 1827 as having over £10,000 in shares, as was Charles Pascoe Grenfell, while other members of their families held smaller amounts. The shareholders were almost entirely London based though Hardman Earle of Liverpool and members of his family, Thomas Entwistle of Manchester and Kirkman Finlay of Glasgow held substantial sums.[52]

The first directors of the company included Glyn, but not any of the Barings. The interest of the Grenfell family was represented not by Pascoe himself, but by his son Charles Pascoe. The first meeting of the Board took place on 16 June. Thomas Tooke was appointed chairman with Larpent as deputy chairman, William Tooke, solicitor (Thomas's brother) and Thomas Telford, engineer, with Philip Hardwick as surveyor and architect, both the latter at salaries of £500 per annum. Soon afterwards Peter Logan who had

50 Quoted in Broadbent, 1, 156–157.

51 *The Times*, 30 Jun. 1825.

52 MDL Archives, St Katharine's Dock, 96.

been working on Dundee Harbour was appointed resident engineer at the same salary.[53]

Glyn was appointed Treasurer and Glyn's were invited to be Treasurers to the undertaking so involving the bank as well as Glyn himself. Every year the minutes were to note with approval the payment of £10.10s customary Christmas gratuity to the Clerks of Glyn Mills & Co. Glyn was initially a member of the Building Works and Compensation Committee which had the general supervision of the purchases, works, and contracts, though that was soon split and Glyn became a member of the Compensation rather than the Building Committee. He was soon to be a member of the Finance Committee and the Systems, Establishment and Rates Committee. He was thus in a powerful position in the Company, his concerns going beyond narrow financial issues. When the Dock Committee was formed in 1828 under the chairmanship of Thomas Tooke himself Glyn was a member and regularly attended the weekly meetings and occasionally took the chair.[54]

The Dock was based on outline plan drawn up by Telford and Philip Hardwick. Telford had done little work in London and had played no part in the building of the earlier London docks. William Jessop was responsible for the West India Docks and John Rennie the London Docks, and, in association with Ralph Walker, the East India Docks. The plans for St Katharine's Dock had been drawn up in 1824. The site was cleared by May 1826. Telford had completed Menai Bridge earlier in that year, but he was now 67 years of age with many other commitments and he relied heavily on Thomas Rhodes who had worked with him on the Caledonian Canal and on the Menai. Rhodes was initially inspecting foreman engineer, but was appointed resident engineer in 1828. In contrast to Telford Philip Hardwick was in the early stages of his career. He had begun his independent practice in 1816 as surveyor to the Bethlehem Hospital which had moved to a new building in St George's Fields, Southwark the previous year. Glyn's father, Sir Richard, had laid the foundation stone when he was President of the Hospital and Glyn himself was later on the court of governors.[55] St Katharine's Dock was Hardwick's first major commission. His first role was that of surveyor in the negotiations to purchase the site. His success with the dock warehouses was to lead to other commissions in the City including Goldsmith's Hall, the City Club and the hall and library at Lincoln's Inn. The connections he made led him to designing country houses for city bankers. An early example was the rebuilding of Chadacre Hall for Thomas Hallifax. By then he had been

[53] Unlike Telford he would be expected to be full time on this contract or virtually so.

[54] MDL Archives, 117, St Katharine's Dock, Dock Committee minutes.

[55] Jonathon Andrews et al, *The History of Bethlem*, 1997, 409.

appointed surveyor to the London and Birmingham Railway, like Glyn and others being associated with both dock and railway, though originally his work for the railway was expected to be 'quite occasional'.[56] While retained by the railway the Globe Insurance building in Pall Mall was rebuilt from his designs.

The plans drawn up in 1824 were generally followed in the construction of the Dock. The main problem was how to fit the most dock accommodation into a restricted and awkwardly shaped site. When space had been allowed for warehouses the area of water available for the dock basins was only ten acres. Telford was only able to fit two basins to the site and in doing so had to abandon the rigid rectangular shapes adopted by Jessop and Rennie in the earlier docks. He provided an entrance basin of 1¾ acres, 180 feet in length between gates and 45 feet wide with a single pair of gates from the river. The entrance was deeper than that of the London Dock. Two basins each with a single lock from the entrance basin rather than one large one were provided. The locks allowed the entry of ships of no larger size than the West India Dock designed in 1799. The water area of the west dock was 4 acres and the east dock 4¼ acres. There were to be lofty warehouses surrounding the docks on three sides, the warehouses having their front wall supported on massive iron columns on the edge of the quay. This was in contrast to the West India and London Docks where the warehouses were set back about 50 feet from the water's edge, with a road and a narrow transit shed between the warehouses and the water so that an initial sorting of the goods could be made before they were housed on the warehouse floor. The intention at St Katharine's was to save the labour used in the preliminary sorting by getting the goods from the ship directly on to the warehouse floor. This was effective when the cargoes were of the same kind and destined for the same warehouse but more costly when mixed. This design was not repeated at any of the London docks built subsequently.

Three tenders were received in January 1826. That of George Burge, then only thirty and who was first brought into prominence by his work at the dock, was accepted at only £225.000 in comparison with that of Thomas Townshend for £392,000 and Thomas Thatcher (£345,000).[57] Possibly

[56] TNA, RAIL 1108/89, Glyn to Cropper, 19 Dec. 1833.

[57] Burge later built the timber pier at Herne Bay, undertook tunnel works at Dover and was the principal contractor for Box Tunnel. Townshend was well established by the 1820s having worked for John Rennie. Later ran into difficulties with Tring Cutting on the London and Birmingham Railway. Thatcher had worked on the Kennet and Avon Canal and the City Canal on the Isle of Dogs. *Biographical Dictionary of Civil Engineers in Great Britain and Ireland, 1600–1830*, ed. A. Skempton, 1, 2002, 105, 712–713 and 695–697.

Burge put in a very low tender to undercut more established contractors. Progress at first was slow as Burge was hampered by lack of room but by October eight pile engines were at work on the coffer dam. By the middle of January 1827 work on the cofferdam had probably finished and so excavation could take place below tide level. The soil excavated for the construction of the dock was removed in barges to Millbank and provided a firm base for Thomas Cubitt's buildings in Belgravia. One witness said that a thousand men were employed on the excavations. In June 1828 the directors reported that the dock would be ready to receive ships by October and the rest of the works would be completed by the end of 1829. The formal opening of the basin, west dock and a large shed facing the basin took place on Saturday 25 October 1828, when the first nine ships entered the dock two years and six months after the start of the excavations.[58] Telford later wrote 'As a practical engineer I must protest against such haste, pregnant as it was and ever will be, with risks, which in more instances than one severely tasked all my experience and skill, involving dangerously the reputation of the directors and their engineer.'[59]

However the east dock was still unfinished. The money was running out as by 1828 costs had overrun by 7½ per cent. A total cost of £1,827,000 was then estimated including some additions to the project.[60] Costs had risen initially because the sums required for compensation of householders and businesses in the parish of St Katharine were almost always greater than expected. Some 11,000 people were displaced by the works. About £125,000 was paid to the Hospital for its land and interests with a further £36,000 for replacement buildings for the hospital chapel and residences near Gloucester Gate in Regent's Park. Loans therefore had to be raised in the final stage of construction. An arrangement was entered into in April and May with Glyn's to meet the engagement of the Dock Co. between April and the end of 1828 whereby the last two calls of 10 per cent would be delayed until later in the year. The loan amounted to £100,000 with interest at 4 per cent. £25,000 was borrowed in April, £40,000 more by June and £35,000 in October. In June it was agreed to raise a loan of £500,000 for which authority had been given in the 1825 Act. In December a loan of £200,000 was agreed with the Bank of England, half of which was advanced against a debenture and half against promissory notes from eight directors. £50,000 went towards paying off the £100,000 borrowed from Glyn's who then extended the remaining £50,000 of their loan which was repaid in June 1829. The Bank of England

[58] A.W. Skempton, *Civil Engineers and Engineering in Britain, 1600–1830*, 1996, 82–85.

[59] Autobiography, quoted in L.T.C. Rolt, *Thomas Telford*, 1958, 144.

[60] MDL Archives, 96/1.

was repaid in June and August 1829. Fortunately these demands came at a time when the money market was easy.

Burge completed the contract and water was ready to be admitted to the East Dock on 27 November 1829, but the warehouses round the east dock were only completed in 1830. However the financial position was still difficult. In January 1830 a special meeting of the proprietors had been called as although expenditure was within the revised estimate they would still have to find nearly £200,000 and in view of the possibility of an additional warehouse being needed the meeting agreed to seek parliamentary sanction for loans of £300,000. The necessary Act received Royal Assent on 8 April and it was agreed that £200,000 should be borrowed immediately. Tooke, Larpent and Glyn were asked to arrange the disposal of these debentures. Within a week £132,700 had been placed at 3 per cent. In late October Glyn was authorised to place a further £50,000 debentures on the most advantageous terms but not under par. Another loan from the Bank was taken out in December, and renewed in March 1831 which the company succeeded in repaying by the following July, though in November a £60,000 mortgage was to be taken by the chairman and deputy chairman at not more than 4½ per cent.[61]

By May 1830 four years after the start of construction virtually all work on St Katharine's Dock had been finished. The Company possessed a dock fully open for traffic conforming to the best contemporary principles of dock design. However although the dock was moderately successful commercially, it never quite lived up to its founders' expectations. When it opened there was not sufficient business in the Port of London to fill all the docks and the competition led to lower rates for the traffic secured, though some business was diverted to St Katharine's from the older docks which had lost their protection.[62] Consequently for the first three years after opening St Katharine's only 3 per cent was paid and then for two years the dividend was as low as 2½ per cent. This was followed by a gradual improvement and in 1838 5 per cent was reached at which level it remained until 1846. St Katharine's was not alone in making only a modest return. The London Dock did little better and even the West India Dock company which had maintained a 10 per cent dividend until 1829 paid only 5 per cent in 1832 and 4½ per cent in 1837 just before their amalgamation with the East India Dock Company. By then the latter Company had lost its monopoly of Indian trade and ceased to be a trading concern with its own ships. As the East India

61 MDL Archives, 126/1.

62 R.R. Ashbee, George Carr Glyn and St Katharine's Dock, *Three Banks Review*, 129, 1981, 52.

Company had its own warehouses in the City, none had been built at their Docks, and so the accommodation was not suitable for many other traders.

It gradually became clear that St Katharine's Dock had distinct limitations. Its capital cost was relatively high. The dock companies were highly competitive and overall there was too much capacity so raising the rates was not feasible. They had to search for business. Something of the rivalry between the London docks can be seen from a report by the former boarding clerk for St Katharine's Dock Company resident at Gravesend for nine years. He had boarded, frequently with unexpected success to his employer from an open boat, 17 feet 10 inches in length, no fewer than 20,710 vessels from foreign parts and on them had sailed the equivalent of more than once round the world.[63] Unloading direct into a warehouse was only an advantage if the whole of the cargo could be dealt with in the area where the ship docked. The design was more relevant to the needs of the 1820s and earlier decades than the 1830s and certainly than the 1840s. As free trade grew there was much less need to use bonding facilities in warehouses or what were known as Legal Quays. Built mainly to accommodate cargoes of low bulk and high value, they had not sufficient space to deal conveniently with bulk cargoes particularly timber from Northern Europe which had to be stored and seasoned in raff yards adjacent to the dock to avoid the labour and cost of further handling. In two crucial respects St Katharine's was poorly placed to take advantage of progress into the age of steam. Steamships increased rapidly in number and more importantly in size and St Katharine's was so far up river to make access difficult, even more so than the West India Dock, and it also had difficulty in accommodating the larger vessels. In 1840 it was calculated a dock built to cater for 140 'normal' sailing ships of 300 tons could only accommodate 35 foreign going steamers.[64] Moreover both the site and design of St Katharine's meant that it could not be linked with the growing railway system which by the 1840s was linking London with almost all large provincial towns.

Generally therefore the experience of investors in the dock companies after 1828 did not encourage the promotion of other dock companies in London or investment in the existing ones. At St Katharine's there was little change in the composition of the board. By the end of 1834, ten years after the board had been formed, there were only two new faces. Glyn retained the Treasurership and took the chair on occasions, apparently as the unofficial vice-chairman. Glyn's made temporary advances from time to time to enable dividends to be paid and lent £30,000 in 1847 to pay off a

[63] *The Times*, 3 Dec. 1842.

[64] Evidence of James Walker on the Hull Dock Bill, 15 Jun. 1840.

debenture. In 1847 Sir George Barclay, C.P. Grenfell, Larpent and Palmer, all on the original board were still serving as directors while Tooke and John Hall, continued as chairman and secretary until the mid 1850s. Glyn still attended directors' meetings regularly and kept up an active interest in the progress of the dock.[65] In the 1850s there were major changes in the board. Tooke stepped down and W.S. Gladstone became chairman. Glyn's name appeared less and less frequently among those listed as attending the board and not at all in the 1860s.[66]

In 1846–48 an average of 688 ships from foreign parts bearing 172,000 tons docked in St Katharine's, while 132,000 tons were loaded. Traffic improved slightly in the 1850s. St Katharine's began work on extra warehousing in 1852. Two buildings were added on the south side of the entrance basin designed by George Aitchison, Hardwick's colleague. However in the mid-1850s, in contrast to the 1,400 merchant ships a year envisaged in the prospectus, the number averaged 960 and although by then the vessels may on average have been larger, the amount in the warehouses was less than half the capacity stated in the prospectus at least on the year-end dates for which data is available. Traffic to the dock was not assisted by the Customs Consolidation Act of 1853 which sanctioned the use of legal quays and bonded warehouses outside the docks. Gladstone's free trade policy meant that the number of goods requiring customs clearance was reduced from 1052 to 48. In this period dividends amounted to about 4 per cent.

New docks in London adapted to the steam age were overdue. The breakthrough came with the Victoria Dock, not inspired by the railway shareholders, their boards or the existing dock companies, but by railway contractors, particularly Peto who with Betts and Brassey obtained an Act of Parliament in 1850 to build on a dock on Plaistow Marshes on the north bank of the Thames, further downstream than existing docks but directly linked with the railway system. The first dock built expressly for steamships, it had an entrance and area of water surface larger than any existing dock in a great rectangle, with half a mile of quays on either side. The entrance locks gave 28 feet of depth so taking steamships of up to 8,000 tons comfortably. In 1860 the dock received 854,000 tons of shipping, double that of the London Dock, four times that of St Katharine's and 70 per cent more than the East and West India Docks combined. In 1864 the Millwall Dock Company was incorporated. In the same year the St Katharine Dock Company amalgamated with the London Dock Company, its dividend having gradually declined from 5 per cent of 1845 to 3½ per cent in 1863.

[65] MDLA, 131.

[66] Ashbee, 53.

Although Glyn with Tooke, Barclay, Lubbock, Larpent and others continued for so long as directors of St Katharine's Dock, the construction of the dock had hardly been completed before they were vigorously engaged in promoting and then constructing and running the country's first main line railway from London to the Midlands. By the end of 1830 not only was George Carr Glyn a director and the Treasurer of the London and Birmingham Railway, his associates on the St Katharine's Dock Board, Barclay and Larpent had been to examine the Liverpool and Manchester Railway on the new company's behalf. It is not recorded whether at that stage they foresaw any of the factors which were to make their dock project rather anachronistic. The railway of the 1830s was not open to this criticism.

CHAPTER FIVE

The London and Birmingham Railway – Development and Management

IT WOULD BE an exaggeration to say that the origins of the London and Birmingham Railway were to be found in St Katharine's Dock, but the London merchants and bankers concerned with the financing and management of the Dock played a prominent part in the foundation of the railway. The boom of 1824–25 which saw the birth of the Dock also resulted in the promotion of a number of railway projects, some realistic, some not.

The heady atmosphere was encapsulated by Robert Stephenson & Co., a firm established in 1823, which in January 1825 drew up a proposed allocation of duties of the firm's surveyors between the London and Northern Railroad, the Liverpool and Manchester, Liverpool and Birmingham, and London and South Wales.[1] This proved to be premature as most projects envisaged during the boom disappeared when the crash came in December 1825. The main exception was the Liverpool and Manchester Railway (LMR) though it only secured Parliamentary approval in 1826, having failed as a result of the opposition of landed and canal interests in 1825. The breakthrough in the development of mainline railways came with the success of the LMR. Soon after it opened in 1830 the LMR was exceeding the quantities of traffic estimated by the promoters, particularly of passengers, which had been based on existing levels of traffic on roads and canals so demonstrating that railways could create new traffic. Moreover it was accomplished by the successful completion of a line of 36 miles, including the engineering feats of crossing Chat Moss and excavating the cutting and tunnels into Liverpool, and by the convincing demonstration of the effectiveness of steam locomotive haulage. A standard of performance by

[1] J.G.H. Warren, *A Century of Locomotive Building by Robert Stephenson & Co., 1823–1923*, 1923, 64.

locomotives was achieved, initially at the Rainhill trials and subsequently by the daily running of trains, not previously regarded as within the realms of practicality. Property was damaged less than feared and the value of adjacent land tended to increase.

This meant that by 1830 interest in railways revived despite the state of trade, depressed after the 1824–25 boom, which only slightly improved in the early 1830s and the unsettled political situation in Parliament and the country at large in the period leading up to the Reform Bill of 1832. Several of the first proposals for railways were aborted when the Government fell on 2 April 1831 and the short session of the new Parliament after the election meant that the more ambitious schemes had insufficient time to complete their course. But a boom in railway promotion and construction followed in the mid-1830s which owed very little to fluctuations in the general state of trade but almost everything to the successful example of the LMR.[2]

Of the projects which had come to nothing in the 1820s and which were now were revived, the first, and in many ways the most important was the London and Birmingham Railway. Schemes for linking the two towns had been mooted in the 1820s. William James had projected a Central Junction Railway in 1820 from London to Birmingham via Uxbridge, Amersham, Thame, Oxford, Moreton-in-the-Marsh and Stratford-on-Avon, though the Act of 1821 only authorised the Stratford-upon-Avon to Moreton-in-the-Marsh section, opened in 1826.[3]

In September 1824 a prospectus was issued for the Birmingham and London Railroad Company which appointed John Rennie as engineer in February 1825.[4] For much of 1825 John Grantham and his brother Edward surveyed on Rennie's behalf a route from the West and East India Docks which skirted central London and went via Watford, Tring, Bicester and Banbury to Coventry.[5] A Bill was brought before Parliament in 1826, but like the bills for a line from Birmingham to Liverpool brought forward in both 1824 and 1825 it was decisively rejected.[6] The pressure for the railway was stronger in Birmingham than in London, as between 1750 and 1831 the former's population had increased from 50,000 to 110,000, and its products were known all over the world. The demand for transport was growing – in 1800 there were only 8 coaches daily to London, taking 18 to 20 hours, but by 1831 there were 22, taking some 12 hours. By canal the quickest

[2] R.C.O. Matthews, *A Study in Trade Cycle History*, 1954, 108–109.

[3] Miles MacNair, *William James (1771–1837)*, 2007, 53–54, 99.

[4] *Aris Birmingham Gazette*, 6, 13 and 20 Sept. 1824, and 14 Mar. 1825.

[5] For Grantham see Skempton, 1, 265–266.

[6] Norman W. Webster, *Britain's First Trunk Line, The Grand Junction Railway*, 1972, 15–17.

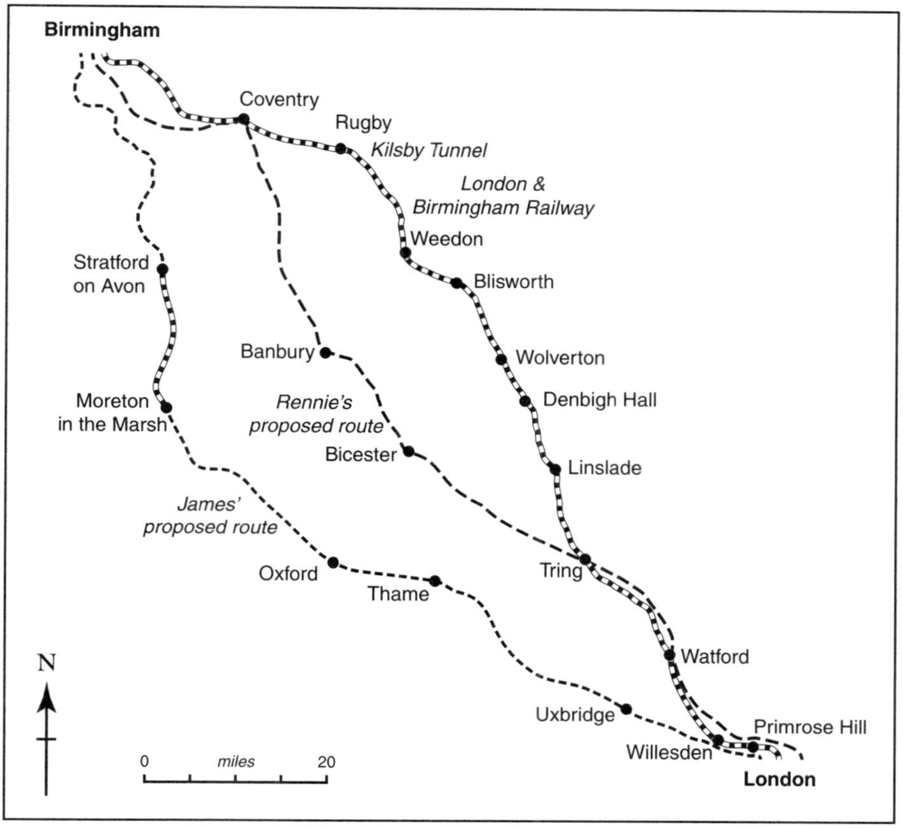

Map 1: Proposed railway routes from London to Birmingham:
William James 1820; John Rennie 1825; Robert Stephenson 1833, the adopted route.

journey to or from London took three days. Birmingham manufacturers felt they were losing out to their continental competitors as goods could not be delivered quickly enough.

In 1830 'the progress of the Liverpool and Manchester line renewed the spirit of the projectors'.[7] Two rival groups were formed with most of the impetus initially coming from Birmingham rather than London – the London, Coventry and Birmingham Railway (LCBR) and the London and Birmingham Railway (LBR). It was the former project with which Glyn, Mills, Hallifax were associated. The LCBR promoters, who met in Birmingham on 24 April and in London on 28 April favoured a route from Islington, via

[7] *Osborne's London and Birmingham Railway Guide*, 1840, 46.

Hornsey, East Barnet, South Mimms, the Dagnall gap, Leighton Buzzard, Fenny Stratford, Rugby, Coventry and on to Birmingham, then being surveyed by Frank Giles, who had earlier worked for Rennie. They later explained that this route was chosen because it deviated less than any other from the direct route between Liverpool and London, passed through the large manufacturing city of Coventry with access by the Coventry Canal to the Warwickshire coalfield and offered the great agricultural counties of Leicester and Northampton additional facilities for the conveyance of corn and cattle to Birmingham, London and other markets. It was claimed that the route presented no variations of level which could not readily be accommodated by the use of locomotive steam engines. The company stated that the conveyance of passengers and light merchandise by coaches and other carriers between Birmingham and London was supposed to cost £300,000 per annum and that of heavier articles by canal and otherwise £500,000. Consequently even if there were no additional intercourse there would be ample remuneration for a capital of £1.6 or £1.8 million. On 27 August a meeting was told that a considerable amount of shares had already been subscribed. Applications for them could be made to Glyn Mills, to the Bank of England branch in Birmingham, or to Haltons and James. Quite why Glyn Mills were associated with the LCBR rather than the London and Birmingham is not clear.[8]

The provisional committee of the LBR issued a prospectus in May. Those initially involved were primarily Birmingham orientated. The provisional committee in Birmingham had 17 members in contrast to London's five. Significantly 13 of them were also members of the provisional committee of the Liverpool and Birmingham which project was announced simultaneously. William Tooke was the solicitor to whom applications for shares in London were to be made. The proposals were referred to John Rennie, and John Grantham and his sons revised the route via Oxford and Banbury put forward in 1825. The committees met again on 19 July when they affirmed they were going ahead.

The LCBR particularly envisaged themselves as the start of a national system. Should the LMR realise the expectations that were generally entertained 'it must be highly important for all the principal towns to possess this cheap and rapid means of intercourse with the seaports, and especially with the Metropolis, and this line for the first sixty miles, more than half its extent, proceeds in the direction most convenient for all the largest towns and most important manufacturing districts in the kingdom.'

[8] *Derby Mercury*, 14 Jul. 1830; *Aris Birmingham Gazette*, 30 Aug. 1830.

From the neighbourhood of Northampton, a northern branch might proceed by Leicester to Derby where it would meet the Railway already projected by way of Belper to Manchester,[9] and form a railway communication between the great centre of cotton manufacture and London, while another branch might proceed, by way of Sheffield, to Leeds and the West Riding of Yorkshire. For these sixty miles it would be the channel through which materials landed at the Port of London would pass to the Midlands and the North and through which woollens, cotton, earthenware, coal and iron would be conveyed to London. In August they announced that in the execution of this great national work, they would have the services of Mr George Stephenson, so highly appreciated by the directors of the Manchester and Liverpool Railway, as well as those of Mr Giles.[10]

The LBR too emphasised the precedent of the LMR which was nearly completed and its success would decide whether the agency of steam could be as efficiently employed for the purposes of land carriage as for maritime power. On 26 August a deputation reported that the works on the LMR, which was to open on 13 September, were in such a state as to leave no doubt that they would fully realise 'the expectations entertained of the superiority of this mode of carriage over every other at present known'. A capital of £2,000,000 would be raised.[11]

Stephenson may have played a major part in bringing the two projects together for although the LBR committee decided on 30 August to apply to Parliament for powers to make the line from London to Birmingham, the two projects, the LBR and the LCBR soon combined. On 11, 18 and 24 September meetings of deputations from the provisional committees of the two companies, the first two meetings consisting of only Birmingham based members, were held in Birmingham with Edmund Peel from the LCBR, brother of Sir Robert Peel, then Home Secretary, in the chair. Peel was to be chairman and the LBR was to nominate the deputy. They soon agreed that eight from London should be added to the committee. Consequently Thomas Tooke, chairman of the St Katharine's Dock board, G.P. Barclay a director, and Isaac Solly, another London merchant who was chairman of the London Dock Company, were elected 'for better enabling them to establish an efficient board of management in London'. They were later appointed the first members of the London Committee,[12] but Peel,

[9] In the event only in 1863 was it possible to travel to Manchester from Derby via Belper and the Peak District.

[10] *Liverpool Mercury*, 20 Aug. 1830; *Aris Birmingham Gazette*, 30 Aug. 1830.

[11] *Aris Birmingham Gazette*, 30 Aug. 1830.

[12] TNA, RAIL 384/26, meetings of 11, 18 and 24 Sept. 1830.

Ledsam and Barker[13] later went to London with a view to increasing the London-based members.

Moilliet, Smith, Pearson and Moilliet, and the Birmingham Banking Co. were to be bankers in Birmingham and Glyn, Mills Hallifax and Co. in London. Stephenson and Son were to be the engineers. Messrs George Barker and Sons, Messrs Corrie and Carter, and William Tooke were appointed solicitors. The company was to have a capital of £2 million, 7,000 shares were to be reserved for land owners and canal proprietors on the line of the intended railway, 1,000 for the committee and 12,000 for general subscribers. It was agreed the title should be the London and Birmingham Railway and that 'an eastern line be kept in view', i.e. the route via Oxford was not favoured.

The effective inauguration of the amalgamated company came on 13 October when the Birmingham and London Committees met at the London Tavern and decided that the Company would be governed by a general committee with 20 London and 20 Birmingham representatives. The £100 shares were to be allocated to London, Birmingham and Liverpool, each of which were to have 4,000, the two committees 1,000 each, land owners and canal interests 5,000, with 1,000 in reserve. Thus even at this stage Liverpool was to be apportioned shares on the same basis as the terminal towns, though as will be seen this division between geographical areas did not work out in practice. The London members present on 13 October were all except one directors of St Katharine's Docks, and three more soon joined them.[14] It was at this meeting that Messrs Glyn & Co. were recognised as bankers in London on the understanding that one of their firm would consent to be a member of the Committee. Glyn had not been involved earlier with railways except that in 1829 he had signed the Newcastle and Carlisle subscription contract, possibly because of his links with Newcastle bankers.[15] He was not at the meeting on 13 October but came to that on 21 October and was added to the Committee on 24 October. This meant that virtually from the start the LBR had the backing of this leading City bank and George Carr Glyn started an association with a pioneering railway venture behind which he put his full weight and and which he was soon to lead. While a number joined the board who were not associated with the Dock Company, Thomas Tooke, Sir John Lubbock[16] (chairman and deputy

[13] Joseph Frederick Ledsam of Thomas Ledsam, button manufacturers, and also partner in the Birmingham Banking Co. George Barker was a prominent Birmingham solicitor.

[14] TNA, RAIL 384/1, 13 Oct. 1830.

[15] M.C. Reed, Investment in Railways in Britain, 1820–1844, 1975, 208.

[16] His London bank was the London agent of the Birmingham Banking Company.

chairman of St Katharine's), George Larpent, Barclay, and Henry Rowles as well as Glyn, remained a powerful influence on the London committee which was soon to take the lead over its counterpart in Birmingham particularly on financial matters.[17] Tooke was to serve on the board until April 1844 when his colleagues noted he was one of the few remaining directors named in the Act of Incorporation. In December 1830 a Finance Committee was established. Glyn, Lubbock, Larpent and Tooke were members. They were, inter alia, to audit all bills and accounts and to report to the board as to their expediency.[18] Peel, whose presence in the chair at the inaugural meeting had doubtless enhanced the launch of the combined company, gave way to Isaac Solly, as chairman of the Board. Solly was a Baltic trader and timber merchant, whose firm was of long-standing in the Danzig and Memel trade, and which in the Napoleonic wars had secured large contracts to supply government dockyards with Polish and Prussian oak and Russian hemp. He was sufficiently prosperous to take up £423,000 of the Prussian loan of 1818 organized by Rothschilds.[19] He was chairman of the London Dock Company for 20 years and of the British and American Steam Navigation Company, and was a member of the court of Royal Exchange Assurance.[20] Indeed that company had strong links with the LBR. Lubbock succeeded Pascoe Grenfell as Governor in 1838, and he was succeeded by Thomas Tooke. Riversdale Grenfell replaced his father on the court.[21]

The board, at this stage in practice the London Committee, was soon looking into finance, asking the Birmingham Committee for all the data upon which they based their estimate that £2 million would be sufficient capital as the Liverpool and Manchester cost £30,000 per mile. They also wished to see the estimate from which they had calculated the income to be 'derived from the work'.[22] £2 million turned out to be a compromise between the estimate of Giles and Stephenson of £1,650,000 at about £12,000 per mile and £2,500,000 which some members of the Birmingham Committee thought would be necessary. Stephenson said

17 TNA, RAIL 384/1, 13 Oct. 1830. Rowles was a major London builder and on the board of St Katharine's Dock. He was also a director of Globe Insurance from 1828. Pascoe St Leger Grenfell joined the board. He was a half brother of C.P. Grenfell who was on the dock board.

18 TNA, RAIL 384/1, 21 and 27 Oct., 6 Nov. and 11 and 24 Dec. 1830, 7 Jan. 1831.

19 S.D. Chapman, *The Rise of Merchant Banking*, 1984, 83.

20 Henry Solly, *These Eighty Years or the Story of an Unfinished Life*, 1893, 1, 6–7.

21 Supple, *Royal Exchange Assurance*, 352.

22 TNA, RAIL 384/1, 21 Oct. 1830.

there would be no dependable information until they had completed the survey on which they were engaged, which was taking Giles' route as its basis. The line he proposed was from Birmingham to Stonebridge, then through Coventry to Rugby and Weedon Beck, through Stoke Bruerne, east of Stony Stratford and west of Fenny Stratford, to Leighton Buzzard, from which place the line to Watford would either be through Ivinghoe and Berkhamsted or the Dagnall Gap and Hemel Hempstead and from Watford east or west of Harrow to the junction of the Regent's Canal with the Paddington Canal.[23] The committee discussed how many tracks were needed. Stephenson reported that a quadruple line for the first 30 miles or so from London would cost £30,000 a mile with £15–20,000 a mile for the rest of the route, while quadruple lines throughout would cost £20–25 000 a mile with additional land costs. The Committee decided on quadruple lines throughout so the line would need capital of £3,000,000. In February 1831 the estimate for construction etc came to £2,842,000 with a further £239,000 for the carrying department, warehouses, engines and carriages, making £3,081,000 in all. Meanwhile anxious to build on the experience of the LMR three directors (Wilson, Barclay and Larpent) visited that line in December.

In February 1831 the directors decided not to introduce a bill in that session of Parliament. They were not ready with the necessary data. They also thought that postponement would give abundant opportunities for acquiring such information and time for negotiations which might convert enemies into friends. They could profit by another year's experience of the LMR and stimulate the commercial and monied classes of the Metropolis to a more zealous support. They were also conscious of the pressure of public business in Parliament – Lord Grey's Whig government had only taken office in November 1830, following the general election on the accession of William IV and was about to introduce the first Reform Bill.[24] This delay did not diminish enthusiasm for the project. George Stephenson told W.T. Salvin that 'as an investment for money you cannot have a better than the London and Birmingham'. He later advised Salvin on the good prospects for a number of other lines, including the GWR, so not confining his recommendations to lines with which he was involved.[25]

Richard Creed had been appointed secretary in London while Captain Moorsom was his opposite number in Birmingham. Moorsom had substantial

[23] Ibid, 5 Nov. 1830.

[24] Ibid, 18 and 24 Feb. 1831.

[25] Letter of 21 Sept. 1831, quoted in M.C. Reed, George Stephenson and W.T. Salvin: the Early Capital Market at Work, *Transport History*, 1, 1986, 14–15.

naval experience, most recently as flag captain to the commander in chief at Chatham. Creed had considerable business experience as a member of Creed and Fauntleroy, Army and Navy agents in London, and had acted as agent and banker to his uncle, William Haig, the naval instructor to William IV when Duke of Clarence.[26] Initially appointed to look after the finance and audit department, he soon became more generally involved. In May the board asked him, together with George Hennet, to look at the route within 30 miles of London and the possibility of carrying the line to the east of London for the convenience of trade and avoiding the parks of the Earls of Essex and Clarendon near Watford 'whose objections could not be removed and were too important to be disregarded.' In addition the board thought it desirable that the railway should terminate near the port of London. They did produce such a plan, with the line running from a depot for general trade near Limehouse Cut to Kentish Town and Kilburn and then west of Harrow and east of Watford, so avoiding the parks of the two Earls. A passenger station would be provided near Battle Bridge on the Regent's Canal, served by a branch from Kentish Town. This was ruled out and the line finally decided upon did touch the parks of these great landowners, though it was much mitigated by Creed's plan for a tunnel to avoid Cassiobury Park and adjoining plantations belonging to Lord Essex, to which Stephenson agreed. Solly was deeply indignant, like the rest of the directors, that the company was obliged to pay Essex £30,000 for a small part of Cassiobury Park as the price of his consent.[27]

On 31 January 1832, before the Bill entered its Parliamentary course, the company issued a circular,[28] stating that detailed and accurate information had been obtained. The excavations and embankments had been reduced and the inclines were smaller in no case exceeding 1 in 330. Another variation was the occasional use of tunnels, ten in number which the engineers believed could be traversed by locomotive engines without the least inconvenience to passengers. The circular mentioned particularly the three largest, Primrose Hill (half a mile), north of Watford, one mile and Kilsby, a mile and a quarter. They would all be 25 feet high, well lighted and ought to be called galleries rather than tunnels. It was now thought that four lines were not necessary. Two would be sufficient for any probable extent

[26] Henry Booth, states that Creed was dissatisfied with the partnership and so dissolved it. A few years later one of the partners was found guilty of malpractices during the period when Creed was a partner. As a result he lost £40,000. (Henry Booth, *Henry Booth*, 1980, 157–180).

[27] TNA, RAIL 384/1, 13 May and 29 Jul. and 21 Sept. 1832; Solly, 9.

[28] TNA, RAIL 1110/260.

of traffic.[29] Consequently the estimated expense had been greatly reduced to £2,400,000, so the parliamentary estimate was adjusted to £2,500,000 instead of the £3 million a year earlier. The estimated income from traffic on roads and canals was £671,000, based on the actual returns of the current traffic by canals and coach: passengers £331,000 by coaches and posting, £112,500 from goods by vans, stage waggons and market carts and £227,330 from goods by flyboat, but no account was taken of iron, coal or bricks or livestock then carried by canal. In the light of the experience of the LMR, half the expected gross income could be expected to cover expenses.[30] In the summer of 1837 when £3,102,000 had been spent, a sub-committee examined likely receipts in more detail and concluded that total annual receipts from existing modes of transport amounted to £894,339, though neither estimate stated what proportion of existing traffic the railway was expected to take over or how much new traffic would be generated.[31]

From the outset there were warnings of substantial opposition in Parliament, despite the changes already made. After hearing from Lawrence and Moss, the chairman and deputy chairman of the LMR, Barker warned the board that the Bill would succeed in the Commons but not in the Lords unless the number of dissents from landowners were reduced. In Barker's judgement £100,000 would be adequate to secure this. The Bill was introduced on 16 February 1832. There were petitions against it from numerous aristocratic landowners as well the head of the place where the aristocrats were educated, the Provost of Eton, a substantial landowner in North West London, and from road and canal interests. Nevertheless the Bill passed the House of Commons where it received a second reading by 146 to 125, and a majority in Committee of 15 (24 to 9).[32] Although some powerful landowners who had originally opposed the LMR now saw the advantages of railways including the Earl of Sefton and Lord Derby, the Bill was defeated in the Lords, as Barker had predicted but not Robert Stephenson who had been elated by the 'capital majority' in the Commons and had added that 'it seems doubtful whether our opponents will persist in pursuing us in the Lords.' In fact the opponents pursued George Stephenson personally and he was subject of three days of intensive questioning, even being caught out by counsel on the matter of the material in the Tring ridge and the angle of

[29] TNA, RAIL 1110/260, circular of 31 Jan. 1832.

[30] Ibid.

[31] TNA, RAIL 1110/260, report for half-year ending 30 Jun. 1837.

[32] Curiously, one of the tellers for the Noes in the division on second reading was the Marquess of Chandos, the father of the Marquess of Chandos, chairman of the LNWR from 1853 to 1861.

the proposed cutting. The committee rejected the Bill as it did not appear to them that a case had been made which would 'warrant forcing of the railway through the lands and property of so great a proportion of dissentient landowners and proprietors.'

The reaction was swift. 'By God, it is one of the damnedest, rascally things I ever saw in my whole political existence,' said one noble lord on coming out of the Committee room, although Lord Wharncliffe who had taken the chair, while agreeing that there was no doubt that it was to the apprehensions of landowners that failure had to be attributed, said that he had pointed out to those who consulted him beforehand the extent of the opposition. He himself thought the line a great national measure but the landowners could not be forced; they had to be wooed and won.[33] The defeat was immediately followed by a public meeting at the Thatched House Tavern when 16 peers and 33 members of the House of Commons resolved that a railway from London to Birmingham would be productive of very great national benefit and that it must be believed that the failure of the bill in the House of Lords had arisen from apprehensions on the part of landowners and proprietors respecting its probable effect on their estates which the meeting firmly and conscientiously believed to be ill-founded.

The railway therefore concentrated on conciliating the landowners. In effect they were bought off. By November the Duke of Grafton and the Earl of Essex had withdrawn their opposition, others had taken up a neutral position and negotiations were pending with the Countess of Bridgewater and Lord Southampton. By the following January when the bill was reintroduced 21 landowners had withdrawn their dissents covering 20 miles of the route. The Company made much of the changed situation in the circular issued. 'Nearly all those who were the most active and formidable have been conciliated.'[34]

The landowners appeased, the LBR was successful in 1833 and obtained its Act for a railway with a share capital of £2,500.000 and power to raise £835,000 by mortgage for a railway commencing on the west side of the high road leading from London to Hampstead, ie Chalk Farm. The line onwards to Euston had been the object of particular opposition in 1832 so that had to wait.

1833 effectively marked the beginning of main line railways in Britain as not only did the LBR secure Parliamentary authority but so did the Grand Junction, which was the successor of earlier schemes to link Birmingham and Liverpool, but now instead of ending in Birkenhead it was to run to Warrington where a line had been opened in 1833 to connect that town

33 Peter Lecount, *The History of the Railway between London and Birmingham*, 1839, 21.

34 Circular 23rd Jan. 1833 included in TNA, RAIL 384/260.

with the LMR. Thus railways were authorised with the potential to form a continuous line of nearly 200 miles though not under common ownership. 1834 saw the authorisation of the London and Southampton and 1835 the Great Western. These were major financial and engineering projects of an unprecedented size. Glyn was to comment later on the tendency to underrate and undervalue the exertions of those on whom devolved the responsibility for these great undertakings (referring to the constituents of the LNWR).

After the railway had been authorised by Parliament in 1833 a London subcommittee of Finance and Treasury was established. Solly was chairman; the other four members – Glyn, Barclay, Grenfell and Lubbock – were all directors of St Katherine's Dock and the group immediately asked the secretary to write to the London and St Katharine's docks to find out how they registered shares and delivered certificates.[35] Glyn doubtless remained close to his colleagues on the St Katharine's board, but crucial to the future of the railway company and our understanding of Glyn's views and the policies he pursued on the LBR board were his links with a number of directors in Liverpool and also with Joseph Langton, the Secretary of the Bank of Liverpool, which was one of the country banks for which Glyn's were the London agent. Langton was, with James Loch, one of the directors of the LMR nominated by the Duke of Sutherland. These letters show much more clearly than the LBR's board and committee minutes the considerable influence which Glyn wielded even before he became chairman in 1837.

Correspondence survives from the early days of the board between Glyn and two Liverpool Directors, William Rathbone and Edward Cropper in which they discussed various issues arising from company business. Both were Quakers and their families had close links. William Rathbone's father, also William, had been a partner in Cropper, Benson, with Edward's father, James, but in 1809 on William senior's death, the younger William and his brother Richard had set up as commission agents. Cropper Benson in addition to trading with Ireland, North America, India and China established the first line of packet ships to carry mail to North America. They also undertook joint trading ventures with Rathbone Bros. James Cropper and William Rathbone were directors of the LMR, and substantial shareholders. Their experience and that of other shareholders in the LMR must have greatly encouraged them to purchase shares in the LBR and in the GJR where Edward's brother John was a director. Thomas Tooke in his *History of Prices* attributed the predominance of Lancashire capital in the LBR to the greater knowledge they possessed of the nature of such undertakings as well as to the

[35] TNA, RAIL 384/57, 20 May 1833.

extraordinary accumulation of capital in that district which greatly exceeded the amount which could be profitably reinvested in the cotton industry, great and increasing as that had been.[36] This was exemplified by the Croppers. A year after the LMR opened James Cropper noted that the weekly revenue from passengers was £3,600 and from goods £1,000. 'I think there is a probability that the gross earnings of the first three months of this quarter will be at least £52,000 and next I think it will be £39,000. If the expenses are the same as last year half year say £35.000, it would leave £56,000 net or dividend of £7 a share.' Thus from this source alone, he noted, he would receive an income of nearly £2,800 per annum.[37]

The Act specified that at least ten of the 24 directors had to live within 20 mlles of London and ten within 10 miles of Birmingham. Rathbone and Edward Cropper, with Robert Garnett of Manchester, were the three non-resident directors.[38] They also spoke for the many Liverpool and Lancashire shareholders as well as being experienced business men on whom Glyn could rely. It seems that the correspondence started in 1833 following confidential discussions about the officers of the company when Rathbone and Cropper were in London. Glyn emphasised to Cropper that it was confidential – he had already put himself in a position of much delicacy – but that it was to be equally open to Rathbone and Garnett.[39]

In September 1833 Robert Stephenson was appointed engineer-in-chief. He quickly recommended to the directors that John Dixon and William Crosley, a very experienced canal engineer, should be appointed assistant engineers at the London end and Thomas Gooch, who had started his career as an apprentice of George Stephenson, at the Birmingham end. It was the appointment of Dixon which raised difficulties as he was employed by the LMR and Robert Stephenson does not seem to have approached that company before recommending him to the LBR board. Cropper told Glyn of the problems with the LMR arising from Stephenson's approach to Dixon which Glyn passed on to the Committee by which, he told Cropper 'we are much annoyed but from the absence of Stephenson who is in Liverpool, we cannot before next week act out more fully upon its suggestions.' Glyn was very critical of Stephenson's handling of the matter:

36 Thomas Tooke, *History of Prices and the State of the Circulation*, 1858, 2, 275.

37 Liverpool Maritime Museum, Cropper MSS, D/CR/10/58, James Cropper to Eliza Cropper, 9 Aug. 1831. He added that most of it would be to spare for other purposes than 'our living or accumulation'. Among other charitable activities the Croppers were building an orphan house.

38 This provision was repealed in 1835.

39 TNA, RAIL 384/376, 25 Apr. 1833.

> This first start of Stephenson is a very bad one and shows great want of tact on his part. We (the London Committee) were aware of the great delicacy of the step as regards Dixon's appointment and had a personal explanation with Stephenson upon it. He has been misled or at any rate misinformed … for it was understood by him to be with the knowledge of the LMR that Dixon was offered the appointment and added in confirmation that Dixon would take it up in three weeks.

However Glyn was then surprised to find that Dixon had taken advantage of the situation to raise his terms with the LMR with whom he remained. The LBR had wished to have Dixon to superintend the work at Watford tunnel in view of his experience at Liverpool. Glyn pointed to the board's difficulty in its relations with its engineer 'We feel a disinclination to interfere much with Stephenson in his selection of his sub-engineers so that he may be left without any diminution of his entire responsibility for the perfect execution of the work.' Glyn was better versed in the way professional engineers worked than Cropper. In his desire for economy the latter had suggested had suggested that the assistant engineers should be required to hand over to the company any premiums they may receive from young men, in fact apprentices. Glyn advised him, perhaps based on his experience with St Katharine's Dock, that this would totally inadmissible and at variance with all professional usage. The nomination of engineers rested with Stephenson, but the committee had to approve as appointment and dismissal rested with the committee. Glyn concluded that this was sufficient check on the Engineer-in-chief without in any way interfering with his responsibilities.[40]

The new company also had to learn to deal with lawyers. Glyn told Cropper that as they were entering negotiations for obtaining possession the land required the question of payment to the Solicitors for this business arose. Several suggestions had already been made as to how their costs could be adjusted, but they risked making difficulty with the lawyers. He would be glad to receive further ideas. Something had to be done. Glyn thought that if they could not do better than the principle of taxation. A favourite idea of his was to use one or two general deeds of conveyance instead of a separate deed for each, so saving much money. He asked Cropper to consult any practical men of the Committee about this possibility. He added that the lawyers rejected it but that had not convinced him of its impracticability. A week later he reported that after some difficulty they had come to an arrangement with the lawyers. Rowles had suggested paying the lawyers a fixed salary,

[40] TNA, RAIL 1008/92, Glyn to Edward Cropper, 3 and 10 Oct. 1833.

which course the LNWR was to adopt in 1861 but Glyn thought there was a strong case against it. He had not found any precedent for such a course in any of the large undertakings or private concerns. He ended on a point which illustrated the difficulty of operating largely through separate London and Birmingham committees – 'I suppose the Birmingham committee will be able to bring their Solicitor to a similar contract.'[41]

The Liverpool banks were also the subject of correspondence between Glyn and Langton and Cropper. As early as February 1832 Glyn told Langton that he had recommended that the balance of Liverpool deposits should be transferred to the Bank of Liverpool from Moss, of Moss, Rogers and Moss. It might lead to the placing with that bank the subscription for the continuation of the line from 'Birmingham to your town which must eventually take effect.' Moss was perhaps Liverpool's foremost banker, as well as being a director of the LMR and the chairman of the Grand Junction on its formation in 1832. In July however Glyn told Langton that this message was premature and it was September 1833 before the Finance Committee accepted this recommendation. He told Langton that no doubt it would excite the anger of Mr Moss, but though entertaining the proper feelings for one commercial man to another, nothing ever justified the removal of a connection. In this case he thought justification existed because of the steps taken by Moss when the Birmingham Bill was before Parliament.[42] He told Cropper that Moss had not assisted the undertaking in any way, and added that the Finance Committee had inserted the Bank of Liverpool in the list of banks where calls on shares could be made.[43]

Glyn was also critical of the banking arrangements of the Birmingham Committee who had appointed two banks and so were maintaining balances which in his view were too large. He tried to find an acceptable solution to the division among the board members of the £1,000 a year allocated for their remuneration, apparently made difficult by the need to pay expenses to the Liverpool and Manchester directors. He reminded Cropper that it was common practice in London for the chairman to receive a better remuneration than the members as he had more onerous duties to perform and consultations and arrangements to make. When Cropper offered to help by giving up part of his allowance he told him that this was out of the question and that he regretted the division of opinion on such a paltry subject.[44]

[41] Ibid, 15 and 21 Nov. 1833.

[42] Barclays Archives, 25/265, Langton Papers (LP), 11, 18 and 41, 29 Feb. and 16 Jul. 1832, and 30 Sept. 1833.

[43] TNA, RAIL, 384/276, 25 Sept. 1833.

[44] TNA, RAIL 384/276, 25 Sept. and 15 Nov. 1833 and 10 Apr. 1834.

The press of business from the registration of shares and receipt of payments for the call upon the shares 'was so great on this office that we have relieved Creed by adjourning specially until 23rd.' Later he told Cropper that registration had proceeded satisfactorily. Great credit was due to Creed's arrangements with efficient support from Captain Moorsom.

The Dixon episode did not mean that the LBR was less interested in the progress of the LMR. Glyn asked Cropper whether there was any truth in the reports of a falling off in the number of passengers on the LMR compared with the same period of last year. When Glyn saw the figures he said they were on the whole very satisfactory. He also noted with some satisfaction that the Grand Junction Canal experiments to speed up their boats had mixed results. Although a speed of 10 miles an hour had been attained the water rushed over the banks. The number of locks must make it impracticable and such competition was not to be feared by the railroad.[45] In 1835 Glyn reported the agreement of the Admiralty to experiments on railway bars at Woolwich Yard. Professor Barlow was asked to visit the LMR to advise on the weight of rails, the design of chairs, the distance between supports and the size of the blocks.[46]

The engineers and other staff having been appointed the work of construction went ahead. Stephenson recognised that there were not sufficient large contractors capable of taking on lengthy sections of the line and so 30 contracts were let. The first three were let in May 1834 for the 16 miles from Camden to Watford. Eight more were let by November and by February 1835 work was proceeding on more than half the line. All contracts had been let by November 1835. Meanwhile it had been decided to extend to Euston, as originally intended.

In February 1835 the London Committee had considered a report from Creed which recommended that the extension to Euston should be exclusively for the conveyance of passengers. The report and subsequent discussion are of interest in showing the economic and financial considerations brought to bear on the decision. Goods were still to be received and delivered at Camden. The additional mile of line would only bring in £5754 which obviously would not afford adequate compensation for the expense of the extension. However the estimate did not take into account passengers to and from places between London and Edgware. Moreover the advantage of rail over road lay in 'cheapness, certainty and expedition.' Seven minutes would be gained on each

[45] Ibid, 8 Nov. 1833.

[46] TNA, RAIL 384/41, 7 Feb. and 384/2, 6 Aug. 1835. Peter Barlow, scientist and engineer, professor at the Royal Military Academy, who about 1830 became interested in testing rail sections and the effects of gradients and curves.

journey so the advantage would increase. To a person who had a journey of 100 miles to make it might be of little importance that it should take 4 hours 53 minutes rather than 5 hours, but when the journey is only ten or twenty miles the saving of time became important. To Watford and back there would be a saving of 14 minutes on an hour and a half. This would be particularly the case with persons whose business took them daily into London. Access from the frequented New Road would decide many to resort to excursions of pleasure, who would never exert themselves to go to Camden Town, and Euston was more conveniently situated for business or amusement. An estimate of the general increase of traffic was difficult but from every person induced to go ten miles the return would be the same as ten persons going the single mile. 70 passengers daily for 11.2 miles would bring in £11,965, ten per cent on the estimate. Delay to another Session might mean the opportunity of carrying the railway over open ground could be lost as it might be built on. Other railways might avail themselves of the proposed line of approach – presumably the GWR was the company in mind. On the other hand other companies might want to make use of the line which would reduce the cost to the LBR. Finally the note advised against seeking power to charge a higher rate of toll:

> Looking to the benefits which the steam packets are reaping from the low price system, and to the fact that passengers are conveyed by one engine, the less will be the average expense of power upon the whole number conveyed. There appears to be every inducement to make the charge for passengers at the lowest remunerating rate with a view to attracting the greatest number.[47]

The necessary Act of Parliament was secured in July and the plans approved in November. Work on the extension started in December 1835. In 1836 Hardwick was commissioned to erect the great portico. In February 1837 proprietors were told his plan had been adopted because 'the entrance to Euston opens immediately on what will necessarily become the grand avenue for travelling between the Metropolis and the Midland and Northern parts of the Kingdom'.[48]

Meanwhile the work of construction on the rest of the line was going ahead. There is however little evidence of Glyn's interest in the work of construction in the early stages but he does seem to have kept a careful eye on the build-up of the workforce, and the progress of the works, often in conjunction with the Liverpool members of the board. Edward Cropper must

47 TNA, RAIL 384/41, 7 Feb. 1835.

48 TNA, RAIL 384/12, 7 Feb. 1835.

have criticised the level of expenses in the preliminary stages of the railway as Glyn told him he was quite aware that the expenditure of the LBR had been large, but he thought unavoidable, from many obvious causes which could not occur again, but did not warrant the imputation of extravagance.[49]

In April 1834 he noted that Stephenson had deservedly received much commendation from those who had seen the specification plans for their clearness, accuracy and fullness. In May he wrote 'I hope our contractors will take advantage of this beautiful season.' In July he considered that on the whole things had gone very satisfactorily under all heads. He had no reason to complain of serious deviations from estimates even under the head of land purchases. They were however obliged to keep an eye on contract no 1 but they were getting it into better order.[50]

Stephenson had in fact reported to the London Committee on 18 June that contracts 1 to 3 were proceeding satisfactorily. Glyn told Cropper they would very soon be in a position to bring the Tring contract forward, a point on which Stephenson was very anxious as it was the most difficult part of the whole line and requiring the greatest engineering skill. He had advised then not to advertise, but to apply to 12 contractors who were entitled to tender on account of their means and qualifications, telling them the company would not accept any of their offers if they above the LBR's calculations of costs. He added:

> I am always for open bidding but under the circumstances of this case and the difficulties of the ground, decidedly acquiesce in the alternative in which we hope you and your colleagues will agree. Any failure in the work on this portion of the line either in execution or time would be fatal and it ought not to be trusted to any but the most practised hands.[51]

However despite the logic of appointing many contractors this did not prevent over a third failing, including those engaged on all of the most difficult work, as a result of rising prices technical difficulties, inexperience and sometimes taking on too much. Some were replaced by others but often the railway company took over. On average over 12,000 men worked on the 112 mile line for three years.

It is not easy from the formal minutes to establish how important Glyn's contribution had been to this point, apart from acting as a banker – Glyn's offered a loan of £12,000 for a week when the fifth instalment on shares

[49] TNA, RAIL 1008/92, Glyn to Cropper, 10 Oct. 1833.

[50] TNA, RAIL 384/276, Glyn to Cropper, 10 Apr., 15 May, and 24 Jul. 1834.

[51] Ibid, 10 Apr., 15 May and 23 Jul. 1834.

was expected in few days when it was not expedient to sell Exchequer bills or order a transfer from the Bank of Liverpool.[52] Nevertheless there clearly were key areas in company management where he played a vital part. First as has been seen he built effective links with the Liverpool directors and shareholders and his correspondence with the northern directors shows his wide ranging interest in the business of the company. His correspondence with Joseph Langton, secretary of the Bank of Liverpool, while mainly about banking matters, contained references to the railways affairs and Langton was also used as a link with the railway interest in Liverpool. Second he had strong views on the structure of management and in ensuring its effectiveness.

The importance of the Liverpool shareholders and their representatives on the board grew rather than diminished in the early years of the LBR. Already in October 1833 the non-resident directors were planning to meet in Liverpool, assisted by their own secretary, though in practice there seem at this stage to have been few meetings at least of which records were made. In December 1834 Glyn was canvassing the best way of facilitating the membership of Hardman Earle, but was doubtful about removing Young, or Gibson[53] for this purpose as they had friends on the board. If Lefevre resigned after the annual meeting in February then 'I think we could introduce Earle without difficulty aided by our Liverpool friends.'[54]

By 1836 there was a dichotomy between the geographical distribution

[52] TNA, RAIL 384/41, 2 Apr. 1835.

[53] LP 91, 18 Dec. 1834. James Gibson was one of the directors appointed on incorporation. Thomas Young, briefly listed as a director in 1830, joined the board after he ceased to be private secretary to Lord Melbourne on the fall of the Whig ministry in November 1834, but first attended the LBR board in May 1835. He was formally appointed as a replacement for Shaw Lefevre in Aug. 1835, by which time Melbourne was Prime Minister again. Young's background was most unusual for a private secretary to a Prime Minister or a railway director. Recommended to Melbourne by the duke of Devonshire, as a shrewd handy sort of man whom he had found as purser of his yacht more serviceable than men of better breeding. Melbourne regarded him as his weather gauge, 'Through him I will be able to look down below.' Reputed to have persuaded Melbourne to accept the Premiership in June 1834. 'If it only lasts three months, it will be worthwhile to have been Prime Minister of England.' Glyn referred to 'our three friends Prevost, Grenfell and Young' in a letter to Langton (LP 138, 20 Feb.1836). Young was appointed Receiver General of the Post Office by Melbourne. He remained a director of the LBR until the LNWR was formed and was appointed to the latter board. (David Cecil, *Lord M.*,1954, 45, 111; L.G. Mitchell, *Lord Melbourne, 1779–1848*, 1997, 128–129 and n70; David Hodgkins, Railway Rhymes, *Journal of the Railway and Canal Historical Society*, 38, 2015, 227–234.)

[54] LP 91, 18 Dec. 1834. Hardman Earle, broker and also partner in Earles & Carter, a seed crushing firm. Reputed to have sold all his shares in water companies to invest in the LMR. Married Joseph Langton's sister, Mary.

of the shareholders and that of the board which remained mainly London and Birmingham based. Despite the substantial interest in the line in both Birmingham and the City of London and the appointment of bankers from both places, in 1833 Liverpool shareholders held more shares than those from Birmingham and London combined: 32 per cent, compared with 16 and 13 per cent respectively. Manchester had 15 per cent. In contrast to shareholders on the LMR and the Grand Junction many did not retain their shares and despite the increase in capital of over 50 per cent, the number of shareholders barely increased from 1833 to 1837. In particular Birmingham's share diminished sharply: by 1837 it was only 3 per cent, and the London share was down to 8 per cent, while the proportions held in Liverpool and Manchester rose to 40 and 18 per cent respectively, with a further 12 per cent held elsewhere in the north-west.[55] Although the London directors were highly influential their combined holding in 1835 only amounted to 139 shares, an amount exceeded by Cropper and Rathbone taken together. Glyn and St Leger Grenfell only held 10 each.[56] However the position was very different with debentures, Glyn himself told the Select Committee in 1839 that the capital raised in 1837 came not so much from Lancashire as through the Stock Exchange.[57]

By late 1835 and early 1836 the Liverpool interest was becoming very dissatisfied with their limited voice in the company's affairs. Indeed in February 1836 Laurence Heyworth proposed to the board that there should be six directors from Liverpool elected at the expense of London. The board expressed unqualified surprise as they thought Cropper, Rathbone and Garnett had satisfactorily represented the interests of Liverpool shareholders. Glyn told Langton that he had had a very disagreeable correspondence with Heyworth, but it ended with his writing a very proper disclaimer. In the event the immediate change was more limited. Hardman Earle was elected in place of Copeland, a London director,[58] 'We all felt the greatest satisfaction at the prospect of having him added to us,' wrote Glyn.[59] Heyworth's proposals

[55] M.C. Reed, *Investment in Railways in Britain, 1820–1844*, 1975, 133–138.

[56] TNA, RAIL 384/149. In the record Cropper is included as a London director, but his holding has been excluded from the London directors' total given above. In 1839 Glyn held 20 shares; Cropper 203 plus a holding of 200 jointly with David Hodgson. In both 1835 and 1839 Garnett was the largest shareholder with 704 and 900, though in 1839 Edward Wilson, a Liverpool merchant and director of the Bank of Liverpool, elected in 1838 had 800. Only two others had more than 250. The Bristol Committee of the GWR (a comparable body to the London directors of the LBR) held £130,600 in shares in their company in 1835–36.

[57] Select Committee on Railway Communication, PP, 1839, x, Q76.

[58] William Copeland was a porcelain manufacturer of Stoke-on-Trent, but was also a London merchant and Lord Mayor in 1835.

[59] LP 139, 24 Feb. 1836.

were defeated at the board. Prevost, St Leger Grenfell and Young, the retiring directors who would have had to drop out, were re-elected, three very efficient directors, the board noted.[60] In February 1837 Hodgson of Liverpool and Cooke and Houldsworth of Manchester replaced three London and Birmingham directors. When Solly resigned in May 1837 he was replaced by Boothby, a very active Liverpool shareholder. All four new directors attended the meetings of the non-resident directors who continued to meet at Newton from time to time. In 1837 they met to consider what course it might be advisable to adopt over the present feelings of alarm and want of confidence amongst the proprietors.[61] Glyn was sympathetic to Liverpool shareholders in that their critics forgot that many in Liverpool held shares in every railway and seemed to be incapable of giving any credit to them for acting conscientiously upon the trust confided in them by the proprietors.[62] However he was quick to move when Liverpool interests were critical, wanting to know who was the scribbler 'in this day's *Times*'.[63] In 1837 Glyn seems to have thought that the non-resident directors were trespassing on the functions of the main board and committees, for Hodgson was asked to write to Glyn to explain that the resolutions adopted by the non-resident directors were only understood by them to convey their opinions and recommendations and were of course entirely subject to the constitutional authority vested in the regularly appointed committees and with the sincerest desire to assist the other directors for the general benefit of the company. Nevertheless by March 1838 some members of the group were themselves uneasy about the position and they agreed that future meetings would only be held on special occasions. Indeed there is no record of a meeting thereafter.[64]

Glyn pursued with Cropper and Rathbone questions of economy. In 1833 he told Cropper that it appeared very important to him to concentrate as much as possible on the details of the business and to avoid the multiplication of work and entries. He therefore asked whether Cropper agreed with the desirability of arranging at once that the registry and transfer of certificates should be confined entirely to London. He added that if the suggestion was worth acting upon the proposal must come from Cropper or Rathbone as colleagues in Birmingham were already quite jealous of the

60 TNA, RAIL, 384/2, 22 Feb. 1836. John Lewis Prevost was a London merchant. He was agent and consul general for Switzerland. He served on the LBR board from its inception and then on the LNWR. A member of the Political Economy Club.

61 TNA, RAIL 384/2, 24 Mar. 1837.

62 LP 141, 29 Feb. 1836.

63 LP 193, 24 Sept. 1836.

64 TNA, RAIL 384/62, 7 Oct. 1837 and 10 Mar. 1838.

London committee.[65] On another occasion he criticised the Birmingham Committee for proposing to charge interest on calls not paid by a certain date; the London Committee thought this sharp practice as no notice had been given and so fixed a later date, though he thought the principle right. When concerned about the Company's position over a purchase of land from Lord Howe he wished that Rathbone as a member of the Birmingham Committee would bring his energy to bear on this question and bring it to termination. He stressed he was writing as an individual as it had not been mentioned in the London Committee. Later he told Cropper that he would be very glad to hear that the Birmingham Committee had settled for their station 'and on moderate terms, but I fear.'[66] He awaited the reports of the four engineers on the type of rail to be used and hoped that would be resolved before he went on a month's holiday.[67]

Like the Stockton and Darlington Railway the LBR at this stage had no locomotive building capacity of its own. Economy was one of the issues when it came to the manufacture and system of operation of locomotives. Joseph Pease, chairman of the SDR, told the LBR, directors they were right in not taking that troublesome department into their own hands and sent figures derived for the actual costs on the LMR which, he said, proved that the cost of locomotive power greatly increased when the management was in the company's hands. He also thought that the contract should be let for one year only. Few engine manufacturers were yet acquainted with the expense of working engines though he was satisfied that great improvements were now taking place. 'Did or could we have supposed six months ago that a steam engine travelling 25 miles an hour and taking 200 passengers would cost less per mile than a post chaise with a pair of horses.'[68]

However by 1835 who was to supply the LBR's locomotives had become a controversial matter particularly between Stephenson and the non-resident directors. Robert was now taking the same line as his father on the LMR who had claimed that he alone should determine the type of locomotive used on the line. James Cropper and other directors had criticised this as giving rise to a conflict between his interests as chief engineer and manufacturer. In this Cropper was consistent in that he had earlier been concerned with Princes

[65] TNA, 384/6, 8 Nov. and 19 Dec. 1833.

[66] Ibid, 10 Apr., 23 Apr. and 22 May 1834. Lord Howe succeeded in that he was paid nearly £18,000 at £2,080 an acre for some unproductive garden property on a proposed branch line. R.W. Kostal, *English Railway Capitalism, 1825–1875*, 1994, 150; RAIL 384/99, 8 Sept. 1834.

[67] Ibid, 2 Oct. 1834.

[68] TNA, RAIL 1008/111, R349, Joseph Pease to the directors of the LBR, 1835 (no precise date).

Dock, Liverpool which had cost £600,000 compared with the £684,000 which the Clarence and five other docks with an acreage twice that of Princes had cost. This was in part due to overcharging, corruption, and grossly inefficient engineering management leading to high costs and delays. Cropper had secured the resignation of the engineer, John Foster in 1824 and the appointment of Jesse Hartley, appointed on conditions that excluded outside business commitments which might lead to the conflicts of interests which characterised the corruption of the Foster regime.[69] Other manufacturers were being attracted to diversify into the business of locomotive manufacture, notably Edward Bury, but Stephenson successfully denied him the opportunity to sell engines to the LMR by rejecting his designs as not meeting his specification modelled on the Planet, the locomotive built immediately before the opening of the LMR and a class of which many examples were built by R.W. Hawthorn, the firm in Newcastle on Tyne in which Robert Stephenson was a partner.

Difficulties on the LBR arose as early as December 1834 when locomotives were required to assist the contractors in the London Division. It was thought they could be obtained second hand from the LMR but Rathbone and Creed ascertained not only that the LMR had none for disposal but they could not be obtained from any other quarter. Stephenson gave Creed some names of manufacturers including Bury, and Creed on his own initiative had written to R.W. Hawthorn. The London Committee then ordered one engine from Tayleur's Vulcan Foundry and one from Newcastle, both firms in which Stephenson had a substantial interest.[70] Edward Cropper and Rathbone took exception to this, but Stephenson took this as a personal attack and told his partner Longridge that they half intimated that he should withdraw either from the Railway or from engine building. Longridge suggested that he dispose of his shares to his father temporarily. Although Stephenson said the other directors supported him, by February the board had approved Rathbone and Cropper's resolution that no director, secretary, engineer sub-engineer or servant of the company could be a contractor.[71]

However it seems that Stephenson continued as a partner of R.W. Hawthorn, and when later in 1835 it was necessary to order locomotives for the opening of the line he recommended that ten locomotives to his

69 Adrian Jarvis, James Cropper, Liverpool Docks and the Liverpool and Manchester Railway, *Journal of Transport History*, 19, 1998, 26.

70 TNA, RAIL 384/40, 10 and 24 Dec. 1834.

71 TNA, RAIL 384/40, 7, 13 and 27 Jan. 1835; Stephenson to Longridge, 26 Jan. and Longridge's reply of 4 Feb, quoted at length in Michael R. Bailey, *Robert Stephenson, the Eminent Engineer,* 2003, 178.

Patentee six wheel specification be purchased for the first part of the line from Camden to Watford. The tender on this basis was agreed, but did not find favour with Cropper and his colleagues partly because it included a royalty for Stephenson's patent. Stephenson then proposed that Tayleur should have a contract to provide and maintain the locomotives, but this was objected to as Stephenson was a partner in Tayleur too though shortly afterwards he ended that association.[72] Other tenders were sought and examined and when Bury put forward an exclusive contract it was accepted despite Stephenson making clear his preference for six wheeled locomotives. The London Committee put the question to Sir Marc Brunel, John Farey and Roberts, though not delaying the Bury contract.[73] When Rathbone reported that Bury could not provide engines in time for the opening the directors agreed to the purchase of twelve Patentees to ensure that locomotives were available for the opening of the line but Cropper and Rathbone, who had not been present at the London meeting, persuaded the Birmingham Committee to reverse the decision and the London directors effectively gave way.[74] Boothby urged Rathbone on. He wrote 'I believe Bury to be the most competent man in the country for the undertaking and I know him to be actuated as much by a spirit of emulation as by any hope of profit.'[75] The contract with Bury was signed in May 1836. Bury moved to Wolverton in charge of the operation and maintenance of the locomotives on a contract basis while retaining his interest in his works in Liverpool. Bury and Stephenson had to co-exist until Stephenson ceased to be engineer-in-chief at the end of 1838 following the opening of the entire line.[76]

Stephenson immediately signed an agreement with the North Midland Railway under which he was appointed locomotive superintendent with responsibility for supplying locomotives and their operational and maintenance facilities and recruitment and training of footplate staff, though he tended to delegate most of his functions. Although he remained a partner in the largest locomotive manufacturer he agreed to remain impartial and by August 1842 when his appointment ended 44 locomotives had been

[72] TNA, RAIL 384/41, 9 Sept. and 14 Oct. 1835.

[73] TNA, RAIL 384/2, resolution of board endorsing recommendation to London Committee. Mr Roberts is not further identified in the minutes but presumably he was Richard Roberts, partner in Sharp Roberts, Manchester which began locomotive manufacture in 1833. John Farey was an active member of the ICE and in this period a consulting engineer (Skempton, 1, 223–224).

[74] TNA, RAIL 384/41, 5, 6, 18 Nov., 2 and 9 Dec. 1835; RAIL 384/42, 23 Dec. 1835, 7, 15 and 27 Jan. and 11 May 1836.

[75] TNA, RAIL 1008/92, Boothby to Rathbone, 18 Dec. 1835.

[76] Bailey, 182.

introduced from nine different manufacturers, all to his specifications.[77] It is not clear what part Glyn played in all this. He was not chairman of the LBR at the time of the dispute between Stephenson and the non-resident directors, but by 1839 he was chairman of both the LBR and the NMR. It seems unlikely that Stephenson would have achieved his all-powerful position on the NMR without Glyn's whole-hearted support. Certainly Glyn had some doubts about Bury for as late as Saturday 15 July 1837 when he hoped that the LBR would certainly be open for the public on the following Thursday from Euston to Boxmoor he told Langton that if it did not, the blame would rest on the absence of Mr Bury's engines.[78]

The new railways were business enterprises of unprecedented size and more geographically dispersed than most existing businesses. Before the railway was opened Glyn, like others, had to travel to other points on the railway particularly Birmingham. He went to Birmingham with some of his colleagues in November 1835 starting on Wednesday but hoped to be back by noon on the Saturday. In May 1837 he hoped to get away on Thursday to attend a meeting on Friday and leave everything in London happily settled. When Thursday came he said he was 'most reluctantly just setting off'.[79] He also went occasionally to Liverpool and in February 1835 combined LBR business with meeting the Bank of Liverpool directors.[80]

In 1825 there were only two firms with capital with a market value of more than £3 million – the Trent & Mersey Canal with £5.4 million and the Grand Junction Canal with £3.4 million.[81] The LBR's initial authorised capital of £3.3 million thus exceeded that of almost all earlier companies but little consideration had been given to management structures and lines of responsibility. There was little directly relevant experience, and no generalised management expertise or principles had been developed. Industries had developed their own management structures to suit their particular needs. Railways therefore had to a large extent to devise their own systems of management. The LBR was the largest railway company to be established but others started in the 1830s were larger than the largest companies of the pre-railway age. By 1839 Peter Lecount in his Treatise on Railways recognised that while little progress had been made

77 Bailey, 183.

78 LP 314, 15 Jul. 1837.

79 LP 121, 291 and 292, 2 Nov. 1835 and 27, 31 May 1837.

80 LP 92 and 103, 25 Jan. and 18 Feb. 1835.

81 Charles R. Hickson, John D. Turner and Qing Ye, The Rate of Return on Equity across industrial sectors on the British Stock Market, *Economic History Review* (*EcHR*), 64, 2011, 1226, for the 1825 figures.

to perfect management, the present system of directors was on the whole the most suitable for managing a commercial concern, possibly based on his knowledge of the LBR. 'For proper management everything should centre on the committee of direction. These may with advantage subdivide themselves into smaller bodies for particular purposes with nothing finally concluded till brought before the general body.' He warned that 'a body consisting of many individuals is utterly unfitted for executive functions. Every board has someone to whom is entrusted the entire superintendence and control.'[82]

Even before he became chairman Glyn had been working on these lines. In his Memorandum of Management Division of 1836 he stated that the natural division of the Company was six departments – Finance including audit and necessary checks (Creed); Police (Moorsom); Engineering (Stephenson); Locomotives (Bury); Coaching (Bagster); and Goods Carrying (Baxendale).[83] Glyn said the management of the details of the business in each department (with the power of punishment and dismissal in certain cases) should be left to the Head of Department. Each department should from time to time report to the Committee of Management and suggest such changes in the arrangements as might appear expedient to the Committee of Management, from which each head would receive his orders and instructions.

Glyn recognised that the Committee of Management by itself could not effectively check the operation and arrangements of an undertaking such as the LBR so it needed a confidential superior officer, whose principal duty would be to superintend the working of the system and to observe the working and operations of each outdoor department. Nevertheless all orders should go direct to the head of department. The officer would be sent a copy of the Committee's orders. The confidential officer should be the outdoor secretary. Although not stated in his memorandum, the LBR had in effect two outdoor secretaries: Creed and Moorsom in that they were respectively the London and Birmingham Secretaries and as a result acted as coordinators on behalf of the board. The great object in view is to establish an efficient system of inspection and at the same time to prevent the interference of any officer of the company with the head of any department. Glyn also wrote instructions for the storekeeper. He was to be under the direction of the Secretary, who was to be given a list of all stores to be contracted for. He had to be very attentive that the stock in hand.

Soon after Glyn became chairman; he was to build on these principles.

82 Peter Lecount, *A Practical Treatise on Railways*, 1839, 253–254. He wrote his *History of the London & Birmingham Railway* in the same year.

83 TNA, RAIL, 1008/104. The names of the Heads of Departments were added in pencil to the list.

CHAPTER SIX

Glyn and Banking in the 1830s

In the 1830s the business of Glyn's expanded considerably. Assets and liabilities continued to grow reaching £2,042,000 by 1833. Though country business increased and by 1835 Glyn's was the centre of a network of 57 local banks, by 1840 country account balances accounted for only a sixth of the total. On the assets side the high proportion of discounted bills remained, representing four-fifths of the assets in 1833. The average ratio of cash to liabilities in the seven years for which data has survived at 12.5 was much less than in the 1820s. Surprisingly railway current accounts are entered separately from as early as 1829 when they amounted to £250. In 1830 they reached £14,700, which was the LBR's credit balance, the only railway client, a figure not surpassed until 1834. It seems curious that railway accounts were recognised as a separate class of business so quickly and as the entries for a considerable period are in the same copperplate handwriting it is likely that the totals were classified later.[1]

Currie later wrote that Glyn displayed in business great ambition. He desired to make his house the first in London, and to perpetuate a long line of bankers. He was bold without rashness, prudent almost to a fault with his own expenditure. He was a great admirer of the 3 per cents and eschewed investments which offered high interest. 'Get hold of the right sort of people and let them have what they want.'[2]

It was in the 1830s that George Glyn became recognised as the leading partner in the bank, though not the senior partner. His father had become the father of the Corporation in 1829. His wife Mary died in 1832 and by 1834 he was residing almost entirely in Dorset and did not often come to London. In 1835 he resigned as alderman, and a deed of 1 January 1835 marked his retirement from the Bank. As Charles Mills the

1 RBS Archives, GM/718.

2 Currie, 1, 95.

elder had died in 1826, Thomas Hallifax the younger and Edward Mills, another nephew of Charles Mills the elder, were made partners, though the partnership were bound for £100,000 against any public liability for want of public notice of Sir Richard's retirement.[3] In December 1836 George, preoccupied with banking matters, was made anxious by accounts from Dorset of his father's health, though it improved somewhat and George did not then have to travel to Dorset. He did go down the following July and again in October.[4] He told Moorsom on 11 April 1838 he hoped to get down to Birmingham towards the end of the following week to look about if the perilous state of his father's health at 83 would allow him,[5] but his father, Sir Richard Carr Glyn, died at his London home in Arlington Street six days later. George's elder brother Richard Plumptre Glyn inherited the title and the Dorset properties and became the senior partner. The will required his brother to lend to George £4,500 for the purpose of augmenting the capital of the banking house. His father bequeathed £60,000 in the three per cents to Richard Plumptre and George Carr for the purpose of the banking house.[6]

Glyn was appointed a deputy lieutenant of the City of London in 1831. He was one of five leading London private bankers who formed a Country Bankers Association to adopt measures for their mutual protection against the various species of robbery, forgery and fraud.[7] By the early 1830s Glyn was well regarded in Government circles, though in the 1830s Glyn's public involvement was largely confined to banking matters. He was known to Charles Greville, clerk to the Privy Council, well enough to be asked in Pall Mall his opinion about the situation in the city when there was an expectation of a great riot. He was made one of the Commissioners for the issue of Exchequer Bills for public works when Edward Ellice, Secretary to the Treasury and Government whip, thought that the Commission was getting in the hands of a clique.[8]

Glyn was elected a member of Brooks's in March 1828, proposed by Lord Lansdowne, who had just resigned as Home Secretary on the fall of Goderich's ministry and seconded by Sir Matthew White Ridley. After the

3 RBS Archives, GM/881/4, deed of 1 Jan. 1835.

4 Barclays Archives, 25/265, Langton Papers (LP) 79, 235, 236, 321 and 328, 2 Oct. 1834, 15 and 16 Dec. 1837, 28 Jul. and 14 Oct. 1837.

5 RBS Archives, GM/237, Glyn to Moorsom, 24 Apr. 1838.

6 TNA, PROB 11/1895, f 133, Will of Sir Richard Carr Glyn.

7 *The Circular to Bankers*, 29 Jan. 1830.

8 *Greville Diaries* (10 Nov. 1830) ed. P.W. Wilson, 1927, 1, 331–332; Edward Ellice to Loyd, 1 Sept. 1831, D.P. O'Brien, ed., *The Correspondence of Lord Overstone*, 1971, 1, 201.

Reform Act radicals wanted an alternative to Brooks's which was not Liberal enough, too expensive and not a dining club.[9] Glyn was a committed Liberal – in 1830 he recommended a candidate for the election to Robinson Pease at the Hull Bank and when the Reform Club was established in 1836 by those radicals who sought to emulate the Tory Carlton founded in 1832 and avoid the embrace of the Whig element in what became the Liberal party, Glyn became a founder member. The Club had 237 MPs in membership at the end of 1836. He remained a member of Brooks's, but later resigned, though he was re-elected in 1849 after he became an MP.[10]

Another matter in which he was involved and where he seems to have been brought in because of his experience rather any endeavour on his part to build business for Glyn's was the proposal for a Bank of India. Another stage was reached in the abolition of the trading privileges of long established monopolistic companies when in 1833 the East India Charter Act ended the East India Company's commercial life while maintaining its political governing function, so making it largely an agency of government. This followed a period of major changes in the trading patterns between Britain and India which coupled with other factors, some internal to the firms, led to the collapse of a number of trading houses, notably John Palmer & Co. George Larpent was widely involved in Anglo-Asian commercial politics. His firm, Cockerell and Trail, had precipitated the fall of Palmers as it had called in Palmer's debts to its London partner. Larpent however saw the weaknesses of the agency houses and he was convinced that they should not be permitted to engage in banking on their own account. His firm did not permit their new sister house in Calcutta to do so.[11]

In 1833 Larpent put forward the idea of a British based joint-stock bank for India where banking facilities were limited. He circulated a paper to leading City bankers and merchants, including Thomas Tooke, John Hodgson, J.H. Palmer, George Carr Glyn, Lefevre, Nathaniel Rothschild, William Crawford, and Samuel Gurney, who met on 1 November to discuss the establishment of a Bank of India. Larpent argued that the failures of merchant houses trading with China and 'the derangement of commercial

[9] *The Life of the Rt Hon Sir William Molesworth*, Mrs Fawcett, 1901, 74, letter to his mother, 19 Feb. 1835.

[10] Hull History Centre C/DPF/1171, Glyn to Pease 6 Jul. 1830; *Memorials of Brooks's: from the foundation of the club 1764 to the close of the nineteenth century: compiled from the records of the club*, ed. J.F. Webb-Prosser, 1907, 111 and 161; information from Simon Blundell, Librarian of the Reform Club. In 1849 Glyn was sponsored by the Duke of Bedford and Edward Ellice.

[11] Anthony Webster, *The Twilight of the East India Company, The evolution of Anglo-Asian Commerce and Politics, 1790–1860*, 2009, 104–107.

credit in the country exhibit in a strong light the mischievous effect of the union of banking and commercial business and call for their separation.' Loan capital was needed to develop the produce and manufactures of India. The Bank would oil the wheels of international commerce by providing credit to merchants in India and Canton. It would also be a mechanism for the transmission of East India Company funds to London. An initial paid-up capital of £1,000,000 was proposed with subscribed capital of a further £1,000,000. The decision to end the East India Company's monopoly of the China tea trade from April 1834 would give an opportunity which would be difficult to take in ordinary times. Branches in Calcutta, Bombay and Madras were envisaged. Thomas Tooke strongly supported the proposal, but Palmer, who in addition to being governor of the Bank of England was now heavily involved in the China trade through the house of Palmer, Dent, McKillop & Co. dissented. Though not opposed to a bank he thought the scheme totally impracticable and would adversely affect existing arrangements.[12]

Glyn does not seem to have shared Palmer's view as he was asked to draw up a petition to Lord Althorp, the Chancellor of the Exchequer, for a royal charter which Palmer did not sign, though his partner McKillop did with Lefevre, Tooke, Hodgson, Gurney, Glyn, Larpent, and Crawford.[13] The project did not come to anything in 1833, but was revived in 1836 following the establishment of the London East India and China Association which Larpent chaired. Glyn does not seem to have been involved. However the Glasgow, and Liverpool East India and China Associations were opposed to the proposal, fearing it meant a revival of London dominance. Palmer reiterated his opposition and the impetus for the project faded.[14]

As the Bank of England's charter was due for renewal in 1833, a parliamentary committee was set up in 1832 to report on the working of the Bank. At issue were the questions of the power of the Bank of England, and whether the creation of joint-stock banks should be made easier, as they were thought to have the advantage over the private banks in that their liability was spread over many shareholders rather than over six partners at most. Horsley Palmer summed up the Bank's function:

[12] University of London Library, Larpent Papers, MS 172, (i), (ii) and (xi). John Horsley Palmer was a director of the Bank from 1811 to 1857 and Deputy Governor 1828–30 and Governor 1830–33.

[13] Ibid (iii). The document is attributed to Richard Carr Glyn, but is in George Carr Glyn's handwriting.

[14] Ibid (xiii); Webster, 109–111.

> The Bank of England is required to provide a requisite supply of paper money for the average circulation of the sphere in which it acts, and to uphold public and private credit when called upon. When commercial credit is affected, it is in such times that the credit of a great body like the Bank of England is available and has the power to uphold the credit of the country.

Palmer believed in the need for a fixed principle of operations by the Bank, subject to a discretionary relaxation in cases of emergency – the Palmer Rule –

> the reserve held by the Bank should be such that when the exchange rate was just about to become adverse (i.e. gold was just about to flow out) one-third of its liabilities should be matched by coin and bullion; and that it should thereafter maintain its securities unchanged, so that any loss of gold would equally reduce the notes or the deposits.[15]

Glyn, with George Grote, was the chief spokesman of the private London bankers. Glyn was very much in favour of a single bank of issue in London. It meant that the private banker only had to hold in reserve notes from the one bank. A multiplicity of notes would effectively diminish deposits and make assistance to the second class of trader more difficult. Witnesses were questioned about the impact of changes in the circulation of Bank notes on commodity prices and the exchanges. Glyn doubted whether credit restrictions by the Bank reduced commodity prices. The Bank was competing more actively with them than it used to do, but, though it opened private accounts as readily as the private banks, it made advances less freely. He accepted that on the whole the Bank had exercised a very wise and liberal discretion with respect to advances made by discount, but did not think the private bankers felt the slightest dependence on the Bank. They considered themselves the best customers the Bank had except for the Government.[16] He favoured the abolition of the new rule that notes or bills for less than £50 should not be payable in London, and the reduction of the Bank's monopoly radius of 65 miles to, say 25 miles.[17] He expressed hostility to joint stock bankers. The Country Bankers Association had said 'All Joint Stock Banking Companies aim at making all cases conform to their established rules; while

[15] Horsefield, The Opinions of Horsley Palmer.

[16] Committee of Secrecy on Expediency of Renewing Charter of Bank of England, PP, 1831–2, vi, Q. 2894.

[17] Ibid, Qs 2828–31.

the very essence of a Private Banker is that he makes a rule for every case.' Glyn explained that the London private banker had relationships with businesses which were none too soundly established. No public body could have access to those sources of information enjoyed by the private banks on which the decision to grant or withhold a loan was based. Customers with established businesses would often come to Glyn's without the least notice and say 'Put for £5,000 or £10,000 to my account'. He did not think that such arrangements could be made with the requisite speed and secrecy by public establishments.

He went so far as to say that you never can get that done by a secretary or a board of directors, which you can have done by six individuals in partnership. 'I should draw this distinction generally, that you cannot get a director to do that for his proprietors, which a private banker will not do for himself.' He opposed joint-stock banks issuing their own notes because he felt that this would add to fluctuations in the volume of currency. He also thought that commercial leaders would not come forward for loans with the same confidence and alacrity if they knew that their claim was to be considered by a board of directors which included their business rivals. He argued that joint-stock banks were not suited to London 'the largest centre to which all the money transactions of the Empire point.' He added that he was not speaking for banks like Drummonds and Coutts, the gentlemanly banks mainly west of Temple Bar which principally held the accounts of individuals. City business was essentially different from West End business. 'I should say our reserved deposit was necessarily a much larger one than the deposit at the west end of the town banker.'[18]

To some extent debate about the issues raised was limited by the preoccupation of the Government and Parliament with the Reform Bill, and the committee never made a report. Glyn's consolation was that the Chancellor of the Exchequer, Lord Althorp wrote to say that he considered the evidence of Glyn and Samuel Gurney was the best practical evidence the Committee had, and he was confident the public would think so generally.

However Peel, Lord John Russell, Sir James Graham were on the committee and radicals like Thomas Attwood, a witness and Sir Henry Parnell, a committee member, carried little weight and there was no serious opposition to the renewal of the charter. In 1833 the charter was renewed for 21 years with liberty for the Government to 'break the lease' at the end of ten. The sixty-five mile radius remained. Bank notes were to become full legal tender except at the Bank itself and its branches, although Peel and

[18] Ibid, qq. 2828–31, 2883, 2892, 2928, 2942–4, 3063, and 3113.

others voted against this provision. Dealings in bills and notes with less than three months to run were exempted from the limit of 5 per cent in the Usury laws so that in future the Bank was able to raise its rate to more than 5 per cent to respond to crises. All banks were required to make returns of their circulation and were authorised to issue notes for less than £50 payable in London. Joint stock banks were permitted in London provided they issued no notes. Ten days after royal assent the final draft of the prospectus of the London and Westminster Bank was issued. The National Provincial and the London Joint Stock Banks soon followed.

Apart from serving on the committee Glyn was a very interested observer of developments in banking and financial policy and, as David Kynaston put it, one of the sharpest commentators.[19] His comments survive in large measure because of his close banking links with Liverpool and he regularly wrote to Joseph Langton, to keep him abreast of the situation in London. He was the deputy agent of the Bank of England's branch in Liverpool until appointed as manager of the Bank of Liverpool when it was formed as a joint stock bank in 1831 largely as a matter of civic pride following the establishment in Liverpool of branches of the Bank of England and the Manchester and Liverpool District Bank. Glyn's letters demonstrate the kind of relationship which a London banker enjoyed with his country correspondents though they were probably more frequent and more informative on matters not related to banking business than was general. Indeed Glyn said that Samuel Hope of S. Hope & Co, another Liverpool bank, for which Glyn's were the London agents was 'most unreasonably jealous of my correspondence with you.'[20] The correspondence buttressed Glyn's connections with the strong Liverpool party on the LBR and later the LNWR. Successive chairmen and directors were active in commercial and public life in Liverpool. Joseph Hornby was chairman of the Bank of Liverpool from 1839 to 1843 and later Joseph Ewart and Hardman Earle were directors and in the 1850s chairmen. All were directors of the LNWR at various times. Glyn's were appointed agents when the bank began business. Glyn then accepted an annual payment of £600, but this rose over the years as the business of the Bank of Liverpool increased. In 1865 Glyn's commission for keeping the London account was raised form £1,250 to £2,000 a year.[21]

The letters sometimes contained political comments in which Glyn did not hesitate to express his Liberal views. 'Nothing whatever is known as

19 Kynaston, 107.

20 LP 330, 23 Oct. 1837.

21 George Chandler, *Four Centuries of Banking*, 1964, I, 294.

to the new administration, but that the Duke of Wellington has his way,' he wrote in November 1834 in the hiatus following the fall of the Whig ministry, and commented the following month that he scarcely thought that Lord Stanley would take office under Peel. He told Langton that he was glad he had done so well in the first elections in Liverpool following the Municipal Reform Act, and added that the Council would occupy David Hodgson, a director of the LMR who had become a director of the LBR in 1837, which he probably regarded as a welcome distraction. At the Parliamentary election of 1837 he thought that Sandon and Ewart would be the best return for Liverpool and its business and was much vexed at the result for though Ewart was not the best member for the requirements of such a constituency, his successor was no improvement in that respect and was a Tory.[22]

Some of Glyn's letters were responses to enquires from Langton about the soundness of clients or prospective clients, an important aspect of the relationship between a country banker and his agent in London, and the flow of information was two way. These were mostly succinct and to the point – 'We believe Mr Smith is a very respectable man'; 'the parties are said to be the most respectably connected in Scotland'; 'Messrs K and L are in very good credit in the corn market and are generally considered very steady people'; 'we do not believe him to be a person of much property'; and perhaps the ultimate put down 'the person is dead, very insolvent and cannot pay'.[23]

The upswing of the economy from 1833 not only led to renewed interest in railways but also in joint stock banks, 44 of which were formed in 1832–35 and another 59 in the first half of 1836.[24] Glyn remained hostile to joint stock banks. He thought Langton should know that Cunliffe & Co were much entangled with a bill broker's house which had recently failed. 'It is most difficult to explain the mode in which he has been taken in, but it is another proof of the risk incurred by those who, not having been bred up to the arts of London business, engage in it under the idea of increased profit'.[25] In 1834 he was seriously alarmed at the overeagerness for banking

[22] LP 88, 332, 318 and 320, 18 Nov. 1834, 4 Nov. 1837, and 24 and 26 Jul. 1837. Viscount Sandon, later the Earl of Harrowby, a supporter of Peel and a free trader was MP for Liverpool from 1831 to 1847. William Ewart was a Liberal who had succeeded Huskisson as MP for Liverpool in 1830. He was defeated by a Tory lawyer, Cresswell Cresswell.

[23] LP 5, 14, 15, 29 and 133, 3 Nov. 1831, 14 and 16 Apr. 1832, 13 May 1833 and 1 Feb. 1836.

[24] Baker and Collins, in *Monetary and Banking History*, 52.

[25] LP 43, 26 Oct. 1833.

projects, as were the directors of the Bank of Liverpool and the Bank of Manchester who mounted pressure for more regulation of bank creation.[26] In 1835 he specifically referred to the London and Westminster. 'Every day confirms the opinion of those who think that private banking is more suited to the peculiar wants of this City and consequently the new establishment makes no way. Not one mercantile house of any eminence or large business has opened with it.'[27] Indeed the London and Westminster had been refused admission to the London Bankers Clearing House.

He wrote in October 1834 that the Derby Bank might be added to the list of joint stock banks which are suffering from improvident advances. There is something wrong in the system of management in many of them.[28] He was extremely critical of the policies of the Bank of Manchester. Its decision to issue its own notes was 'the subject of real regret to me on many accounts' he told Langton confidentially.[29] A month later he hoped that this very disagreeable subject would end in the adoption of a better system and their giving up the issue of their own notes. Two days later a communication from the Bank of Manchester left 'little hope of any satisfactory accommodation between us', and by 18 November he was telling Langton that the Manchester Bank had made an arrangement with Denison's & Co. for its London agency – 'it is a great relief to us to be released from a connection requiring such a large number of floating acceptances'.[30] This led to difficulties. After the manager of the Manchester Bank persuaded the directors of the Bank of Liverpool of the reasonableness of his case, Glyn had to visit Liverpool to explain his bank's position. This he did, taking care to emphasise that Glyn's would, if required, stand by the Bank of Liverpool to the extent of a cash advance of £50,000, would accept to the full all bills and securities in the Bank of Liverpool's possession, if generally held by bankers and would accept uncovered for up to £150,000. Glyn's judgement was correct about the excess of paper credit.[31] He was also concerned about the tendency of some of the new banks to develop extensive branch systems without what he considered to be adequate capital reserves. He declined the accounts of

26 LP 72, 25 Aug. 1834; P.L Cottrell and Lucy Newton, Banking in England and Wales, in *Banking Liberalisation*, ed. R. Sylla, R. Tilly and G. Tortelli, 1999, 97.

27 LP 93, 20 Feb. 1835.

28 LP 72 and 81, 25 Aug. and 6 Oct. 1834.

29 LP 83, 6 Oct. 1834. The Bank of Manchester had started business in 1829, despite the opposition of many of the leaders of the Manchester business community. It began to issue its own notes in 1834. The bank narrowly survived disaster in 1836, but was wound up in 1842.

30 LP 86, 87 and 88, 4, 6 and 18 Nov. 1834.

31 Chandler, 1, 260.

exponents of this type of banking,[32] a message he repeated a number of times in 1836, predicting great mischief and complaining he heard of nothing but new banking companies especially in Lancashire.[33] On the other hand he had considerable trust in the Bank of Liverpool, telling Langton that if old Mr Heywood drops 'you will receive a large accession of business and of the best quality'.[34] He declined offers from the new Royal Bank and from the South Lancashire to become their London agents, but was prepared to take on the Union Bank of Manchester, as the directors took the Bank of Liverpool as their prototype.[35] He moved on from outright opposition to joint-stock banks and by 1836 thought they should be obliged to conform to a particular set of wholesome regulations.[36] He agreed with William Clay that no joint stock bank should be allowed to begin business until at least its capital, management and constitution had been approved by some form of sanctioning board, and earlier he had pressed Lord Althorp when Chancellor of the Exchequer to accept this idea.[37] Although he personally did not give evidence to the Parliamentary Committees which looked into joint-stock banking in 1836, 1837 and 1838, initially instigated by William Clay, he did encourage the Bank of Liverpool to put forward their ideas for reform. Public supervision of banking companies was to be one of the reforms incorporated in the 1844 Act.

An unusual item of business occurred following the Abolition of Slavery Act in 1833 when Glyn and Thomas Hallifax acted as agents in collecting slave compensation on behalf of the Bernard family of Bristol, and William Heath and his wife of Jamaica, but their role was a formal one, as distinct from Currie & Raikes or Smith, Payne & Smiths who were engaged as mortgagees of West Indian estates.[38]

Glyn's were very ready to assist in City emergencies. In 1835 in the Spanish panic in the Carlist war Spanish stock fell in one week from 72 to 50. It seriously affected at least half the membership of the London Stock Exchange. There was an emergency whip-round in the City. Glyn wrote that the exertions which have been made in which we have felt it our duty

[32] LP 228 and 230, 3 and 7 Dec. 1836.

[33] LP 143 and 153, 2 Mar. and 14 Apr. 1836.

[34] LP 113, 23 Sept. 1835.

[35] LP 153 and 154, 14 and 18 Apr. 1836.

[36] LP 160, 11 May 1836.

[37] LP 163, 164 and 168, 13, 16 and 30 May 1836. William Clay was Liberal MP for Tower Hamlets.

[38] N. Draper, The City of London and Slavery: evidence from the first dock companies, 1795–1800, *EHR*, 61, 2008, 450.

to contribute to the utmost with prudence would, he trusted, prevent much further mischief.[39] As explained in chapter 8 Glyn was also concerned about speculation in railway stocks in the boom which started later in 1835 and the number of promotions.

Glyn's correspondence with the Bank of Liverpool shows that he was not a committed follower of either the Banking or Currency schools of thought, but a pragmatist ready to support discretionary and common sense policy to maintain confidence in the money market. Although the Bank of England's policies in general received his support he saw inconsistencies as the financial pressure developed in 1836–37. Four-fifths of the Court of the Bank in this period were merchants[40] but it was finely balanced between those currency theorists who believed that a general contraction of the note supply was the appropriate remedy for unfavourable foreign exchange rates, irrespective of the needs of the public and those who while accepting the need for contraction of the money supply were more conscious of the Bank's public responsibilities. In October 1835 the Bank decided not to make advances on bills endorsed by joint-stock banks of issue. This was a move against rival note issuers in an attempt to control the money supply more effectively. Glyn was not opposed to the general principle but he thought it a very strong measure clearly aimed at the Northern and Central Bank and the Bank of Manchester which might result in serious consequences for the bill brokers who would not be able to supply their wants with this restriction especially as money was already tight in the market. It was not expedient and not fair to turn round upon the issuing joint-stock banks and discount houses which held many bills of this kind without some previous and sufficient notice.[41]

Glyn's were not very exposed to the 1836–37 crisis which largely had its origins in the American trade, and acutely affected those houses involved in that trade, particularly Timothy Wiggins, Thomas Wilson and George Wildes, but it had more general repercussions partly because of the policies of the Bank of which Glyn was often critical. As early as May 1836 he noted that there was an increasing apprehension in the money market of a great scarcity of money, in part caused by the East India Company receiving a large sum which meant that it was locked up at the Bank and not employed. The discount brokers had been pushed but the Bank had behaved very well in accommodating them. Money however remained tight. In July 1836 he reported that the stock of gold in the Bank had diminished but

39 LP 104, 28 May 1834.

40 Anthony Howe, From 'Old Corruption' to 'New Probity': The Bank of England and its Directors in the Age of Reform, *Financial History Review*, 1, 1994, 25.

41 LP 117 and 118, 8 and 12 Oct. 1835.

he had not heard of any general export of it to the US. A fortnight later he wrote that the amount of American bills was very large, especially on Morrison, Cryder and Co. They were shippers of bullion to the States, but were the only house doing so. As a result the Bank of England were getting 'very fidgetty' about 'the American houses.'[42] At the end of August the Bank ordered a considerable reduction in the holdings of bills accepted by the major merchants in the Anglo-American trade. Thus the banks and discount houses holding large quantities of American bills found the liquidity of their assets reduced overnight. The Bank of Liverpool, closely connected to such merchants, especially W. & J. Brown (William Brown had been its first chairman), sent a deputation to the Bank to plead for a relaxation of the new ruling. As a result the Bank permitted the discounting of American bills drawn against the actual transfer of goods. Glyn congratulated Langton on their action in bringing the deputation so speedily and commented that he could scarcely imagine any act more calculated to produce confusion and less likely to attain the object which the Bank desired. He concluded that the rate of interest was the proper mode of effecting an improvement in the foreign exchanges and was sure in time to produce its effects without essential inconveniences.[43] He therefore welcomed the rise in interest rates but was dismayed by the continuing poor foreign exchanges. He was particularly critical of the Bank's refusal to discount first class American bills on a number of occasions, a view also taken by Overend & Gurney. Glyn's had tried to counteract this policy by keeping up supplies to the discount houses to prevent them from having recourse to the Bank.[44] He was also critical of the Bank's making available quarterly loans in September at 3½ per cent. In late October in easier money market conditions the Bank relaxed its restrictions on American bills so removing, as Glyn put it, the odious distinction against the American merchants.[45] Glyn himself had been the medium of communication between the Bank and some of the American houses informing them that the Bank was ready to take any amount of paper.[46] Commenting on a series of dealings on a bill of which the Governor, now James Pattison, had been critical, Glyn said 'the fact is the Governor will not or cannot understand that the transactions are perfectly legitimate.'[47]

42 LP 181 and 185, 2 and 16 Jul. 1836.
43 LP 187, 6 Sept. 1836.
44 LP 191, 193 and 195, 20, 24 Sept. and 8 Oct. 1836.
45 LP 206, 28 Oct. 1836.
46 LP 205, 24 Oct. 1836.
47 LP 191, 20 Sept. 1836.

In the autumn however he remained generally optimistic, though fearful of exorbitant interest rates and the subsequent loss of capital abroad. This was not the case as in November there was run on the Irish banks, particularly the Commercial and Agricultural Bank of Ireland. Much gold was shipped from Britain to Ireland. Glyn hoped the Government would act to support the market in public securities. He appreciated the difficult position in which the Bank was placed and told Langton 'we must make great allowance for the Bank, they have a most difficult card to play – the demand for bullion from Ireland has been very large, which upon their diminished stock of bullion is serious.' On 14 November he told Langton that he had been with Spring Rice, the Chancellor of the Exchequer, that morning and he was fully satisfied of every needful co-operation on the part of Government to counteract any tendency towards internal panic. He expected Spring Rice, to 'take a step by which the money and exchange markets would be relieved.'[48] The Commercial and Agricultural Bank failed, followed by a decision to raise the rate to 2½ per cent, a long overdue measure in Glyn's opinion.[49] At the end of November there were rumours that the Northern and Central Bank of England was insolvent, and the Bank of England while pursuing a generally liberal discount policy was refusing some bills such as those bearing the names of issuing joint-stock banks and was anxious to discourage the circulation of three month bankers drafts which had risen during the pressure for cash. Glyn supported these measures 'provided there was little inconvenience to general business'.[50]

He saw the difficulties of the Northern and Central as confirming his opposition to joint-stock banks issuing their own notes and particularly those with large branch systems, 'the district banks' as they were known. Indeed the Northern and Central had been regarded as the 'boom bank' with its rapid opening of 36 branches.[51] Again he and other bankers were consulted by the Bank of England which he praised for supporting the Northern and Central despite the deception of its directors. In acting for the general good the Bank had saved many particularly in Lancashire from insolvency.[52]

Glyn was more directly involved in another rescue operation taken by the Bank. Sir James Esdaile, Esdaile, Grenfell, Thomas & Co. was a London bank which was agent to seventy-two country banks. As early as July 1836 when Esdailes problems began Glyn was telling Langton that the subject of

[48] LP 213, 215 and 217, 11, 14 and 16 Nov. 1836.
[49] LP 219, 19 Nov. 1836.
[50] LP 224, 28 Nov. 1836.
[51] Cottrell and Newton, 97.
[52] LP 227, 237, 238 and 240, 1, 17, 19 and 22 Dec. 1836.

Esdailes had caused him regret and annoyance especially as his brother in law, Pascoe St Leger Grenfell, a partner in Esdailes, was one of his oldest and best friends and the groundless loss of his connection had been most vexatious. His conviction at that time based upon the best information was that Esdailes were perfectly sound and possessed ready means to a considerable extent. Old Mr Esdaile was decidedly a man of property but Glyn nevertheless had urged the expediency of adding to the partnership a man of property who might satisfy the world of the ill nature of the surmises about the bank's difficulties.[53]

American finance and banking were less highly developed than the British. The first effects of the American crisis of late 1836 were felt by local banks in areas which traded heavily with America. Esdailes was soon caught in their correspondents' difficulties. In December 1836. Glyn and several other bankers had been so concerned that they had seen Esdailes' books and then wrote to the governor of the Bank of England to say that in their opinion after every proper deduction they were solvent and upon a liquidation there would be a considerable surplus, but a large amount of assets were so locked up that they could not be realised or rendered available for Esdailes within any reasonable period. The Bank had already advanced £140,000 and Glyn advised that it did not look as if the 'house could be conducted with ease and safety without a further advance. A very slight pressure would render it necessary to apply for further aid.' Although Esdailes struggled on into the New Year, by mid-January they were in difficulties. The repercussions of a failure would be great because of its links with so many country banks. Their position had been very unpleasant during the two previous months, wrote Glyn.[54] He now thought it unlikely that the Bank would increase its advance by the amount needed and with other private bankers offered to contribute £100,000 which would be repaid after the Bank had been repaid. He emphasised to the Bank that the consequence of even a temporary stoppage of such a house as Esdailes in the present unsettled state of public credit would be so fearful that 'we deem it right to press upon the Bank in the most urgent manner the necessity of interfering to prevent such a calamity'. It was thought that £500,000 in all would be necessary. Most of the leading houses were prepared to go along with this, and ten banks signed. Freshfield, the Bank's lawyer, questioned whether the Bank ought to undertake the liquidation of a London banking house. He had great difficulty in conceding the principle. The Court met the following day and at first was reluctant to help but the private bankers offered to contribute rather more.

[53] LP 182, 4 Jul. 1836.

[54] LP 254, 12 Jan. 1837.

In the event they and the Bank seem to have contributed £142,000 and £166,000 respectively. 'We have had a great struggle but have succeeded in carrying the immediate liquidation,' Glyn commented. He later added that if they had not forced the arrangement on the Bank such a sensation would have been raised throughout the country that every sovereign would have been drained form the Bank. Only three days after the liquidation he was reporting that all Esdaile's country banks were taken up except for one.[55] Glyn and John Masterman were appointed inspectors and completed most of their task quickly. They were assisted in 1838 when as Glyn put it 'good arises frequently out of mischief'. The total destruction by fire of the Royal Exchange, including the offices of the Royal Exchange Assurance Co. on the night of 10–11 January enabled them to sell to the insurance company the newly built and commodious premises of Esdailes at 21 Lombard Street for £16,000.[56] Esdaile's paid a dividend of 13s 6d in the pound, but the inspectors found it impossible to get a landowner, Sir John Owen, to settle a debt to the bank of nearly £40,000, so a further 6½d was not paid until early 1873 just before Glyn's death. Glyn's benefited immediately when nine country banks who had used Esdailes as their London agents transferred to Glyn's including Bacon, Cobbold of Ipswich, the Birmingham Banking Co. and Lacon, Youell & Co. of Great Yarmouth.[57] Three country bankers who had Esdailes as their London agents however failed in 1836 and 1837 as a result of the collapse.[58] Glyn's also benefited when they took over Ladbroke, Kingscote and Gillman when Felix Ladbroke decided to retire. 290 accounts were transferred to Glyn's. Robert Ladbroke and Henry Kingscote continued to receive a proportion of the interest on the transferred accounts, and Kingscote was subsequently involved in a number of banking ventures associated with Glyn's.[59]

Glyn's doubts about the Bank of England's policy increased considerably in 1837. He agreed with the Bank on the need to contract the money-supply, in practice the note-supply, to secure an improvement in the foreign exchanges and to attract gold to London. But he had different views on the best means to employ. He believed that rationing discounts or raising the bank rate

[55] LP 256, 258 and 259, 17, 20 and 21 Jan. 1837.

[56] LP 342, 11 Jan. 1838; *Morning Post* 12 and 13 Jan. 1838.

[57] Anon, The Esdaile Crisis, *Three Banks Review*, 70, June 1966, 39–48; Fulford, Appendix III, and RBS Archives, GM/234.

[58] Margaret Dawes and C.N. Ward-Perkins, *Country banks of England and Wales : private provincial banks and bankers, 1688–1953*, 2000, 27.

[59] Royal Bank of Scotland Heritage Hub, Ladbroke and Co., 1730–1841. (http://heritagearchives.rbs.com/companies/list/ladbroke-and-co.html).

above 5 per cent would undermine confidence and cause an internal demand for cash. He thought the best method was for the Bank to sell its holdings of Government securities, known as the deadweight. If the Bank did not employ the proceeds of the sale the circulation would be reduced. It would also check the rise in stock prices and so 'prevent boats full of foreign bonds arriving again to the detriment of the gold reserve.' However he complained that the directors of the Bank 'stick to the deadweight with a pertinacity arising from their requiring to pay it to their dividend and will not offer it on reasonable terms'. Instead the Bank restricted its accommodation.[60] He later said that

> I had been a firm advocate for their general line of policy but latterly there has been so much vacillation and sudden alteration in the proceedings, both in their conduct towards individuals and the general system, that I am rather distrustful and am strongly confirmed in my idea of having parliamentary commissioners to look after their acts. Though they might be right in principle yet towards the bill brokers they have acted harshly and without proper notice.[61]

One of Glyn's main concerns was that too many of the Bank of England's directors were impregnated with political economy doctrines. He placed great reliance on the 'practical knowledge' of Horsley Palmer to overcome these insufficiently pragmatic tendencies.[62] In February he saw Palmer and explained his thinking. He told Langton that Palmer said he 'was much counteracted recently' a reference to his colleagues (i e those of the currency school) who did not share his views.[63] However Glyn was soon explaining to Langton that improved confidence in the London market and less pressure for cash was due to 'Palmer's firmness in the Bank and his practical knowledge had gained ascendancy over the doctrinaires by whom our worthy governor was led'.[64] However the Bank was soon faced with the problems of Anglo-American merchants who had over extended in the boom of 1836, and their position worsened with the scarcity of cash and the high interest rates. Wildes', Wiggins' and Wilson's, the weakest of the American houses, approached the Bank for special aid. Though Glyn was initially confident that help would be forthcoming, the Bank vacillated and

60 LP 248, 261 and 264, 5, 25 and 30 Jan. 1837.
61 LP 272, 11 Feb. 1837.
62 LP 277, 18 Feb. 1837.
63 LP 273, 13 Feb. 1837.
64 LP 277, 18 Feb. 1836.

then refused help.[65] Two directors of the Bank of Liverpool wrote to the Governor of the 'great embarrassment which prevails in Lancashire both in the Mercantile and Manufacturing interests, arising chiefly from the want of confidence occasioned by the doubt and discredit thrown upon American paper', adding that 'unless immediate steps are taken to restore confidence and mercantile credit, we must soon inevitably witness the most awful crisis ever known in this or any other country'. They appealed to James Pattison, the outgoing Governor, to be instrumental in preserving the country from the calamities now threatened.[66]

The merchants were considering appealing to the Government when the Bank granted to each of the three firms £200,000 of abnormal discounts on personal and other commitments which enabled them to meet their immediate obligations. Glyn had been called with other London bankers to the Treasury committee of the Bank before the decision was taken and told Langton:

> I may tell you that had it not been for the firmness of Horsley Palmer and the Deputy Governor, (Timothy Curtis), the Governor (James Pattison) and his party in the Court would have brought down every American house and involved every mercantile and manufacturing connexion in general confusion. I really think the Governor is mad upon this subject. He and I have been brought into disagreeable collision, but acting under the advice of Curtis and Palmer, and knowing his reign is over in three months, they advised me to have no notion.

It was already known that J.R. Reid was to be the Bank's deputy governor 'though it is the fashion to decry him … I have always found him a very reasonable man, fully alive to the duties of the Bank, and not too much impregnated with political economy doctrines – he, Curtis and Palmer fall well together'.[67]

For his part Glyn hoped that a larger view of the Bank's responsibilities would more readily prevail under Curtis, but it was soon tested again. By May the three Ws were in difficulties again. Remittances from the United

65 LP 282 and 284, 25 Feb. and 2 Mar. 1836.

66 Bank of England, G4/59, 21 Mar. 1837 quoted in Kynaston, 108.

67 LP 286, 6 Mar. 1838. The Governor and Deputy Governor were only appointed for two year terms. Sir John Reid was senior partner in East and West India merchants Reid, Irving & Co. and MP for Dover. Pattison was Liberal MP for the City. Timothy Curtis, then deputy Governor, succeeded Pattison. Curtis was an engineer, who had been a governor of the Bank since 1820.

States were few and many bills were arriving only to be dishonoured, while those accepted were difficult to discount. At the height of the crisis on 24th May with the three main Anglo-American houses in severe difficulties Glyn wrote that 'we all entertain the strongest hopes of the Bank taking the decisive step and determining to carry these houses' and adding the next day that 'everything was progressing very satisfactorily with the Americans'.[68] As the Bank continued to delay its decision he grew more pessimistic. 'From what Mr Palmer tells me I fear the result.' He was confident of Curtis and Reid, but not of most of the rest of the Court.[69] The Court asked the governor and deputy governor to lay before the Prime Minister, Melbourne, and Chancellor, Spring-Rice, the applications from Wilson and Wiggin for further relief, and to state to them the apprehension of the Directors. Ministers admitted they were impressed with the public inconvenience which would result to the manufacturing and commercial interests from a suspension of the houses engaged in the American trade. They were most anxious if it could be done with safety that these calamities should be mitigated if not averted, but it was not within their province to direct or influence the decision of the Bank as they possessed neither the data nor the knowledge by which the solvency of commercial houses could be ascertained. The buck therefore was passed back to the Bank, which refused to intervene as the affairs of the three firms were such as prevent their continuing further support and forced them to suspend business. Glyn said the annoyance felt and expressed by Horsley Palmer was not disguised. The proposal was lost against the Governor and his deputy by one vote.[70] Wildes', Wiggins' and Wilson's went and a number of small firms also fell. However the fact that the news reached England that specie payment in the United States had been suspended helped restore confidence in London. Bills due could now be paid in notes.

Two more Liverpool firms were now in difficulties: Morrison, Cryder and Browns. Glyn noted 'I believe that Morrison has taken his deeds and parchments to the Bank. It must have been a bitter step.' The Bank was willing on the security offered to lend £325,000.[71] A week later the Bank also bailed out Browns which had been helped to negotiate with the Bank by the Bank of Liverpool.

The 1837 crisis had one extremely important consequence for George Glyn personally and for Glyn's Bank. As will be seen in chapter 15 on Glyn's

[68] LP 289 and 290, 24 and 25 May 1836.

[69] LP 292, 31 May 1836.

[70] LP 293, 3 Jun. 1836.

[71] LP 297, 8 Jun. 1836.

international activities, the imminent prospect of Wilsons' failure who were the London agents for both the Province of Upper Canada and for the Bank of Upper Canada led to an approach to George Carr Glyn by the Bank of Upper Canada to become their agent. George was able to use the situation to secure also the joint agency with Barings of the Province of Upper Canada. Glyn was directly involved with one follow-up to the crisis, which led to a long term involvement in Canada. Meanwhile at a meeting of the principal creditors of Wilsons on 5 June he was appointed with Palmer, Bates and John Cryder one of the inspectors to look into the company's assets and debts to establish how much could be paid to the creditors.[72]

Glyn remained critical of Bank policy. In September he expressed surprise that with the reserves still relatively low, the Bank should offer its quarterly loans at the low rate of 4 per cent. 'I fear it is tending to give currency to the expectation of money being very cheap and too much inclination to the spirit of speculation.'[73]

Later in 1837 another American development concerned Glyn. This was the attempt by Nicholas Biddle, president of the Bank of the United States, to bolster the cotton market. He built up large holdings of cotton which was exported to Liverpool where his agents released only a little at a time. The operation was financed by borrowing and by the sale of American stock on the London market by the Bank of the United State's London agent, Samuel Jaudon. The Bank of England and others were concerned at what they saw as a distortion of the proper working of the market. Glyn told Langton of his own disapproval and that of the Bank, saying that, if co-operation in London and Liverpool could be relied on, Jaudon's proceedings would soon be checked. Glyn's themselves had refused Jaudon's account as they were certain that 'the day will come when Mr J. will require pretty considerable support and advances'.[74]

By the end of the decade Glyn's was one of the largest private banks. Figures for business passed through the Clearing House for 1840 show three banks with over £100,000,000 of business – Barclays, £107,000,000, Glyn's £105,000,000 and Jones Loyd, £104,000,000. Together they accounted for almost a third of the total of £978,000,000 and only Masterman (£90,000,000) and Robarts (£80,000,000) approached them.[75] The number

[72] LP 295, 6 Jun. 1836; *The Times*, 6 Jun. 1837.

[73] LP 325, 7 Sept. 1837.

[74] LP 335, 20 Nov. 1837.

[75] *Bankers Magazine*, July 1844, 261. In 1839 the total cleared was £954,401,600 for which notes of £66,275,000 were required for settlement. (Robert Martin Holland, *The London Bankers Clearing House*, 1910, 269, also D.M. Evans, *City Men and City Manners*, 1852).

of country banks for which Glyn's acted as London agents had increased from 49 in 1830 to 68 by 1840: the increase being assisted by the failure of Esdailes, but was particularly marked in the Midlands which now accounted for almost a quarter of such banks.[76]

[76] Derived from Fulford, Appendix III. In August 1844 the *Bankers Magazine* published lists of country banks and their London agents. Glyn's total was 50 but a number on Fulford's list were not included.

CHAPTER SEVEN

Chairman of the London and Birmingham

Before the London and Birmingham Railway opened for traffic Glyn unexpectedly became chairman. Solly had to resign in April 1837 because he had been declared bankrupt and so was disqualified from being a Director and Chairman of the Company. The heavy duties on Baltic timber maintained by the British government to protect the Canadian timber trade meant that he and, particularly, his son diversified into riskier business – hemp, corn and especially tallow. Solly had also advanced £40,000 to save one of his brothers from bankruptcy which led to a lawsuit.[1] His colleagues on the LBR board regretted his departure. They said he had carried out his duties with exemplary assiduity and ability, and with a constant zeal for the interests of the Company. They then resolved unanimously that Glyn be appointed chairman in his place. This was a crucial time in the development of the railway. Much had been done but the work of construction was incomplete and the enterprise had still to prove it would be a successful operation. John Francis stressed the novelty of the railway world. Everything was untried. The result was that the directors were at fault.

> They were good governors of a dock corporation, and they were capital managers of an assurance company; but they too often made the mistake of thinking that railways required a new mode of business. Mr Glyn … applied the ordinary rules of business and was awarded by success.[2]

Glyn immediately introduced two new mechanisms for overseeing the development of the line. First two station committees were appointed,

1 Solly, ii, 271.
2 *John Francis, History of the English Railway*, 1851, 2, 4.

one for each end of the line, to superintend and carry into effect every arrangement connected with the practical opening of the railway. Second in a novel development he gave individual directors a role in the supervision of the construction works. To this end individual directors were appointed for the eleven sections into which the line was divided. They were specially charged with regular inspections and superintendence of all contracts for the works of the railway and of the executed portions of such works. The secretaries were to provide them with details statements from the engineers' reports of the total quantity of work to be performed by the contractor and of the quantities of excavation, etc which should be executed week by week, with the number of men who ought to be employed on each separate work to ensure the completion of the whole by the appointed times. The directors were to compare every fortnight work which ought to be performed, and that completed, to visit the works from time to time and to report to the appropriate LBR Committee any deficiency on the rate of progress, to authorise summarily any steps needed except those of a more serious character which should be reported to the appropriate Committee with recommendations. Thus Euston and Camden Stations and the Extension Line to Euston were assigned to Calvert; Tring to Earle; Coventry to Garnett; and Berkswell, Yardley and Saltley Viaduct to Rathbone.[3]

Glyn was presumably led to this course by what he regarded as an insufficiency of control of the contractors by the management, but he was giving responsibilities to the directors which later would be regarded as falling within the sphere of the officers though at this date the lines between them were not drawn clearly. He safeguarded the position of the engineers by insisting that all instructions from the superintending directors to the assistant engineers had to be made through the Engineer-in-Chief, Robert Stephenson.

Glyn's efforts to give the directors a more active role in the management of the company continued. In October 1837 it was decided to draw up a rota for the daily attendance of directors at Euston. Glyn did not think this arrangement was likely to last, but thought that his idea of a director attending at Euston daily with weekly committee meetings was better than having new committee men as managing directors. He hoped the non-resident directors would 'make this sacrifice until the details of our system are matured' as he thought it right not to impose on those living at a distance.[4] However two days after his comments to Langton the Board decided on a more formal

[3] TNA, RAIL 384/2, 12 Apr. 1837, where a complete list of the directors assigned to sections of the line can be found.

[4] Barclays Archives, 25/265, Langton Papers (LP) 335, 20 Nov. 1837.

arrangement which showed that, under pressure from the non-resident directors, they were not content to leave matters to directors conveniently placed in London. In the following month the duties of the Committee of Management were defined as follows–

1. to superintend and carry into effect the laws and resolutions of the board, and bye-laws and regulations of the Company.

2. to recommend to the board appointments of officers and the higher class of servants and all additions to the numbers of inferior servants and workmen, and to hear and decide upon all complaints.

3. to inspect and sanction all orders for stocks and stores.

4. to constitute an audit for the effective examination of all bills and charges previous to payment.

5. to receive the reports of the secretariat and other heads of departments and superintendents and to give advice, assistance and direction in all cases of emergency and difficulty.

All orders were to be conveyed to the Outdoor Department through Moorsom and to the Indoor Department through Creed.[5]

The intention was that this committee should meet daily at Euston for an hour. It was to consist of two from London, two from Birmingham and two from Lancashire. One of Glyn's motives may well have been to reduce the workload falling on him personally. He unexpectedly took on the chairmanship some months before the first part of the line opened and at the same time had to deal with banking crises including the fall of the three American houses and helping Browns avoid bankruptcy. He told Langton that 'I could not have gone on long as it has worked out lately.'[6]

For a time this committee did meet daily, usually under Glyn's chairmanship. Glyn seems to have been an active chairman, taking the lead on a number of matters and not hesitating to intervene with officials when necessary. He told Creed that Moorsom said nothing about the arrangements at Birmingham for passengers to and from the GJR station. This should be arranged. On the other hand he told Moorsom that he was content that he

5 TNA, RAIL 384/45, 22 Nov. 1837. London Committee resolution in concurrence with the Birmingham Committee. 384/62, 21 Oct. 1837 for the non-resident directors views.

6 LP 333, 7 Nov. 1837.

and Creed should follow their own course in working out the details of the arrangements he had transmitted to him.[7]

In 1840 Glyn assured proprietors that duties of the directors had not diminished with the progress of the undertaking. New responsibilities had been created and new obligations placed on them arising from the enormous establishment 'that you have been pleased to entrust to our management.'[8] In 1842 the number of directors had been reduced to 18 but in 1845 it reverted to 24, the number allowed by statute, One reason was to increase their Parliamentary force as Glyn put it, adding that there were several MPs willing to join them.

The Grand Junction Railway had opened its line on 4 July 1837 with through trains from Liverpool and Manchester to Birmingham which ran to their temporary station at Vauxhall Birmingham about a mile away, from the LBR's Curzon Street terminus and the interchange at Birmingham was unsatisfactory for some time. The two companies had failed to agree on joint station arrangements in 1835, and the LBR would not accept the GJR's proposal for a direct connection east of Curzon Street which would have allowed through running without reversal. Thus the LBR and GJR had separate stations in Birmingham. Before the LBR's line was opened for through traffic from London to Birmingham Glyn complained to Creed that Moorsom had said nothing about the arrangements for passengers to and from the GJR station and this should be put in hand.[9] It was November 1838 before the GJR opened its own terminus in Curzon Street, adjacent to, but separate from, the LBR's.

Three days later after the opening of the GJR's line to Birmingham Glyn noted that two postal deliveries from Liverpool and Manchester began that day. He commented that the public convenience would be very great but when the whole distance was completed it would bring about an extraordinary change. Next day however he was put out when the second delivery was a full hour late, as a result of the late arrival of the GJR train in Birmingham. He asked Langton 'what and where were the hindrances'. By 11 July he was hoping that the GJR would improve 'or it will tend to impair confidence in railways and the mode of travelling.' Doubtless he was concerned about the expected opening of the LBR which he told Langton on 15 July he 'hoped' would 'certainly' open on Thursday (20), but the irregularity of the GJR was against us although no one ever thought of

[7] RBS Archives, GM/237, Glyn to Creed, 21 Apr. (a Saturday) and to Moorsom 21 Jun. 1838.

[8] TNA, RAIL 1160/260, 7 Feb. 1840.

[9] RBS Archives, GM/237, 21 Apr. 1838.

making those allowances which were fairly due in a new establishment.[10] The LBR did indeed open from Euston to Boxmoor on 20 July 1837 'for traffic derived from excursions of pleasure and curiosity as few reside locally,' showing how little immediate possibility there was of suburban traffic. There were three trains a day from each end and 39 855 passengers were conveyed on the first 28 days.[11] On 16 October the line opened from Boxmoor to Tring.

However temporary arrangements had to be made at Euston as the winding engines and associated equipment to haul trains up the steep bank from Euston to Camden were not ready and until 14 October steam locomotives were used for that purpose. William Fotheringham Cooke and Charles Wheatstone had already suggested using their primitive electric telegraph on the LMR to communicate from one end of a tunnel to the other, but the directors thought it too complex for sending the few signals required. They now learned that the winding house at the top of the Camden bank would need to know when a train was ready to start. They approached the LBR and met Glyn and Creed and then Stephenson at the end of June and were given the use of the carriage shed at Euston for their experiments. A demonstration to about 20 directors of the LBR went well and by 17 July the circuit had been extended to Camden. Stephenson was satisfied with the results, so much so that following the introduction of better instruments, he decided to recommend strongly a trial on an extended scale. Glyn reported that Cooke was full of enthusiasm for extending the telegraph to Birmingham with an immediate extension to Harrow. The Station sub-committee asked Cooke and Stephenson for an estimate, but the LBR was not destined to be the successful innovator in this instance. The non-resident directors said they were not prepared to undertake further expenditure on trials without clear evidence of its usefulness, and the London committee accepted their view and confined the trial to the Euston to Camden section.[12] A more extensive use of the telegraph had to await the GWR's installation of the system between Paddington and Hanwell in 1839.

There was a double opening on 9 April 1838 when the line was extended from Tring to Denbigh Hall, north of Bletchley and from Curzon Street, Birmingham, to Rugby. The main engineering problem had arisen

[10] LP 308–10, 314, 7, 8, 11, and 14 Jul. 1837.

[11] TNA, RAIL 384/12, 18 Aug. 1838.

[12] John Liffen, Introduction of the electric telegraph in Britain, *Journal for the History of Engineering and Technology*, 80, 2010, 275; TNA, RAIL 384/35, 26 Sept. and 3 and 11 Oct., 384/62, 30 Sept. and 7 Oct.1837.

in boring Kilsby tunnel and neither it nor Blisworth cutting was completed. In February Chaplin and Horne[13] had been asked to make arrangements for the conveyance of passengers and luggage between Denbigh Hall and Rugby with through bookings. They provided coaches to cover the missing section though trains departed from Rugby 4½ hours after the connecting train had arrived at Denbigh Hall, so a journey between London and Birmingham took some 8½ hours.[14] Even then it was difficult to provide an adequate number of coaches for the public, but the reception by the public on the whole fully equalled the expectations of the Board. In July 1838 Marshal Soult was conveyed to Birmingham, reaching Denbigh Hall in one hour thirty-five minutes and breakfasting with the officers at Weedon Barracks before going on to Rugby for the train to Birmingham. He then proceeded by the GJR to Manchester, the entire journey taking ten hours. Glyn commented to Moorsom 'I hear the Marshal was really very pleased with us.'

The complex interplay of the new railway and the coach trade was explained by Chaplin to Glyn. The former was satisfied with LBR's handling of his company's coach trade to Boxmoor and Tring, but advised that it would worthwhile for the railway to encourage the coaching trade to come on the line. While the coaches based in Coventry and Birmingham were likely to act as a body and pursue a losing trade for some time, their coaches between Birmingham and London 'are just now earning an above average mileage' and so were unwilling to direct the trade onto the line. Many of them had no alternative between 'coaching or no coaching', while others were putting on 'a new coach from Leicester to Manchester whereas I have just removed one.' They were encouraged by hearing of grants of money to improve the Holyhead road – £9,000 now under contract at Dunstable, and by the fact that the provincial towns off the railway must have communication. Chaplin advocated that until the line was complete or almost so the LBR should charge per coach load between the railheads regardless of passengers or parcels. This would give the coach owners an incentive to bring traffic to the line.[15]

[13] Chaplin was head of Chaplin and Horne, except for Pickfords the largest road transport firm, who also owned hotels. Chaplin foreseeing the effects of railways sold most of his stock of coaches and horses retaining only what was necessary to contract for the railway companies for services to places not on the railway line. He briefly went to Switzerland and returned to make a large investment in the LSWR. He was soon a director and from 1842 chairman. *Frasers Magazine*, 36, 1847, 223.

[14] TNA, RAIL 384/5, 15 Jan. 1838.

[15] TNA, RAIL 1008/92, Chaplin to Glyn, 16 Oct. 1837.

It was soon possible to start single track working through Kilsby tunnel on Sundays and the first train ran from London to Birmingham on 24 June 1838. Other trains followed and Euston became an attraction. Lady Charlotte Guest recorded that 'after dinner Mr Price drove with us to see he London and Birmingham Railway, where we saw the Mails go off. There is a large carriage attached to the Train which forms a moveable Post Office, and in which all the letters to be left on the line are to be sorted as they go.'[16] Glyn was able to tell shareholders on 21 August 'yesterday a train had passed over the entire length of line in five hours.' However he warned that they were determined to moderate the speed of trains as they were anxious to secure the safety of passengers rather than achieve the maximum speed. Consequently trains would take six hours in the winter months until the embankments had acquired a proper degree of stability.[17]

The full passenger service had to wait until 17 September, when a private train carrying Glyn, the directors, Creed and Stephenson ran from Euston to Birmingham, a journey which took 4 hours 48 minutes including 34 minutes of stoppages. The duke of Sussex, Queen Victoria's uncle, and his suite were conveyed in two carriages as far as Rugby. There were crowds to see the train at all the stations. The first train to convey the public took much longer, leaving at 8.10 am and arriving just before 2 pm, partly as a result of longer stops at stations.[18]

However in June the following year Glyn told the Select Committee on Railways that cuttings were still a problem though the embankments generally were satisfactory, but agreed that while the earthworks were still consolidating it was in the interests of the company to reduce speed to keep down costs, though the speed of the mail train and the first class train had been increased to 25 mph from 22½ mph exclusive of stops.[19] From May 1839 the first class trains were scheduled to do the run in 5½ hours including seven stops.

Notwithstanding the problems associated with the completion of the line, the scale of the achievement was enormous. This was recognised by contemporaries. 'The London and Birmingham Railway is unquestionably the greatest public work ever executed either in ancient or modern times' rhapsodised one periodical, which went on to say that by measure of the

16 *Lady Charlotte Guest, Extracts from Her Journal*, 1833–1852, ed., the Earl of Bessborough, 1950, 72, entry for 5 Jul. 1838.

17 TNA, RAIL 1110/260.

18 *The Times*, 18 Sept. 1838.

19 Select Committee into State of Communication by Railways, First Report, PP, 1839, x, Qs 211, 311 and 316, 18 Apr. 1839.

labour alone the Great Wall of China might compete with it, but considering the outlay of capital required, together with the unprecedented engineering difficulties, the gigantic work of the Chinese sinks totally into the shade.[20] At Euston Station the functional train shed attracted few admirers, but Hardwick's Doric portico or Propylaeum, emulating that on the Acropolis in Athens, 72 feet in height, was huge. With its four fluted columns, each eight and a half feet in diameter, it formed a symbolic gateway to the places served by the railway in a form which evoked security, safety and stability and a monument to its achievement.[21] This was matched by the four massive Ionic columns with a square pediment bearing the arms of London and Birmingham which fronted the Birmingham terminus in Curzon Street, also designed by Hardwick.

Euston soon gained hotel accommodation. A pair of buildings were erected at the entrance flanking the great portico. Like the portico the hotels were designed by Philip Hardwick, but the two buildings arguably ruined the portico's main effect – the vista from the Euston Road The western building, the Victoria provided sleeping accommodation and an unlicensed coffee house; on the east the Adelaide was intended to serve more as a respectable club-house than as an ordinary hotel perhaps to emulate the recently opened clubs in Pall Mall, including the Reform of which Glyn was member. Glyn was closely involved in this. He was a trustee of the London and Birmingham Hotel Company and he, Garnett and Boothby let the construction contract to Thomas Grissell and Partner.[22] When built they leased it for 21 years to Joseph Dethier, a Belgian and Zennini Vantini who is said to have come from Corsica.[23] The venture met the needs of travellers, arriving and departing from a station that was some distance from any established place of refreshment, inn or hotel. It was soon paying a steady dividend of six per cent.[24] The board soon saw the need for a comparable facility at the Birmingham end of the line. In March 1839 the directors asked Hardwick to investigate the possibilities and he proposed to convert the board room in the main terminus building at Curzon Street for use as a hotel. This work was

[20] What will Parliament Do with the Railways, 1836, 4, quoted in Micheline Nilsen, *Railways and the Western European Capitals: Studies of implantation in London, Paris, Berlin and Brussels*, 2008, 53.

[21] Nilsen, 53–54.

[22] Grissell was in partnership with Samuel Morton Peto, his brother-in-law, but he tended to concentrate on buildings and Peto on railways.

[23] TNA, AN 1464 and 1467, Jul. 1838 and Nov. 1839.

[24] Jack Simmons, Railways and Hotels in Britain, 1839–1914, in *The Express Train*, 1994, 40.

complete by December 1839, but the demand was so great that a wing was added in 1840–41 designed by Dockray, the company's engineer.[25]

When the railway was up and running there was another look at the Committee system. The Board decided that to arrange 'an efficient system of management and of assisting the superior officers of the Company in the discharge of the duties of their departments' the following committees be appointed – Finance and Indoor Establishment; Audit; Coaching; Locomotive; Goods (carrying); Works and Permanent Way.

The heads of the departments concerned were required to lay before the respective committee all reports connected with the business of the Department, and any alterations and suggestions they wished to bring forward. The Committees were to meet at least once a month and the Chairman and Deputy Chairman were to be members of each.[26]

Glyn, though prepared to stand up for what he saw as the genuine concerns of the railway, was always less concerned about the possible outcome of Parliamentary enquiries than the shareholders. He told them in 1839 that he believed that many looked upon the appointment of the Select Committee on Railway Communication with apprehension and dismay, but in his mind there was never any ground for doubt or alarm. On the contrary the LBR would have an opportunity of repelling the many aspersions and claims that had been so industriously and so unjustly heaped upon them. There was no reason to fear that the management of the company would be wrested from the hands of the directors. He told the proprietors in August 1839 that no legislation would result 'which was not conducive to the interests of the public and consequently to yours the company, for it is quite evident that the safety of the public is inseparably connected with your permanent advantage'.[27]

Glyn was the natural link between the company and politicians. When the LBR's 1837 Bill was in the Lords, he was in touch with the Duke of Richmond and concluded that the Bill was likely to pass the third time without any embarrassment to the company.[28] In 1838 he spent considerable time combating the Government's: The Railway (Conveyance of Mails Bill). 'My times have been so fully occupied with the proceedings rendered imperative by the extraordinary enactments of Mr Labouchere that I have not been able to attend at the Euston station. I confidently expect

[25] Christopher Monkhouse, Railway Hotels in *Railway Architecture*, ed. Marcus Binney and David Pearce, 1979, 120.

[26] TNA, RAIL 384/4, 6 Dec. 1839.

[27] TNA, RAIL 1110/260, 2 Aug. 1839.

[28] TNA, RAIL 384/3, 2 Jun. 1833.

that we shall get out of the obnoxious clauses.'[29] Laing sent him privately an outline of the 1842 Railway Bill and he was warned of the change in the Passenger Duty.[30]

One fundamental question relating to railways was the extent to which outsiders would run trains or act as carriers on the railway companies tracks. There were a number of firms which were carriers on road or canals or both. When the LMR started up the carriers assumed that they would operate on the railway. Unlike most canals the LMR had a common carrier obligation. After an investigation by a committee into the question of whether foregoing the carrier's income was preferable to incurring expenditure on wagons and warehouses, the LMR decided that the railway company should itself be a carrier of general merchandise, and only rarely came to satisfactory terms with carriers. Andrew Comber, Pickford's agent in Liverpool, was recruited by the LMR to act as their goods manager in Liverpool.[31] The GJR followed this practice, though in March 1838, agreed to set aside wagons for Pickfords' exclusive use.

The LBR's initial solution to the problem of freight carrying was to link with companies like Pickfords which had carried by road or canal. A central figure in the early years of the carriage of goods traffic by the LBR and indeed by other railways was Joseph Baxendale. He had reinvigorated the carrying business of Pickfords on roads and canals. By the mid 1830s he was taking on roles outside the firm, joining the board of the Regent's Canal Company in 1836. But he recognised that the future both for him personally and for Pickfords lay with the railways.[32] In June 1837 Glyn, Boothby, Calvert and Cropper were asked to communicate with Baxendale, but there were still hesitations about involving the carriers When Bagster told Creed of the rates for potatoes from Watford to London and for manure in the reverse direction, Creed commented 'If the business of the railway should go on smoothly after the opening to Tring, it is probable that the company will be induced to make an essay of carriers but we must decline anything of the sort for the present'.[33] It was only in December that Glyn told the Management Committee that after various conferences terms had been agreed for Baxendale's appointment

[29] RBS Archives, GM/237, Glyn to Ledsam, 23 Jun. 1838.

[30] TNA, RAIL 384/3, 2 Jun. 1837; 384/5, 10 Feb. and 13 May 1842.

[31] Gerard L. Turnbull, *Traffic and Transport, An Economic History of Pickfords,* 1979, 108–109.

[32] By the end of the 1830s he had joined the board of the South Eastern Railway and soon became deputy chairman and later chairman. He acted as adviser for the construction of the Belgian State Railways, was a director of the Amiens and Boulogne Railway and was connected with the Nord.

[33] TNA, RAIL 1008/92, Baster to Creed, 6 Oct. 1837.

as superintendent of the carrying department. The railway provided power and wagons and any buildings needed at the stations.[34] Baxendale explained to the Select Committee on Railways in 1839 that prior to March he had been superintending the railway's carrying business but then became a salaried officer and lately had been the general superintendent of the railway but he soon gave up the latter as it over-taxed him.[35]

Before goods traffic fully started Pickfords became a carrier on the LBR largely through adventitious reasons though no doubt Baxendale's foresight played a part. In the summer of 1838 he anticipated a water shortage on the Grand Junction Canal at the summit level, and so negotiated an agreement to transfer some of the traffic to the railway if a drought occurred. This it did in September and Pickford's Birmingham traffic was transferred to rail. Other firms applied but only two more were admitted to send a small amount of traffic. The agreement with Pickfords was temporary and the company did envisage that when the necessary warehouse, wagons and locomotive power were available and goods traffic commenced the line would be open to all carriers on equal terms The LBR was heavily criticised for this and Glyn had to give publicity to Creed's letter explaining that the restrictions on the number of carriers were temporary.[36]

By the following February shareholders were told that when the line was open to all carriers the company itself would undertake goods traffic to ensure that fair rates were charged. However the LBR was slow to cater for goods traffic only becoming fully operational for this purpose in April 1839 and up to that point traffic from the GJR bound for London had to be transhipped to the canal at Birmingham. Interchange of trucks at Birmingham between the two rail companies was then agreed. By the end of 1839 Pickfords was undertaking daily rail services between London, Birmingham and Liverpool and Manchester. However relations between the GJR and Pickfords were never satisfactory and following a number of disputes the GJR refused to renew Pickfords' contract in September 1840 though that with Chaplin and Horne continued.[37]

Baxendale resigned his appointment with the LBR in November 1839.[38] He told the Select Committee that for the LBR to become carriers would crush a large body of small capitalists. Nevertheless the LBR had not given

34 TNA, RAIL 384/3, 30 Jun.; RAIL 384/85, 6 Dec. 1837 and 9 and 31 Jan. 1838.

35 Select Committee on Railways, second report, PP, 1839, x, Baxendale's evidence Qs 2376–9, 2457.

36 TNA, RAIL 1110/260, 1 Feb. 1839.

37 Turnbull, 109–112.

38 TNA, RAIL 1008/94, 14 Nov. 1839.

up the idea of carrying goods themselves as in February 1840 Baxendale wrote to the LBR directors 'Should the company contemplate becoming carriers it would be far worse than folly for private individuals entering into competition.' He wanted reassurance that he would not lose the capital he was about to invest in premises for the railway's traffic.[39] Pickfords did not have a monopoly of LBR goods traffic, but they were by far the most important carrier and occupied a site at the LBR's freight terminus at Camden Town. Because Baxendale believed that the railway had seriously underestimated the future level of traffic, and because Pickfords existing terminus for canal traffic at the City Road basin needed replacing to cope with rail traffic, he bought land on the south bank of the Regent's Canal adjacent to the LBR's own goods depot and built an administrative headquarters, warehousing and stables. There was a private dock and lay-by on the canal and a private bridge over the railway tracks to give access to the LBR's line. Later a siding was added adjoining the railway's own depot.

The LBR was slow to develop coal traffic. It was only in December 1844 that the LBR agreed to convey Stephenson's coal from Rugby to Kilburn. George Hudson, by now chairman of the amalgamated Midland Railway, came to the LBR board in January 1845 to discuss a proposed agreement on freight between the two companies with special rates for train loads. The LBR then agreed that engines of much greater power were needed for freight traffic.[40]

Glyn while responsible for the company's policy was ready to intervene on matters such as the timing and frequency of trains. He told Creed that there was a case for starting the 10.00 am train at 9.30 but asked him to take Chaplin into his counsels for the form of the advertisement for he was thoroughly versed in the art of putting the matter before the public. The advertisement should draw attention to the 7.30 morning as the train for Lancashire passengers and to the two subsequent ones, 9.30 or 10 and 11 o'clock, as the trains for the convenience of Birmingham, its neighbourhood and intermediate places. The through trains for the convenience of the 'short passengers' must call at the intermediate stations but they should keep their present time of 18 mph and this should be made known in the advertisement. The third through train should commence without delay, and he thought a fourth might be needed before long.[41]

Arrangements were made for particular types of passengers. In 1842 100 pauper emigrants from Nottingham were conveyed at the same rate as

[39] TNA, RAIL 1133/149, Baxendale to LBR board, 5 Feb. 1840.

[40] TNA, RAIL 384/6, 13 Dec. 1844 and 10 Jan. 1845.

[41] RBS Archives, GM/237, 21 Apr. 1838.

soldiers as were parties of at least 80 convicts. Servants out of livery and female servants travelling with their employers by first class trains were charged only second class fares but were required to travel in the compartment reserved for livery servants. Children under 2 when riding on the knee of a passenger were to be conveyed free.[42]

The running of trains on Sundays posed difficult issues for the company. In 1837 before the line opened Glyn complained to Langton that there had been a very animated discussion at the proprietors' meeting not on the creation of shares but on the shutting up of the railway on Sundays. A great deal of wrangling took place before it was agreed that the railway could be opened for four hours on Sunday, the hours to be chosen by the directors.[43] They decided on 11 to 1 and 3 to 5. In August it was noted that an account of receipts on Sunday and of the net profit of Sunday travelling had been kept separate according to the plan of the LMR. The profits from Sunday travel were used for the maintenance and repairs of places of divine worship under the direction of the Churches and Schools Committee, a practice which continued under the LNWR. In February 1838, a memorial was received from the station clerks and police and porters of the London division stating the inconvenience to which they were personally exposed from working on the Sabbath.[44] This continued to be an issue. Glyn's own views were made clear in a letter to Ledsam.

> Though I entertain strong opinions upon the Sabbath question by which I hope always to regulate my own family and arrangements, yet I must not make myself a judge of the actions of others and having accepted from the legislature a trust for the public I conceive our duty requires us to provide sufficient accommodation on Sundays for the demands of passengers.

He added there appeared to be ample reasons for the case which was made out for arrangements best calculated to avoid unnecessary labour on that day.[45] Goods trains were not allowed on Sundays. Later the problem of overnight goods traffic at the weekend arose. The board decided that Saturday night goods trains with deliveries to carriers on Sunday mornings would violate the principle laid down by the proprietors regarding the running of goods trains on Sundays but orders would be given for the wagons arriving on

42 TNA, RAIL 384/5, 10 Feb., 13 May and 11 Aug. 1842.

43 LP 308, 30 Jun. 1837.

44 TNA, RAIL 384/2, 14 Jun., 1 Jul. and 17 Aug. 1837, 20 Feb. 1838.

45 RBS Archives, GM/237, 23 Jun. 1838.

Saturday night to to proceed direct to the shed of the carriers to which the goods belonged.[46]

Sir Robert Peel had declined to introduce the LBR Bill in 1832, but after Glyn became chairman there were a number of occasions when he was in contact with Peel. In September 1842 Glyn wrote 'Will you allow me to take the liberty of mentioning to you that the 11 o'clock down train is now diverted to stop at Hampton where it will meet a Birmingham to Derby train and thus you have a communication with Tamworth after the receipt of letters in London.' He added that if for any reason Peel required at any time a special train the directors had instructed the officers to attend to his wishes. Peel simply said he wished he would be able to profit by it but had no immediate prospect of doing so.[47]

When Marshall Soult, the special representative of France at Queen Victoria's coronation, toured industrial England, Glyn took a personal interest in his journey from Euston. He supervised the arrangements for the Dowager Queen Adelaide's journey, and later for Queen Victoria and Prince Albert when they travelled from Watford to Tamworth to stay with Peel at Drayton Manor, near Tamworth. The LBR commissioned two special carriages for the use of the royal family in 1842 and 1843 – one was for the use of the dowager Queen Adelaide and one for Queen Victoria and Prince Albert which was used throughout their journey to the Midlands in 1843. Before the Victoria's first journey on the LBR Peel asked him to get in touch with Lord Jersey, the Master of the Horse to learn of the proposed movements of the Queen and Prince Albert – from Watford where she proposed to be at 11.30 to Tamworth on 28 November to visit Sir Robert Peel at Drayton Manor, on 1 December from Tamworth to Chesterfield for Chatsworth to stay with the Devonshires, from Chesterfield to Nottingham to visit the Rutlands at Bevoir Castle and on from Belvoir Castle to Watford via Syston and Leicester on 8 December. Peel asked for a room for the Queen on arrival at Watford and how the Queen should leave Tamworth station as it was on an embankment. Glyn accompanied the train to Tamworth.[48]

The LBR exceeded its estimates of the cost of construction by a wide margin and finances became tight during the period when construction was being completed. The report of the directors for the second half of

[46] TNA, RAIL 384/5 10 Feb. 1842.

[47] BL, Add Mss 40488, Glyn to Peel, 13 Sept. and Peel to Glyn, 17 Sept. 1841.

[48] BL, Add Mss 40536, Glyn to Peel, 17 Nov., and Peel to Glyn, 19 and 22 Nov. 1843. The Queen had previously travelled from Windsor to London. The royal couple travelled to Watford from Windsor by coach. David Hodgkins, A Prime Minister and his constituency: Sir Robert Peel and Tamworth Railways, *JCRHS*, 226, 2016, 478–485.

1836 attracted much criticism as it revealed that 'the contemplated works in the carrying department, as well as the road itself' would require nearly £2 million more than the Parliamentary estimate (£4,332,322 instead of £2,500,000), which included £255,000 for the cost of the Euston extension and station. The estimate for land and compensation had doubled from £250,000 to £506,000, in part because more land was needed, though despite Lord Howe and others, this accounted for only about 13 per cent of the total of the excess and 11 per cent of all expenditure, as Harold Pollins pointed out. Works, roads and stations gave rise to 72 per cent of the excess.[49] Robert Stephenson said that a large part of the excess rose from the cost of stations, some £600,000, and he was supported by Creed who claimed that was one expense which no engineer could estimate, and they had arrived at a most fearful excess.[50] However the stations were rather primitive by later standards and even at Euston the station buildings such as ticket offices were in a different architectural world from Hardwick's arch. An article in the *Mechanics Magazine*, possibly inspired by the railway as it was reproduced as an annex to the report of the half yearly meeting, argued that the estimate was what ought to have been paid and that the company had been forced to purchase 800 acres more than they needed. The works for forming the road had cost £423,238 above the estimate due in part it was alleged to an increase in the width of the road because of a prudential regard for the theory lately propounded by the engineer of the Great Western Railway that the only proper width for railways was seven feet and the increased cost of the tunnels. In the case of Kilsby and Primrose Hill tunnels where there were unprecedented difficulties the company had to take up the contracts themselves. The cost of rails had risen due to increases in the price of iron; that of stations in part because of the traffic expected from other railways. There was no reason why the estimate for revenue should not also be doubled to £750,000 and so a profit of 15 per cent was feasible even with a total cost of £5,000,000. The magazine's view was that profit would fall not much short of a million in view of the link up with the GJR and the potential of their Irish traffic.[51]

The directors succeeded in getting Parliamentary authority to raise another £1,000,000 (£625,000 in shares and £375,000 in debentures). Glyn had to explain to the Select Committee in 1839 that they had called up £125,000 in shares with a £25 share being offered to every holder of a

[49] Harold Pollins, A Note on Railway Construction Costs, 1825–1850, *Economica*, 19, 1952, 404–406.

[50] Select Committee on Railways, PP, 1839, x, Creed's evidence Q. 259; Stephenson's evidence Qs 4692–4.

[51] *Mechanics Magazine*, 4 Mar., reproduced in *Birmingham Herald*, 9 Mar. 1837.

£100 share, and borrowed £500,000 by loans partly based on prospective calls on shares. £100,000 of the latter was borrowed from Glyn's Bank. He explained they had put the emphasis on debentures rather than shares because of the financial situation in Lancashire and pressure on the money market arising from trade with America.[52] Even six months later the directors were not as sanguine as the *Mechanics Magazine.* A sub-committee had looked into the likely revenue and concluded that it would be £17,229 a week, or £894,868 a year. In the event receipts for 1839 were £614,131. In 1840 they increased to £748,235 and to £811,475 in 1842 with expenditure falling from 42 to 36 per cent of receipts.

Nevertheless the LBR was highly profitable. The first dividend paid for the second half of 1838 was 3¾ per cent, followed by 8⁵⁄₁₆ for 1839, 8¾ for 1840 and 10 per cent thereafter except for 1842 when it was 11⅕ per cent, though as Glyn pointed out, the half yearly dividend paid then was the first 5 per cent paid clearly and fairly out of profits – previous dividends had been assisted by the sale of shares which fell to the general propriety.[53] In August 1843 it was agreed to raise £1,375,000 in £25 shares and to consolidate £4,125,000 of stock into a general capital stock.[54] The Company distributed £281,204 for the six months ending 31 December 1843, an annual rate of return of over 9 per cent on its total paid up capital of £6,325,865. The nominal rate for ordinary shareholders was 10 per cent on the paid up share capital of £4,307,020.[55]

Glyn had confidence in the company's potential. He told Creed in April 1838 that the shares had fallen £5, but this was evidence of the absurdity of the market.[56] In August 1841 Glyn told shareholders 'I had not expected so favourable result after the creation of a considerable number of new shares.' When in August 1842 a dividend of 5 per cent for the half year was announced the *Railway Times* commented that there was every reason to believe that in no future half year would a smaller return be secured to the enterprising individuals who had constructed the most important work in Europe. It also called attention to the sound and enlightened views of the chairman on some matters of importance to railway proprietors at large.[57]

52 Select Committee on Railways, PP, 1839, x, Glyn's evidence Qs 16–22.

53 TNA, RAIL 1110/260, 10 Feb. 1843.

54 TNA, RAIL 384/5, 11 Aug. 1843.

55 In fact the average rate on the share capital was over 11 per cent as some full dividends were paid on shares not fully called up (Reed, 62 and 64)

56 RBS Archives, GM/237, Glyn to Creed, 21 Apr. 1838.

57 *Railway Times*, 13 Aug. 1842.

The LBR was soon faced with the problem of how to provide financially for the depreciation of locomotive and rolling stock. In June 1838 the LBR established a Reserved Fund for Depreciation of Stock, with £3,500 for depreciation of Locomotive Engine Stock and £2,000 for carriage stock. From 1839 the Company regularised the depreciation at 5 per cent each half year on the actual cost. In February 1842 he told shareholders that a detailed and careful examination of the Company's stock fully convinced the Directors that the half yearly reserve of 5 per cent for depreciation was the lowest the company would be justified in making if their carrying stock was to be maintained in an efficient state and represent the value for which it was charged in the capital account.[58]

In 1842 Glyn thought it desirable for a general review of the state of the Company's affairs to take place. Each Committee reported on the practicability of amalgamating offices in their Departments, and of effecting savings in expenses without impairing the efficiency of the general establishment. They were also to report on the numbers employed and on wages and salaries.[59] The outcome was reported to the board by Glyn himself. Little change was recommended. He was against the proposed amalgamation of the Audit and Account departments. The former had provided a most salutary and beneficial place for the general security of the proprietors. More generally he concluded that each Committee earnestly desired to reduce the expenses of its department with extra efficiency in the service. Pushing the system of economy to a greater extent might tend to interfere with the first duty of the directors towards the proprietors and the public, and the full efficiency and proper management of the whole. A reduction in expenditure would not be possible until Edmonson's ticket system was introduced at the company's stations.[60]

The LBR was always interested in the practices of other lines. Boothby and Hodgson reported that they had collected considerable information concerning coke and had authorised the preparation of some at Darlington. They had seen a very useful sort of open carriage on the Newcastle & Carlisle

[58] TNA, RAIL 1110/260, accounts for 30 Jun. 1838, 31 Dec. 1839 and meetings of 13 Aug. 1841 and 10. Feb. 1842. Harold Pollins, Aspects of Railway Accounting before 1868, in *Studies in the history of Accounting*, ed. A.C. Littleton and B.S. Yamey, 1956, 347–348. Pollins points out that while Glyn said the plan was followed in almost every company, this was not the case – perhaps an example of Glyn defending the industry rather praising his own company.

[59] TNA, RAIL 384/5, 9 Dec. 1842.

[60] RBS Archives, GM/237, 12 Jan. 1843. Thomas Edmonson had pioneered the system of serially numbered tickets ready to be sold to the public which was introduced on railways from 1839.

and had ordered one of the same pattern as well as a truck and a wagon which they considered showed some improvement over those in use on other railways.[61]

He was often ready to leave matters to officers. Following a difference about how to deal with a member of staff where a committee were not as strict as Moorsom would have liked Glyn told him that he mainly agreed with his practices and observance of discipline, yet in such cases he thought that the paramount authority of a committee should be regarded. He added that he did not quite agree with Moorsom in thinking the regulations of the Navy quite in point under the LBR, but it would always give him great satisfaction to co-operate with him on the maintenance of any proper rules for the due performance of 'our service'.[62] Ledsam had mentioned that there was not any officer at Birmingham corresponding to Mr Bagster. Glyn asked 'Would it not add to your efficiency if such an appointment was made in the person of an active intelligent man.'[63]

Wolverton soon became a place of considerable importance to the LBR. About half way between London and Birmingham it was soon designated as the boundary between the spheres of the London and Birmingham Committees.[64] In practice it was for many years a genuine frontier station. All trains stopped there for ten minutes and locomotives were changed. The latter needed to be serviced and passengers refreshed after their three hour journey from London or Birmingham. Glyn took a keen interest in Wolverton's development.

In 1831 the parish of Wolverton had a population of only 417, mainly in Old Wolverton about a mile from the LBR's station. Wolverton was part of the estate bought by the famous physician, Dr John Radcliffe, who on his death in 1714 left it in trust for the benefit of University College, Oxford.[65] The Trust was a powerful body with Viscount Sidmouth and Sir Robert Peel serving successively as chairman with land owners William Ralph Cartwright, MP for Aynho, William Henry Ashurst, MP for Oxfordshire from 1815–30 and Thomas Bucknell, MP for Oxford University as fellow members.[66] Initially the railway paid £1,622 to the Trust for 27 acres (£60

61 TNA, RAIL 384/3, 17 Aug. 1837.

62 RBS Archives, GM/237, 11 Apr. 1838.

63 A. Bagster had been superintendent of the Leicester and Swannington. He also had coaching experience (Gourvish 29).

64 TNA, RAIL 384/2, 5 May 1833.

65 Nikolaus Pevsner and Elizabeth Williamson, *Buildings of England, Buckinghamshire,* 1994, 544 and 564.

66 Ivor Guest, *Dr John Radcliffe and his Trust,* 1991, 482–483.

an acre) with £2,114 compensation. The Trust persuaded Stephenson to add a fourth arch to the viaduct over the Ouse as flood protection, but by the time the line was completed Stephenson had found it necessary to divert the river and add two more arches. In 1837 the Trust sold eight more acres which the company needed for the station for £1,600 making it clear that the matter was not negotiable.[67]

The LBR's activities at Wolverton soon expanded beyond the station. Although the first locomotives were bought from private contractors, maintenance shops were needed and the company decided to site these at Wolverton. Glyn was concerned about developments there. He wrote to Creed a few months before the railway opened 'I wish clearly to understand our present doings at Wolverton. Am I wrong in thinking that work is now going on under Goodall or some other of the Company's people, if so to what is this work confined and how much has been expended?' He also asked 'Where is Bury? I wish you would enquire of him which portion of the Wolverton works buildings he wishes to have finished and ready first. I should like to hear by Monday.'[68] The first engine shed was completed in 1838. This was much more than a shed to stable the locomotives. It was a comprehensive repair shop with an erecting shop and iron and brass smithies.[69] In 1840 13½ acres were purchased for £1565 for workshops and housing – the little streets as they were known, including Creed Street and Glyn Square, though it was only in 1842 that the board directed the Estates Committee to name the streets and number the houses, possibly to meet the needs of the new postal service.[70] The three-sided Glyn Square had terraces of six houses on the north and south sides and a terrace of 20 on the east. The railway line made up the fourth side of the square. The streets were laid out and houses constructed by local builders, particularly Dunkley of Blisworth.[71]

Glyn was very conscious of the scale of the LBR's activities. In 1840 he said 'At Wolverton, our central station, which not long ago was little more than an open field, we have now established what may almost be called a town, wanting however, I regret to say many of the advantages usually possessed by populous placed in other situations.'[72] It was on his

[67] Guest, 398 and 403.

[68] RBS Archives, GM/237, 21 Apr. 1838.

[69] Described in detail by Francis Whishaw, *The Railways of Great Britain and Ireland*, 1842, 234–238. He visited Wolverton in 1840.

[70] TNA, RAIL 384/ 5, 14 Oct. 1842.

[71] Bryan Dunleavy, *The Lost Streets of Wolverton*, 2012, 96–99.

[72] TNA, RAIL 1110/260, 7 Feb. 1840.

recommendation that the company planned to provide two schools for the moral and religious improvement of the residents, one for infants and the other for persons of a mature age. Glyn took a personal interest in the schools and church at Wolverton. The Trustees leased at a peppercorn rent an acre of land at the corner of Creed Street for the infants school. Glyn defended this course on grounds of self interest in that the company and the public would benefit from moral and well conducted servants but also from higher motives of duty towards the people they employed.[73] He visited the schools in 1842.[74]

The Trustees were ready to donate 2½ acres for a church in the hope that the company would bear the cost of building it, a hope that did not materialise. The latter limited its donation to £1,000, though the church with the vicarage was to cost £5,000 when completed in 1844. The Trustees were not satisfied with this and the LBR raised a further £1,000 by subscriptions from shareholders. Prior to the building of the church the Bishop of Lincoln appointed the Revd George Weight as resident chaplain and services were held in a large room. The church itself, St George the Martyr, was consecrated in May 1844 by the Bishop. The Radcliffe Trust endowed the living with £150 for the vicar's salary.[75] Glyn himself presented an elegant set of silver communion plate, chalice, patens and large flagon.

Glyn was proud of the way that the LBR was developing Wolverton, but also anxious to justify to shareholders the necessity of doing so, particularly in contributing to the church. In 1842 he said:

> We are beginning to find more fully the economical result of the establishment at Wolverton. Attendance at the places of worship and the schools is most satisfactory and numerous. The result is more important than the mere comfort of the Company's servants there. It has a result which not only acts on our profits, but also most materially on the convenience and safety of the public.

A year later he said 'You will reap the benefit of this, for I am sure that there is not a single person attached to that establishment who would not willingly and gladly come forward and perform extra service in order to meet occasional emergency.'[76] In 1844 he said the railway had been obliged

[73] TNA, RAIL 384/4, 20 Dec. 1839; 1160/260, 10 Feb.1840.
[74] TNA, RAIL 384/5, 10 Jun. 1842.
[75] TNA, RAIL 384/4, 16 Oct. 1839; 1160/260, 10 Feb. and 7 Aug. 1840.
[76] TNA, RAIL 1110/260, 10 Feb. 1842 and 8 Feb. 1843.

to collect a population from nearly every part of the kingdom who settled there without any local attachment.[77]

The schools were the more necessary because in a new industry in a new town the population was very young. Francis Head in 1849 drew attention to the extraordinary number of young couples and young children. He said that 638 of the population of 1405 were below 16 years of age. He also pointed to number of young widows, and a considerable number of men who had lost a finger, hand, arm or leg. However he said all of them looked to support to the company, and 'not only their services and their thoughts but also their parts of speech are more or less devoted to it, for instance the pronoun "she" almost invariably alludes to some locomotive, "he" to the chairman, and "it" to the London board'.[78] A reading room and library were also provided by the company.

Glyn believed that all this helped provide a loyal workforce. In October 1839 Glyn was asked to give his attention to the creation of a superannuation or friendly society for the company's servants. For the workers at Wolverton a Friendly Society was established to which the company contributed because a certain degree of hazard which no calculation can foresee nor prudence guard against was inseparable from the nature of the employment of many of these individuals. In July 1842 he pointed out that the share of payments to engine drivers, switchmen and policemen dependent on their good behaviour had greatly increased in the previous half year. He attributed this in great measure to the success of Wolverton which placed the workers in a degree of comfort. In the second part of 1842 gratuities for good conduct amounting to £3,423 were paid to engine drivers and firemen.[79] In the locomotive department by 1843 the average pay bill had been reduced since 1840 with fewer workmen and less overtime, and the wages of the less important workmen reduced. Although a small further reduction was recommended, Glyn endorsed the view that there were in the locomotive department especially amongst those at Wolverton a number of sensible and well conducted working men attached to the service of the company and grateful for the advantages, moral and social, which the Board had placed within their reach; the hope of rendering this a well instructed and moral community rested on its population being settled rather than fluctuating. The company should therefore hold on to the higher rates as the ultimate

77 TNA, RAIL 1110/260, 9 Feb. 1844.

78 Sir Francis Bond Head, *Stokers and Pokers, or the London and North Western Railway*, 1849, 82.

79 TNA, RAIL 1110/260, 1 Jul. 1842; 384/5, 10 Mar. 1843.

reward for good conduct and lengthened service, but wait for the occurrence of vacancies as they arose in the ordinary course.[80]

The episode over the financing of the church was only one example where relations between the Radcliffe Trust and company were uneasy.[81] Difficulties arose over allotments which the workers themselves seem to have started on the Trust's land which the trustees then fenced off and sold to the LBR.[82] The Trust spent £1,600 on stables, coach houses and a taproom for the sale of beer, but before this was completed a beer shop had been opened on the station premises. Glyn assured them that the beer shop would close as soon as a tenant of the trustees opened a public house accessible to the families of the residents, but the first station had not been intended to be permanent and in 1840 the LBR decided to rebuild it on a new site with a refreshment rooms on both up and down platforms. The trustees' public house, the Radcliffe Arms, was therefore left isolated and the trustees had to reduce the rent and provide the lessees with a site for another pub, the Royal Engineer.[83] The new station was built in five months, had kitchens and cellars, and even an ice-house, a piggery and small vegetable garden. The refreshment rooms were let to Joseph Dethier and Zenoni Vantini of the hotels at Euston. They had a staff of 28 in 1848. They attracted much attention.[84]

In 1847 Lipscomb said that this station might be considered one of the wonders of modern times in connexion with railway enterprise. 'The land which a few years ago was covered with rich crops is now overspread with extensive premises and streets.' He described the settlement as very compactly and regularly built, with seven streets, a church, schools, a market house and about 200 houses accommodating nearly 1,000 people.[85]

By 1852 Wolverton was not providing sufficient housing for the increasing number of workers. The Radcliffe Trust refused to sell any more land in Wolverton and so the LNWR bought 19 acres from Earl Spencer in Stantonbury to the south of Wolverton, which at that time consisted of a few farm-houses and cottages. The initial tender was for 104 cottages and

80 TNA, RAIL 1110/260, 8 Feb. 1843.

81 For the church see the report in *The Times,* 29 May, and the letter from George Bramwell, solicitor to the Trustees, ibid, 1 Jun. 1844. *The Times* attributed the whole cost of building the church to the LBR.

82 Report to the Radcliffe Trustees of 17 Apr. 1847, quoted by Bryan Dunleavy in a post on 28 Feb. 2012 on wolverton.past.co.uk.

83 Dunleavy, 130.

84 TNA, AN 109/1471, contract of 1 Dec. 1840; Head, 85.

85 G. Lipscomb, *History and Antiquities of Buckingham*, 1847, iv, 419.

four houses in what became New Bradwell. Some were to replace houses in Wolverton demolished to make room for the expansion of the workshops. The two storeyed terraces of houses had at each end a three storeyed house for foremen, engine drivers and their peers. By 1854 there were 500 to 600 persons in the new settlement.[86] Even the cottages were a substantial improvement on the first houses in Wolverton where according to the 1851 census there were cases of one up and one down cottages being occupied by a family of six with four or five adult lodgers.

[86] TNA, RAIL 410/222, 22 Feb. and 410/287, 9 Mar. 1853; *The Buildings of England, Buckinghamshire*, 1994, 541; RAIL 410/576, 9 Feb. 1854.

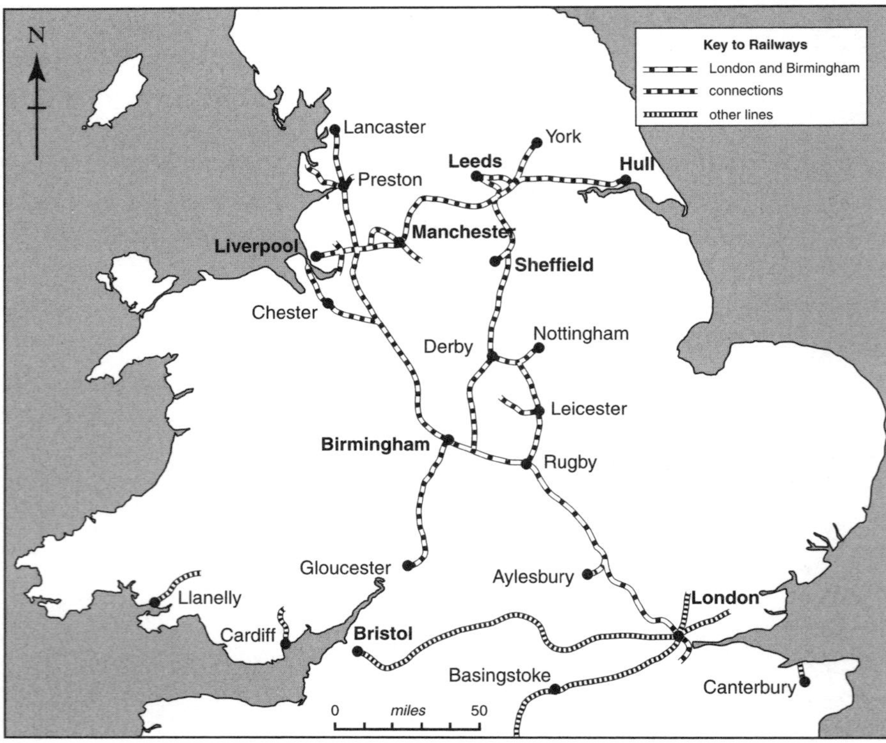

Map 2: The London and Birmingham Railway
and its connections, 1841.

CHAPTER EIGHT

The London and Birmingham – Gateway to the Midlands and the North

LONG BEFORE the railway service between London and Birmingham started in 1838 a number of questions about the relationship of the LBR to other lines were raised and decided in ways which were to have important consequences for the national railway network. These questions and the part played by George Carr Glyn, initially as director and then as chairman, are examined in this chapter.

The first to be determined was whether the Great Western Railway projected from London to Bristol should enter London by the LBR's route from Acton and share their terminal at Euston, a course strongly favoured by Glyn as it would provide a common portal for traffic to and from London to the west and north and possibly encourage any future lines to the north to follow suit. Its failure also meant that the broad gauge system developed as a more self-contained network.

Second the nearly simultaneous approval of the Grand Junction Railway from Birmingham to Liverpool meant that the LBR would not function in isolation from other railways in the West Midlands and the Northwest, though the details of the link in Birmingham and the extent and terms on which there was to be through traffic would have to be worked out.

Third, at a very early stage an opportunity for the LBR to serve as the link between London, the East Midlands and the North East was taken with the formation of the Midlands Counties Railway which joined the LBR at Rugby and served Leicester, Nottingham and Derby, and of the rival route the Birmingham and Derby Junction with proposed links to the LBR at Hampton and Birmingham itself. Both joined the North Midland at Derby which ran to Leeds with a link to York via the York and North Midland. Glyn himself was chairman of the North Midland. While Euston was being constructed Glyn told shareholders that the station opened on what would necessarily become the grand avenue of travelling between the Metropolis and the Midland and Northern parts of the kingdom.[1]

In the 1830s the position of the LBR as the link between London and the north was unchallenged. In the 1840s some of Glyn's energies were devoted to trying to maintain that position by building links from the LBR line to districts east and west of their main line and by resisting companies which tried to establish alternative routes to London. This can be seen both as an attempt to create a rational national system and to retain the LBR's monopoly created by being first in the field.

A bold attempt to secure the primacy of Euston by making it the portal for the west as well as the north came when the GWR was in the early stages of planning its line. The GWR was slow to settle on a London terminus. When their first plan was published in August 1833 the directors explained that no route had yet been adopted.[2] In the Parliamentary plans deposited in November the plan was for a terminus situated on the west side of the Vauxhall Bridge Road, next to the Thames and the works of the Equitable Gas Company, of which the company's then chairman, Benjamin Shaw, was a director. The line would continue via Pimlico, Brompton and Hammersmith to South Acton.[3] However that plan soon ran into difficulties. Although the Bill passed the Commons in March 1834, 'by a triumphant majority', as Shaw put it,[4] strong opposition came from the landowners in Pimlico, Chelsea and Brompton, particularly Earl Cadogan and the Marquess of Westminster, especially as a considerable part of the railway was to be constructed on viaducts. To secure their position in the Lords

[1] TNA, RAIL 384/12, 3 Feb. 1837.

[2] TNA, RAIL 250/1, 30 Aug. 1833. The various plans and negotiations for the GWR's London terminus, including the proposal to use Euston are described in David Hodgkins, The GWR comes to London – Why Paddington?, *RCHS Journal*, 36, 2010, 40–50. See also E.T. MacDermott, *History of the Great Western Railway*, 1927, 1 (part 1), 10, 14–16, 27–28, 34–36; Michael Tutton, *Paddington Station, 1833–1854*, 1999, 7–15.

[3] TNA, RAIL 250/84, London Committee of Management, 7 Sept., 5 and 26 Oct. 1833. The GWR did not seek authority at this stage for a complete line from Bristol to London because of the difficulty of raising sufficient capital in time and because they wanted to pre-empt the rival project from London to Windsor (TNA, RAIL 250/96 (Bristol Committee) 1 Oct. 1833).

[4] In a letter to shareholders, *The Times*, 11 Mar. 1834. Shaw of Cornhill, London, had chaired the abortive London, Portsmouth and Southampton Railway in 1825 (ibid, 26 Jan. 1825). He was the first chairman of the GWR – according to MacDermott (1, 50), 'a shadowy figure of whom little more than his name is recorded.' His other claim to distinction is that with two other City figures he purchased and donated the land for University College, London when it was founded in 1826 (*The Survey of London*, 21, 87–90).

the GWR decided on a terminus at Brompton at the rear of the Hoop and Toy public house at the western end of Thurloe Place close to the site of the future South Kensington station.[5] The Turnpike Commissioners of the Metropolis[6] opposed this as they were very concerned about the impact of the new railways on the roads for which they were responsible, particularly because the proposed bridge over the narrow Old Brompton Road would leave insufficient room for access to the proposed station.

The Turnpike Commissioners therefore petitioned Parliament. In their view one railway entering London from the Acton area would be sufficient. Their solicitor asked the LBR if the GWR could enter London by the LBR route and if so where they could join it. Glyn told Edward Cropper of this idea and added that he had 'urged this suggestion on the Great Western six months back and its adoption would have saved that body much opposition and expense, but the Bristoleans did not like it.'[7] Glyn had close links with the GWR. Edward Wheeler Mills, the brother of Charles Mills, Glyn's partner in Glyn, Hallifax & Mills and himself a partner from 1835, had taken the chair at the first joint meeting of the GWR's Bristol and London Committees and was a director of the GWR from 1834 until 1863. Glyn, Hallifax & Mills were appointed the GWR's bankers in London. Glyn's brother-in-law, Riversdale William Grenfell was also a director, and both he and his brother, Pascoe St Leger, a director of the LBR, held shares, though their father, Pascoe Grenfell did not, despite his support for the London Northern Railroad in the 1820s and the fact that the GWR cut a swathe through his land at Taplow. Glyn himself with 65 shares was a rather larger shareholder than the two younger Grenfells, but never became a member of the GWR board. He was appointed Treasurer in October 1835, though he soon withdrew because of the difficulties it would cause his banking business.[8]

Glyn seems to have been on good terms with Saunders, the secretary of the GWR. In 1835 when the GWR's bill was before Parliament he told him that the previous day he had travelled by the first locomotive ever in

[5] TNA, RAIL 250/1, 3 May 1834.

[6] In 1826 the metropolitan turnpike trusts north of the Thames had been consolidated into one commission with James McAdam as surveyor-general. *The Survey of London*, 21; T.C. Barker and Michael Robbins, *A History of London Transport*, 1963, 1, 13.

[7] TNA, RAIL 384/276, Glyn to Cropper, 15 May 1834.

[8] TNA, RAIL 250/1, 24 and 27 Aug. 1833; RAIL 250/2, 30 Oct. 1835; RAIL 251/1, 1835–6; R. Fulford, *Glyn's*, 1953, 81; Penny Watts-Russell, Travelling Steam: Pascoe Grenfell and the Great Western Railway, *JCRHS*, 217, 12–16, 2013; Geoffrey Channon, *Railways in Britain and the United States, 1830–1940*, 2001, 168–169, 171.

use near London, but he mainly wrote to contrast the hostile attitude of Eton to the GWR with that of the headmaster of Harrow, whose school was only 10 miles from London and any evil, if there were any such, would be increased by the nearness of the metropolis. Nevertheless 'the enlightened head of Harrow never raised a word against us.'[9]

Glyn now told Cropper that the Turnpike Commissioners' idea was of the greatest importance and required serious consideration. It could be a source of much profit if not attended with too much increase of business for the LBR's purpose. He mentioned in confidence 'that the proposition now came with a job, not to the LBR's cost, hanging to it, but it would be entertained or not according to the recommendation of our practical officers and put with a single view to our proprietors. It is the joint offspring, I suspect, of one of our colleagues and the Commissioners.'[10] Cropper replied that he and Rathbone, agreed it was very desirable to encourage the idea. It would be a source of profit and advantage would be derived 'from making our station the starting point for all roads North and West.'[11]

Stephenson considered that a junction might very conveniently be made 4½ miles from the depot at Camden Town[12] at the intersection of the road from Harlesden Green to Acton. Four lines from the junction to the depot would not be necessary. The difficulties of traffic would be confined to the depot. The passengers might be accommodated but he was doubtful about the possibility of bringing the whole of the goods to the LBR depot though not prepared to offer any decided opinion.[13] When the Bill came before the Lords the Turnpike Commissioners opposed the Bill but the decisive voice was Cadogan, who objected on various grounds despite Lord Wharncliffe, who had introduced the bill for the GWR, pointing out that the company had already altered its proposals because of his opposition. 'After preventing it coming to London, the noble Earl ought not to turn round and object to the whole measure,' but the Lords rejected it by 47 to 30.

The idea of using the LBR's proposed terminal now came to the fore. Glyn asked Rathbone for any information on the terms and conditions which it was intended the Grand Junction should use the LMR. He added that he would be inclined to treat the Western Company in the most liberal way

[9] TNA, RAIL 1014/3, letter of 24 Jun. 1835.

[10] I have not traced any indication of the nature of the 'job', or of the name of Glyn's colleague. Rowles, a major London builder, is the most likely. (Oxford DNB, 48, 17.)

[11] TNA, RAIL 384/257 19 May 1834.

[12] The decision to continue the line to Euston had not then been taken.

[13] TNA, RAIL 384/276, letter of 22 May 1834; RAIL 384/257 for Stephenson's report of 15 May 1834.

consistent with the LBR's interests and 'to leave them as much unshackled as we can in the use of our line. They would require a portion of our land for a station, which might be leased of us without interfering with any of our arrangements.'[14]

This set in train a series of protracted and complicated negotiations, the first stage of which took place in the autumn of 1834. In discussions in which Glyn was involved, an annual rent of £25,000 was agreed based on construction and maintenance costs with access for the GWR to a separate depot at Camden Town, and at Euston if the LBR extended there. At first exclusive rights of access for each company at particular times of the day were suggested, but that was soon abandoned.

At this stage Glyn was optimistic. He told Rathbone that they had come to an arrangement on an equitable basis. He thought there was good ground for supposing that 'in passengers it (the GWR) would fully equal our expectation, but in traffic the LBR would probably exceed them.'[15] The LBR refused to make a formal agreement with the GWR as the latter was not yet incorporated, but the GWR was prepared to rely on this.[16] Their Bill thus went ahead and their prospectus said that the station in London for passengers was intended to be near the New Road as the LBR plans for an extension to Euston were now going forward.[17]

The matter was only revived after the GWR obtained their Act on 31 August 1835. Two new cross currents then developed which complicated and eventually were to wreck the proposal. First, before further negotiations with the LBR started Brunel had begun to mount his case for a wider gauge than 4 ft 8½ in. Second and more fundamental the powerful Liverpool interest in the LBR took the line that a joint station was inimical to the interests of the LBR.

Brunel was now insisting that the broad gauge was vital to his plan for the GWR and wanted a decision on the Euston terminus in time to submit a Bill for the 1836 Session. The junction with the LBR was the only real obstacle to his plan for broad gauge as an additional rail to each railway would have to be laid down. He did not foresee any difficulty in this but if the LBR objected, the Euston plan would have to be abandoned. On 29 October

14 TNA, RAIL 384/276. This letter bears no date, but has been attributed to circa April 1834 in RAIL 384/276. However it was certainly written after the defeat of the Bill in the Lords on 25 Jul. 1834. Rathbone was a director of the LMR, as was James Cropper's son John, Edward's brother.

15 TNA, RAIL 384/276, 2 Oct. 1834.

16 TNA, RAIL 250/83, 5 Nov. 1834.

17 TNA, RAIL 250/83 and 384/51, 5 Nov. 1834.

the GWR Board decided in favour of the broad gauge, and told Robert Bright, the deputy chairman,[18] who was to meet the LBR at Birmingham, that if they did not succeed in gaining their object the company would apply to Parliament for another terminus for the GWR.

Stephenson following discussions with Brunel was now doubtful. Although he told Creed that the Primrose Hill and Kensal Green tunnels were sufficiently wide for the broad gauge, and arranging the rails for carriages of different widths was practicable, great inconvenience would result with more expense from maintenance and repairs. He continued 'one of the chief advantages of a junction would be neutralised because the land necessary for a depot would no longer be rendered mutually useful – the business of the two railways must be conducted as distinct and would require as much land as if the depots were in different parts of London.' He had advocated a joint entrance to London, but the adoption of different widths made this questionable, though the depot at Euston Grove would be fully equal to the accommodation of any imaginable traffic.[19]

The two companies then agreed on tariffs for traffic on the LBR and that the arrangement would be terminable on 2 years notice by either party.[20] The GWR clearly believed that this agreement on 'pecuniary terms' did not affect the allotment of land at Euston and Camden. They wanted to acquire the land by purchase, or at least a building lease.[21]

Meanwhile the LBR board was running into serious internal opposition from its powerful Liverpool shareholders. This was probably part of a wider move to exercise their muscle as the proportion of the company's shares they held rose. A hint of difficulties to come had been given when Garnett wrote to Creed in October 1834 opining that the compensation contemplated 'by our London friends' was far too low. He did not attach much importance to the GWR taking off the LBR's hands any of the land at the London station because he had no doubt its value would greatly increase very soon after the line was in operation. Several proprietors had spoken to him about the issue.[22] When the agreement was under discussion again the following autumn, Boothby wrote to Cropper, Rathbone and Garnett setting out several objections. The GWR should apply to Parliament and try to obtain another entrance to London and see what it would cost. He did not believe the GWR could get an equally good entrance to London

18 And also George Gibbs' business partner in Bristol.

19 TNA, RAIL 1009/92, Stephenson to Creed, 31 Oct. 1835.

20 TNA, RAIL 250/97, 5 and 6 Nov. 1835.

21 Ibid, 10 Nov. 1835.

22 TNA, RAIL 1008/ 92, Garnett to Creed, 15 Oct. 1834.

for less than £500,000. A junction with the GWR was not desirable, and he regarded the rent agreed as paltry compared with the risks to the LBR's traffic. It would not bring any traffic and might take some away especially journeys for short distances and excursions of pleasure. Somewhat illogically he added that the room at the station might be wanted for other companies 'more beneficial to our traffic' such as a line from Cambridge or Portsmouth, or a connecting line round London for the convenience of forwarding goods from the southern ports, nearly all of which, from Dover to Plymouth, would probably have a railway communication with London in a few years. Extra lines might be needed because on the GWR short distance traffic would predominate requiring trains every hour or even every half hour in the morning and evening with delay to the LBR trains and risk of accidents.[23]

This was followed by a meeting of some of the largest shareholders in Liverpool on 16 November 1835 under the chairmanship of David Hodgson. Cropper and Rathbone were present and 21 shareholders including Boothby, as well as Richard, James, and Edward, Moon.[24] The committee they set up agreed that the proposals were not so framed as to obviate many difficulties which might ensue to the LBR, nor founded on a safe or proper basis with reference to other traffic which might thereafter develop. They suggested a fixed toll of 2d per ton of merchandise per mile on all traffic with a discount of 50 per cent when £3,000 was reached, limited to two years, at the end of which a more permanent obligation might be entered into, founded on the experience of both parties and in a spirit of equity, mutual interest and accommodation. It was altogether undesirable to part with any of the land by sale or by lease comprising the stations at Camden Town and Euston Grove. Buildings required should be let.

It was this last point which the London Committee of the LBR accepted and which became the major stumbling block between the two companies. The GWR were told they 'shall have the best accommodation we can afford for the traffic of their line at our depots but the cession of any part of the stations at Camden Town or Euston Grove for their exclusive use, whether by sale or lease, is inadmissible. We will build workshops for their use on fair terms but not give up any portion of the ground for a distinct establishment.' Creed told Moorsom it seemed that they had imbibed a

23 TNA, RAIL 385/257, 26 Oct. 1835.

24 TNA, RAIL 1008/92, Creed to Moorsom, 10 Dec., RAIL 385/52, 16 Dec. 1835. The Moons were Liverpool merchants. Richard Moon was the father of the future chairman of the LNWR, also Richard Moon, born 1815. James and Edward were his uncles.

notion that they can come to Euston Grove cheek by jowl and keep one half of the ground for themselves.[25]

Negotiations now came to a head. The GWR asked for a lease of 21 years, but when the LBR board met on 17 February 1836 they decided that a portion of Euston station should be exclusively allotted for the use of the GWR but it would be subject to 2 years notice to quit on the part of the GWR and five years on the LBR's.[26] This was not quite what the Liverpool party had advocated but it was very close to their view. The GWR board declined to accede to the conditions proposed for the land at Euston Square. They told their proprietors that the permanency of the junction would be defeated by such conditions. They were informed that a large and influential body of 'distant' LBR proprietors were pressing their directors to retain the power to break any lease at the shortest possible notice in the hope that better financial terms might be obtained, and some also feared that there would not be room for both lines at the depots. In deciding against going to Euston the GWR were reinforced by their confidence that an excellent and independent terminal could be secured without much difficulty in the next session of Parliament.[27] Significantly the GWR did not mention the question of the difference in gauge, nor had the Liverpool objectors in their representations. However one leading GWR director saw it differently. George Henry Gibbs told his brother that he regretted the loss of a good entrance to London. He was critical of the influence of the Liverpool party, both on the LBR and the GWR, where they were also trying to secure a seat on the board. 'We are in the power of a set of fellows who hold a large number of shares and who have no other merit to recommend them.'[28]

The GWR's decision was clearly a disappointment to Glyn though he does not seem to have been bitter, telling Langton in January that he thought the GWR directors were excellent men of business. He had a foot in both camps: a month later he was telling Langton that he was about to be assailed for holding GWR shares. Later he seems to have assisted

[25] TNA, RAIL 250/83 and 384/51, 5 Nov. 1834.

[26] TNA, RAIL 384/2, 17 Feb. 1836.

[27] TNA, RAIL 250/2 and 1110/264, half yearly report, 25 Feb. 1836.

[28] *The Birth of the Great Western Railway, Extracts from the Diary and Correspondence of George Henry Gibbs*, ed. Jack Simmons, 1971, 49 and 79. Gibbs was offered the chairmanship when Benjamin Shaw retired in 1837 but declined, Gibbs illustrates the problems the Bristol and London directors had with the Liverpool party on company matters in several entries in the diary and their attempts to get a seat on the board (Gibbs, entries for 2 and 27 Nov., 57 and 58).

the GWR to make an arrangement with the Bank of Liverpool.[29] Once the GWR had declined to go to Euston on the terms offered there seems to have been little examination of the matter by either party. However in 1839 both Saunders and Stephenson gave their views on the episode to the Select Committee on Railways. Saunders was quite clear that what prevented agreement was not money, but the position the GWR would have in Euston and the conditions on which they were to hold their tenure. William Sims, by then Chairman of the GWR, added that the LBR were glad to get rid of them.[30] Saunders also said that when the proposal was made the general view was decidedly in favour of several lines running to the same terminus, but this quickly changed with further practical knowledge of railways. Stephenson had made the same point. He denied however that there would have been problems at Euston. Half the space at Euston was still vacant. The site was designed 'by me for two distinct stations.' The location of Euston would have been more advantageous for the GWR and the public. LBR passengers could have had access to the GWR without leaving the station. As there were four lines from Camden Town any danger would have arisen at the junction and despite the gauge problem he thought it all could have been managed without danger to the public. Indeed when Euston opened it was served by four tracks, only two of which were equipped for cable haulage by stationary engines, the normal means of exit from the station until 1844.[31]

Neither Saunders nor Stephenson blamed the 'distant proprietors' of the LBR, but it is hard to escape the conclusion that it was their determination to put what they perceived to be the interest and profitability of the LBR before wider considerations which ruled out bringing the GWR closer to London than Paddington, a defect only remedied a quarter of a century later by the opening of the Metropolitan Railway in 1863. Glyn later maintained that if it had not been for the co-operation of the LBR in making the arrangement

[29] Barclays Archives, 25/265, Langton Papers (LP) 129, 141, 259 and 261, 9 Jan. and 29 Feb. 1836, and 21 and 25 Jan. 1837.

[30] Sims was on the original London Committee and was closely involved in the negotiations with the LBR, 'another shadowy figure today' according to MacDermott (1, 50), but he was a partner in Jacob Sims & Co., India merchants, a director of the Bank of England, chairman of the Glenarvon Iron Co, and a director of insurance companies. He committed suicide on 15 November 1839: 'destroyed himself in a fit of temporary insanity', according to the coroner's jury. Financially sound according to E.W. Mills, he had told his solicitor he had too many irons in the fire and was depressed following his sister's mental illness (*The Times*, 18 Nov. 1839). Gibbs expressed doubts about his judgment.

[31] Select Committee on Railways, PP, 1839, x, Qs 931–3 and 1018–19, for the evidence of Saunders and Sims; Qs 4695–4708, for Stephenson's.

for the use of Euston station the GWR's bill would have failed in Parliament in 1835.[32]

When the GWR obtained its Act in July 1835 there were only 21 companies officially listed on the Stock Exchange but the number almost trebled in the next twelve months. Glyn was nervous about the extent of speculation. He regretted the great increase in railway schemes. 'Some are very good and well conceived, but many are mere speculations. I have done everything to stop the gambling in our shares, not to the satisfaction of the stock exchange here or of the share brokers elsewhere.' In February 1836 George Gibbs could not understand why the GWR shares had advanced so much, 'I connot discover one fact bearing upon their value on which any rise could reasonably be built', with one alarming exception: the patronage of the Stock Exchange.[33] In February 1836 the *Circular to Bankers* noted that the whole active interest of the Stock Exchange had been lately directed almost exclusively to shares in railways, adding that the operations and purchases in them had been greatly accelerated by orders from the country, especially from Lancashire.[34] However there was more to the boom than froth. It established a market in non-government securities through the establishment of home rails as a readily marketable security on the London Stock Exchange. 1835 also saw the birth of the stock exchanges in Manchester and Liverpool.

Moves to connect the LBR with the East and North Midlands were being made. Here Glyn had been co-operating with George and Robert Stephenson who had built the Leicester and Swannington Railway and sunk pits at Snibston, near Coalville.[35] According to Clement Strettton, early in 1832 a number of George Stephenson's friends and associates visited Alton Grange near Ashby-de-la-Zouche, now Stephenson's home, to discuss further railway projects. They included not only Glyn but Cropper, Henry Booth and Joseph Sandars of Liverpool, John and Joseph Ellis of Leicester, Edward Pease of Darlington, Charles Sturge and Samuel Beale of Birmingham, William Vickers of Sheffield and Henry Houldsworth of Manchester. Immediately afterwards George Stephenson attended a meeting at Glyn's bank where it was decided that he and Robert should examine routes for several lines.[36] However later that year the Erewash coalmasters, concerned

[32] TNA, RAIL 1110/269, 20 Feb. 1852.

[33] LP 120, 23 Oct. 1835; *The Birth of the Great Western Railway*, 78.

[34] *Circular to Bankers*, 26 Feb. 1836.

[35] Glyn subscribed to the Leicester and Swannington, but only in 1837 (Leicestershire Record Office, 31'15/104).

[36] Clement E. Stretton, *The History of the Midland Railway*, 1901, 47.

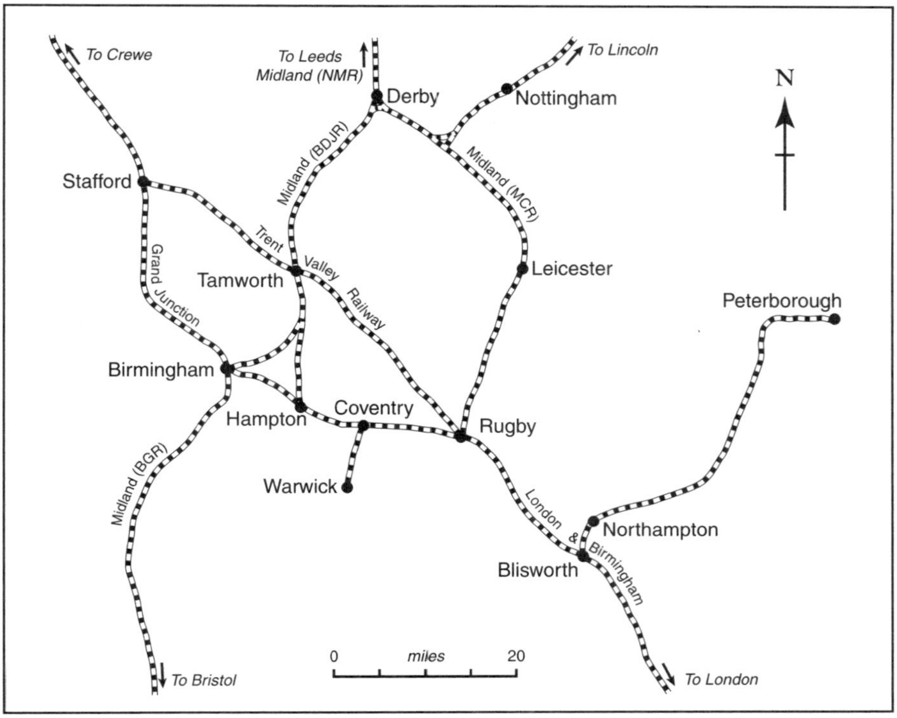

Map 3: The network in the Midlands showing the constituent lines of the Midland formed in 1844 and the London and Birmingham and Grand Junction which became part of the LNWR formed in 1846, as did the Trent Valley, opened in 1847.

that they would lose their market for coal in Leicester to the Leicester and Swannington Railway, took the first steps to form what became the Midland Counties Railway from Rugby to Leicester, Nottingham and Derby. Glyn was therefore only involved in the North Midland Railway from Derby to Leeds, though a shareholder in the Midland Counties.

These extensions would mean that by 1836 firm plans had been laid for through routes from London to the East Midlands and the North East so that the largest cities in England would be linked by rail to London, four of them to Euston – Birmingham, Liverpool, Manchester and Leeds, while Sheffield was to be linked to the system by a branch line to Rotherham. Only Bristol was served by a separate line to London. All three of the main constituents of the future Midland Railway (the Midland Counties, the Birmingham and Derby Junction and the North Midland) were incorporated in 1836 when 29 companies with a total mileage of 955 were sanctioned by Parliament, three times as much as in any previous year and not to be exceeded until

1845.[37] The MCR and the BDJR both linked with the LBR and at Derby with the North Midland to provide through routes to Leeds. In addition the Birmingham and Gloucester, also incorporated in 1836, would provide a link from the BDJR and the LBR to the Southwest, using the latter's station in Birmingham.

As we have seen such links were one aim of the LBR from the outset.[38] The gestation of the first of these – the Midland Counties Railway took some years. In 1832 the Erewash Valley coal owners proposed the extension of the Mansfield and Pinxton Tramway to Leicester. By August 1833 a somewhat different proposal had emerged which concentrated on linking Derby, Nottingham and Leicester and connecting them all to London by a line to Rugby. The hope was to complete the line in time for the opening of the LBR. A provisional Committee was formed with Leicestershire, Derbyshire and Nottinghamshire members, but the scheme was again postponed largely so that full surveys be completed.

On 12 February 1835 a deputation from the MCR urged upon the LBR board the advantages of a junction at Rugby and the LBR's Liverpool shareholders asked the directors to lend their support to the MCR project.[39] Various controversies, particularly whether the line should join the LBR at much greater cost at Blisworth via Northampton rather than Rugby and whether the line should extend from Trent to Pinxton and to Chesterfield and beyond meant it was June 1836 before the Bill was passed. Both these variations had to be dropped.[40] The financial support largely came instead from sources other than local. Of the £786,500 subscribed at 1 March 1836 only £299,000 had come from 270 local shareholders. The remaining £486,000 had come from 231 outsiders.[41] Among them were those with a strong interest in the LBR: Glyn himself, Joseph and Daniel Ledsam, Edward Cropper, Theodore Rathbone and Robert Garnett with others from Liverpool and Manchester: Robert Benson, John Cropper, Laurence Heyworth, Thomas and Henry Houldsworth, William Garnett, and Edward Wilson.[42]

The Liverpool influence was evident. In 1838 three of the Lancashire directors were asked by the North of Trent Works Committee to advise

[37] H.G. Lewin, *Early British Railways*, 1925, Table 1, 186.

[38] *Leeds Mercury*, 29 Aug. 1840, reporting half yearly meeting on 26 Aug. 1840.

[39] TNA, RAIL 384/2, 12 Feb. and *Derby Mercury*, 25 Feb. 1835.

[40] V.A. Hatley, Northampton hoodwinked? How a main line of railway missed the town a second time, *Journal of Transport History*, 7, 160–172.

[41] *Derby Mercury*, 11 May 1836.

[42] Midland Counties Railway Act, 1836.

upon the type of locomotives and carriages required, and suggest suitable builders. As might have been expected from their attitude on the LBR they championed Edward Bury's inside cylinder four-wheeled design as used on that line. Rathbone expressed particularly strong views to the Committee and six locomotives of the Bury type were ordered immediately. Twenty-three more such locomotives were ordered in January 1839. When the MCR locomotives were handed over to the Midland Railway in 1844 only seven of the fleet of forty-seven were not built by Bury or to his design. Bury did however decline to tender to work the railway as he was too busy.[43]

The Birmingham & Derby Junction Railway originated in schemes discussed in Birmingham in 1834. George Stephenson surveyed the route and suggested a junction with the LBR at Stechford to enable trains from Derby to use the LBR's station in Birmingham also to be used by trains on the Birmingham and Gloucester then under consideration. He also proposed a branch from the BDJR's main line at Nether Whitacre to the LBR's line near Hampton to accommodate traffic to and from the London direction. The BDJR was above all a Birmingham company though the original directors included the Burton brewers, Samuel Allsopp, William Worthington and Thomas Bass. Daniel Ledsam, William Francis and James Pearson were directors of both the BDJR and LBR.

The MCR had seen itself as the provider of the route from the north to London and therefore objected to the Hampton branch of the BDJR as competitive with their own route by Rugby. Moreover the NMR objected to the MCR's proposal to continue northwards from Trent up the Erewash valley. The three companies agreed before their Bills were considered in Parliament to remove both branches, but whether by accident or design the MCR Bill contained the line to Pinxton. As the BDJR Bill could not be amended they put forward a separate bill for the Hampton line which they were able to consolidate with their main bill during the parliamentary passage. The BDJR Bill provided for a share capital of £600,000. In September 1836 the Board decided to concentrate their efforts on building the Derby and Hampton line with a view to completing their connection to the London line before the Midland Counties could build to Rugby. The Derby to Birmingham line via Hampton, with a need to reverse trains there, was opened to the public on 12 August 1839, though in late September the LBR board decided that their locomotives would haul the trains from

43 TNA, RAIL 490/13, Committee for the Works North of the Trent, 13 Mar., and 490/7, the Acting Committee, 10 Apr. and 30 Nov. 1838 and 11 Jan. 1839; J.B. Radford, *Introduction to The Nottingham and Derby Railway Companion*, 1839, vi, vii and x, 1979 reprint; TNA, RAIL 384/4, 20 Dec. 1839.

Hampton to Birmingham. By December BDJR were complaining about the cost of extra engines for forwarding passengers by special trains consequent on the late arrival of LBR trains at Hampton.[44]

The combination of such tolls and charges for the use of Birmingham station, the fact that the BDJR and the BGR did not open to Birmingham until 1840, and only reached the LBR station in 1841 meant the BDJR's revenue was unsatisfactory. By June 1840 the MCR route was near enough to Rugby for a short road link to be provided to the LBR. Relations between the BDJR and the MCR were never easy and were exacerbated by a secret agreement between the MCR and NMR whereby all the latter's traffic to Rugby and on to the south would be sent by the MCR route from Derby to the exclusion of the BDJR. The BDJR succeeded in having this agreement declared void, but then embarked on reducing fares to enable them to compete. The result was a price war, though in 1843 the MCR secured a writ compelling the BDJR to abandon their differential scales.[45]

The NMR with Glyn in the chair seems to have been hostile to the BDJR refusing all but the most grudging co-operation in matters such as through fares for passengers and rates for goods and maintaining connections between trains at Derby. On the other hand the LBR also with Glyn in the chair seems to have done its best to remain outside the squabble. In August 1840, following an approach from the BDJR stating that they would promote traffic from the LBR by an acceleration of the trains to the north and requested the LBR to maintain strict impartiality, Glyn told shareholders that the directors had not favoured either company though it might be in their interest to favour the BDJR from the larger toll they would receive. They had however a higher duty to perform: namely a duty to the public.[46] Creed wrote to the BDJR directors 'although the Company is interested in promoting the traffic which will pass over the longest portion of their line, they feel it their duty in booking passengers through, whether by the Birmingham and Derby or by other lines, to act towards all with the most strict impartiality.'[47] In 1842 following negotiations between the LBR, BDJR and MCR, Dicey, the MCR chairman, recognised the principle that the LBR and BDR companies be treated as one line from Rugby to Derby via Hampton and tendering an annual payment of £6,000 per annum as a full compensation for their existing joint interest in the traffic.[48]

[44] TNA, RAIL 384/4, 20 Dec. 1839.

[45] E.G. Barnes, *The Rise of the Midland Railway*, 1844–74, 1966, 60.

[46] TNA, RAIL 36/2, 2 Jul. 1840; RAIL 1110/260, 7 Aug. 1840.

[47] TNA, RAIL 36/2, 2 Jul. 1840.

[48] RAIL 384/5, 9 Dec. 1842.

Glyn was much more closely involved with the North Midland Railway though it was the furthest from London of the three future constituents of the Midland Railway. A committee was formed in Leeds, but Londoners were dominant. As Joseph Pease put it 'the railway has been taken out of the county. It is a London railway with a London Committee.'[49] Glyn was on the London Provisional Committee and both Charles and E.W. Mills were shareholders as were other bankers, Frederick Huth, and Kirkman Hodgson, as well as merchants James Morrison and William Leaf. Glyn told Langton that he hoped his Liverpool friends would support the line, which he thought they would start in conjunction with the Midland, taking up their line at Derby. He introduced to him 'his friend Mr Huth' whom he asked to be introduced to Edward Wilson. He also said he was very anxious about the Leeds (the NMR) joining the LBR and much wished Wilson would write to the partners at Leicester to promote a junction between the Midland Counties Railroad and the Leeds line. To oppose each other would be crass.[50] By 5 October Glyn was telling Langton that the NMR subscription list was full.[51]

George Stephenson surveyed the route from Derby to Leeds in September 1835. In successfully advocating the route to the east of Sheffield, Barnsley and Wakefield, he avoided the South Yorkshire hills and chose to follow river valleys. However this led to a difficult passage in Parliament where Vignoles, backed by Lord Wharncliffe with his extensive interests in South Yorkshire coal, argued in favour of extending the Midland Counties to Chesterfield and then pushing northwards through the hills to Leeds. The Aire and Calder Navigation also strenuously opposed the Bill. 'That body', said Glyn 'was perhaps the most opulent and influential of all that were connected with canals. They might be said to possess almost a monopoly of the traffic of a large part of Yorkshire. They were very naturally very unwilling to encounter rivalry and he did not blame them for it.' They had accordingly provided the most inveterate opposition both in Parliament and elsewhere particularly in the Lords where they secured the inclusion of restrictive clauses which the NMR had to negotiate its way round later. Glyn called their conduct in demanding reimbursement of the expenses of their opposition as like that of schoolmasters who extracted from the pockets of the pupils the cost of the rod by which they themselves were to be flogged and said the directors could

49 *Durham County Advertiser*, 1 Jan. 1836, quoted in Reed, 82.

50 LP 111, 12 Sept. 1835. Frederick Huth was on the London Committee of the NMR. Huths were soon to establish an office in Liverpool. Edward Wilson was simply described as 'gentleman' in Gore's directory of Liverpool. Later a director of the LBR.

51 LP 112, 114 and 116, 12, 25 Sept. and 5 Oct. 1835.

not accede to terms so unjust and extravagant.[52] Stephenson later regarded his route as the finest piece of engineering associated with his name. Though expensive it was cheaper to build than the alternative route and was well placed to tap the coal to be found in the hills rising from the valleys, which potential Stephenson had spotted just as he had at Swannington.

Stephenson not only took up residence at Tapton House just outside Chesterfield, on which he took a 10 year lease in March 1838, but in 1837 formed the Clay Cross Company with Robert Stephenson, Sir Joshua Walmsley, Sandars, George Hudson and Glyn.[53] Each had an initial investment of £2,500 in the company. These substantially increased in the early years of the venture. By the end of 1841 each had invested £15,000, and Glyn's brother Sir Richard with others had invested £10,000, so the company's capital stood at £110,000 compared with only £20,000 at the end of 1839, reflecting a rapid expansion of the collieries at Clay Cross and Tapton, and of limestone quarrying and burning at Crich near the line at Ambergate. It represented major investments in land, coke ovens and railways and above all in wagons which accounted for almost a third of the total expenditure. £11,115 was gained from the sale of coal in the first half of 1841, with £2,299 from lime and £1,858 from coke, giving a profit of £1,007.[54] Glyn's investment might have been intended to provide traffic for the LBR, but until 1844 the LBR would not carry coal. Until then it was taken to Rugby by rail and then by canal to London. Given his interest in Stephenson's similar venture at Snibston, there was probably an element of wishing to back the Stephensons and share in their success. Glyn sold his share, described as a twelfth of the increased capital of £180,000, to George Stephenson for £15,000 in June 1846.[55]

The NMR Bill received royal assent in July 1836. Glyn was elected chairman of the board, an office he held until September 1841. There were London and Leeds committees of the board. The London group included Kirkman Hodgson, Frederick Huth, Ralph Fenwick, William Leaf, Thomas French and William Newton (though he was a banker and alderman of Derby), as well as Glyn, but not Morrison. Riversdale Grenfell, Charles and E.W. Mills and John Hodgson were shareholders. George and Robert Stephenson were appointed joint engineers and were instructed to take the necessary steps for staking out the line and for making the earliest arrangements for letting the

[52] Frederick S. Williams, *The Midland Railway: Its Rise and Progress*, 1886 edition, 46–47.

[53] Skeat, *George Stephenson*, 1973, 205 and 208.

[54] Institution of Mechanical Engineers archives, IMS152, Clay Cross Company balance sheets for half years ending December 1839 to December 1841.

[55] RBS Archives, GM/1263, bond of indemnity relating to the sale, 30 Jun. 1846.

contracts for the mile-long Clay Cross tunnel, the most difficult engineering task.[56] The Leeds Committee, which included J.B. Pease and William Beckett, another of the country bankers linked to Glyn's, were highly appreciative of the part Glyn played in initiating the North Midland. They felt deeply how much the interest of that great manufacturing district were indebted to him for the original suggestion that the NMR should be brought to Leeds and for Glyn's able and increasing exertions in assisting to obtain the sanction of the legislature to this important measure.

It was Glyn who brought before board the question of the mode of the working the company's locomotive power and the Board agreed to contract it out. Robert Stephenson's proposal to manage the locomotive power and receive remuneration by a percentage upon the amount of profits after a dividend had been declared was agreed in principle.[57] 144 locomotives were purchased, all to Stephenson's specifications. It was not however until May 1840 that the forty miles of railway between Derby and Rotherham were opened. The section between Rotherham and Leeds followed seven weeks later.

George Hudson had pleaded unsuccessfully with Stephenson to make York the terminus of the NMR line rather than Leeds. Instead Hudson backed a line to connect with the North Midland at Altofts near Normanton: the York and North Midland which received Parliamentary authority in 1836. Though Glyn was not directly concerned with this project, when in 1833 George Hudson and his associates in York formed the York Union Bank, a joint stock bank, Glyn's became the bank's London correspondents. The YNMR was partially opened in 1839 and to the junction with the NMR on 1 July 1840, the same day as the latter opened to Leeds. Thus York, as well as Leeds was linked with London. At a dinner that evening not only was a toast drunk to Mrs Glyn, who does not seem to have been present at many of her husband's railways celebration, and the ladies, but a glee 'Here's a health to all good lasses' was sung.

Glyn later said his original intention had been to resign on the completion of the works and the opening of the line. From his experience he was convinced that the management of a railway must be entrusted to directors resident on or near the line, competent from local knowledge to deal with the various considerations and causes which must influence the traffic and regulations of every line, and able to give regular attention to the practical working of each department through a system of committees and to whom the officers of the company could have frequent reference. However

56 TNA, RAIL 530/2, 16 Jul. 1836.

57 Ibid, 3 Oct. 1838.

the solicitations of friends connected with the Company and his own feelings with regard to its general and financial position induced him to delay his resignation.

Glyn's sentiments about the line's finances were fully justified. As a result of its heavy earthworks and seven tunnels the cost of construction amounted to £40,000 a mile compared with £26,000 on the Midland Counties and £20,000 on the York and North Midland. Financially the line quickly turned out to be a disappointment, despite the newly opened Ambergate ironworks and Clay Cross colliery. The mineral wealth of South Yorkshire and North East Derbyshire was largely untapped and the coal traffic to London not yet developed.

The NMR attracted traffic but not on a scale which made it a ten per cent line. Although by 1842 26 passenger and freight trains were running daily between Derby and Leeds and additional traffic came from Clay Cross and Ambergate, Glyn had to rebut charges made by a substantial Liverpool shareholder that Stephenson's Clay Cross company had been granted favourable rates. The same rates were applicable to other colliery owners: Earl Fitzwilliam, the duke of Devonshire and Sir Henry Hunloke.[58] Working expenses were high at 47 per cent of gross receipts and the NMR had substantial debts, some incurred from expansion beyond the original plans, like the new joint station at Normanton. In 1839 it was decided to apply to Parliament for permission to raise £500,000 in shares and to borrow £500,000.[59] Consequently although the line was fully open in the second half of 1840, it paid no dividend for that period. 3½ per cent was paid in 1841, but only one per cent in the first half of 1842. While this compared badly with the LBR and GJR, the BDJR paid less than 2 per cent in 1840, 1842 and 1843, and 2½ per cent in 1841, while the MCR paid 4 per cent in 1841 but 3 per cent and 3⅖ per cent in the two following years. More shares were issued by the NMR in 1841 at a 35 per cent discount.

Glyn felt able to resign in 1841 because of the improved aspect of the company's affairs, in part because of savings in working expenses of about £13,000. His decision was influenced by the removal of the Secretary's office from London to Derby. Slightly defensively he said in his resignation letter that, while he looked back on his intimate connection with the North Midland with pleasure, he appreciated that the expectations of its promoters might not yet have been realised. However they had contributed to the carrying out of this great public work whereby the welfare and future prospects of a part of England connected with a most important branch of

58 *Derby Mercury*, 1 Sept. 1841, report of meeting of 26 Aug.

59 TNA, RAIL 530/2, 5 Feb. 1839.

the manufacturing interests would be most materially promoted. From the manner in which the work had been executed unless all calculation failed it would eventually remunerate the proprietors. He added that he would remain a proprietor and if at any time his railway connections could be the means of furnishing information or affording any facility he would be ready to do so.[60]

He was succeeded by William Newton. Prosperity however was not close at hand for the NMR. The economic depression of 1842 made improvement more difficult. Coal was being carried at a rate which was probably uneconomic. The £100 shares dropped to £70 by September 1841. The poor financial performance of the NMR led to the setting up of a shareholders' committee of enquiry almost immediately after Glyn's resignation. It proposed a series of economies, including reductions in wages. These were regarded by the *Railway Times* as cheeseparing and led to frustration and anger by the shareholders and the setting up of another committee. Hudson was a member although it was chaired by Peter Brancker, a Liverpool shareholder, whose appointment as director, Hudson had successfully opposed in 1841. The main recommendation was that staff numbers and wages should be reduced to bring a fall in the wage and salary bill from £40,600 to £22,800. The board proposed less severe savings as they believed the committee's proposals would risk the welfare of the establishment and endanger the safety of passengers. Six directors resigned and Hudson and Brancker became members of the board.

Hudson, now the most influential director, brought in Thomas Cabry as engineer and Peter Clark as secretary, both from his York and North Midland. Wages were reduced, and workers who protested dismissed. This attracted hostile criticism particularly from Vincit in the *Railway Times* who predicted serious accidents would result particularly from the employment of inexperienced drivers in place of those dismissed. The company's case that the men recruited were all competent rang less true when within a few weeks two collisions occurred. The driver of one of the trains was sent for trial at the inquest, and the Railway Department of the Board of Trade found that the accident had been caused in part due to long hours, a novel intervention accompanied by a threat to take greater powers if companies withheld information from the Railway Department as the North Midland had attempted to do.[61] Though Newton and Hudson – often from the chair of the YNMR where he had more opportunities, defended the wage cuts,

[60] TNA, RAIL 530/2, Glyn to Henry Patteson, 24 Sept. 1841.

[61] M. Robbins, The North Midland Railway and its Enginemen, *Journal of Transport History*, 4, 1960, 180–182.

fares were increased so reducing revenue and the annual rate of dividend only rose to 3 per cent in 1843. The root of the matter was the high capital expenditure of the line and cuts in costs could not radically change the overall picture. The situation was only improved by the amalgamation of the three Midland companies in mid-1844. The MCR was reluctant to be a party to his but Hudson was able to force the amalgamation by threatening that the NMR would lease the BDJR and force all trains to take that route to Rugby. In the end MCR shareholders were convinced they should join because while their own line was cheaper to run, they were always competing against the rival BDJR.

One of the consequences of the opening of the Midland lines and the through route to York was an increase in traffic on the line from Euston to Rugby. In 1841 the attention of the board was drawn to the limited accommodation at Euston, and in March 1842 the erection of an entirely new station was only abandoned on the ground of expense in favour of further additions and improvements. The original Euston had only one departure platform, so the problem was only resolved when an Act to empower the LNWR to enlarge their station in London was passed in 1846. Glyn said,

> we have been obliged to buy streets – streets, gentlemen – to give the public the accommodation they require ... when these buildings are finished – buildings which I assure you are erected without a single ornament, and without the slightest unnecessary expense – we shall not have one foot of ground more than is necessary at the present moment.[62]

Compared with the developments in the Midlands the 1836–37 boom left relatively little mark on the areas adjacent to the LBR's main line. There were attempts to make links from the LBR near London to the City and to the GWR itself. The LBR also established a few branch lines. A proposed extension to the west led to a conflict with the GWR which heralded the graver disputes of the 1840s, as did the threat of lines from Manchester to the LBR which cut out part of its route to the north west.

In the 1830s the LBR did not seem particularly interested in reaching the City and the London docks, despite the proposal in 1835 for a London Grand Junction Railway to start at Camden Town and go on to Battle Bridge (on the Regent's Canal), Snow Hill and the Thames, 'thus forming a magnificent and uninterrupted entrance to the city of London and the Thames from the North and the West of England'. A capital of £750,000

[62] G. Royde Smith, *Old Euston*, 1938, 26–27.

was proposed. It was thought that four out of ten passengers on the GWR and the LBR would use the line as well as some omnibus users. It could convey cattle to Smithfield, goods from the Regent's Canal and suburban traffic.[63] However the provisional committee did not contain anybody from the LBR or even from St Katharine's Dock. The proposal was authorised by Parliament in 1836 and in 1837 reached the stage of advertising for tenders for a viaduct over Gray's Inn Lane.[64] The LBR in June 1837 wished them every success but offered no assistance. In early 1838 Sir Samuel Whalley, chairman of the LGJR, called on Glyn but this brought no change in the LBR's attitude. When the LGJR brought forward a bill to extend its powers the LBR board instructed the Committee of Management to oppose it. The bill was thrown out.[65]

At the same time the Birmingham, Bristol and Thames Junction Railway succeeded in Parliament. Despite its grand title this was a three mile railway from Willesden to cross and connect with the GWR main line and proceed to the Kensington Canal basin. It opened in 1840 but was not a financial success. The LBR refused to purchase it in 1844, and only agreed to lease it when the company was in danger of liquidation, so gaining access to the Thames via the Chelsea basin of the Kensington Canal.

The LBR was happy to make the necessary connections to the Midland Counties at Rugby and to the GJR and BDR at or near Birmingham because those lines were in effect extensions of the LBR and their London traffic was fed into Euston. There was no question of any of those companies attempting to establish a rival route to London, at least not until 1844 and 1845 when the GJR came near with its overtures to the GWR. However the threat of a more direct line from Manchester, at least to Rugby, arose with the complaints of Manchester merchants just before the passing of the Grand Junction Act in 1833 that it would give them a very roundabout way to London – by the LMR to Newton and then the GJR and LBR. In 1834 they demanded a more direct route which would avoid Birmingham. The GJR was unresponsive, and by 1836 two rival schemes for lines from Manchester were put forward: the Manchester and South Union to Rugby via Lichfield, and the Manchester and Cheshire Junction to Crewe, supported by the GJR. Neither succeeded in Parliament in 1836, or in 1837, but the companies then merged with the result that the Manchester and Birmingham Railway Act was authorised with a main line from Manchester through the Potteries to Chebsey, north of Stafford, and branches to Crewe and Macclesfield.

63 *The Times*, 16 Sept., 4 and 31 Oct. 1835.

64 *The Times*, 30 Jan. and 18 Feb. 1837.

65 TNA, RAIL 384/3, 2 Jun. 1837 and 11 Apr. 1838; 384/45, 3 and 10 Jan. 1838.

Fearing that the GJR would not co-operate fully, the MBR then promoted a subsidiary company entitled the Manchester and Birmingham Extension to run from Stone to Rugby, via the Trent Valley. The GJR was offered a joint share in the line but rejected this when they found that they would be in a minority on the joint board.

Glyn was not opposed to this development, but wanted it to go ahead on the LBR's terms. In November 1838 he told Boothby, now a director, that the opposition of the LBR, GJR, MCR and probably the NMR might have succeeded in stopping the Trent extension line for the following year. Nevertheless it remained important that this extension should take place and 'that our position and any proposal made to us should receive the deliberate and material consideration of the board … with knowledge of the steps taken by the GJR. We must be very cautious and not hasty in incurring the expense of parliamentary opposition.'[66] In the event the GJR and LBR did oppose the scheme, but there was not time for the Bill to finish all its stages in the 1839 Parliament.

The MBR reached an agreement with John Moss and Charles Lawrence, chairman and deputy chairman of the GJR, in October 1839 which guaranteed the GJR use of the Trent Valley line if it was ever built, but did not commit the GJR to supporting it. The MBR decided to concentrate on building the junction with the GJR at Crewe. In early November 1839 the LBR board again expressed its hostility to the making of a line from Stone to Rugby. This meant it was some years before serious attention was directed to a Trent Valley line.

The matter came up again in 1843, when Glyn expressed doubts to Moss. The line would only be desirable to either of their undertakings by the necessity of a measure of protection to the existing lines. Moss replied that if he knew how to preserve the Irish and other traffic to the existing lines 'I should not entertain for a moment the Trent Valley project.'[67]

Opposition to the Trent Valley line was in line with Glyn's policy of keeping other companies from making rival lines and from tapping the sources of LBR's traffic in what the LBR regarded as their natural district, though this term was not precisely defined at a time when extensive areas were still bereft of railways. Until the mid-1840s Glyn was prepared to go far from the LBR's main line both to provide more feeder lines and as a means of keeping out others, while some could be safely encouraged as candidates for the Euston empire.

[66] RBS Archives, GM/237, Glyn to Boothby, 30 Nov. 1838.

[67] TNA, RAIL 1008/108, Glyn to Moss, 26 Jul. 1843 and Glyn's reply, both quoted in Moss's letter to Glyn of March 1844.

A partial exception which went beyond the LBR's district was to the west of its main line where in 1837 the LBR supported a proposal for a Cheltenham inspired line from Cheltenham, via Oxford, to Tring on the LBR main line – the Cheltenham, Oxford and London and Birmingham Union Railway with a capital of £1,400,000. The LBR board agreed to assist as they envisaged the line as carrying traffic for South Wales and even southern Ireland, but It ran into obstacles with landowners. At the same time the GWR was backing a line from Cheltenham to join its line at Swindon – the Cheltenham and Great Western Union, to which the GWR had offered an initial loan of £5,000. George Henry Gibbs called on Glyn in Lombard Street to remonstrate against his lending his sanction to the line to Tring, a scheme so hostile to the GWR's interests, so ill-founded in every respect. Next day at E.W Mills suggestion Gibbs went to the Bank again and asked for Charles Mills, E.W. Mills elder brother, 'who saw the force of our argument and promised that our representation would be attended to.' E.W. Mills told Gibbs afterwards that Glyn had offered to do everything in his power to redeem the false step he had taken and that he had written a very strong letter to Cropper. Gibbs thought that the Tring line would deprive the GWR of a great source of traffic and a few days later he noted that the Tring line 'by our attacking Glyn's banking feelings and by the result of the meeting at Oxford (to support the GWR's branch to Oxford from Didcot) appeared to be knocked on the head.'[68] This episode demonstrates Glyn's influence in the LBR before he became chairman. When the Lords approved the GWR's line from Cheltenham to Swindon they declared the Cheltenham to Tring was not a competing line, and it was expected to go ahead in the following session, but the impetus had gone, despite claims that it was significantly shorter than the GWR route.[69]

Though frustrated on that front the LBR took effective steps to serve towns adjacent to its main line – Leamington, Aylesbury and Northampton. Indeed before the main line was opened a branch to Leamington was envisaged, one of the most attractive destinations in close proximity to it. The town was then expanding rapidly and in 1838 Queen Victoria was to authorise the name Royal Leamington Spa. By 1841 its population reached 15,700, having been a mere 315 in 1801. The LBR surveyed a line from Coventry to Leamington in 1836, but Glyn reported in 1837 that the great majority of landowners were opposed to the project which had therefore been abandoned, though the company hoped to return to it. This they did in

[68] *The Birth of the Great Western Railway*, 12, 14 and 17 Mar. 1837, 18–19; TNA, RAIL 384/2, 3 Feb. 1837; *The Times*, 7 Apr., 30 Jul. and 7 Dec. 1836.

[69] *The Times*, 16 Sept. and 31 Oct. 1835.

1842 though the lead was taken by local promoters who formed the Warwick and Leamington Union Railway and approached the LBR for support. This was given, though in March 1842 Glyn reported that a further subscription was needed to carry the bill into Parliament in the current session and he thought that the board should offer this. After the Bill succeeded the LBR purchased the line and Glyn and other LBR directors took seats on the board.[70] The Aylesbury Branch was successful more immediately. Local interests promoted a single track branch from Cheddington to Aylesbury in 1836. A separate undertaking, it was built under Robert Stephenson's supervision but when opened in 1839 it was worked by the LBR under a rental agreement.

The branch to Leamington was only nine miles long and that to Aylesbury seven. The line from Blisworth to Peterborough, authorised in 1843, was a very different proposition. It was 47 miles long, though one of its purposes was to connect Northampton, only four miles from Blisworth, to the LBR main line. Northampton was a substantial town whose population had increased from 7,000 in 1801 to 15,000 in 1831 with the rapid expansion of the boot and shoe industry. However situated in the valley of the Nene with hills on all sides except the east it was not well suited for a station on a through route from south to north. The Grand Union Canal had bypassed it, though a heavily locked branch reached the town in 1814 to connect with the Nene. Robert Stephenson had recommended that the LBR should pass to the west of Northampton and despite strong representations from Northampton interests, his plan was adhered to, thus avoiding a sharp drop into the Nene Valley and possible difficulties with the Spencers at Althorp whose estate a line out of Northampton to the north would have had to cross.[71] The line's destination was Peterborough because the LBR intended to tap the traffic of East Anglia by linking up with the Eastern Counties Railway (ECR). The line was initially proposed by a group of local people but Glyn was asked with other directors to negotiate with the parties as the LBR was willing to pay for the preliminary proceedings. The Bill ran into difficulties in the Lords but the LBR was assisted by Lord Clarendon because according to Glyn he was annoyed that others were trying to stifle a debate about the merits of the undertaking. The line brought the LBR into what was then an area without railways. The ECR ran to Cambridge

[70] TNA, RAIL 384/5, 13 Feb. and 8 Jul. 1842.

[71] The legend that Northampton interests were largely and strongly opposed to the LBR entering the town is discussed with reference to the extensive literature on the matter in the chapter The Town that Missed the Railway in Robin Leleux, *East Midlands, Regional History of the Railways of Great Britain*, 9, 1976, 43–52.

but there was nothing between there and Peterborough until the ECR was authorised to build a line from Ely to join the LBR at Peterborough, completed in 1846. Glyn saw the Blisworth-Peterborough line as a branch which would itself be beneficial to the LBR but which was much more important as a link in the chain of railway communication between east and west.[72]

No sooner had the Bill been obtained than the situation in eastern England changed rapidly. In February 1844 Glyn referred to Peterborough as 'our eastern terminus'. He was somewhat taken by surprise by the extraordinary activity shown by the amalgamated eastern lines in contrast to what he regarded as the state of apathy in which they had existed for many years apparently without any intention of occupying the part of the country which might have been said to belong to them.[73] He recognised that the branch lines proposed must interfere with the direct traffic which might otherwise pass via Peterborough to London, though he hoped to find a new traffic from the 80 mile branch line which was then opening from Norwich to Peterborough.[74] It now seems curious that even at that date Glyn apparently took granted that traffic between Peterborough and London would focus on Euston, 109 mile from the station which the LBR shared with the ECR at Peterborough via Blisworth compared with 76 on the future Great Northern.

In March 1844 the LBR board decided to co-operate with the ECR in opposing a railway from Cambridge to Peterborough and on to Lincoln and recognised that this stance meant they could not consistently support a line from Boston to Lincoln. At the same time they supported Hudson's Midland Railway line from Nottingham to Lincoln. Even the line from Bletchley to Bedford, backed by the duke of Bedford was supported as a valuable feeder opening up communication with London and the northern districts, though Glyn had to insist to a deputation that the LBR were prepared to pay 4 per cent on the estimate of £120,000 but not on more.[75]

Like the other branches the Blisworth to Peterborough was planned as a cheap line with single track, level crossings rather than bridges where possible and avoiding heavy earthworks. However by the time the line was opened for goods traffic in December 1845 it had been decided to make the line double track in pursuit of Glyn's strategy. The idea that the LBR could serve Peterborough from Euston was by then being submerged by new developments and the LBR was supporting Hudson in the Midland's bid for

[72] TNA, RAIL 1160/260, 11 Aug. 1843.

[73] The Eastern Counties leased the Northern and Eastern.

[74] TNA, RAIL 1160/260, 9 Feb. 1844.

[75] TNA, RAIL 384/24, 12 Jun. 1844.

a line from Lincoln to Cambridge and Peterborough as a way of deterring the London–York direct.

Meanwhile the LBR was conscious that Euston could become the gateway to Scotland as well as to the North of England. Indeed in May 1841 a steamship service was begun between the new port of Fleetwood, a town created by the Preston and Wyre Railway in conjunction with the local landowner, reached by railway the previous year, and Ardrossan, already linked by rail with Glasgow. By then however the extension of the trunk railway to Scotland had become a practical possibility. In October 1842 the LBR board took the view that it was in their interest that the proposed line from Lancaster to Carlisle should be made and thus desirable that the LBR should co-operate on the measure on an equitable principle,[76] The Government's largely laissez-faire approach to railway routes did not extend to those to Scotland and Ireland which were regarded as of strategic importance, and as important links between London and Dublin and Edinburgh, not least for postal traffic. Lieutenant-General Sir Frederic Smith of the Royal Engineers and Professor Peter Barlow had been commissioned by the Government in 1839 to examine the best means of completing railway communication between London and Dublin, Edinburgh and Glasgow. In the case of Scotland it was generally accepted that one trunk line would be sufficient for traffic and Smith and Barlow in a series of reports published in 1840 and 1841 found in favour of the west coast route. The North Union under the chairmanship of Rathbone already linked the GJR with Preston and its continuation northwards in the form of the Preston and Lancaster had been authorised in 1837. Beyond Lancaster Joseph Locke at the behest of the GJR made a number of surveys favouring the Lune Valley route. Smith and Barlow in 1841 decisively rejected a route proposed by George Stephenson which would have crossed Morecambe Bay and followed the Cumberland coast. Locke's route with some variations, including the abandonment of a summit tunnel in favour of the route over Shap, was chosen. The LBR subscribed £100,000 which with £250,000 from the GJR and other lesser subscriptions meant that the Bill was able to go before Parliament in 1844 and received approval in June. The capital was to be £900,000 with £300,000 more if a double line was built.

The LBR found that its support for the Lancaster and Carlisle attracted criticism from the eastern companies. Their complaints were referred to Glyn who was authorised to take any steps he might deem expedient for the protection of LBR's huge interests in the arrangements then going forward in the Eastern Counties, keeping in view the importance of connecting any

[76] TNA, RAIL 384/5, 14 Oct. 1842.

extension from Norwich with a line via Wisbech to Peterborough, and by Bury or Ipswich to London. Despite the LBR's subscription to the LCR, when the board received a deputation from the proposed Caledonian Railway they were told it appeared indispensably necessary for the company to persevere in the course of strict neutrality hitherto followed relative to the respective lines of communication with Scotland. Later when the question of opposing the North British Railway arose because it was an east coast rival to the west coast Caledonian, the board refused to abandon its policy of neutrality.[77] Nevertheless their support for the latter continued, Hodgson and Rathbone being appointed proxies for the LBR's votes, though the provisional committee of the CR did not contain a LBR representative.[78]

Following the union of the Parliaments of Great Britain and Ireland in 1801 the UK Government had a strong interest in establishing a fast and secure route for passengers and goods and for the Royal Mail from London to Dublin. In the years immediately before the coming of the main line railways the London to Holyhead road had been much improved by Telford, not least by the two bridges at Conway and Menai, both completed in 1826. Steam packets from Holyhead had been introduced in 1819 worked by the Admiralty on behalf of the Post Office. When the railway link from London to Liverpool came into operation in 1838 the London to Dublin postal traffic was sent via Liverpool. However the government had appointed commissioners to consider the provision of railways in Ireland and their report in 1838 covered proposals for Welsh harbours, narrowing the choice to Holyhead and Porth Dinllaen on the Lleyn peninsula. Further reports in 1840 and 1842,[79] influenced by the naval assessors on the Commission, led the Government to plump for Holyhead with which a rail link had still to be formed, though the 1842 report favoured a route along the coast rather than inland like the road. A company formed in 1839 published a prospectus but it was 1843 before the Chester and Holyhead was promoted. To succeed, support was necessary from the English main line companies and from the Post Office. The CHR seems to have approached the LBR rather than the GJR which had taken over the Chester and Crewe. One factor was that the GJR resented the CHR's attempt to take over the Chester and Birkenhead. Peel, now Prime Minister, had been Chief Secretary for Ireland from 1812 to 1818 and was keenly interested in improving communications with Dublin. In 1843 naval officers were appointed to make further surveys of the harbours at Holyhead

[77] Ibid, 12 Jan. and 8 Mar. 1844.

[78] TNA, RAIL 384/6, 22 Oct. 1845.

[79] Select Committee of the House of Commons on Post Office communication with Ireland, PP, 1842, ix.

and Porth Dynllaen and James Walker was asked for his observations. He reported the following month, having received much help from Glyn, Creed and Bury regarding the approach through Chester and Crewe. Glyn wrote to Moss to say it was essential for the interests of the LBR and GJR and other existing lines connected therewith that arrangements should be made by which the traffic of the proposed CHR should be permanently retained and continued upon those lines. Moss however thought that to secure the Irish traffic 'our two companies should make the line'.[80] Glyn reported on a meeting at Sir Robert Peel's of promoters of the proposed line to Holyhead via Chester at which he was present.[81] Nevertheless Glyn did not treat this as a matter for the LBR alone – indeed they could only obtain access to the proposed line via the GJR – and was in touch with Moss, as the plan had a bearing on the interests of both companies. The LBR was soon committed to allowing the CHR a third share in the undertaking while the GJR had envisaged it would share the project solely with the LBR.[82] Nevertheless as the LBR board would not go back on its negotiations with the CHR which was beginning the process of securing a Bill and was talking to the government about the mail contract the GJR reluctantly agreed to accept a one-third share. Differences over the CHR were one of the main ingredients which resulted in a period of antagonistic relations between the LBR and GJR only resolved by their amalgamation agreed in 1845.

80 TNA, RAIL 1008/102, Glyn to Moss, 16 Nov. and Moss's reply of 17 Nov. 1843.

81 Peel was accompanied by Sir James Graham and the Chancellor of the Exchequer. Moss accompanied Glyn and J. Walker was also present. *The Times*, 11 Jan. 1844.

82 TNA, RAIL 384/5, 1 Dec. 1843 with extract from minutes of GJR directors meeting of 24 Nov.

CHAPTER NINE

Glyn and the National Railway System

THE MAIL CONTRACT and the routes to Scotland and Ireland were unusual as in the 1830s and early 1840s most railway matters did not involve the Government. Parliamentary approval was a necessary precondition to the birth of a railway, but the approval of the Government was not. A railway's Act of Parliament was essentially to mediate between the railway and those affected by its construction, including other railway companies, not to impose standards which had to be adhered to. Moreover Britain was quite unlike France where the state was given from the start control of every aspect of railway construction, charges and operation with the corps de ponts et chaussées even planning the routes.[1] In Belgium there was an early decision to build a public rail system. In Britain, though a passenger duty was introduced in 1832, this was solely to raise revenue and put railways on the same basis as stage coaches. Questions of monopoly and indeed safety were largely ignored by the Whig Government, despite a number of MPs and peers arguing strongly for limitations on the monopoly of railways. In 1836 Poulett Thomson, President of the Board of Trade said that the Government would not make any proposal for preferring one line of railway to another or even for pointing out any rule for the adoption of the House on this subject. The most cogent speech came from James Morrison who argued strongly for intervention.[2] He compared the case of

[1] Frank Dobbin, *Forging Industrial Policy, The United States, Britain and France in the Railway Age*, 1994, 105, and more generally, for a comparison of the divergent approaches in the three countries to the planning and control of railways.

[2] Morrison was a retail and wholesale textile merchant. Left over £3 million. MP 1830–37 and 1840–47. He had been associated with the LBR, but declined to invest to any extent in British railway companies as it would be incompatible with his role as a critic, which may have encouraged him into partnership with John Cryder in the American trade, and extensive investments in US railroads. Chaired the 1846 Committee on Railway Enactments

railways, where Parliament had effectively created a monopoly, with roads with open access (or open to all who paid tolls). Thus no company would be formed in the future to make a new railway between the same places and come into the field under equally favourable circumstances, and if they did succeed despite the capital investment involved, the original company would reduce their charges to get rid of the competition. He therefore proposed that all future railway acts should have a clause in them to protect the public interest, limiting dividends to a certain rate, or that power be reserved to Parliament to revise and fix at the end of every twenty years the tolls chargeable on passengers and goods conveyed. Such a clause should be introduced immediately to avoid shareholders complaining that they had not been warned of this invasion of their property rights. He thought the task should be undertaken by independent commissioners but did not press this, as he thought it not acceptable politically. However he withdrew his bill as there was no chance of it being carried that year.[3] Christopher Foster has commented that Morrison saw the problems of natural monopoly in a nutshell, though leaving the task of review to Parliament would have much weakened his remedy.[4] The Duke of Wellington also argued that some plan ought to be devised to bring the railroads under the supervision of Parliament at some future period. A power to revise the provisions after a certain time was necessary. He secured an amendment giving power to Parliament to revise the terms of a railway Act during the same or succeeding session according the terms of any general Act, but in the event no such provision was passed.[5] Wellington and Morrison were not the only voices in favour of intervention, but neither they nor the Government took up the matter and the issue of monopoly as a general issue was largely dormant until 1844.

Meanwhile Glyn was concerned about other aspects of Government policy. From an early stage he was conscious of the need for his and other companies not to lose the confidence of either public or Government. He began to play a major part in instigating joint action on behalf of the railway companies both in inter-company relations and in their dealings with the government. His personal standing and chairman of the company with links to most of the railways then operating or in course of construction put him in the lead. It was at Euston that representatives of 18 companies

when he grilled Hudson. The recommendations led to the establishment of the Railway Commissioners. He published pamphlets on railways. (R. Gatty, *James Morrison*, 1789–1857, 1977, 258–66; ODNB.)

[3] PD, 33, 977–88, 17 May; PD, 35, 134, 12 Jul. 1836.

[4] C.D. Foster, *Privatisation, Public Ownership and Natural Monopoly*, 1992, 23.

[5] PD, 34, 1–3, 3 Jun. and 498–9, 14 Jun. 1836.

met in May 1838 to consider the proceedings of a Select Committee set up to investigate the carriage of Post Office mail by railway. A committee of railway representatives managed to secure some concessions – the earliest instance of such joint action.[6] Glyn warned LBR shareholders in August 1838 just before the line was fully open that it was highly necessary that their arrangements for an interchange of traffic and for the conveyance of passengers the companies should cherish a feeling of liberality and a regard for the comfort and accommodation of the public. If they did not act thus the cry of monopoly which had already been raised would be revived and increased. He added in support that the LBR's charge for mail was considerably less than the coaches had been.[7]

There were soon complaints from traders at the LBR's exercise of its powers which culminated early in 1839 in a petition to the House of Commons against the high rates they charged. Glyn did not react directly to the petition, but he backed, or perhaps even instigated, an approach by Burke and Venables, railway solicitors of Westminster, who wrote on 7 January to the secretaries of all the railway companies seeking support from their boards for an association of railway companies with a view to protection against any attack on them which might arise in the ensuing session. The companies were invited 'to act in concert in endeavouring to repel any improper interference with their vested rights'. They also thought it prudent to establish the association as 'a scientific society for the encouragement of public improvements' and to give as little publicity as possible to it.

Consequently the first meeting of the Railway Society was held in the office of Burke and Venables on 9 March 1839 with Glyn in the chair. Its purpose was to promote and encourage the scientific improvement of railways throughout the United Kingdom, and probably more significantly, the protection of the general interests of the proprietors. The LBR paid a subscription of £20. Soon the appointment of a Select Committee on Communication by Railways was announced and the Society then set up a committee to watch over all proceedings in Parliament at all likely to affect railway interests. The Society was also recognised by the President of the Board of Trade as the organ through which it would seek any information required on railways.[8] However in December the Society – the first embodiment of the railway interest – was dissolved. The surviving documentation does not make clear why it was so short-lived. It is possible

6 Ibid, 16; *Railway Times*, 5 May and 30 Jun. 1838.

7 TNA, RAIL 1110/260, 21 Aug. 1838.

8 TNA, RAIL 1008/105; *Railway Times*, 13 and 20 Apr. and 22 Jun. 1839; Geoffrey Alderman, *The Railway Interest*, 1973, 16.

that there was not sufficient support to keep it going. Even the NMR, of which Glyn was then chairman, though prepared to entertain the idea favourably, thought it not advisable to stir in this matter unless it was generally entertained by other railways.[9]

Glyn personally gave evidence to the Select Committee. Like Stephenson and Baxendale, by then deputy chairman of the South Eastern Railway, he thought a superintending board annexed to the Board of Trade would be useful to ensure uniformity of bye-laws and signalling arrangements and even to arbitrate in disputes concerning through fares. The Committee tentatively suggested that such a board should be established to control companies' bye-laws to which the public might be subjected and which should be approved in advance.

The Select Committee also observed that it did not appear to have been the intention of Parliament to give to a railway company the complete monopoly of the means of communication on their road. Indeed, provision was made in many Acts of Parliament to enable other persons to run engines and carriages upon the road upon the payment of tolls. Glyn told the Select Committee that several accidents had occurred in consequence of that divided authority. He was quite clear that stations were the private property of a railroad company and others had no right to use fixed engines at a station. There had been applications to put locomotives on the LBR line, but not from parties who seemed to have the means. With the carriage of goods the position was different. Trains were hauled by the company. The Committee concluded that the intention of allowing others to run engines could not be carried into effect in the way contemplated, as the payment of tolls was only a very small part of what was necessary to open all roads to public competition. A person with authority to place an engine and carriages on a railway would be unable to supply the engine with water, or to take up or set down passengers at a station and so all competition would be rendered impossible. The Committee added that the safety of the public also required that there should be one system of management, under one superintending authority with the power to make and enforce all regulations for the protection of passengers and for conducting and maintaining the new mode of communication. It admitted that they would thereby acquire an entire monopoly, but if these extensive powers were granted to private companies it became most important that they should be controlled to secure the public as far as possible from any abuse which might arise.[10]

[9] TNA, RAIL 530/2, 20 Aug. 1839.

[10] Second Report of Select Committee on State of Communication by Railway, PP, 1839, x, Glyn's evidence Qs 110–111, 120 and 124.

The Committee continued its work in 1840 when it reaffirmed its views but again emphasised that it was advisable to interfere with the companies as little as possible and that interference by a Government board with the promotion and choice of routes by railways would be undesirable.[11]

A Railway Regulation Act was then passed, put forward by two members of the committee: Lord Seymour[12] and James Loch.[13] It provided that railways should be inspected before their opening to ensure that their Act had been complied with. The Board of Trade had to approve the company's bye-laws. Consequently the Railway Department of the Board of Trade was set up as a small extension of the Statistics Department. It could call for returns of traffic and of all accidents attended with personal injury. The Board's hand was soon forced by accidents and one in Sonning cutting, when all the passengers in a mixed third class and goods train had been thrown out and six of them killed, awakened the interest of the Department in the whole question of facilities provided for the poor.

In January 1841 when concern was mounting about the number of accidents on railways Glyn took the chair at a meeting in Birmingham of all the principal railway companies in England. Those present thought that by far the greater part of the accidents were due to the neglect and disobedience of orders by railway servants. An improved state of discipline and moral responsibility on their part would reduce accidents. It was decided to set up a general conference to take into account the causes and circumstances of accidents and the means of guarding against their occurrence in the future. Despite the concentration on the responsibility of employees, they emphasised the grave responsibility falling to railway directors and the obligation to adopt all judicious and practicable expedients for ensuring the general accommodation, comfort and safety of the passengers. Therefore the meeting would deprecate any sudden or hasty legislation. But the meeting were not just in favour of discipline, they thought it due to men whose services were so arduous to encourage the requisite discipline, by adequate remuneration and by suitable rewards for extraordinary exertion or long-sustained good conduct. They considered whether a conductor or captain should be placed on the locomotive as well as the driver and fireman but thought this would divide authority and diminish the responsibility of

11 Third Report of Select Committee on State of Communication by Railway, PP, 1840, xiii.

12 MP for Totnes, eldest son of the Duke of Somerset, Lord of the Treasury, 1839–41.

13 MP for Wick. A director of the LMR by virtue of the Marquess of Stafford's large investment. Principal agent for Stafford (created Duke of Sutherland in 1833) and apologist for the family's actions on their Sutherland estates (the Highland Clearances).

the engineman. Finally they considered it desirable for a uniform system of signals recognised and applicable to all railways and drew up rules for the consideration of each railway company.[14]

The Railway Regulation Act 1842 had an easy passage through Parliament. Gladstone discussed the Bill with railway company representatives. It provided for the reporting of accidents on a wider basis and gave the Board power to delay the opening of new lines, to settle disputes between companies and turnpike trustees and others at level crossing gates, and to authorise the companies to enter land to repair cuttings etc when necessary for safety. Gladstone claimed he sought greater powers only where experience showed they were called for. Licensing of drivers was not pursued because of an improvement in the conduct of engine drivers. It would, said Gladstone, lessen the responsibility of directors of railroads.[15]

The next development owed nothing to the state, but was a mechanism established by the railway companies themselves whereby they could settle with each other for fares and rates for through journeys over more than one company's lines: the Railway Clearing House. The need for such an arrangement on the railways had become very apparent by the beginning of the 1840s. By 1840 there were linked railway lines between London and Preston via Birmingham; Liverpool and Hull; London and York; and Gloucester to Leeds. There were numerous obstructions to through communication ranging from refusals to allow other companies wagons on their line with transhipment necessary, exorbitant charges, including those levied on the BDJR by the LBR, difficulties in arranging scales of through charges, and in exchanging wagons.[16] Even when progress was made in these areas there was the problem of 'keeping the accounts' as Baxendale put it to the 1839 Select Committee.[17] Robert Stephenson told the same committee that independent companies were, as often or not, inclined to overreach one another rather than come to a simple understanding. He favoured the creation of an independent board whose intervention would be useful whenever a difference arose between two companies over a bye-law, a signal, or even a price.[18] The Post Office was another influence stressing the importance of through mail traffic.

The railways' main contribution was the establishment of a clearing house. Although the Bankers' Clearing House seems to have been the main

14 *The Times*, 22 Jan. 1841.

15 PD, 60, 166, 8 Feb. 1842.

16 TNA, RAIL 384/4, 20 Dec. 1839.

17 PP, 1839, x, Qs 5720–1.

18 Ibid, Qs 4739–42.

precedent there was a small clearing system for through passenger traffic on the roads operated by the Golden Cross Coach Company. How far the Railway Clearing House established in 1842 was largely Glyn's creation was a matter of some controversy on the occasion of its fiftieth anniversary in 1892. A lengthy article in The *Times* said that the credit of the application to railways of the clearing principle long known in banking was largely due to George Carr Glyn who used his powerful influence in support of the proposal, put to him by Robert Stephenson and Kenneth Morison. A subsequent report in *The Times*, presumably inspired by James Allport, then eighty-one, claimed that the original idea was his.[19] Allport subsequently set out hIs claim to authorship in more detail. When in charge of the traffic arrangements of the BDJR, faced with the difficulties in dividing the receipts with the companies with which it was linked, he had put forward the idea that a system similar to the bankers' clearing house should be set up. He said Robert Stephenson who was present at a meeting of BDJR directors discussed the matter with Glyn. Allport's version was disputed by Sir Edward Watkin, who said the attribution of the origin to Allport was absolutely incorrect and that those who lived in those days knew very well that the suggestor of the clearing house was Glyn. Philip Bagwell found no confirmation of Allport's claims in the records of the BDJR.[20] When the RCH was formed Watkin had not yet joined the railway world, but from 1846 he was closely involved in the central senior management of the LNWR and would have known Morison fairly well. Allport does not seem to have been mentioned as an originator of the clearing house mechanism until his own claim 50 years later.[21]

It is certain that Glyn and Kenneth Morison played a much bigger role than Allport in the starting the RCH and it is very doubtful whether it would have got off the ground at that stage had not Glyn put his weight and that of his company behind the concept. Glyn not only chaired the first meeting, but remained chairman until his death 31 years later. He was of course fully knowledgeable about the Bankers Clearing House, which by 1839 included 29 banks clearing £954 million annually with a daily average of about £4 million.[22] This was also the case with Morison. He had worked

[19] James Allport, joined the BDJR in 1839, manager, BDJR, 1843, Newcastle & Darlington, 1844–50, MSLR, 1850–53, Midland, 1853–80. Knighted 1884.

[20] *The Times*, 26, 27 and 30 Jan., 3 and 9 Feb. 1892; Philip Bagwell, *The Railway Clearing House in the British Economy, 1842–1922*, 1968, 33.

[21] Neither Morison in his *Origins and Results of the Clearing System*, 1846, nor Sir Francis Bond Head in his chapter on the RCH in *Stokers and Pokers*, 1849 make any reference to Allport's role.

[22] Second Report from the Select Committee on Banks of Issue, PP, 1841, v, appendix 31.

for the East India merchants, Babington and Macaulay, until Glyn brought him into the LBR in 1839 as head of the Audit Department. He noted the contrast between the simplicity with which his former employer's accounts were settled through the Bankers' Clearing House and the difficulties and confusion, long delays and angry correspondence associated with the settlement of accounts between railway companies. With the LBR he also had dealings with the Golden Cross Clearing House.[23]

Glyn was in the chair at a meeting of the Coaching and Police Committee of the LBR on 7 April 1841 when it agreed that if booking passengers by the issue of a single ticket to any first class station on the lines connected and working with this company could be brought into use, without much additional expense and trouble, by adopting the system of clearance of tickets at one office in London or Birmingham, the convenience and comfort of the public would be so great as to make it desirable to recommend the same to the Board for adoption.

Creed and Morison were instructed to prepare a plan and system for such an office. This concentrated on passenger traffic, though pointing out that the principles were equally applicable to other traffic, and the plan was sent to the other companies. The key to the scheme was the provision of through tickets by the clearing house for use by the companies' stations and daily returns of tickets sold, fares paid etc. from those stations direct to the clearing house.

Other companies were slow to back the scheme though many did so following visits to secretaries and superintendents by Morison. Hudson's York and North Midland gave its support after initial objections. But the Grand Junction did not, despite their Board's general approval, because they would have to adopt Edmondson's system of consecutively numbered tickets if the scheme were to work smoothly, which they thought too costly. This meant that other companies in the north-west did not take part when the scheme started in January 1842 at 11 Drummond Street, a building near Euston station made available by Glyn. Morison was the part-time Secretary with six clerks. They worked under the direction of the Clearing House Committee consisting of one representative of each of the participating companies. There were initially nine, essentially the LBR and the companies which had through traffics with the LBR and other companies in the Midlands and Yorkshire, though not all attended regularly. There was little doubt that Glyn and the LBR were in the lead. Creed with Morison was in attendance. Glyn was given authority to authorise such expenses

[23] Bagwell, 35.

as might be indisputably necessary and was empowered to call upon the companies to pay their quota of these expenses.[24] Morison reported to the April 1842 meeting that passengers could book through from every town of any importance within the limits embraced by the Clearing House. Companies were charged £5 for each through booking station, with levies on through bookings proportionate to their receipts from such traffic. Much of this income went on salaries for the six people employed and Morison.

Some on the LBR wanted to go further by way of standardisation. The audit committee suggested a central audit for all railways in every part of the kingdom They considered that this would bring economy and many other advantages, though recognised it would need the agreement of other companies. They said one company had already agreed to take advantage of such an arrangement, and suggested that those directors of the LBR who had seats on other railway boards should urge their companies to take part. Glyn more realistically commented that the question was almost beyond the purview of the board. It was not certain that such a plan would commend itself to most of the proprietors, and not very likely that the GJR and YNMR would agree to have all their accounts passed through a central office in London.[25]

Progress with goods traffic took longer. The companies were slow to return information on a uniform basis. In 1843 Glyn complained that the LBR had been subjected to serious inconvenience by the detention and unfair use of their wagons by other companies. He threatened that unless there was an immediate improvement his company would be obliged to restrict the use of its wagons to its own lines.[26] The use of carriers by many of the companies meant it was difficult for the Clearing House to keep track of the multiplicity of carriers. The LBR in the early 1840s had no less than fifteen private carriers for the goods trade between their terminuses. It was only in 1847 that the new LNWR started carrying directly for the public, as for the most part the Grand Junction and Manchester and Birmingham already did. Glyn told shareholders at the February 1848 meeting that the new system had fully answered expectations.

The Railway Regulation Act of 1842 had come in a year when trade was particularly poor, the commodity markets dull, mills closed and unemployment high. It was the year of the Plug Plot. Nevertheless the four leading railway companies were all paying ten per cent and others were

24 TNA, RAIL 1080/2, 26 Apr. 1842.
25 RBS Archives, GM/237, Jan. 1843.
26 TNA, RAIL 1080/2, 15 Mar. 1843.

paying six and seven per cent, though the public thought dividends were too high and that railway directors charged extravagant fares. Just as the success of the LMR in its initial phase of operation had stimulated new companies to emulate it but on a larger scale, so now moves began for other areas to join in the prosperity – towns not yet served by a railway wanted to have the benefits a railway could bring. The fears of the country gentry had been overcome by the gains to the value of their land. In 1842 and 1843 Parliament only authorised railways with a total capital of £8 million. By late 1843 the mood was beginning to change. Glyn told shareholders in February 1844 that it looked very much as if the forthcoming session of Parliament would be memorable for the number of railway projects likely to be brought before it. He hoped it would not be remembered for the mischief arising from ill-considered reckless projects originating in the current state of the money market, encouraged by the representations of parties who ought to have been better informed.[27]

Gladstone, now Vice-President of the Board of Trade, also had concerns about these developments. That his mind was not closed to going further by way of regulation than the 1842 Act is shown by a letter he wrote in December 1843.

> Parliament is, as I think, reasonably averse to interference with railway companies in their efforts to turn their capital to the best account. But there are limits to this principle which have been discerned and deliberately overstepped in the provision made for public safety; and it is not impossible if the companies be found to act in a churlish spirit towards the poorer class of passengers that legislative imposition may go further than it has yet done.[28]

He was also concerned about the increase in mileage which could arise from the current surge of bills.[29] In March 1844 he set up a Select Committee on Railways under his chairmanship to consider whether new provisions ought to be introduced into such railway bills as might come before the House during the present and future sessions for the advantage of the public and the improvement of the railway system. Among the members were Labouchere, President of the Board of Trade from 1839 to 1841 and two MPs closely

[27] TNA, RAIL 1110/260, 9 Feb. 1844.

[28] BL, Add Ms 44092, letter to T.D. Acland, 6 Dec. 1843, friend of Gladstone's at Christ Church, Conservative MP for Somerset, but followed Peel as a Free Trader.

[29] In 1844 the total rose to nearly £18 million embodied in 48 Acts. This was small in comparison with 1845 and 1846, but was a decisive break with the past.

involved in railways, Charles Russell, chairman of the GWR, and Edmund Denison, the leader of the London and York party and future chairman of the Great Northern.[30] The witnesses were largely from railway companies and Gladstone was in effect using the committee as a sounding board for his own proposals with Samuel Laing, then an official in the Railway Department of the Board, as his mouthpiece.

Laing submitted a paper 'Hypothetical Outline of Considerations which May be Given to, and Asked from Railway Companies as Equivalents in an Amicable Settlement' based on Gladstone's ideas. Laing also gave lengthy oral evidence. He suggested two ways in which the railways could help the public: improved accommodation for poorer passengers by requiring the railways to provide some reasonable third class trains at low charges even if uneconomic; and insistence on reduced fares where the companies were making profits above a limit to be defined. The maximum fares set out in companies' acts of parliament could be subject to periodical revision perhaps every twenty years. It was discussion of this proposal in the Committee which led Laing to suggest that the government take out an option to purchase railways at the end of twenty one years to be exercised if the company did not reduce its fares. This would apply only to lines approved in the future. Laing assured Labouchere that the latter part of the scheme had been sent to 'several leading gentlemen of the railway interest', and from some of these he had got a definite expression of assent. The representatives had met Gladstone which resulted in a general agreement on certain points of principle. Others did not dissent but wanted the details left open. The GWR was nearer dissent than any other company.[31]

When Glyn gave evidence on 6 March he concentrated on competition but also commented on the scheme for Government intervention set out by Laing. His evidence showed that he would welcome some degree of government control to ensure that the future railway system was more rational and less wasteful of resources. At the same time however it was clear that he was safeguarding the interests of the LBR in part because he regarded that as the corner stone of such a national system.

When asked by Gladstone whether his knowledge acquired in his professional capacity as a banker, especially the state of the money market and the tendency to commercial speculation, had an influence on his view of the general condition of railway property, he said it induced him to think that railway property as property was in a state of great danger. He looked

30 Russell, a Conservative protectionist, sat for Reading, 1830–37 and 1841–47. Denison was Tory MP for the West Riding, 1841–47 and 1848–49.

31 Report of the Select Committee on Railways, PP, 1844, xi, Qs 1408–12.

forward with apprehension.[32] He took this line because he was essentially defending the status quo and feared what he regarded as illegitimate competition which he did not see as leading to benefits for the public in the form of lower charges. Low fares might prevail for a time but then a combination of the companies would force them up. Generally speaking he thought that the country could be served by branches from existing lines. Competition between main lines meant they were not successful. He instanced the competition between the Midland Counties and the BDJR for the traffic from Derby and the north to London, which put both companies into an inferior position as regards dividends and working stock. He added that some BDJR coaches were so poor that the LBR had to prevent them from coming on to their line for reasons of public safety. The MCR was somewhat better, but 4 per cent at the outside was all it could be expected to pay, hardly a reasonable dividend.[33] Restraint of high dividends by a government board would be preferable to competition by ensuring that the dividends were kept at a fair and adequate ratio, the arrangement for the company being also under the supervision of the Government board as regards the accommodation of the public generally. He went so far as to say that he would rather see a competitive line in the hands of Government than a private company. He emphasised however he was speaking as a railway proprietor, not as a member of the public.[34]

Later he was asked what he meant by illegitimate competition. He explained that existing railways were exposed to two types of competition – direct and indirect; the latter arose from companies which had a traffic of their own to depend on and from motives of profit induced traffic which belonged to a more direct line to pass over theirs at reduced fares. He gave as an example the attempt by the Manchester and Leeds Railway to draw traffic between Manchester and London by their line to Leeds and then by the NMR and MCR at a considerable reduction in fares below the rate they were charging for their general traffic. He would prevent this practice by an equal rates clause.[35] Pressed on the case for another line from Liverpool to Manchester, he was against a new direct route, but if a new line was proposed to serve towns off the direct route, the opportunity to serve these towns should be offered to the existing company to provide branch lines. They would be better placed to do the work and give better accommodation than the new line formed for the purpose of competition. The LBR did not

32 Qs 2966–9.
33 Qs 2976–82.
34 Qs 2985–90.
35 Qs 3066–7.

regard the London to Cambridge as a competing line, but if it were taken on to York it would then become a competing line to the NMR as it would be within 15 miles of it, and much more so in the case of the YNMR.[36] He thought the existing through traffic from Darlington and York to London without going via Leeds was extremely small and he thought it was the excitement of the moment which had led to the formation of the London and York company. He defended the Northampton to Peterborough branch as a west to east connection and the LBR had assured the Eastern Counties that if they went to Cambridge the LBR would not oppose them. They sought the traffic between Norwich and Yarmouth and the Birmingham and Midland districts. A line going to York never entered their calculations.[37] He expressed opposition to the Trent Valley on the ground that there was 57 miles of railway to be made with the saving of six miles with scarcely any new traffic to be introduced, and which would leave several large towns not served by this more direct line.[38]

He did not think an adverse opinion from the Board of Trade on a competing line would be a strong enough protection: the line ought to be stopped by a more effective safeguard. The principle was the protection of existing property. Thomas Gisborne, Whig MP for Nottingham, contested his case for existing companies to be offered the opportunity to make branch lines to places not served. A branch to Lincoln might mean the distance to London was 150 miles; a direct line might be 40 miles less. Would that be sufficient reason to permit it? Glyn argued that the saving to York was 27 miles and so that to Lincoln must be less, perhaps 15. He thought the public ought not be carried an additional 50 miles but that 15 miles was not too much.[39] When asked whether he saw great scope for the legitimate extension of railways he replied that there might be in some cases but repeated that the country would be best served by branches from existing lines. Glyn, though very much from the point of view of avoiding competition to existing lines, including the LBR, favoured direct lines, like several contemporaries, including at that time James Morrison who complained in 1846 that very large masses of people were imperfectly supplied by circuitous routes. Glyn's policy would have resulted in a smaller network than that which eventuated, perhaps on the scale of Mark Casson's counterfactual design for an alternative layout of the British rail network which would have resulted in a network of only 13,000 miles compared

36 Qs 3074–80.

37 Qs 3094–6, 3001–4.

38 Qs 3086–9.

39 Qs 3029–31.

with the 20,000 miles reached in 1914 and a saving of 25 per cent of the construction costs of the actual system.[40] However Glyn did not give any idea how large a branch network would be needed and seems to have assumed that the main purpose of railways would be to carry traffic between the major cities, whereas the actual length of journeys soon tended to be much less than the initial estimates. Moreover Glyn's LBR was unusual in that the only major centre on its 112 miles length was Coventry, and on the LNWR in 1850 well over half the receipts came from under 20 per cent of the passengers, those who travelled 50 miles or more. Nevertheless in the mid-fifties the average distance travelled on the LNWR was only about 25 miles though about 50 for first class passengers.[41]

Not surprisingly Glyn did not think that any benefit would arise form deferring legislation for a year. If the money market continued in its present state 'we shall have such a variety of schemes brought forward that without some check upon the illegitimate competition the existing property in railways will be depreciated to a serious extent'.[42] Speaking as a proprietor rather than as a member of the public he would rather see the Board of Trade having certain powers which would ensure the safety and convenience of the public and the revision of fares provided that did not interfere with the fair right of the existing company. The Government board would improve the performance of the existing company with regard to the public and the capital investment of the competing company would be saved.[43]

He thought it would be for the advantage of railway property if an attempt were made to introduce a plan on the lines suggested, but he was not at all confident that the railway body generally would consent to an arrangement which did not secure to them a much more efficient guarantee against competition than they had yet been able to devise.[44] On Laing's ideas for purchase he thought the acceptability of the option would depend on the number of years; he thought 25 years might be right – this was the period which occurred to him after talking with other directors. On the powers a Government board might have, he agreed with Gladstone that if the right of revision were limited to the matter of charges for passengers other questions could be trusted to the force of public opinion and the self

[40] Mark Casson, *The World's First Railway System, Enterprise, Competition, and Regulation on the Railway Network in Victorian Britain*, 2009, 17.

[41] T.R. Gourvish, *Mark Huish and the London & North Western Railway, a Study of Management*, 1972, 120 and 193.

[42] Q. 2975.

[43] Qs 2991–3.

[44] Qs 3139–40.

interest of the companies though he added that the supervision of the Board would be needed to see they were carried out.[45] Indeed he told Sir John Easthope that in his view the Board should have a decisive rather than a recommendatory role in settling questions in dispute between two railroad companies. He had always been an advocate of a Government department having a degree of control but unless they took the power of absolute management they could not interfere with the time of starting, but under some circumstances they should be allowed to adjudicate on questions of public complaint, the rates of travelling etc.[46] He had considered the possibility of the Government purchasing all the railways and taking the internal management in to their own hands, but he had rejected it as he did not think that Parliament would ever allow such immense machinery to be managed by Government because of patronage and other matters, and thought this obstacle so great he had not concerned himself with other difficulties.[47]

He had a long exchange with Gisborne and others about how Gladstone's plan of future dividend limitation might work. If 10 per cent were fixed as the maximum dividend payable then the dividends for companies paying substantially below that ought not to be revised. He believed that no railway proprietor would get a fair return on his capital unless the dividend were 6 per cent. He was prepared to see this as a floor. Companies paying 8 per cent could be revised down to six par cent and companies above ten per cent to 10 per cent. The details of how it was carried out were the most important part of the scheme and it was almost impossible to commit oneself to them at present.[48] He identified a fundamental weakness in Gladstone's ideas when he told Lord Seymour firmly that the system of revision ought to apply to all railways; he did not see why a railway started in 1838 should be on a different footing from one begun in 1844.[49] Earlier he had stressed that the companies would need an equivalence in the shape of some guarantee by Parliament that the right of revision was conceded for the protection against the chance of competing lines interfering detrimentally with their fair interests.[50]

On the third class he admitted that the LBR had only one third class train at a rather lower speed than the others. It stopped at Roade for

45 Qs 3018–23.
46 Qs 3010–11 and 3023.
47 Qs 3148–9.
48 Q. 3051.
49 Qs 3055–6.
50 Qs 3000–1.

1½hours so that other trains could pass, taking 7¾ hours from London to Birmingham.[51] He did not think that the company could afford to provide the present standard of accommodation which was near to second class though not covered in summer for one penny a mile.[52] At 1d per mile companies would expect some equivalence.

George Hudson was the only witness to take a hostile line. He was in favour of high fares and did not think that profits could be made from third class passengers which the YNMR did not carry. He even argued that third class passengers did not like second class carriages and preferred theirs completely open. Low fares were a dangerous experiment for railways to try and would not substantially increase their revenue. The idea that traffic would double if fares were halved was preposterous. He thought Parliament should refuse to sanction lines whose primary object was to compete with an existing line. If he were given a protection against competition he would seriously consider whether it would not be advisable for the companies to agree to a fair consideration of their case after twenty years. His difficulty was that he could not see that Parliament could give a guarantee that any future Parliament would not authorise a competing line.[53] He did not hide his self-interest. He denounced the proposed York and Cambridge line as unnecessary. Lincoln had no need of more direct communication with London than that provided via Nottingham and the Midland to Rugby and Euston: if an existing line was doing its job properly and there was not sufficient local traffic to support the new line, the competing line ought to be stopped.[54]

On 20 June Gladstone introduced his Railway Regulation Bill which aimed to give statutory backing to the recommendations of the Select Committee. The most controversial part of the Bill were the clauses dealing with the revision of railway charges and the purchase of railways by the state,

[51] Prior to the amalgamation in 1846 3rd class coaches were in a minority on the LBR. Creed told the Metropolitan Railway Commissioners in 1846 that the LBR that the company had 150 1st class coaches, 135 2nd, but only 44 3rd class together with 23 2nd and 3rd class composites (PP, 1846, xvii, 107).

[52] This was a slight improvement on the position in 1842 when Creed had told the BOT in 1842 that 3rd class passengers on the 7 am down train passengers had to wait at Roade from 10.40 to 12.30 to allow other trains to pass and to refresh themselves, and arrived in Birmingham at 3.15pm. The carriages were open, but the company intended to assimilate the construction of the carriages to second class standard with spring buffers. On occasions the carriages which held 24 passengers had been used for horses and cattle (Creed to Board of Trade, 10 Jan. 1842, PRO, MT6/1/51). However 3rd class passengers from London to Manchester and Liverpool had to wait until 6 am next morning for a GTR train.

[53] Qs 4217, 4228–9, 4255, 4347.

[54] Qs 3114–5.

based on the third report of the Committee.[55] The Committee had concluded that many new schemes were likely to come forward and that Parliament had an opportunity not expected to recur for attaching conditions necessary for the public good to avoid monopoly, high fares and unreasonable profits. The position of the legislature should be reserved. Gladstone certainly saw the proposed law as renewing a discretion, excluded by the Acts for existing railways. The bill as presented gave the state two options. First in the case of all new railways, whatever the level of dividend paid, to take powers to purchase, at any time after 15 years from the passing of its Act, on the basis of 25 times its average dividend over the last three years with a maximum of 10 per cent. Second if a company had paid a dividend of 10 per cent over three years the Government could revise its fares and charges so that 10 per cent would not be exceeded, though if as a result dividends were less than 10 per cent the Exchequer would have to make up the loss. In essence what was proposed was an inducement to the railways to declare honest profits of about 10 per cent, as they would not know which option might be brought into play at the end of 15 years. As Foster put it the Act has generally been seen by historians as an aberrant nationalisation proposal in a laissez-faire age, but against the background of the need to regulate the private monopolies created at the end of the twentieth century could be seen as a periodic review of railway profitability on the lines of formula RPI–X where X at a review is changed to give reasonable profitability over the next period, though backed by the threat of purchase.[56]

This proposal went not only further than some of Gladstone's colleagues, including Peel the Prime Minister, wanted to go, but quickly aroused the opposition of the railway community. Peel told Gladstone when his Committee was still at work that it would be unjust and a precedent dangerous to the security of all property to take a power compelling the sale of a particular species of property created by an act of the legislature. There was nothing in the property contrary to equity or the maxims of religion as in the case of slave property. To compel the sale of a great establishment like the London and Birmingham Railway was altogether different from the compulsory sale of land for local improvement or defence. Sir James Graham, the Home Secretary, wrote that the shock this would give to the security of property would not be compensated by any public advantage.[57]

Peel had a more reasonable case than the railway companies. The report had been available since April and it seems it was only the introduction of

[55] PP, 1844, xi, 5.

[56] Foster, 24 and 26.

[57] BL, Add Ms 44650.

the Bill and the imminence of the second reading which led the railway interest to complain strongly. While Glyn had warned that the proposals might be unacceptable to shareholders, others seem not to have anticipated this, and it has been argued that it was this which explained the change in the railways' attitude.[58] It was Hudson, the lone opponent of the proposals on the Committee, who now took the lead with a vehemence which belied the extent to which his fellow railwaymen had been prepared to go along with the proposals and to which they had been consulted. Hudson organised and presided over a meeting of seventeen railway companies on 26 June which drew up a memorial to Peel attacking 'a most inexpedient change in the system under which railways have been hitherto promoted and maintained' and the ex parte nature of the enquiry which did not give the railways an opportunity to respond. The memorial urged that the Bill should not be proceeded with that session. Significantly Glyn did not sign the memorial. Gladstone tried to undermine Hudson and his colleagues by getting Laing to ask George Burke, the solicitor who submitted the document, whether the names were attached by authority of the companies with which those gentlemen were officially connected or by their managing boards. Burke replied that they were affixed at a meeting convened by circular to the principal railway companies but when Laing asked whether meetings of the boards were held, Burke said no special authority had been given to sign any particular memorial, but it was assumed they had authority.[59]

Before the bill was introduced 29 companies sent representatives, with George Hudson in the lead, though Glyn was also present, to an acrimonious meeting on 1 July with Peel and Gladstone, which was preceded and followed by much publicity. Initially this had the effect of strengthening Gladstone's resolve. 'My temper was moved by the proceedings of the railway people today: a kind of sediment of anger remained long after, though the opportunity was good for discipline.'[60] Two days later he wrote to Moss 'More blind and unreasonable conduct I have never yet known. In Parliament I have been viewed with suspicion as being interested in railways, and disposed to sacrifice the public to the companies. But from me those who are leading this

[58] A.J. Arnold and S. McCartney, *George Hudson, The Rise and Fall of the Railway King*, 2004, 130–131.

[59] PD, 76, 504, 8 Jul. 1844; PP, 1844, xli (Copies of any Memorial to Sir Robert Peel by certain directors and others connected with Railway Companies, against the Railway Bill now before this House and of any correspondence thereupon between the Board of Trade and the aforesaid Memorialists).

[60] *The Gladstone Diaries*, 1968–1994, III, ed. M.R.D. Foot and H.C.G. Matthews, 3 Jul. 1844; BL, Misc Ms 44527, Gladstone to Moss, 5 Jul. 1844.

movement, including Mr Glyn, to my amazement, will not obtain one jot or tittle of concession.'[61] He admitted the strength of the railway companies in the House of Commons and the benefits they had conferred on the country, but it was time there should be a trial of strength, which he felt he had made every effort to avoid.

Gisborne and Russell failed in an attempt to delay the second reading on 8 July. Gladstone then vigorously defended the Bill. He told the House it was absurd to represent the bill as an attack on railway property. New companies had been formed since his committee reported. Existing companies had not been adversely affected. GWR shares had risen from 110 on 13 April to 123 on 29 June. He objected to the grossest misrepresentations being put on the Bill. He had originally wanted four directors on the committee but withdrew two after having been accused of packing the committee for the railways. The option to purchase only applied to new railways and would require Parliamentary approval. He said the proposal to refer bills to the Board of Trade had been advocated very strongly by Glyn, Captain Laws, Swift, and Cardwell.[62] The debate was resumed on 11 July when the Government won by 186 to 99, the Conservatives being mostly in favour, and the Liberals 3:2 against.[63]

On the morning of the resumed debate, Hudson, not yet an MP, wrote an open letter to Gladstone, published in that morning's *Times*, arguing that the railways had not misunderstood or misrepresented the Bill. The enquiry had been one-sided being dominated by Laing. They objected particularly to the clause which in their view gave the government absolute power to purchase compulsorily any new railway after fifteen years. The fact that the railways had remained passive until the publication of the Bill should not be taken as acquiescence in the government's intentions. They did not want to take steps prematurely or disrespectful to the Government.[64]

Peel had taken the lead for the Government on the second day of the debate. Although he made it very clear that he still thought it right to take security for

[61] Gladstone's father had substantial holdings in the GJR and his brother Robertson was a director of that line. He had told Moss earlier that it might be as well that he should not be the medium of communication on that particular subject (the GJR's interest in the CHR). BL, Misc Ms 44527, Gladstone to Moss, 23 Nov. 1843.

[62] PD, 76, 675–676 etc, 11 Jul. 1844, for Gladstone. Captain Lawes was Manager of the Manchester and Leeds Railway; Swift, the Solicitor for the GJR and Cardwell, then a Peelite MP for Clitheroe.

[63] An analysis of the vote is set out in Iain Mclean and Christopher Foster, The Political Economy of Regulation, Interests, Ideology and Voters and the UK Regulation of Railways Act, 1844, *Public Administration*, 70, 1992, 325.

[64] *The Times*, 11 Jul. 1844.

the public interest against exaction and abuse, he was more conciliatory to the railways and his attitude seems to have influenced heavily Gladstone's next steps. Gladstone offered to meet Hudson when he 'settled as he hoped the railway enactment in a long conference.'[65] The result of this private meeting was a much more limited bill. The period was increased from 15 to 25 years. More importantly it omitted the precise, but complicated, purchase formula and other provisions which had taken many clauses to set out, but which would now have to be settled in the future. Moreover the provisions allowing the Board of Trade to make reductions in the purchase price for mismanagement and for failing to keep the railway in good repair were discarded. These changes were seen as a victory by the railways. James Morrison pointed to the folly of taking an option to purchase or to revise charges without establishing a systematic control over the method by which profits were calculated. Curiously despite his words about railway directors Gladstone displayed afterwards little animus towards Hudson, describing him much later as a very bold and not at all an unwise railway projector. He was a man of great discernment and possessing a great deal of courage and rich enterprise.[66]

The following month Glyn told shareholders he had not taken any prominent part in the campaign; he was one of a large deputation and though his appearance as the representative of the LBR probably helped, the railway proprietors were indebted to others especially to Hudson, to whose exertions he attributed entirely the railways success. He had acted as chairman throughout and had made a most vigorous stand.[67]

Gladstone's expectation that his Bill would not be regarded as an attack on property was naive. But his theoretical case was strong. Those who sought powers ought to be required to do things in return, like the carriage of mails and conveyance of third class passengers, in decent conditions, speed and price. The effect on competition was feeble, but any strategy which distinguished between lines authorised before and after 1844 was scarcely logical or practical. It eventually meant that sections of mainline routes could be nationalised and others not.

There was less controversy about another of the main recommendations of the Select Committee incorporated in the 1844 Act.[68] The case for cheap fares for third class passengers was accepted, despite Hudson's evidence to the Committee. The Act provided that companies which derived one-third

[65] *The Gladstone Diaries*, III, 17 Jul. 1844.

[66] PD, 325, 1400, 4 May 1888. He also wrote a set of verses or song *The Fall of Hudson* which gave a very balanced view, Hodgkins, Railway Rhymes, 232.

[67] TNA, RAIL 1110/260, 9 Aug. 1844.

[68] Fifth Report, PP, 1844, xi.

or more of their revenue from passengers, the majority, must run at least one 'Parliamentary' train, as they became known, each weekday. They were to stop at every station, to run at a speed of at least twelve miles an hour and the fare was not to exceed 1d per mile. The Board of Trade was also to approve the construction of carriages, which had to protect passengers from the weather effectively and to have seats. Receipts from these trains was not to be subject to the Passenger Duty, provided Board of Trade approval was secured. Although it would be a mistake to regard this as a benefit to the poor: the journey between London and Lancashire or Yorkshire even at parliamentary rates would cost a semi-skilled worker ten days wages, the number of such passengers rapidly increased. By February 1845 Gladstone told Parliament that some 2,500 a week were travelling on the GJR and on the LBR there were 48,000 a quarter compared with the previous 65,000 a year.[69]

The issues raised in the earlier on the LBR about Sunday travel were reflected in Parliament. Though the companies were under an obligation to run mail trains on Sundays, the Bill did not oblige companies to run parliamentary trains. The Bishop of London secured an amendment which precluded parliamentary trains from running on Sunday. In the Commons it was asked why there should be one law for Dives and another for Lazarus, as first and second class passengers could travel. Gladstone responded by saying that the working respectable mechanic would not choose the Lord's Day for travelling and he would not be a party to compelling a company to run certain trains upon Sunday. The observance of the Sabbath was the main support of religion. One MP asked the House to 'place Mr Gladstone in the position of the mechanic. Let him feel the necessity of rest to the worn mind, and of free air to an enfeebled body, and that gentleman will form a very different conclusion.' Gladstone was very annoyed when the Government was defeated by 73 to 41, several Government supporters voting in the majority. After discussion in cabinet it was agreed that there were to be no compulsory parliamentary trains on Sundays but any voluntary trains had to carry third class passengers.[70] Gladstone told Glyn that he realised this meant a choice between abandoning their Sunday trains or running the cheap trains on Sundays as well as week days and would be glad to have his views, but companies did not opt for the first alternative.[71]

69 Jack Simmons makes the point about the relation to wages (*The Railway in England and Wales, 1830–1914, 1, The System and its Working*, 1978, 36); PD, 77, 133, 5 Feb. 1845.

70 John Francis, *A History of the English Railway*, 1851, 2, 118–120; *The Gladstone Diaries*, III, 2, and 29 Jul., 2, 3 and 6 Aug. 1844.

71 BL, Add Ms 44527, Gladstone to Glyn (he also wrote similar letters to Russell, and Moss), 22 Jul. 1844.

CHAPTER TEN

The Formation of the London and North Western Railway

THERE WAS LITTLE SIGN at the end of 1843 of the enormous developments which were to hit the railway world, including the LBR, in the next two years. At the half-yearly meeting in January 1844 Glyn seemed very confident of the LBR's position: 'Every year increases the number of railways in connection with this establishment. From all parties, whether from Lancaster or Darlington we receive the same friendly assurances of co-operation.'[1]

However as Gladstone made clear during the debates on his Bill in June and July 1844, while his committee had been sitting Parliament had to deal with a large number of bills for the construction of new railways. In the Session of 1844 49 railway acts were authorised with a capital of £20 million and a mileage of 805, compared with £15 million and only 160 miles in the first four years of the decade. The revival of interest was made possible by the greater ease of raising capital. It was to culminate in 1845 in the Railway Mania, resulting in a proliferation of companies in areas adjacent to the lines of existing companies, providing competitive lines but also leading to existing companies taking over the newcomers to protect their districts. Thus to an extent the leading existing companies lost control of the situation and had to take decisions as to how far they would themselves construct new lines, whether to back in various ways projects put forward by local parties, and how they would define the geographical area – the district – which they would regard as their own territory. In this new world Glyn and the LBR had to make their way in conjunction with allies. In the 1844 Session the LBR did not put forward any bills of its own, but proposals from other

[1] TNA, RAIL 1110/260, 9 Feb. 1844.

companies meant that the first half of 1844 saw the beginnings of a number of challenges particularly on its northern and western flanks much more serious than it had faced in earlier years. Above all its relationships with the GJR were strained, and Glyn found himself accused of inconsistency.

A natural development from the establishment of the lines between Manchester and Liverpool and London with the end-on junction in Birmingham between the GJR and the LBR would have been an amalgamation between the two companies. The proposal to link the two systems by a line from Rugby to Stafford, first put forward in the 1830s, might have been expected to put more emphasis on the case for union between the companies based in London and Liverpool. The leading protagonists for the line were however, as has been seen, companies based in Manchester interested in a more direct route to London which would duplicate part of the GJR and LBR's route, north of Rugby. Whether and how this was to be accomplished led to acute differences between the LBR and GJR. Relations between the two companies became enmeshed in controversies with others, particularly the GWR and the development of lines to Shrewsbury, but also in debate about the role each was to play in the route to Ireland via Holyhead. Thus the path to union was far from smooth.

The LBR was not only interested in its link with the North West. Its links with the Midland system were equally important, exemplified by Glyn's chairmanship of the North Midland. The arrival of Hudson and the amalgamation of the Midland companies to form the Midland Railway in June 1844 gave them greater emphasis, but the LBR-Midland link to the north became threatened by proposals for a more direct route to the North East.

The revival of proposals for a Trent Valley line was only one of the matters with which the LBR had to deal in 1844, which for a time shattered relationships between the LBR and the GJR before a rapprochement brought about the amalgamation which led the formation of the LNWR in 1846. In principle both LBR and GJR had a common interest in obtaining control of a Trent Valley line which linked their two lines and provided a more direct route to the north west, and in developing the route to Holyhead. Part of the difficulty may have arisen from personal difficulties. Glyn had been critical of Moss's attitude when the LBR bill was in Parliament and the latter was head of a bank which was a rival to the Bank of Liverpool.[2] Moss was also ill at vital times. The final negotiations leading to the amalgamation in 1845 took place when Moss was ill. That the Chester and Holyhead sought an

2 Barclays Archives, 25/265, Langton Papers (LP) 41, 30 Sept. 1833.

alliance with the LBR rather than the GJR, and the lack of the participation of the GJR in the CHR, can be explained by a number of factors, none of which seem fundamental. Perhaps an element was a lack of foresight on the GJR's part. Despite the GJR's agreement to take a share in the CHR Moss told the proprietors as late as January 1844 that the CHR was new to the proprietors and seemed surprised on seeing the GJR described as forming part of a great national trunk route in James Walker's 1844 report on the route to Ireland, apparently oblivious that Walker had used the same expression in his report seven years earlier though he then told shareholders that 'we had better unite with the LBR in making the line.'[3] Glyn's somewhat erratic stance on the TVR is equally hard to comprehend even as a tactic, but there were occasions when he was more inclined to back it than a number of his colleagues on the board. His espousal of the Birmingham to Chester line fitted with the exclusion of the GJR from the CHR, but he must surely have seen it as likely to irritate the GJR. It also sat ill with his view that he thought that the country would be best served by branches from existing lines, which criterion hardly fitted the Birmingham to Chester.[4]

Relations between the companies were not improved by the failure of the three companies to secure what they expected from the Government, effectively a fourth party in the CHR project. Glyn, Moss and the CHR chairman met Peel and ministers in January 1844 to find that instead of a contract worth £80,000 a year, which the CHR promoters had believed necessary to justify building the line, Peel would not even countenance £60,000 and next day the railway representatives agreed to £40,000 provided a separate bridge at Menai was not required. The GJR board then refused to take a third share unless a cheaper inland route was adopted and Moss told shareholders he could see little reward coming from such a line.[5] They also wanted their engineer, Joseph Locke, to be joint engineer with Stephenson, a proposition totally unacceptable to the CHR. Moss was informed by the CHR that it was purchasing the Chester and Birkenhead Railway whose traffic had hitherto been boycotted by the GJR in favour of their own longer route to Liverpool via Warrington. The GJR regarded this as a hostile act and withdrew its support for the CHR probably expecting that this would mean the Bill would be dropped. They thought the railway to Holyhead would not pay, and that their support had been based on a larger government contribution. They also feared a reduction in the traffic to

3 Norman W. Webster, *Britain's First Trunk Line, The Grand Junction Railway*, 1972, 160 quoting Moss's words to shareholders on 30 January 1844.

4 Select Committee on Railways, PP, 1844, xi, 4 Mar. 1844. Q. 2971.

5 TNA, RAIL 225/7, Chairman's address, special general meeting, 31 Jan. 1844.

Ireland through Liverpool. Nevertheless in February 1844 Moss said that he endorsed a recent statement by Glyn that the interests of the two companies were closely identified and gave assurances that the GJR would not impede the CHR. The LBR, which was now represented on the provisional CHR board by Glyn and six others, secured the backing of proprietors for their contribution of £1 million rather than £700,000 towards costs of the CHR. In obtaining this Glyn stressed the risk of a rival route to the LBR-GJR being established. The LBR had expected its partner in the route to Crewe to share in the Holyhead venture.

When the Bill was in the Lords the duke of Wellington had wanted it deferred for the Government to consider further which harbour should be used, but Glyn told the government that if the Bill was lost in 1844 his company would abandon it.[6] The CHR Act received Royal Assent in July 1844 but the provisions dealing with the Menai Bridge only became law in a modified form a year later. Nine of the eighteen CHR directors were nominated by the LBR, including Glyn himself who was closely involved on the CHR board. He was not only engaged in the negotiations with Peel and the Treasury but when the bishop of Bangor opposed the line because it came too near his palace, Glyn suggested that he might be persuaded to set aside his private feelings if he were offered £15,000 for the purpose of founding and endowing a school, a plan thwarted by the Treasury's insistence on changes to the route.

The CHR was not the only cause of dissension between the LBR and GJR, and between Glyn and Moss personally. The TVR project was revived. Moss had approached Glyn to secure the LBR's participation, but LBR board was initially reluctant. They thought that Parliament by rejecting the previous proposals had decided that no benefit would be derived from a railway between Rugby and Stafford avoiding the important towns of Birmingham and Coventry. They added that should it be found necessary to shorten the proposed line to Ireland public convenience would be more effectively be served by a line between Birmingham and Chester.[7] The GJR had already decided to go for a line from Shrewsbury to Stafford with an extension to Alrewas on the BDJR. The LBR's refusal to back the TVR and especially their idea of a line between Birmingham and Chester came as great shocks to the GJR. Moss agreed that the TVR would injure both the LBR and GJR's lines to Birmingham, but asked whether the Government with its troops and mails and the population of Ireland and Scotland and the great manufacturing interests of Lancashire, Liverpool and Wales would

6 TNA, RAIL 1008/102, Glyn to Peel, 1 Jun. 1844.

7 TNA, RAIL 384/5, 8 Mar. 1844.

long remain content 'with ten miles round every journey they took to and from the Metropolis because we have made the road so'. He added 'Are we not called upon with our increasing receipts and our shares at so high a premium to give this most important traffic the best line possible?'[8] A saving of at least half an hour on the journey to London could be secured. He complained about LBR's actions over a broader front, the CHR, and the latter's purchase of the Chester and Birkenhead without consulting the GJR. He stressed that was in the interests of the two companies to unite for all purposes 'offensive and defensive'. Moss made explicit his underlying concern – that LBR might be actively promoting a competing line, or co-operating with another party. He suggested that the GJR and the MBR should join in making the TVR.[9]

The publication of the TVR's prospectus on 11 April made the LBR board think again if only to the extent of being prepared to consider carefully the proposal.[10] Within a fortnight Moss and Lawrence on behalf of the GJR had concluded an agreement with the TVR in which they promised to take a two-ninths share of the capital and to run over the line all their traffic for London and the South East, provided the TVR line started at Stafford. Shortly afterwards Edward Tootal, chairman of the TVR, saw the MBR and then was given authority by the GJR and MBR to conclude an agreement with the LBR.[11]

In May Glyn reported to his board that the GJR had agreed that a third of the capital should be provided by the TVR proprietors themselves and the rest equally divided between the GJR, MBR and LBR. He said that he and Cooke, a Manchester based LBR director, had not committed themselves in any way to these terms, but it appears from Tootal's note to his board that the invitation to the LBR had been made with Glyn's approval. Tootal added he had no fears for the ultimate result. A new line from Rugby to London was inevitable unless the LBR accepted the TVR on their terms. It is not clear whether this threat was made explicitly to Glyn.[12] At the same meeting Glyn reported that the provisional committee of the Shrewsbury and Birmingham (SBR) had brought a deputation to see him and other board members. Ormsby Gore, their chairman, said they had the support of

8 TNA, RAIL 1008/108, Moss to Glyn, dated 'March 1844' but seems to have been written after the LBR's resolution of 12 March had been received.

9 TNA, RAIL 1008/108, letters of 3 and 11 Apr. 1844.

10 TNA, RAIL 384/5, 12 Apr. 1844.

11 TNA, RAIL 699/1, 4 May 1844.

12 TNA, RAIL 1008/108, Tootal to Cleather (Secretary of TVR), marked 'For Board' 17 May 1844.

the local landowners who were opposed to the Shrewsbury to Stafford line. They wanted to join the LBR at Birmingham, but if this proposal did not meet with encouragement they would address themselves to the GWR. The LBR said they would be prepared to lease the line.[13]

The LBR board then asked Glyn and others to negotiate on the basis that the LBR wanted to work the line from Rugby as far as Tamworth and that only traffic specially required for the public convenience would go by that route. The proposed line should be encouraged and indicated they would be prepared to lease the line at 4 per cent.[14] Moss wrote a further hostile letter to Glyn on 17 May as he had learned from an advertisement in a Shrewsbury newspaper that the LBR were planning to lease the Shrewsbury and Birmingham and complained that they were not adhering to the arrangement with the TVR made with Tootal. Glyn, perhaps disingenuously, denied to Tootal that his reference to support applied to the SBR. It was the Shrewsbury to Stafford he had referred to.[15] Tootal went further and told Glyn that as the LBR had withdrawn from an agreement which Glyn had led him to consider acceptable, he had declared the negotiations at an end.[16] Moss secured from shareholders on 21 May a resolution that the line from Shrewsbury to Birmingham and the guarantee on the part of the LBR was an act of direct hostility by the LBR board to the GJR. The LBR should withdraw from that project.[17] These pressures combined to persuade the LBR board to agree that they were unwilling to close the avenue to negotiation and to give power to Glyn's committee to conclude an agreement.[18] They may well have been influenced by Peel, as Glyn reported that the Prime Minister and his brother, William, both of whom lived near Tamworth, had separately urged that the Trent Valley line be made.

Glyn meanwhile attempted to outflank discussions about the TVR by suggesting to Moss a working agreement between the LBR and GJR whereby the net profits from both companies were to be pooled and equal dividends to be paid to the shareholders of each, though the companies and their boards would remain separate. He thought it premature to enter into detail, but hoped that it would be received in the spirit in which it had been offered. He would rejoice if it led to the termination of those differences which were a source of annoyance and anxiety, he was sure to

13 TNA, RAIL 384/5, 10 May 1844.

14 TNA, RAIL 384/5, 10 May 1844.

15 TNA, RAIL 1008/108, 21 May 1844.

16 TNA, RAIL 1008/108, Moss to Glyn and Smith, 17 May; RAIL 699/1, 20 May 1844.

17 TNA, RAIL 220/7, 21 May. 1844.

18 TNA, RAIL 384/5, 22 May 1844.

Moss as well as to himself.[19] The GJR board instantly rejected this proposal as inequitable. They argued that the GJR paid, and would continue to pay 10 per cent whereas in future the LBR would not be able to pay more than 8 per cent.[20]

Later in June Moss attacked Glyn for saying that he expected the MBR to continue to Chester, and asked 'Suppose we were to guarantee a line from Birmingham to Banbury and which would probably be continued to Oxford and so on to London, telling you we did it only in self-defence and it would not be our fault if there were injury to you through it.' Nevertheless he was prepared to meet Glyn to consider a friendly alliance, provided the TVR went ahead and the LBR withdrew its support for the SBR.[21] Glyn claimed to Moss that their support of the SBR was a domestic matter, undertaken in self-defence because the SBR had threatened to enlist the GWR's support.[22]

The meeting took place on 3 July in Birmingham when Glyn and Smith met Moss and Lawrence.[23] They concluded a wide ranging agreement covering the various points at issue. Their two companies would remain separate and independent but unite for mutual defence. The LBR could prosecute the Holyhead and Birkenhead lines and any branches south of Birmingham. The GJR would not make a disproportionate reduction in fares to and from Liverpool or by arrangement with the Irish Steam Navigation compete for the Irish traffic, but leave it to take its natural course. The LBR was prepared to withdraw from its guarantee to the Shrewsbury and Birmingham while the GJR would make a line from Shrewsbury to Wolverhampton and guarantee 4 per cent to the SBR and lease it. The TVR should be leased to the LBR, MBR and GJR jointly on the basis already agreed by Moss and Tootal. Neither company was to engage in any new enterprise without the consent of the other and was to assist each other for the accommodation of the joint traffic. A committee of three directors from each company should be formed to fix the prices over both lines always with reduction in view to do away with any grounds for competing lines. The agreement was endorsed by both the LBR and GJR boards and by the general meeting of the GJR.[24]

19 Text reproduced in *The Times,* 3 Jun. 1844.

20 *The Times,* 10 Jun. 1844.

21 TNA, RAIL 1008/108, 20 Jun. 1844.

22 Ibid.

23 Thomas Smith was a long serving director of the LBR. A Birmingham brass manufacturer.

24 TNA, RAIL 220/7, 1 Aug. 1844.

This could be regarded as settling the TVR question, and might have been thought a preliminary to more formal union of some kind, or at least to herald a period of working together without animosity or suspicion. Given the tenor of the earlier correspondence it is perhaps surprising that agreement had been reached, especially as other major disputes had already arisen, but the LBR accepted the inevitability of the Trent Valley line. However the climate was still uncertain and trust was at a premium. Creed had twice to write to the GJR reassuring them as to the LBR's commitment to the 3 July agreement and particularly to the terms of the tripartite take-over of the TVR. However as will be seen it did not resolve issues with the Shrewsbury and there were comparable developments to the west of the LBR main line which were more complex, the manoeuvrings lasted longer and gave rise to a fierce rivalry with the Great Western, complicated by the battle of the gauges, and delaying any union of the LBR with the GJR.

The LBR itself intended a line from Oxford in a northerly direction by Banbury to its main line and from Oxford in an easterly direction to Aylesbury together with influential local parties and proposed to apply to Parliament in the next session. They were prepared to back a proposed line from Warwick to Worcester.[25] These were rivals to the GWR's lines from Oxford to Banbury and to Rugby and also to Worcester. Glyn met Russell and Brunel in May 1844 to try to reach agreement, but the GWR were not prepared to compromise, only conceding that they would not go further north than Rugby. This essentially was a question of which gauge was preferable. The commercial part of Oxford was in favour of the narrow gauge;[26] the Wolverhampton iron masters came to feel strongly that a route to London independent of the LBR was desirable and so preferred the broad gauge. They backed the Oxford, Worcester and Wolverhampton (OWWR) which would join the Oxford and Rugby near Oxford. The rivalry was increased by a revival of the proposal to construct a line from Worcester to Tring or Weedon. There were uncertainties over the best route and Stephenson changed his original advice after further surveys, but what emerged to put to Parliament in 1845 was the LBR backed the London, Worcester and South Staffordshire (LWSSR) proceeding from Tring to Bicester, Banbury and Pershore to Worcester and on to Wolverhampton via the Severn Valley. The LBR support for the LWSSR increased when they learned that the LSWR were considering a line from Basingstoke to Oxford which would give a connection on the same gauge between the North and Midlands with the

25 TNA, RAIL 384/5, 12 Apr. 1844.

26 TNA, RAIL 384/24, 13 Jun. 1844.

South Coast.[27] This enlarged the area of conflict with the GWR especially as the latter were backing the Berks and Hants Railway line from Reading to Basingstoke.

In the first half of 1844 there were few difficulties in Glyn's relations with the Midland companies which in June were to amalgamate under Hudson's chairmanship. It was in Glyn and the LBR's interests to make common cause with Hudson on a number of issues, principally to defend Euston as the gateway to the north and to maintain and augment the traffic to and from the Midland system. The importance of this was emphasised in June 1844 when the Newcastle and Darlington Junction line was opened from Darlington to Gateshead on the south bank of the Tyne, giving for the first time a through line from London to the Tyne. On 18 June a special train with Glyn and colleagues left Euston at 5 am and reached Gateshead at 2.25 pm. The very light train averaged 37 miles an hour for the journey. Thousands of spectators greeted Glyn, Hudson, and George and Robert Stephenson. It is possible that this celebration brought home to both Glyn and Hudson the reality of the threat to their monopoly of the route to the north posed by the London and York, launched on 3 May, the project of Edmund Denison, MP for Doncaster. When Glyn and Hudson met on 28 June they agreed a number of points arising from the running of trains into Euston and Rugby, but also that because their existing lines were menaced by the projected lines from London to York it would be for their common interest to give the greatest accommodation they could to auxiliary lines to the District through which the projected lines were to pass and therefore to render the latter of no value to the public or to the proprietors. The MCR undertook to turn their attention to the line via Lincoln to Peterborough and the LBR to the communication from Peterborough to the LBR main line in furtherance of their common object.[28]

A further meeting chaired by Robert Kennard, one of the leading directors of the Eastern Counties Railway, was held at the latter's London terminus at Shoreditch at which Glyn, accompanied by Cropper and James Morrison, and Hudson, with Ellis and Beale, were present.[29] A number of far-reaching propositions were agreed. The ECR was not to be extended north of Hitchin and the Bedford and Peterborough branches of the LBR were not to be extended without the consent of the ECR.

27 TNA, RAIL 384/5, 6 and 20 Sept. and 384/6, 10 Oct. 1844.

28 TNA, RAIL 384/24, minutes of conference held at Euston on 28 Jun. 1844.

29 Samuel Beale was a Birmingham iron manufacturer, founder of what became the Midland Bank and later chairman of the Midland Railway.

Further north it was agreed that the Midland would make a line from Swinton, on its Sheffield to Leeds line, to Doncaster, Bawtry, Gainsborough, Lincoln, Boston, Spalding and March and another was to be made from Doncaster northward to join the York and North Midland either by the Midland or the YNMR. The net receipts of the London to York traffic were to be divided equally between the LBR and the ECR. Traffic south of Doncaster was to be sent over the Midland and the ECR. The York and London direct was to be opposed by all four companies (the LBR, MR, YNMR and ECR). The LBR and ECR were to unite to oppose any other company seeking an entrance into London between Shoreditch and Euston stations.[30]

In the autumn it soon became apparent that the July agreement between the LBR and the GJR had not settled all the problems between the companies. The LBR agreed to abandon their support for the SBR line between Birmingham and Wolverhampton, but would not agree to the GJR making the line between Shrewsbury and Wolverhampton. The LBR argued that the Shrewsbury Company was important to the common interests of the GJR and LBR and there was a risk of the Shrewsbury turning elsewhere which might in the end prove highly detrimental to both companies.[31] The GJR relented only to the extent of allowing the SBR to subscribe to half the capital.

A further factor was by now embittering relationships. The Churnet Valley line told the LBR board that the best and most direct route from Manchester to London was for them to connect with the LBR by a line from Stoke to Tamworth. The latter recognised that support for a such line north of Birmingham was ruled out by the July agreement with the GJR but thought that once the Churnet line had been approved they could accommodate its traffic as they did that every other company. Their attempt to be both in a special relationship and to be open to all at the same time meant they had to express their very deep regret that the answer to the Churnet Valley should have given so much umbrage to the GJR.

A key meeting which showed how GJR policy was developing took place in late October between Robertson Gladstone, one of the leading directors of the GJR, and a deputation from the OWWR at the latter's request. The GJR agreed to support the OWWR's Bill and the latter agreed to support the Grand Junction and Shrewsbury. The OWWR was anxious that the GJR should take shares in their company and nominate two directors. The deputation were told that the practicability of adopting the broad gauge was

[30] Ibid, meeting of 9 Jul. 1844.

[31] TNA, RAIL 384/5, 6 Sept. 1844.

under consideration by the GJR, and the question was discussed whether the GWR would bear a portion of the expense if the GJR agreed to lay down the broad gauge. The companies also agreed that the OWWR must not be considered a competing line to the LBR and so no London traffic was to be booked through from the GJR, though a new and important district would be opened up greatly to the advantage of the GJR.[32] All this except the matter of taking shares and seats on the board was immediately accepted by the GJR board and the chairman said he had already asked Norris, the GJR's engineer, to report on the practicability of adopting the broad gauge on the GJR. This was ready for the board at its next meeting but the GJR board declined as they were 'not prepared to go the further length' of having a representative on the OWWR board.[33]

The corridors between the LBR and GJR were still open. In November Glyn, Cropper and Smith met Moss, Gladstone and Hornby to discuss points of difference.[34] Relations were complicated by misunderstandings over a letter which Moss had mislaid or never received, so much so that Moss left the chair while the others debated the matter. A further meeting took place on 10 December when so little progress was made that Moss refused to make any report to shareholders the following day. At the adjourned meeting his feelings were still ruffled by a dispute with Glyn over the missing letter. He spoke at some length to shareholders about this giving the impression that he was according primacy to what he regarded as a personal slight rather than to the substance of the issues, calling this a painful matter, though he did acknowledge that both companies did not now wish to rake over past misunderstandings. What seemed to have touched him on the raw was an imputation that he had shown a lack of foresight in not purchasing the Chester and Birkenhead Railway. Nevertheless his view remained that the LBR were acting outside the terms of the July agreement.[35]

Among the Bills submitted for consideration in Parliament in the 1845 Session there were a number which vitally affected the LBR's interests and their relationships with other companies. Agreement with the GJR had apparently been reached on the TVR, but the GJR was opposed to the Churnet Valley. To the south the LBR backed the LWSSR from Tring to Worcester and Wolverhampton with branches from Bicester to Oxford and Banbury to Rugby, while the GWR supported the OWWR, which to curtail mileage was now to join the Oxford and Rugby at Banbury.

32 TNA, RAIL 220/5, 30 Oct. 1844.

33 TNA, RAIL 220/5, 23 and 30 Oct., 6 Nov. 1844.

34 TNA, RAIL 384/6, 8 Nov. 1844. Joseph Hornby was another GJR director.

35 TNA, RAIL 220/7, 11 Dec. 1844.

These were only a small minority of the 220 bills deposited for consideration by Parliament in 1845. While the complex negotiations which led to these bills were taking place the seeds of the Railway Mania were sown. The events of 1845 had their origins in 1844. Money was then plentiful. The principal trunk lines were paying good dividends and new issues of existing companies were generally available to those who possessed existing shares. Threatened by new proposals the existing companies supported proposals to protect their own interests if possible turning them into feeders to their own line, though when these were in the territory between the existing companies they led to friction. The larger companies were buying or managing small companies and guaranteeing them dividends which if not usually as high as they paid to their own shareholders were often disproportionate to a realistic assessment of the prospects of the new company.

In January 1845 16 new companies were registered; by April the monthly total was 52. Railway stocks rose – the GWR from 155 to 207 from 1 January to 31 May, the Midland Counties 116 to 188, the top-ranked LBR from 229 to 247 and the GJR 225 to 232. The price of pig iron rose by 50 per cent. The provisional committees of the new companies which were advertised contained very extensive lists of names drawn from the City, landowners, barristers, merchants and manufacturers, including many MPs. The number of new companies increased during the summer and early autumn. The increase in the deposit needed for shares from 5 to 10 per cent hardly affected the speculation. In September 457 new projects were registered and the total for the year was 1057. However by October the stocks of the leading established companies had reached or passed their peak and fewer new projects were registered, though hundreds were still in process of formation. Credit became tighter. However the enormous scale of the Mania can be judged by an estimate made in mid-November that while the capital paid up and invested in railways completed amounted to some £70 million, and £67 million had been expended or was required for railways in the course of construction, £563 million would be required for the 620 new schemes then before the public, with a further 643 companies yet to register.[36] Although many of the projects were lost owing to failure to comply with the Board of Trade's regulations, Peel told the House in January 1846 that 815 schemes were deposited.[37]

Gladstone, following the recommendations in the Fifth Report of his Committee on Railways, had established in August 1844 a Railway Board whose function was to examine schemes laid before Parliament and to report

[36] *The Times*, 17 Nov. 1845.

[37] PD, 83, 190, 26 Jan. 1846.

in favour or against for the guidance of the Select Committee. The Railway Department of the Board of Trade was enlarged for this purpose under Lord Dalhousie, vice-president of the Board of Trade, as Gladstone wanted to reduce the load on the President, but also had in mind possible clashes with his personal interest in railways and especially that of his father and brother. The Board, said they would have in mind the ability and bona fide intention of the promoters to prosecute their application; the advantages to be obtained from the national point of view and also for towns and districts immediately affected, the engineering circumstances of the line, the costs of construction, the traffic and working expenses. While not setting out to favour existing companies if more meritorious schemes came from others, in practice existing companies do seem to have been favoured somewhat because they could more readily show their viability. Some more roundabout routes were favoured over direct lines by new parties in an endeavour to reduce capital expenditure. They had to deal with 135 bills in a very limited time. Not all the Board's recommendations were accepted by Parliament, but of the 90 recommended for approval, only 17 were rejected and 14 of the 26 recommended for rejection were turned down.[38] However Dalhousie was not fully supported by ministers, particularly Peel and in the leading case of the OWWR the Prime Minister voted against the Board's report which recommended the break of gauge at Oxford rather than further north and the Board effectively collapsed. This meant that in future Parliamentary Committees on railway bills were even more concerned with local issues rather than any consideration of an overall system.

Another aspect of Dalhousie's policy, which stemmed from the thinking behind the work of the 1844 committee, was to call for the companies to give equivalents, that is reductions in tariffs, in exchange for the limitation of competition. Eight important companies did so. According to Henry Parris, there is little evidence surviving about the extent and effect of Dalhousie's equivalence scheme which had to end with the Railway Board, but certainly political contemporaries believed that he drew up a scheme by which the country would partitioned among the great companies, and Glyn himself referred to this later.[39]

Relations between the LBR and GTR quickly worsened in the early months of 1845, though Moss told his board that he had been informed on good authority that the LBR had no wish to depart from anything that had been agreed at Birmingham.[40] However Glyn dropped a bombshell at the

[38] H.G. Lewin, *The Railway Mania and its Aftermath, 1845–1852*, 1936, 17, Table 2.

[39] Henry Parris, *Government and Railways in the Nineteenth Century*, 1965, 61–89.

[40] TNA, RAIL 220/5, 27 Jan. 1845.

LBR's half yearly meeting on 12 February when he announced that the LBR proposed to amalgamate with the MBR and the Churnet Valley and to lease the TVR, so bringing them under one management. He declared that the time had come when it was advisable that Manchester and London should be put in direct communication with each other, and the Churnet line would provide a slightly shorter route from Tamworth, and via the Churnet to Stoke and Macclesfield and then by the MBR.

The MBR was guaranteed a dividend of 5 per cent and half the surplus profits for three years. In that period either company could require an amalgamation of their mutual stock at the Manchester market price of 6 February 1845 to take effect after the expiry of three years. The TVR agreed to lease their line to the LBR alone after it had been made under the existing agreements with the three companies. Another agreement provided for eventual amalgamation with the Churnet but both were necessarily tentative as the Churnet and TVR had still to be approved by Parliament so the amalgamations could take place were to be on fair and equitable terms in within five years.[41] The negotiations seem to have been a coup in which Glyn himself played the major part. At the next board meeting he was given the special thanks of board for his conduct in the difficult and important negotiations which he had promptly and satisfactorily brought to a conclusion.[42] Moreover as he made clear to shareholders he had secured the general sanction of the Board of Trade to the arrangement and he thought that the Board had agreed as it was evident that four distinct and independent boards must have great difficulty in securing harmonious working. Indeed the Board's Railway Department had reported that they were unaware of any public reasons why the amalgamation should not take place, subject to provisions enabling its use by all traffic on equitable terms. It was an improvement in communication rather than a new integral line and could hardly be maintained as an independent undertaking without neutralising many of the anticipated advantages of superior economy and despatch.[43]

Meanwhile LBR had received a letter from Mark Huish, general manager of the GJR, written before the announcement, asking whether there was any truth in the rumour that the LBR had bought or leased the MBR which the MBR confirmed.[44] When they next met Moss told

[41] TNA, RAIL 384/6, 14 Feb. 1845.

[42] TNA, RAIL 1110/260, 12 Feb. 1845; RAIL 384/6 14 Feb. 1845.

[43] PP, 1845, xxxix, 111. The BOT had earlier made clear to Booth, secretary of the LMR that they were satisfied with the list of maximum charges which were included in the Act amalgamating the GJR and LMR. TNA, MT 11/631, Jul. 1845.

[44] TNA, RAIL 384/6, 14 Feb. 1845; 699/1 11 and 17 Feb. 1845. Captain Mark Huish

his directors that no communication had been received from the LBR, nor was any expected. Moss was ready with his deputy chairman to take any measures necessary to protect GJR interests, He thought the LBR's move was certainly hostile to the GJR's interests as hitherto Manchester to London traffic had been routed via Crewe and then over GJR rails to Birmingham.[45]

There was also an increasing clash of interests between the LBR and GJR, and so with the GWR in the area between Shrewsbury and Birmingham and the districts south of Birmingham in the triangle bounded by the LBR's main line, the GWR and the Birmingham-Bristol line. At the half-yearly meeting in February 1845 Glyn made very clear why the LBR was backing the line from Tring to Worcester and Wolverhampton (the LWSSR). Parties in the north of England thought it would be detrimental to their interests if the broad gauge were brought to Rugby and Wolverhampton. He added 'I shall make no remarks on the extraordinary circumstances of the GWR trying to find themselves in Staffordshire … it certainly struck us that South Staffordshire was a little out of that distinct which according to the natural bearings of the map would appear to belong to the Great Western Company.' In February 1845 it was agreed that Smith would be a director on the LWSSR. The LBR was searching for other counter moves, such as building west from their Warwick and Leamington branch and flirting with the proposed Cheltenham and Oxford.

Meanwhile Robert Gladstone and Booth had purchased shares in the Shrewsbury and Birmingham on behalf of the GJR, but negotiations for an amalgamation of interests with the SBR had come to nothing because the latter insisted on making the line between Dudley and Wolverhampton. Moss and Gladstone after mature deliberation then entered into an alliance with the GWR, offensive and defensive. Under this agreement the GJR agreed to support the Oxford and Rugby as well as the OWWR. Moreover they would not negotiate or enter into any arrangement with any company which might prejudice or affect the ORR or OWWR. The GWR would support the Shrewsbury and Grand Junction Railway and petition Parliament in its favour except in so far as they were pledged to abstain on all matters affecting the SBR which the GJR had with the TVR pledged to oppose.[46]

The routes between Shrewsbury and Birmingham were in indisputable GJR territory. The GJR's next move went well beyond that area. When the

became secretary of the Glasgow, Greenock and Paisley Railway in 1837, after a career in the Indian Army. He became secretary and general manager of the GJR in 1841.

45 TNA, RAIL 220/5, 5 Mar. 1845.

46 TNA, RAIL 220/5, 19 Mar. 1845.

prospectus of the broad gauge Birmingham and Oxford Junction (BOJR) was published in April Moss and three of his colleagues were listed on the provisional committee. How far this was a tactical move by Moss and the general manager, Mark Huish, is unclear. The line to Oxford would give them the prospect of a narrow gauge route to London provided, as seemed to be the intention of the Railway Board, the GWR were required to lay a third rail on its broad gauge.

The Railway Board however was generally favourable to the LBR projects. The Churnet Valley and the SBR were both approved by the Railway Board, as was the Tring scheme which the Railway Board preferred to its GWR rival especially as it was concerned at the implications of extending the broad gauge northwards. In Parliament however matters took a very different turn. The Churnet Valley and SBR schemes were turned down before they reached the Committee stage as they did not comply with Standing Orders. In Committee the preambles of the Oxford and Rugby and the OWWR were proved but that of the LWSSR was not. In committee the GJR supported the GWR backed schemes against those of the LBR. The committee not only ruled in favour of the Birmingham and Oxford scheme but their report on the Oxford, Worcester and Wolverhampton specifically referred to the need to give the GJR an alternative route to the south.

The GJR wanted to enlist support to ensure that the Committee's view was endorsed at the report stage. A circular was drawn up, probably by Huish, but after discussion by the board was revised by Robertson Gladstone and Mozley and Saunders of the GWR, and issued under Huish's signature which stated that the GJR did not anticipate any inconvenience at all from the introduction of the broad gauge among the narrow gauge lines. It would help companies which wished to run high speed trains. They therefore opposed the handing over of the district between London, Bristol and Birmingham to the absolute monopoly of the LBR who were seeking to obtain in addition to their line from London to Birmingham, the entire control from Birmingham to Manchester and Birmingham to Holyhead. They were satisfied that no provision would enable the GJR to compete so successfully with the LBR's extended schemes as effectively as the formation of another line, independent of the LBR.[47]

The LBR board was convinced that the company was bound to act upon the pledges given to occupy the Worcestershire and Staffordshire

[47] TNA, RAIL 220/5, 11 Jun. 1845. The circular is printed in full in MacDermott, 1, 226–228.

district with the narrow gauge.[48] The LBR lobbied Parliament, together with the Midland but to no avail. Parliament approved the broad gauge lines at the expense of the LBR's proposals, though obliging the Oxford and Rugby to add a narrow gauge rail, if called upon to do so by the Board of Trade. Glyn at the general meeting in early August said that the company had been dealt a severe blow with the loss of the Tring and Worcester Bill. This was not because of the superiority of their opponents' line. The real cause of their failure was the principle of competition which for the first time Parliament had adopted, in direct conflict with various resolutions of the House of Commons, and with their own legislative act of the previous session. He did not blame the iron masters of Staffordshire who thought they were acting for their own interests. He was however surprised at their other opponents, the GWR and GJR. The former had tied up the railways in their own district to prevent competition, while the latter had acted in a way their directors had not anticipated – presumably a reference to Huish, particularly the circular of 11 June. He did not refer to the gauge issue as such, but the report of the directors did. The company was disappointed as reasonable expectations had been founded on the able and comprehensive report of the Board of Trade. Prejudicial effects would flow from the introduction of a gauge differing from that which was uniformly laid down through out the country. The action of a narrow gauge company in supporting the broad gauge company might be a matter of surprise but the LBR directors did not feel called upon to enter into a discussion of the grounds on which the GJR had sought to vindicate their proceedings. He added that the contest was over and he hoped with it all angry feeling. The ORR and the OWWR received Royal Assent on 4 August 1845. The LBR had lost the battle and its prospects had also been undermined when the CBR repudiated its agreement with the Holyhead company and approached the GJR. Moreover the MBR shareholders, though committed to amalgamation, were pressing for better terms from the LBR.

At the shareholders meeting a few days later Glyn also listed a number of proposals for lines which the LNWR would propose or support. They included a line from Hampton to Warwick and Leamington, and on to Banbury with the probability that some other company would continue it to Cheltenham and also lines from Banbury via Brackley to Buckingham, Aylesbury and Harrow. Nearer to the heart of the dispute in the previous session he said they had formed a connection with the Birmingham Canal Company with the intention of forming a railway connecting Birmingham

[48] TNA, RAIL 384/5, 13 Jun. 1845.

with Wolverhampton and the Shrewsbury and Wolverhampton line. The directors had no wish whatever not to come to some amicable arrangement with the GJR, notwithstanding what had been said at the last meeting of that company.[49]

Despite Glyn's remarks it seemed as if the prospect of a closer relationship between the LBR and GJR had disappeared, but the denouement was very sudden. Moss had resigned as chairman at the general meeting in August. He was not well and it may be that the absence of his somewhat abrasive personality helped the rapprochement. He was a distinguished banker and contributed much to both the LMR and GJR, but Husskison when MP for Liverpool had observed 'If Moss were less fidgety he might have saved himself and me some trouble'.[50] On 24 September the GJR's select committee met, with only Lawrence and Rotheram of the board present, together with Swift, their solicitor, Booth and Huish. Rotheram seems to have been included in the group because Robertson Gladstone was in Scotland. They discussed together an arrangement of the differences between the GJR and LBR. They had invited Joseph Langton to the meeting. Langton was a director of the GJR, though not particularly prominent in the company's affairs. Following the GJR's merger with the LMR in 1844 he had been appointed a director continuing his role as a representative of the Duke of Sutherland. His presence at this meeting almost certainly arose because as the manager of the Bank of Liverpool, the first joint-stock bank to be based in Liverpool, he was well known to Glyn. It is not clear whether Glyn suggested Langton as an intermediary or whether the initiative came from the GJR side who would have been well aware of Langton's closeness to Glyn. He was authorised to express to Glyn the earnest desire of the committee to consider and carry into effect such a mutual arrangement as might be fair and satisfactory to both companies. Langton does not seem to have taken part in the subsequent negotiations in London between Lawrence and Rotheram on the one hand and Glyn, Cropper and Thomas Smith on the other. No account of the negotiations survives, though the GJR board minutes refer to there having been many conferences, and a copy of the agreement in Glyn's handwriting has survived with the signatures of the five negotiators.[51]

These talks resulted in an agreement on 17 October. It covered the topics in dispute between the companies and so had a considerable influence on the

[49] TNA, RAIL 1110/260, 7 Aug. 1845.

[50] In 1829. Quoted by C.R. Fay in *Huskisson and His Age*, 1951, 376. He also gives a similar quotation from 1825.

[51] London University Library, Ms, 584, xxi.

future map of railways, as well as achieving the amalgamation. The North Staffordshire (NSR) was not a signatory to the agreement though it stated that the NSR line was to be modified. It was to be allowed to construct from Macclesfield to Norton Bridge with branches to Leek and or Congleton. If the Derby and Crewe amalgamated with NSR, the GJR would give up their shares in the Derby and Crewe, and both GJR and LBR would support the amalgamated company. For their part the NSR would not oppose in the next session any of the GJR's plans to improve their communication with Liverpool. The LBR was to be perfectly neutral as to the two lines between Wolverhampton and Shrewsbury with the GJR at liberty to support the Shrewsbury Wolverhampton and South Staffs line. Similarly the LBR was to stand neutral as respects the Shropshire Union Railway.

On the BOJR, the GJR was to be neutral as a company, but the three individual directors of the GJR who were on the board of the BOJR were to remain unfettered. Otherwise all the existing agreements of the GJR and the LBR were to be carried out on mutual account and at mutual risk.

The capital of the amalgamated line was to consist of £5,788,560 from the GJR, their existing capital of £4,822,000, augmented by the addition of £964,760 stock without payment in respect of such new stock and of the LBR at £8,653,750 forming a joint consolidated capitals' fund of £14,442,310. Unpaid capital was to be called up as previously arranged, but no further stock was to be created without the consent of both parties. Receipts were to be considered amalgamated from 1st June with dividends from 1 January 1845.

The agreement created a joint board of 42 (24 LBR, 18 GJR) while making clear that adjustment to cater for the MBR would be necessary. It was to be submitted to the two boards in the following week and to proprietors thereafter. In recommending the agreement for adoption the signatories pledged themselves 'to cease all future connexion with their respective companies and boards' if either the Board of Trade or the company failed to adopt the agreement.[52]

These threats did not have to be used. All seemed to assume that the amalgamation would go through as had the Midland's the previous year, though the title 'Great London and Liverpool Railway,' used during the negotiations, was not adopted.[53] Both boards approved on 22 October. In Liverpool Lawrence and Rotheram were thanked by the GJR board for their persevering exertions in bringing the negotiations to so happy a termination, and the valuable assistance tendered to the Committee by Huish and Swift

52 TNA, RAIL 220/8, GJR Select Committee, 21 Oct. agreement dated 17 Oct. 1845.

53 E. Cleveland Stevens, *English Railways: their Development and Relation to the State*, 1915, 54.

was acknowledged with great satisfaction.[54] At the proprietors' meetings on 7 November there was no difficulty about approval. In London Glyn first announced that the terms of the agreement with MBR had been altered, because of changed circumstances, but did not go into detail. It was the terms of this merger which attracted comment rather than the one with the GJR. William Entwistle, then Conservative MP for South Lancashire and a partner in Jones Loyd, the Manchester bank, thought that the MBR was being treated better than it deserved. It was not on a par with GJR or the LBR: the bargain had been struck more to frustrate rival companies than for the value it represented. Glyn agreed that this had been a factor, but nevertheless the terms were favourable to the LBR. He warned the people of Manchester that this put the amalgamated company in a position to offer terms for traffic which no competitor could meet. He then announced that they had at last succeeded in coming to terms with the GJR. He was sorry that amalgamation had not been agreed when first proposed. It would have removed a good deal of difficulty and saved a great deal of heart-burning and foolish squabbling. The advantages would be great – command of the most direct line to Liverpool and to the north generally under a single management; they would get rid of the threatened competition for the Holyhead traffic and could use the large establishment at Crewe for the mechanical purposes of the whole line. There was little opposition but James Morrison in his *Defects of the English System of Railway Legislation with suggestions for its improvement* asked what could be more injurious to a large and important manufacturing population than the Act amalgamating the Grand Junction and Manchester and Birmingham and one or two other lines. He also commented 'the monopoly of the producers is on the eve of being destroyed and do not let us in the same session confirm a still more odious, more oppressive and far more indefensible monopoly on the part of the public carriers.'[55] But his view that the remedy lay in terminable leases was not widely shared and the new giant company rolled forward. Morrison's only success was to secure the establishment of the short-lived independent Railway Commissioners.[56]

The amalgamation was authorised in 1846, along with lines which were the product of the Railway Mania. But what was Glyn's attitude to the Mania? The LBR did not wish to be involved with speculative lines, which would have been quite contrary to Glyn's financial policy, but it was not possible to stand entirely aside without undermining the position they

[54] TNA, RAIL 220/8, 25 Sept. and 21 Oct.; RAIL 220/5, 22 Oct. 1845.

[55] Morrison, *Defects of the English System of Railway Legislation*, 1846, 37 and 43.

[56] Parris, 104–107.

had already attained. Many of their moves were on the western flank in an attempt to ward off the expansion of the GWR. They were also prepared to help the MR with the losses it incurred on taking over the Birmingham and Bristol. However there were limits. When Boothby tried to interest the board in supporting a line from Swansea via Brecon to Worcester, Glyn told him that the project was deserving of favourable consideration but not in a state to admit of any distinct pledge on the part of the company. Nevertheless six directors lent their names to this project (known as the Welsh Midland), but in Parliament it did not satisfy Standing Orders. In September another proposition came up – the London, Weedon and Kidderminster projected by Rowland Hill and others. The LBR thought this worth their support, though the board rejected the possibility of amalgamation, while not closing the door to a lease. Rathbone and Smith were put forward as directors.

By this time proposals were being launched thick and fast and the board had to discriminate more. They agreed to take shares in the proposed Wolverhampton, Banbury and Cheltenham and were prepared to work the projected line from Hardwick to Blisworth which was to be encouraged if did not clash with other lines. They were approached to support the Reigate and Watford, but felt they should pause before they could pledge themselves. More generally, when seven other lines had been submitted by promoters anxious to obtain the encouragement and support of the LBR, they sensibly resolved that however desirous they might be to encourage lines which in affording increased facilities to the communications of the country which might at the same time promote the interests of the LBR, they could not enter upon the consideration of the projects referred to, or of other in similar circumstances, until they had the opportunity and means of informing themselves as to the general character and features of each line and the effect which they might have on existing railways.

Attention has been paid to the large sums people – landowners, professionals, manufacturers and many others – subscribed to railway companies in the Mania, though since many of the companies did not get off the ground and shares were initially only part paid (often 10 per cent) their actual investment, and consequently any losses would often be much less than the amounts quoted in the Parliamentary returns might suggest. Less attention has been paid to the sums which railway directors in the established companies were prepared to invest in what were effectively extensions of their own lines. Glyn himself, as described in Chapter 11, put down for £126,220 in 1845 and £42,220 in 1846 for such projects, but he was overshadowed by Ledsam with £40.300 and £186,000. Much of Glyn's money went into the Trent Valley. Surprisingly his £92,000 in that company was matched by Tom Young whose means were much more modest – perhaps intended as a speculation, and by Thomas Smith and Joseph Hornby.[57] The TVR shares however quickly made a large profit as in 1846 the newly formed LNWR purchased the line paying £28 for each £20 share on which only £5 had been paid up, a profit of £478,000. The Birmingham, Wolverhampton and Stour Valley, in which Benson, Ledsam and Westhead each put down for £60,000, and Glyn £2,000, was less successful but was leased in perpetuity to the LNWR in 1850. Although the capital was then reduced, shareholders were paid three-quarters of the LNWR dividend. Directors put down for over £200,000 in the London, Worcester and South Staffs in 1846, but this venture never got off the ground. The Buckinghamshire Railway attracted much smaller sums but was leased in 1851 at a rate of 4 per cent.

These railway directors by their subscriptions contributed to some minor extent to the Railway Mania particularly as they backed projects which came to nothing or returned much lower dividends than forecast. In this they conformed to the recent analysis by Andrew Odlyzko that the malpractices of paying dividends out of capital or fraudulent accounting which were certainly present, and gave the Mania an inescapable aura both at the time and subsequently, did not account for the investment disaster which was due to overoptimistic business plans which forecast lower costs and higher rates of return than could be realised.[58]

[57] Director of the GJR, and of the LNWR on amalgamation. He also put down for £60,400 in the new Liverpool and Manchester project as did his colleagues Hardman Earle and John Cropper, and Robert Benson Jun. of the MBR.

[58] Andrew Odlyzko, The Railway Mania, Fraud, Disappointed Expectations, and the Modern Economy, *JRCHS*, 215, 2012, 2–11.

CHAPTER ELEVEN

Glyn's in the 1840s – the Railway Bank

The *Bankers Magazine* in 1849 said Glyn's probably had the largest business of any of the London banks. The magazine believed the number of private accounts must be enormous and that it had more public companies banking with it than any other establishment in the City. It appeared to act as London agent for about 60 country banks, one half of which were joint stock banks. The staff of clerks in the town and country departments was, the magazine believed, second only to the Bank of England. In 1846 further premises were added on Change Alley. Half a million sterling was said to be 'no uncommon sum' for Glyn's to settle at the Clearing House of an afternoon.[1] The article commented that Glyn was now regarded as the leading railway financier of his time and it was by no means improbable that his experience of the management of important monetary operations in his own bank had enabled him to conduct those of the North Western with so much ability and success. This in turn led to the prosperity of the bank. D.M Evans pointed out in 1852 that Glyn's within the last five years had largely increased their operations by being favoured with the accounts of many of the first-rate railway companies. The high standing which Mr Glyn had as chairman of the LNWR had merited the confidence of the directors of railway companies.[2] By then it might have been questioned whether Glyn was primarily a railwayman or a banker. There was considerable interdependence. As Bertram Currie later put it 'the sagacity and courage with which he threw himself into the railway movement contributed largely to the fortunes of his house.'[3] Stanley Chapman has commented that in the City only Glyn's showed continuous interest in transport and industrial concerns.[4]

1 *Bankers Magazine*, 9, 1849, 252–253. Glyn's employed 70 clerks in 1843.

2 D.M. Evans, *City Men and City Manners*, 1852, 10.

3 Currie, 1, 95.

4 Chapman, *Merchant Banking*, 35.

That Glyn's were the bankers to the LBR and the GWR is not surprising. From the start George Carr Glyn was a director of the former and Edward Mills of the latter. Indeed until the early 1850s Glyn's were the only bankers in London to the GWR who then decided to open an account with a joint stock bank. Spencer Walpole, then the GWR chairman said that in that time on no occasion had Glyn's ever hesitated or declined to render any pecuniary accommodation or assistance, which had been required or solicited. Mills, consulted his partners, who agreed that advantages were to be gained by the GWR in opening the new account.

Although by 1833 Glyn's were bankers to these two of principal railway companies they were not bankers to the first main line railways in the North and North West – the LMR and the GJR, nor were they bankers to the GNR, LSWR, LYR or the Caledonian. But these were exceptions. All the other main line companies had an account with Glyn's and the number of railways banking with them grew rapidly: 22 in 1843, 56 in 1844 and 110 in 1845, when railway companies' deposits amounted to £1.4 million, 30 per cent of Glyn's total. The bank records now available do not show how these totals of railway company accounts were arrived at and the total of 110 for 1845 must have included a significant number of companies which were projected in the Mania but did not come to fruition. 137 British and 84 overseas companies were listed in Appendix IV to Fulford's *Glyn's* as having accounts with the bank. However this list seems to be an inclusive list of all the railway companies which banked with Glyn's – thus it includes the North Midland which became part of the Midland (also listed) in 1844 and both the Manchester, Sheffield and Lincolnshire and the Great Central which was the former's title after 1893. The list does however illustrate the wide range of Glyn's interests. In Britain they ranged from the Cornwall Railway to the Deeside and several Irish companies banked with Glyn's.

In 1840 railway credit balances with Glyn's were £142,000 out of total deposits with Glyn's of £2,437,000. They then rose steeply to £293,000 in 1841, and after a drop in 1842, to £655,000 in 1844 and a peak of £1,402,000 out of total deposits of £4,649,000 at the end of 1845 before reducing to £1,024,000 in 1846 and to £546,000 in 1849. Railway balances therefore increased from 6 per cent of the total in 1841 to 30 per cent in 1845.[5] By 1872 the total amount of railway deposits grew to more than £4 million, over a third of Glyn's deposits. Lines also had one or more local bankers – Glyn's were the London agents. The extent of the impact of railways on every day business can be gauged from the list of dividend and interest payments due on

[5] RBS Archives, GM/718.

particular dates. In 1864 the dividends of the North Eastern were payable on 19 August, the LNWR on 25 and the North Staffordshire on 26 August with eight other companies' payments due that month. On September 1 alone, the dividends of the Midland, some Great Western stock, the Great South Western of Ireland and seven other companies were payable.[6] Masterman, Peters, Mildred Masterman & Co. and a number of other banks also banked for railway companies but not on a scale approximating to Glyn's.

The scale of the traffic was large. The LBR at times accumulated large cash balances, a proportion of which were kept at Glyn's: £59,000 out of £277,000 in March 1838. The remainder was at their Birmingham and Liverpool bankers, the former for expenditure especially on construction, but the latter was because money on debentures and shares tended to be received there, and was transferred to Glyn's or Birmingham as the need arose. At one stage Glyn's were asked to transfer £18,000 weekly to the Birmingham bankers. Glyn's were also asked from time to time to place money on loan, and to lend money to the LBR on a short term basis. In May 1837 they were first asked to place £20,000 on loan and then at the end of the month lent the company £20,000, which was followed by further loans in July. The work done by Glyn's increased in January 1838 when the task of paying half-yearly dividends to debenture holders was transferred from the LBR offices to the bank.[7] The LBR placed a fifth (£100,000) of its 1838 issue of loan notes with Glyn's.

The work done by Glyn's increased from the growth in the number of companies which banked with them but also from the size of the transactions. In February 1848 the LNWR's balance at Glyn's was £319,000. When the LNWR sent cash received at Birmingham, Chester and Manchester direct to London instead of to the Bank of Liverpool, Glyn's refused Langton's request that their commission rate be raised from ⅛ to ¼ per cent in compensation for the expected halving of the traffic to £400,000 per annum.[8]

In 1847 Glyn's were asked by Creed to place £20,000 to the LNWR's account with the Bank of Liverpool that day and £30,000 three days later and to call in £150,000 of the amount out on loan to meet these payments and others 'which would be required on Monday.'[9] The LNWR obtained a guarantee from Glyn's that money placed on loan for short periods would be paid at the time specified. A premium of 1/16 of the amount of interest

[6] RBS Archives, GM/136, Notebook containing the accounts and debentures of various railway companies, 1856–71.

[7] TNA, RAIL 384/57, 10 and 31 May, 5 and 12 Jul. and 3 Jan. 1838.

[8] TNA, RAIL 410/332, 10 Nov. and 15 Dec. 1849, 12 Jan. 1849.

[9] RBS Archives, GM/139, 16 Apr. 1847.

was paid, and this became the normal practice.[10] In November Glyn's told Charles Stewart, Creed's successor, that they had placed £100,000 on loan at 4½ per cent for two months.[11] Some loans were on call – the Midland asked Glyn's to invest £40,000 at call in October 1849 and next month to place £20,000 on deposit with the London & Westminster. Pares, the Leicester bank, one of the Midland's local bankers, transferred £10,000 to Glyn's and also lent the Midland £10,000 for 2 years and paid the money to Glyn's. In February 1851 Glyn's lent the Midland £20,000 'for a few weeks' and again in December which was repaid after three weeks.[12]

The extent of Glyn's business in acting as a conduit of funds from clients and from country banks to railways is not clear. In 1842 however the SER received £100,783 remitted from various bankers on account of instalments on shares. The largest single item (£64,707) came from Glyn's, the company's bankers.[13] The South Wales Railway banked with Glyn's. Their cash book shows a considerable flow of funds with the receipt of instalments on shares and loans from the GWR briefly reaching £200,000 in mid-1847.[14]

Glyn said that the original intention of loans in debentures was to introduce into the railway system a different class of money dealers. When railways were first established, there were a good many people, particularly in the Metropolis, who did not know what the railways were; who disliked the security of the shares; and yet were willing to advance their money upon railway debentures.[15] Reed suggests that on the MBR at least, people in trade supplied most of the share capital but the largest group of lenders were gentlemen and women and professionals.[16]

Insurance companies were another source of loan capital for railways. The Globe with which Glyn was concerned lent £19,860 to the LBR in 1844 as well as other sums to the London and Blackwall, the BDJR, the Northern and Eastern, and the Newcastle and North Shields. In the early 1850s the Globe made loans in the form of debentures to the Newcastle and Berwick, the Whitehaven and Furness and the South Eastern. The Royal Exchange lent £30,000 to the LBR in 1838 and the Sun £5,000 in 1844 and advanced

10 TNA, RAIL 410/332, 9 Jun. and 15 Dec. 1848.

11 RBS Archives, GM/139, from Creed, 16 Apr. 1847; GM/139, to Stewart, 7 Nov. 1854.

12 TNA, RAIL 491/40, 31 Oct. and 14 Nov. 1849, 20 Feb. and 6 Mar. 1850, 26 Feb. and 24 Dec. 1851, 14 Jan. 1852.

13 Quoted in M.C. Reed, *Railways and the Growth of the Capital Market in the Victorian Economy*, ed. M.C. Reed, 1969, 175.

14 TNA, RAIL 640/92.

15 Select Committee on Railway Acts, PP, 1846, xiv, Q. 1960.

16 Reed (1975), 256–257.

£66,000 to the Preston and Wyre in 1847, about a tenth of its capital.[17] The Guardian Assurance and Albion Assurance both lent £50,000 to the GWR in 1847.[18] The Alliance lent £50,000 and the London Life £100,000 to the LYR in 1852 at 3½ per cent and renewed the loan at 5 per cent in 1857. It has been estimated that as much as 8 per cent of all life offices' funds was invested in railway debentures during the 1850s and 14 per cent in the case of Rock Life.[19]

The Bank of England was another source. In 1837 Glyn himself had attempted to get a loan of £250,000 from the Bank of England for the LBR, and later that year he proposed to the Governor a loan of £200,000 secured on the company's debentures. The application was withdrawn as the Bank 'manifested disinclination'.[20] The Bank of England from 1842 did lend up to £250,000 against the debentures of particular companies. Initially Cazenove and Pearce were the intermediary though they do not appear themselves to have been active in the railway market. The brokers made proposals to the Bank based on a railway company's request for short term money. Loans were usually £100,000 at par with the brokers charging 3/16 per cent, and by 1851 the capital account of the Bank included £3,070,000 of debentures of eleven railway and two canal companies.[21] In December 1848 the Bank had renewed a loan of £200,000 to the LNWR until January 1852 and £100,000 to July 1852. Another loan of £120,000 at 2½ per cent was renewed on 5 December until 10 January at 2 per cent with a guarantee from Glyn's.[22] By then the LNWR and one or two other big companies were dealing directly with the Bank.[23]

It must be emphasised that although regarded as the railway bank Glyn's were bankers, the keepers of accounts and providers of credit, and not investors. In this they followed the practice of most British banks. The main exceptions were the provincial Quaker bankers involved in the Stockton and Darlington and other railways in the North East. Not only did the Peases, the financial driving force behind the SDR, when they could not raise sufficient capital locally turn to fellow Quakers for finance, particularly the Gurneys, bankers in Norwich, they were bankers and directors of this and

17 Ibid, 245; S.A. Broadbridge, *Studies in Railway Expansion and the Capital Markets in England, 1825–1873*, 1970, 91.

18 TNA, RAIL 250/193, 8 and 22 Apr. 1847.

19 Supple, *Royal Exchange*, 315, 327–328.

20 TNA, RAIL 384/57, 2 Aug. and 4 and 11 Oct. 1837.

21 Clapham, *Bank of England*, II, 193.

22 TNA, RAIL 410/332, 15 Dec. 1848.

23 David Kynaston, *Cazenove & Co.*, 1991, 38 and 194.

other lines in the North East. Indeed for the first twenty years of its existence bankers were the group with the largest amount of capital in the SDR. John Moss, as we have seen was a private banker, heavily involved from the start in the LMR and GJR. Cunliffe, Brooks & Co and Loyds, Entwistle had significant shareholdings in the Manchester and Leeds (later Lancashire & Yorkshire) and Samuel Brooks chaired the first board meeting of the MLR. Both the Cunliffe and Loyd families, and their banks, and the Manchester and Liverpool District Bank, provided short term loans to the LYR which in the 1850s and 1860s was almost always overdrawn when the bi-annual dividends had to be paid.[24] Charles Mangles and his brother Ross Donnelly were respectively, chairman of the LSWR and director of the LNWR, and were partners in the West Surrey bank at Guildford, but the bank was only founded in 1836, two years after the railway had been authorised and was not a banker to the LSWR.[25] Geoffrey Channon rightly points to the lack of any equivalent in British railway history to the part carried out by American bankers and financiers who played a pivotal role in railway affairs from the 1850s and later in many instances a controlling one. He regards Glyn's proposal to merge the LNWR, GWR and LSWR as the only occasion when financial capital sought directly to shape the railway industry. This attempt, described in Chapter 13, was not however a close parallel with the American experience. Glyn was not using his clout as a banker, but that of his company, the largest in the country, in which he had a relatively small personal financial stake.[26]

Glyn, as has been shown, was only a modest investor in the LBR and GWR but he invested more heavily in railways during the period of the mania. According to the Parliamentary returns for 1845 he was prepared to invest £155,870 spread over a number of companies but by far the largest sum was £94,200 in the TVR. A number of his other investments were also in lines associated in some way with the LBR, which amounted in all to £126,220 – the Bedford and London and Birmingham (£4,000) the LWSSR (£24,000) and the Chester, Manchester and Liverpool Junction (£4,000), but he also was listed as interested in two railways in Ireland and a number of small lines in Norfolk and Suffolk, as well as the Midland's Ely to Lincoln line (£2,400). He may well have seen these eastern lines as providing traffic

[24] Reed (1975), 172–175; Broadbridge, 92, 94, 99.

[25] Cassis, in Youseff Cassis and Philip L. Cottrell, *Private Banking in Europe, Rise, Retreat and Resurgence*, 2015, 38 regards the Mangles case as comparable to the Peases, but their involvement was much less intensive, though Charles had extensive interests in docks and shipping.

[26] Geoffrey Channon, *Railways in Britain and the United States*, 2001, 37–38, 168.

for the LBR's branch from Blisworth to Peterborough. A similar pattern can be seen in 1846 when he put down to take £47,720 shares, but £35,150 was in lines in what was regarded actually or potentially as the LNWR's district: the Buckinghamshire, including the Oxford to Tring; the Welsh Midland, the Shrewsbury and Birmingham; and the Stour Valley line. There was only one investment elsewhere, again in Norfolk.[27] Two of his partners at the bank invested much smaller amounts: Charles Mills, £3,000 in 1845 and £22,000 in 1846, and E.W. Mills only £2,750 and £8,750. However the partners' investments were personal and were not made on behalf of the bank.

Glyn's were bankers to the Norfolk Railway. Glyn seems to have soon sold his shares in the Norfolk Railway at a small loss. In 1847 the railway informed Glyn's that they were taking a mortgage of £50,000 but 'before they take steps to borrow this money they wish to know if you or your friends desire to lend any part of the sum.' The Bank's reply has not been traced.[28]

The fact that London banks did not provide capital for railways has often been commented on. Disraeli found it remarkable that in the 1840s the great leaders of the financial world, (firms such as Rothschilds and Barings) took no part in raising capital for railways:

> The mighty loan-mongers, on whose fiat the fate of kings and empires sometimes depended, seemed like men who, witnessing some eccentricity of nature, watch it with mixed feelings of curiosity and alarm. Even Lombard Street, which was never more wanted, was inactive, and it was only by the irresistible pressure of circumstances that a banking firm, which had an extensive country connection, was ultimately forced to take the leading part that was required and almost unconsciously to lay the foundation of the vast fortunes which it has realised and organised the varied connection which it now commands. All seemed to come from the provinces and from unknown people in the provinces.[29]

Once he had moved to London Nathaniel Rothschild had virtually nothing to do with industrial finance, and, like Richard Plumptre Glyn, did not take to travel by train. He declined to meet his son Lionel at Calais as 'railway travelling makes my head ache so terribly that I cannot make up my mind to a 30 hour shaking.' There were a few regrets. James Rothschild, of the Paris house on a visit to the north of England in 1843 on seeing the traffic on the LMR did comment 'What is happening here with the railways is

27 PP, 1845, xl, 52, 189, and 341; PP, 1846, xxxviii, 116.

28 RBS Archives, GM/118, 21 Feb. 1847.

29 Benjamin Disraeli, *Endymion*, 1881, 356–357.

quite amazing and had I come here earlier we would almost certainly have built this railway. It must yield enormous sums. Never have I seen so many people as [are travelling] between Liverpool and Manchester,' but Nathan in London preferred generally to concentrate on the business he knew best. The English Rothschilds saw railway shares as surrogate government bonds.[30]

This was a contrast to the Continent where the French and Austrian Rothschild Houses were active, unlike the German and London houses, though Nathan in London was prepared to recommend operations to his brother James in Paris, who played a major part in French companies, especially the Nord, which had eight English directors including two Barings, John Moss, Masterman and Chaplin. After the establishment of the main French system Rothschilds financed lines in Italy, Spain and Austria. British engineers and contractors were responsible for many French railways, but as Platt warns it did not follow that a contract for construction of a railway abroad brought in British investors beyond the modest extent of whatever the contractor and his friends could mobilise for themselves. However some contractors did go beyond what this generalisation might suggest. In the case of the Paris to Rouen which was closely associated with the London and Southampton, Mackenzie the contractor brought together a group including representatives of Denison, Heywood, Kennard & Co., J. Barned & Co., William Gladstone and Thomas Weguelin, merchant bankers, and the ubiquitous Alderman Thompson. Moss and Lawrence of the GJR were among the directors. The support for the Rouen-Havre Railway included John Masterman who formed companies to seek other concessions in France as well as the Dutch Rhenish. He backed several companies in which Benson had invested.[31] It has been stated that two-thirds of share capital in railways in France was subscribed by the British, but others have more realistically suggested 200 to 300 million francs (£8 to 12,000,000). Only in the case of the Nord was it substantial.[32]

Glyn's Bank was described in some detail by Daniel Hardcastle in 1842. He said it was a complete contrast to Coutts. At Glyn's, in addition to a large portion of the accounts of the nobility and landed gentry, was the greatest number of commercial accounts in London. Scenes of bustle and animation took place daily. About three o'clock all was activity and vigour – the place was a fair and far more like a great change than the Royal Exchange itself used to be. The counters were packed with clerks, as close as they could

[30] Niall Ferguson, *The World's Banker: The History of the House of Rothschild*, 1998, 430–431, 433.

[31] Jehanne Wake, *Kleinwort Benson: The history of Two Families in Banking*, 1997, 59.

[32] L.H. Jenks, *The Migration of British Capital to 1875*, 1927, 143–144 and 148.

stand together, but people might have to wait for twenty minutes before being served. Two mighty streams of money flowed in and out. 'The rapid progress of modern discoveries, the exploring genius, the accumulated strength and ponderous force of the inventions and improvements of the nineteenth century are all represented in this one Bank and not to an equal extent in any other.' This was possible because of talent of a high order which combined intelligence of the most vivid character and judgment of the keenest power. It draws more on mental than pecuniary resources, great as the latter unquestionably were. The partners had turned the spirit of the age to their profit without violating in any known instance the established principles of sound and legitimate banking. Hardcastle concluded that if there were half a dozen houses in London such as Glyn's one would be inclined to think that private banking had not reached the climax of its prosperity, but the number of such banks was declining every year and joint stock banks were everywhere on the increase.[33]

Glyn's laid stress on the fact that 'Rapidity and clearness of handwriting, facility in the formation of legible figures and expedition and accuracy in the performance of extensive additions are indispensable.' All clerks had to provide a fidelity bond for no less than £1,000 as security in case he should 'lose, embezzle, purloin, consume, misspend or unlawfully make away with, detain or keep any Money, Bond or Bonds, Bill or Bills, Note or Notes, Paper or Papers, Goods, Chattels, Effects or other Thing or Things Whatsoever that shall be entrusted with him' and the rule went on to describe the types of fraud and deceit. However from 1842 a new guarantee scheme was established in the City which provided the necessary security by the clerk on payment of a premium of 6s. per cent per annum.

In 1815 over 30 clerks were employed. By 1843 the staff had increased to 70. A sample of the new entrants to the bank between 1810 and 1840 shows that most of them were described as the sons of a 'Gentleman'. It sounds odd to our ears that others were recorded as coming from families of farmers, surgeons, merchants, brokers etc. Only about a third came from homes in London; others from the Home Counties but some from Devon, Cornwall, Yorkshire and Cumberland. Some of the latter were probably recommended by banks for which Glyn's were the London agents. Certainly a few clerks left Glyn's to go to country banks and Glyn's sometimes lent staff to assist country banks in difficulty. The age limit for entry was 18–20 years but there was a waiting list so applications need to be made from 16 onwards. It was the practice on entering the bank to live on the premises and junior

[33] Daniel Hardcastle, *Banks and Bankers*, 1842, 37–38.

clerks continued to live in until 1912. The remainder initially lived close to the bank within walking distance or a very short journey by horse bus. By the 1850s clerks lived as far away as Woolwich, Blackheath, Sutton and Croydon. Work started at 9 am, but although the bank closed to the public at 4 pm it was often 5.30 or 6 pm before the seniors left and 7 or 8 before juniors left. Staff worked a full six day week, but there were annual holidays – from about 1817 at a rate of a week a year. This was not increased during George Carr Glyn's time, nor were there any definite pension arrangements though special arrangements were made in a few cases.[34] It was said that new faces from Glyn's at the Clearing House were greeted with the cry 'Another victim for the Slaughter House' though there is evidence to show that there were social activities and a good deal of esprit de corps.[35]

From 1815 the starting salary was £75 for fully qualified clerks. In 1841 it was increased to £80 but was later reduced to the earlier level. Salaries were reviewed at Christmas. Increases beyond the minimum were 'rigidly dependent on the periodical investigations of efficiency and conduct', though a rise of £5 a year up to £100 was normal. Thereafter increases were entirely on merit. Few average clerks reached more than £200–250 per annum. Salaries were augmented from the Staff Christmas Fund, made up of contributions from customers. Country banks provided some 15 per cent of the total. In the first half of the century the clerks' Christmas money was from a third to a half of their annual salary, though the proportion was reduced as the century advanced. In 1820 the 32 staff received £3,688 in salary and £1,237 in Christmas money; by 1840 64 staff received £7,776 and £2,852. The fund was divided according to length of service, so a long serving clerk who had not progressed far up the salary level could receive up to half a year's salary.

D.M. Evans compared the characteristics of private and joint-stock banks. In the former one met cashiers and clerks peering through spectacles with a steady and staid appearance, whose only enquiries were about the weather and the prospects of business. In the latter the chief study of clerks was to give effect to checkered neckerchiefs, showy chains and mogul pins. Their showy buildings were also a contrast to the sober business-looking establishments with anciently fashioned railed counters usually found in private banks.[36]

[34] The holiday provision was less generous than at the Bank of England which in 1849 introduced an entitlement from 9 days to 3 weeks according to length of service, *Bankers Magazine*, 1849, 499.

[35] Anon, The Nineteenth-Century Bankers Clerk, *Three Banks Review*, 36, 1957.

[36] D.M. Evans, *City Men*, 10.

There were setbacks at Glyn's. In 1844 they suffered a fraud by one of their officers, and the partners were said to have been engaged the entire night making a security examination of their bank. The sum was trifling in comparison with the extravagant amounts mentioned in the rumours.[37] On the other hand trouble was avoided. When in 1841 a large number of forged Exchequer bills were presented, Sidney Smith commented,

> I am much frightened about Exchequer Bills, having £1,200 in that sort of paper, but they all proved to be good. Coutts, the banker, is got into a scrape which is not considered very creditable to him; he suffers in false bills to the amount of £40,000; the same bargain had been offered to Glyn and Masterman and had been rejected by them.[38]

The number of country banks for which Glyn's acted as agents declined from 68 in 1840 to 55 in 1850, but the change in numbers included amalgamations as well as failures. The geographical coverage was virtually unchanged. The end of Esdailes and Ladbrokes epitomised a trend in private banking in the City. By 1839 only 29 of the 45 private banks which had been members of the London Clearing House in 1810 remained. The number declined further by 1854 when there were 25 private banks in membership. Five joint stock banks were then admitted but had no share in the management. It was only after 1864 that a single committee was created for private and joint stock banks.[39]

In 1841 a select committee of the House of Lords was appointed to inquire into the effect of the alterations in the laws regulating the interest on money. Glyn and other bankers gave evidence. Glyn took the view that the limitation of the rate on bills of up to three months to 5 per cent had been an inconvenience and that its removal had not led to any great disadvantage. It had been unhelpful to Glyn's in that previously when the actual market value of money exceeded five per cent they had been prevented from carrying on their usual system of discount for a particular class of customers, shopkeepers, factors and retail dealers. Those who were not regarded as high class mercantile security could now be lent money at a rate of over five per cent. He thought that about a quarter of bills discounted in London were

37 *Bankers Magazine*, November 1844, 111.

38 *Selected Letters of Sidney Smith*, ed. Nowell C. Smith, 1953, 2, 741, Smith to Lady Grey, 15 Nov. 1841.

39 Robert Martin Holland, *The London Bankers Clearing House*, 1910, in The National Monetary Commission's report on The English Banking System, Washington DC, 1910, 270 and 276.

for over three months. It was not the case that parties had been ruined by the higher rate. When the rate was limited to five per cent money was still borrowed but commission was charged. Now they were not driven into the hands of intermediate parties whose commission was eating them up. As far as he could say the change had been a great relief in both manufacturing and agricultural districts. The change had been beneficial to trade and in some degree had equalised the supply and demand for money by drawing into the discount market funds from insurance companies and other bodies in the City who would otherwise have employed them in the public funds. Moreover it had diverted money otherwise employed on foreign securities into the discount market.[40]

The Bank of England's charter was due for renewal in 1844 against the background of the debate between two schools of thought – the banking and currency schools. Horsley Palmer spoke for the first when in 1837 he blamed the joint-stock banks and excessive speculation in foreign securities for the recent pressure in the money market and wanted bankers to have discretionary powers over the volume of currency. This was countered by Samuel Lloyd Jones who was strongly against leaving the power to issue currency in the hands of the banks and wanted a strict limitation on the ability to issue currency, with a separation of the Bank's issuing and banking functions. The debate continued with increasingly more weight being given to the approach of the currency school as there was considerable dissatisfaction with the Bank of England's record. This was a view to which Peel was inclined and following consultation with William Cotton, the governor and Benjamin Heath, his deputy, he introduced his Bill which provided for the separation of the Bank's note issue from its banking operations, a fixed ratio between notes and bullion and a fixed issue of £14,000,000 notes which might be issued against securities. The Bill also inhibited the formation of new joint stock banks by prohibiting new note issues and limited the size of individual English bank note issues to those existing in 1844.

The Bank itself supported the Bill, but Horsley Palmer was not content and asked Peel to increase the limit to £16,000,000. Peel's refusal led to a meeting of thirty private bankers, including Glyn, who sent a memorandum to Peel. They thought the absence from the Bill of a clause which would enable the Bank to go beyond the limit of £14 million would create a general feeling of uneasiness through out the country and so deprive the scheme of the advantages it possessed and restrict the business of the country by tending to withhold legitimate accommodation. This was signed by 21 City

[40] Select Committee into laws regulating the interest on money. PP, 1841, xii, Q. 110 et seq.

banks, including Barclays, Smith Payne and Curries, as well as Glyn's, though seven refused, including of course Jones Lloyd.[41] Peel however was adamant in his views and the protest was completely unsuccessful.

In January 1846 Glyn was concerned about the demands of the Railway Mania on the banks. He told George Moffat[42] that he had letters from the country, Liverpool, Manchester and Glasgow, complaining of lost production and stagnation. 'I speak disinterestedly for we have our deposit business with the Bank of England. If anything is settled it would be only prudent and fair to the mercantile class to announce it.' Moffat passed this on to Peel under cover of a letter relating to the proposition to amend standing orders so that parliamentary deposits on Railway Bills would be lodged with the Clerk of the House before the first reading instead of when the petitions were presented. He added that the proposal was very popular in the City and in monetary circles. The amount subscribed for railway deposits had been for several months past been employed by the town and country bankers in commerce and agriculture – the sudden withdrawal of so large a sum was pressing with great severity in the monetary operations of both these classes and consequently on the value of their stocks. About £9 million was now required, but this would be reduced by two-thirds if the deposits only had to be found when standing orders had been complied. with. The change would also have the advantage that payments and therefore withdrawals from the banks would be spread as the days of first reading days would vary. The effect concluded Moffat would be imperceptible in comparison with £9 million at once when the Bills were submitted. The change was unlikely to increase speculation, as Parliament had wisely doubled the deposit. He added it was urgent, but could hardly be proposed in the House without Peel's sanction. Peel replied direct to Glyn that when the Government had resolved to interfere in matters of this particular nature the announcement should be general and as far as possible all parties affected by interference should be simultaneously informed. Glyn responded by confirming that there had been disquietude in the money market both in Liverpool where the sale of colonial produce had been under great difficulty, and in Manchester but added that the Bank of England appeared disposed to meet funds as far as they can with prudence.[43]

It was the following year before the country was hit by a commercial crisis in part brought about by the consequences of the Railway Mania. By

[41] The memorandum was published in *The Times*, 11 Jun. 1844.

[42] Partner in Moffat & Co., wholesale tea dealers in London and Liverpool. Liberal MP for Dartmouth, 1844–52 and later for other constituencies.

[43] BL, Add Ms 40482, Moffat to Peel and Glyn to Moffat, 19 Jan.; Peel to Glyn and Glyn to Peel, 21 Jan. 1846. The timing of the deposits was not changed.

April 1847 the Bank's reserves had fallen had to £6.2 million. On 8 April the Bank raised the rate to 5 per cent and restricted the range of bills it discounted. Arguably it should have done so about a fortnight earlier, but the government was raising funds for Irish famine relief and meanwhile a rise in interest rates in New York led to a large flow of bullion abroad. On 27 April after William Brown and Adam Hodgson had seen Peel who stated he could not recommend the Government to intervene, Langton saw the Governor and Langton and Glyn saw the Chancellor of the Exchequer and pointed out that banks could not assist the public unless they could obtain equivalent discounts from the Bank of England. The pressure was however short-lived and during May and June the money market recovered its buoyancy.[44]

A second crisis occurred in October. The rate was increased to 5½ per cent and no further advances would be made for the time being on Exchequer Bills. Failures of grain importers and of the Royal Bank of Liverpool led to extreme tightness in the market with the Bank almost the sole source of money, but its own reserves declined to £2,376,000 by 22 October. Lord John Russell sent for Glyn and other bankers on the evening of Friday, 22 October and they emerged persuaded that he would do something.[45] The following day Glyn was part of the deputation of London bankers which urged the Chancellor to suspend the Act, and issue three or four million more bank notes for the next three months stating the case of the country trade. The Governor wrote to say although the Bank could still maintain itself within the confines of the Act, nevertheless some securities might have to be sold or accommodation limited on discounts. The Bank thought it wise to defer to the Government on whether the Bank Act should be suspended. By 1 pm on the following Monday the letter from the Government authorising relaxation was announced after discussions with the Governor.[46] The Bank was allowed to enlarge the amount of their discount and advances upon approved security, but at a minimum rate of 8 per cent. The Government did not formally suspend the Act, but assured the Bank that if this policy led to any infringement of the law an Act of Indemnity would be placed before

44 Chandler, I, 277; *The Greville Memoirs*, ed. Lytton Strachey and Roger Fulford, 1938, V, 464; H.M. Boot, *The Commercial Crisis of 1847*, 1984, 51.

45 Thomas Baring to Francis Baring, 23 Oct. 1847, reproduced in *Journals and Correspondence from 1808 to 1852 of Sir Francis Thornhill Baring*, edited by his son the Earl of Northbrook, 1905, 239.

46 Wood showed his long reasoned draft to Peel late on the evening of 22 October who much reduced it in length, Norman Gash, *Sir Robert Peel: The Life of Sir Robert Peel after 1830*, 1972, 628.

Parliament. This ended the crisis and by 2 December the rate was reduced to 6 per cent and to 4 per cent on 4 January 1848. At the end of the year the reserve had increased to £8.4 million.

There was considerable controversy about the causes of the crisis and criticism of the Bank of England, whose case was not assisted by the bankruptcy of the firm of the Governor, W.R. Robinson, following imprudent operations in corn. The Chancellor Sir Charles Wood wrote to Loyd on 9 August that he had heard that George Glyn within the last week had become a convert to the necessity of repealing the Act of 1844 to which Loyd replied that the demand for capital by the railroad companies was now telling with powerful effect to which he mainly attributed the present high rate of interest. The opportunities of advantageous investment in railway shares and bonds, he suspected, was gradually exhausting the resources of many country bankers. There was severe competition between the old channels of trade and the new field of railroad enterprise and so the rate of interest would necessarily be high for some time. This was natural and intelligible to all who were willing to understand it but the results would all be charged to the poor Bill of 1844, the scapegoat to which all parties wanted to lay their grievances – whether the unavoidable result of the course of events or the consequence of their own blindness or imprudence. He included Glyn in his criticism – 'I know nothing of G. Glyn's opinions or of his conversion. He is engaged in a very extended banking concern and surrounded by all the influences of railroad vanity and speculation.' In this spirit Wood in December asked Loyd whether Glyn's judgment was not warped by the difficulties in which he was placed. 'Could you expect men who believe that an issue of paper would have saved them to think so much of the general good as of their own?'[47]

Nevertheless Glyn was appointed, only a few months after his election as MP for Kendal, to the Select Committee which under F.T. Baring's chairmanship was set up to look into the commercial distress of 1847 and how far it had been affected by the laws regulating the issue of bank notes. It was a large committee including, Wood, Labouchere, President of the Board of Trade, Peel, Graham, Disraeli, Ricardo and Hume as well as Tom Baring, Drummond and Alderman Thompson from the City, and Russell and Hudson from the railway world.[48] Glyn also gave evidence to the Lords committee under the chairmanship of the Lord President, the Marquess of Lansdowne, which gave him an opportunity to set out his views in detail which are of importance as he was a major player as chairman of the largest

[47] Wood to Loyd, 9 Aug. and 17 Dec., Loyd to Wood, 10 Aug. 1847, *Overstone*, 1971, 1, 387–388 and 402.

[48] Select Committee on Commercial Distress, PP, 1847–8, viii, i.

railway company and a leading private banker with the biggest interest in railways.[49]

Discussion of the crisis by historians has tended to concentrate on three main areas: the role of the Bank of England and the effect of the Bank Act of 1844 in monetary affairs; the impact of harvest failures in Britain and particularly Ireland on British trade and the balance of payments; and the impact of railway investment on income, investment and consumption.[50]

The Bank's policy has been criticised in two respects. First it was argued that after the 1844 Act it abandoned its traditional responsibility for the general state of money and credit and began instead to compete vigorously with the rest of the market in discounting bills of exchange by reducing bank rate to at least 1½ per cent lower than any rate it had previously charged, a move which took the monetary world completely by surprise.[51] As a result interest rates were depressed below the rate which would have prevailed under previous policies. To these critics the division of the Bank into two departments left the Banking Department free to develop its own policies as if it were a commercial bank. The Act did not establish any rules for the Department. It has however been suggested that the Bank adopted its new discount policies to control the demand for discounts which it saw as a flexible means of adjusting its reserves. Certainly it discounted a higher volume of bills, but historians now see the low interest rates as products of the strong balance of payments and large bullion influx between 1843 and August 1846 rather than the result of action by the Bank.

Glyn however largely agreed with the criticism of the Bank. He thought the low rate of interest in 1847 was an encouragement to speculation and attributed the lowness of the rate to the fact that under the 1844 Act the Bank of England had ceased to be regulators of the currency and became merely bankers (by the separation of the Issue Department from the Banking department). They sought discounts and employment for money, competing in the money market with the usual suppliers of money to the mercantile classes, discounting bills which previously they were not in the habit of discounting. The Bank's rate went as low as the brokers for discounts so forcing the brokers to go lower.[52] There were larger fluctuations than previously in the rate of interest in 1847; the high rate had not caused the failures which in addition to the corn trade were in the East India trade where Glyn believed credit had been overextended for some time. The Mauritius failures arose

49 Select Committee of the House of Lords on Commercial Distress, PP, 1847–8, viii, ii.

50 H.M. Boot, *The Commercial Crisis of 1847*, 1984, 81–3.

51 *Bankers Magazine*, Oct. 1844, 57.

52 Commercial Distress, Lords, Qs 1669–71, 1683 and 1693.

because of the large amounts locked up in mortgages which could not be realised.

He thought the panic in the third week of October had arisen because of the hoarding that had gone on and parties having property did not think they could obtain Bank of England notes for that property. There were upwards of twenty million notes in circulation on 23 October but the notes were doing much less work than sixteen million would have done in normal circumstances. The Bank could not meet demand because it had only £1,000,000 in notes and £400,000 of bullion in reserve. If the Act of 1844 had not been in operation the Bank would have extended its facilities as it did following the letter of the Government issued on 25 October. There would have been no danger because the exchanges with both the US and Europe were very much in favour of Britain. This would not have stopped insolvencies but the fear in October was for solvent houses. The fact that the Act of 1844 limited the circulation of the country banks, meant that if they were obliged to accommodate their district with more notes they had to buy from the Bank or in the money market.[53]

He thought it better to revert to the old system under which the bank managed the circulation than to continue under the £14 million limitation. It was a mistake to invest the Bank with a public character and put them in a position of holding enormous public deposits which gave them huge influence over the monetary system, and then to tell them that they could act as any private Bank would for the advantage of their proprietors. He added that he did not think the constitution and system of the Bank Court were exactly what they ought to be for the due administration of the circulation.[54] Generally the directors had been a highly respectable body and had conducted their affairs extremely well, but he regarded it as a great evil when matters such as fixing the rate of interest and the general regulation of the circulation were determined by a majority. A majority one week could be upset the following week. He would like to see the whole responsibility for circulation in the hands of the Bank rather than divided between Bank and Government. On the Bank Court there should be commissioners not elected by the proprietors, appointed for, say, three years, under Act of Parliament, not immediately by the Government or the proprietors, and not removable by the Government. They should not have an absolute veto on the proceedings of the Court, but if they dissented from the majority their reasons should be submitted in writing, and laid before Parliament. He also saw no reason for the exclusion of bankers from the Court, but would rather the commissioners

53 Qs 1720 and 1723–6.

54 It was still predominantly composed of merchants, Howe, 1994, 25.

were not engaged in trade. He thought that the Bank should have power to exceed £14 million when demanded by the adverse state of the exchanges, but the circumstance when such discretion should be exercised could not be defined in regulation. He thought that on the whole the Bank had been fairly managed by the governing body.[55]

He had changed his view on the desirability of separating the Issue department from the Banking department. The events of 1847 proved it was an experiment which had failed.[56] He disapproved of the clause in the Act which restricted silver bullion to a fifth of the reserve. It had caused difficulties for merchants from the Pacific who found no market in London for their silver and had to send it over to Paris to obtain bills of exchange. The rigid proportion complicated operations as a rise in gold or notes would render the proportions wrong. On the other hand he approved of the restriction on the circulation of country banks introduced in 1844 as bringing the regulation of the circulation under the Bank.[57]

Secondly discussion has concentrated on trade. The need to import large quantities of corn in 1847 destroyed the balance of payments equilibrium and caused the large outflow of bullion which heralded the crisis of April while the collapse of the price of imported corn in the third quarter of 1847 started the chain of bankruptcies which marked the onset of the October crisis. This followed panic buying in May pushing prices to high levels, with merchants possibly hoping to sell to Ireland, or to re-export to the Continent. In June the price collapsed. Speculation has also been blamed for other failures, but it was perhaps more misjudgment as for five years consumption had grown rapidly and importers had difficulty in keeping up with demand. In 1847 the growth suddenly stopped as did the usual accommodating credit which was essential for the operation of international trade. Merchants in the long distance trades found themselves extremely illiquid and this was made worse in the East India trade where there was serious credit abuse.[58]

Glyn would not have dissented from this analysis. He saw the cause of the April 'Pressure' as Lansdowne, the chairman of the Lords Committee, called it, as strikingly different from that of October. The first was caused by the necessary importation of corn and other foodstuffs, but the Bank helped those affected, and the foreign demand for gold was met by raising the rate of interest and the foreign exchanges quickly adjusted and by the early autumn were favourable. But in August and September, with the good harvest,

[55] Commercial Distress, Lords, Qs 1777, 1782–6 and 1795.

[56] Qs 1815–6.

[57] Qs 1826 and 1748.

[58] Boot, 64–72.

there were large failures among those who had speculated in corn. This affected other merchants, and by October there was a more general lack of confidence, very much increased by the failure of banks in Liverpool and elsewhere. The situation, he thought, resembled closely that of 1825. The lack of confidence was so great that merchants feared that the reserves of the Bank would be driven so low that they would be unable to convert their assets into Bank of England notes. However the 1825 crisis was a banking one; that of 1847 was a commercial one.[59]

On the impact of railway investment, in 1844–47 Parliament authorised the raising of £256 million for railway construction compared with £15 million in the period 1840–43. Of course not all projects were completed and or even started, but it is estimated that the gross expenditure on railway capital formation in the UK, excluding land, amounted in 1845 to £13.2 million, in 1846 £32.7 million and in 1847 £36.8 million.[60] By mid-1847 3,907 miles of track were under construction employing 256,509 workers and £4.3 million a month in capital was raised. Indeed by mid-year expenditure was exceeding the amount the companies could currently raise and by August the reserves built up in 1846 had been exhausted. There had been increasing difficulty in servicing capital. Unpaid calls increased from less than 2 per cent in the first half of 1846 to 12 per cent in the second half. This led to heavier borrowing in 1847 despite higher interest rates, to lower dividends and to the suspension of schemes. Companies found that many of the new schemes were likely to be less profitable than earlier one, an outcome more likely when, after the October crisis the government required that no new construction contract was to be entered into for the year commencing in November 1847 unless agreed by three-fifths of the shareholders.[61] Railway investment had reinforced the panic as it followed the drawing of reserves to maintain construction at a time of a declining supply of funds. This meant a flow from London to the provinces and a strengthening of their reserves, so that the country banks were able to command very large sums in October and were able to escape the crisis without much harm.

The general view held by contemporaries was that excessive demand for railway funds drove up interest rates to a point where both investment in other activities and in railways at that level could not be maintained at the same time. Historians have taken different views but Boot in his study concluded that railway demand for capital did have a significant effect on interest rates, particularly in the years before 1847. The impact of railway

59 Qs 1648 and 1744.

60 Figures based on Table 1, H.M. Boot, *The Commercial Crisis of 1847*, 1984, 5.

61 The Railways Extension of Time Act, 1847.

investment on income and consumption has also given rise to divergent opinion. James Wilson in the *Economist* argued that railway investment stimulated consumption in the short run but left the economy unable to satisfy this increased demand or to maintain its supply of capital goods for railways. Others, including Tooke, argued that railway investment led to a fall in consumption which triggered the collapse of prices in the crisis of October 1847. Modern historians have suggested that consumer expenditure fell as investment rose, but a more recent view is that consumption was well maintained though the impact of high food prices must have reduced real income of the poor, but consumer expenditure did not fall severely. The main reason seems to have been the high level of investment and activity in railways and related industries. This was a point of view Glyn endorsed and he had firm views on how the demand for capital had a ripple effect throughout the economy.

He thought the increased demand for money caused by the railway boom with the employment of large numbers of railway labourers at high wages, and in iron manufacture, added to the amount of imports, by a greater demand for food. However railway demand for capital had a limited effect. It added to the pressure on the mercantile sector as many shopkeepers and small manufacturers went into railways to a much greater extent than they were warranted in doing. However the capital called up circulated rapidly, as the railway directors paid it to ironmasters and contractors, who paid it to labourers who spent the money with shopkeepers through the country and as every ten or twenty miles of railway was opened a large quantity of fixed capital was released by enabling shopkeepers in all the towns to hold comparatively short stocks of goods. Indeed he pointed to this as a factor which had operated since the opening of railways counterbalancing in a great degree the capital transferred from floating to fixed. He did not think it possible to estimate how much capital had been saved by this more hand to mouth business, but his view was based on questions he had put to dealers in some of the principal towns. He saw this as more important than the saving in the cost of transport. That so many more people were in employment because of the railway boom might have increased the consumption of food, but it also reduced the number falling on the poor rate for support.[62] Earlier he had told LNWR shareholders he did not wish to argue how far the transfer of fluctuating capital to fixed capital in the course of railway enterprise had taken place and whether this had been mischievous or otherwise to the commercial world. He left that to political economists.

[62] Commercial Distress, Lords, Qs 1649–52, and 1657–8.

However he came near to answering the first question when he asserted that railway companies by freeing an enormous amount of capital that was locked up in warehouses, shops, counting houses had done more to release the capital of the country than anything which had taken place for years. The blame for what happened in 1847 should 'fall on those who in 1845 and 1846 opened the door of the legislature to projects simply designed for the purpose of competition … who forced us to defence … to undertake schemes which otherwise would never have entered into our heads.'[63]

Glyn's suggestions for introducing an independent element in the Bank of England's governing body were not adopted, but it was decided that the Court would in principle recommend to the proprietors candidates they considered most fitted for the job, so those of a mature age could be considered whereas previously younger candidates had been appointed so they would not be too old when their turn came to serve as Deputy or Governor. Private bankers however continued to be ineligible to serve on the Court, but the Bank gradually disengaged itself from active participation in the discount market.[64]

The 1840s with their years of depression at both the beginning and end of the decade meant that country banks found that it more prudent to lend less locally so they had funds to place in London which they increasingly placed them more widely in the London market particularly with bill brokers especially Overend and Gurney. Barnett, Hoare in 1849 advised the Liverpool Union Bank that 'with many of our country friends we have arranged, whenever their balances exceed a certain amount, to hand over the surplus to Messrs Overend & Co.'. Glyn's apparently adopted a similar practice at this stage.[65]

By 1845 Glyn's total liabilities and assets had reached £4,649,000 with country accounts at £533,000 being only a fifth of the town level. Funds at the Bank of England amounted to £242,000, while the debts owed to Glyn's on current accounts had risen from £261,000 in 1844 to £732,000 the rise being particularly steep in the country office. Of course this peak, reached at the height of the Railway Mania, was not sustained. Following a slight drop overall in 1846, when the fall in railway balances was offset by a rise in the country office balances, there was a steep fall in 1847 with the railway balances were down to £703,000 and country balances to £419,000. The changes in the town balances in this period were small – in 1847 only 11 per

[63] TNA, RAIL 1160/269, 19 Feb. 1848.

[64] Elizabeth Hennessy, The Governors, Directors and Management, in *The Bank of England, Money, Power and Influence*, ed. Richard Roberts and David Kynaston, 1995, 190–191.

[65] R.S. Sayers, *Lloyds Bank in the history of English banking*, 1957, 181.

cent lower than the 1845 peak. The main fall was in bills discounted, down from a peak of £3,325,000 in 1846 to £2,045,000 in 1848 and country accounts overdrawn rising to more than £500,000 in both 1847 and 1848. The total balance at the end of 1849 was £3,727,000, over 40 per cent above the 1841 level. In the 1840s the average cash to liabilities ratio dropped slightly to 11.8 per cent though reaching 13 per cent in 1845.

CHAPTER TWELVE

The London and North Western – Management

On 22 July 1846 the amalgamation act creating the LNWR received the royal assent. The board immediately elected Glyn chairman with Charles Lawrence of the Grand Junction as his deputy. The fact that John Moss, chairman of the GJR, had retired due to ill health ensured that Glyn's appointment was uncontested but in any case Glyn had strong claims as head of the largest element in the new company. His position was fortified by the reputation he had gained in representing the railways generally and by his links with the City and politicians. This chapter reviews Glyn's achievements in the management of the new company.

At the first general meeting of the new company held on 7 August Glyn said that perhaps the only wonder was that the amalgamation had not taken place before, and that it had been the original intention of the promoters of both the LBR and GJR to carry on the two concerns conjointly, but the difficulties of carrying on the two undertakings at the start precluded this.[1] He emphasised the success of the constituent companies, the difficulties with which they had to struggle in carrying out what in the first instance had been nothing but an experiment on the largest scale, and that they had achieved this unaided. He and the board were very conscious of what the new company owed to the two engineers who had been so largely responsible for bringing its two main constituents to the state in which they were merged. Glyn successfully moved that a testimonial worth 1,000 guineas (£1,050) be presented to both Stephenson and Locke. He told shareholders that if the

[1] TNA, RAIL 1110/269, 7 Aug. 1846. There does not seem to be other firm evidence for this intention, though the prospectus for the Grand Junction Railway stated that 'united with the projected line from London to Birmingham it will form the main channel of communication from North to South.' (RAIL 1075/1254)

Kilsby tunnel had proved too much for the talent of Stephenson, or Boxhill for that of Brunel or St George's Hill for Locke, the companies would have found no government coming to their assistance, as they had found the landowners in every part of the country diametrically opposed to the objects in view.[2] He saw the advantages of railways. There were many like him, he told shareholders in 1850, who had suffered from being three nights in a mail coach to get to Glasgow. The rising generation would become so used to railways that they would forget the hardship of that journey and travel to Glasgow comfortably in fourteen hours. He also emphasised the saving of capital by wholesalers and retailers who no longer needed to hold the same amount of stock as previously. 'Interest was saved as the transmission of money took less time, and above all the penny post would not have been possible without the railways'.[3]

The new company was to face new and unprecedented challenges in the aftermath of the Railway Mania which brought consequences for the whole railway system. At the end of 1845 2,345 miles of railway were open with average receipts per mile of £2,690. By the end of 1852, shortly after Glyn's resignation as chairman, mileage had increased to 7272, but receipts had fallen to £2,160 per mile.[4] This reflected the lower profitability of many of the new lines and the sharp reduction in economic activity, especially in the early part of the period. By the end of 1845 there was a downturn and in 1846 and 1847 several major sectors of the economy were depressed as described in chapter 11. This meant that under Glyn's chairmanship the LNWR had not only to adjust to changes in the economy but also to face considerable hostility from critics who on the whole exaggerated the weaknesses in the company's performance. More was expected of a company with a quarter of the traffic receipts of British railways and an eighth of the miles of railway then open.

Even in more robust economic circumstances the task facing Glyn and the new company would have been huge in both financial and management terms. The unprecedentedly large company had a capital of £17,242,310 and borrowing powers of £5,747,000. The LBR was the largest element in the new company. £8,653,750 of the capital was allocated to LBR shareholders who took eight of the 18 seats on the new central board, £5,788,560 to the GJR, with six seats and £2,800,000 to the MBR with three seats. The duke of Sutherland's representative took the other seat. However much of the

2 TNA, RAIL 1110/269, 7 Aug. 1846 and 12 Aug. 1847.

3 TNA, RAIL 1110/269, Feb. 1850. The penny post was introduced by Rowland Hill in 1840. Hill was chairman of the London, Brighton and South Coast Railway from 1842–46.

4 H.G. Lewin, *The Railway Mania and its Aftermath 1845–1852*, 1936, 114, Table VIII.

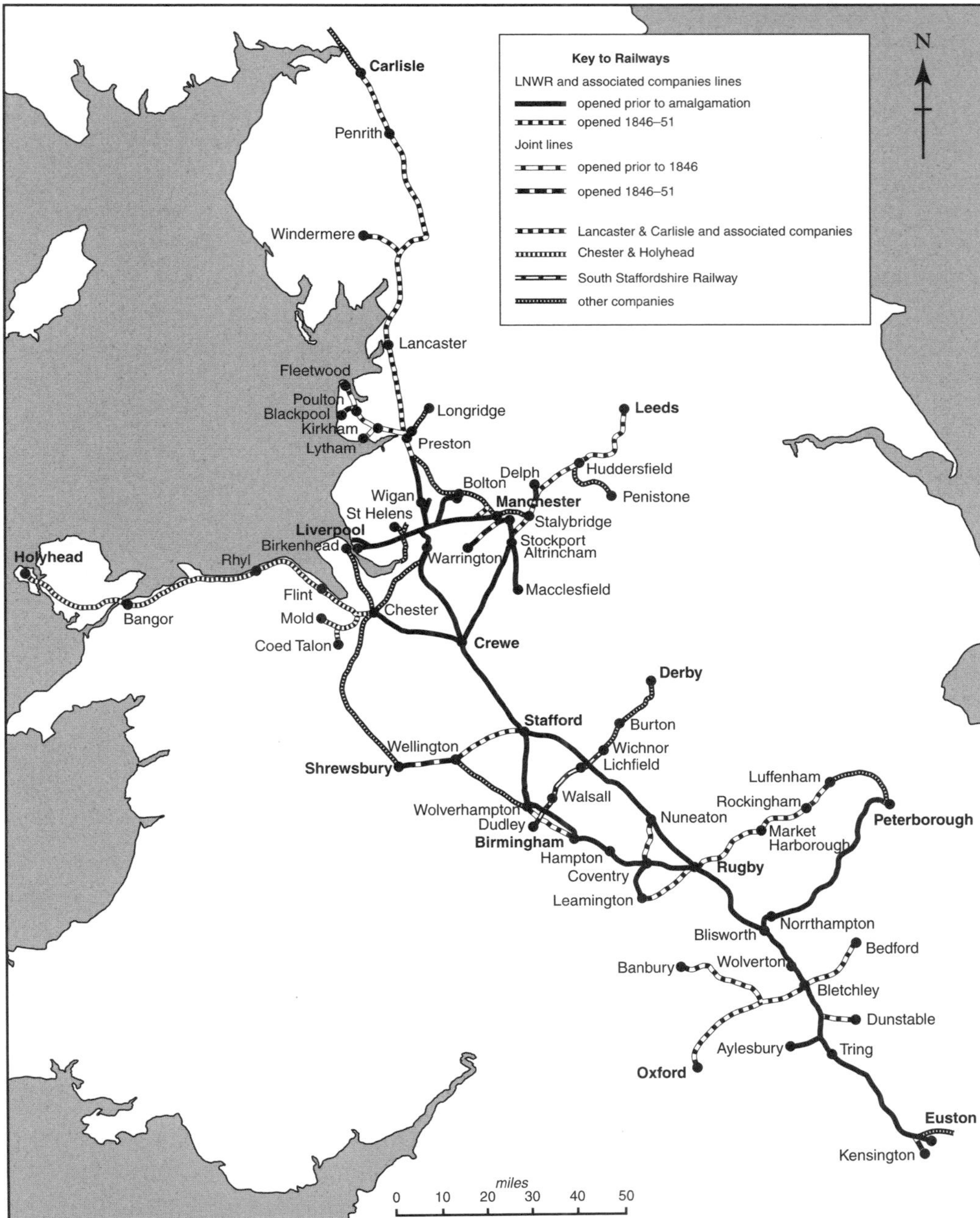

Map 4: The LNWR under Glyn's Chairmanship, 1846–52.

organisation of the constituent companies was retained at levels below the central board though a general manager was appointed later in 1846.

The amalgamation did not take place because any of the three companies was weak separately. They had been paying good dividends – in 1844 both the GJR and the LBR paid 10 per cent[5] which the LNWR was to pay in its first year, a level never again attained. The demand for more capital was foreseen from the start. At its first meeting in December 1845 the board asked for all obligations beyond the current share capital to be listed. Projects going forward in the current session of Parliament were reviewed in April 1846. In August the new board was informed that £4,587,000 was needed for new works authorised by Parliament in that Session, roughly a third for each of the LBR, the GJR and the Trent Valley lines. It was agreed to issue £25 shares with a £2 call immediately to raise £1,375,000.[6] Indeed Glyn warned shareholders that his personal opinion was that it was impossible to expect that future profits would produce such large returns to the shareholders, as the return on the newer investments would not match the old for they were much more of a protective character. He added that many of his colleagues were sanguine enough to look for an increased dividend. His remarks led immediately to a sharp drop in LNWR shares. Glyn proved to be right – capital increased to £29,000,000 by 1851, but the dividends decreased.

The Amalgamation Act prescribed lower rates and fares than previously allowed and in 1844 the running of parliamentary third class trains had been made compulsory. Thus while both goods and passenger traffic on the LNWR kept up surprisingly well in the difficult years of the late 1840s, passenger revenue was reduced despite an upward trend in the number of journeys. Goods traffic was promoted vigorously. It was contributing 50.9 per cent of total receipts in 1851 compared with 41.5 per cent in 1846, a remarkable transformation, though one paralleled on other railways.[7] The LNWR was helped in this period by its low proportion of third class passengers – 39 per cent, compared with 72 on the LYR, 65 on the Midland and 50 on the Eastern Counties, though the number of such passengers was increasing much faster that for first and second class.[8] Symptomatic of its attitude was that the board learned with regret that the LYR was to have third class

5 Only equalled by Hudson's York and North Midland.

6 TNA, RAIL 410/20, 6 Aug. 1846.

7 T.R. Gourvish, *Mark Huish and the London & North Western Railway, A Study in Management*, 276. According to Lewin, the corresponding national figures were 47.1 and 37.6 per cent (*Railway Mania*, 114, Table VIII)

8 S. Salt, *Facts and Figures, principally relating to Railways and Commerce*, 1848, 34. The GWR however had only 16 per cent.

carriages on all their trains between Liverpool and Manchester. The board judged that it would reduce fares and disturb existing arrangements. In 1846 Creed had gone so far as to say that increasing the third class was considered generally objectionable to the other passengers, though claiming credit for being the first company to have covered carriages for the third class.[9]

In July 1846 Glyn headed a committee to consider the new scale of fares which would require a 'nice adjustment to make them substantially conformable to the new law', and the group was 'requested to do the needful conferring with the executive officers on the subject.'[10] The maximum fares were reduced to 2½d per mile express, 2d first, 1½d second and 1d third. Fares were made uniform over the whole system in June 1847, and fixed at the legal maximum for the main line. However this suggests a more rigid regime than was the case in practice. When the board was particularly concerned about the fall in Liverpool-Manchester receipts in 1849, fares were reduced as an experiment for six months.[11] On the other hand day tickets where the uptake had been disappointing were increased in price from two-thirds to three-quarters of the full fare. Local fares were reduced in the face of competition. Overall Wyndham Harding calculated that between 1843 and 1847, LNWR fares had reduced by 35 per cent in first class, 40 per cent in second and 29 per cent in third, compared with respectively 22, 24 and 25 per cent in seven large companies. He did not distinguish between the effect of the Act and other causes.[12] Glyn however warned in 1846 that the increase in traffic was not in proportion to the reduction in fares.[13] Later he did not see much scope for increasing fares as he was unconvinced that such a step would bring in more revenue.[14] Meanwhile express trains were improved and journey times reduced partly as a result of the opening of the Trent Valley line. *The Times* claimed this brought most important advantages to a very large class of commercial men who leaving by the 6.15 am from Euston would have an extra two hours in Manchester or Liverpool to transact their business before returning on the evening train.[15] The evening express from London only took 5 hours and in May 1848 a service to Scotland began with

9 TNA, RAIL 410/21, 9 Jun. 1849; Report of Select Committee on Railway Acts, PP, 1846, xiv, Qs 1747, 1758 and 1765.

10 TNA, RAIL 410/20, 13 Dec. 1845, 14 Feb., 14 Apr. and 11 Jul. 1846.

11 TNA, RAIL 410/21, 14 Feb. 1850.

12 Wyndham Harding, Facts bearing on the Progress of the Railway System, *Journal of the Statistical Society of London*, XI, 1848, 32.

13 Select Committee on Railway Acts, PP, 1846, xiv, Q. 1751.

14 TNA, RAIL 1110/269, 22 Feb. 1850.

15 *The Times*, 22 Jun. 1847.

the journey to Glasgow and Edinburgh taking only 12½ hours. Mrs Gaskell recorded in December 1847 that they left 'Manchester at 26 minutes to 10 and from that time until we got to London last night we never stirred out of the railway carriage. For we went through the Trent Valley which does not pass through Birmingham.'[16] The opening of the TVR was also the occasion of the introduction of railway time by the Post Office, the principal railway companies and the municipal authorities in the most important towns, a cause strongly advocated by Henry Booth.[17]

On the freight side it was not simply a matter of adjusting rates to meet the terms of the Act. Independent carriers had been excluded from the GJR but allowed on the LBR. A uniform policy had to be adopted. Glyn headed a committee of directors set up in February 1846 to consider freight tolls, and in July a committee under Moorsom was appointed to consider the arrangements for rates and fares with Pickfords and generally in the merchandise department. This became the Goods Committee. In August Huish and Creed, who had respectively been the secretaries of the GJR and LBR were asked to see Baxendale about arrangements to be made for the future of the freight business. At the same time they were asked to consider the question of appointing a single manager for the whole traffic department. By October 1846 Glyn reported that the negotiations with both Pickfords and Chaplin & Horne were nearly satisfactorily completed. The result would involve great changes in the company's carrying business, which required a general manager in the department as did the harmonious working of the whole of the traffic on the line. It was therefore the need to harmonise arrangements on the freight side which formally at least gave rise to the appointment of a general manager. Glyn told the board that he believed there would be no difference of opinion as to the gentleman to be selected and begged therefore to propose Captain Mark Huish, the general manager of the GJR, as general manager for the company.[18] It was later agreed that his salary should be £2,000, a considerable advance on the £1,250 he had been paid by the GJR. The company began to carry over the whole line in February 1847 and an agency agreement resulted in Pickfords and Chaplin & Horne, carrying out the collection and delivery functions for the southern division an arrangement similar to that made earlier by the GJR.

Although Glyn had been involved with George Stephenson in his collieries in Leicestershire and then Derbyshire, the LBR and LNWR were slow to develop the coal traffic, especially as Stephenson had been

[16] *The Letters of Mrs Gaskell,* ed. J.A.V. Chapple and Arthur Pollard, 1966, 49.

[17] Booth, 159; TNA, RAIL 1110/269, 14 Feb. 1848.

[18] TNA, RAIL 410/20, 10 Oct. 1846. Gourvish, *Huish,* 108.

moved to write to the Prime Minister in 1846 to suggest a railway should be constructed for supplying the Metropolis and the southern and south eastern counties with cheap coal, coke and lime from Derbyshire, Leicestershire and Warwickshire. He thought the Government might take an interest but it could be carried out with the assistance of some Londoners and his friends. Peel told him it was not for the Government to do this and no more seems to have been heard of it.[19] Doubtless even Stephenson saw it was not a practicable proposition in the late 1840s. However the LNWR's coal traffic did increase substantially. It produced only £30,000 in 1845 but £105,000 in 1852. An example of the effort made to encourage traffic can be seen in the agreement made with the Clay Cross Company in 1849. The LNWR would carry coal at ¾d. per ton per mile over the 80 miles from Rugby to London, including stations on the West London line. Clay Cross had to send 45,000 tons a year and to pay for 3,750 tons within 30 days of the end of every month. If they met this they would be allowed a drawback of ¼d. per ton per mile and any excess of 45,000 tons would be charged at ¼d. per mile. Wagons were to carry at least 4½ tons, had to be approved by the railway and empties had to be returned or a fine paid for wasting power.[20]

After the first half year of working as an amalgamated company Glyn was able to report a substantial rise in the number of passengers carried amounting to 17 per cent (3,277,590 in the second half of 1846 compared to 2,793,372 in the corresponding period in 1845) but the gross receipts from passengers was less on account of the reductions in fares, while the expenses had been higher. This was therefore a benefit to the public but not to shareholders. While reductions in expenditure could be made, competition from other companies could put further pressure on fares.[21] In the first half of 1847 the number of passengers travelling diminished, particularly as a result of the Irish famine. This also caused such a drop in the pig traffic that the total of livestock carried fell although other classes increased.

Despite these difficulties the new company still had ambitious ideas. Quadrupling the lines between London and Rugby was considered but Stephenson told the board that the cost would be about £2,000,000. In January 1847 however the board approved a more limited proposal when Glyn himself proposed two extra tracks from Primrose Hill to Watford to cater partly for traffic to and from the proposed Buckinghamshire lines and the Birmingham and Oxford to cost £350,000.[22] In the event even this was

19 BL, Add Ms 40590, Stephenson to Peel, April (no day) and Peel's reply, 21 Apr. 1846.

20 IMS, 454/3.

21 TNA, RAIL 1110/269, 12 Feb. 1847.

22 TNA, RAIL 1110/269, 12 Feb. 1847.

abandoned as the provision of further sidings and other facilities for goods traffic meant that the existing two tracks would suffice.[23]

At the general meeting in August 1846 Glyn stressed the importance of securing bills for the improvement of the stations in Manchester, Birmingham, London and Liverpool, but as money became tighter the contractor for the East and West India Docks Railway was asked to postpone construction for six months, and the bill for the Warwick to Hampton line giving a more direct route to Birmingham was repeatedly deferred. However that did not prevent Glyn from proposing a line from Bletchley to Wellingborough. In March 1848 the abandonment of the EWIDBJR and the Hampton line was considered but it was thought that the shareholders of the former would not agree, and it was not clear if it was practicable to abandon the Warwick line. Nevertheless Glyn had been able to tell shareholders that, except for one small branch to which they were committed to coal owners near Coventry, the company was not putting forward any bills in 1848.[24] Neither the Warwick line nor that projected to Wellingborough came to fruition.

In August 1849 Glyn defended the company. If the company had known what they did now they could have built bigger stations and sidings and saved a good deal of capital. With the knowledge of 1849 they could have avoided getting into many projects and doing many acts which the competition and the unwise legislation of 1845–46 forced upon them. But all that had been done was with a view to the profit of the whole concern.[25]

The extension from the original terminus in Birmingham in Curzon Street to the New Street station was certainly an improvement but the line which was less than a mile long cost £350,000. Another source of financial pressure was the price which had to be paid to subsidiary lines which the LNWR had either encouraged or needed to form part of its network as feeders or simply to prevent them falling into the hands of competitors. The Warwick and Leamington line obtained £125 a share The Leeds and Dewsbury line pushed the LNWR to exchange £70 of their stock for every £100 worth of LNWR stock. The Stour Valley was leased at two-thirds of the LNWR dividend. The LNWR took a third of the lease of the Preston and Wyre with the Manchester and Leeds holding the major share. The LNWR did turn down offers to take over the Warwick and Birmingham, and Warwick and Napton canals, and decided that the Warwick and Stratford line should be

[23] Two additional lines for goods from Primrose Hill to Willesden and one up line on to Bletchley were provided in 1859.

[24] TNA, RAIL 410/20, 9 Oct. 1847 and 11 Mar. 1848; RAIL 1110/269, 18 Feb. 1848.

[25] TNA, RAIL 1110/269, 17 Aug. 1849.

pursued by private parties. Later their interest in South and Central Wales meant that Moon and Tootal were appointed to the board of the Swansea Junction and the company agreed to work the proposed Shrewsbury and Aberystwyth, though the latter did not get off the ground.[26]

The LNWR interest in subsidiary companies was substantial, amounting to £3 million by 1848 and expected to rise to nearly £5 million by 1852. Stakes were often secured, at least initially, not by the LNWR itself putting up the necessary capital, but by directors personally investing in the concern, though holding the shares in trust for the LNWR. Thus Glyn in 1849 held 5,000 shares in the EWIDR, 1,000 in the Leeds and Dewsbury, and 7,810 with Ledsam in the South Staffordshire. and 2,000 with Creed in the Caledonian.[27] Later 13,500 shares in the Coventry, Nuneaton, Birmingham and Leicester were transferred from board members to the LNWR, 1336 from Glyn himself. This procedure did not generally cause difficulties, as the subsidiary companies were only too pleased to have these injections of capital and more generally the LNWR interest and influence, but as will be seen the device was heavily criticised when used for hostile purposes. Glyn was on the boards of a number of subsidiary companies though he did not attend regularly. They included the Coventry, Nuneaton, Birmingham and Leicester, the Buckinghamshire and the CHR. Although the chairmen were usually locals, the boards were dominated by LNWR representatives.

By 1848 the need for economy and improved efficiency led Glyn to propose the appointment of a committee to investigate the establishment under Moorsom.[28] This Committee produced a series of reports which were generally approved by the board and implemented. They included the merger of the audit and accounts departments, which made it convenient to release Morison to head the Railway Clearing House on a full-time basis. To keep commitments to future expenditure under control, they proposed an experienced officer should be appointed to communicate with the boards of the companies with which the LNWR was in communication. Booth was given this task. They also recommended that the company adhere to the principle of obtaining stores by public tender. Engineers and architects were asked to avoid all unnecessary and expensive ornament. Expenditure on the Manchester and South Junction was restrained until experience of the traffic had been gained. In the following January the Finance Committee

[26] TNA, RAIL 410/20, 15 Aug., 10 Oct., 4 Nov. 1846, 9 Jan., 11 Feb. 1847; RAIL 410/21, 10 Jul., 12 Sept., 3 Nov. 1852.

[27] TNA, RAIL 410/20, 14 Apr. 1847.

[28] TNA, RAIL 410/20, 11 Mar. 1848. The reports are at RAIL 410/50.

was authorised to dispose of a portion of the company's interest in branches and subsidiary lines as opportunity offered.[29]

Other reports dealt with staffing matters, particularly as the wages bill was a major concern. Glyn himself specified firemen's wages, permanent way maintenance, locomotive power and coke as problems needing attention. In December 1848 the LNWR had 10.263 employees, including 966 clerks, 3,054 porters, 3354 artificers and 738 drivers and firemen. Wages were relatively high, even porters on under £1 a week were substantially better off than agricultural labourers, and drivers, long in short supply, commanded more than most skilled workers.[30] While a superannuation fund was now recommended, other changes were largely detrimental to the interests of the workers, and displayed a highly paternalistic attitude which Glyn largely shared. This had been seen earlier in 1848 during the Chartist demonstrations when McConnell told Glyn that he had caused the workmen in the locomotive department to sign a declaration of their willingness to serve as special constables and 478 workmen were sworn in at Crewe works. The directors noted with satisfaction the readiness and zeal with which the servants of the company declared their determination to exert themselves for the maintenance of order and the protection of property. On the other hand the conduct of some of the company's servants under similar circumstances which had not been equally satisfactory was referred to the Grand Junction directors to deal with as they should deem expedient. Three were dismissed but were later reinstated having agreed to serve when required in future.[31]

Following the Moorsom report the apprentice scheme was to continue but the authority of the board was needed before the numbers could be increased. Payment of overtime to clerks was to be dispensed with. Gratuities for drivers and police on whose steady conduct the safety of trains might depend were to continue, but a gradual reduction in the wages of artificers in the locomotive, carriage and wagon shops was approved.[32] The Company quickly ran into difficulties with the locomotive men who provided an early example of railwaymen's group solidarity. The practice of the LBR of making progress to maximum salary based on ability and good conduct rather than on length of service was adopted, but the introduction

[29] TNA, RAIL 410/20, 13 Jan. 1849.

[30] *Quarterly Review*, Dec. 1848; Philip S. Bagwell, *The Railwaymen: The History of the National Union of Railwaymen*, 1963, 20.

[31] F.C. Mather, The Railways, the Electric Telegraph, and Public Order during the Chartist Period, *History*, xxxviii, 47,193; TNA, RAIL 410/20,15 Apr. 1848.

[32] TNA, RAIL 410/20, 13 May and 10 Jun. 1848.

of a new system of classification, approved by Glyn and the board, meant that the numbers in the top grade were limited and so whereas a driver could have reasonably expect to move from 5s. 6d. a day to 8s. after 8 or so years service, in future it might take 25 to 30 years. Almost all the locomotive men at Camden stopped work from 7 to 23 August 1848. They were members of the Locomotive Steam Engine and Firemen's Friendly Society which during the strike met daily at the Railway Tavern. Apart from the basic issue they distrusted McConnell, the locomotive superintendent for the southern division, and contrasted their treatment with what they regarded as the more liberal regime enjoyed by the former GJR locomotive men. They were quickly replaced by men transferred from the northern division, guards, or brought in from elsewhere. Creed denied that the reclassification was intended to reduce wages. The dispute coincided with the half yearly meeting and Glyn also had to intervene when the matter was raised in the House. On both occasions he firmly maintained the company line. In Parliament he said that he was sure members would be anxious to ensure that no surrender should be made by the company to the men in their service. The men's case and their meetings were reported in some detail in the press as were two accidents involving inexperienced substitute drivers. The men lobbied the MPs for Marylebone. Apparently through the offices of Madigan, the permanent way superintendent, some 20 men saw Glyn and they agreed to return to their duties leaving the settlement of their grievances in his hands. Glyn told them they would have no cause to regret the confidence they had placed in him. The resolution to return to work included thanks to Glyn for his kindness. Creed confirmed that their wages would not be prejudiced in any way and their interests in other respects would be fully protected. Glyn despite his kindness, reported to the board in September that no concessions had been made to the engine men. Moreover they had been told that in future they must enter into engagements for 3 months rather than 14 days. A gratuity was then awarded for the sense of good conduct displayed by those who undertook extra duty during the strike.[33] The men seem to have regarded Glyn as the deus ex machina above their battle with management, but only in so far as their concerns were based on misunderstandings was their trust justified. These changes brought results. By the second half of 1849 expenses in the locomotive department had been reduced from £13,019 to £10,743 because 'more duty had been performed in proportion to the wages paid.'[34]

[33] TNA, RAIL 410/20, 15 Jul., 6 Aug., 9 Sept. 1848. *The Times*, 8, 14, 15, and 23 Aug. 1848. Bagwell, 31–32.

[34] Bagwell, 33.

At the end of 1850 there was another dispute when Trevithick, locomotive superintendent of the northern division, lengthened the requirement for notice for future employees, allegedly to make industrial action more difficult. The men petitioned Glyn, but Earle, chairman of the northern Locomotive Committee, told them it was not intended to apply to men then in the service of the company and would not involve any reduction in wages: the intention was to obviate a sudden stoppage of the line with consequent disruption to commercial and postal services.[35] The temperature rose when the men at Camden threatened to take action to support their colleagues in the North. This led to reports in the press and editorials in *The Times* which argued that the company's stance was fully justified. The pitmen of the North or the Manchester cotton spinners might turn out tomorrow without any danger to human life and stocks of calico and coal would suffice until order was restored, but certainty of communication was essential and the public were perfectly willing to pay for this through wages. It was thought that there were a large number of engine drivers currently out of employment who would be willing to work. A deputation saw Glyn and wanted him to mediate in the North with the threat that they would support their colleagues there. The company responded firmly. Each man on going to get his wages at Camden station saw McConnell and Edward Watkin (the assistant secretary), was given a copy of a warning and asked to sign immediately. Almost all refused. Next day notice was given to about six men and the men quickly dropped their support for the northerners.

Treatment of company officers was rather different. In 1850 the twenty senior executive officers met to consider a voluntary surrender of a percentage of their salaries in consequence of the depressed state of railway property. The reductions initially proposed ranged from one per cent on salaries of £100 to ten per cent on salaries above £1,000, but the offer was limited to salaries of £200 or more. However a week later the board turned down the offer, though they were according to Dockray much pleased with the spirit shown, but refused to accept it as they did not consider the staff overpaid.[36]

The single board and general manager did not mean that the LNWR started as a highly centralised organisation. Of the officials only Huish had company-wide responsibilities. There were separate secretaries, Creed and Henry Booth, and superintendents, locomotive superintendents and goods managers for the Southern and Northern divisions corresponding

[35] TNA, RAIL 410/221, 13 Dec. and 410/20, 14 Dec. 1850.

[36] TNA, RAIL 410/20, 16 Dec. 1848, 15 Apr. 1849, RAIL 410/21, 9 Mar. 1850. M. Robbins, ed., Dockray's Diary, *Journal of Transport History*, vii, 1965, 3 (11 Mar. 1850).

to the two main constituent companies with the MBR forming part of the northern division.[37] However giving freedom to the divisions based on the old companies did not always work. In March 1847 Glyn was surprised that an advertisement for a loan had appeared without the sanction of the main board, and he concluded that to control systematically the financial condition of the company a joint finance committee was needed to superintend the receipts and expenditure of the three divisions. Such a committee was accordingly created.

In September 1848 Creed retired from the secretaryship and was made a director. Glyn was anxious to bring in a successor from outside the company and consulted Sir Charles Trevelyan, then assistant secretary at the Treasury. He recommended Charles Stewart. The son of a collector of customs at Falmouth, Stewart had run away to sea and became the owner of a ship trading in opium between Hong Kong and Shanghai. He then became Financial Secretary and Treasurer to Sir Henry Pottinger's expedition to China.[38] Stewart was to display some of the qualities of his life in the East, not always to the advantage of the reputation of the LNWR. When some members of Parliament sought an injunction to prevent trees being taken down in Haydon Square, as the goods station there was being extended, he went to the Square and the trees were cut down while the case was being heard. He was also personally involved in the fracas at Wolverhampton in December 1851 when the line was blocked by a derailed locomotive and the rails taken up to prevent access by the SBR to the Stour Valley line.

The LNWR's structure was complex and formed when there was little precedent for an organisation which had daily operations over a wide part of the country. Apart from the central board to which the company-wide committees reported, there were local committees concerned with some aspect of the work of a division or in many cases with a subsidiary company. In 1852 there were ten national committees chaired by different directors – Locomotive; Road and Traffic; Works, Construction and Estate; Audit; Rates and Taxes; Capital Expenditure; Finance; Stores; Church and Schools; and Parliamentary, as well as the Special Affairs which dealt largely with relations with other companies.[39] Although by then there were

[37] With the opening of the Leeds and Dewsbury line a north-eastern division was formed for locomotive and goods purposes in 1849.

[38] G. Royde Smith, *Old Euston*, 1938, 61–63. Stewart was later to become chairman of the Atlantic Telegraph Company.

[39] TNA, RAIL 410/1267. Ledsam chaired both the Works, Construction and Estate, and the Church and School, Committees though the latter was hardly a burden. Glyn chaired Special Affairs.

30 directors to draw on, Benson[40] was on seven committees and Tootal, Edward Cropper and Lyon were each members of a significant number. There were also many ad hoc committees, some set up to negotiate with other companies with an official, often Huish, supporting them. The London-based committees normally met on the Thursday afternoon and Friday preceding the Saturday when the monthly meeting of the board was held – Board Week as it was known to the staff, who spent most of the week preparing for these meetings. Dockray called this an intermittent management 'and wondered how such a concern as a railway went on at all under such a state of things. It could only be because it could not stop'.[41] This seems to be a much exaggerated view and he was no doubt implicitly emphasising the role of the full-time professional staff in contrast to the amateur part-time directors, but the system did enable board members, most of whom had substantial commercial or other relevant experience, to be involved in the effective management of the company. Officers had their own hierarchy but there was much joint working and while supervision was effected principally by the committees and the board, no doubt the influence of Huish and other officials was strong especially when they were working with only one or two directors. Nevertheless directors were not ciphers and this was especially true of Glyn, though he had considerable faith in the officers. He told a shareholder in 1848 who had urged the appointment of directors who could give their whole time to management that he little knew the great anxiety and trouble connected with the vast undertaking. It had grown with the years. It had become a machine which it was almost impossible for any set of men to manage without assiduous attention. Because 'the directors are not giving their whole time to it, does he suppose that therefore the affairs of the railway are neglected. What is our staff for? I would rather have a paid officer doing duty at the head of the establishment than an unpaid director, even if they gave the whole of their time to the concern.' The railway happened to have some of the most competent railway officers which were ever collected.[42]

The structure proved to be sound and was emulated by other companies. As Terry Gourvish has pointed out the management of the LNWR in its heyday in the later nineteenth century differed only in a reorganisation of

[40] Robert Benson junior. His father, also Robert, was a partner in the Liverpool merchant house, Cropper Benson and a director of the LMR. Robert junior succeeded his father as a director and after a period in textiles established Robert Benson & Co, bankers, in London in 1852. He married Moorsom's daughter Eleanor.

[41] Robbins, Dockray's Diary, 2 (8 Jan. 1850). Dockray was a cousin of Benson's.

[42] TNA, RAIL 1110/269, 18 Feb. 1848.

committees, an increase in divisions and the creation of officers' meetings from the system in Glyn's time.[43]

One reason why the system worked was because of the position of general manager who was expected to report to the board on the general working of the line. Huish's reports also covered the work of the committees, many of which he personally attended and he often formed a link between them. This mode of operation put Huish in a powerful position and made it difficult for the board to resist his recommendations. Nevertheless he operated in close consultation with the board and as Gourvish put it in his study of Huish 'we must not follow other writers in underestimating the role of the company's successive chairmen, especially Glyn and Chandos, and of other prominent directors.'[44] Huish, however, had his critics in the company from an early stage. Dockray in 1850 drew a parallel with Bury, who had just resigned, whom he thought did not act sufficiently upon general principles to enlist the sympathy of a large section of those by whose assistance alone can any management be successful and thought that Huish would fall in the same way – when the pinch comes he would find everybody ready to give him a kick, to rejoice in his failure and displacement. Some years after Glyn's chairmanship these failings were a factor leading to his dismissal.[45]

Although the first meeting of a joint LBR and GJR board had taken place on 18 December 1845 in anticipation of the merger, both boards continued to meet separately though after the passage of the Act in July 1846 as permanent local committees. This was done for two reasons. First the Board of Trade had concerns about an over-powerful company. They considered that the companies had sufficient identification of interest to be allowed to amalgamate, but it did not follow that an entire and permanent fusion was absolutely necessary to allow them to effect all they desired. At the very first meeting of the combined boards it was agreed that the proceedings of the local boards would be interfered with as little as possible.[46] Glyn said it would be irrational, rash and unwise to move too hastily in adjusting the system. Later he stressed that it was a prudent and just step that the great interests at Liverpool, Manchester and elsewhere should retain their local committees.[47]

Members of both the main board and the local boards thus had considerable experience on the boards of the constituent companies, some having served since their companies started. There were six from the GJR: Charles

43 Gourvish, *Huish*, 113.

44 Ibid, 165.

45 Robbins, Dockray's Diary, *JTH*, vii, 1965, 111.

46 TNA, RAIL 410/20, 13 Dec. 1845.

47 TNA, RAIL 1110/269, 7 Aug. 1846 and 16 Feb. 1849.

Lawrence, of Wavertree Hall, where he entertained Peel on his visit to Liverpool in 1847, a West India merchant and Mayor of Liverpool in 1825, who was the first chairman of the LMR; William Rotheram, another Liverpool merchant, had been on the first board of the LMR; Hardman Earle, broker and seed crusher of Liverpool had been a director of both the LMR and GJR; Joseph Hornby, a Liverpool merchant also involved in insurance and slate quarrying, who had been on the board of the GJR since it was authorised; George Grant, John Gladstone's partner since 1812 and a director of the GJR despite Gladstone regarding his directorship as an unwarranted breach of the articles of partnership, and prohibiting him from engaging in other business without his consent; and Lewin Mozley, a Liverpool banker in Barned & Co.[48] Edward Cropper and Ledsam, like Glyn, had been on the LBR board from the start. The others from the LBR were Moorsom, one of the first secretaries of the LBR, Thomas Smith, Thomas Young, George Anson, and John Lewis Prevost. The three from the MBR all became prominent on the LNWR board – Joshua Porter Westhead, Robert Benson Jnr and Richard Barrow. The other member was George Loch, the Duke of Sutherland's representative as he was on the LMR latterly on the GJR board.

In the years following the Railway Mania it became increasingly untenable to think of railway directors as fly-by-night characters bent on making quick profits. Indeed from the outset this was hardly the case with the major companies outside Hudson's orbit. Hudson was a man of humble origins who created a large empire by reckless and corrupt means, and was regarded in the satirical press as the archetypical railway director, though he was an exception.[49] Geoffrey Channon has shown that in the period 1836–55 the directors of the GWR whose social origins are known were from the landed classes, higher professionals and big business, and were occupied in land and agriculture, commerce and finance, and the professions and administration. Denison, chairman of the GNR 1847–64, was the son of a baronet, Laing was a Cambridge educated lawyer who became chairman of the London and Brighton. The LNWR board was similarly constituted, though only Anson was from the landed class, but Loch represented a duke and Glyn was the son of baronet who was a significant landowner. However there were seven merchants and four manufacturers, with three bankers, one naval officer and the unclassifiable Tom Young.[50]

[48] S.G. Checkland, *The Gladstones, A Family Biography, 1764–1851*, 1971, 60, 179 and 327.

[49] James Taylor, Business in Pictures: Representations of Railway Enterprise in the Satirical Press in Britain, 1845–1870, *Past and Present*, 189, 2005, 120–121, 126.

[50] As will be seen from the descriptions of individual members of the board several were both merchants and manufacturers (Barrow, Earle and Hornby) so the classification is to

In 1848 or early 1849 Tom Young penned some verses entitled *The Board*, a poem dedicated without permission to the 'Shareholders of the L&NW Rly by their Obedient Humble Servant, The Author' which sheds light on the characters of Glyn and his fellow board members. Four more verses were added in 1849 by H E (Hardman Earle) so all eighteen members of the original main board are mentioned.[51]

First Glyn, the Chairman, quick of speech,
On any given text can preach,
Lawrence, the vice, next in the van,
'A fine Old English Gentleman'.

Tom Smith, who in himself comprised,
All that good and great and wise is,
And though strange fancies oft has uttered,
He knows which side his bread is buttered.

Ledsam, though silent as a door,
Like the Welshman's parrot thinks the more.
Then there's the wavering Prevost
Who loves to vote both yes and no.

Anson who makes, not writes, a book,
And Loch who represents the Duke
Both ornamental in their way,
But less disposed to work than play.

Barrow from Stavely (not Odillon),[52]
And Mozley who glories in a million
Whose eloquence is nothing but
A Steam Engine to crack a nut.

some extent arbitrary. Geoffrey Channon, *Railways in Britain and the United States, 1830–1840*, 2001, 178–186, especially Tables 8.1 and 8.4.

51 TNA, RAIL 1057/3335, Lord Wolverton, 'biographical material probably collected at time of his death' mostly obituaries. The Ms has not survived. The text is in typescript and seems to have been typed in the 1920s.

52 Richard Barrow retired as a London overseas merchant in 1840 and bought the Staveley Coal and Iron Co. in which his elder brother was involved. He was a director of the MBR and then of the LNWR until 1861. 'Not Odillon' is a topical reference to Odillon Barrot, who from December 1848 to October 1849 was the Prime Minister of France in the Second Republic under Louis Napoleon.

Then there's Tom Young, who's called also
For brevity TY HO,[53]
George Grant, the chief of all the Grants
With pockets filled he nothing wants
But for his native mountain pants.
Tom Young Home Office

There's Cropper too, who having made
His fortune has retired from Trade,
And Benson, who with honest zeal
(Though somewhat fierce) the public weal
Pursues, or sits he for the nonce
In ten Committees all at once.

Rotheram, a pecker in Finance,
Who never throws away a chance.
There's Moorsom, Captain in the Navy,
And Hornby, a dealer in Polldavey;
(A sort of canvas this, thats sent em
From their factory at Bentham.)

And then there's Westhead, Knaresborough's pride,
A new M.P.,[54] and there's beside
One Earle, a draft from the Grand Junction,
A hardman he without compunction,
Of whom least said is soonest mended,
And now my list and poem is ended.
H.E. 1849

The other directors from the constituent companies were local directors which enabled them serve in various capacities. The board contained a

[53] It is not clear why Young describes himself as HO in the verse and Home Office at the end, since in 1848–49 he was Receiver General at the Post Office. Possibly PO was misread by whoever typed the verses. In court in 1848 a letter was produced signed with the initials TY HO and Young was asked what they meant (*The Times*, 7 Oct.1848). Young may have been teased about this by members of the board and so included it in the verse, but it is odd that he put Home Office as his address.

[54] Joshua Brown-Westhead, Manchester textile manufacturer, director of the MBR and of LNWR until 1850. Elected Liberal MP for Knaresborough 1847. Returned to LNWR board 1861 and deputy chairman 1861–72.

number of members of Parliament. Glyn himself was elected MP for Kendal in 1847. Of the directors in the early 1850s Ross Mangles of the Bengal civil service, who in 1847 became a director of the East India Company and later its chairman, was Liberal MP for Guildford, James Heywood, whose brothers ran the Manchester bank, was MP for North Lancashire, while Sir Charles Douglas was a Peelite Conservative who later became a Liberal, and John Ellis, a farmer before he became involved in coal, lime and corn and the Leicester and Swannington Railway, was Liberal MP for Leicester. He was also on the Midland board and had succeeded George Hudson as chairman in May 1849. The army officers, General Anson and Captain Carnegie were also MPs.

In 1850 Glyn proposed that the proprietors should appoint a committee to confer with the board on the most suitable persons to fill these directorships. Dockray commented that he hoped this would have the effect of confirming Glyn's influence over the proprietors, an influence which he observed had always been used most disinterestedly, often in restraining them from plunging into crude schemes.[55] The committee thought that the existing directors, deprived of the local committees would be wholly inadequate to the performance of the duties devolving on the members. Glyn himself regretted that the Amalgamation Act did not allow the system to go on until the old committeemen would have ceased to hold office and so agreed to the proposal from the committee that the board should be thirty strong. He did not believe that a smaller number would be able to properly and efficiently carry on the business.[56]

The powers of the committees were surprisingly wide and sometimes limited what today would seem to be as executive prerogatives. In April 1847 the board concluded that as a general rule appointments and dismissals of porters and subordinate officers should rest with the committee and not with the superintendent.[57] In June 1852 it was agreed that every third vacancy should be filled by the chairman and deputy chairman from a list of applicants to be kept for that purpose. A subcommittee of the Traffic Committee was to work out the system of allotments.[58]

The part Glyn played in the affairs of the LNWR was a wide-ranging one despite his formal position as a non-executive chairman. That he was directly involved with so many issues means that the role of the General Manager should not be exaggerated. Much of the high-level representation

55 TNA, RAIL 1110/269, 22 Feb. 1850; Robbins, Dockray's Diary, II, 113 (23 Feb. 1850).

56 TNA, RAIL 1110/269, 21 Feb. 1851.

57 TNA, RAIL 410/20, 10 Apr. 1847.

58 TNA, RAIL 410/22, 12 Jun. 1852.

work fell to Glyn. He met other company chairmen head to head. He came to an agreement with Ricardo, the chairman of the NSR about their traffic over LNWR rails to avoid a hostile petition against amalgamation. He undertook negotiations with Pickfords and Chaplins when the changes in the company's carrying policy were being carried through. He went with two northern directors to discuss the proposed Runcorn Bridge with the Duke of Bridgewater.[59] He could act within areas of a committee's remit. In 1851 Huish told the Rates and Traffic Committee that Glyn himself had authorised a travel concession.[60] In the autumn of 1846 he had several discussions with Russell over the gauge question and other matters, and the following year he was asked to take charge of discussions with Lord Redesdale about the Railway Commission and matters relating to the gauge question on the Birmingham and Oxford line with the help of Carter and Swift, the two solicitors. He entered into an agreement for the purchase of the Priory at Warwick and the adjacent land but financial constraints led to the extension to Warwick being abandoned and one landowner had to be paid £5,000 to release the company from the contract.[61]

Glyn was on the board of the Buckinghamshire Railway, which was controlled by the LBR, and took a close interest in relations with the duke of Buckingham. When the LNWR planned to cross his estates, Smith the Duke's agent, sent in a claim for £25,000, saying that 'unless the entire interests are compensated I do not think the duke of Buckingham's support can be fairly anticipated or relied on'. Glyn replied to the Duke 'I shall undertake the claim made by your Grace's steward, in consideration of the powerful, friendly and active support which the undertaking has received from Your Grace; it should be arranged by Your Grace and me, not to be known beyond us.' Glyn did not often attend the Buckinghamshire board but was present at several meetings in 1850 when there was a dispute over the site of the proposed station at Buckingham. He told the board that he considered the company bound in honour to provide a passenger station at the Cross Keys if the Duke insisted and he would not be a party to any deviation.[62] Peel's family wished to have Peel's hearse to be placed upon a truck and conveyed to Tamworth on a mail train. Officials told them it was not the usual practice and passengers would object to travelling on the same

[59] TNA, RAIL 410/20, 14 Apr., 13 Jun., 10 Oct. 1846.

[60] TNA, RAIL 410/145, 11 Jul. 1851.

[61] TNA, RAIL 410/20, 14 Nov. 1846, 10 Jul., 9 Oct. 1847.

[62] F.B. Heath, The Grenvilles in the nineteenth century: the emergence of commercial affiliations, *Huntingdon Library Quarterly*, XXV, 1961–62, 44–45; TNA, RAIL 86/3, 10 May 1849.

train. Huish referred the matter to Glyn with the result that the family's wishes were met.[63]

The board was not reluctant to look at organisational problems. In 1850 Glyn headed a committee to consider the arrangements necessary and best calculated to ensure the efficient performance, with due regard to economy, of the ordinary legal business of the company.[64] Glyn's view was not always upheld. In February 1851 he objected to a proposal from a group of directors that only four of the six board members retiring each year should be eligible for re-election, but the half yearly meeting in February 1851 upheld the view of the majority of the board.[65]

Glyn himself always had strong views on organisation and just before he retired from the chairmanship he warned the board that at the next meeting he would put a proposal on the expediency of appointing an executive committee. It was then agreed to appoint three members of the Special Affairs Committee to consider together with the chairman and deputy chairman questions of urgency between board meetings.[66]

Glyn and the LNWR, though strongly opposed to government interference with railway's practices took a keen interest in accounting and audit. The requirements relating to audit were still very limited. The Companies Clauses Consolidation Act, 1845 required directors of all companies, including railways, to cause full and true accounts to be kept of money received or expended on behalf of the company and all persons employed by them. The Act also required balance sheets. There were relevant provisions in the Acts of individual companies and some more general provisions as a by-product of legislation for other purposes. Books of passenger receipts had to be kept for the purpose of the Railway Passenger Duty Act of 1842. However there was no provision for independent audit.

There was a lengthy struggle between the railway interest and Parliament over audit. Initially former ministers made the running rather than the Government. It started when Lord Monteagle presented his bill for to provide for the more effectual audit of railway accounts on 20 December 1847.[67] Monteagle, argued that the existing system of audit by persons connected with the governing body must be open to suspicion.

63 *Westmorland Gazette*, 13 Jul. 1850.

64 TNA, RAIL 410/21, 12 Jan. 1850.

65 Ibid, 14 Dec. 1850.

66 TNA, RAIL, 410/22, 12 Jun. and 10 Jul. 1852.

67 Thomas Spring Rice, 1790–1866, created first Baron Monteagle, 1839. Colonial Secretary 1834–35, Chancellor of the Exchequer, 1835–39. Now held the sinecure post of Comptroller of the Exchequer.

Accounts were periodically published which proved to be utterly fallacious. He proposed that on application by a given number of shareholders directors should be compelled to submit their accounts to an inspector appointed by the Railway Commissioners. The Bill passed the Lords without a division and was introduced in the Commons by Sir F.T. Baring, the future Lord Northbrook, Monteagle's successor as Chancellor. Labouchere, the President of the Board of Trade was in favour of the principle of the bill but it attracted only 38 votes while the bill's opponents mustered 100, including Glyn and a number of other railway directors. When Monteagle first put forward his bill Glyn's had deprecated it strongly as Government interference[68] Arthur Smith in *Bubble of the Age* alleged that Glyn meant to resign if the Bill were carried.[69] Glyn, who had not spoken on second reading, not only denied that but said that the bill had been lost not so much through the railway interest as by the independent majority who agreed that the Bill was taking out of the hands of the proprietors the power that legitimately belonged to them. It was not that the directors objected to investigation of their accounts – but they did object to the Government having the control while they had all the responsibility.[70]

Notwithstanding their opposition to Government interference the LNWR was one of the more advanced companies in matters of accounting and audit. The LBR had been a pioneer in the field of railway accounting. It introduced a balance sheet in August 1840. By 1845 it was still the only company so to do.[71] Some further steps was forced on them. Because of the erroneous statements and calculations which had appeared in newspapers regarding the current and prospective financial position of the LNWR, in October 1848 the directors caused a detailed account of the engagements and liabilities to be sent to shareholders and the press. The aim was to show that when all the share capital was called up, probably in 1852, provided weekly income had increased from £42,194 to £48,725 the company would still be able to pay 7 per cent on its shares.[72] The statement set out the

[68] TNA, RAIL 1110/269, 18 Feb., 16 Aug. 1848.

[69] Arthur Smith, *Bubble of the Age, or the Fallacies of Railway Investments, Railway Accounts, and Railway Dividends,* 1848, 60.

[70] TNA, RAIL 1110/269, 16 Aug. 1848.

[71] S. McCartney and A.J. Arnold, Financial reporting in the context of crisis: reconsidering the impact of the 'mania' on early railway accounting, *The European Accounting Review,* 11, 2002, 411.

[72] *Morning Chronicle,* 28 Oct. 1848 published the table which was amended by Stewart's letter of 28 Oct. published on 30 Oct. In December *Fraser's Magazine* (38, 1848, 714–715) welcomed circumstantial accounts of other railway companies following the LNWR's example.

capital received from stocks and shares and debentures for the main line and branches with the totals expended, and the sums required to complete the works with expenditure on stock listed separately. Branch lines being built were listed as were subsidiary lines, with capital contribution, and the amount guaranteed. This set the standard for other companies. Indeed Ellis the chairman of the Midland in 1849, regretted that they had not been able to give shareholders a more lucid statement of the accounts. It had been their intention to have rendered as complete an account as the LNWR's which 'I regard as a model for all companies'.[73]

The critics were far from silenced. In November 1848 John Whitehead, a member of the Stock Exchange, published a letter to Glyn in which he stated that the LNWR was hiding the facts from shareholders and in particular the abandonment of the tolls system with its carriers had resulted in great losses, which were being met from the profits of the passenger traffic.[74] The new system had encouraged ruinous canal competition and goods rates should be doubled which would mean that unprofitable traffic would transfer to canal or sea. Whitehead received much publicity. His demand for detailed analyses of profit and loss on each description of traffic was unrealistic and his attempt to prove losses by comparing the respective earning capacities of a passenger carriage and a goods truck was far-fetched. The *Morning Herald* and particularly the *Morning Chronicle* defended the LNWR, with articles – especially those in the *Chronicle*, clearly written after close personal contact with Huish. The charge soon became one of making a loss on goods traffic. Huish set out his answer in a pamphlet: *A Letter to George Carr Glyn on some points of Railway Management.* His arguments were generally convincing: he exposed the fallacy of doubling the rates to increase receipts and stressed the need for high volume low profit traffic such as coal, but he over-emphasised his case and claimed too much. Contrary to his statements the LNWR had reduced rates though this did not prove financial losses. *The Times* commented that the calculations and statements of Mr Huish were clearly given and his pamphlet was not undisfigured by that taunting tone which characterises railway discussions and renders allusions to them at all times disagreeable.[75] This meant Whitehead wrote two more letters to Glyn on which comment appeared in the press, but Huish did not publish another refutation. Some of Whitehead's criticism was valid and the charge that the company was conducting goods traffic at a loss led to steps to measure the costs attributable to that sector.

[73] Quoted in McCartney and Arnold, 413.

[74] J. Whitehead, *Railway Management, A Letter to George Carr Glyn Esq., Chairman of the London and North Western Railway,* 1848.

[75] *The Times,* 30 Nov. 1848.

However Whitehead's criticisms did not mean that the confidence of the City was lost. Commenting on the company's report for the second half of 1848 the *Bankers' Magazine* said that the shareholder in the LNWR possessed by far the soundest and best property of the kind in the country, while warning of further capital expenditure and competition. Two months later in a note on Glyn it said he had filled the arduous duty of his office with great ability. The poof of the confidence reposed in his direction lay in the fact that, while shareholders of all the other important lines exhibit anxiety on the subject of the capital accounts, the LNWR had escaped every suspicion of mismanagement and it was firmly believed that the dividends had been fairly earned.[76]

The discussion of audit continued. In 1849 Monteagle secured a select committee of the House of Lords which concluded that there was no adequate means of enforcing the prohibition on the payment of dividends out of capital as required by the 1845 Act, nor of confining the spending of capital to the purposes set out in the Act. They drew attention to the want of uniformity of railway companies accounts and recommended standard formats. They also recommended the establishment of a reserve or depreciation fund, and more controversially that one of the two auditors for each company should be appointed by the Railway Commissioners. However they did not mention the conceptual basis that companies should adopt in preparing those accounts.

Monteagle brought in a bill based on his committee's recommendations. Rushed through the Lords late in the session, it received a first reading in the Commons on 9 July, but the railway companies bypassed further parliamentary debate. On 17 July the LNWR held a special meeting of proprietors. Glyn took the chair, a somewhat ambivalent role as he said it was not for him as a director to make any observations but proceeded to make clear his opposition as a proprietor. He then read out the powers in the LNWR Act on the appointment and duties of auditors and claimed that if other companies had availed themselves of the large powers given to them their property would be in a much better position and much of the present confusion and want of confidence in the accounts would have been avoided. Only Richard Dean, a barrister, did not oppose the Bill outright, seeking instead amendments to the detail. This attracted only one supporter and Dean was told by Glyn that he would have been surprised had any commercial man taken that line.

The railway companies then went direct to the Prime Minister, Lord John Russell, who told the deputation, including Glyn, that if the railway

[76] *Bankers' Magazine*, Mar. and May 1849, 162 and 252–253.

1 Sir Richard Carr Glyn by Colin Gill

2 Pascoe Grenfell by Samuel Cousins, after Sir Martin Shee

3 Richard Plumtre Glyn by an unknown artist

(courtesy of the Royal Bank of Scotland)

4 Sir Charles Mills

(© Royal Bank of Scotland)

5 Gaunts, as rebuilt in 1809
(courtesy of Dorset History Centre)

6 St Kenelm Church,
Hinton Parva
(© Kim Parker, Dorset OPC)

7 St Andrews Church,
Fontmell Magna
(courtesy of David Bailey, Dovecote Press)

8 St Katharine's Dock, progress of works, January 1828
(© Museum of London)

9 The opening of St Katharine's Dock, 25 October 1828
(© Museum of London)

Drawn by T. H. Shepherd.

Pl 70.

ST. EDMOND THE KING, LOMBARD STREET.

10 Lombard Street by T.H. Shpeherd, 1829

(author's collection)

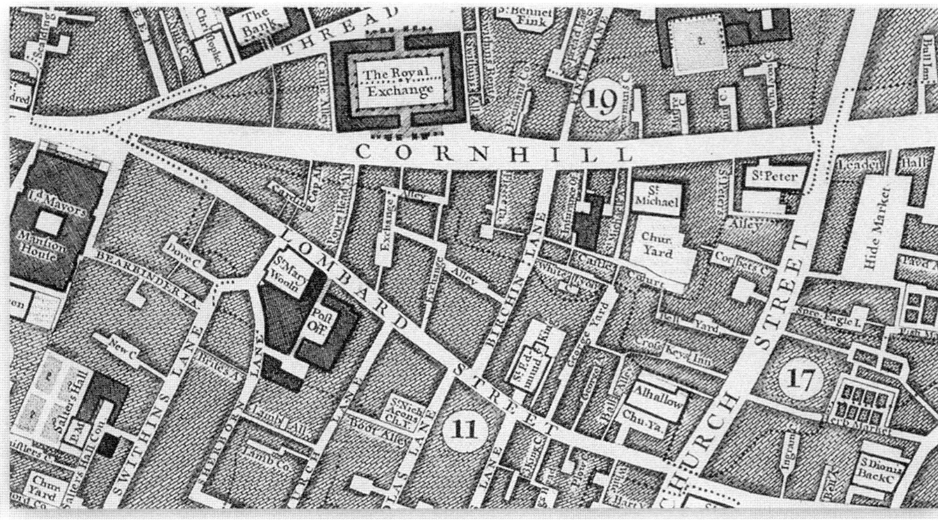

11 The City in 1747 just before the foundation of Glyn's (section of Roque's Map, the numbers refer to the City wards – 11 Langbourne, 17 Bridge Within, 19 Cornhill)

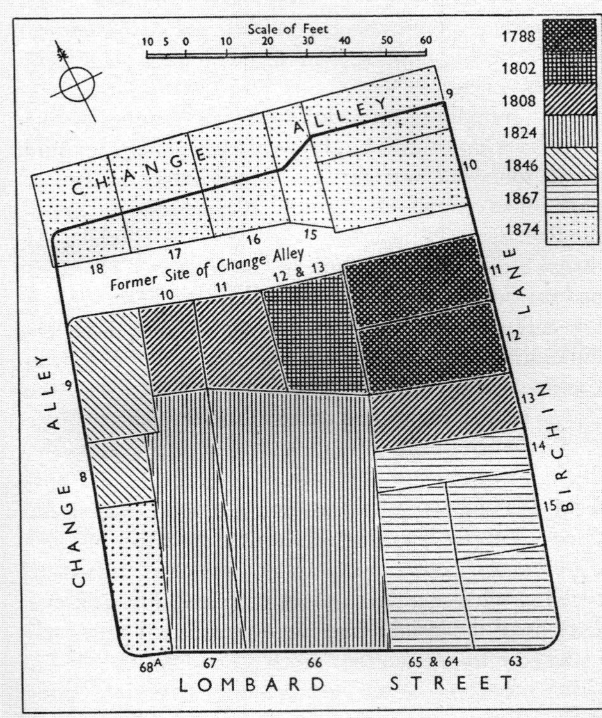

PLAN OF SITE OF NO. 67 LOMBARD STREET

Showing the dates of the acquisition of the various properties within the island site, bounded by Lombard Street to the south, Birchin Lane to the east and Change Alley to the north and west

Note.—Nos. 11, 12 and 13 Birchin Lane were relinquished in 1824. Nos. 11 and 12 were repurchased in 1857 and No. 13 in 1867

12 Plan of Glyn's site at 67 Lombard Street, showing the stages of development

(reproduced from Roger Fulford, *Glyn's*)

13 Bankers Clearing House
(courtesy of the British Newspaper Library)

14 Garroway's Coffee House
(Thornbury's Old and New London, 1897)

Extracts from Glyn's Bank notebook concerning the accounts and debentures of various railway companies

(© Royal Bank of Scotland)

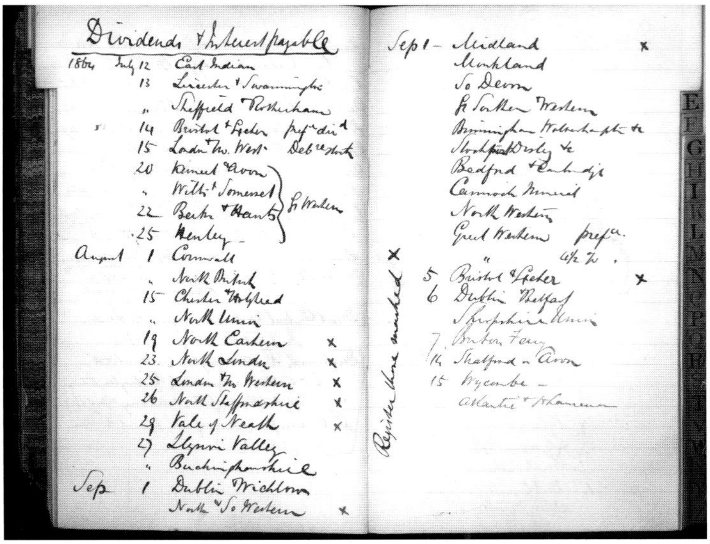

Dividends & Interest payable

1864 July 12 East Indian
13 Leicester & Swannington
" Sheffield & Rotherham
14 Bristol & Exeter pref. div.
15 London & N. West Deb. stock
20 Kennet & Avon
" Wilts & Somerset } Gt Western
22 Berks & Hants
25 Henley
August 1 Cornwall
" North British
15 Chester & Holyhead
" North Union
19 North Eastern x
23 North London x
25 London & N. Western x
26 North Staffordshire x
29 Vale of Neath x
27 Llynvi Valley
" Buckinghamshire
Sep 1 Dublin Wicklow
North & So Western x

Register those marked x

Sep 1 – Midland x
Monkland
So Devon
Gt [illegible] Western
Birmingham Wolverhampton &c
Stockport Disley &c
Bedford & Cambridge
Cannock Mineral
North Western
Great Western pref. 4½ %
5 Bristol & Exeter x
6 Dublin Belfast
Shropshire Union
7 Burton Ferry
14 Stratford on Avon
15 Wycombe –
[illegible]

15 Companies for which dividends and interest payable 12 July to 15 September 1864

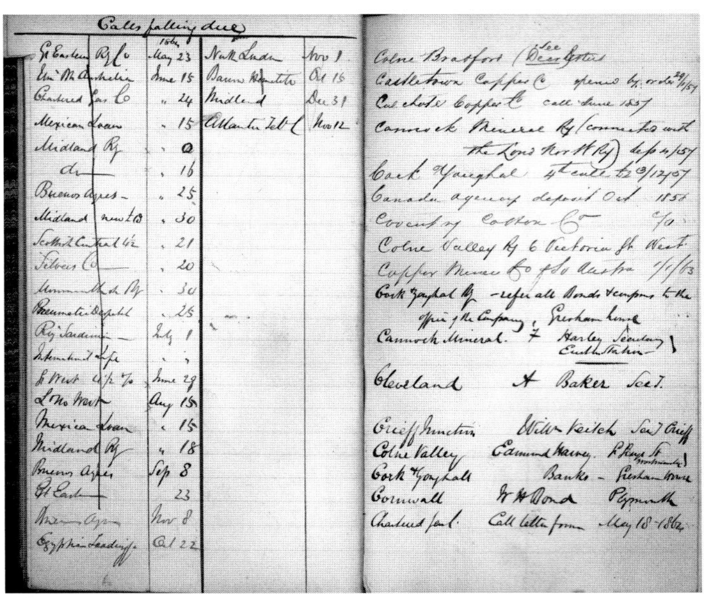

Calls falling due

Gt Eastern Ry Co	1864 May 23	North London	Nov 1
[illegible]	June 15	[illegible]	Oct 16
Chartered Gas Co	" 24	Midland	Dec 31
Mexican Loan	" 15	Atlantic Tel Co	Nov 12
Midland Ry	" [illegible]		
do	" 16		
Buenos Ayres	" 25		
Midland new £10	" 30		
Scottish Central 4½	" 21		
Silvers Co	" 20		
Monmouthshire Ry	" 30		
Pneumatic Despatch	" 25		
Ry Sardinia	July 1		
International Life	"		
Gt West 4½ %	June 29		
L & N West	Aug 15		
Mexican Loan	" 15		
Midland Ry	" 18		
Buenos Ayres	Sep 8		
Gt Eastern	23		
Buenos Ayres	Nov 8		
Egyptian Trading	Oct 22		

Colne Bradford (see Letters)
Castletown Copper Co opened by order 29/1/57
[illegible] Copper Co call June 1857
Cannock Mineral Ry (connected with the Lond Nor W Ry) Sept 4/57
Cork & Youghal 4th call £2 3/12/57
Canada agency deposit Oct 1856
Coventry Cotton Co [illegible]
Colne Valley Ry & Victoria Gt West
Copper Mines Co of So Australia 1/1/63
Cork Youghal Ry – refer all Bonds & coupons to the office of the Company, Gresham House
Cannock Mineral. 7 Harley Secretary Euston Station
Cleveland A Baker Secy.
Crieff Junction Wm Keith Secy Crieff
Colne Valley Edmund Harvey [illegible]
Cork & Youghall Banks – Gresham House
Cornwall W H Bond Plymouth
Chartered Gas Call letter from May 18 1862

16 Calls falling due, May to Decemeber 1864 and list of companies with contacts

Two bank notes issued by country banks for which Glyn's was the London agent

(© Royal Bank of Scotland)

17 Batson, Berry & Co, Tweed Bank, Berwick £5 note

18 Cyfartha and Hirwain Bank £5 note

19 Entrance Front of the London Station by C.F. Cheffens, 1837
(The *Mirror*, 8 April 1837, published before the works were completed)

20 Euston Station by J.T. Bury, 1837
(© City of London Corporation)

21 View taken from under the Hampstead Road Bridge, looking towards the station at Euston Square, by T.T. Bury, 1837.

(© City of London Corporation)

22 The shaft for shooting the earth over the mouth of Primrose Hill Tunnel looking across the site of the future South Hampstead station to Loudoun Road and Kilburn Priory bridges. Hampstead, 11 August 1837, by R.B. Schnebbelie, 1837

(© Camden Local Studies and Archives Centre)

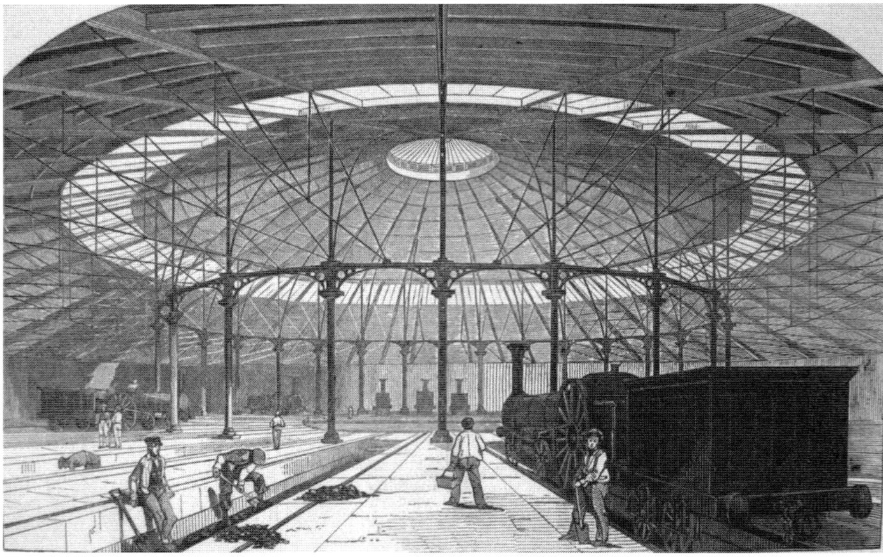

23 Interior of the new great circular engine-house at the Camden Town depot of the North Western Railway, 1847

(author's collection)

24 Interior of Pickford's Parcel depot, Camden Town, London, c. 1860

(© Science and Society Picture Library)

25 Curzon Street, Birmingham, by John C. Bourne
(author's collection)

26 Ackermann Prospect of 1847: entrance to the London and Birmingham Railway
(reproduced with the permission of the Library of Birmingham)

27 Oil painting of steam train passing near Leighton Buzzard 1837 by Thomas Cresswick

(© Senate House Library, University of London)

28 Early engraving of Wolverton viaduct
showing a wooden Haversham Bridge
(courtesy of Wolverton Past)

29 Coventry Station
(© British Library)

30 Robert Stephenson by John Lucas
(courtesy of The Literary and Philosophical Society of Newcastle upon Tyne)

31 Richard Creed by Edward McInnes after Henry Wyndham Philips
(© National Portrait Gallery, London)

32 Wolverton, the Little Houses and Wolverton works with Glyn Square, Young Street and Ledsam Street indicated shortly before demolition in 1960
(courtesy of Brian Dunleavy, Wolverton Past)

33 Stanmore Park
(courtesy of the Stanmore Tourist Board)

Stations	DOWN TRAINS. Derby to Leeds.								Sundays		
Departure from	Miles.	1 Mail.	2	3	4	5	6	7	8 Mail.	9	10
		P. M.	A. M.	A. M.	A. M.	A. M.	A. M.	A. M.	P. M.	A. M.	A. M.
LONDON	...	9. 0	...	...	6. 0	9.15	...	11. 0	9. 0	...	8. 0
		A. M.				P. M.		P. M.	A. M.		
BIRMINGHAM	...	12.40	...	7. 0	10.30	1.15	...	3.45	12.40	...	...
		A. M.	A. M.	A. M.	P. M.	P. M.	P. M.	P. M.	A. M.	A. M.	P. M.
DERBY	0	3.19	...	9.15	12.45	3.45	4. 0	6. 0	3.19	7. 0	3. 0
Arrival at											
DUFFIELD	5¼	...	...	9.29	...	...	4.14	...	...	7.14	3.14
BELPER	7¼	...	...	9.37	1. 4	...	4.22	6.19	...	7.22	3.22
AMBERGATE (For Matlock, Buxton, &c.)	10½	...	...	9.47	...	...	4.32	6.29	...	7.32	3,32
WINGFIELD (For Alfreton.)	14	...	...	9.58	...	...	4.43	6.40	...	7.43	3.43
STRETTON	17¾	...	...	10. 9	...	...	4.54	...	...	7.54	3.54
CLAY CROSS	20	...	...	10.16	...	...	5. 1	...	...	8. 1	4. 1
CHESTERFIELD	24	4.12	...	10.26	1.40	4.37	5.11	7. 3	4 12	8.11	4.11
STAVELEY	27¾	...	...	10.37	...	...	5.22	...	...	8.22	4.22
ECKINGTON (For Worksop, Newark, &c.)	30¼	...	...	10.44	1.55	...	5.29	7.18	...	8.29	4.29
KILLAMARSH	32¼	...	...	10.50	...	...	5.35	...	...	8.35	4.35
BEIGHTON	34	...	...	10.56	...	...	5.41	...	...	8.41	4 41
WOODHOUSE MILL	35¼	...	...	11. 2	...	...	5.47	7.33	...	8.47	4.47
TREETON	36¾	...	...	11. 8	...	...	5.53	...	...	8.53	4.53
MASBRO (For Rotherham & Sheffield.)	40	4.43	8. 3	11.18	2.12	5.10	6. 3	7.44	4.43	9. 3	5. 3
SHEFFIELD	45	5. 0	..	11.45	2.45	5.30	6.30	8.15	5. 0	9.45	5.30
Ditto Departure from	45	...	7.35	10.45	2. 0	4.50	5.30	7.30	...	8.45	4.45
KILNHURST	43¾	...	8.19	11.34	...	...	6.19	...	...	9.19	5.19
SWINTON (For Doncaster.)	45	...	8.25	11.40	...	5.29	6.25	8. 3	...	9.25	5.25
WATH	47	...	8.32	11.47	...	...	6·32	...	...	9.32	5.32
DARFIELD	49¼	...	8.40	11.55	...	...	6.40	8.15	...	9.40	5.40
BARNSLEY	53	5.16	8.51	12. 6	2.48	5.48	6.51	8.26	5.16	9.51	5,51
ROYSTON & NOTTON	56¼	...	9. 2	12.17	...	...	7. 2	...	...	10. 2	6. 2
OAKENSHAW (For Wakefield.)	60	5.35	9.12	12.27	...	...	7.12	8 45	5.35	10.12	6.12
NORMANTON (For Manchester, York, &c.)	63¼	5.44	9.23	12.38	3.14	6.14	7.23	8.56	5,44	10.23	6,23
METHLEY	66¼	...	9.42	12.57	...	...	7.42	...	...	10.42	6.42
WOODLESFORD	68	...	9.48	1. 3	...	...	7.48	9.18	...	10.48	6.48
LEEDS	72¾	6.19	10.15	1.30	4. 0	7. 0	8.15	9.45	6.19	11.15	7.15
		A.M.	A. M.	P. M.	P. M.	P. M.	P. M.	P. M.	A. M.	A. M.	P. M.
MANCHESTER	113	8.30	11.45	0	6.35	8.45	10. 0	...	...	1. 1	9.30
YORK	87	6.40	11. 0	2. 0	4.45	7.45	...	...	6.40	12. 0	8. 0
HULL	111	8.36	12.30	3.40	6.45	9.10	...	...	8.36	3·45	9. 0
DARLINGTON	132	9.20	1.45	5.15	7. 0	...	...	...	9.20	...	...

34 North Midland Timetable for Down Trains showing connections from London and Birmingham at Derby and to Manchester (via Manchester and Leeds Railway), York and Darlington (via the York and North Midland and the Great North of England at Leeds) 1 May 1842

(author's collection)

35 Grand Trunk Railway, snow plough Saint Agapit, Quebec, 1869
(courtesy of Toronto Public Library)

36 Grand Trunk Railway advertisement, 1857
(courtesy of Toronto Public Library)

37 Grand Trunk Railway, 'Trevithic' no. 209, old type of wood burning locomotive, c. 1860
(courtesy of Toronto Public Library)

38 The Victoria Bridge over the St Lawrence construction – the first train across, 17 December 1859
(courtesy of Toronto Public Library)

39 The Victoria Bridge in winter
(courtesy of Toronto Public Library)

40 Alexander Galt
(coutesy of Library and Archives Canada)

41 Thomas Ridout
(courtesy of Toronto Public Library)

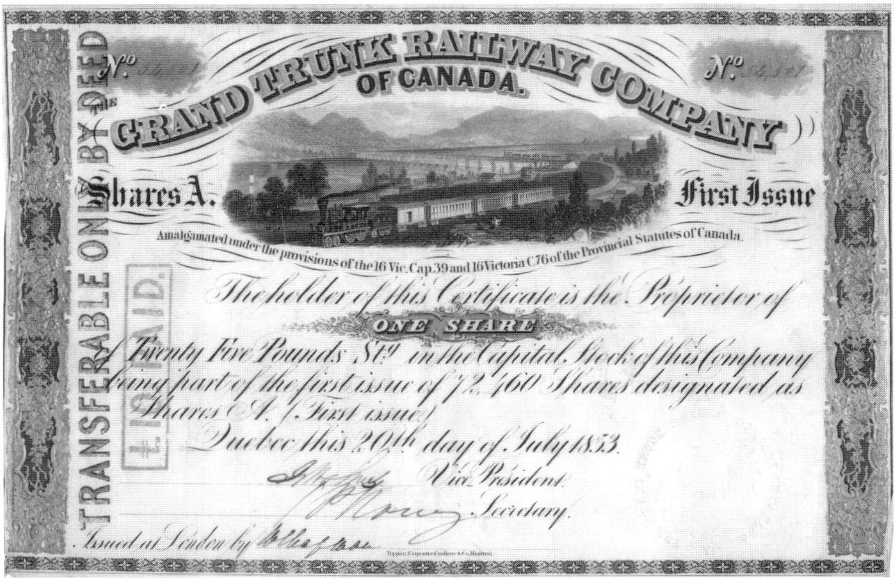

TRANSFERABLE ONLY BY DEED

THE GRAND TRUNK RAILWAY COMPANY OF CANADA.

Shares A. First Issue

Amalgamated under the provisions of the 16 Vic. Cap. 39 and 16 Victoria C. 76 of the Provincial Statutes of Canada.

The holder of this Certificate is the Proprietor of

ONE SHARE

of Twenty Five Pounds St.g in the Capital Stock of this Company being part of the first issue of 72,460 Shares designated as Shares A. (First issue)

Quebec this 20th day of July 1853.

Vice President.

Secretary.

Issued at London by

£ 10 PAID.

42 Grand Trunk of Canada share certificate
(© Royal Bank of Scotland)

43 John Moss
by an unknown artist
(courtesy of Liverpool
Public Library)

44 George Carr Glyn
by A. Wyvil
(*Bankers Magazine*)

45 Charles Russell
by an unknown artist
(courtesy of Steam, Museum of the Great Western Railway)

46 George Hudson
by Sir Francis Grant
(© National Portrait Gallery, London)

47 Joseph Langton
(courtesy of Barclays Archives)

48 Bank of Liverpool, Water Street, Liverpool
(courtesy of Barclays Archives)

49 Thomas Tooke,
by an unknown artist

50 Bertram Currie
by an unknown artist
(© Royal Bank of Scotland)

51 William Newmarch
(courtesy of Royal Statistical Soctety)

52 Thomas Baring
by an unknown artist
(courtesy of the National Trust,
Hughenden Manor)

53 Constantine Moorsom
by an unknown artist

54 Mark Huish,
General Manager of
the London and North
Western Railway
(*Illustrated London News*)

55 Marquis of Chandos
(later 3rd Duke of Buckingham)
Chairman of the LNWR
(Sir Charles Lawson, *Memories of Madras*)

56 George Carr Glyn
by Sir Francis Grant
(National Railway Museum)

57 George Grenfell Glyn
(© Royal Bank of Scotland)

58 His wife Georgiana Tufnell
by Robert Thorburn
(courtesy of National Museum
Stockholm)

59 St Leger Glyn by Camille Silvy
(© National Portrait Gallery, London)

60 Pascoe Glyn
(© Royal Bank of Scotland)

companies were prepared to take the measure of additional audit into their own hands he was not the man to bring railway companies under the control of Government for that purpose.[77] The bill was therefore withdrawn on the understanding that the railway companies would introduce a Bill into Parliament in the next session. Glyn at the half yearly meeting in August was much exercised by the imputations made against accountants chosen by railway companies as auditors: they were not the mere tools of the company.[78]

The LNWR then consulted shareholders. Gladstone apparently wrote to Glyn about the outcome as Glyn in his letter of 17 December said he did not agree with Gladstone's view. He said more replies had been received than from any previous circular to shareholders and they manifested a confirmed determination against any government interference. Only 12 per cent were for the Government. He added that he was proposing an Audit Bill which he hoped would carry the general feelings of others.[79] A committee of LNWR shareholders reported to the half-yearly meeting in February 1850 and submitted a draft bill containing some proposals for improvement of audit but emphasised the need for auditors and accountants to be independent of directors and shareholders. Glyn did not comment on the details of the bill but wanted room to negotiate with other companies. The ensuing consultations led to continued opposition against any interference by Government but no consensus on a measure that would meet their wishes.

In the next Session of Parliament there was some confusion as two bills were put forward, but in 1851 Joseph Locke, the engineer who was now Liberal MP for Honiton, was asked by the railway companies to bring forward a bill. Labouchere did not oppose the Bill, but made it clear that the audit of railway accounts should be founded on some principle beyond the railway companies. Audit should not necessarily by Government, but Locke's Bill did not give shareholders any better protection than they already had. Glyn, the only railway representative to speak at that stage, supported the Bill but thought some changes should be made. Later in Committee he opposed an amendment to require auditors to examine and refer if necessary to a competent person all sums paid to engineers. Edward Ellice argued that the exorbitant sums extracted for professional services had been greater than fraud. Glyn objected that this was an interference with the common discretionary power of the directors. He thought that the Bill as a whole would work well for railway companies which encouraged Labouchere to say that though the bill did not go as far as he would have liked it could be welcomed

77 TNA, RAIL 1110/269, 16 Aug. 1849.

78 Ibid.

79 BL, Add Ms 44368, Glyn to Gladstone, 17 Dec. 1849.

as an improvement. However E.B. Denison and Packe, the former the son of the current chairman and the latter a future chairman of the Great Northern wanted the bill to be rejected much to the annoyance of Locke who acting for the shareholders now found directors against him. Glyn expressed surprise at the stance taken by Denison and others and defended the line taken by Locke, as did Peto, but Packe and Denison persisted and effectively killed the Bill.

This was the end of more than a decade of attempts to impose audit by statute. Standard accounts had to await the Regulation of Railways Act, 1868. The LNWR took its own steps to improve matters. The committee of proprietors established the previous year to look into the question of legislation had appointed a professional auditor, J.E. Coleman, and now became a standing audit committee, a step Locke applauded as the adoption of the principle in his bill. Coleman who had been employed by the Bank of England and other public bodies told the proprietors the arrangements were so perfect and systematic that he had no hesitation in recommending their continuance.[80]

Glyn took the lead in many Parliamentary matters. In March 1847 he and Hudson saw the Chancellor of the Exchequer about Edward Strutt's Railway Bill. This had been proposed when the Commisioners of Railways (Strutt was their president) were set up in 1846 and merely extended the Commissioners powers somewhat, largely to make reports on railway bills. The Government withdrew the Bill pleading lack of time but the underlying reason was the opposition of the railway interest. Nine of the leading companies formed a committee which organised extensive lobbying.[81] In 1848 the board took the view that the report of the Royal Commission on the gauge question contained numerous errors and an unfair view of the capabilities of the narrow gauge and performance on the LNWR.[82] The LNWR and other companies successfully urged the Government to incorporate in the Criminal Prosecution Bill a clause enabling those who attempted to throw trains off the line to be sentenced to transportation for life.[83]

[80] TNA, RAIL 1110/260, report of 15 Feb. presented to the half-yearly meeting on 22 Feb. 1850. Gladstone however was somewhat critical of Coleman's work elsewhere, though Glyn, while making clear that he had been appointed by the auditor, Abel Payton, defended him, saying too much had been expected of him, as his work was based mainly on the figures. 'A sound mercantile man would have caught more than the best accountant.' BL, Add Ms 44368, Glyn to Gladstone, 22 Dec. 1849.

[81] TNA, RAIL 410/20, 6 Mar. 1847; Henry Parris, *Government and the Railways in Nineteenth Century Britain,* 1965, 125–126.

[82] Ibid, 10 Jun. 1848.

[83] TNA, RAIL 410/21, 10 May 1851.

One government measure on which Glyn was specifically consulted was the Act to facilitate the dissolution of railway companies which enabled companies incorporated in the Mania to go into voluntary liquidation. Dalhousie explained to Peel that he had seen Glyn and found him fully satisfied of the advantage of the measure 'which you propose'. Glyn told Dalhousie that his ideas coincided very much with the scheme, but pointed to the difficulty of restricting the right of voting to holders of stock purchased by a certain day, because of lack of effective proof of the date of purchase. Somewhat surprisingly in view of earlier contacts between Peel and Glyn, Dalhousie had to reassure the Prime Minister 'Glyn is a gentleman and I am sure will give us safe information and good sense.'[84]

The British Electric Telegraph Company Bill sought power to carry their lines beside any railway. This was presented as an attempt to establish a national system of telegraphic communication and would override the wishes of individual railway companies, some of whom were refusing access. Glyn said he was very much in favour of telegraphic communication, lines for which already existed on the principal lines of railway, but opposed the bill on the ground that compulsory powers were being conferred on the telegraph company which could lead to conflicts with the railways. Although it was given a second reading in the Commons, it did not succeed in the Lords.'.[85]

The early mainline railway companies had to establish ways of allowing for depreciation, and as described in Chapter 7 the LBR had been a pioneer. Glyn was fully behind the moves which first the LBR and then the LNWR made. Indeed he drew a parallel with the practice which life assurance offices employed to meet the contingent liabilities on a life policy.[86] The LNWR on formation did not make an allowance for depreciation, but did so in 1847 for both rails and stock. Glyn told shareholders in February 1848 that composed of mercantile men the board had thought from the first that the question was of serious import and would press upon all railways, however much in their first years they might overlook its effects. He gave as an example when new rails of greater weight were purchased the cost of the original rails was charged to revenue and the cost of the increased weight (ie the improvement) was charged to capital. Replacement engines would be charged to revenue and additional engines to work on new lines would be charged to capital.[87] However when Huish was asked to look its

[84] BL, Add Ms 40589, Dalhousie to Peel, 9 Apr. 1846.

[85] PD, 119, 961–7, 12 Mar. 1852.

[86] TNA, RAIL 1110/269, 13 Aug. 1849.

[87] TNA, RAIL 1110/269, 18 Feb. 1848.

application to rolling stock he had doubts about this procedure, especially in the absence of data and any acknowledged principles of ascertaining the annual cost of deterioration. He concluded that it was wrong to set up a fund for rolling stock as in practice it was not reducing in value and its effective value was maintained in the workshops. He had grasped the modern conception of valuing plant in relation to its earning capacity.[88] In a further report he recommended that the sum set aside for the deterioration of the permanent way should be increased, as unlike rolling stock it deteriorated slowly and evenly and so could produce a sudden cost burden. The calculations were reviewed in 1853. It was found that by then rails were more costly but better able to cope with heavier loads and locomotives, and positive additions to the track's capability should be charged to capital but making good wear and tear were to be charged to revenue.[89]

Glyn continued as chairman of the Railway Clearing House, the membership of which widened considerably. In October 1848 19 companies were represented at the RCH Committee and nearly 30 in March 1849. In September 1847, not only was the Earl of Yarborough, chairman of the MSLR, present under Glyn's chairmanship but so was a gentleman simply recorded as the Rt Hon the Lord Mayor of York (Hudson). Morison was appointed full-time manager of the RCH at a salary of £800. Receipts for through traffic in 1847 amounted to £583,202. Successful though the clearing house was, the financial panic of 1847 meant that the organisation needed a legal rather than a voluntary basis and Glyn proposed a Deed of Association to enable action to be taken against those member companies who defaulted on their obligations. The deed was prepared but members concluded that statutory powers were advisable and the outcome was the Railway Clearing Act of 1850.

The Act meant the actions of the Clearing House were constricted by statute instead of by what the companies voluntarily agreed. This was shown two years later when Chaplin, now a director of the LSWR, proposed that the RCH committee should try to persuade Parliament to abolish the Passenger Duty on all fares under a penny a mile. Glyn, objected to the motion as not within the limits to which the Committee should be confined. He thought the Committee would act wisely by rigorously limiting themselves to those functions. The Committee backed Glyn and the RCH accepted its more limited role, though by then receipts for through traffic amounted to £3,391,958. The question was pursued by a separate group, the forerunner of the Railway Companies Association, to which in future political matters

[88] Gourvish, *Huish*, 143.

[89] Huish's reports are at TNA, ZLIB, 15/1/19 and RAIL 410/7/19/4.

were left. In 1855 when some members wished the RCH to persuade railway companies to adopt a standard form of accounts. Glyn ruled that this too was 'beyond the province of the Clearing House'. While Morison was secretary clerks were recruited on the recommendation of companies. From 1842–49 75 of the 142 clerks were recommended by Glyn. Later it was alleged in the press that preference in new appointments had been given to men from Kendal, Glyn's constituency.

As on the LBR Glyn continued to steer between the strict Sabbatarians and those who wanted people to be able to travel on Sundays. In February 1849 a shareholder moved that no LNWR trains should run on the Lord's Day except where required by Act of Parliament, or in cases of necessity. He believed such trains were unremunerative, though his main objection was the need for the company to set an example to others, as they had with the provision of churches and schools. Glyn replied that every proprietor had the right to express his conscientious opinion. He did not think that providing churches and schools was much to boast about, and in fact the Sunday trains were well filled. Glyn reminded the meeting of the resolution of the LBR in 1838, the policy still followed. He added that he had then ascertained the opinions of some of the most distinguished members of the church and the dissenting community and they were decidedly in favour of providing some accommodation to the public on Sundays.[90] The board later received a complaint that there was no train from London to the North on Sundays between the 10 am, which was inconveniently heavy, and about 9 pm. The Traffic Committee recommended that in view of the probable increase of traffic during the summer and the want of accommodation for 'passengers from foreign countries or elsewhere' an afternoon train should be put on from London to Liverpool and Manchester which they thought within the scope of the general meeting's resolution. The vote was tied 11:11 but was carried on Glyn's casting vote.[91]

In February 1847 Glyn outlined the company's policy on schools. The money for the existing schools came from subscriptions, not grants from the company. In fact the directors individually had borne most of the burden. However his personal view was that property has its duties as well as its advantages, but this applied to the proprietors as well as to the directors and he sought their agreement to providing it.[92] Glyn then commissioned Watkin to produce a report on the schools in the localities where the company's workers lived, and the company later gave small grants to schools from the

[90] TNA, RAIL 1110/269, 16 Feb. 1849.

[91] TNA, RAIL 410/21, 10 May 1851.

[92] TNA, RAIL 1110/269, 18 Feb. 1847.

fund established from the profits of Sunday travel. The company turned down requests for contributions to a new chapel and a Roman Catholic church at Crewe, but were prepared to approve a school at Longsight as well as those already existing in Crewe and Wolverton.[93]

[93] TNA, RAIL 410/20, 9 Aug. and 9 Sept.1848; RAIL 410/22, 15 May 1852. Watkin's report is at RAIL 1008/109.

CHAPTER THIRTEEN

The London and North Western – Expansion, Monopoly and Competition

THE AMALGAMATION solved a number of problems which had beset Glyn's LBR. Awkwardnesses over the interface with the GJR were removed at least at the company level, particularly as the TVR became an integral part of the new company. Instead of debating with Moss, Glyn could help meet Peel's wishes on the siting of a new approach road to Tamworth station in his constituency where Peel had consulted the mayor and was anxious to promote the general welfare of the town. The railway had not taken powers to purchase the land necessary, but the mayor assured Peel that two of the landowners concerned were members of the Town Council and the third was also willing to sell. Peel also wrote to the Postmaster General, Lord St Germans, about siting a post office sorting office at Tamworth, as it was at the intersection of two important railway lines. Glyn and Tootal, the chairman of the still independent TVR, were willing to assist, but the Post Office decided against this proposal for, as Glyn told Peel, the existing sorting office in Birmingham and the Travelling Post Office sufficed.[1]

Fears that the GJR might come south in conjunction with the GWR and concerns that the LBR might penetrate GJR territory were removed but the GJR's part in supporting the Oxford and Rugby ensured that the earlier rivalry with the GWR continued and this was exacerbated by

[1] BL, Add Ms 40591, Peel to the Mayor, 1 May, Mayor to Peel, 6 and 18 May, Peel to Glyn, 7 May, Peel to Lord St Germans, 7 May, Glyn to Peel, 14 May and 24 Jun. 1846, Tootal to Peel, 26 May. Peel told St Germans 'I have no other wish that is such an establishment be made the place shall be that which will be the most conducive to the convenience of the public and the interests of the public service.' The comparative advantages of the sites including those of Tamworth should be duly weighed.

the gauge war. A Royal Commission was appointed in 1845 to enquire whether in future Acts of Parliament for railway construction a uniform gauge ought to be specified, whether means could be adopted of bringing existing railways into uniformity or whether there were other ways of obviating the difficulties of break of gauge. The Commission took evidence from Stephenson and others, and concluded that all railways constructed in Great Britain, including those already under way, should have a gauge of 4 ft 8½ in. and if this was adopted some equitable arrangement be found for producing uniformity. The Board of Trade was less decisive. The Act allowed the South Wales and the adjacent Monmouth and Hereford railways to be laid with the broad gauge as provided in their Acts and broad gauge railways already sanctioned south of the London to Bristol main line to be constructed on that basis. While the Act stated that no railway should be constructed except on the narrow gauge it stipulated that any railway constructed under a present or future act could contain a special provision defining the gauge of such railway.

The BOJR which the GJR had backed, and which local parties, particularly traders in the Birmingham area, saw as necessary to give access to London independent of the LBR, had not been abandoned, though in view of the success of the Oxford and Rugby in the 1845 Session, it was now to join that line at Fenny Compton. In December 1845 the LNWR decided to oppose it, unless some satisfactory compromise could be reached. Protracted negotiations took place, and Carter thought a satisfactory arrangement had been made with Brunel but unexpectedly the GWR had rejected it. The LNWR, mainly to counter the BOJR, had put forward proposals for lines under two subsidiary companies – the Buckinghamshire and the Warwickshire and London, to create a nexus of lines in those counties. The latter included a line from Worcester to Weedon similar to the LWSSR proposal lost in 1845, but it failed to command Parliamentary support in 1846 and only the Oxford to Bletchley section of the ambitious Buckinghamshire project was accepted. On the other hand the BOJR Bill succeeded, mainly because it would supply healthy competition to the LNWR. Moreover the Act included a power to lease or sell the line to the GWR.

In November 1846 Glyn asked his colleagues if they were satisfied with the position reached or whether they should apply to Parliament in 1847 to amend that position. Russell had written about improvements to Leamington station which gave Glyn an opening for a discussion of mutual interests. He was already thinking of a bid for the BOJR as he told colleagues that he understood the GWR had offered 8 per cent to the BOJR and also to the Birmingham and Dudley. Thus any LNWR offer had to be nearer 10 per cent. Russell replied that he was weary of war but the GWR had to be allowed to carry out the plans it had openly professed. He believed any discussion should be confined to a definite point while Glyn thought that it would be better to discuss a broad and general arrangement on the basis that the gauges question was settled by Parliament. Opinion among LNWR board members diverged considerably. They agreed that the most desirable result would be a friendly arrangement with the GWR based on the status quo on gauges, but if this was not possible, Glyn was given discretion to offer a lease to BOJR with a payment equal to the LNWR's dividend.[2]

Glyn had several discussions with Russell, but the subsequent talks between Swift and Saunders did not get far, as Saunders insisted on the broad gauge on the Birmingham and Wolverhampton and Dudley, linked to the BOJR. Soon the BOJR itself took a more hostile stance when they told Glyn that the interests of trade and of the public called for the exclusion of the LNWR's influence in any second line northward from London.[3] The LNWR received petitions from shareholders in the BOJR, particularly in Lancashire, dissatisfied with the terms offered by the GWR and arguing that the LNWR had the same interest as the GJR in providing continuous communication between Lancashire, Oxford and the South. Glyn told them that the LNWR would be prepared to negotiate a joint lease with the GWR which would give the public the advantage of the lower rates fixed by the LNWR's amalgamation Act. Russell refused to meet Glyn as if the LNWR could convince the shareholders of the BOJR and subsequently Parliament to rescind the agreement with the GWR, the GWR would submit.[4]

Despite the fact that the GWR had signed an agreement to buy the BOJR, the LNWR began to encourage directors and shareholders to buy its shares. This was raised in a debate in the Lords by Lords Ripon and Lyndhurst. It was asked whether a declared intention of Parliament could be overturned by the free market in shares. Ripon presented a petition from the BOJR and BWDR complaining that the LNWR had collusively purchased shares in the BOJR thereby defeating the object which Parliament had in view when they authorised the GWR to purchase the BOJR. This line was taken strongly by Lord Lyndhurst who alleged the LNWR had bought £38,000 of the £50,000 shares, distributed them, and then called a meeting to add to the number of directors. The BOJR had then refused to complete the sale to the GWR. The duke of Buckingham doubted whether the House should interfere with the matter. The shares were bought and sold on the

2 TNA, RAIL 410/20, 4 Nov. 1846.

3 Ibid, 14 Nov. 1846 and 7 Jan. 1847.

4 TNA, RAIL 39/208, Glyn to Russell, 2 Dec., enclosing his reply to the memorialists, and Russel's reply, 3 Dec. 1846.

open market, a line taken by Earl St Germans speaking for the LNWR directors, supported by Lord Stanley. The company only wanted joint use. Lyndhurst argued that if the LNWR were admitted then 'all ideas of competition would be futile.' Hatherton claimed that the iron masters of the Midlands were threatened by Scottish and Welsh competition. To admit the LNWR would destroy competition as the LNWR would send slow goods trains by this route and impede the GWR's traffic.[5] The House agreed to set up a committee, but it never met as the LNWR board decided to refer the question of the legality of the sale of the BOJR to the GWR to the Lord Chancellor but judgment was given against them with costs, and the GWR obtained an injunction from the Court of Chancery to compel the BOJR to carry out their agreement, and to restrain LNWR interference.

Before this case was heard Henry Crosfield raised the matter at the proprietors meeting in August 1847 and said that as the courts had decided that there was nothing illegal in the practice of buying shares he would encourage those who had not done so to secure an interest in the BOJR. He praised Mozley for his efforts in this. Glyn who had not commented in his chairman's report then said it was not for him 'in this room' to say a word about the BOJR line. The LNWR had not been involved in its corporate capacity, though despite this denial it is hard to see that the purchases would have taken place without the goodwill of the board even if there was no explicit encouragement. Glyn added that the company had made an offer to use it as a second line to Birmingham without interfering with the GWR's rights. They wanted joint tenure of the line.[6] Nevertheless Glyn later paid tribute to his colleagues who had incurred liabilities that must have been voluntarily undertaken.[7] Although the GWR successfully introduced a Bill to give them power to lay the broad gauge on the BOJR, the LNWR did succeed in obtaining running powers between Banbury and Birmingham, though they were never used.

There was also rivalry with the GWR in adjacent areas. In the 1846 Session the GWR backed the Cheltenham and Oxford planned to join the OWWR at Shipton, but the Bill was withdrawn following difficulties over the estimates. A rival narrow gauge scheme was defeated. The schemes were expected to be revived and LNWR decided that it should be involved. They

[5] PD, 97, 15–16, 16 Mar. 1847.

[6] TNA, RAIL 1110/269, 13 Aug. 1847. Henry Crosfield, a food importer and grocery wholesaler in Liverpool. A substantial shareholder and for many years one of the auditors of the LNWR.

[7] TNA, RAIL 1110/269, 21 Feb. 1851. Although not argued in the Lords, the LNWR would probably have purchased the shares from the individual directors.

quickly worked out a possible arrangement which would mean a guarantee of 4½ per cent on a quarter of the capital of £1,200,000, and the line was to run, not just from Cheltenham to Oxford, via Northleach and Witney, but continue via Aylesbury to Tring. The board was by no means unanimous. Boothby in particular took an unfavourable view, and it was agreed that they should not take any decided and prominent part in the undertaking. However in January 1847 the LNWR gave the requested declaration of support to the local company. The Bill however was lost, while the GWR Bill was passed on condition that narrow gauge rails should be added if subsequently required by the Railway Commissioners. Shortage of capital meant that construction of this line was never started. The LNWR did not again attempt to reach Cheltenham. Indeed Glyn went so far as to tell shareholders that it was not a line the loss of which he very much regretted. Huish was instructed to compete for the London and Cheltenham traffic even though the opening of the Bristol–Gloucester line gave a better connection at Bristol than the Birmingham route.

Glyn's position on the undesirability of competition had been strengthened rather than weakened by the events of 1845 and 1846. As chairman of the LNWR Glyn held consistently to his view that competition was inadvisable and at times came near to prophesying disaster as a result of its introduction. If Parliament had exercised a wise discretion they would have acted on the doctrine laid down by the Board of Trade and would have encouraged by proper regulation the completion of the existing system of railways rather than have promoted the dangerous and, he believed, futile doctrine of railway competition. He had taken this line in evidence to the Select Committee on Railway Acts in 1846. By August 1847 he was arguing that the reduction in rates required by the Amalgamation Act had already resulted in an effect similar to competition. Further competition would involve two companies competing for the same amount of traffic from one point, and so force directors to reduce fares to the lowest possible point and require two establishments to be kept up kept up, two capitals employed and only one 'receipt' to be divided on those two capitals. The proprietors in search of greater returns would force their directors to reduce their establishments, servants would be discharged and machinery not kept up and he asked what would become of public safety. This in turn might mean that those who had hitherto been willing to serve as directors would no longer do so.[8]

In February 1848 he said if Parliament continued to encourage the doctrine of competition he would consider railway property as an uncertain

[8] TNA, RAIL 1160/269, 7 Aug. 1846 and 13 Aug. 1847.

and inconvenient tenure which no man would desire his family or widow would hold. But if they could return to the system so strongly recommended by Lord Dalhousie, if instead of trying to destroy each others interest, railway companies could be brought to unite, Parliament would impose on all railways a proper system of fares and charges so as to secure the public welfare and give the existing interests the protection for the money they have laid out, this and other old existing lines railways would continue to be a safe and sound investment.[9]

This was against the background of falling dividends. By the late summer of 1848 the LNWR had experienced three consecutive half years when the dividend had fallen; there were also considerable reductions in dividends of other companies.

Annual rate of dividends 1846 to first half of 1848

	1st half 1846	*2nd half 1846*	*1st half 1847*	*2nd half 1847*	*1st half 1848*
LNWR	10	10	9	8	7
GWR	8	8	7	7	7
LSWR	7.5	8.5	7.5	8	6

The LNWR shares had dropped from 202 in September 1846 to 120 in July 1848. The GWR's had not fallen so much (146 to 95), but the LSWR had fallen from the equivalent of 180[10] to 92. It was these three companies which were the parties in a proposed major amalgamation.

Early in September 1848 Glyn, Russell of the GWR and Chaplin of the LSWR embarked on a series of discussions. They explained this was because of the unprecedented demand for additional capital for the simultaneous construction of many new lines not immediately or imperatively required; the prejudicial effect of this demand on the commercial and manufacturing interests, and the resulting serious depletion of investments in railways. They wanted to adopt for the sake of both the public and the proprietors some immediate and effective measure for counteracting such results. Later that month Glyn explained to Sir James Graham[11] that the reaction to the excitement of 1845 and 1846 had been most complete and its results most

[9] Ibid, 18 Feb. 1848.

[10] LSWR shares were not then fully paid up.

[11] Sir James Graham, Home Secretary in Peel's administration, but now out of office.

extensive. He had been endeavouring with the GWR and LSWR companies (those, he said, most engaged in contests to redress the follies and legislation of 1845 and 1846) by some mutual pecuniary arrangement for the future by which further outlay for duplicate and unnecessary lines might be avoided but there were great difficulties and many problems.[12]

On 9 September 1848 the LNWR board appointed a committee of Glyn, Mangles (brother to the chairman of the LSWR), Grant, Smith (a director both of the LNWR and LSWR), and Westhead to negotiate with a view to effecting an arrangement by which an entire union of interests between them might be produced and at the same time be of advantage to the public. Many proprietors personally urged Glyn to see whether the end of the dispute over the BOJR afforded an opportunity of getting rid of expensive contests. Liverpool shareholders sent a memorandum to the board urging a similar course. Some commentators saw it as a conspiracy against the travelling public.[13] A meeting was arranged at Glyn's Bank on 22 September. The LSWR board decided that every question in dispute had to be settled before proceeding to Parliament. In October the LNWR team explained to the board where things stood – and urged that if the LSWR withdrew they should proceed with the GWR alone.[14] On 1 November representatives of the three companies agreed it was important to make arrangements for uniting the interests of the three companies to prevent wasteful expenditure in unnecessary schemes or parliamentary contests, while providing a fairly remunerative income for the safety and accommodation of the public through efficient establishments under a well organised system of management. This could best be achieved by creating a permanent and absolute identity of interests among the shareholders of the three companies under the sanction of the legislature. Meanwhile arrangements should forthwith be made for placing the expenditure of the companies under control and facilitating the use of stations and working of lines in the interests of the public. A board of control should be appointed of seven directors from each company, decisions to be taken by a majority of those present. This board was to have charge of the Bill but if at least five of the directors from any one company objected the matter should be referred to arbitrators.

12 BL, Add Ms 40452, Glyn to Graham, 29 Sept. 1848.

13 'In Mr Glyn's banking house these great dictators of the railway world came together … and swore amity and agreement. They were seeking to arrange their rivalries which had cost them so much treasure to diminish expenses and increase their dividends. It means smashing the traveller or grinding the employed', *Fraser's Magazine*, 38, 1848, 472–473.

14 TNA, RAIL 410/20, 14 Oct. 1848.

No new pecuniary engagements were to be entered into without the agreement of the other two companies (except for the LSWR's extension to Windsor, to which the GWR objected) but existing liabilities could not be overruled. The broad gauge lines already built or sanctioned could be maintained. The companies should be represented equally on the united board. Amalgamation could go ahead between the GWR and LNWR or the GWR and LSWR (but not between the two narrow gauge companies, the LNWR and LSWR) if an amalgamation of the three companies proved not to be possible. General meetings of the three companies were to be called for 13 December to consider the arrangement and to approve the draft Bill. Glyn had earlier explained to Graham that the difficulties had been almost insuperable from jealousies and doubts, but GWR and LSWR, both hitherto stout advocates for competition, had assented to apply to Parliament. He added that this plan might give the opportunity to carry out the view to which Graham had referred of the establishment of a large railway corporation, independent of the government but under sufficient public control.[15]

However Glyn was proved to be too optimistic, and perhaps unrealistic, as the scheme failed both in matters of detail and principle. Jealousy won. The document drew a speedy response from the LSWR which objected to anything which precluded them from reaching Windsor and more broadly to the GWR's condition that questions relating to the broad gauge on future lines should be excluded from the remit of the board of control.[16] The LSWR also objected to the ban on their company amalgamating with the LNWR alone. The GWR and LSWR objected to the clause which prevented new commitments to expenditure being entered into without the consent of the board of control. For its part the LNWR directors when they met on 11 November refused to agree to equality of representation on the board in view of their much larger paid-up capital: £14 million with an annual revenue of over £2 million compared with the GWR's £7 million and £820,000. This was the sticking point as neither the GWR or the LSWR would accept greater representation of the LNWR on the board. The GWR argued that in the absence of equality the union or amalgamation would amount to a sale or transfer of the other undertakings to the LNWR who would exercise the power of exclusive control by virtue of the majority of their representatives, though of course this exaggerated the power of the LNWR as under the initial scheme at least the company would find it hard to get a majority unless one of the other companies sided with it.

15 BL, Add Ms 40452, 26 Oct.1848.

16 TNA, RAIL 411/3, 13 Oct. and 10 Nov. 1848.

But essentially the question of board representation was an argument about power and principle as much as numbers and consequently the LNWR broke off negotiations on 25 November. The proprietors meeting therefore never took place.[17]

Glyn said the rupture involved no ill feeling. He also told shareholders that he thought that in the present state of railway property great advantage must arise not merely from an amalgamation of the three companies but also from a larger one if railway undertakings could be brought together under one head and one management to a greater extent.[18] The *Railway Times* did not doubt that the parties were sincere in their aims, but they were mutually distrustful, too individual, too equally self-willed to continue long to act in the spirit of their resolutions. Identity of interest between these three companies was to be expected only in the railway millennium.'[19]

While the negotiations were still continuing Glyn revealed to Graham how far he would be prepared to go towards a less competitive and more centralised system. Graham had laid it down as a principle that direct government interference and possession of railways were incompatible with the character and feeling of the country. This was very much Glyn's own view. Glyn had told shareholders in 1848 that it was impossible that 'we should condescend to work under government superintendence.' If a proprietor desires that the lines should be a mere government machine 'Let me give him notice to quit'. He added that he would not regret the day that would allow him to sit in his own counting house in more quiet.[20] He suggested to Graham that railway stock would be converted into government guaranteed security on the application of the railway company after a trial of the line for a given period, the price of the government stock being so many years purchase of the average dividend. The government would appoint a director to act in the management of the line during the probation period; when converted into guaranteed stock the proprietors would name two-thirds of the direction and the government one-third. After satisfying from the net earnings the guaranteed dividend the surplus profits would be divided between the government and the proprietors. Glyn said the result of such a plan would be to place every railway in the hands of government by the act of the proprietors as very much the best market for their work under these terms. What was wanted was a concentration and control which would prevent the useless and wasteful outlay of capital.

17 The correspondence was reproduced in *The Times*, 28 Nov. 1848.

18 TNA, RAIL 1110/269, 16 Feb. 1849.

19 *Railway Times*, 2 Dec. 1848.

20 TNA, RAIL 1110/269, 18 Feb. 1848.

However Glyn in practice did not think there was a better plan than to allow a bill to pass to permit amalgamations between companies under certain conditions. Nothing short of amalgamation or a union would prevent the renewal in ensuing times of this folly of competition and consequent expenditure. Graham had also raised the possibility of temporary aid to companies to allow the completion of works which could not be stopped without total loss. Glyn thought this would be sufficiently met by occasional loans though the Exchequer Bill Loans Commissioners. Glyn concluded by emphasising that the expenditure forced upon the LNWR, utterly unprofitable and arising mainly from the caprice of parliament, was several millions but much might still be saved.[21]

Glyn came back to this issue from time to time. When he wrote to Gladstone to thank him for an arbitration (the Six Towns award) he asked whether, having had the question of competition directly and indirectly before him with all its ramifications and effects on the public service and on the returns for investments, he thought there would be a hope of Parliamentary regulation and control allowing the existing companies in particular districts to throw the whole of their receipts for division upon their capital and the arrangements for working under one body and giving them protection against future interference. Without some attempt to arrive at territorial settlement between the competing bodies he feared the evil would continue to increase to the detriment of property, and without any permanent advantages. He added that he was inclined to think that many of the companies are disposed to this view.[22] Nevertheless what Bagehot was to call a 'system of competing monopolies' prevailed.[23]

The failure of the attempts to secure a widely based amalgamation resulted in the LNWR turning to rates agreements and pooling agreements. They have sometimes been seen by historians as the manifestations of the policies of the wicked Huish, the General Manager of the LNWR, trying to preserve the hegemony of the LNWR, rather than a natural development in the economic and financial circumstances in which companies found themselves. After all 'people of the same trade seldom meet together, even for merriment and diversion, but the conversation ends with a conspiracy against the public, or in some contrivance to raise prices.'[24] Nor do the critics

21 BL, Add Ms 40452, letter of 1 Nov. 1848.

22 BL, Add Ms 44370, Glyn to Gladstone, 26 Sept. 1851.

23 *The Economist*, 18 Feb. 1863, reproduced in *The Collected Works of Walter Bagehot*, ed. Norman St John Stevens, X, 1978, 443.

24 Adam Smith, *Inquiry into the Nature and Causes of the Wealth of Nations*, ed. W.B. Todd, 1976, I, x, c, 27.

of the practices of the 1850s usually recognise that such agreements were almost normative behaviour by railway companies until 1948, though work by Channon, Cain and Butterfield has done much to shed light on this rather murky area.[25]

Such agreements had no place in the early mainline railway system as in general lines were not in competition with each other for traffic. The Midland Counties and the BDJR conducted a rates war, but this was speedily ended by their inclusion in the Midland merger. The first pool was probably when the Midland, allied with the Manchester and Leeds, began to compete with the GJR for the Lancashire to London traffic. The three companies arranged a percentage division of the receipts under which the development of business on both the GJR route and the Midland route became the common interest of all three companies.[26] This agreement was maintained for the following years, with the exclusion of the Manchester, Sheffield and Lincolnshire whose line had been opened in November 1845 from all through traffic. In December 1848 Huish reported to the board on his correspondence with Ellis of the Midland, who had appointed a committee to confer with the LNWR. The latter's group included Glyn and in August 1849 he told shareholders that arrangements had been concluded with the Midland for the working of a considerable portion of the traffic. He said it did not amount to an amalgamation, but was 'to use a mercantile expression on joint account'.[27] By October a formal LNWR-Midland joint committee had been established which agreed additionally that goods traffic between the two companies should take the shortest route. In August 1850 the LNWR reached a more formal agreement to end competition in freight rates and fares between London and York, Doncaster, Lincoln, Leeds, Sheffield and Wakefield, but this did not take account of the forthcoming opening of the GNR. In 1849 James Allport had been appointed general manager of the MSLR and not only did that company wish to have a share in the traffic from Lancashire and Yorkshire to the south, other companies such as the North Staffordshire and East Lancashire had opened lines which were important links in through routes and competitors to the existing routes.

[25] Geoffrey Channon, Railways Companies and Pooling in Britain before 1900, in *Railways in Britain and the United States*, 2001, 110–127, and 150–151; P.J. Cain, Railway Combination and Government, 1900–1914, *EcHR*, 25, 1972, 623–641; P. Butterfield, Grouping, Pooling and Competition: the Passenger Policy of the London & North Eastern Railway, *JTH*, 7, 1985, 21–47.

[26] Charles H. Grinling, *The History of the Great Northern Railway*, 1903 edition, 92.

[27] TNA, RAIL 1110/269, 17 Aug. 1849.

In 1846 Glyn to avoid a hostile petition from the newly formed North Staffordshire Railway had agreed with J.L. Ricardo, the chairman,[28] that the NSR should have every reasonable facility for transmission of traffic over LNWR while the LNWR could use the NSR route for their direct Manchester traffic.[29] The NSR opened southwards to Colwich and northwards to Macclesfield in 1849 and claimed that as the successor to the Churnet Valley the LNWR was bound to the agreements made with that line and in particular to allow them a share in the Manchester to Euston traffic. Glyn acted with Huish to resolve the dispute, but there had to be further talks the following year.[30] In 1850 a traffic agreement was negotiated but the NSR raised problems which were only resolved after arbitration.[31]

Meanwhile Ricardo introduced a Railway Traffic bill which while general in application was mainly designed to serve the interests of his own company which he thought was being bypassed by the monopolistic LNWR. He wanted better connections and through coaches. Railways would be required to stop for passengers and trucks at every junction. He also wanted equal rates. He was opposed by Glyn who pointed out that the favourite trains for passengers were the express trains and a train from London to Carlisle might need to make eleven unnecessary stops. Labouchere incurred Gladstone's displeasure for suggesting that the bill might be read a second time and then referred to a select committee, and Ricardo eventually withdrew it.[32] Relationships with the NSR however remained difficult.

However the major challenge to the LNWR was the opening of a second route from the north into the capital. In the late 1840s the Midland was still dependent on the LNWR for entry to London, so traffic from the Midlands, Yorkshire and the Northeast had to use the line from Rugby to Euston. In August 1850 the GNR began services from its temporary station in London and so became the main prospective competitor with the LNWR for traffic to the north, particularly Scotland. Initially however it was not in a good position to compete. The building of its direct line from Peterborough to Retford had been deferred and it relied on the MSLR for the Lincoln to Retford portion of its circuitous route and the York and North Midland for its entry to York, via Knottingley.

[28] MP for Stoke 1841 until his death in 1862. Free Trader and opponent of the Navigation Laws. Chairman of the Electric Telegraph Company 1846–56. A neighbour of Glyn's in Upper Ecclestone Street and a fellow trustee of the Royal Danish Railway.

[29] TNA, RAIL 410/20, 13 Jun. 1846.

[30] TNA, RAIL 410/20, 17 Feb. 1848 and 410/21, 9 Jun. 1849.

[31] TNA, RAIL 1110/269, Directors report to Half-Yearly Meeting, 21 Feb. 1851.

[32] PD, 111, 1066–1081, 1 May 1850.

Initially the LNWR's response was to strengthen the arrangement with the Midland and LYR (formerly the Manchester and Leeds) already known as the Euston Square Confederacy by the inclusion of the MSLR, previously excluded. While the MSLR derived some advantages for its Hull traffic it was specifically excluded from arrangements with the GNR for London to Manchester traffic and from accepting through rates. The agreement was concluded in Manchester in December 1849.[33] While this meant that running of Manchester to Kings Cross trains was ruled out Allport was prepared to accept this as an alternative to the LNWR's previous policy of restriction. The companies shared Manchester London Road station and the ownership of the Manchester, Altrincham and South Junction Railway. Lord Yarborough, the MSLR chairman, said that to repudiate the agreement with the LNWR would cost the company £1,200 from prospective reprisals by the LNWR whereas they would gain only £800 by an amicable agreement with the GNR.[34] The LNWR also had an agreement with the LYR whereby the GNR were excluded from Manchester, Rochdale, Burnley, Todmorden, Halifax, Huddersfield, Bradford to London traffic. In return the LNWR agreed to send traffic for Newcastle and Edinburgh via Normanton.

With the opening of the GNR the search for a wider agreement raised some fundamental issues in the negotiations to avoid 'ruinous competition' as the current phrase had it. A division of territory was impracticable because it would have cut across the powers which companies had been granted by Parliament. Consequently the companies concentrated on what was later known as pooling which had the advantage of making rate-cutting a much less attractive policy. The LNWR and its allies argued that the GNR was entitled to share in that traffic for which it had effective arrangements while the latter asserted its right to a portion of all traffic for which its lines formed part of a reasonably good route. This led to the Octuple agreement which to a considerable extent protected the existing interests of the LNWR and its allies. It covered the eight companies involved in London to Edinburgh traffic on the West Coast route, and the two East Coast routes: the GNR route and the Midland via Rugby, Normanton and York. Traffic was to be divided equally between the West and East coast routes, while the East Coast route was to be divided initially one-third to the GNR route and two thirds to the Midland. However the split was to be 63:37 when the direct line for Peterborough to Retford was opened and goods traffic was to be split 50:50 from the start. Equal rates and fares were to be charged. At the same time the Sextuple Agreement was made dealing with other traffic to Scotland

33 George Dow, *Great Central*, 1, 1959, 144.

34 Grinling, 452.

– to Glasgow and from intermediate places to Edinburgh. The negotiations for these agreements resulted in the attainment of the LNWR's goals. The LNWR was also in alliance with the Edinburgh and Glasgow Railway so that the East Coast route was unable to have through connections to Perth and Aberdeen.

The LNWR and Midland's differed with the GNR over the terms of a separate agreement to cover traffic to Lincoln, Doncaster, Sheffield, Wakefield, Leeds and York and Gladstone was asked to arbitrate on what became known as the Six Towns agreement. He met Glyn, Ellis, and Denison. Glyn reported that Gladstone told them that although he was not justified in deciding anything other than the division of traffic of the six named towns, such a confined reference which did not embrace the general question of a division of territory would be nugatory and futile. If asked he would enlarge the arbitration to cover this, but at the next meeting of the Joint Committee Glyn said that the minutes of the previous meeting exaggerated Gladstone's remarks. He had not directly suggested a division of territory and his award did not venture on to that ground.[35] It marginally favoured the GNR.

The GNR accepted these agreements because the spectre of ruinous competition haunted the railway world, including GNR shareholders, a view strengthened by the competitive reductions in fares to London for the Great Exhibition which had developed before Gladstone delivered his opinion. In August in the middle of the fare reductions, Glyn said the fares charged were ridiculous. It was folly to think it could continue. It must lead to combination, and to a division of the whole territory and district among the companies according to their respective positions.[36] Denison, the GNR chairman, said of the Octuple Agreement 'unless he had put very great value on peace, harmony and quietness, I should not have made such concessions.' He said he did so because he was apprehensive of the consequences of a severe contest.[37] In the event complete price stability was short lived as Huish encouraged re-booking at Normanton, though when the GNR challenged this the dispute was referred to Gladstone who ruled in the GNR's favour.

As we have seen Glyn took the lead in the initial talks with the Midland. While the pooling agreements were the work of Huish in essence and were an extension of his pioneer work with GJR they carried forward Glyn's view that precedence should be given to existing lines and they needed protecting from unfair competition. 'We have always advocated one principle – that competition is not the rule of railway management but it is by connecting

[35] TNA, RAIL 406/3, 2 and 23 Jul. 1851.

[36] TNA, RAIL 1110/269, 15 Aug. 1851.

[37] At the March 1851 proprietors meeting, quoted in Grinling, 99.

the various links together in union and harmonious working for the benefit of all that the public can be efficiently served.' He went on to say that this principle was recognised by the GNR and some other companies with which the LNWR was brought into contact. 'It was that principle which would preserve railway proprietors safe and unscathed, the other way injures to a degree we can scarcely estimate.'[38] Glyn was well aware of what was going on and the idea that he was too busy with his banking activities to restrain Huish is quite incompatible with his wide and often detailed involvement in the LNWR's affairs and his generally shrewd attitude.[39]

These agreements were only able to operate successfully because the Railway Clearing House provided a mechanism which the companies could accept as independent. The agreements stated that the receipts were to be divided in the proportions 'recognised and acted upon in the Clearing House'. The committees of the companies operating the agreements met at the Clearing House where at the first meeting of the Octuple Agreement Committee Morison who was acting as secretary produced examples of the mode of dividing the receipts,' which were approved.[40]

Although the attempt to amalgamate with the GWR in 1848 failed the potential for conflict between the LNWR and GWR had been reduced and there was tacit acceptance that the LNWR and GWR would not set competitive fares where their systems came in to contact.[41] Both were more restricted financially and less willing to take on commitments, but the advent of two ambitious local companies in the area between Birmingham and Chester (the Shrewsbury and Birmingham and the Shrewsbury and Chester) which the LNWR regarded as its own district, but into which the GWR wished to expand, changed the situation and led to extensive and bitter disputes. The SBR had failed to get its bill in both 1844 and 1845, but before the 1846 Session its provisional committee agreed with the LBR that its own line would be confined to the portion between Shrewsbury and Wolverhampton, leaving the extension to Birmingham to be provided by the Birmingham, Wolverhampton and Stour Valley line in which it would have a quarter share with the LBR and others. This was immediately before

38 TNA, RAIL 1110/269, 21 Feb. 1851.

39 'With Glyn immersed in banking affairs Huish wielded for more power than his contemporaries.' Dow, 1, 136. Grinling, 434, took a similar line. As pointed out above Huish had to work with a powerful and able board. His power outside the company rested on the dominant position of his company in the market as well as on his personal abilities. Moreover other railway chairmen were not full-time.

40 Bagwell, 251–252.

41 M.C. Reed, *The London & North Western Railway*, 1996, 53.

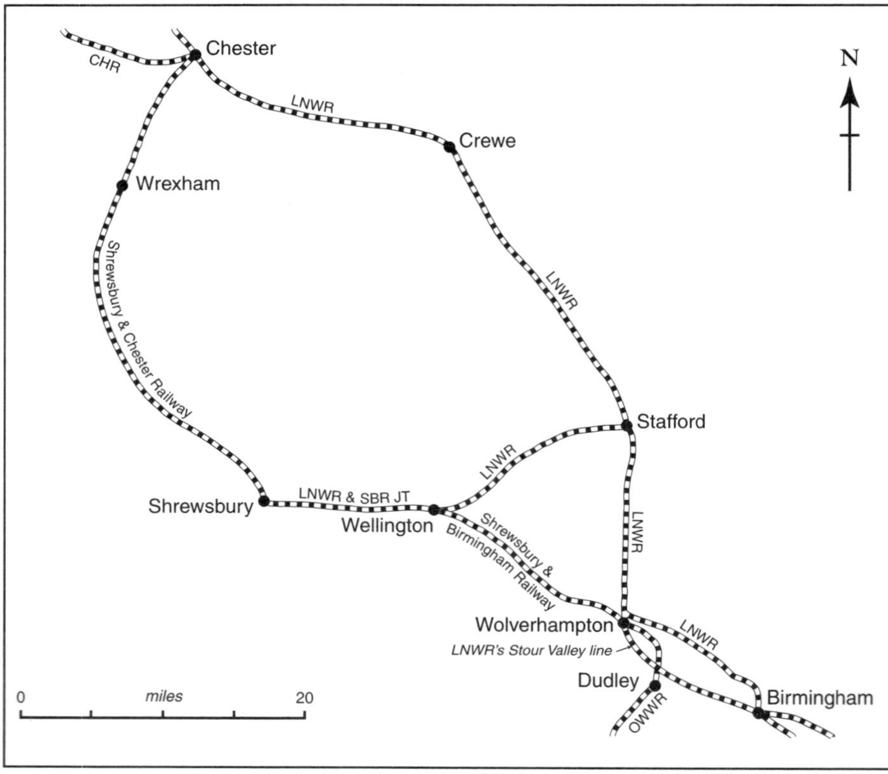

Map 5: The Shrewsburys.

the formation of the LNWR and the LBR had to fend off a rival project backed by the GJR. However the two companies came to a compromise in the Commons Committee on the understanding that both bills would be passed but only one line constructed. The SBR line was chosen, but the section from Shrewsbury to Wellington was to be made jointly with the Shropshire Union, an LBR subsidiary. The Shrewsbury and Chester had been authorised in 1845.

Initially the LNWR seems to have regarded the two Shrewsbury lines as local enterprises having close affinities with them. However they not only soon amalgamated, but announced that they would be prepared to carry both passenger and freight traffic between Birmingham, Wolverhampton and Birkenhead at rates less than those charged by the LNWR over its route, and convey their passengers from Wolverhampton to Birmingham by coach rather than on the LNWR's Stour Valley line. This does not seem to have been preceded by any diplomatic moves to come to any agreement with the much more powerful company. Huish warned Roy, the Shrewsbury secretary, that if the Shrewsbury companies were unwise enough to proceed the result would be a general fight. The board too issued a warning.[42] The Shrewsburys were not deterred. The LNWR retaliated by excluding their booking clerk from the joint station at Chester to prevent the sale of tickets and brought pressure on the Chester and Birkenhead to refuse interchange of traffic with the Shrewsbury Companies. Other steps were taken by the LNWR to delay the Shrewsbury's traffic such as preventing a siding being built to give access to the Birmingham Canal when the Riot Act had to be read. Very large reductions in fares were made, the Shrewsburys' being matched by the LNWR. To what extent the tactics were approved in any detail by Glyn personally or the LNWR Board is not clear. In Parliament when the CHR Bill was debated Ormsby Gore, chairman of the SBR and also MP for Shropshire, sought to defend his company's and his county's interests by moving a clause to prevent the LNWR, which 'exercised a large and unjust monopoly', stopping the traffic of the SCR at Chester, but this move, opposed by Glyn, was not successful.[43]

There were proposals, counter proposals and appeals to the courts, while fare-cutting continued. This led the LNWR board in January 1851 to authorise the Special Affairs Committee to determine the measures necessary for the protection of the company's interest affected by the aggressive proceedings of the SBR and SCR. The Committee 'after mature consideration' decided it was inconsistent with the interests of the LNWR to refrain from following the Shrewsbury companies in their measures of aggression and that the Traffic Committee should act accordingly. The reduction in fares should be immediate and confined for the time being to the line between Birmingham, Wolverhampton and Shrewsbury. Glyn was not present at that meeting of the SAC but he was at subsequent meetings when the Shrewsbury issues were pursued and he certainly did not dissent from the general lines of the policy though was probably not behind some of the more extreme measures the staff resorted to. By March, the LNWR was offering 3 per cent initially, rising to 4 per cent after 4 years on a capital limited to £1,000,000 to the SCR which they rejected as they wanted 4 per cent from the outset.[44]

Divisions then emerged among the SCR shareholders. One faction of the shareholders assured the LNWR board that their company had not sanctioned any agreement for amalgamation with the GWR and they were free to enter an agreement whereby 9/11 of the dividend payable to LNWR

[42] TNA, RAIL 410/21, 19 Nov. 1849.

[43] PD, 110, 383–387, 27 May 1850.

[44] TNA, RAIL 410/21, 11 Jan. 1851; RAIL 410/77, 13 Jan. and 8 Mar. 1851.

shareholders would be secured to the SCR. Parity of fares was agreed from Liverpool and Birkenhead to Wolverhampton and Birmingham. Meanwhile getting nowhere with the LNWR, Ormsby Gore, chairman of the SCR and the joint SBR–SCR committee, turned to the GWR, and also to the OWWR in an attempt to secure an independent route to the south.

The agreement with the GWR needed the explicit consent of the shareholders of both Shrewsbury companies. A series of rowdy meetings took place complicated by the LNWR through their directors and staff buying shares. It was alleged that there were 144 SCR shareholders with addresses within one mile of Euston and Camden stations. This led to a debate in the Lords with complaints that the intention of allowing a second competing line to the Northwest was being thwarted with Lord Lyndhurst again criticising the LNWR for buying up stock. The LNWR denied this though admitted that LNWR officers and others connected with the company had invested some £10,000. Glyn told proprietors that it was not for him to say how far it was wise of them to do so, but regretted that although they acted solely to protecting the proprietors interests they gave a handle, though a feeble one, to be used against them. In August Huish remained optimistic telling the SAC that the LNWR party was in a decided majority and four new directors had been elected and that anti-LNWR directors were now likely to change their allegiance.[45] But the attempt to persuade shareholders that they could get better terms with the LNWR failed despite those present at the meeting telegraphing Stewart to see if the LNWR would give a 4½ per cent guarantee. The Shrewsburys not surprisingly then accepted a traffic agreement with the GWR, which offered future amalgamation and a guaranteed dividend. The LNWR nevertheless continued to resist SBR's wish to use the Stour Valley line from Wolverhampton to Birmingham and delayed opening the line, in December allegedly blocking the line when the SBR tried to run a train, no doubt acting in the spirit of the SAC's resolution in January. Stewart not only warned the SBR but was present on the morning of the incident.[46]

The long running difficulties with the NSR came to a head in 1852, when negotiations for traffic arrangements with the LNWR were broken off and the NSR decided to promote bills for new lines from Colwich to Wolverhampton, duplicating the LNWR's line and linking with its competitor, the GWR's line to the south, and to extend the Sandbach branch to Warrington with a view to reaching Liverpool. The new lines were to be mixed gauge so giving the

45 TNA, RAIL 410/77, 14 Aug. 1851.

46 G. Body, *Great Railway Battles*, 1994, 62.

GWR access to the Potteries and indirectly to Liverpool.[47] The LNWR then agreed to a further arbitration and Robert Stephenson was appointed with James Hope-Scott QC. The main issue was running rights for the LNWR over the NSR. The arbitrators went well beyond the terms of the reference. They recommended the LNWR should acquire all the assets of the NSR and pay a guaranteed dividend on its share capital. In October the LNWR board accepted their recommendations and the arbitrators were asked to use their good offices to bring this about. Although the shareholders of both companies approved Stephenson's proposal, action was suspended pending the report of the Cardwell Committee, appointed by the Government to consider the principle of amalgamation as applied to railway bills. Ricardo became a member of the LNWR board, another example of the cross membership of railway boards, common in this period. There was a further arbitration in 1854 and three separate attempts at amalgamation in 1853, 1854 and 1855, all of which were quickly rejected by Parliament.[48]

Meanwhile the LNWR monopoly of the Birmingham traffic was broken when the GWR's service from Paddington to Birmingham started in September 1852. In the 1852 Session a number of bills which passed adversely affected the interests of the LNWR and the one by which the LNWR intended to connect their Buckinghamshire line with the OWWR was thrown out by the Lords, 'on what grounds I am a loss to conceive, for there was nothing to object to in the Bill' said Glyn. The SAC recommended to the board to take steps for a line from Shrewsbury to Crewe and showed the concern of the directors with the growing power of the GWR. They thought that with the broad gauge lines opened to Birmingham and the GWR intending to apply for powers to lay down that gauge to Birkenhead and into Lancashire, the LNWR Board would become all the more determined to prosecute and encourage narrow gauge lines throughout South Wales: the chief source of the through traffic of the GWR which notoriously was thought heretofore to end at Bristol.[49]

In August Glyn told proprietors that he had not considered it the proper time to move on the general question of relations with the GWR, but as soon as the Session ended, the directors unanimously supported an approach to Russell. Glyn wrote on 4 August 1852 to propose amalgamation. He argued this would be in the interests of both public and shareholders who imperatively called for mutual co-operation between the two companies

47 Rex Christiansen, The Growing Pains of a Railway, *JRCHS*, xxvi, 1980, 34–46, for the complex relationships between the LNWR and NSR in the 1850s.

48 TNA, RAIL 410/23, 11 Aug. 1855.

49 TNA, RAIL 410/54, 8 Jul. 1852.

and an end to the costly and harassing strife which had unhappily long distracted the attention of the two boards. These desirable results could only be attained by an absolute amalgamation. He proposed that a bill be introduced in the next session, but meanwhile a joint committee be set up to draw it up and to settle differences. Ordinary stock would be converted in the proportion of 100 for the LNWR and 75 to 80 for the GWR, as agreed or settled by arbitration, with preference stock carried forward. As in the case of the merger between the LBR and the GJR the new company was to be managed for the first three or five years by the existing boards as local committees under a general board. Finally the Midland was to be invited to 'concur in this arrangement generally in manner and on terms to be settled with them'.

Russell called a special meeting of his board for 10 August. In his reply later that day he expressed considerable doubt whether Parliament would approve such an amalgamation though he told shareholders next day that if it were allowed, he would hail such a change as most beneficial to railroads and the public. Nevertheless the GWR directors did not accept that absolute amalgamation was the only or the better way of attaining an end to strife. To commit to one large company undivided control and power over nearly one half of England was inconsistent when trade required extension rather than a limitation of railway accommodation. More particularly they could not agree to going back on their existing agreements with the two Shrewsbury companies. They feared that the outcome could well be the diversion of traffic north of Wolverhampton over the LNWR lines. The matter of the Shrewsbury would deter them from accepting the proposal even if the financial terms were satisfactory. The GWR had not yet received any financial advantage from their northern lines.

Russell made some counterproposals. Agreements on which they differed should be settled in court. Some division of net proceeds could be made. This would give the public two distinctive lines of railway to afford ample scope to the traffic of all districts and allow the full development of the mineral and manufacturing resource of the country without obstruction or hindrance. Other companies should be invited to join in the agreement for equal charges.

Following a board meeting Glyn replied on 12 August. He said that they would not have made their proposal if they had not thought that the GWR agreed it was the best way of effecting the public and private objects. The money terms were very reluctantly agreed by his board, and only for the sake of peace. While the GWR's traffic might increase on some lines, there was risk of losing traffic on others, The Shrewsbury lines would involve a further charge against the GWR's revenue: 3 to 4 million of capital on which they would have to pay interest.[50] He thought that the difficulties with Parliament would not be severe. Russell's proposition was unacceptable. It too would require parliamentary sanction. It would not meet the difficulties in relation to third parties, and it was contingent on the assent of other companies. Moreover it was vague and general in character.[51]

This was virtually the end of the negotiations. The failure was not popular with many Liverpool shareholders who met and resolved that the hostile attitude and fruitless negotiations of these gentlemen (Glyn and Russell) should be discontinued and a conference of those interested in both railways should be formed to meet the directors.[52]

The possibility of amalgamating with the Midland remained with whom a general traffic agreement had been concluded with in August 1849. In the autumn of 1851 the Midland, anxious to become permanently identified with a company having a line to, and a terminus in, London took the initiative.[53] In the years following the Railway Mania the Midland's dividends reduced more sharply than those of the other leading companies. 7 per cent in 1847, it was down to 2.1 per cent in 1850 and to 2.5 per cent in 1851. The Midland approached the LNWR and the two companies nearly reached an agreement. Glyn himself was not in the negotiating group, but it was rumoured that the LNWR board was divided, one party anxious to buy or lease the Midland, with the others led by Glyn against, though this hardly seems compatible with his general attitude to the prospect of amalgamation.[54] Following negotiations Smith recommended to the board that the LNWR should pay £60 for each Midland £100 share, but Benson moved that in view of the relative values of locomotive and carrying stock only £57½ be paid. This was carried by 14 votes to 10. The Midland held out for £60 and on 25 November their board declined the LNWR offer.[55] Negotiations continued but Ellis thought that it would be wrong to behave as if their line was about to be broken up in a year or two and if they laid low for a while they could expect their position to improve. They were in any case on good terms with the LNWR and so he felt as satisfied as if the amalgamation had actually been effected. For its part the LNWR felt that even if the terms had been agreed there could have been difficulties with Parliament. The existing

50 They were amalgamated with the GWR in 1854.

51 *Railway Times*, 14 Aug. 1852, and TNA, RAIL 1110/269, 13 Aug. 1852.

52 *Preston Guardian*, 9 Oct. 1852.

53 Francis Carbutt wrote to Glyn (TNA, RAIL 410/77, 7 Aug. 1851).

54 W.L. Steel, *History of the London and North Western Railway*, 1914, 189 quoting the *Derbyshire Advertiser* of 7 Nov. 1851.

55 TNA, RAIL 410/77, Special Affairs Committee, 11 Dec. 1851.

agreement fused the receipts from merchandise and they offered to enter into a permanent agreement to guarantee the Midland's access to London with exclusive use of offices at Euston.[56]

Despite Ellis's protestations that the Midland remained on good terms with the LNWR (he was at this time on the LNWR board), in the face of the failure of the amalgamation negotiations, the Midland soon returned to its plan for an entry to London independent of Euston, by means of a line from Leicester to Hitchin, which would give access to Kings Cross via the Great Northern. Such a line had been promoted by Hudson and authorised by Parliament in the heady days of 1847 but it had not been built in the subsequent depression and the powers had lapsed. Now the principal landowners in the neighbourhoods of Market Harborough, Kettering and Bedford, including William Whitbread whose family owned about one-eight of the land needed, threatened to support an independent line if the Midland did not act. Another factor was that ironstone had been discovered on the route in Northamptonshire. For these reasons the Midland decided to go ahead and informed the LNWR. They offered the LNWR a share in the capital. The latter regarded the line as inconsistent with their agreement which precluded taking measures calculated to divert traffic from the other's line.[57] Glyn and others saw Whitbread and Ellis and the LNWR decided to explore possible lines from Northampton to Leicester via Market Harborough and from Northampton to Bedford and Hitchin.[58]

Further talks led to a renewal of discussions about the possibility of a closer union or amalgamation of the two companies. At the same time the publication of the correspondence between Glyn and Russell caused Denison, chairman of the GNR to suggest to Ellis, that an amalgamation of the GNR and the Midland would be a natural development given that they duplicated stations at several towns and two trains ran where one would suffice. He also suggested that the Midland terminus should be King's Cross. The philosophy of the companies in this period can be illustrated by a letter from Ellis to Denison – 'If again we look to the practical working of the railway system we find that competition has invariably after a short and violent struggle terminated in an agreement for a division of the traffic.'[59]

Smith led the LNWR group when they met representatives of the Midland board in Birmingham on 3 and 4 September when Smith proposed amalgamation of the two companies with Parliamentary authority to be

[56] TNA, RAIL 410/21, 10 Jan. 1852.

[57] TNA, RAIL 410/77, 13 May and 410/21, 15 May 1852.

[58] TNA, RAIL 410/77, 10 Jun. 1852.

[59] Grinling, 122–123 for Denison's letter of 16 Aug; TNA, RAIL 406/7, 22 Sept. 1852.

secured in the 1853 or 1854 session. The relative values of the two companies would be fixed by arbitrators. The LNWR proposed that arrangements should be made which would satisfy the landowners between Leicester and Hitchin but the Midland refused to countenance this as they were already pledged to the landowners and the LNWR had to agree.[60]

Ellis told Glyn on 9 October that the Midland and the LNWR were willing to come to an extended arrangement with the GNR and would be prepared to consider further if Denison wished to propose a bill to authorise a more complete and lasting union of interest between the Great Northern and the united LNWR and Midland companies. Glyn played little part in subsequent developments on this front. Ellis secured a resolution at the Midland's meeting of shareholders on 3 November for an amalgamation of the LNWR and MR on the basis that the relative value of the two undertakings be ascertained and fixed by referees of high standing, though the GNR were still considering its position.

On the same day the LNWR general meeting, with Smith in the chair, resolved it was expedient to effect a permanent union of interest between the LNWR and Midland on the basis proposed by Ellis but if the first application to Parliament failed further application should be made in the following and ensuing sessions. A draft bill was examined by a joint committee of directors on 28 November and they even decided on a title – London, Midland and North Western.[61]

However the fears expressed earlier about the attitude of government to amalgamations of major companies were fully justified when in December a committee was appointed and so all proposals for amalgamation then pending were deferred. Although initially not on the committee Edward Cardwell was soon appointed as a member and then became chairman. Glyn and other chairmen were not called to give evidence. The Committee relied on Huish and other general managers. Huish reflected Glyn's thinking and argued that combination was inevitable and it was better for the public that the companies should be permitted under certain restrictions and control to protect public interests in security than not knowing what parliament would do next session. He was in favour of giving a power to the Board of Trade to decide whether new lines should be given to an existing operator in that district. He had no objection to Government audit provided the expense were not thrown upon the companies. They would feel protected against those who did not conduct themselves with the same rectitude. Companies should compete in facilities and convenience rather than rates.

60 TNA, RAIL 410/77, 3 and 4 Sept. 1852.

61 TNA, RAIL 491/3, 3 Nov.; RAIL 410/1, 3 Nov.; RAIL 406/3, 23 and 28 Dec. 1852.

The committee concluded that between Liverpool and Manchester five companies, including the canals, more or less had a common understanding with each other and no rivalry existed bearing any resemblance to keen competition. The LNWR and GNR divided the whole country according to a fixed plan and the GNR did likewise with the GER. If amalgamation were conceded Parliament would part with a power which it might exercise in order to secure for the country freedom and economy of transit. In its final report it recommended that while working arrangements between companies for the regulation of traffic and the division of profits should be sanctioned under proper conditions and for limited periods no further amalgamation should be sanctioned except in minor or special cases. Cardwell, by then a Minister, moved a number of resolutions in the House of Commons which would be instructions to select committees considering railway bills to avoid conflicting rulings. Glyn approved of all the resolutions but complained that the Committee's report contained no reference to the gauge question which was connected very intimately with the safety of the public in that the highest engineering authorities in England had given it as their deliberate opinion that no more ingenious method could be devised for adding to the insecurity of railway travelling than to have a mixed gauge. Cardwell answered that the subject though important had not been prominent enough before the committee to warrant a special instruction to Select Committees on future bills.[62]

This policy of not permitting further amalgamations was not followed rigorously by Parliament in the next few years. In 1854 the North Eastern was formed from the York, Newcastle and Berwick, and the York and North Midland, and a working agreement was made by the Eastern Counties and the East Anglian and Norfolk companies to form the Eastern Union, the precursor of the Great Eastern. In the LNWR-Midland case there had been an attempt in the summer of 1853 to combine the traffic receipts of the two companies which would be apportioned at the end of each half year on a basis to be agreed. The proposals were rejected by the Midland board which also turned down arbitration, at which the LNWR board expressed surprise and regret.[63] The LNWR consoled itself that receipts were already fused on merchandise. It was 'a sufficient bond of union to ensure the hearty cooperation of both for general objects'. The LNWR board were ready to enter into a permanent agreement for transit of MR's traffic to and from

[62] Select Committee on the Principle of Amalgamation applied to Railway or Railway and Canal Bills, PP, 1852–3, xxxviii; PD, 125, 1200 and 1207–8, 15 Apr. 1853.

[63] Ibid, 11 Jun. and 15 Oct. 1853.

London and to give them exclusive use of offices at Euston.[64] In September 1854 the board considered heads of a ten-year traffic agreement with the Midland which was approved in November.[65]

In Glyn's period as chairman developments in London, and of the Irish and Scottish traffic developed largely outside the framework of rivalry though government policy tended to have more say.

Immediately before amalgamation the LBR board had recognised that they lacked access to the Docks. They saw the City as the great focus of business and contemplated an eastwards extension from Camden to Faringdon Street chiefly for goods traffic with an eastern goods terminal, though morning and evening business trains might run. The preliminary estimate was £600–700,000, but, as Glyn explained to the Commission on Metropolitan Railways in 1846, the LBR had not presented their Camden to Faringdon Bill because the cost of a tunnel under Skinner Street and the land for a station adjoining Snow Hill, would cost much more than the estimate and he did not think that long distance passengers would want to change trains at Camden for the City. Instead they put up two-thirds of the capital for the East and West India Docks and Birmingham Junction Railway (EWIDBJR) to run from the goods station at Camden to West India Dock at Blackwall. Although Stephenson's estimate for land proved too low, nevertheless it was built round the then periphery of urban development and would have cost much more only a decade later. Glyn told the Commission that EWIDBJR would be better than the line to Faringdon as goods could be taken direct from the docks to Manchester. The line was completed in 1852 and renamed the North London Railway. By 1856 it was paying a dividend of 4¾ per cent. Although primarily intended as a goods line, it proved popular with passengers, particularly after 1865 when it secured a more direct access to the London and Blackwall's Fenchurch Street terminus. Glyn was on the board only for the first few years of the company's existence, but the LNWR nominated a majority of the directors.

Glyn also told the Commission on Metropolitan Railways they were doubling their space at Euston from 6 to 12 acres. They now had 30 acres at Camden while Pickfords had 2 more. All carriers for the north had establishments at Camden. Glyn who had been a strong advocate of opening Euston to the GWR now told the commission that a central terminus would not be advantageous as companies wanted separate facilities. There might be savings on clerks, but distribution from a central point would cause congestion.[66]

64 TNA, RAIL 410/21, 10 Jan. 1852.

65 Ibid, 9 Sept. and 11 Nov. 1854.

66 Report of the Royal Commission on Metropolitan Termini, PP, 1846, xvii, 90–93.

The line which brought the LNWR most frequently into contact with the Government was the Chester and Holyhead. The Government was keenly interested in ensuring that the land and sea connections between London and Dublin were as good as possible and in maintaining frequent and reliable postal services. The LNWR which provided the chairman, Moorsom, and several directors, sought an adequate return on its investment in the CHR, but did not wish to spend to the extent that the CHR itself did. However by 1847 the LNWR had agreed to work the line, supplying engines, carriages and wagons and related staff. The CHR was anxious to run its own steamers as a natural extension of the rail service. The building of their two vessels was at first financed by two directors personally in the absence of statutory backing, which was not obtained until 1848 in a bill which enabled the CHR to raise £250,000 and the LNWR to subscribe £120,000. Hudson, Gladstone and Labouchere spoke in its favour.[67] The CHR opened from Chester to Bangor in May 1848 with the completion of the Conway tubular bridge. In August the line from Holyhead to Llanfair PG was opened which enabled the Irish mail trains to start running, albeit with a coach connection over Telford's Menai suspension bridge. With the opening of this route the Admiralty overnight packet service was transferred from Liverpool to Holyhead, and the CHR began a fast daytime service to Kingstown from Holyhead. The government thought the terms proposed for the conveyance of mails were exorbitant and annoyed that the CHR had gone ahead with its steamers without consulting them and before the harbour works were completed.[68] In January 1849 the negotiations with the Admiralty over the steam packet arrangements were not going well. The CHR's financial position was desperate. Despite a further loan of £100,000 from the LNWR, they had to mortgage the steamers raising £35,000 from Glyn's. In February it was suggested at the LNWR board that Glyn should be the chairman of the CHR. Glyn was prepared to take this on if he were persuaded it was expedient and necessary but the board agreed that it was not then the case. However the board threatened to re-open the contract with the Post Office.[69]

In July the Government opted for public tender for the mail services. Both the CHR tender and one put forward by Betts, in conjunction with William Jackson, a very large shareholder in the CHR, and Peto, were rejected. A bid from the City of Dublin Steam Packet Company which had previously operated the Liverpool to Dublin service succeeded. The CHR

[67] PD, 97, 1050, 27 Mar. 1848; *The Times*, 28 Mar. 1848.

[68] TNA, RAIL 1008/102, H.G. Ward, Admiralty, Devonport to Glyn, 22 Sept. 1848.

[69] TNA, RAIL 410/20, 9 Oct. 1847; 13 Jan. and 15 Feb. 1849.

withdrew their steamer service immediately and following the opening the line over the Menai Bridge with the first Holyhead-Euston express running on 18 March 1850,[70] sought power to enable them to lease their line to the LNWR. Glyn made it clear that the Bill had not originated with the LNWR and was only an enabling measure. A lease would need specific approval from the proprietors. Shareholders objected as the LNWR had not yet had even a sixpence return for its investments in the line. The CHR was defended by Jackson who admitted the line was in difficulties but had been offered £200,000 from three men. One was undoubtedly Samuel Morton Peto who had been elected to the board in August 1850, and had already underwritten interest payments when he became chairman in February 1851 in place of Moorsom. The Bill was approved by LNWR shareholders by roughly 5 to 1 and Glyn discussed terms with a deputation from the CHR. However in the face of amendments proposed in Parliament including one to give the GWR running powers, the Bill was withdrawn.[71] The CHR was however paid £200,000 by the government towards the construction of a new harbour at Holyhead.[72] In February 1851 the LNWR agreed to take up £120,000 in preference shares in the CHR. Again this was challenged. Glyn said the subscription had been possible for some time but was being made then because it was thought that the preference shares would soon be paying a regular dividend. They did so but only from the first half of 1855.[73]

In January 1851 Glyn with Smith and Rotheram met Peto and Jackson to complete the agreement with the CHR and the Dublin Steam Packet Company. In March the board decided to develop fully the mineral, cattle and goods traffic to and from the CHR. In January 1852 £180,000 was advanced to the CHR on the deposit of their unissued second preference shares at a rate of 5 per cent.[74]

Control of the route to Ireland was relatively straightforward compared with that to Scotland, north of the border. The LNWR itself fully owned the route as far as Preston; onwards to Carlisle the Lancaster and Carlisle Railway (LCR) managed the Lancaster and Preston Railway. The LNWR had a stake of £326,000 in the LCR itself and nominated 7 of the 17 directors. The line to Carlisle had been completed in December 1846

70 TNA, RAIL 410/21, 29 Dec. 1849, 12 Jan. and 9 Mar. 1850.

71 TNA, RAIL 1110/269, 14 Feb. 1850; RAIL 410/21, 22 Feb., 13 Jul. and 16 Aug. 1850.

72 TNA, RAIL 1008/102, Sir Charles Wood (Chancellor of the Exchequer) to the Chairman, CHR, 18 and 31 Jul. 1850.

73 TNA, RAIL 1110/269, 21 Feb. 1851.

74 TNA, RAIL 410/21, 11 Jan. and 13 Sept. 1851; 10 Jan. 1852; RAIL 410/22, 13 Mar.1852.

and the Caledonian's from Carlisle to Beattock in September 1847 and on to Glasgow and Edinburgh in 1848. It was important to the West Coast companies to keep out intruders from the east and the board backed the LCR in opposing the leasing of the Newcastle and Carlisle and the Maryport and Carlisle to the York, Newcastle and Berwick, which Hudson had achieved with doubtful legality in 1848. The companies themselves managed to free themselves from this lease in 1850, leaving Hudson himself as the sole guarantor. Glyn himself was asked to adjudicate on the cost of termination of the lease, He awarded the Newcastle and Carlisle only £3,000, much to the disappointment of their shareholders.[75]

Relations with the Caledonian were difficult and complex. The line itself was an impressive engineering feat, but it was in considerable financial difficulties arising from the cost of construction, and from financing mergers with smaller companies in Central Scotland by guaranteeing dividends. In 1848 the through trains from London in 12½ hours encouraged the Post Office to transfer the London-Edinburgh mails from the East Coast route, then still with road connections across the Tyne and Wear, to the West Coast main line. However travel on the latter had its disadvantages. The Lancaster and Carlisle called the LNWR board's attention to the inconvenience to passengers on the West Coast route caused by the lack of good hotels, such as those found at Newcastle, York and Derby.[76] By 1848 the LNWR had an extensive interest not just in the Caledonian itself but in its affiliates. In June 1846 it had agreed to lease the Scottish Central jointly with the LCR and CR at 6 per cent. In 1848 Glyn advocated making an agreement with the Aberdeen Company without guaranteeing the shares. The LNWR would provide the moving stock in return for purchasing the Aberdeen company's mileage rate, though this was not proceeded with.[77]

The LNWR wished to be able to exercise more influence on the CR but in its corporate capacity could not nominate directors. Glyn and Creed, both shareholders in the CR, were nominated as individuals. The board's attempt get Poole, the goods manager for the Northern Division, to take on the superintendence of the CR's traffic failed as he said he was fully occupied.[78] The CR's financial position deteriorated as it could not meet its obligations on its guaranteed and preferred stocks. The LNWR thought it

[75] RBS Archives, GM/138, Glyn to John Clayton (Solicitor to the Newcastle and Carlisle), 3 Mar. 1851; A.J. Peacock, *George Hudson, 1800–71, The Railway King*, 1989, 2, 306 and 439; *Railway Times*, 1851, 353 and 462.

[76] TNA, RAIL 410/21, 13 Apr. 1850.

[77] TNA, RAIL 410/20, 13 Jun. 1846 and 15 Jul. 1848.

[78] TNA, RAIL 410/20, 12 Aug. 1847.

had reduced its fares to a ruinously low level. Huish asked whether they should make an effort to coerce the company or continue their policy of neutrality. The board decided on the latter.[79] In September 1849 a committee of CR shareholders was set up to investigate the company's affairs. In the following month Glyn and Hope Johnstone, the Caledonian chairman and Tory MP for Dumfriesshire who had extensive estates in Annandale, discussed the possibility of the LNWR taking over the working of the Caledonian. It was agreed that the line could be worked on the basis of a deferred payment of up to £200,000 secured by the transfer of CR stock, but difficulties arose over the CR directors' personal obligations, and the LNWR declined to go ahead, no doubt fearing they would be dragged into the CR's internal disputes.[80] In February 1850 Hope Johnstone resigned together with most of the board, but his successor, Captain J.E. Plunkett, was equally unsuccessful in resolving the CR's financial position.

The LNWR found it difficult to stand aside completely. Its main link with the CR's board was broken when Fox Maule, who was a director of the LNWR and of the LCR and CR, resigned all three directorships because of his ministerial duties as Secretary at War in Lord John Russell's Government. In August 1850 Glyn was asked whether the company had guaranteed the CR which was in a state of bankruptcy. He replied that if the LNWR had guaranteed the CR it would not be in a state of bankruptcy. Watkin was sent to Scotland to investigate the CR's finances and its affiliates. He reported that they needed to raise more capital and make economies but the board was inexperienced and divided and he could not see any chance of such developments without a new spirit in the management of the whole concern.[81]

In September the LNWR board offered to mediate in the CR's complicated questions. The Scottish company turned this down, Glyn told Plunkett that some of his colleagues practically versed in railway matters were ready to help. The CR board appointed Carnegie as a director, the LNWR arranging to transfer stock from the company to Carnegie personally to give him the necessary qualification. Rotheram and Booth were also nominated by the LNWR to assist the CR temporarily and secured seats on the board. but even with their participation there was no agreement with the shareholders. A month later Carnegie reported failure and the three LNWR directors resigned in December.[82] Captain Coddington, the

79 TNA, RAIL 410/20, 15 Jul. 1848.

80 TNA, RAIL 410/21, 13 Oct. and 10 Nov. 1849.

81 TNA, RAIL 410/77, 24 Aug. 1850.

82 TNA, RAIL 410/21, 14 Sept., 12 Oct., 9 Nov., and 14 Dec. 1850.

secretary of the CR, wrote to say that the CR board strongly hoped that LNWR directors would not desert the CR shareholders in this crisis.[83] In 1851 the CR by Act of Parliament restructured its capital and adjusted its obligations. In January 1852 it paid its first dividend since January 1849, but only of ½ per cent and the LNWR advanced £180,000 to the Caledonian at 5 per cent on the deposit of preference shares.[84] The LNWR investment in the CR, while very modest in relation to its total capital, was far from remunerative, even if at least partially offset by securing the Caledonian's traffic to and from England. It is however surprising, given that the majority of Caledonian shares were held in England, that the shareholders did not insist on more direct LNWR participation at an earlier stage and that Glyn and others were content with a velvet glove approach. English money, but not English control, was welcome.

There is little evidence of conflict between Glyn and colleagues on the board, but his wishes were not invariably adopted by his fellow directors. In February 1850 he proposed a dividend of 2½ per cent – 6 per cent for the year 1849. Lawrence however thought it should be 2¾ per cent and he carried the day in the board by a single vote (8 to 7). At the proprietors meeting Glyn said circumstances had been more adverse than he had foreseen, so it would have been safer to take a 2½ per cent dividend with a larger reserve. However when Glyn moved the larger dividend recommended by the directors, Richard Moon, not yet on the board, moved an amendment for 2½ per cent and he was supported by Peyton, Mozley, Garnett and Mark Philips, the influential MP for Manchester. Hardman Earle and Robert Bright justified the rate proposed by the directors as profits ought to be divided, not kept for the future. The amendment was put to the vote and the lower rate for which Glyn had argued on the board was carried by 96 to 78.

August 1850 brought a further debate when the board, this time unanimously, proposed to maintain the 5 per cent level for the full year, retaining £145,000 to assist the maintenance of a 5 per cent dividend in future. Several proprietors took a different view, and Hardman Earle, though making it clear that he had not voted for more than 5 per cent on the board, said he had been in favour of a larger dividend, Glyn said the had obtained the opinion of the Solicitor General and counsel who assured them that the practice of carrying such a sum forward was legal. The amendment for a higher rate was lost by 90 to 58. It was at this meeting Glyn that explained he did not receive the slightest benefit in his individual capacity in the City, nor was he on the Finance Committee. Though he was always willing to advise

83 TNA, RAIL 1008/111, Coddington to secretary of the LNWR.

84 TNA, RAIL 410/21, 10 Jan. 1852.

when asked his opinion on the state of the money market or similar matters, he had no voice in questions of banking and deposit. He commended Stewart and the Finance Committee for discounting debentures before they became due. It was 'just what we as bankers would have done with money left in our hands'.

In February 1851 Glyn again was more cautious than his colleagues. If he had been administering his own private affairs he would have preferred not to make any increase in the dividend but to wait until he had seen the effects of the competition now coming from various quarters, but as there was a balance of about £150,000 to be carried forward the recommendation of 2¾ per cent was carried unanimously. A year later the company was able to pay 3 per cent for the second half of 1851 largely because of the additional traffic arising from the Great Exhibition.

In June 1852 Glyn suggested the appointment of an executive committee of directors.[85] There was no discussion of his proposal in July or August, perhaps because of preoccupations with the negotiations with the GWR. Glyn resigned as chairman on 9 September 1852, and refused to reconsider the matter following the board meeting of 12 September. He last chaired the board on 10 August. His reason was ill health. He told colleagues that if he had attended to the urgent representations of his friends and medical advisers he would have resigned long ago. Indeed Smith said that when he had wished to resign in February because of illness in his family Glyn dissuaded him as his own state of health would shortly compel him to retire though he would try to remain until after the end of the Parliamentary Session. In the event Smith resigned in September because of renewed affliction in his family so the LNWR lost both the Chairman and his deputy at the same time.[86]

Glyn said his views had not altered on the need for some organic change in the distribution of the functions of the executive which he had put to the board in June. He wished however to leave the question entirely open for his successor. He suggested that the board should replace him with a successor able to devote his whole time to, and be more capable of sustaining, the increased responsibility of the position.[87] Managing the amalgamated company particularly through the thirty strong board was undoubtedly a heavy load, and the failure of his attempt to amalgamate with the GWR may well have added to his concerns.

Glyn's resignation came at a time when there was considerable criticism of the LNWR. The *Railway Times* said that the large board of thirty

85 TNA, RAIL 410/22, 12 Jun. 1852.

86 TNA, RAIL 410/22, Smith to the Board, 18 Sept. 1852.

87 Ibid, Glyn to Board, 9 and 13 Sept., Board minutes, 12 Sept.

directors meant that Glyn had responsibility without power. 'Soldiers and sailors, tinkers and tailors' were brought together once a month for a few hours. Thus the railway was in the hands of officials who had power without responsibility. They ought to form a council under the chairman. I believe that Mr Glyn would not object to an office so constituted.' wrote their correspondent.[88]

A fortnight later the *Railway Times* was speculating who would be appointed to succeed Glyn. Brown Westhead, the MP for Knaresborough, who had been a member of the MBR board, was regarded as a strong candidate who would have the unanimous support of the Manchester section of the board. Dalhousie, then Governor General of India, was mentioned as he was expected to return to the UK,[89] as was Fox Maule, now Lord Panmure, and now back on the LNWR board. Wharncliffe, Granville, Kinnaird, Strutt, Shaw Lefevre, James Wilson and Laing were all mentioned though the *Railway Times* favoured Peto. By this time Glyn and Anson had been charged by the board to convey to Panmure the unanimous wish of the board that he would accept the chair. Glyn told him there was a general move in thinking that the role should be lightened as much as possible. He did not see a way 'out of our present dilemma unless you will accept. You know enough of the constitution of our board to be aware that there must always be some feeling of jealousy. You alone can unite all these suffrages. To the Railway Interest in general it would be of the greatest benefit.' Glyn said it would give him satisfaction to serve under Panmure. He did not have that opportunity as Panmure declined the offer as his private affairs took so much of his time. His father, with whom he had scarcely any contact in his adult life, had died six months earlier leaving him considerable estates in Scotland. He told Glyn that it was the most flattering compliment he could have received to find he possessed the confidence of so influential body of men. Panmure thought the chairmanship gave rise to sufficient work for the whole undivided attention of time for the most active man of business.

Glyn's response was almost one of despair. His colleagues were determined to continue in the old ways and would not think of adopting the plan of appointing a Chairman who would give all his time and receive remuneration, so providing more direct supervision of the officers and departments. He did not know what the board would do bearing in mind the connection with the Duke of Sutherland and the vast stake he had in the undertaking. He wished Lord Granville would think of it, though he

88 *Railway Times*, 25 Sept. 1852.

89 He did not return from India until 1856, as his term of office was extended.

was certain he would not. He added 'the jealousies are great and present difficulties almost insuperable. The officers do not like any change which would interfere with their patrimonies.'[90] Whether Panmure would have borne out Glyn's hopes may be doubted. John Sweetman in the ODNB comments on his political career 'Panmure had an unhappy knack of offending too many people.'

The failure of the attempt to persuade Panmure to take the chairmanship led the board to appoint one of their own. On 3 November they unanimously agreed to the proposal by Sir Charles Douglas and Glyn that Anson, should be elected. Tom Young's comment in the verses quoted above that 'he makes, not writes a book' and was 'less disposed to work than play' suggests that he may have been put forward as an aristocratic figurehead to avoid more controversial and more powerful personalities, whereas Glyn seems to have wanted a strong personality to control the board.

Glyn established a considerable reputation as chairman of the LNWR. Edward Watkin who worked closely with Glyn on a number of matters, said on Glyn's death, he had revered him as a kind of old master and constant friend. Under his chairmanship he first acquired a sound working knowledge of railway working and policy.[91] Glyn himself admitted his relative moderation. When the NSR had put forward the bills for lines to Wolverhampton and Sandbach which he regarded as extremely hostile to the interests of the LNWR, he told shareholders, in what turned out to be his final meeting as chairman, that he knew it was a matter of surprise that he had never taken upon himself to answer the statements of Ricardo. He refrained not from any difficulty he had in replying but because he did not think it becoming that persons occupying the chairs of great companies should indulge in a system of vituperation that could do no good and must do much harm. In any case he had successfully proposed that the dispute should be referred to Stephenson and Hope.[92]

[90] Scottish Record Office GD45/14/680, Anson to Panmure, and Glyn to Panmure, both 9 Oct. Panmure to Glyn 22 Oct., Glyn to Panmure 19 and 25 Oct. 1852. It is not clear why the Sutherland investments, which stemmed from the second Marquess of Stafford's purchase of £100,000 shares in the LMR and subsequently added to, were regarded as such an obstacle by Glyn. According to Eric Richards, *The Leviathan of Wealth*, 1972, 147. Sutherland periodically sold shares to develop Dunrobin Castle (rebuilt by Barry in 1845) and to relieve the acute distress in Sutherland, but he held £205,000 shares at par in 1846 then worth £526,593. That number of shares would have been worth about £240,000 on 1 October 1852. Granville, like the Duke of Sutherland, was a grandson of the first Marquess of Stafford.

[91] TNA, RAIL 635/11, 24 Jul. 1873.

[92] TNA, RAIL 1110/269, 13 Aug. 1852.

CHAPTER FOURTEEN

Glyn's in the 1850s

GLYN'S LEVEL OF BUSINESS, following the drop in the late 1840s, remained low until 1852 when it reached £5,257,000, the highest until 1857. In 1852 there was a big increase in railway and country balances and on the other side an unprecedented rise in investments as well as a big increase in bills discounted. In the immediately following years, particularly as on one side country balances and on the other bills discounted were much lower, the overall balance was lower though not reverting to the level experienced in the late 1840s. Glyn's made increasing use of deposits with the Bank of England which reached £86,000 in 1839 and over £200,000 in the three years 1845 to 1847 at the time of the railway boom. After dropping off until 1854 when such deposits amounted to £261,000 and for the first time exceeded cash at Glyn's which continued to be the norm. Deposits at the Bank continued to rise to £714,000 in 1858 and while not continuing at that level, over £400,000 was usual. The close of 1857 saw a rise of over a quarter in the town balances, with an almost six-fold rise to £1,308,000 in country account debts. The balance at the Bank of England stood at £862,000. However these figures, derived from the Periodical Returns Book, relate only to the end-year figures in the Yearly Statement of Assets and Liabilities and are no indication of the scale and nature of Glyn's transactions with the Bank. Overall balances over the next few years varied little, though railway balances dropped. From 1856 there was a separate entry for deposit accounts on which interest began to be paid. In that year they amounted to £570,000, and except in 1859 when the total was over £1,000,000 it was about £500 to 600,000, though remaining a small proportion of total balances: about 14 per cent compared with 37 per cent in Collins' sample of banks in the 1850s. The ratio of cash to liabilities averaged 11.8, much higher than in Collins' sample.[1]

[1] Michael Collins, The Business of Banking: English Bank Balance Sheets, 1840–1880,

There were few changes in the partnership. Thomas Hallifax junior, a wealthy and much travelled bachelor who lived in Berkeley Square died after a long illness on 5 October 1849 at his father's home at Chadacre Hall at Hartest near Long Melford in Suffolk. Like his father he was a member of the Royal Yacht Squadron, purchasing Camilla, a schooner of 147 tons in 1841.[2] He frequently went to Western Europe – France and the Netherlands in 1820, France, Switzerland and Italy in 1822, and Vienna, Adrianople and Constantinople in 1827. He took his two sisters to France in 1834 and was in Italy in 1836.[3] His father Thomas Hallifax who had been a partner for more than half a century died only five months later on 5 March 1850 aged 76.[4] He was the last Hallifax to be a partner as his only surviving son was a clergyman. It seems Thomas Hallifax senior had retired from an active participation in the partnership some years earlier as George Carr Glyn's eldest son, George Grenfell Glyn became a partner on his coming of age in 1845. Charles Henry Mills, the son of Charles Mills, became a partner in 1852, aged twenty-two after Eton and Christ Church. A year later he married Louisa Isabella Lascelles, daughter of the Earl of Harewood, reflecting the Mills' social status and increasing integration in the upper classes exemplified by their life at Camelford House.[5] While the other partners did not have family links with the aristocracy their addresses illustrate their social standing. In 1858 E.W. Mills lived in Bryanston Square, and George Carr Glyn in Upper Ecclestone Street, his brother, Sir Richard, in Upper Brook Street and his son George Grenfell in Upper Belgrave Street.

Charles Mills though as a partner senior to George Carr Glyn left the principal management of the bank to him.[6] George's elder brother, Sir Richard Plumptre Glyn became senior partner on Thomas Hallifax senior's death, but `senior' related to Richard Plumptre's length of service rather than his impact on the bank's business. He lived at Gaunts in Hinton Parva,

Business History, XXVI, 1984, 46. Such comparisons have limited value because of lack of comparable data. However Collins notes that perhaps London bankers held a relatively high proportion on current account.

[2] Montague Guest and William B. Boulton, *The Royal Yacht Squadron: Memorials of its Members,* 1903, 482.

[3] Suffolk Record Office, Bury St Edmunds, passports and other documents relating to these visits, HA519/129, 130, 133, 136–137, 140, 142–143, 152, and 156.

[4] *Morning Post,* 8 Oct. and *Ipswich Journal*, 13 Oct.1849; *Daily News,* 11 Mar. 1850.

[5] C.H. Mills' connection with the Harewoods led to his becoming MP for Northallerton in 1866, but he was unseated as his agent had bribed without his knowledge, though Mills himself had bought property to obtain the tenants votes. His brother-in-law, Egremont William Lascelles was elected in his place. From 1868 to 1885 he was MP for West Kent.

[6] Currie, 1, 83.

Dorset where he was lord of the manor and had the gift of the living, of which Rev John Carr Glyn was the incumbent.[7] The fact that the bank remained a private undertaking was emphasised in the late 1850s when George Carr Glyn's fourth son, St Leger, became a partner, making four Glyn's and three Mills.[8] In the debate on the Banking Bill Glyn himself had argued that as Parliament had legislated for the benefit of joint stock banks, private banks were entitled to some consideration. They were prevented from strengthening themselves beyond six partners. He did not favour unlimited partnerships but private banks should have power to have ten or twelve partners[9] His doubts about banks with limited liability persisted. He was not at all satisfied that they had been attended with favourable results. They had not been sufficiently tested in England to enable persons to speak with confidence of the operation of limited liability, while in the United States, its application had been decidedly unfavourable and unsatisfactory.[10]

In many respects Glyn's was a typical private bank. The private banks in London were attracting increased competition from the larger joint-stock banks, though the strength of the private banks was not to be judged by the amount of capital in the bank itself, which was usually much less than that of joint stock banks. This could be a relatively small proportion of the wealth of the partners and the reputation of the firm depended significantly on the other assets of the partners: whether country estates, urban property or investments in government railway or commercial stocks. There was a general, if not precise, awareness of these assets which was a source of public confidence in the bank and was particularly important as the partners liability was unlimited. Thomas Coutts insisted that a reserve fund at the bank was not necessary as he himself always kept a reserve fund of at least £100,000.[11] The private banks tended to be run by a small number of partners in the same family who had inherited their position and intended to hand over to their sons. In 1853 the *Bankers Magazine* analysed the twenty-five private banks in the City who were members of the Clearing House. They had 104 partners between them, of whom 67 had the same name as other partners. Five of the six partners in Smith, Payne and Smiths were called Smith. At Curries all six bore the name of

[7] *Post Office Directory of Dorset*, 1855, 44.

[8] It is not clear from surviving records precisely when St Leger became a partner but he was not listed as a partner in the Bankers Almanack for 1858.

[9] PD, 147, 121, 21 Jul. 1857. The limit on the number of partners was raised from six to ten later in 1857.

[10] Ibid, 127.

[11] Edna Healey, *Coutts & Co., 1692–1992, The Portrait of a Private Bank*, 1992, 294.

Currie.[12] Opening the door to others was not helped by the maintenance of the legal limit of six until 1857. The family emphasis tended to result in some partners regarding banking as something of a part-time occupation and to concentrate on other fields. It also probably led to a conservative attitude to business and an unwillingness to innovate. Unlike the joint stock banks they usually refused to pay interest on deposit accounts, though Glyn's began to do so in 1856. Coutts only did so to special customers with large deposits.[13] As late as 1864 George Grenfell Glyn who must personally have gained an enormous amount of business for the bank remarked 'it is apparently the fashion of the day boldly to ask for accounts, but I confess that is a course I cannot bring myself to adopt unless in the case of personal friendship.'[14]

Glyn was in touch with Gladstone over various railway matters, notably the arbitration Gladstone undertook in 1851 when out of office. Following the fall of the Derby government and his appointment as Chancellor of the Exchequer in December 1852, Glyn told Gladstone that he had troubled him so frequently on railway matters that the least he could do was to assure him that if at any time he could be useful to him in the City for the purpose of acquiring information or otherwise he was freely and faithfully at Gladstone's command. He added that if the Continent remained quiet there was every chance of being able to effect in the Spring a successful funding operation towards the retirement of a portion of the Debt.[15] Indeed Gladstone in his great budget of 1853, which reduced income tax to 7d immediately and promised its elimination within five years, did create new stocks at a lower rate of interest and gave the option of conversion to existing holders. Though new money was raised at a lower rate the conversion proved to have no appeal to existing holders and the redemption of the South Sea stock proved expensive to the Exchequer. The changes of 1853 were soon overshadowed by the effects on the finances of the outbreak of the Crimean War so in March 1854, Gladstone raised income tax from 7d and in May raised it to 14d, telling the House that it was the duty and the policy of the country to make in the first instance a great effort from its own resources. Glyn was in touch with Gladstone at the time advising him in late March that there was no chance of funding bills at 3¼, but 4 per cent would probably suffice if it were accompanied by a guarantee of that rate for, say, ten years. When both 3½ and 4 per cent bonds were being issued in 1854 he thought this

12 *Bankers Magazine*, 1853, 352–361.

13 Healey, 294.

14 Fulford, 162.

15 BL, Add Ms 44373, Glyn to Gladstone, 30 Dec. 1852.

complicated matters for dealers and they all ought to have been at 4 per cent.[16] While generally critical of measures which raised cost or presented obstacles to trade, he approved of the government's plan to levy stamp duty on foreign bills to raise revenue in the Crimean War. He did not think that at the rate proposed it would have a material effect on business. In this he differed from Masterman, MP for the City of London, though both claimed to be speaking for the City.[17]

Gladstone's desire to reduce pressure on the Exchequer caused him to challenge the charging policies of the Bank of England, a cause which Glyn fully supported. Gladstone was concerned about the cost of issuing deficiency bills which represented advances to the Treasury in anticipation of the quarter's revenue and were paid off within the quarter. It counteracted the volatile effects of quarterly payments on revenue account into the Bank. Gladstone now limited deficiency bills to the amount needed at that time, taking into account the balance held by the Treasury, rather than the total needed for dividend payment in the whole quarter, so reducing significantly the amount of interest the Treasury would have to pay. The Bank held this to be illegal, claimed the whole amount required and asked him to take the opinion of the law officers. Gladstone did so and the law officers backed him. The Bank then consulted their own counsel who recommended that the Bank take their grievance to the Prime Minister, Lord Aberdeen. This angered Gladstone particularly as it was the Bank which had invited him to consult the law officers and by which he would have been bound had their opinion been adverse. He told Aberdeen that it would have been 'poltoonery of the first water' to refuse a fight.[18] Indeed the episode meant that Gladstone never forgave the Bank for its obstructive attitude, and in 1861 the Bank reluctantly accepted the heavy reductions in their charges which Gladstone then proposed.[19]

Glyn told Gladstone that the Bank's case, which he regarded as Freshfields' (the Bank's solicitors), was biased in that it suggested that the security of the public's creditors was the sole object whereas the real issue was whether the bills should be limited to what was actually required on that day. This question was independent of the matter of the proper remuneration of the Bank. He added that other questions connected with the Bank: the

[16] BL, Add Ms 44373, Glyn to Gladstone, 25 Mar.; PD, 133, 1122, 29 May 1854.

[17] PD, 133, 1364–6, 12 Jun. 1854.

[18] Letter of 18 October, 1854, quoted in Clapham, *The Bank of England, A History*, 1944, II, 254.

[19] David Kynaston, The Bank and the Government in *The Bank of England, Money, Power and Influence, 1694–1914*, ed. Richard Roberts and David Kynaston, 1995, 23; Clapham II, 256.

public deposits, the circulation and the Act of 1844, would arise before long. He hoped to see Gladstone taking on these difficult questions and putting them on a sound footing. He ended by saying that he could not help but feel that Peel, had he been spared, would have undertaken the amendment of the Act.[20]

Gladstone then sent Glyn the proposals he had sent to W.G. Anderson, the Assistant Paymaster General at the Treasury, whom he had asked to examine the cost of the Bank's management of the public accounts and the improvements which might be made in the Bank or Treasury rules. He also asked Anderson to enquire into the charge of managing the public debt, and the cost of regulating and conducting the issue of notes with a view to adjustments of the profits of such issue. More basic questions could then be looked at – the amount of issue the Bank could forward on securities; the amount of payment the Bank should make to the state in respect of the issues; whether any change should be made in the terms on which the Bank managed the national debt; and what would be a just remuneration to the Bank for management of the Public Account – to be treated as a whole; and finally a number of points on deficiency bills.

Glyn had a number of immediate comments on these issues. He hoped that the first enquiry would be general and that Gladstone would undertake some arrangement which would separate more distinctly the Issue Department in the Bank and lay the ground work for a gradual improvement and sounder circulation for the country bankers. In deciding how much should be paid to the Bank, regard should be to the advantage derived by the Bank from the use of the Government balances and from the monopoly on this and other public accounts which the Bank held e g the Court of Chancery, Court of Bankruptcy, Ecclesiastical Commissioners, Exchequer Bill Commission etc. Glyn thought the total of such deposits must be very large. He really believed that the Treasury and funding work should be done by the Bank for very little indeed in consequence of all the advantages falling to the Bank by the public demands.[21]

Later that year Glyn himself sent a scheme which he had thrown together to Sir James Graham, now First Lord of the Admiralty, for his and Gladstone's consideration. He was not aware that any sound objection could be raised to managing and securing the convertibility of the Note and the Store of Bullion by the rate of interest, and by it some of evil effects of the Act of 1844 would be overcome. He still thought it would have

[20] BL, Add Ms 44380, Glyn to Gladstone, 21 Apr. 1854.

[21] BL, Add Ms 44381, Gladstone to W.G. Anderson, 21 Jul. and Glyn to Gladstone, 22 Jul. 1854.

worked better to have left the entire management of the Note Circulation in the hands of the Bank of England subject only to certain Parliamentary control, but was prepared to reconsider the matter. In theory when the Issue and Banking departments were separate, as the demand for bullion rose there should be a corresponding decrease in the amount of notes in active circulation. In practice this did not happen because though bullion was taken in exchange for notes, the latter in the hands of the public had always been more than replaced by drawings from the Bullion Reserve and the effect on the circulation generally neutralised. The fixed maximum of £14 million had brought another evil as during an influx of bullion money was in too much abundance, but in times of imminent pressure an internal panic arose from the knowledge that there was a fixed amount beyond which no issue can be made.

Glyn then set out his own scheme. The Issue department should be separated entirely from the Bank. Control should be vested in Commissioners appointed by Parliament or in a board composed of some executive members of government. In consideration of the debt of £11m due to the Bank by the public, that amount of national notes should be issued without reference to bullion so long as this debt remains unpaid. The other issues should be made and controlled by the Commission. The bullion in the coffers of the Bank should be handed over to the Commission. The amount in store would be the Regulator of the amount of interest to be charged upon the National Notes to be issued. The rate of interest should be varied inversely as to the amount of bullion in the public coffers, for which he suggested a scale, ranging from not less than 3 per cent when there was £20 million of bullion to not less than 4½ per cent when £14 million of bullion, to 6½ per cent when £10 million with such further increases as the Commissioners might deem necessary below £10 million. The Commission should make annual reports to Parliament and have power to issue the national notes on Government Stock, Exchequer Bills and Bonds subject to such regulations as might from time to time be made. The provisions of the 1844 Act on country banks and joint-stock banks should remain in force, and no interference with existing issues should be allowed, but the Commissioners should be empowered to issue National Notes to the banks entitled to issue their own notes in substitution of such circulation at a lower rate of interest than that fixed for other circulations.[22]

In November Gladstone sent Glyn another letter covering the same ground. In reply Glyn said he was glad to find Gladstone agreed that the

[22] BL, Add Ms 44382, Glyn to Graham, 28 Sept. 1854.

store of bullion could be managed and secured by the rate of interest, so it followed that the statutory limitation of notes was not necessary and as it was attended with evil which required extraordinary contortions to overcome there was no reason why to continue it. He was also pleased to find Gladstone admitted to the value of a 'safety valve'. He admitted the constitution of the commission presented a difficulty, but it could not be insuperable. The present machinery in the Bank for the Issue Department meant antagonism between the duties of banking and money supply. He had always considered the plan of the 1844 Act for the gradual but not fixed extinction of the country banks circulation and for its replacement a very valuable portion of the law, though most defective in its mode of working as it was now left to the Bank and some new machinery was now needed. Later he emphasised to Gladstone that no system for the regulation of the currency in a country like England could be devised which did not carry with it the admission of the necessity of periodical recession; it was required by the very nature of things and had in fact been admitted in all recent legislation on the subject. He added he was not disposed to fear the discovery of gold. The growth of production in the country was always stimulated directly to keep pace with the surfeit of bullion. He wrote again later that day to say that two bodies of people had been at him. The country bankers of England wanted the 1844 Act altered to allow them as before to enlarge the issue of their own notes. He added on that he and Gladstone agreed that the Act stood very properly and worked well. The Scottish banks wanted to be allowed to increase their note issue upon deposits instead of bullion. He thought that might be worth consideration in connection with Gladstone's general plan of issuing securities at regulated rates of interest. He added that in both cases he had declined to act for them. He concluded 'If you want any question put about your intention I am at your service when bidden for I am not an interpolator by profession and never mean mischief, though just now am very angry with one department of the administration which has used me hardly.'[23]

By the time Gladstone and Glyn had concluded their correspondence a public debate had started about the renewal of the Bank's charter. Criticism by the Birmingham Chamber of Commerce and others such as Thomas Tooke, originally a supporter of the currency school but since 1844 an advocate of the principles of the banking school, concentrated on the £14 million, though as the *Bankers Magazine* put it when it is agreeable for the public to vent their dissatisfaction the Birmingham Chamber of Commerce and its imitators lift their heads and multitudes are ready to be persuaded

[23] BL, Add Ms 44382, Glyn to Gladstone, 4 Nov. and 9 Dec. 1854.

that the measure of Sir Robert Peel was the cause of all their suffering, but there was no agreement on what should replace it. What people wanted was a discretionary power to exceed the £14 million limit, but it was the desire to avoid that discretion that involved the judgment of individuals which had caused Peel to legislate.[24] In February 1856 Glyn asked Gladstone whether any steps had been taken preparatory to the revision of the Bank's charter and whether they intended to set up an inquiry into the workings of the 1844 Act, Gladstone in effect said the Government had no intention of revising the charter and particularly in the circumstances of the Crimean War did not favour an inquiry.[25] Later that month George Frederick Muntz the tory radical MP for Birmingham moved for a wide ranging committee. Glyn objected to this. He thought the question for enquiry was whether the limit should be £14,000,000 or whether there should be any limit at all. The panic of 1847 was not produced by fear of the convertability of the bank note but by the knowledge that there was a fixed sum of £14,000,000 beyond which the Bank could not issue notes and those with ample security of the very best character could not convert it into bank notes. This was resolved by the letter of indemnity which meant that those who had hoarded notes because of the scarcity threw them onto the market.[26]

In the event the Government took no steps to change the legislation governing the Bank. Critics of the Bank Act believed that in wartime conditions with heavy borrowing and higher taxes the currency system only survived because of imports of gold. D.B. Chapman of Overend and Gurney said in 1857 'We have looked to the arrival of steamers from Australia, as much as to almost anything else, to know whether we are safe in going on with our business'.[27]

During the recess in the autumn of 1857 a major financial crisis blew up. This started in the US where trust companies and banks failed in September and in October 150 banks stopped payment in just four eastern states. Bank rates rose in Europe. In London it was raised to 6 per cent in early October and to 8 per cent on 19 October. The Liverpool Borough Bank failed on 27 October and two days later Overend and Gurney's asked the Bank for unlimited assistance should the firm be pressed. There were major difficulties in Scotland including fears for the Union Bank of Glasgow which had close connections with Dennistoun's, American bankers and exchanger brokers of Liverpool, London, Glasgow, New York and New Orleans, who suspended

24 *Bankers' Magazine*, 1855, 797–799.
25 PD, 140, 222–3, 5 Feb. 1856.
26 PD, 140, 1509–11, 28 Feb. 1856.
27 Select Committee on the Bank Acts, PP, 1857, x, Qs 1423 and 5310.

payments as did Sanderson's, the bill-brokers. The Bank Rate was raised to 9 per cent on 5 November and to 10 per cent four days later. In Scotland the Western Bank had long carried from year to year a growing volume of bad and doubtful debt. By July 1857 they were faced with hopelessly bad debts of £452,000 and there were also further imprudent advances to America. By 9 November the Western Bank had closed its doors. The Union Bank of Glasgow now came under pressure. They sent a delegation to London to see the Bank of England which agreed to discount bills to a total of £2 million. Glyn's were the Union Bank's London agents and proved to be an important intermediary with Threadneedle Street, and themselves provided £200,000. The Union Bank was strongly supported by the Edinburgh banks anxious not to see another Scottish bank fail.[28]

On 11 November the brokers, Sandersons collapsed with liabilities of £5 million but it was only on the following day that the Governor, Sheffield Neave, admitted that members of the Court were coming round to the view that a repetition of the Chancellor's letter of 1847 was necessary, having earlier thought that their high Bank rate was bringing in sufficient funds. The chancellor, Cornewall Lewis, decided to issue a letter without a formal request from the Bank, which he did later that day. He told Overstone, who thought that Chapman of Overend Gurney had threatened the Bank to secure the suspension of the Act, that no pressure was applied to the government which they could not have easily resisted; the pressure applied was the pressure of facts By 14 November over £500,000 of notes beyond the 1844 limit had been put into circulation and the excess reached a maximum of £920,000 on 20 November as difficulties continued. By the end of the month no excess notes remained in circulation. The rate was reduced to 8 per cent on 24 December and to 6 per cent on 6 January and progressively to 3 per cent as early as 11 February.

Glyn spoke in the debate on the Bank Issues Indemnity Bill on 4 December.[29] He told Lord Grey 'It has been a terrible crisis, worse than 1847,'[30] and said in the House that the 1847 and 1857 crises were very similar in their causes. In 1847 it was brought about by overtrading with India and large speculations in Europe in the corn trade, together with internal pressure on the Bank. In 1857 the parts of the world from which the pressure arose were different, the United States and Northern Europe where the system of credit had broken down, but the causes were identical. To this was added the

[28] Richard Saville, *Bank of Scotland: A History 1695–1995*, 392–393, 500–501.

[29] Because the increase in circulation went beyond the limit of the 1844 Act, an Indemnity Bill was necessary to regularise the excess.

[30] Durham University Library, Grey Papers, GRE/B132/15, Glyn to Grey, 28 Nov. 1857.

extraordinary over-banking in Scotland. These results could not be traced to the 1844 Act in any way consistent with just reasoning. However Glyn distinguished between the causes of the crisis and the effect of the Act when the pressure had arisen. This tended to reduce the reserves of the Bank, but men who were not speculators but needed a supply of currency could not obtain it or thought they would be unable to do so. The government had acted correctly to issue the letter. He had doubts whether the power should remain with the government as it was exercised without rules and depended entirely on the feeling of those who for the time being were entrusted with the administration of the affairs of the country. He saw no reason why under appropriate regulations the Governor of the Bank should not be vested with such a power.[31]

The result was that a Select Committee was set up. Glyn was a member, but the committee did not publish a report that Session but only the evidence. The Committee resumed its sittings in 1858. In its report it proposed no change in the Bank Act, sharing Glyn's view that the causes of the crisis could hardly be traced to British currency law. The Committee seemed to have been impressed by the Bank's argument that whatever the law's defects it had safeguarded the ultimate reserve of bullion and kept notes convertible. The Committee put the crisis down to the great abuse of credit and consequent over-trading.

Glyn supported Disraeli's Budget of 1858 which included the remission of the war level of income tax and the abolition of the War Sinking Fund, except that he protested against the stamp duty of one penny imposed on cheques.[32] Two years later when Gladstone was preparing his budget Glyn wrote to ask him to consider before determining the Stamp Duty on endorsements whether it was provident to counter the claims of the commercial constituency which might be raised against it. He feared it would be a severe impediment to business. He would be sorry to see the popularity of Gladstone's budget marred by this experiment.[33]

In 1860 he suggested to Gladstone two savings in the Bank of England's charges. Later that year he was challenging the Treasury's definition of a public account. The Chancery and Bankruptcy accounts and the East India Government account should be included. A proper definition of a public account should be those which by statute are opened at the Bank of England because Parliament had directed it or were in some way interested, as they were all part of the Bank's aggregate balance. In 1862 Gladstone was still

31 PD, 148, 185–8, 4 Dec. 1857.
32 PD, 149, 1308, 19 Apr. 1858.
33 BL, Add Ms 44393, Glyn to Gladstone, 2 Feb. 1860.

encouraging Glyn to give him the benefit of his views though they differed on the importance of stock payable to bearer.[34]

In 1854 the Bankers Clearing House was still confined to the private banks: there were 25 in membership, but after pressure from the joint stock banks led by David Salomons of the London & Westminster they decided to admit five joint-stock banks but not to give them any share in the management.[35] The process of settlement was simplified as cheques on the Bank of England replaced banknotes. Nevertheless any competitive advantage over the joint stock banks derived by the private banks from the Clearing House disappeared. Glyn's personal standing in the City was emphasised in 1858 when he succeeded Robarts as chairman of the Bankers Clearing House, a position he held until 1867 when he resigned because of ill health.[36]

Glyn was of course also deeply engaged in the affairs of Glyn's bank. He dealt with some of the principal customers himself. In 1845 Lord Howick, soon to succeed his father Earl Grey, was puzzled to know why the Bank had sent him a bond prepared for signature, when he had only called on Glyn to find out whether he would lend him the money and on what terms. He now thought he could get the money at 4 or 4½ per cent in Northumberland (Glyn had apparently offered 4 to 5 per cent according to the Bank Rate). He was concerned lest a prepared bond would attract stamp duty. Glyn replied the same day saying that he himself had left the bond at Howick's house – he lived in Eaton Place, very near Glyn's house in Belgravia – in case the bond was needed as he was going away for a day or two. If not executed it would not attract stamp duty. He ended the letter 'a loan on the terms stated by me will be at your lordship's command at any time if you find it expedient to take that course.'[37]

[34] Glyn to Gladstone, 21 Aug. and 13 Oct. 1860; BL, Add Ms 44394, Gladstone to Glyn, 5 Dec. 1862, Add Ms 44399.

[35] Albert M. Hyamson, *David Salamons*, 1939, 97.

[36] LMA, MS 32006/002.

[37] Grey Papers, GRE/B132/15, Howick to Glyn, 7 Jul. 1842, and Glyn's reply of the same day. The correspondence does not cover Howick's interest in railways. Howick objected to Hudson's Newcastle to Berwick passing very close to his property and backed the rival Northumberland Railway with Brunel as the engineer. This line was opposed by other landowners and the Board of Trade found Hudson's line preferable. (A.J. Arnold and S. McCartney, *George Hudson*, 2004, 67–70.) Sidney Smith wrote to Howick's mother Lady Grey 'I hear that Howick's atmospheric railroad is vigorously opposed by the retired linen draper but powerful railroader, Mr Hudson, but I do not think that Howick would embark on such a novelty without much previous examination.' (nd but ascribed to Sept. 1844, *Letters of Sidney Smith*, ed. Nowell C. Smith, 1953, II, 852–853.)

It is noteworthy that Glyn, who was chairman of the largest railway company in the country, could show such subservience in writing to one of his aristocratic customers. Replying to Grey in 1845 when he requested a statement of his account to be prepared and accounts to be consolidated. Glyn told him that this would be done and then added:

> It will give us very great pleasure to be in any way useful to your Lordship and I beg you will draw on your account for any sums which you may require and will not hesitate to avail yourself of this facility until you adopt any other arrangement which may be more convenient to your Lordship.

He advised Grey on his investments, and told him in 1857 that it would be better for him to take an advance on his Canadian bonds, as the rate of interest was very low. This would be better than selling the bonds as the price had been temporarily lowered by an operation of the Canadian Government. He added 'I do not like to make an offer from Glyn and Co for in these hard times we have such a number of commercial people waiting and desiring of support that I feel it a duty to do our best for them but we will manage this matter for you somehow.' In late December he told Grey that they would credit his account with a loan of £4,000 and mentioned that Canadian debentures were now 108½ to 109. In January 1859 Glyn thought Grey might like to know that among the Canadian debentures held by him £13,000 fell due on 1 July and would be paid off. Grey might wish to look out for another investment in the interval. In June Grey had still not decided because Glyn told him that the Nova Scotia debentures were about 108. The debt was not large but it was a poor country. South Australian Bonds were also 108 – the Victorian about the same price. In 1867 Grey was still investing in colonial securities. Glyn told him he agreed with his preference for one or other of the two colonies named by him. He had suggested to his friends in Lombard Street that they should procure an investment between them for the sum named by Grey and he had also instructed them to employ for him at interest the sum of £7,000 which could remain out until required – 10 days notice would be quite enough. The rate of interest was very low. He agreed with Grey about the probable rise in good colonial securities. The only drawback in holding them was that if they suddenly required to be realised it was not always easy to do so without some sacrifice, but with sufficient time that could generally be avoided. He concluded by saying 'I am always glad of an opportunity of attending to your wishes.'[38]

38 Ibid, Glyn to Grey, 5 Aug. 1845, 28 Nov. and 18 Dec. 1857, 7 Jan. and 9 Jun. 1859, 4 Jan. 1867.

Quite apart from dealing with Hudson in railway matters, Glyn's dealt with some of his financial affairs. The bank wrote to Francis Taylor of Hudson's Union Bank at York in May 1849 to say it would be very desirable that 'we should have a personal interview with yourself or one of the directors of the Union Bank. So much excitement exists as to the affairs in your District that it would be satisfactory to us and might do much good if we were enabled on authority to disabuse the public mind of all erroneous impressions.' The following day they wrote again to say we, presumably George Carr Glyn, had seen Hudson who fully explained the resources of the Bank and the monies he was about to raise. Glyn's were ready to offer any reasonable assistance to the bank should any run take place but trusted from the precaution the Union Bank had taken that nothing of the sort would recur. In November Taylor was told that Glyn's had been instructed by Hudson to sell his stock (it is not clear which) and to place the £50,000 with the Yorkshire Union Bank. There were further difficulties with Hudson. Fulford quotes the letter of 31 July 1851 when Glyn's called Hudson's attention to the fact that his account was overdrawn to the extent of £2,000, and mentioned that they had no means of preventing it being known to their clerks whose attention was called to the fact when cheques were presented for payment. Fulford regarded this as a masterpiece of tact and good feeling. It did not seem so to George Carr Glyn who wrote two days later a letter to which Fulford does not refer to explain that he was not the writer of the letter about which Hudson had complained. He had asked for the bills listed in Hudson's note amounting to £3,250 to be placed under discount. The bank understood that the two loans of £1,000 would be repaid in the first week of October. Difficulties however continued. In November Glyn returned bills of £3,445 sent to them by Hudson, saying 'that we do not understand this transaction and must decline to discount them.' By December Glyn's were calling attention to the two loans of £1,000 and asking Hudson to make arrangements for their liquidation before the end of the year. In January 1853 Hudson's account was £1,915 in debit and the bank would not consent to any further overdraft. In April the bank refused an advance in the absence of any knowledge of the value of the deeds to which Hudson alluded. The documents were returned. Meanwhile the Globe at a meeting of the Treasury Committee at which Glyn was present refused to lend Hudson £30,000 on certain houses and land in Whitby but agreed to £25,000 for which there was safe security, particularly as a considerable amount of fire insurance would follow.[39] William Jackson, the

[39] LMA, 11658/5, 19 Feb. 1852.

contractor, was another to whom stiff letters were written. In May 1856 he was told that the recent advance had been made on condition that no overdraft would be allowed. 'We regret the painful necessity of making this communication.' Jackson thought he had found a way round the limit but was told this loophole was only for insurance costs.[40]

On the other hand transactions for the major railway companies usually proceeded smoothly. Glyn's were quite ready to advance the Midland £20,000 on hearing from Bell, secretary of the Midland, and a year later placed £50,000 on call at 2 per cent, though in 1853 the advance to the Midland was limited to £50,000 in view of the state of the money market.[41]

Glyn's may not have provided investment funds for British manufacturing firms but they did enable the country banks to assist manufacturers with working capital. The Leeds Old Bank said in August 1854 that their customers attending the wool sales in London were drawing on them heavily for cash and they had to provide them with £40 to 50,000. They would therefore be glad to know whether Glyn's would take their bills at 2 to 3 per cent. Three years later £50,000 had been lent by Glyn's, presumably for the same purpose. The Old Bank repaid £25,000 in October.[42]

The Central Bank of Scotland asked Glyn's for their opinion of discount acceptances they had been offered by Messrs Strachan and Paul in the Strand to contractors, mostly in France, generally at longish dates and so to be paid by instalments. Later the Central Bank's agent in Aberfeldy wished to have the account of a Devonshire Baronet who had taken a lease of Castle Menzies and asked Glyn's if they could do anything for them without too much trouble. They ended their letter by 'PS is this dear money to last long?'[43] Langton in Liverpool said some valued constituents were anxious to obtain information about the Asiatic Insurance Co. Later his sub-manager wrote that some friends were desirous of investing in South Carolina bonds, expiring in 1858 to the extent of £10,000 at 98. If Glyn was in a position to know of any offer on these terms through any private channel, they would be glad to know. Although as will be seen in chapter 15 Glyn's sometimes had difficulty in selling Canadian bonds for which they were agents in 1860 the Canterbury Bank thanked them for securing £10,000 and the Wilts and Dorset applied for £80,000 of the same issue.

40 RBS Archives, GM/4/1, to Francis Taylor, 17 May, 18 May and 29 Nov. 1849; GM/4/2, to Hudson 31 Jul., 2 Aug.,15 Nov. and 3 Dec. 1851, 9 Apr. 1853; GM/4/3, to Jackson, 13 and 14 May 1856.

41 RBS Archives, GM/2, to J.F. Bell, 22 Sept. 1853.

42 RBS Archives, GM/429/30, 12 Aug. 1854 and 3 Oct. 1857.

43 Ibid, GM/429/14, 15 Jan. 1855 and 16 Apr. 1860.

In this decade the cost of telegraph services was falling. Techniques for money transactions by wire were developed. Coded messages reduced costs and enhanced security. At the end of 1855 there were difficulties over codes. The Bank of Liverpool wanted the simplest possible used when ordering from Glyn's by telegraph the unconditional payment of money without waiting for written advice, so messages should end with a, e, i, o or y according to the day of the week, a code changed in 1862. To some extent such procedures replaced the relationship based on bills of exchange. Nevertheless personal relationships remained important. When Langton died in December 1855, his successor, Samuel Smith, was obliged by Glyn's assurance that they would extend to him the same courtesy and confidence in their future intercourse which their much lamented friend so long enjoyed from Glyn's.[44] Moreover bills were still convenient for transaction processing and short term credit purposes, though increasingly accepting and discounting bills became more the province of merchant bankers than of the clearing banks.

The Norfolk bank, Lacon, Youell & Co. had two unusual dealings with Glyn. In 1855 they instructed Glyn's not to pay drafts without special advice as a clerk had absconded with two signed drafts. Glyn's were asked to detain anyone applying for money on these drafts. The clerk 'may immediately be identified by his eyebrows which meet on his nose.' In 1865 they made the arrangements and sent to London for sale a vessel called Sir Francis Drake on which Glyn's had a mortgage.[45]

Payment of interest on funds deposited by country banks with Glyn's does not seem to have been a major issue in the 1850s, but G.M. Moore of the Stone Bank mentioned to Glyn the low rate of interest that they were receiving on their bank account. He then wrote to say that he trusted that, as the rate of interest was now generally higher, the interest on the Stone account would be advanced in the same proportion. On the back of the letter is a note that on 1 January, Bank rate was 2 per cent, 7 Jan. 2½, 21 Jan, 3 so the Stone Bank should be allowed 1¼, 1½ and 2 per cent respectively.[46] In 1858 the York Union Bank said they were pleased that Glyn's would allow sums in their hands beyond £10,000, but having asked what the rate of interest would be went on to say that the chief portion of the balance would be required in ten days time for the payment of interest.[47]

[44] Ibid, GM/429//31, 15 Jan. 1855 from the Manager to Messrs Glyn; 16 Oct. 1854, 18 Nov., 11, 13 and 29 Dec. 1855.

[45] R.S. Sayers, *Lloyds*, 118 and 135.

[46] RBS Archives, GM/429/52, 20 May 1853.

[47] Ibid, GM429/67, 5 Jan. 1858.

Wentworth Grey, a young city merchant found himself in difficulties in 1860 when his partner and brother was in the West Indies. He had a balance at Glyn's for £1,600 but found it necessary to borrow to meet commitments. He went to Glyn's and stated his case to Williams, one of the clerks, and Mills, but they could do nothing for him and told him it was 'quite against the rules of this house to advance money on wharf orders etc'. That afternoon he called again by appointment to see Mr Glyn who said although it was against their rules to make such advances yet in the present instance they would consent to break their rule and make an advance of £3,000'.[48]

Fulford records that in some time of panic Glyn sold a part of his consols at a fraction under the price of the day to help a customer while S.J. Loyd, chuckling to himself as he bought the consols cheap buttoned up his pockets and allowed a perfectly solvent firm which banked with him to suspend payment.[49] This was in keeping with other dealings by George Carr Glyn.

[48] Kynaston, *City of London*, 208 quoting from the Charles Williams and Wentworth Grey records in the Guildhall Library.

[49] Fulford, 116. Croker states that S.J. Loyd bought £100,000 LNWR debentures at 25 per cent discount when a manufacturer was in desperate need for cash in 1847. (Kynaston, 159, quoting Louis J. Jennings, ed. *The Croker Papers*, 1884, III, 152).

CHAPTER FIFTEEN

Glyn's Overseas – mainly Canada

Early Overseas business

For much of the first half of the nineteenth century Glyn's played little part in arranging loans and bonds for overseas governments, institutions or enterprises, unlike Barings who from the late eighteenth century had been so engaged and in 1803 had financed the Louisiana purchase. Glyn's did introduce circular letters of credit which took the form of a document signed by one of the bank's partners addressed to the bank's correspondents abroad, generally empowering the bearer to draw up to the sum fixed in the letter. These had been pioneered by Robert Herries of Herries and Co. a generation earlier as a service to individual clients travelling on business or pleasure. It is more likely that Thomas Hallifax or Charles Mills was responsible for this innovation than Glyn as they were much travelled. It was such a letter of credit which was the subject of a notorious case of fraud when Allen Bogle, a partner in a bank in Florence abstracted it from the bank for a short time, and copied it on a printing machine used to make copies of Florentine pictures. Many copies were cashed successfully until identical letters were presented in two nearby Belgian towns on successive days and the Belgian bankers had the presenter arrested. Bogle sued *The Times* for libel when in May 1840 the paper printed letters by the so-called Marquis de Bourbelle, Bogle's partner in crime, which had been seized by the French Government. Bogle was awarded a farthing's damages, and Glyn's, Rothschilds, and Barings met to discuss raising a fund to reimburse *The Times* for the considerable expenses it had incurred in the case. *The Times* however declined to accept the £2,700 offered and the money was used to endow a scholarship at Christ's Hospital and another at the City of London School. In 1846 a tablet was unveiled at Lloyds at a dinner commemorating the episode.[1]

Glyn's also ran into trouble when in 1833 Dom Miguel of Portugal raised a loan of £3,400 which included some bills of exchange drawn on and accepted by Glyn's. His niece, Donna Maria the Queen of Portugal, expelled him and seized his treasure. Glyn's then brought an action against the Queen to determine her right to cash the bills. The case was eventually decided in the House of Lords in favour of the Queen as a bill of discovery could not be filed against the Queen who was not a party to the action, though Lord Wynford, in a dissenting judgment, said a fouler fraud was never committed on the merchants of Great Britain. Glyn's then pursued Soares, the Portuguese minister, who had endorsed the bills.[2]

Unlike most private banks Glyn's were not merely a retail bank but carried out some of the functions of a merchant bank. From the 1850s they were involved in public issues and accepting house business. They were also involved in the establishment of joint-stock banks abroad. A foretaste came in the 1830s though Glyn's overseas interests were then small, confined to the British Empire and to a link with one Australian bank and the start of an agency for the Bank of Upper Canada.

The Bank of New South Wales had been started as early as 1817, and the Bank of Australasia set up by royal charter in 1833. That bank was in competition with the small local Tamar Bank in Tasmania so the latter sent Philip Oakden, one of its partners, to London to see whether the bank's position could be strengthened. This led to the setting up of the Union Bank with a capital of £500,000. George Carr Glyn was one of the original subscribers and one of the three trustees. George Fife Angas, involved in shipping, banks and the South Australian Land company, was on the board and Edward W Mills, Glyn's partner, and Jacob B. Montefiore, one of Australia's largest merchants, were among the subscribers. The English directors were not all City figures. They included Robert Gardner of Manchester, Thomas Sands of Liverpool, and bankers Christopher Rawson of Halifax, Charles Hindley MP of Birmingham and Charles Mangles MP of Guildford. The aim was to meet the increased demand for capital in the Australasian colonies. The directors looked forward to good dividends as bank interest in Australia was 8 per cent and the dividends of other colonial banks had averaged 15 per cent. Shares were rapidly taken up, 7,000 of the 20,000 being purchased in Australia, and in this respect the Union Bank was rather more successful

1 *The History of The Times, 1, The Thunderer in the Making, 1785–1841,* 1935, 417; Fulford, 137–140; RBS Archives, GM/991/2 and 3.

2 *Morning Post,* 28 Feb. 1837, *The Times,* 23 Jan. 1841.

than the smaller Bank of Australasia. Glyn's were the Union Bank's London bankers. In 1838 its paid up capital was £143,000 with only £4,712 profits but by 1843 its profits were £84,465, with a capital of £806,000, making it more profitable than the Bank of Australasia. By 1839 it had establishments in the chief towns of eastern Australia and arrangements were being made for a branch in New Zealand. The Glyn family links were strengthened in 1854 when St Leger Glyn was elected a director.[3] George Carr Glyn remained a trustee – in 1858 he was signing a request to the Bank of England to hold £184,000 New Zealand 4 per cents at the disposal of the Union Bank.[4] By 1873 it became a limited company.[5]

The start of Glyn's Canadian Business

Australia was not to be the main overseas interest of Glyn's, but Canada, where their interest began in a small way in the 1830s, and grew until that country presented perhaps the most intractable problems which Glyn's and George Carr Glyn personally had to face. They were involved on three levels: first, jointly with Barings, as London agents of the Province of Canada; second as London agents of the Bank of Upper Canada; and third with the Grand Trunk Railway where Glyn and Baring were both on the London board. These simple statements of the relationship between Glyn's and the Canadian bodies do not bring out the complexity of the situation as from 1850 the Bank of Upper Canada was the banker to the Canadian Government and also banker to the Grand Trunk Railway from its formation in 1853. In the railway's early years a majority of the directors on the Canadian board of the railway were members of the Canadian government, which had major financial interests in that concern.

Glyn's first became involved in Canada following the failure of the Anglo-American house, Thomas Wilson and Co., who closed their doors on 2 June 1837. Wilson's and Barings had been the main houses specialising in the American and Canadian markets, and were the joint financial agents in London for Upper Canada, though Barings had shown no enthusiasm for being involved in Canadian government finance. It was only in 1835, when money was particularly plentiful and US securities had become the growth

[3] *Morning Post*, 4 Jul. 1854. He retired as a director in June 1864 (*Morning Post*, 30 Jun. 1864.)

[4] RBS Archives, GM/492, 24 Feb. 1858.

[5] A.S.J. Baster, *The Imperial Banks*, 1929, 63–67; S.J. Butlin, The *Australia and New Zealand Bank: The Bank of Australasia and the Union Bank of Australia, 1829–1951*, 1961, 53.

stock of the day, that Barings tendered for a loan of £400,000 at 5 per cent to Upper Canada for public works, mostly for canal construction. They split the loan with Wilson's who had also tendered, though much of the loan was left on deposit with Wilson's and Barings and when Wilson's failed they had £90,000 credited to the account of the Bank of Upper Canada, for whom Wilson's were the London agents.[6] The Bank founded in 1812 and based in Toronto transferred their agency to Glyn's in 1837 just before Wilson's failed. George Glyn seems to have been approached by an intermediary, possibly Robert Gillespie of Gillespie, Moffat and Co., the largest import house in Montreal. Glyn wrote to Sir George Grey, the Under Secretary at the Colonial Office, to say that the Bank of Upper Canada without any approach from Glyn's had paid them the compliment of selecting them as agents for the Bank. He told Grey that he would like to add the financial agency for the province which Wilson's had held, 'which comprehends the payment of the dividends on the debentures for the loan raised here some time back'[7] Grey and Glyn then met and the position was confirmed, though John H. Dunn, the Receiver General of Upper Canada had intended that Barings should take over the whole agency, but after seeing Grey, he agreed to appoint Glyn's as joint agents.[8] Glyn wrote to Grey again on 12 June to say his colleagues agreed to the proposal, and they would be able to advance temporarily the money necessary for the payment of dividends.[9] Glyn doubtless was the more willing to advance money to the province because like Barings they wanted to avoid Upper Canada seeking a writ against Wilson's assets. Barings and Glyn's were also Wilson's creditors. Fulford suggests that Grey would have preferred Glyn's to Barings because the former was Whig and the latter Tory, but it seems more likely that Grey wanted to meet the Canadian wishes and appreciated that Glyn's were reputable successors to Wilson's. Barings reaction at the time seems to have been one of acquiescence, rather than the mortification suggested by Fulford.[10] They still had £60,000 of the loan stock on their hands. Baring and Glyn chaired the committee of creditors. In 1838 the Bank of Upper Canada received £28,500, but £59,436 was never

[6] Michael J. Piva, Financing the Union: The Upper Canadian Debt and Financial Administration in the Canadas, 1837–45, *Journal of Canadian Studies*, 25, 1990–91, 82–83.

[7] Glyn said the post itself carried no salary or emolument but it was 'a feather'. Glyn initially was not clear whether the appointment was to be personal to him or to the firm. TNA, CO 422/222, Glyn to Grey, 10 Jun. 1837 reproduced in Fulford 145–146.

[8] TNA, CO 422/222; Fulford, 145–147; John Ireland, John Dunn and the Bankers, *Ontario History*, LXII, 1970, 83–100.

[9] TNA, CO 22/224.

[10] Fulford, 148.

repaid. Thomas Ward, Barings long-standing agent in the USA, approved of Glyn's involvement. In 1841 he told Joshua Bates they appear to be thriving in Canada and 'to be a frugal, good sort of people.' At the end of 1848 Hincks, the recently appointed Inspector General of Finance, told Barings that the Canadian government had declined in 1837 to make Barings the sole agents. While there was no dissatisfaction with Glyn's, 'a divided agency is not worth the attention either of your house or Messrs Glyn's', and he 'did not believe that any house would be so likely to advance our interest as yours,'[11] and thought Barings should now take over the whole agency, but they refused out of friendship to Glyn's. Indeed they went so far as to say that if the Canadians insisted on a sole agency then Glyn's were as able and willing as they were promote the interests of the colony.[12] The agency continued to be joint.[13]

The Earl of Durham was sent out as Governor following the Mackenzie rebellion and in his report recommended the union of the provinces of Upper and Lower Canada to form the province of Canada, achieved in 1840. In 1842 Barings and Glyn's jointly raised £1.5 million at 5 per cent for public works in the province, mainly the Welland Canal. This growth in investment in Canada coincided with disillusionment in the City with US securities especially following the default of Pennsylvania. In 1847 Glyn's advanced £40,000 on the security of £80,000 provincial debentures deposited with the bank. In September 1848 Hincks told Baring that they had experienced some temporary embarrassment and wanted £40,000 to meet the January dividends. Baring and Glyn jointly met that request as Glyn had done in 1847, but Baring pointed out that they would have preferred not to do so, if maintenance of the credit of the colony had not required it. They could find more advantageous employment for their money.[14] For his part Glyn told Hincks later that month that the price of Canadian bonds continued very low and quotations were nearly nominal.[15]

Until 1847–48 much of the finance needed for the modest rate of progress in the Canadian economy could be found locally. Canada then experienced

[11] Francis Hincks, *Canada: Its Financial Position and Resources*, 1849, 6–12 (Hincks to Barings, 20 Dec. 1848).

[12] Philip Ziegler, *The Sixth Great Power, Barings, 1762–1929*, 1988, 157, quoting Thomas Baring to Francis Hincks, 12 January 1849 (Baring Archives, HC1.20).

[13] Ibid, 157 (NAC, MG 24 D21).

[14] D.C.M. Platt and Jeremy Adelman, London Merchant Bankers in the First Phase of Heavy Borrowing: The Grand Trunk Railway of Canada, *The Journal of Imperial and Commonwealth History*, 18,1990, 213, LAC, frame nos 148–9, 151–3, 155–7, 70210 and 70320.

[15] RBS Archives, GM/4/1, 29 Sept. 1848.

a financial crisis which meant the provincial banks could not find sufficient funds for private investment or to accommodate Government needs so they turned to London, though initially without much success. In 1848 Dunn did not succeed in negotiating a £200,000 loan with Barings. Hincks wrote to Baring –

> Our bonds are not recommended as an investment, while those of the USA are: indeed I have felt mortified to find that the price of Canadian bonds is never quoted in the list of stocks, although those of each of the United States, as well as of all other foreign governments, are kept constantly before the public.[16]

Hincks personally visited London in 1849 to try to raise a £500,000 loan, but it was not possible to place the debentures in any quantity, though Glyn's and Barings agreed to sell them on commission. Glyn told Hincks that he shared his surprise at the comparative indifference shown by investors in Britain to the Canadian debt. He blamed recent events in Canada, including the Mackenzie rebellion and the expectation of annexation by the United States in the American newspapers. 'A little time and a more general knowledge of the contrary feeling in Canada will tend to remove this impression' he wrote, but urged Hincks to influence the British press to lead the public to a fair consideration of the Province's financial position and exhibit the actual figures and results of her increasing revenue and resources.[17]

The mechanism for marketing provincial securities in London was improved in 1849, when Hincks officially appointed Barings and Glyn's as agents under the new Act for the Better Management of Public Debt.[18] The two bankers were frequently to find themselves in the position where a decision on strict commercial grounds was not possible because they were also agents for the colony, and as such became the unofficial controllers and regulators of the flow of Canadian credit and of public funds. Baring and Glyn worked closely together and generally were of a common mind on issues. That Baring, unlike his brother, was a Conservative MP who was twice urged to accept the office of Chancellor of the Exchequer, while Glyn was a Liberal, did not affect their relationship.[19] Currie wrote that Baring

[16] Hincks, 11, letter of 12 Dec. 1848.

[17] RBS Archives, GM/4/1, Glyn to Hincks, 10 Aug. 1849.

[18] Michael J. Piva, Community and Crisis: Francis Hincks and Canadian Economic Policy, *Canadian Historical Review*, 66, 1985, 194–195.

[19] Baring was chairman of Lloyds, 1830–68 and a member of the court of the Bank of England, 1848–67. MP for Huntingdon from 1844.

was certainly a proof, if any were wanting, that a merchant may be as good gentleman as an acred lord or squire and he was wisely content with and proud of his trade.'[20] Glyn told Hincks 'I have seen Thomas Baring and wish it were in my power to report that his opinion did not coincide with mine … I believe his opinion is founded, as mine is, upon the opinion of some of the best informed people in the stock market.'[21] By this time Glyn's were the London agents of other Canadian banks including the Bank of Montreal which agency they shared with the Union Bank, and the Gore Bank who appointed Glyn's when their London agent, Reid, Irving & Co failed in the 1847 crisis.

As the demand for capital grew, it was not matched by increases in the abilities of the Canadian banks to provide it, so the agency soon attracted a much increased volume of business, of which railways were the main ingredient. Indeed Barings and Glyn's became vital players in the financing of Canadian railways which developed slowly compared to Britain and the United States. Only 68 miles were open in the Province in 1850, compared with 6,000 in Great Britain and 9,000 in the United States. By 1860 however there were 1,600 miles open. The population of the Province was 1.8 million in 1851, almost equally divided between the French speaking Lower Canada and Upper Canada. The cities were small and the distances between them great. Montreal, the largest city had only 90,000 people but it was about twice the size of Toronto, 350 miles to the west, or Quebec, more than 150 miles to the East. To the west of Upper Canada there was a small settler population of some 25,000 and about 100,000 natives. This land was under control of the Hudson's Bay Company which was more interested in maintaining its business based on hunting than opening up the territory to others. The economy of Canada itself was largely reliant on timber and wheat, but good land was becoming scarce. The Great Lakes, rivers and associated canals provided a very adequate network for water transport except during the long hard winters when they were frozen.

The Earl of Durham had recommended the construction of a railway from Halifax to Quebec to give the people of Canada 'the far more certain and speedy communication throughout the winter that they possess in summer.'[22] The only railway then operating in Canada was a short line between the St Lawrence, opposite Montreal, to Lake Champlain. Canadian interests were keen to develop an alternative to water transport. They thought a Canadian railway would take traffic from the rapidly growing

20 Currie, I, 43.

21 RBS Archives, GM/4/1, 10 Aug. 1849.

22 *Lord Durham's Report on the Affairs of British North America,* ed. C.P. Lucas, 1912, 1, 319.

American grain areas to the Atlantic, and feared the rapidly growing US railroad network would take traffic from Canada to New York and Boston. Another factor was that they found it difficult to enter US markets because of the high tariffs and so sought their own routes to the Atlantic. Although projects were put forward no railway was built in part because of the boundary dispute with the USA.

It was 1845 before the St Lawrence and Atlantic Railway was founded in Montreal with a capital of £600,000 designed to run to the Maine border where it would link with the Atlantic and St Lawrence projected from Portland. A key figure in the development of Canada was Alexander Galt who saw Montreal as funnelling capital between Great Britain and the American west. Active in real estate and later insurance, by 1844 he was the chief officer of the British based colonisation company, North American Land. He and his associates in Montreal invested in the St Lawrence and Atlantic, but to raise sufficient capital Galt went to London, where at the height of the railway mania he found sufficient English investors to fill the gap, though a year later many were unable to pay their calls. Other projects were put forward including the Great Western from Niagara to Windsor, but little was constructed in the 1840s.

The lack of a rail connection to the open sea was even more acutely felt by Montreal businessmen during the very severe winter of 1848–49. The shortage of capital for projects led to sufficient pressure on the Government for it to bring in the Guarantee Act in 1849 which provided that for any company building a railway at least 75 miles long, of which half had been completed, interest of up to 6 per cent on funds raised to complete the line would be guaranteed by the government. In return the Government would take a mortgage on the property.

There were tensions between the Canadian Government and the London bankers. When Baring and Glyn agreed to try to dispose of £500,000 securities for Hincks in 1849 they sought assurances that he would not allow the public debt to increase beyond £500,000 for any purpose whatever. The St Lawrence and Atlantic met the criteria of the Guarantee Act, and at the end of 1850 proposed to issue debentures to the extent of £400,000. In a joint letter Glyn and Baring explained that such debentures would be very difficult to sell; they could only be marketed at such a ruinously price as would alarm existing holders of Canadian bonds.

> We are desirous not only to prevent such an occurrence, but to aid to the utmost of our powers in the advancement of every work likely to promote the prosperity of the province. … We see no other mode therefore than to purchase a portion ourselves … to try to give confidence to others, as

> well as to meet your immediate wants, and though not anxious to buy a security for which we see as yet no chance of resale, we consent ... to buy debentures to the extent of £100,000 nominal capital.[23]

Glyn and Baring were also concerned with the ease with which railways could qualify for help under the Guarantee Act. Faced with the possibility of other open-ended commitments to finance the growing number of Canadian railway projects they asked the Government to repeal the Act and to set a limit on the amount of future Government liabilities for public works, which they suggested should be £1,000,000 or an annual interest of £60,000.[24] The Act was not repealed but the provincial government agreed that guarantees would be limited to capital and to main lines and the debentures guaranteed would be company rather than government ones.[25] This enabled Barings and Glyn to arrange for Canadian securities to be quoted in the official Stock Exchange lists.[26] Consequently Glyn and Baring in 1851 contracted to sell £467,500 in 6 per cent debentures, all for the St Lawrence and Atlantic.

The amount of Canadian business transacted by Glyn's and Barings both for the Government itself and for the growing number of railways increased considerably. In 1852 the two London houses were marketing £200,000 Upper Canada debentures issued for the Great Western and £100,000 for the Ontario, Simcoe and Hudson Railway.[27] From 1853 to 1855 Glyn's and Barings sold a further £570,000 for the Great Western and £375,000 for the Ontario, Simcoe and Huron. This was in addition to £2.7 million sold for the Grand Trunk. The close relationship of government and railway finances was illustrated when Hincks borrowed from Glyn's on his personal account to buy bonds in the Ontario, Simcoe and Huron, though the Parliamentary committee which investigated this decided that he had not used his influence as a cabinet minister to make a profit.[28]

Over the next few years Glyn's sold further debentures – £356,000 from the autumn of 1855 to early 1857. In August of that year they received £200,000 more for sale and notice of another £400,000 of Municipal Loan

[23] The Canadian Financial Agency, *The Three Banks Review*, 32, Glyn's and Barings to Hincks, 10 Jan. 1851 (RBS Archives, GM/4/1).

[24] Ibid, 32–33.

[25] Piva, 1985, 203.

[26] RBS Archives, GM/4/1, Glyn Mills to Hincks, 27 Jul. 1852.

[27] R. Hidy, *The House of Baring in American Trade and Finance*, 1949, 414–415.

[28] R.S. Longley, *Sir Francis Hincks, A Study of Canadian Politics, Railways and Finance in the Nineteenth Century*, 1943, 238–239.

Fund debentures. They began to doubt their ability to maintain sales of these securities above par, especially as on occasion the two London houses needed to advance funds for interest payments.[29]

Although the Grand Trunk was quickly to become the major problem in Canada facing Glyn's and Barings, the provincial agency was not without its difficulties. On the day following the suspension of the Bank Charter Act in 1857 Glyn told the Receiver General that the Province's debentures were quite unsaleable in the existing state of money pressure and financial difficulty. The Province had been advanced £301,939 against which Glyn's held only £199,650 in unsold provincial and municipal loan bonds.[30] On 1 July 1858 the amount of interest due and payable at the London agents was £205,105. Glyn's and Barings were able to sell £350,000 6 per cent bonds within a week in 1859, but the advance from Glyn's was well in excess of this sum. It was possible in late 1859 to give holders of the £11,600,000 liabilities of the Province the option of converting to a 25 year 5 per cent stock. Some £2,000,000 was converted within six months and in addition an issue of £2,800,000 at 6 per cent was oversubscribed and was soon selling at a small premium. This enabled the advances made by Glyn's and Barings to be repaid, but the position soon deteriorated. In December 1861 the bankers were disappointed not to have received any communication from Galt saying how he intended to make provision for the dividends payable on 1 January 1862, about £148,000 by each of Barings and Glyn's. In May 1862 Galt was asking for a temporary loan to meet the payments due in July and proposed to issue $4,000,000 in Exchequer bills, payable in two years.[31] Galt's departure when the John Macdonald-Cartier government fell meant that while the projected deficit was somewhat reduced the basic problems remained.

Glyn's and Barings continued to act as agents for the Province and from 1867 for the Dominion of Canada. The creation of the Dominion led to an increased volume of Canadian securities being handled by the agents, but there was no repetition of the severe problems encountered during the early days of the agency. Moreover difficult though it sometimes was to sell Canadian bonds both Glyn's and Barings were receiving commission on bonds sold. It was 1893 before the agency was transferred from Glyn's and Barings to the Bank of Montreal.

[29] Hidy, 432–433.

[30] The Canadian Financial Agency, 33–34, Glyn to Morrison, 13 Nov. 1857.

[31] In this period the dollar was worth 4.5 to 5 dollars.

Canadian Railways – The Grand Trunk

Meanwhile with the signing of the Webster-Ashburton Treaty, which settled the boundary dispute on the Canadian frontier with Maine and Vermont, the British government became interested in making a military road from the Maritime Provinces to the St Lawrence, but the governments of the Provinces preferred a railroad – the Intercolonial. In 1847 Grey, the colonial secretary, who had received a number of petitions for a railroad, told Elgin, the governor-in-chief of North America,[32] that if the Provincial governments agreed on a mature scheme the British Government might be justified in applying to Parliament for some assistance in carrying it into effect. However Grey only a fortnight later, while admitting that a Quebec–Halifax railway would be of infinite benefit to the whole empire, was much more doubtful of helping except possibly in return for the conveyance of mails and troops at cost price.[33] Proposals were made for a line costing £5 million. Apart from the strategic interest Grey wanted to encourage emigration from England and Ireland, but his enthusiasm was soon replaced by doubts as the British Railway Commissioners reported that the Intercolonial could not for a long time to come yield a commercial return and could be justified only on the grounds of emigration and defence. He did not think he could carry the Commons, particularly in the face of Cobden's anti-imperialism and the likelihood that Peel, Graham and Gladstone would oppose such expenditure by the Government.[34]

There was talk of government construction to be financed by borrowing on the London market. Baring and Glyn warned the provincial government that Canada's credit in London was not high enough to warrant such a large-scale government venture.[35] In 1849 and 1850 two Canadian leaders came separately to London to press their case. Hincks in 1849 failed to persuade the British Government to assist with the building of railways. He desired continuing imperial aid for emigration programmes because Britain should be concerned not only in getting rid of redundant population but in securing extensive markets for her manufactures.[36] Joseph Howe, the premier

[32] That is all the Canadian provinces.

[33] *The Elgin-Grey Papers, 1847–1852*, ed. Sir Arthur Doughty, 1, 24–27, letters of 19 Apr. and 3 May 1847.

[34] Ibid, 1, 351–352, Grey to Elgin, 18 May 1849.

[35] Anon, Glyn's and the Grand Trunk Railway, *Three Banks Review*, 52, Dec. 1961, 28.

[36] Piva, 1985, 188, quoting *A Memorandum on Immigration* by Hincks, 20 Dec. 1848. He spoke strongly against protection at the railway jubilee in Boston in 1851 and in 1854 negotiated successfully the Reciprocity Treaty with the USA.

of Nova Scotia, advocated a railway from Halifax to Windsor, Nova Scotia, which could become a section of a longer line to Quebec. He saw it is a duty of government to be in advance of the social, political and industrial energies which they had undertaken to lead. Howe visited London in late 1850 and early 1851 to ask the imperial government to guarantee the necessary capital. He secured the support of several London newspapers and influential people and addressed a large massed meeting at Southampton. Grey said Howe was very energetic in his endeavours to get a favourable reception for the railway and he was hoping that after all he would be able to succeed in getting the railway taken up by the government.[37] Howe saw Morton Peto, the contractor, who offered to build the line himself if the Colonial Office provided half the capital. He himself would put up £100,000.[38] In March ministers decided that they would guarantee the interest on a sum necessary to build the railway provided it formed a complete line from Halifax to Quebec or Montreal.[39]

There were very sharp differences over the choice of route. For military reasons the British government wanted the line away from the US frontier.[40] New Brunswick much preferred a route via St John, while Howe, like the British, favoured the northern route to Halifax along the north shore of New Brunswick. Both he and those in New Brunswick were anxious to secure the European and North American Railway projected to link Nova Scotia and New Brunswick with the United States. Upper Canada was less interested in the Intercolonial than in a line from Montreal to Toronto. These differences resulted in a conference of the Canadian provinces in Toronto where Hincks insisted that the proposed railway be extended westwards from Quebec to Montreal and on to Windsor (Ontario) or Sarnia. He introduced a bill to cover both the Intercolonial to Halifax and the trunk line in Canada. Grey now prevaricated: personally he seemed open to the Intercolonial as it would at least promote colonisation, but he was not ready to commend it to Parliament. Hincks then went to London. By the time he arrived the Russell government had fallen and Sir John Pakenham was Colonial Secretary in the new Derby government. Hincks, in the expectation that the loan would be refused, asked Pakenham to give him a final answer in a fortnight as he was returning to Canada shortly.[41] Hincks before sending his ultimatum had

[37] Doughty, 2, 782, Grey to Elgin, 17 Jan. 1851.

[38] John G. Cox, *Samuel Morton Peto, 1809–1889*, 2008, 81.

[39] Doughty, 4, 1590–1593, Grey to Elgin, 14 Mar. 1851.

[40] This was the route surveyed by Major W. Robinson in 1849 which became the basis on which subsequent negotiations for the Intercolonial were based.

[41] Further correspondence relative to the projected railway from Halifax to Quebec, PP, 1852, xlviii, 503, Hincks to Pakington, 1 May 1852.

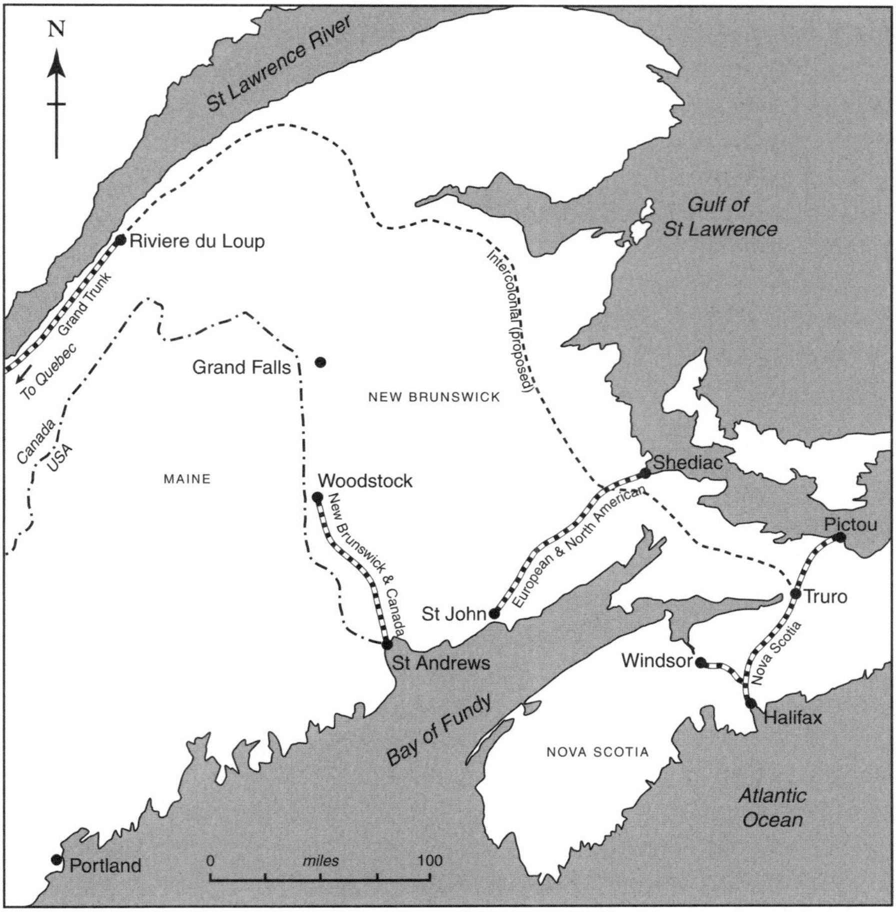

Map 6: The Proposed Intercolonial.

learned that Peto, Brassey, Betts & Jackson, the largest railway contractors in England were still anxious to build both the Intercolonial and the European and North American. They were looking for business as there were now few opportunities in England and they were subject to much more competition from European contractors on the Continent. Hincks, despite his declarations in the recent past that the construction of railways in British North America by private enterprise was both impolitic and impossible now listened to proposals from William Jackson for a line from Montreal to Hamilton or beyond.[42]

[42] Longley, 220.

The Colonial Office then rejected the proposal to guarantee the interest because of the inability of the provinces to agree to the route favoured by the British government and insufficient exploration of the St John's route. *The Times*, while regretting the indignant remonstrance, as it called Hincks' letter, pointed out that the Canadian representations received less attention than that commonly shown to the emission of any petty European principality or South American republic.[43] Jackson returned with Hincks and had discussions with politicians and commercial interest. In August Hincks discussed the possibility of a contract for the Quebec and Richmond which would link with the St Lawrence and Atlantic from Montreal at Richmond for Peto, Brassey and Betts. By the autumn of 1852 these contractors had undertaken to construct the Quebec and Richmond Railway, and a contract for the European and North American from St John to the Maine boundary had been let to Jackson.[44] Whereas the former would shortly become part of the extended Grand Trunk Railway, the latter was only completed from St John to Shadiac in 1860 and it was 1871 before the US section came into operation.[45]

Meanwhile Hincks had caused a proclamation to be issued setting out proposals for the construction of the Grand Trunk and introduced a bill for a company with a capital of £3,000,000. The new company was to construct a railroad from Montreal to Hamilton with a guarantee of £3,000 per mile from the government.[46] At its eastern end it would link with the Montreal to Portland line (the St Lawrence and Atlantic) and in the west with the Great Western then being built between Hamilton and Windsor. From the start the Grand Trunk attracted controversy in Canada. Alexander Galt preferred local lines and keeping them in Canadian hands. From 1849 he was not only president of the St Lawrence and Atlantic but had a major interest in other lines. With Gzowski, a Canadian contractor,[47] he had acquired a charter to build a line from Kingston to Montreal, so linking the Great Lakes with the St Lawrence and Atlantic. Hincks only succeeded in overcoming Galt's opposition to the Grand Trunk by persuading him to merge his lines with

43 *The Times*, 31 May 1852.

44 *The Times*, 11 Aug., 11 and 19 Oct. 1852.

45 Despite the fact that Lady Head, wife of the Lieutenant Governor of New Brunswick, cut the first sod, in the presence of Jackson and Betts on 14 Sept. 1853 (*Morning Chronicle*, 11 Oct. 1853).

46 Longley, 223–224. Proclamation of 4 Aug. 1852.

47 Gzowski was a Polish army officer and military engineer, lawyer in Pennsylvania, public works superintendent, engineer in charge of St Lawrence and Atlantic. Set up contracting and manufacturing business with Galt, Holton and Macpherson.

the Grand Trunk. This came at a heavy price, as purchasing the rival charters led to Gzowski's company, in which Galt, Holton and Macpherson participated, securing an expensive contract for building the Montreal to Kingston section of the Grand Trunk. As H.V. Nelles put it Gzowski brought the skills of a Yankee lawyer to the rough and tumble of Canadian railway contracting.[48] There was also the huge cost of bridging the St Lawrence at Montreal, the 6 per cent guaranteed to the Atlantic and St Lawrence for leasing the line, on which Galt insisted, and the purchase of the St Lawrence and Atlantic, and the Quebec and Richmond.

The amalgamation and consolidation of these lines was achieved in drawn out negotiations in London in early 1853 in which John Ross, Canadian solicitor general and president of the company, Baring and Glyn took part. The mileage was increased from 345, the distance between Montreal and Toronto, to over 1,100 and the capital from £3 million to £9 million, as a result of the purchases of the Galt lines and extensions westwards from Toronto to Sarnia and eastwards to Riviere du Loup. The latter was hardly viable without further extension – it was envisaged as part of a route to Halifax. Glyn hoped that that the latter would be sanctioned to make the Grand Trunk's eastern section profitable.[49] The Atlantic and St Lawrence was particularly speculative, as it depended on the development of Portland, Maine as a port, and the line's ability to generate grain and timber traffic to the port.

It was this enlarged railway which was advertised in 1853 in the prospectus. Glyn and Baring, somewhat reluctantly had agreed to be involved, though Hincks alleged that in 1852 he had found that Barings and Glyn Mills were anxious for new Canadian investments and that Baring informed him that the railway could be built through the sale of private stock and the Guarantee Act of 1849. He also said that it was at Baring's suggestion that he wrote to his colleagues in Canada to ask them to order further surveys along the proposed route between Quebec and Lake Huron.[50] However when Barings were asked whether any of their partners would like to become a director, they refused because 'the connection would be somewhat foreign to our usual business'.[51] They had previously turned down similar approaches from other railways which they had assisted financially. Barings were then surprised to receive a letter from Ross with

48 Dictionary of Canadian Biography (DCB), XII. Sir Casimir Gzowski.

49 Glyn papers, LAC, Glyn to Galt, 8 Oct. 1857.

50 Longley, 220–221, based on LAC Series E (Executive Council Minutes of United Canada. April–June 1852, 6).

51 Platt and Adelman, 216–217.

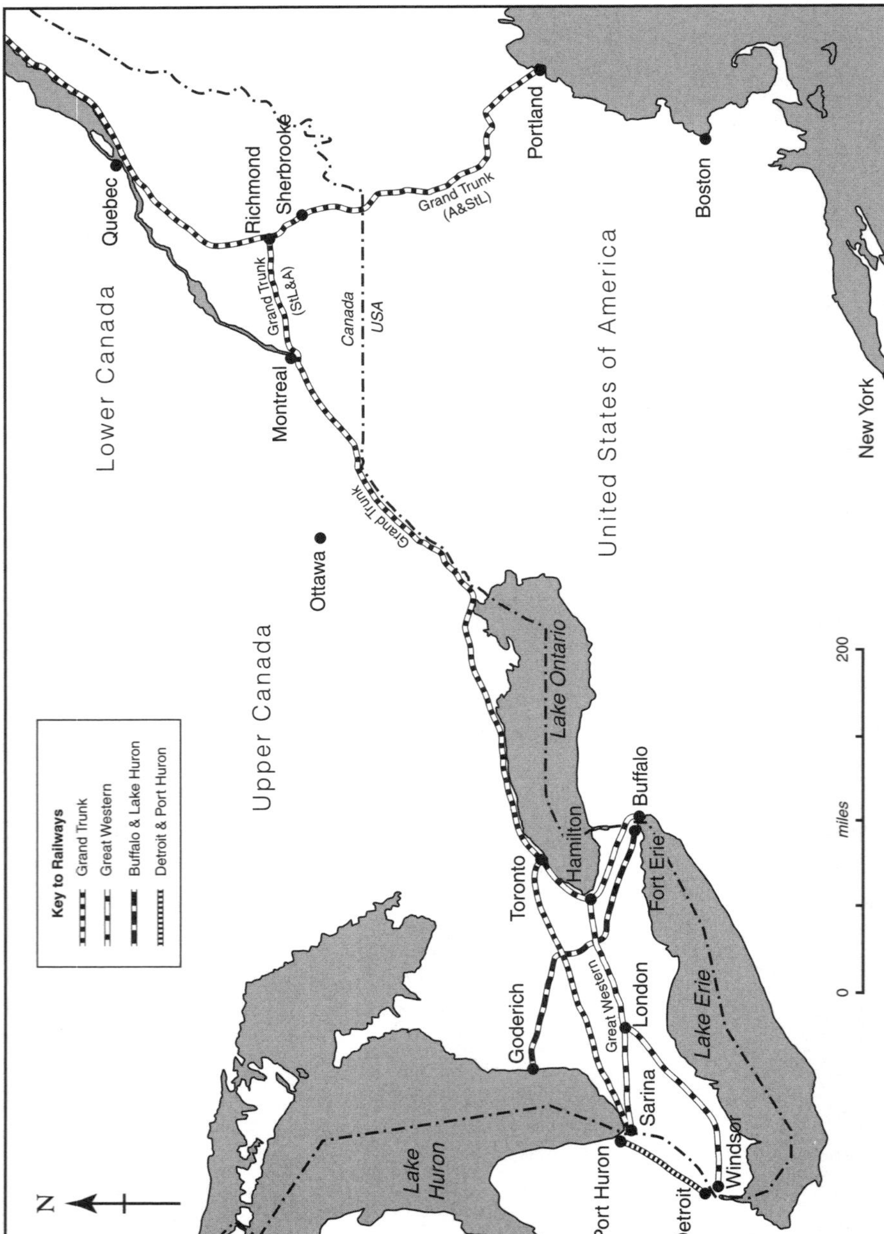

Map 7: The Grand Trunk Railway.

a prospectus which not only conveyed the impression that Lord Elgin had endorsed the railway, but also displayed the names of Thomas Baring and George Glyn as 'Agents of the Province of Canada, and Directors of the Company on behalf of the Canadian Government'[52] Ross pointed out that they would be keeping company with the entire cabinet of Upper Canada, and they accepted reluctantly as the specific representatives of the Canadian government. They were concerned lest their involvement in this way would suggest to prospective investors that they were recommending the project. Glyn's were also the company's bankers in London.

If the presence of Baring and Glyn did not provide sufficient evidence of the validity of the project, they were joined on the London board by William Thompson, Glyn's colleague on the original board of St Katharine's Dock of which he was now chairman, and a prominent and rich City figure whose fortune was considered to be on a par with those of James Morrison and Nathan Rothschild.[53] The other two London directors were Kirkman Hodgson, senior partner in Finlay Hodgson and later Governor of the Bank of England from 1863–65 and a partner in Barings with which his firm merged in 1867, and Woolaston Blake, a colleague of Glyn's on the LNWR board. After Thompson's death in 1854 they were joined by Robert McColmont, a Liverpool merchant, The Canadian government appointed six of their ministers and officials as members of the Canadian board. Thomas Baring took the chairmanship of the London board, a slightly surprising development in view of his bank's long-standing policy of avoiding involvement in the management of client firms, especially in view of Glyn's unrivalled experience of railway management and knowledge of the railway world. No reason has been traced, but perhaps Glyn having pleaded ill health when he relinquished the chairmanship of the LNWR in the previous year, did not wish to take this on. Moreover Baring himself had made a business trip to the United States in the autumn of 1852 where he saw President Martin Fillmore, but went to some lengths to make clear that there was no connection between his visit and political affairs – it was thought he was charged by the Foreign Secretary with special duties in connection with fishing. Though he does not seem to have gone to Canada he must have had talks in the US with Bates, his American partner and others about Canadian developments including railways.[54] Baring and Glyn were concerned about the growth in the size of the project and about a week before the prospectus was issued told Hincks that they would float all the debentures but only

52 Ross to Baring, 6 Apr., Baring to Ross, 8 Apr., LAC, frame, 72310–12.

53 Martin Daunton, William Thompson *ODNB*.

54 *The Times*, 18 Aug., 8 and 12 Oct. and 26 Nov., *New York Times*, 26 Aug. 1852.

half the stock; the contractors had to take the rest. Baring certainly later regretted his involvement. In 1868 he told shareholders they had on their hands a concern which, as a man of business, he was now willing to admit, having later events to guide him, they ought never to have entered into.[55]

The prospectus presented a dazzling future for the railway with dividends of 11½ per cent. The historian of the Grand Trunk, A.W. Currie, argues that this was credible because of the high dividends paid by British railways such as the London & Birmingham and Liverpool & Manchester but their successor the LNWR had not paid more than 6 per cent since 1849 and in 1852 the average dividend of the twelve principal British companies was 3.3 per cent.[56] The capital required was £9.5 million, of which £3,623,000 was in £25 shares, half of which were issued immediately. Robert Stephenson, appointed consulting engineer, visited in 1853 with Betts and Jackson and on his return said the line offered the certainty of a great traffic. Joshua Bates assured Thomas Baring 'The Grand Trunk will go right, I think'.[57] In the following month the New York correspondent of *The Times* thought that the capital under British management would ensure the vigorous prosecution and early completion of this stupendous work.[58]

It did not work out like that. Though the shares were initially at a premium, by October 1853 they were selling at a 4 per cent discount and by the following June at 82, though debentures were then 94.[59] As early as June 1853 Baring was expressing concern over the financial future of the enterprise and complaining of the lack of consultation with the British board.[60] He sent a fierce letter in October complaining of mismanagement and blunders which even a child would avoid.[61] Soon after the issue of the prospectus the financial situation in Britain deteriorated with moves by Russia and Turkey which led to the Crimean War. In June the Bank rate rose to 3½ per cent. A quarter of the stock was earmarked for Canada, but hardly any of the stock sold there was held for investment, most being defaulted on or resold in London at depreciated prices.[62] The Canadian

[55] *Morning Post*, 1 May 1868, report of meeting on 30 Apr.

[56] A.W. Currie, *The History of the Grand Trunk Railway of Canada*, 1957, 21.

[57] 27 Aug. 1853, Baring Archive, DEP 193, 39, quoted in Ziegler, 223.

[58] *The Times*, 4 Oct. 1853 (article headed New York, 21 Sept.).

[59] Ann M. Carlos and Frank D. Lewis, The Creative Financing of an Unprofitable Enterprise: The Grand Trunk Railway of Canada, 1853–1881, *Explorations in Economic History*, 32, 1995, Table 4, 290, for the prices of Grand Trunk securities at 30 Jun. 1853–81.

[60] Longley, 231 (Baring's letter of June, unreferenced).

[61] Baring to Hincks, 10 Oct. 1853.

[62] Platt and Adelman, 219–220.

government's contribution on the basis of £3,000 a mile was limited to £3,111,500, reached by 1858, and raised by government debentures sold in England which cost the Government about £180,000 a year in interest. The *Economist* later pointed this was partly offset by the revenue gained from high import duties on material imported for the railway and commodities consumed by the construction workers.[63] Many shareholders must have been in the position of Francis Mills, the brother of Charles and Edward. When he died in 1855 his executors had to sell shares and large amounts of stock in parcels in the course of 1857, much of the latter at 40–42.[64] By 1860 Baring thought it might have been better if the Grand Trunk had received no assistance from the Canadian government. The company would have stood more chance of a profit if it had been allowed to limit the extent of its line to commercial necessity.[65]

By early 1854 Baring and Glyn were convinced that the mileage the Grand Trunk had undertaken to build was beyond its resources and asked Hincks to obtain Parliamentary agreement to change the Grand Trunk's charter. The Province agreed to delay completion of over 200 miles of line but to accelerate completion of the rest. Political developments in Canada did not help. Hincks, defeated in the general election, resigned the premiership in September 1854 and was succeeded by Sir Allan MacNab, president of the Great Western with which the Grand Trunk was competing for traffic west of Toronto. MacNab was a Hamilton lawyer, land speculator, and business man. Based in Hamilton he was less interested in links with the Atlantic.

A committee of the legislature investigated Hincks's financial dealings with the railway and though he was generally absolved from wrong doing, the prestige of the Grand Trunk was lessened. In 1855 Baring and Glyn asked the Province to give the Grand Trunk the same support as it gave to other lines under the Guarantee Act.[66] While Canadian ministers did not go that far, they did guarantee 20 year bonds at 6 per cent with a par value of £900,000 which was equivalent to the amount of shares reserved for Canadians but not taken up by them. The progress of the line was hit by lack of funds. By 1855 construction was at a standstill for a period and

[63] £2,793,000 by 1856. Carlos and Lewis, Table 1, 280.

[64] RBS Archives, GM/1362/7/4. Mills, a director of Consolidated Copper Mines of Cobre, had also purchased long leases of a pub and 33 houses off Poplar High Street near the Blackwall Railway and the docks which were bring in £1,250 a year (*Morning Chronicle*, 19 Jan. 1855).

[65] *The Economist*, 3 Feb. 1866, Baring to Galt, 13 Dec. 1860, Ottawa, frame 74935–6.

[66] Baring and Glyn to Cayley, 10 Feb. published in *Herapath's Journal*, 16 Feb. 1855.

interest on debentures was suspended. The London board sent an emissary to Canada to ask for a guarantee on the share capital in return for which the line would revert to the Province after 99 years. This was turned down but the government made a loan of £800,000 towards the cost of the Victoria Bridge which was to cross the St Lawrence at Montreal, obtained by issuing Provincial 6 per cent debentures which were gradually sold in the London market in small amounts to banks and insurance companies, the proceeds being credited to the Grand Trunk's account with Glyn's. Threats from the contractors led to pressure in the legislature. By June 1856 £4,562,300 in debentures had been created; by June 1859 the total was £8,350,400.[67]

Edward Betts was the resident agent. A.M. Ross was the chief engineer who had considerable experience on the Chester and Holyhead including the Conway and Menai bridges under Robert Stephenson. An agent was appointed for each of the four sections, one of which was the Victoria Bridge under James Hodges. Work on the different sections was carried out simultaneously rather than consecutively, thereby foregoing income that might have been earned by early opening of completed sections. The cost of land, raw material and labour cost increased, in part because of the demands of the railway itself. Such was the shortage of labour that about 3,000 men had to be brought over from England who were paid much more than they would have earned at home. Labour was used intensively rather than the mechanical techniques already successfully developed in the United States. Brassey when he went to Canada was surprised to find how far the railway was built on British rather than American lines. When travelling in the States he had particularly noted the advantages of timber trestle bridges and the avoidance of stone bridges and solid embankments.[68] However the contract had stipulated that the line should be superior to any American or Canadian railway 'now known or used' and the permanence of structure and substantiality of the work equal to the first-class English railways. The contractors were exposed to the harsh and lengthy Canadian winters which proved a particular problem with the Victoria Bridge, though Hodges eventually devised a method whereby the ice was used to position the central deck of the bridge and the tubular structure. Despite the success of British contractors on the continent of Europe, the company might with advantage have employed American contractors but this would have been a step too far for Canadians as a principal reason for the line was to secure the country's independence from the US. American know-how in rolling

[67] Carlos and Lewis, 280.

[68] C. Walker, *Thomas Brassey: Railway Builder*, 1969, 93.

stock might have been more directly employed. Most of the rolling stock and the iron work for the Victoria Bridge was built at Jackson's Canada Works at Birkenhead, for which Peto put up a third of the £270,000 capital, but with morticing and planing machines supplied by American manufacturers and two mechanics were sent to the US to see how similar rolling stock was constructed.[69]

Further adverse publicity arose when Captain Galton of the Railway Department of the Board of Trade, having ridden over the main line from Montreal to Brockville (about 130 miles), declared that the line was no better than a track. The London directors sent out their own engineer, Charles Hutton Gregory,[70] who denied Galton's charge that the contractors work had been inadequate. He pointed to marked increases in wages and materials which made the estimates insufficient.[71]

In July 1856 the Legislature passed the Relief Act to grant additional aid and the Company was later authorised to issue £2 million in first preference bonds, all of which had been issued by 1859. The proceeds of the bonds were to be deposited with Glyn's and released from time to time to pay for the work as it was completed. Stephenson and other engineers reported that no material reduction in costs could be made. In 1856 McColmont resigned over the cost of the St Lawrence bridge, then estimated at £1.4 million. He alleged that the company was being led blindfold on the bridge. He tried to enlist the support of his fellow directors for an examination of alternative types of bridges and obtained a report from Charles Liddell who criticised the high cost of the materials and the design. He recommended a trussed girder bridge at a cost of £400,000 in the light of his experience with the Crumlin viaduct in South Wales, but Stephenson refused to discuss the matter with him.[72] McColmont was replaced by William Chapman.

Nevertheless the line from Quebec to Toronto was opened in November 1856. Baring and Glyn could not see the Grand Trunk in isolation from developments in Canadian politics and the finances of the Provincial Government and banks. In 1857 a bank crisis in Montreal was accompanied

[69] A. Helps, *Life and Labours of Mr Brassey*, 1878, 190–191.

[70] Gregory had worked with Robert Stephenson on the Manchester and Birmingham and succeeded Brunel as chief engineer on the Bristol and Exeter.

[71] Currie, 53–54.

[72] RBS Archives, GM/86. Charles Liddell (1813–1894) had worked on a number of railways under the Stephensons before becoming engineer to the Newport, Abergavenny and Hereford, and its extension to Aberdare which included the Crumlin viaduct. Still active in the 1890s when engaged on the future Great Central's London extension.

by a decline in trade and disappointing crops. Traffic fell, but in any case the line was not getting sufficient traffic from Canadian farmers or attracting incoming traffic from Europe or the US whose shippers used American lines, despite Galt's raising of duties on imported goods to encourage the east-west flow of goods and deter traffic to and from the USA. In June 1857 Baring told William Cayley, Canada's Inspector-General:

> by the public Act now passed Mr Glyn and myself are released from the direction after the next general meeting, and we shall both be glad even at a money sacrifice to be relieved from all the obligations and disappointments which we have encountered if we can leave the Company with credit to ourselves but we fear we may be blamed for deserting a sinking concern.[73]

In fact they did not leave – their desire to help the Empire and avoid damage to their reputations was too great.

The railway, always a political issue in Canada became especially so at the general election of 1857. The opposition with some justification accused ministers on the board of lining their own pockets. Baring thought the Canadian directors should refuse to sanction acts which were unjustifiable, but it was hard for Blackwell, the general manager, to translate this admirable precept into action when the offending directors were members of the Government on whose good will the company was reliant. George Brown, owner of the Toronto Globe and leader of the True Grits, was a bitter opponent of the Grand Trunk, seeing it as the creation of Montreal interests.

In November 1857 at the height of the financial crisis in Britain Glyn told Galt who had just entered the McDonald-Cartier government as Finance Minister:

> that he was sorry to perceive that he did not think it possible for the Government to bring forward any measures of further relief in the Grand Trunk matter. If this really is the case I fear the concern must collapse for it is entirely out of the question attempting to move any of the Grand Trunk securities in this market. The state of the traffic returns is so discouraging that no one is disposed to touch the bonds at any price. … We have in vain tried to sell for you, without restrictions as to price, some of the new 7 per cent debentures, but no one will look at them.[74]

[73] Baring to Cayley, 12 and 16 Jun. 1857, Ottawa, frames 73608 and 73614–5.

[74] Fulford, 154, for extract from letter.

Indeed the following day Glyn told Ross, then Solicitor General in the provincial government and President of the Grand Trunk, to consider whether it would not be wiser and on the whole as easy as any other measure of relief, and possibly more popular, for Government to 'take the whole concern' having the undertaking made over with its liabilities and paying off the stockholders by debentures running for 20 years at a low rate of interest – certainly not above 4 per cent. This would be a complete measure.[75] He returned to the point three years later.[76] He asked Galt whether he had ever considered whether the plan generally adopted by the continental governments assisting railway undertakings could be adopted by him as likely to conciliate the legislature viz., that certain relief being granted, the railway works etc. should at the expiration of a certain number of years fall into their hands, and become the property of the Province. The term of years varied, being sometimes 50 and sometimes as long as 80 or 90 years.[77]

While Glyn and Baring do not seem to have differed over what action they should take, Baring, at least in the 1850s does seem to have been more sanguine attitude than Glyn, perhaps because Glyn had to deal with the Bank of Upper Canada as well as the railway. In early 1859 Baring consoled himself that '1858 had certainly been a wonderful year for profits. Luckily it has been an expensive one and we have Grand Trunk and Weardale or we should become too fat and saucy.'[78] He was sympathetic towards Canada. He told Cayley, that 'we do not wish and feel we ought not to enforce our full right on such a valued and valuable connection as that with the Province.'[79] This was when the house of Baring itself, quite apart from the private holdings of the partners, had £351,500 tied up in Grand Trunk shares and debentures, with company debts in current account of a further £125,000. In 1859 a further £1,111,500 in 6 per cent preferential bonds was authorised to fund the outstanding debt held by the contractors. Barings and Glyn's had to take up most of the issue. In 1859 Glyn's had refused a number of drafts for £100,000 as the Grand Trunk Board had not the funds to meet repayment.[80]

75 Anon, Glyn's and the Grand Trunk Railway, *Three Banks R*eview 52, 1961, 32–33.

76 Ibid, 35–36, Glyn to Cayley, 31 Oct. 1860.

77 Ibid, 37.

78 Ziegler,179, Baring to Bates, 30 Jan. 1859, The Baring Archive, HC1 20.4; Weardale was an unprofitable iron works in County Durham in which Barings were losing money on their investment despite selling rails to the Grand Trunk.

79 Ziegler, 224, LAC, MG24 D21 and 24, 18 Jan. 1858.

80 Currie, 91–92, based on the first report of the Canadian Financial and Departmental Commission, 1863.

It was 1859 before the Toronto to Sarnia section was opened which linked with the Detroit and Lake Huron so providing a route to the mid-western United States. However the Grand Trunk was built to a gauge of 5 feet 6 inches making interchange with US lines which were built to the standard 4 feet 8½ inches difficult, a weakness not remedied until the line was rebuilt to standard gauge between 1872 and 1885. The cost of the whole line, £11,000 per mile, was low by British standards but high in relation to the return as it ran through much less populated country. Revenue per mile was initially only £11 per week instead of the estimated £25. Traffic was heavily dependent on a volatile trade in staples, particularly timber and cereals, and was usually in low value goods over long hauls to distant markets and so was open to undercutting by waterborne traffic. Only in 1860 was the Victoria bridge at Montreal ready for traffic. It was then the longest bridge in the world, but its magnificent engineering was not matched by its affordability, for it cost some £2 million over budget. Cobden regarded it as a tremendous monument of engineering skill and wasted capital.[81] The opening of the bridge by the Prince of Wales brought a fleeting moment of optimism. Glyn told Baring that Laurence, a partner in Cazenoves, said that now was the time for a pot of fire in the Grand Trunk bonds. Very little would bring them up to par.[82] The London board still found it difficult to exert control over the Canadian board, who, Baring complained to Sir Edmund Head who had succeed Elgin as Governor-in-chief in 1854, seemed unfortunately to have supposed that as much money as might be wanted could be found in London.[83] In Canada most wanted the railway but regarded its difficulties as the responsibility of British financiers and contractors.

By March 1860 when the accounts with the contractors were settled, the capital of the railway stood at almost £13 million. As only about a third of the capital was in shares the company had to pay the fixed interest charges on the remainder which were for a long time greater than its earnings.[84] By 1860 the company had no funds to meet the bills drawn to pay the contractors, 'a difficulty which must be surmounted. It is a moral obligation on the board, though its weight would fall as usual on us.' wrote Glyn.[85]

81 *The American Diaries of Richard Cobden*, ed. Elizabeth Hoon Cawley, 1952, 211.

82 Glyn to Baring, Mar. 1859, quoted in Kynaston, *Cazenove*, 38–39.

83 Platt and Adelman, 218, letter of July 1856, LAC, frame 73442. Jackson, whose activities were mainly confined to the initial financial negotiations, is said to have set the tone for the whole company with his ostentatious manner of living and desire to impress the colonials (Walker, *Brassey*, 87).

84 Currie, 53–54.

85 Glyn's and the Grand Trunk Railway, 33.

An appeal for Government assistance in July 1860 did not succeed. Barings and Glyns had to take up the larger part of the second preference issue of debentures, as little was applied for by the public. They also took a first lien on the company's rolling stock, as a security and to prevent seizure by other creditors. Apart from their holdings of shares and debentures Barings were then owed £297,000 and Glyn's £279,000 with a further £50,000 to Glyn personally, £627,000 in all.[86] Glyn's and Barings obtained judgment in the Canadian courts as creditors but at the request of the Canadian government, the attachment in respect of rolling stock was transferred to the Bank of Upper Canada to try to boost the Bank's resources. As will be seen the Bank was another problem with which Glyn had to deal.

Financial considerations, while important, were not the only factors governing the course of action of Glyn and Baring in this period. Glyn wrote to Baring in November 1860 –

> You and I have done much and suffered so much together that it would take a great deal to interfere with the feeling which I entertain towards you and to the end of this extraordinary business I shall hope to row in your boat and under your steering; I think we shall eventually land it successfully in spite of obloquy and difficulty.[87]

In short while Baring and Glyn were anxious to make the Grand Trunk successful financially if at all possible, they were prepared to let the strategic and political considerations have priority.

Baring expressed his annoyance with the Canadian politicians and press several times. To Galt he wrote that he wished the Government's sympathy could be translated into action. Canada had reaped all the benefits and the English capitalists nothing but losses. He and Glyn regretted every day that they had ever been induced by the Canadian Government to connect themselves with the undertaking. Later he asked Galt how anyone could imagine that the power of the Grand Trunk had been employed to the public injury of Canada when daily experience confirmed that the railway, although of the greatest benefit to the province of Canada, had been the source of serious loss for those who had furnished the means of its construction.[88] His protests did not alter the perspective of Canadians.

86 Ibid, 33.

87 Platt and Adelman, 223, LAC, frame 1367.

88 Platt and Adelman, 219, Baring to Galt, 3 Apr. and 19 Jun. 1860, Ottawa 74617 and 74662–5.

A few months later Baring told Bates that their unpopularity was awful and hoped that they might not be the cause of the stoppage of the road. 'We should be as much abused in England as in Canada.'[89] Glyn too was sympathetic towards Canada. He told Cayley in October 1860 that:

> it would have been easier for us to have declined 14 months ago to make further advances, but Messrs Barings and ourselves, having had the promise of the assignment of the rolling stock, and buoyed up by continual representations of increasing traffic consented to go on and finish the work which had we declined to do must have fallen on others, probably on the province itself. We have carried out the completion of this great undertaking and we cannot believe that the Canadians will allow those who been have so bona fide to be sufferers for their determination.[90]

Moreover the expected increase in traffic with the opening of the Victoria Bridge did not result. A series of investigatory committees was set up. English shareholders in both London and Liverpool set to work, concerned that Baring and Glyn's lien on rolling stock was detrimental to bondholders' interests. When London investors met in January 1861, Baring told them that the company needed £2.5 million, two-thirds for interest in London, 14 per cent for interest in Canada and the rest for improvements. A Committee of Seven share- and bondholders was formed which included William Newmarch, still with Globe Insurance, but well known to Glyn, as well as Henry Cleaver Chapman from Liverpool, a persistent critic of the Grand Trunk. The Governor-General, Head, who sympathised with Glyn and Baring and the British investors, was in London in late 1860 and early 1861 when he discussed with Baring various plans including receivership, but on his return found the Canadian administration nervous of any major action at least before the general election in the summer. Instead they appointed a royal commission under John Langton, a Canadian business man and government auditor. Langton found inefficiency particularly in rolling stock, and that the capital needed to be increased by £500,000, but the aim must be to reduce the bonded debt to the point where interest charges would not exceed the average annual earnings. The Committee of Seven largely agreed. They identified a considerable number of improvements needed and recommended a preferential mortgage for equipment, a watering down of creditors claims, and the Canadian government was to

89 Ziegler, 227, Baring to Bates, 26 Mar. 1861, The Baring Archive, HC1 20.8.

90 Glyn's and the Grand Trunk Railway, 35–36, Glyn to Cayley, 31 Oct. 1860.

be asked for £1.5 million in bonds, repaid over a long period by receipts through the carriage of mail, troops and military supplies. They also recommended that someone of great skill, experience and energy to go out to Canada to take over the supervision of the company and negotiations with the government.

Edward Watkin was the man chosen, undoubtedly on Glyn's recommendation. He had been assistant secretary on the LNWR until he left to take up the general managership of the MSLR in January 1854. Consequently he was well known to Glyn and in 1855 Glyn had wanted Watkin to go out to Canada for not more than two months to put the company in order. The Earl of Yarborough, chairman of the MSLR, said his board was not justified in letting Watkin, who was only in his second year in post, go so far away for so long.[91] Baring lent Watkin a number of documents including two memoranda by J.W. Brooks, President of the Michigan Central, who had examined the cost of working the line. Watkin's mission was enhanced by an interview with the Duke of Newcastle, the Colonial Secretary who had accompanied the Prince of Wales to Canada in 1860. He asked Watkin to be an unofficial emissary on wider matters and encouraged him to examine the possibilities for an intercolonial railway, which the Duke thought was a preliminary necessity for the union of all the provinces and territories into 'one great British North America'.[92]

Watkin's immediate reaction when he arrived in Montreal was that Glyn and Baring had been deceived by over-sanguine estimates. He clearly was better placed than others to understand the position both of the London financiers and the Canadians responsible for the management of the railway and so could negotiate with the government from a surer base. He quickly found savings, reorganising the stores department and discharging more than half the professional engineers, saving their salaries but also avoiding the expense of 'various experiments which an excess of such gentlemen was likely to cause'.[93] He told Glyn 'if anyone wants to see the miserable consequences of years of ignorant and weak management, let him come here.'[94] He took steps to reduce breakage of rails, and began negotiations for an ambitious merger with the Great Western, and the Buffalo and Lake Huron. The Fusion Bill was brought in for that purpose. The top management was changed. To succeed Blackwell, the managing director who had been

[91] David Hodgkins, *The Second Railway King, The Life and Times of Sir Edward Watkin, 1819–1901*, 2002, 131.

[92] Hodgkins, 194–196.

[93] *Herapath's Railway Journal*, 21 Nov. 1861.

[94] The Baring Archive HC5.15.47, 1508, Watkin to Glyn, 28 Mar. 1862.

in ill health, he brought in the general manger of the Great Western, C.J. Brydges as superintendent in December 1861, with the intention that he should jointly manage both companies on merger. The chief engineer, Walter Shanley, who had also been the general manager, resigned in June 1862 to Watkin's relief. In late 1861 the Canadian courts had thrown out a suit by a Canadian creditor for the appointment of a receiver.

Three measures were looked for from the Canadian Government – a bill to rearrange the company's finances, an agreement on payments for postal services and the Fusion Bill, but the fall of the John Macdonald-Cartier government in May 1862, radically changed the position. The cronyism was broken. No longer were members of the government on the Grand Trunk board. Sandfield Macdonald, supported by George Brown opposed the influence of British capitalists while wanting to maintain the political links with Britain. The borrow and spend policy of previous administrations had placed the province at the mercy of Lombard Street, wrote the *Globe*, Brown's newspaper.[95] While Glyn did not comment publicly on the change of government he conveyed to Thomas Galt, Alexander Galt's brother, his regret at the change and expressed his appreciation of Galt's efforts as Finance Minister on behalf of the Grand Trunk. Galt continued to have a private account with Glyn's.[96]

Under the Sandfield Macdonald administration the Fusion Bill was rejected as bringing about monopoly, arbitration over postal rates was refused and a settlement long delayed. Although the Grand Trunk Arrangements Act was passed the terms were not as helpful as the Grand Trunk hoped, though it provided a breathing space. The Act provided for reductions of interest in 1862–64 by 23 per cent and a smaller reduction in the period 1865–66, compensated by higher payments thereafter. Unpaid dividends were to be added to the stock, which subsequently became extremely burdensome to the company giving priority to payments to share- and bondholders rather than to the needs of the railway. The annual receipts for carrying mail and troops were to go direct to the judgment creditors, Baring and Glyn. However without the Act Watkin thought that the British creditors could not hope to salvage more than 7s. 6d. in the pound.

Sandfield Macdonald offered to settle the postal dispute at a higher rate on the condition that the Grand Trunk threw its weight behind his party at the general election in May 1863, but Brydges refused as the company

95 *The Globe*, 20 Sept. 1862, quoted in Andrew Smith, *British Businessmen and Canadian Confederation: constitution making in an era of Anglo-globalisation*, 2008, 80.

96 LAC, Glyn Mills Fonds, Glyn to Thomas Galt, 4 Jun. 1862; RBS Archives, GM/37, Galt to Glyn's, 12 Nov. 1862.

could not depart from their position of absolute political neutrality. When Macdonald reconstructed his ministry in May 1863 Luther Holton became Finance Minister. He was concerned about the scale of government expenditure and though he wrote to Glyn and Barings hoping that they would extend the same measure of confidence and support that his predecessors had uniformly received at their hands, he explained that the government might not be in a position to remit sufficient funds for the payment of the dividends on its bonds due on 30 June, and later wrote to say they were 'reluctantly compelled to devolve upon you the burden of providing for our July engagements.'[97] This did not prevent Holton, writing to Glyn later in the year, saying that the Government could hardly be expected to view with complacency the attempts of the resident agents of a distant proprietary to wield the influence of an enormous corporation in favour of our political opponents.[98] Glyn explained that the depreciation of Canadian securities was caused by stringency in the London money market and not by any design by bankers or the railway board.[99]

By 1862 Glyn's liability alone had risen to £736,000, £54,000 of which was to George Carr Glyn personally. Part of this debt was covered by unsold bonds but they were of doubtful value. When Glyn's settled their accounts for 1862 they set up a reserve fund of £263,000, almost all of it on the Canadian account. The fund was increased in 1863.[100] Baring told Watkin that he had the remainder of stock in the Bank of England in his and Glyn's name to avoid attachment. Later he told George Grenfell Glyn that the Canadians have this habit of bleeding us.[101] Better results were reported in 1862 – net profits were up 60 per cent in the first half compared with 1861, partly because of a reduction in operating costs. In November 1862 Watkin succeeded Baring as president who had only recently taken over from Ross. Baring remained on the London board. Whatever the rights and wrongs of the controversy, Glyn and Baring, while not withdrawing from the company, from the mid-1860s generally played a secondary role.

There were improvements in service. It was soon possible to travel from Toronto to Montreal in 15 hours and to Hamilton in 90 minutes. The Grand Trunk gained access to central Montreal and the docks, and

97 The Canadian Financial Agency, 38, Holton to Glyn Mills and Baring Bros, 22 May 1863.

98 Currie 90, LAC, Glyn Mills letter book, Holton to Glyn, 31 Oct. 1863.

99 Ibid, 94, LAC, Glyn Mills letter book, Glyn to Holton, 26 Dec. 1863.

100 Glyn's and The Grand Trunk Railway, 38.

101 LAC, MG24 D21, Baring to Watkin, 27 Mar. 1862; RBS Archives, GM/99, Baring to G.G. Glyn, 20 Sept. 1862.

improved connections with Boston and New York through amalgamation with the Montreal and Champlain Railway which ran to the Vermont border. Although the Civil War in the United States badly affected business, and the depreciation of the US dollar meant lower earnings from US traffic, gross annual revenue rose from £766,000 in 1861 to £912,000 in 1863. Working expenses were now only 60 per cent of revenue compared with 77 per cent in 1861, though the capital rose from £12,245,000 in 1862 to £16,758,000 in 1864, not least because of the capitalised arrears of interest permitted under the Arrangements Act. At the end of 1863 the best offer the Grand Trunk could obtain for a loan of £50,000 for four months was 8½ per cent through Cazenove. Watkin told Baring that they had until 3.15 the following day to consider whether they should pay so large a price.[102]

An improvement to the revenue was seen in 1864 with passenger traffic rising by 15 per cent enabling revenue to increase to £1,146,000. Much of the cost of renewals and improvements had been met from revenue, but this left little or no money for distribution and to complaints that capital expenditure was being improperly met from revenue. In May 1864 Watkin told Baring and Glyn the he 'could not conceal from you the anxiety I feel in respect to finances. They need £287,000 to the end of the year. How are we to get it?' Watkin said he was quite ready to give way to any gentleman whose influence in financial circles would command the capital they required.[103] The capital position was still dire. Second preference bonds were unsaleable and Baring was asked to continue to assist with short term loans. Shareholder pressure meant the company decided to raise capital for new equipment but even at 7 per cent most of the New Equipment Mortgage Bonds could not be sold. It was a hand to mouth existence. In April 1865 Watkin, who was ill, asked Grant, the London secretary to see Glyn and Baring about the £7,500 interest due the following Saturday. Glyn thought that he could find a market for £10,000 of bonds, but if not a loan could be negotiated with one of the financial companies until 30 June. £30,000 would carry the company through to September.[104] Later in the year the railway borrowed £190,000 from Canadian institutions to purchase equipment without which the railway could not increase its revenue. At long last there was a settlement on postal rates with the new Tache-John Macdonald government.

Revenue increased to £1,356,000 in 1865, but speculation in the company's shares engineered by a Glasgow syndicate and the continuing

[102] The Baring Archive, HC5.15.47, 29 Dec. 1863.

[103] Ibid, 13 May 1864.

[104] Ibid, HC5.15.42, Grant to Baring, 10 Apr. 1865.

effects of the Civil War led to difficult shareholder meetings. New bonds were issued again in 1866 but there was difficulty in marketing them. Watkin from Manchester told Baring he was sounding out 'our friends here' as to taking them up. Meanwhile he had established that Glyn would be ready to join Baring in each lending £50,000 of the £200,000 required for four to six months.[105]

In 1866 and 1867 there was little or no improvement in revenue. With revenue continuing to be spent on renewals there was never enough to service the capital. Arrears continued to mount. Watkin told shareholders in February 1867 that it was necessary to raise capital to pay for new locomotives. He was heavily criticised not least by Captain Henry Tyler, then chief inspecting officer of railways in the United Kingdom, who pointed to the high operating costs and the inadequate expenditure on renewals. Tyler then agreed to go to Canada, and while there became convinced that the management's analysis was correct. He recommended the investment of £1 million over the next seven or eight years. He argued that because Canada was deriving infinite advantages from the railroad, the people and government should be asked for such reasonable assistance, probably a guarantee of bond interest, as would improve the company's credit. Watkin however thought that until the railway had been placed on a sound financial basis it should neither pay interest in cash, nor capitalise it. He was opposed to the further watering down of stock, though he did not go so far as to propose a reduction of the existing capital. Both Baring and Glyn stated that they were prepared to resign if requested, but warned that abuse of the management did not improve the company's earning power.[106] Watkin, now MP for Stockport, as well as chairman of two main line railways in England, who had stayed on at the request of Baring and Glyn, finally refused re-election in October 1868. He was then in uncertain health, though this did not turn out to be a long-term problem. The verdict on Canadian railways which he delivered at his final meeting, no doubt particularly with the Grand Trunk in mind was that it was all unsatisfactory, 'because the Canadian railway system has been made before its time. Instead of making railways where you have population and development, you have railways to bring population and development.' This view has been very much endorsed by recent historians, who thought the Grand Trunk's rate of return would have been reasonable had its construction been delayed until 1861.[107]

105 Ibid, HC5.15.47, Watkin to Baring, 27 and 31 Dec. 1866.

106 Currie, 113.

107 *Morning Post*, 23 Oct. 1868; A.M. Carlos and F. Lewis, The Profitability of Early Canadian Railroads: Evidence from the Grand Trunk and Great Western Railway Companies, in

Watkin's departure and the succession of Richard Potter did not materially change the fundamental problems of the Grand Trunk, nor the position of its bankers, Glyn and Baring. From 1868 to 1872 unpaid interest continued to accumulate, now converted into preference securities rather than special certificates. There was little new funding although capital increased as a result of the purchase of the near-bankrupt Buffalo and Huron. With the expiry in 1872 of the Arrangements Act of 1862, it was agreed that dividends should be paid only from earnings. However by 1873 the capital had reached £29,732,000 compared with the £15,625,000 in 1863, though debentures now only accounted for a quarter of the capital compared with over 80 per cent. By 1881 the main addition to capital was a new 5 per cent perpetual debenture. In 1882 the Grand Trunk amalgamated with the Great Western.

The Grand Trunk was certainly unprofitable but its impact on the Canadian economy was large. Even in the mid-1850s the railway was Canada's largest employer with a $110,000 payroll for 2,600 workers. The company and its rival, the Great Western, were large vertically integrated companies with sizeable repair shops and able to build their own locomotives, the Grand Trunk's expenditure on manufacturing reaching $600,000 a year in the 1860s.[108]

Although Glyn resigned from the LNWR in 1870, he remained a director of the Grand Trunk until his death in 1873. Baring stayed on until his death only a few weeks after Glyn died, while convalescing at Glyn's house in Bournemouth. His holding in Grand Trunk securities was then a nominal £600,000.[109] Their firms continued to be represented on the board by Kirkman Hodgson and William Newmarch.

The Bank of Upper Canada

By the mid-1850s the years of prosperity of the Bank of Upper Canada were over. Founded in 1832 it had soon acquired a share of Canadian government business. It generally prospered and in 1850 the Government's account was transferred to it. However the bank had been poorly managed and after 1850 was drawing on Glyn's for amounts considerably in excess

C. Golin and H. Rockoff, eds, *Strategic Factors in Nineteenth-century American Economic History*, 1992, 413–414.

108 A.A. den Otter, *The Philosophy of Railways: The Transcontinental Railway Idea in British North America*, 1997, 218.

109 Ziegler, 226.

of its remittances. The Bank's manager Thomas Ridout promised this was only a temporary phase but the situation deteriorated, exacerbated after 1857 by the difficulties of its client the Grand Trunk, and by the growth of other banks in Canada. While in its early days it had benefited from flexible standards and informal relationships, this became a disadvantage when it came under accumulated pressures and the Government and Glyn were only partially successful in their push for better systems and management, while at the same time Galt and the Grand Trunk continued to press the faltering bank in traditional ways.[110] Glyn himself had not hesitated to give Ridout advice from time to time, whether on an individual account or on fundamental policy. He told him not to give any further indulgence to Sir Alan MacNab, and a year later that the time had come to put MacNab's mortgaged property up for sale.[111] In 1855 and 1856 the bank made a number of loans to the Grand Trunk and to subsidiary lines. The London bankers to protect their interests had Ridout appointed to the Canadian board of the Grand Trunk, but Glyn in September 1857 was urging Ridout 'not to depend in your operations on such large advances from us'.[112] In 1859 Glyn suggested to the directors that the working capital should be increased and that they should consider amalgamating with another bank.[113] He told a shareholder that the management of the Bank had not kept up with the requirements of the times.[114] A contemporary view was that it was managed by two old men, Ridout and William Proudfoot, the President, and assorted cantankerous noodles.[115] Glyn also sought information from William Cayley, the Province's Inspector General from 1854–58, who was now assistant manager of the Bank, as to the true position of the Bank. Cayley took this post though he told Glyn he was as little prepared for the job as the gardeners for the frost on Saturday last.[116] Glyn told him that the bank directors must not expect any money 'from this side for Grand Trunk purposes'.[117] The Bank had run into difficulties over the affairs of the

[110] Peter Baskerville, ed., *The Bank of Upper Canada, A Collection of Documents*, The Champlain Society, 1987, cxviii.

[111] RBS Archives, GM/4/1, 20 Apr. 1848 and 20 Jul. 1849. The Bank of Upper Canada later made large loans to the Great Western.

[112] PAC, GM papers, Glyn to Ridout, 18 Sept. 1857.

[113] RBS Archives, GM/4/1, 20 Apr. 1848 and 20 Jul. 1849; Anon, Glyn's and the Bank of Upper Canada, *Three Banks Review*, 55, Sept. 1962, 42.

[114] PAC, GM papers, A543, Glyn Mills (but presumably approved if not written by Glyn) to R. Riddell, 7 Sept. 1859.

[115] David Lewis Macpherson, quoted in Peter Baskerville, Cassels, DCB, XI.

[116] PAC, GM papers, A542 Cayley to Glyn, 8 Jun. 1859.

[117] PAC, GM papers, A540, 2 Jun. 1860.

Zimmerman debt. Zimmerman was a railroad contractor who had set up a bank. When he died in a train crash, the bank had no funds to repay the Government funds deposited by a minister. Glyn offered to take securities from the Zimmerman Estate as cover for a loan of £200,000 at 6 per cent to be repaid in half yearly instalments of £25,000, Matters worsened and in May 1860 Ridout was told that half the uncovered balance of £178,000 had to be paid off by 1 October and the rest by 1 January, or Glyn's would cease to accept the drafts of the Bank.[118] Ridout responded 'he hoped their recent remittances and upwards of £50,000 by this mail would satisfy you that every exertion is being made to improve the account.'[119] The bank was in a poor shape; its stock, 83 in 1860, by the end of 1861 had dropped to 47 while the other Canadian banks remained above par. Too many of its assets were locked in overdue or unsaleable assets.[120] Glyn's held shares in the Bank, though they were in George Grenfell Glyn's name. Nevertheless his father wrote to Ross proposing to give him Power of Attorney to sell the shares to show the directors what he thought of their conduct but decided not do so as it would be wrong for him, with inside information, to shift the loss upon others less favourably placed. 'I can afford to lose money, but not reputation.'[121] Despite his letter to Ridout Glyn reluctantly agreed to meet drafts of £50,000 to enable the Bank to increase its stock of gold.

The Bank continued under pressure. A Mr Hopkins, a dismissed clerk, petitioned the House of Assembly to call on the Government to remove their account. The Bank of Commerce in New York refused to endorse the Bank's drafts on Glyn's.[122] At the end of November 1860 Galt told Glyn it would be as well if his son George could visit Canada and look into the Bank's affairs. Some changes in the management of the Bank were needed – in the president certainly. The government could not very well interfere in the personnel of the bank but you could do so with perfect propriety, and 'I could consult with your son … confidentially'.[123] Galt later said that the Bank was so weak it could not stand any change indicating 'even a partial withdrawal of our confidence.'[124] Cayley told Glyn on 4 March 1861 that the Bank had no alternative to drawing upon you to meet the requirements of the Government, or explicitly stating to the Minister of Finance that they

118 Ibid, Glyn to Ridout, 12 May 1860.
119 RBS Archives, GM/69, 11 Jun. 1860.
120 Baskerville, cxxix.
121 LAC, GM papers, A542, Glyn to John Ross, 19 May 1860.
122 RBS Archives, GM/69, Cayley to Glyn, 26 Oct. 1860.
123 PAC, GM papers, A545, Galt to Glyn (private), 30 Nov. 1860.
124 PAC, GM papers, A543, Galt to Glyn (confidential), 4 Feb. 1861.

were unable to meet his demands. Glyn then wrote to Galt pointing out that Glyn's had only continued to support the Bank 'departing from our general rule of business in this case, knowing that the Government was also supporting it. Any withdrawal of that support would have disastrous effect on the province.' Galt agreed to keep a minimum Government balance of $1.2m at the bank. Galt secured that Proudfoot was replaced by Cayley, and Ridout went too. By August 1860 the debt to Glyn's had been reduced from $2.6m to $1.5m, but the improvement did not last and later that year the attachment in respect of rolling stock of the Grand Trunk in the names of Glyn's and Baring was transferred to the bank to bolster their securities.

Cayley was soon replaced by Robert Cassels who had thirty years experience in the Bank of British North America. He came with a guaranteed salary of $10,000 for eight years and the promise of absolute control. He carried out a full audit which established that the loss amounted to $1.25m. Cassels arranged an increase in capital for which Glyn had long argued by raising £500,000 in preference stock, a considerable amount of which was taken up quickly in Canada. He also chased debtors more vigorously though this yielded relatively little. Edward Watkin now refused to admit that the Bank should be given rights prior to those of the Grand Trunk's London creditors. In this he was supported by Baring who had no stake in the bank, while Glyn wanted the Grand Trunk to pay the bank.[125]

Cassels lost his political connections when Sandfield Macdonald replaced John Macdonald. Holton was much less sympathetic to the Bank than Galt had been. In November 1863 most of the Government's funds were transferred to the Bank of Montreal and its account at the Bank of Upper Canada was closed from 1 January 1864. Holton told Glyn and Baring that the Bank of Upper Canada would be treated with the utmost consideration so that no shock be given to its credit. The sole object was to secure to the government the services of an institution possessing resources so ample that without restricting its ordinary operations it could greatly facilitate the financial operations of the government.[126] When Galt returned to office he did not give the account back. The Bank carried on until September 1866 when a run on the Bank developed, caused in part by the Bank of Montreal's demand that their holding of Bank of Upper Canada notes be paid immediately in gold. Business was suspended on 18 September. The shareholders' entire capital of £3,100,000 was lost and the

[125] Baskerville, cxlii, who points out that Glyn's shares could hardly be a major consideration, set against the sums owed to Glyn.

[126] Baskerville, 293 (LAC, RG 19 EIA, v 3376), Holton to Glyn and Baring Brothers, 11 Nov. 1863.

government only received about ten per cent of more than £1 million owed to it. How private depositors fared is less clear as the records were destroyed. The impact on the general financial community in Canada was not great. Although Glyn's held securities which covered the overdraft of £450,000 these consisted partly of mortgages on real estate in western Canada but at the government's request these were given up for Grand Trunk postal subsidy bonds. A trust estate in G.G. Glyn's name was created to cover the remainder, originally £61,500 ($299,300) which was gradually reduced as assets were sold. Hickson, the Grand Trunk manager thought in 1869 that real estate transferred to G.G. Glyn would pay off the Bank's debt to Glyn's, then standing at $114,600 provided the expenses, about which there was concern, were not exorbitant, but progress was slow. In 1875 it was stated that all the mortgages were expected to be paid by 1877.[127]

Other Canadian developments

The Grand Trunk was not the only development in British North America which was the object of interest by British investors as well as Canadian business men and politicians. The Intercolonial Railway, the development of the Hudson's Bay territories in the West and eventually the Federation of the Canadian provinces could conceivably have been pursued as separate projects, but these questions were under consideration at the same time so they became interrelated. Not all protagonists were like Watkin, a whole hearted worker for all three causes. Glyn for the most part rarely allowed himself to be drawn into such matters, especially the attempts to develop the Intercolonial Railway and the purchase of the Hudson's Bay Company. Doubtless he thought that the Grand Trunk Railway, the Agency and the Bank of Upper Canada were more than sufficient for his bank to digest, and did not want to put more funds at risk. However his goodwill towards Canada did permit an interest in the development of communications into the vast undeveloped territory to the west of Upper Canada and members of his family and to a lesser extent the Bank were involved in projects.

A Canadian Agency Association had been set up in 1851 to negotiate the prompt investment in freehold mortgages in Canada. Interest was payable at 7 per cent. Viscount Bury and Pascoe Glyn were on the board and Glyn's were the bankers.[128] Other ventures included the Trust and Loan Company

[127] Ibid, cxlvii; Glyn's and the Bank of Upper Canada, 52; Royal Statistical Society, Newmarch papers, DP003, 3, 4 and 13.

[128] *Bankers Magazine*, May 1853.

of Upper Canada which lent British money to Canadians on landed security, taking advantage of the higher rate of interest prevailing in Canada. Baring and Glyn were the trustees as they were of the British North American Land Company of which E.W. Mills was chairman in 1859.[129]

Pressure for the Intercontinental grew in the late 1850s. John Rose accompanied John Macdonald to London in 1857 to try to get support from Palmerston's government. In conjunction with Allan MacNab, a group of London financiers including Samuel Cunard, Joseph Nelson, Captain W.W. Fitzwilliam, Viscount Bury and George Grenfell Glyn were subscribers to the Halifax and Quebec Railway. Bury may have been the stimulus for this. He had served Governor Head as civil secretary and superintendent for Indian Affairs from 1854 to 1856. He believed that a railway across Canada would give the British Empire a line of communication with India and the East better than the Suez route (the canal had not then been built) or the Cape of Good Hope. Some of those supporting the Halifax and Quebec were bondholders in the Grand Trunk, hoping that this connection would bring more traffic. The promoters sought a grant of £60,000 from the British Government to match subsidies they hoped to obtain from the Canadian provinces. Bury and George Grenfell Glyn were members of a deputation to Bulwer-Lytton, then Colonial Secretary, in June 1858. Not surprisingly no grant was forthcoming and that was the end of that particular project though soon to be replaced by the intercolonial railway.[130]

The unsuccessful North Western Transportation Company, a purely Canadian venture, set up to carry mail to Red River, in what later became Manitoba, attracted Bury's attention. The result was the North West Transit Company whose shareholders included MacNab, Fitzwilliam and Pascoe Glyn, who was then a junior partner in Bensons who became the London agents. The first directors of the company were MacNab, Bury and Henry Glyn, (now on half pay following his successful Crimean War, but holding no official position in the family bank).[131]

Joseph Nelson revived the interest in a railway to Nova Scotia in 1861 when he took a deputation of London financiers including Bury, Pascoe Glyn and Henry Glyn to present a memorial to the duke of Newcastle, the Colonial Secretary. A public meeting to generate support followed.

[129] *Daily News*, 7 Apr. 1851; *The Times*, 29 Mar. 1859.

[130] John S. Galbraith, *The Hudson's Bay Company as an Imperial Factor, 1821–1869*, 1959, 362–363.

[131] Galbraith, 363–364. Henry Glyn had been promoted to Commander in the Crimean War, but then had no appointment for some years, until he served as captain of the Miranda screw steamship on the Australian station in 1860.

This was just before Newcastle's interview with Watkin encouraged him to work towards an intercolonial railway when the problem of opening up the land of the Hudson's Bay Company was also raised. In December Joseph Howe wrote to Baring, asking him to show his letter to Glyn, to propose the formation of an association to promote communication between British and British North American capitalists and to influence public opinion in Britain.[132] Howe doubtless thought it a useful vehicle for pushing for financial support for the Intercolonial and the promotion of colonial union.

Glyn and Baring were both present at the inaugural meeting of the British North America Association on 30 January 1862 and their banks each subscribed 50 guineas. R.W. Crawford (MP for the City of London) took the chair. It had a few influential Canadian members – Howe himself, Gzowski, representatives of the Allen line and Samuel Cunard from the other main transatlantic shipping line, but a much greater number of City notables. Benson, Hodgson, and Newmarch were members as were the stockbrokers, Cazenove, Capel and Chapman, all of whom had been involved in Grand Trunk stock issues. 17 British MPs were members, including John Roebuck who had close ties with Canada.[133] That Glyn himself was not directly involved in moves towards an intercolonial railway did not prevent him from supporting the BNAA. Extension from Riviere du Loup to Halifax would undoubtedly benefit the Grand Trunk if they did not have to bear the cost, and Watkin at this stage clearly envisaged the Grand Trunk, Great Western and Intercolonial as one system from Windsor and Sarnia in the west to Portland and Halifax in the east.[134]

The membership of the BNAA illustrates the point that the British Empire was primarily run in the interests of the City at the expense of industrialists. In Canada the John Macdonald government, though pro-British, pursued tariff policies detrimental to the interests of British manufacturers. In the late 1850s only 2.74 per cent of British exports went to British North America and 3.3 per cent of British imports came from that source. Many manufacturers saw Canada and other colonies as an unnecessary expense, especially as garrisons had to be maintained there. British investment in British North America in this period was much higher per capita than in the US where foreign investment was an extra rather than a necessity. One estimate gave Canadian imports of capital at $100 million between 1850 and 1859.

132 Howe to Baring, 31 Dec. 1861, LAC, Joseph Howe Fonds, 3, 365, quoted in Smith, 63.

133 Smith, 65.

134 Watkin (from SS Asia) to Newcastle, 2 Feb. 1862, Nottingham University Library, Newcastle Papers, 1162.

Initially the BNAA organised petitions from the City and other centres in Britain pressing for the Intercolonial which helped give the project a certain sense of urgency.[135] Indeed the British cabinet did agree on terms for assistance for the Intercolonial, but Gladstone had insisted that the capital to be repaid by annual instalments into a sinking fund. The BNAA was also influential in giving momentum to the cause of a federal Canada, calling for a colonial union. In July 1862 the Colonial Office, hitherto at best indifferent to confederation, invited the provinces to consider the possibility and conferences were held at Charlottetown in New Brunswick and Quebec. Thereafter the BNAA had a much lower profile as a group.

Meanwhile pressure for expansion to the west at the expense of the Hudson's Bay Company was growing. The chartered company was regarded as an anachronism by free traders, a view which gained strength with the demise of the East India Company in 1858 after the Indian Mutiny. The Canadian government believed that unless Canadians established communications with the west, Americans would swarm into the territory and British rule would become a nullity. Newcastle recognised this, but told the Commons that Hudson's Bay had said that if Saskatchewan were taken by the government the proper thing to do was to buy out the Company altogether, because they would be deprived of their hunting grounds. Edward (Bear) Ellice, the Chairman of Hudson's Bay, had indicated to Labouchere as long ago as 1858 that the company would be willing to sell all its land and establishments.

Members of the BNAA were instrumental in taking up the question of telegraphic communication across the continent. Four of the London directors of the Grand Trunk – Baring, Glyn, Kirkman Hodgson, and William Chapman, together with R.W. Crawford and George Grenfell Glyn, wrote to Newcastle about the formation of a company for this purpose and to provide a road route alongside the telegraph. They hoped that a considerable grant of land, if not money, might be made. Rogers, the permanent secretary at the Colonial Office, said the government could not offer pecuniary assistance and had no power to grant land, but wrote to the Hudson's Bay Company to ask whether they would concede a line of land to such a company. Berens, the company's governor, replied that they were not opposed in principle but refused to say what width of land they would grant until they knew more about the route.[136]

A preliminary survey of part of the route was undertaken and evidence of practicability was provided by the opening of the US Pacific Telegraph

135 Den Otter, 116.

136 LAC, Watkin Papers, M24, E17, A 519, letter to the Duke of Newcastle, 5 Jul. and Rogers reply of 31 Jul. 1862; PP, 1863, xxxviii, 87–8, for Baring's letters of 11 Aug. and 5 Sept. 1862.

to San Francisco in November 1861. Watkin pressed more ambitious alternatives on Newcastle, including a steam railway throughout. Matters were further advanced in December 1862 when Howland and Sicotte from the Canadian government met Howe from Nova Scotia and Tilley from New Brunswick at Glyn's Bank. Benson, Chapman, Newmarch and Watkin were present at the meeting, as were George Grenfell and Henry Glyn, but not their father, though Sicotte had written to Glyn and Baring before he arrived in London. The representatives of Canada would guarantee interest on a third of the capital, provided the whole did not exceed £500,000, and provided the Imperial and other colonial governments guaranteed the other two-thirds.

Watkin was instrumental in setting up and following through these discussions. The Atlantic & Pacific Postal Telegraph Company was formed with a capital of £500,000. The board included Benson, Woolaston Blake, and Sir James Fergusson, all of whom were directors of the LNWR, Richard Potter, a timber merchant who was soon to become chairman of the English Great Western Railway, and John Pender, MP, one of the driving forces behind the Atlantic telegraph, as well as George Grenfell Glyn, but not his father or Baring.[137] Indeed the latter told Watkin that, if the Duke wanted these great efforts made he must make them on behalf of the Government, he must not leave private persons to take the risk of Imperial work.[138] Watkin tried to persuade Baring to change his mind. The scheme would make a vast difference to the value of the Grand Trunk and suggested that he and Glyn should be trustees of the company. G.G. Glyn indicated to Baring that his father would sign the letter which Watkin had prepared to send to Berens as would Crawford, if Baring would do so.[139] Watkin tried to dissuade Baring from the view that Newcastle was making use of them to fight a battle with the Hudson's Bay Company. The absence of his signature and that of Glyn would place Newcastle and himself in a very unpleasant position. Baring was not persuaded and neither he or Glyn signed. They thought the telegraph premature and that the plans for the North West were not crucial to the survival of the Grand Trunk.

However Watkin was determined not to let the Imperial work flag, as he put it. He with G.G. Glyn and Henry Glyn, Newmarch, Benson and

[137] LAC, Watkin Papers, M24, E17, A 519, for prospectus of the company, originally known as the Atlantic & Pacific Transit Telegraph Company. The title was changed at Watkin's instigation, as it resembled an earlier venture which had failed. Newmarch Papers, DP001/4/4, Wood to Newmarch, 19 May 1863.

[138] E.W. Watkin, *Canada and the States, Recollections, 1851–1887*, 1887, 124.

[139] The Baring Archive, 5.15.1602 and 1606, 4 and 5 Nov. 1862.

Blake met Berens on 1 December 1862. Berens was only prepared to sell sufficient ground for telegraph poles and a road, while Watkin and his colleagues wanted sufficient width for settlers, but Berens at the end of the meeting offered to sell the company for £1.5 million. Watkin went ahead and secured an examination of the books. G.G. Glyn was closely involved in the detailed negotiations. For some time Watkin believed, despite warnings from Gladstone, that the Government would bear at least part of the cost and not lose the chance of a further crown colony being created from the Hudson's Bay territory.

On finding that this was not the case and that Baring and Glyn would not assist, Watkin's first thought was that a syndicate of 15 people including himself could put up £100,000 each but this fell through because Hudson's Bay insisted on a cash settlement. Instead through the medium of Richard Potter the International Financial Society was approached. It had only just been formed with a capital of £3 million, but it now purchased the company. The IFS banked with Glyn's, but the latter was not among the City firms which had formed the company. Newcastle rather disingenuously played down the extent to which the Government was aware of this development, despite the scepticism of Labouchere, now Lord Taunton.[140] The HBC came under new management but to Watkin's disappointment the new chairman, Sir Edmund Head, despite the fact that his appointment had been suggested by the Duke of Newcastle, proved to be almost as conservative as his predecessors and quickly withdrew support from Watkin's mission to the West after he had engaged Captain Synge, RE,[141] and Henry Glyn to carry out surveys. It was 1870 before the position changed fundamentally when, partly under the influence of the declaration of British Columbia as a British colony, the Company sold its proprietorial interest in the vast intermediate area of Prince Rupert's Land to Canada while continuing as a trading company. As Curries had long been bankers to the HBC, when they merged with Glyn's in 1864 the merged bank became bankers to the HBC.

Glyn's were also the bankers to the Foreign and Colonial Government Trust set up in 1868 to invest £1,000,000 in a wide range of in dividend bearing foreign and colonial government securities, with not more than £100,000 in the stock of any one government. Certificates for a nominal

140 PD, 172, 5–62, 2 Jul. 1863.

141 Captain Millington Henry Synge had long taken a close interest in the Canadian west and in 1852 had published *Great Britain One Empire, On the union of the Dominions of Great Britain by intercommunication with the Pacific and the East via British North America with suggestions for the profitable colonisation of that wealthy territory.*

£100 paying 6 per cent were issued at 85. Currie was a trustee. The sums subscribed were mainly in the £15 to £20,000 range with a few of £50,000 or £100,000. By the end of the year this novel scheme was regarded as having met with fair success.[142]

The failure to make a radical change in the Hudson's Bay Company did not prevent the move to Canadian federation from going ahead, despite opposition. Indeed some of its opponents in Canada saw the Grand Trunk and the London capitalists as foisting federation on Canada at Canada's expense and to the bankers' gain. It was probably for that reason that Glyn and Baring, both members of the House of Commons, unlike other MPs who were members of the BNAA, played no part in debates on the British North American Bill when it was considered and approved in 1867. Another reason may have been their status as financial agents to the provincial government. There is a possibility, but not conclusive evidence, that they may have assisted the passage of the Bill as they may have covered the cost of printing hand bills in support of the Bill.[143] However though the City regarded federation favourably this did not mean that they foisted it on Canada. The City had little impact on the key conferences where the Canadians drew up their proposals on which the British North America Act was largely based.

Other Overseas interests

Apart from the Grand Trunk Railway and associated lines Glyn's played little direct part in overseas railways though acting as bankers for many such companies. One exception was the Royal Danish Railway. This was a railway of 69 miles from Rendsburg on the southern frontier of Schleswig, already linked to Hamburg, to the port of Flensburg on the Baltic, with a branch line of 34 miles to Tonning on the North Sea, so that it both linked with the German system and gave a connection from the North Sea to the Baltic. The prospectus envisaged Tonning would become the principal western port of Denmark. The entire territory traversed by the line, which opened in 1855, became part of Prussia following the war of 1864.[144]

The line had been surveyed by Robert Stephenson and George Bidder, and the latter was appointed the engineer. Peto, Betts and Brassey agreed to lease the line for 14 years from when it opened, paying the shareholders a minimum of 6 per cent. The initial capital was £540,000. As security the

[142] *Morning Post*, 20 Mar. and 31 Dec. 1868.

[143] The evidence is discussed in Smith, 112–113.

[144] *Bradshaw's Shareholders' Guide* 1857; Cox, *Peto*, 2008, 80.

contractors were to place £100,000 in the hands of the three trustees – George Carr Glyn, the Earl of Yarborough, chairman of the Manchester, Sheffield and Lincolnshire, and Ricardo, the chairman of the North Staffordshire. George Grenfell Glyn was the chairman, with five other English directors: John Anderson, director of the Oxford, Worcester and Wolverhampton, Ellis and Beale of the Midland, Edward Cropper and William Gordon Thompson, deputy chairman of both the South Eastern and South Yorkshire. There were also five Danish directors. The concession from the King of Denmark included a clause ruling out the establishment of any competing line for 100 years. Following the Prussian conquest the company was purchased by a Prussian bank and eventually incorporated in the Prussian state system. Glyn's were bankers to this line as they were to the North Schleswig Railway of 1863 and to the East Indian of which George Grenfell was also a director. In all Glyn's at one time or another were bankers to 84 overseas railway companies, of which only nine were in Europe.[145]

Until the 1850s British overseas banks were all concentrated in the Empire, and Glyn's banking interests were still confined to Canada, Australia and New Zealand. This changed in the mid-1850s with the setting up of the Bank of Egypt and the Ottoman Bank.

There were already substantial British trading interests in the Eastern Mediterranean particularly arising from the Suez Isthmus route to India, and the area was also a source of raw materials, but it was the Crimean War which aroused the interest of British bankers in Egypt and Turkey, particularly with the prospect of a rejuvenated Turkey. The Turks issued a charter of reforms (the Hatti-Humayoun) which stated that measures would be taken to establish banks and similar institutions to reform of the financial and monetary system, and create funds to increase the Ottoman Empire's source of public and material wealth.

In Egypt the lead was taken by Peter Pasquali, an Egyptian merchant of Symnra (Izmir) and London. Despite his failure in 1855 to obtain any exclusive privileges from the Ottoman government, the British government issued a royal charter for the Bank of Egypt. The Bank's prospectus, issued in January 1856, proposed a capital of £250,000 with power to increase to £1,000,000. Glyn's were the bankers and St Leger Glyn was on the board, as were four members of Parliament, John Cater of Bensons and Peter Pasquali. The shares initially went to a small premium, but by the end of 1856 had declined to a small discount. Cater went out to Alexandria in July when it opened for business.[146]

[145] Fulford, 258–259 for list of companies.

[146] *The Times*, 15 Nov. 1855, 26 Jan., 15 Feb., 18 Apr., 17 Jul. and 3 Oct. 1856.

Pasquali and a City associate, Stephen Sleigh, wished to form the British Bank of the Levant and sought British incorporation. Edward Zohrab, the long standing Turkish consul general in London, sought a firman from the Sultan. A Royal Charter was initially ruled out by British officials as the capital was to be used outside British jurisdiction. Pasquali and Sleigh wanted a big name as chairman and backing from a substantial city bank. Sleigh succeeded in attracting A.H. Layard who not only had the excavations at Nineveh to his name but had travelled extensively in the Near East and had been attached to the embassy at Constantinople for two years, before returning to be elected MP for Aylesbury, serving as a junior minister in the Foreign Office in the short-lived Derby government of 1852. Sleigh also recruited Henry Kingscote, a partner in Ladbroke, Kingscote & Gillman, taken over by Glyn's in 1841, when Felix Ladbroke retired, and was now a well known philanthropist. Kingscote, who still received a proportion of the interest on the accounts transferred to Glyn's from Ladbrokes, approached Glyn, who thought the Ottoman Empire a very attractive area of investment for banking and would be more than willing to support it if a charter and firman were forthcoming.[147] The charter was obtained in August. Thereafter George Grenfell Glyn took the lead, though at a meeting in October 1855 asked for a prospectus to show his father.[148] His father and the firm agreed to the project and G.G. told Sleigh that he himself would gladly become a director, but that the composition of the board must await a firman. W.R. Drake, a solicitor closely connected with Glyn's and a partner in Birchams, Dalrymple and Drake, now acted as an intermediary. Layard, James John Cummins, chairman of the Union Bank of Australia and Robert Campbell, a director of that bank, also became directors. The name was changed to the Ottoman Bank in February 1856, and while Glyn senior was not listed as a director in the prospectus then issued, he was present at a meeting under Layard's chairmanship on 11 February when the board was constituted. Pasquali and Zohrab were omitted and Sleigh decided to withdraw The firman issued to a rival group which aimed to establish a National Bank of Turkey was purchased for £7,000. The original proposers of the bank lost out. None of the 25,000 shares were allotted to Sleigh, Pasquali or Zohrab. Sleigh had 'the pain of seeing them freely awarded to strangers'.[149] Steps were taken through Clarendon, the Foreign Secretary and Stratford de Redcliffe, the Ambassador in Constantinople to stop the firman being awarded to Zohrab. Indeed G.G. Glyn accompanied

[147] Edhem Eldem, *A History of the Ottoman Bank*, 1999, 33–34.

[148] Ibid, 38.

[149] Quoted in Eldem, 44. The text of the charter is at 454–459.

Layard and Hankey to a meeting in Paris at which Clarendon and Cowley, the British ambassador to France, were present as well as representatives of the Turkish Government. A loan of £150,000 to the Sultan was negotiated at about 5 per cent, much lower than the rate prevailing in Constantinople but never made, in part because the Turkish Government proposed to establish a National Ottoman Bank.

A group led by Wilkin, a London capitalist, and including Samuel Laing, was initially successful in spite of competition from the Ottoman Bank and the Rothschilds but that was abandoned and another venture the Banque de Turkie failed to take off. Sleigh published anonymously, *Extracts from a private diary and correspondence 1855–1856* which sought to prove duplicity on the part of Glyn's and their associates. While it was an ex parte account Edhem Eldem, the historian of the Ottoman Bank, considers that most of the documents which Sleigh published tie in with other evidence. He comments 'it would not be the first case of an adventurous maverick being ousted form his own scheme by well-implanted and powerful members and companies of the financial establishment.'[150] Clearly the City directing group did not consider his presence on the board desirable, perhaps seeing him and Pasquali as likely to involve the Bank in the complex political world of the Ottoman Empire and being unwilling to be tied to the Bank of Egypt. In May 1856 Queen Victoria granted a Royal Charter in the names of Layard, Bruce, G.T. Clark, Cummins, Glyn, Hankey and Kingscote. Zohrab had meanwhile obtained a firman, but the board decided this was unnecessary, and an attempt at a rapprochement was frustrated when Pasquali made unreasonable demands.[151] The London bankers' judgement was confirmed when Pasquali had to resign from the Bank of Egypt in 1860 as he had lent £120,000 to a member of the Egyptian ruling family and made other risky loans. His efforts to recover it led to the Viceroy closing the account. His methods may have more typical of the commerce of the Near East than of the City. In their report to shareholders in 1861 the directors said that the bank had made its way in spite of opposition 'marked by an amount of unscrupulousness, intrigue, and mystification, which was altogether unknown in England.'[152] By 1869 the bank was chaired by William Tite who had been chairman of the Globe, with John Bramley Moore, a director of the LNWR as deputy. St Leger Glyn was a director and John Cater remained on the board.

[150] Eldem, 29–30, note 2.

[151] Eldem, 52.

[152] Quoted in David S. Landes, *International Finance and Economic Imperialism in Egypt*, 1958, 62.

The Ottoman Bank was only been able to issue £3 million of a £5 million loan in 1858, but was able to issue the balance in 1860 when economic conditions in Turkey improved. The prosperity did not last. Disturbances in Syria led to the Ottoman Bank placing the books of its branch there on a man-of-war. Inflation grew and the National Bank virtually collapsed, losing a large sum on the Ottoman loan of 1860. The finances of the Turkish Government deteriorated rapidly. The Ottoman Bank survived and in March 1861 declared a dividend of 8 per cent and had a reserve fund of £63,000. The failure of the National Bank to establish itself meant the Ottoman Bank was in practice the only bank to which the Turkish Government could turn and it issued a very large Turkish government loan in 1862 amounting to £8 million nominal (£5,440,000 at 68) to redeem the floating debt, which was oversubscribed seven times, in conjunction with Charles Devaux & Co. and Glyn's. The commission on this loan enabled the Ottoman Bank to raise its dividend to 10 per cent. It was also a huge benefit to Glyn's where enormous deposits were made, brokers dealing with £2 million in a single day.[153] The concession for a National Bank was opened to competition and was awarded to a syndicate formed by the Ottoman Bank, the Credit Mobilier and its associated Parisian banc d'affaires. This led in March 1863 to the creation of the Imperial Ottoman Bank. Shareholders of the Ottoman received two shares of the Imperial Ottoman for each Ottoman share they held. G.G. Glyn however had resigned in March 1862 because of the pressure of business in his own bank, and Layard too resigned, their places being taken by the Hon. T.C. Bruce, and Pascoe du Pre Grenfell, an associate of Glyn's and a cousin of G.G. Glyn.[154] Glyn's remained bankers.

George Grenfell Glyn then had to devote his attention to the London & Brazilian Bank founded because of the rapid increase of the commercial relations between Brazil and Great Britain. The prospectus issued on 6 May 1862 emphasised the high rate of interest prevailing in Brazil. Trade with Brazil was growing, one influence being the cotton famine caused by the American Civil War. Glyn's were the bankers, but the lead was taken by Bensons as not only was Cater the first Chairman but Pascoe Glyn, still working for Bensons, was heavily involved and later was to become chairman. The capital of £1,000,000 was raised very quickly. Unlike his brother Pascoe, GG was not on the first board, but took 20 shares.[155] In 1863

153 D.M. Evans, 1864, 90.

154 P.L. Cottrell, The Coalescence of a Cluster of Corporate International Banks, 1855–75, *Business History*, 33, 1991, 40.

155 D.M. Joslin, *A Century of Banking in South America*, 1963, 65–66, 155.

it acquired the recently formed Anglo-Portuguese Bank. By 1864 it had four branches in Brazil.

Rothschilds had played a dominant role in Austro-Hungarian state finance monopolising the raising of loans for the House of Hapsburg, crucial to the Empire's finances as the state exchequer had run a deficit each year between 1817 and 1867. Although some English capital had gone to industry in the Empire, not until the 1860s did London capitalists challenge the French monopoly of the region's finances. A concession for the Union Bank of Austria was sold to a group English capitalists. The syndicate included Lord Fermoy, possibly as a titled figurehead, and James Lyster O'Brienne who probably represented Overend Gurney. Although it was announced that the capital of the bank had been subscribed by shareholders whose names appeared to be of the most solid character, the Bank never started business.

Meanwhile George Grenfell Glyn had been in contact with the Austrian cabinet through Samuel Beaumont, MP for Newcastle, who was probably the source of his information that the Austrian Government had decided against using the House of Rothschild to raise a loan which would enable Austria to resume cash payments. Glyn then wrote to Thomas Baring to propose the founding of a bank and raising the loan. This was an opportunity to break into new financial territory, and has been regarded as the most serious threat to Rothschilds' interests that area. Other newcomers were thought by Nathaniel Rothschild to do a great amount of rash business[156] As a Gladstonian liberal GG could hardly approve of the reactionary Austrian Empire, but he told Baring 'Pray observe that I by no means surrender my political opinions … but I allow my commercial interests to take precedence in the present case.'[157] An agent was needed to go to Vienna. GG suggested Madame du Bury, 'a lady no doubt well known to you as having considerable influence in political circles.' On this, as with Hudson's Bay, Tom Baring was unwilling to go along with the younger Glyn's proposal. They were interested in the loan, but not in setting up a bank. G.E. Seymour, a partner in a London stockbroking firm, who worked closely with Glyn's, was to follow Madame du Bury to Vienna as soon as she indicated that the ground had been prepared. Seymour's brief stated that the project was dependent on the proposed bank having close connections with the Government to whom it would give advances. It would carry out normal commercial operations and be active in industrial investment. The directorate was to consist of two committees, one in London and the other in Vienna. The Anglo-Austrian was successfully established as a joint stock company with an authorised

156 Ferguson, House of Rothschild, 607.
157 RBS Archives, GM/13, 7 Jan. 1863.

capital of £2,000,000.[158] The loan however was taken up by Rothschilds and proved to be a failure, as Austria's relations with Prussia deteriorated and only half the sum sought was taken up.

Glyn's also had some involvement in the unprofitable world of Mexican bonds. Following independence in 1821 successive Mexican governments floated loans in other countries when other sources of revenue failed to meet their needs. In the late 1830s Francisco Lizardi & Co were the financial agents for Mexico in London. They re-organised Mexico's debt without much success in 1837 by a conversion and consolidation in which an outstanding bond and its arrears would be exchanged for a new bond plus a land warrant, but the land was the subject of dispute with the United States and the financial crisis of 1837 meant that there was little interest in implementing the conversion. Further attempts were made in 1842, and in 1845, following the revolution against the Santa Anna government, Lizardis lost the financial agency to John Schneider. By 1857 nominal claims on the 1842 issue amounted to £517,554, more than half of which were held by Barings, Hope & Co and Glyn's. It is not clear how they were acquired by Glyn's, or to what extent they had an active or passive role.[159]

Glyn's certainly had an active and for them an unusual role in 1864, following the establishment of Archduke Maximilien, the younger brother of Emperor Franz Joseph I of Austria as Emperor, as it was only in the cases of Mexico and Turkey that in this period they acted as an issue house for foreign bonds.[160] Whether it arose from any previous connection with Mexico or, as suggested by Philip Cottrell, from their contacts with the Hapsburgs through the Anglo-Austrian Bank is not clear. Possibly the last was influential as it was reported that Barings, who had been heavily involved in Mexico at earlier stages, were not interested. The suspension of the servicing of Mexico's external debt for two years by the Mexican Congress in July 1862 led to the Tripartite Treaty on the parts of the United Kingdom, France and Spain and to military intervention, from which the Spanish and British withdrew when the French made clear they were pursuing Napoleon III's aim of a Mexican Empire headed by Maximilien, an aim only made possible by the Civil War in the United States.[161] By 1864

[158] P.L. Cottrell, The Anglo-Austrian Bank, *Business History*, 11, 1969.

[159] Richard Salvucci, *Politics, Markets and Mexico's "London Debt" 1823–1887*, 2009, 137–138, 165, and 177.

[160] Jenks (Appendix C, 422–4) lists nearly over 180 government loans issued in London from 1865 to 1875. The Mexican and Turkish loans were the only instances where Glyn's acted as the issuing house.

[161] Salvucci, 34, 236.

the Mexican bond market had recovered to some extent with the prospect of firmer rule from the new Emperor and the backing of France. Even the *Economist*, while pointing out the small total revenue available in Mexico to pay interest on bonds which before the advent of Maximilien bonds had stood at 33, thought that the Emperor could succeed and achieve at least part of what Pedro I had done for Brazil.[162]

The Emperor began by converting the arrears on the earlier bonds included in the Conversion of 1850 at the rate of £100 bonds for £60 in coupons. These were to pay 3 per cent and the negotiations were carried out by James Capel, as chairman of the London Committee of Bondholders,[163] with Thomas Baring and G.G. Glyn, Glyn's acting on behalf of the International Financial Society. This conversion was an essential condition to raising more money from Europe. Initially the lead for a new loan seems to have been taken by the International Financial Society and the Credit Mobilier in Paris, and on 20 March a contract was signed for a loan to be issued in London and Paris within a fortnight of Maximilien receiving the Mexican crown.[164] At the time James Rothschild was sorry to see the loan go to Credit Mobilier and Glyn's.[165] After complex discussions IFS came to a new agreement with Credit Mobilier. Glyn's, with the IFS and the Credit Mobilier in Paris, would issue bonds to a nominal value of £12,365,000 at 63 per cent (£7,790,000) bearing interest at 6 per cent (a yield of 9.3 per cent). £8,000,000 was for the Government of Mexico and the remaining £4,365,000 for the French to repay their military and other expenses.[166] The issue was unsuccessful but much more so in London than Paris where faith in the future of the Mexican empire was much greater. In London it attracted only 115 applicants who took £500,000 nominal, while in Paris there were 801,702 applicants for £5,000,000 nominal. G.G. Glyn wrote to Charles Mallet 'I cannot disguise it, the affair has been a total failure and must be so considered. You carry it through in Paris on terms which we cannot here accept.'[167]

The French Government forewent its portion of the loan and Credit Mobilier with its close links to the French government took the unsubscribed portion of the loan, but both Glyn's and the IFS refused to take any share

[162] *The Economist*, 2 Apr. 1864.

[163] *The Standard*, 12 Apr. 1864.

[164] P.L. Cottrell, I*nvestment Banking in England, A Case Study of the International Financial Society* 1985, 1, 308–309.

[165] Ferguson, 632.

[166] *The Times*, 18 Apr. 1864 for the prospectus.

[167] Cottrell, *Investment Banking*, 310; RBS Archives, GM/13, 29 Apr. 1864.

though they offered to surrender all profit in the matter. By June Glyn's and the IFS had passed the servicing of the loan to Baring's, the Mexican government's financial agents.[168] But the hope that bondholders placed in a reconstruction of Mexico quickly vanished. By July bond prices had fallen sharply and did not recover, dropping to a new low when in May 1866 Napoleon III announced his intention to withdraw all French troops from Mexico. In June 1867 Maximilien was executed. For two years Glyn's paid the interest on the conversion of 1864, but payments to the London bondholders ceased after July 1866.[169]

Thus Glyn's main initiatives in international banking were not carried forward by George Carr Glyn, but by his successors, particularly initially George Grenfell and also Pascoe. There is no reason to suppose that he disapproved in principle of such developments, even if as was seen with the International Finance Society he may well have been sceptical of some of them. What Philip Cottrell has called the 'Glyn group' continued to play a central role in the founding of Anglo-international corporate banks in the late nineteenth century, though largely as a promotional bloc, but one that provided senior non-executive management through directorships to the various banks set up.[170] Glyn's often acted as bankers to the new ventures even though, as in the Anglo-Italian founded in 1863, the partners in the Bank took no direct part. Other banks had links with others of the 'Glyn group', such as the Bank of Roumania with directors of the Ottoman Bank on its board and the Anglo-Hungarian, linked to the Anglo-Austrian. City associates of Glyn's promoted the London and San Francisco in 1865, the German bank of London, 1871, the Mercantile Bank of the River Plate, 1872 and the Banque de Constantinople, 1872.[171] George Carr Glyn's successors were closely involved in the promotions of these banks. C.H. Mills was chairman of the Imperial Ottoman, and of the Union Bank of Australia. His son, C.W. Mills, was a director of both these banks and of the Anglo-Austrian, as was Bertram Currie. Members of the Grenfell family were also involved. Charles Seymour Grenfell was a director of the London and Brazilian Bank with Pascoe Glyn and Pascoe Dupre Grenfell who was also on the board of the Imperial Ottoman Bank. Sidney Carr Glyn was a director of the Bank of Egypt with Arthur Riversdale Grenfell.[172]

168 Ibid, 311.

169 Salvucci, 252.

170 P.L. Cottrell, Coalescence, 46.

171 Ibid, 43–46.

172 Youssef Cassis, *City Bankers*, 1994, 223–224.

CHAPTER SIXTEEN

Parliamentarian, Landowner and Family Man

THE LATE 1840s and 1850s brought major changes to Glyn's life. In 1847 he became an MP. His family were moving into adulthood. Indeed his eldest son, George Grenfell, on graduating from University College Oxford in 1845 became a partner in Glyn's at the age of 21 and for many years took an active part in the family bank. This did not mean Glyn was relieved from the responsibility of educating his children. His large Victorian family meant that his last child, Edward, born in 1843, only went up to University College Oxford in 1863.

Glyn was 50 before he became an MP. His constituency was Kendal, one of the 20 new boroughs enfranchised in 1832 which returned one member each, since when it had returned a Liberal MP in every election, in contrast to the County of Westmorland in which it was situated. Although the town was reliant on the manufacture of textiles: woollens, lindseys, worsted and carpets, and to a lesser extent on leather, rope and a marble works, it was not booming in this period. The population was virtually static – 11,577 in 1831 and 11,829 in 1851. The registered electors numbered less than 400. No one had a commanding influence in the seat, though both the Earl of Thanet (Sir Richard Tufton) and the Earl of Lonsdale had some. From 1837 Kendal's MP had been George William Wood, a prominent Manchester merchant, but he died in 1843 and at the ensuing by-election George Warburton, the Liberal candidate, beat G.W.P. Bentinck, the Conservative by 182 to 110 in what turned out to be the only contested election in the constituency between the Reform Act and 1874. Warburton did not stand in the general election of 1847, due to ill health and Glyn was elected unopposed, as he was in four further elections before he decided not to stand again in 1868.

It is not clear why Glyn chose to stand for Kendal rather than any other constituency. In October 1850 he declined to preside at the dinner of the

Kendal Agricultural Society on the ground that he did not possess a single acre of land in the county, though he agreed to do so in 1851.[1] He told the Westmorland Society in 1850 that he had for the greater part of his life been intimately associated with gentlemen who came from Kendal as well as from other parts of Westmorland and who were deeply engaged in the mercantile pursuits of the City of London.[2] These gentleman certainly included William Thompson as well as the Croppers. Glyn had known Thompson from the early days of St Katharine's Dock, and from 1835 they were colleagues on the board of Globe Insurance. Thompson had been born at Grayrigg House near Kendal and became a substantial landowner in Westmorland. By the 1840s he was in a different political camp from Glyn. Originally a Whig he wanted to retain the Navigation Acts and the Corn Laws and in 1841 had been elected as the Tory MP for the county, and became the leader of City Conservatism. James Cropper, John's son, recalled how when the Lancaster and Carlisle Railway was being planned as a youth he drove with three of the promoters to see local landowners including Thompson at his estate at Underley near Kirkby Lonsdale who told them nothing would induce him to entertain the thought of a railway through his property, though he soon became a large investor in railway shares.[3] However the opening of the Kendal and Windermere Railway in April 1847, which joined the Lancaster and Carlisle at Oxenholme near Kendal and was then worked by the LNWR certainly assisted Glyn, as John Whitwell, a carpet manufacturer, who seconded Glyn's nomination was its deputy chairman. He was also several times mayor of Kendal. There were also strong links between Liverpool and Kendal, particularly through the Cropper family and Glyn may well have been introduced to Kendal by the Croppers. Both Edward Cropper, and his brother John had married daughters of John and Mary Wakefield of Sedgwick House, Kendal,[4] though Edward's wife had died in 1830. The Wakefields were an influential Kendal family. John Wakefield, brother-in-law to the Cropper brothers, owned a gunpowder factory and was a partner in Wakefield Crewdson, one of the local banks. John Cropper had become a director of the Lancaster and Carlisle. His elder son James, went to live near Kendal when he married into the same family in 1845, in which year he took

[1] *Preston Guardian*, 17 May and 4 Oct. 1851; *Kendal Mercury*, 5 Oct. 1850.

[2] *Kendal Mercury*, 18 May 1850. Brougham was another member of the Society. He told the meeting that Kendal's choice of Glyn as their MP had vastly removed his antipathy to the existence of small parliamentary boroughs.

[3] *ODNB*; James Cropper, *Notes and Memories*, 1900, 110.

[4] Edward Cropper's subsequently married Thomas Babington Macaulay's sister, Margaret, and after her early death the widow of her brother, Henry, also Margaret.

up paper manufacture by leasing the Cowen Head and Burneside Mills, the latter situated next to the Kendal and Windermere line. He succeeded his father on the board of the LCR in March 1852.

At the election meeting on 30 July Glyn was proposed by Thomson Bindloss, (an alderman and chair of Glyn's Committee) and seconded by Whitwell, with the Mayor and returning officer, John Wakefield in the chair.[5] The uncontested election was formal and elaborate. The Court, as it was called, was opened by Wakefield in the town hall followed by an adjournment to a commodious hustings erected in the market place to which Glyn repaired with his friends in procession. The windows of the adjoining houses from which it was possible to hear the proceedings were filled with ladies including Mrs Glyn and two of the Glyns' sons. Whitwell laid emphasis in the great changes in policy in the previous parliament. Many were elected as protectionists, but many had come round and voted for the repeal of the corn laws. It was not clear what the next seven years might bring. It therefore behoved them to elect a man, who acquainted with great commercial and monetary interests, could nevertheless be the stern and unflinching advocate of civil and religious liberties, who was pledged to nothing but would never the sacrifice the interests of the people to any other interest whatsoever. Glyn's speech is of interest in summarizing his stance on various issues. He stood as the representative of one of the most free and independent boroughs in the kingdom. He was returned by no particular section. He was not returned through any extraneous influence but appeared after a full discussion of principles on a variety of occasions without being pledged to particular measures. He would not forget the kindness with which he had been received by the Liberal party in Kendal whose banners and badges he trusted he would wear till his dying day.

Although not opposed at the election two objections to his becoming a member had been voiced. One was that he was too closely connected with railways. He denied the charge. He only had to appeal to the evidence he had given to Parliament and to the acts of the company over which he presided to show that his interests as a railway director were not likely to interfere with any measure conducive to the public safety or convenience. He would however uphold the rights of railway proprietors as he would those of his constituents and his own against any encroachment by government. Those who taunted him with going into parliament in the railway interest did him very great injustice. He regarded the other objection as being of a more serious nature. He had been accused of being lukewarm in the cause

5 *Kendal Mercury*, 31 Jul. 1847. Glyn's links with Kendal do not seem to have arisen through his banking connections. Glyn's were not the London agents for either of the Kendal banks.

of protestantism. It was the faith 'in which I live and to which I am attached more than to life.' He was a member of the Church of England but was also a member of that larger church, the Church of Christ. He found nothing in the faith which they all held which authorised him to turn round and inflict pains and penalties on those who differed from him. There was no class of fellows citizens which was not entitled to equal, civil and religious rights with the rest. He was strongly opposed to the doctrines of Romanism but that was no reason why he should place a sect under terrors of persecution. He was also against church rates falling on those who stood aloof from the communion of the Church of England. He was not bound to any minister but would support Lord John Russell to whom the country owed a huge debt of gratitude. It was the duty of liberals to rally round him. At the very least they had to ensure that he did his duty and that recent measures were not reversed. He praised Cobden and also Fox Maule for his bill ameliorating conditions in the British Army. He regretted the failure of the bill on sanitary reform and also could not see why the City in which he had spent the greater part of his life should be exempt from its operation. He was against taxation which fell on articles of daily consumption, increased their cost and made it difficult for the poor to obtain them. The load of taxation ought to be borne by the rich and powerful.

At the subsequent lengthy dinner for 300 in the Assembly Room, with Wakefield in the chair, Mrs Glyn was with Miss Wakefield in the orchestra, presumably an area reserved for the ladies. There were a large number of toasts, and after the chairman and vice-chairman retired there were more unreported toasts and sentiments suitable to the festivity of the occasion and many songs were sung, the hilarity being kept up until a late hour. It is not clear how late Glyn, or indeed Mrs Glyn, chose to grace the occasion.

The *Morning Chronicle* described Glyn as being in the enviable position of being thought well of by two strongly opposed parties. His polices were Whig, but he was seeking a seat in Parliament not as a supporter of one party, but as a leading member of that new interest which though lately come into existence was already powerful.[6] Indeed at this election the number of MPs who were railway directors, engineers and contractors was considerably increased. Russell had been MP for Reading from 1832 though he was now defeated, and Hudson had been first elected for Sunderland in 1845, but he was now joined not only by Glyn but by Chaplin (LSWR) and Charles Pascoe Grenfell (LBSCR) among the chairmen, the engineers Robert Stephenson and Joseph Locke and contractors Jackson and William Cubitt,

[6] *Morning Chronicle*, 28 Jul. 1847.

as well as a number of directors. The *Illustrated London News* commented that as a banker Glyn had the reputation of being one of the most liberal in London in his mode of conducting business, and had very active and energetic habits. As a railway spokesman he would rank in the House next to Hudson.

Glyn visited his constituency several times. In August 1851 he and Mrs Glyn stayed for a short time in Kendal on their way back from Edinburgh to London. In April 1851 Glyn with Alderman Thompson, John Whitwell and others took a deputation from Kendal and Westmorland to ask that the assizes for that county should be moved from Appleby to Kendal.[7] He became a patron of the cricket club and subscribed to various local appeals including £500 for a school or chapel on Kendal Moor.

In August 1852 he, his wife, two daughters and three sons stayed at the Windermere Hotel.[8] He spoke about the desirability of extending the franchise – before endowing the people with power it was highly necessary to give them the means of wielding it with proper effect which meant imparting to them a moral and religious education. He emphasised his free trade principles which by 1851 had resulted in the disappearance of the old antagonism between commerce and agriculture and to which he attributed the general prosperity of the City.[9]

In 1851 when an election was proposed, a meeting in Kendal made clear that he would be supported again and the following year he was duly elected unopposed. At the last minute he was unable to travel to Kendal because of an attack of bronchitis so severe that his physician advised that the journey would endanger his life. His son George Grenfell Glyn, then aged 27, made what he called his first public speech to accept the nomination on his father's behalf. The absence of the prospective MP had only been known on the morning before the poll and so it made little difference to the planned ceremonies which took the same form as in 1847. Glyn was praised by Wakefield who particularly emphasised his opposition to the Militia Bill which he thought after thirty-five years of peace was a measure calculated to revive an unhealthy military spirit in the community. Whitwell pointed to Glyn's interest in and loyalty to Kendal when there were so many other places which would be glad to have him: only a few days previously a deputation from a most important and influential constituency had attempted to persuade him stand as their member. George's speech had little political content except to underline his father's attachment to free trade and desire

7 *The Times*, 21 Jun. 1851.

8 *Kendal Mercury*, 28 Aug. 1852.

9 *Westmorland Gazette*, 12 Oct. 1861.

to see constitutional progression steadily developed, not going too fast, but up with the wants and necessities of the age. There was again a dinner, this time for 200, when George replied to James Cropper's toast to his father, as a true reformer. His credentials as a reformer were enhanced when in 1853 he voted for the ballot.

Before the election in 1857 it was reported that there was no probability of any opposition to Glyn. He had presented a petition from Kendal, telling Whitwell, then the mayor, that he trusted that the financial position of the country would allow Parliament materially to redeem and modify the income tax. As a constituency MP he gave a silver cup worth five guineas to the Kendal Poultry Show for the best pair of Black Spanish. Later he was a patron of a local exhibition, listed with aristocrats such as Devonshire, Lonsdale and Brougham.[10] He was criticised for giving utterance to sentiments purely of the Manchester School at what the complainant regarded as a private occasion – the dinner of the Kendal Agricultural Society.[11] At the adoption meeting in 1857, he again denied that his interests as a railway director were likely to interfere with any measure conducive to the public safety or convenience. Although several whose political opinions were opposed to Glyn were present, a resolution approving his parliamentary conduct and inviting him to stand again was unanimously adopted and he was elected unopposed. Lord Palmerston's policy was praised and those in the Cobden camp who opposed Britain's action in China were criticised. When a meeting of Non-Electors resolved that the time had arrived for the extension of the franchise and the growing intelligence of the people fully justified such a step, Glyn courteously received the resultant deputation and agreed with their objective.[12]

He was again unopposed at the general election in 1859. His election meeting on 28 April passed off without much excitement, being followed by lunch with the mayor and corporation.[13] Indeed the local paper seemed more moved by Henry Glyn's account of his 200 mile ride to the bridge over the Danube in the Crimean War.[14]

In July 1865 the *Preston Guardian* reported that the Liberal views of Mr Glyn suited the opinions of the bulk of the constituency so well that no opponent was likely to be in the field. Glyn was re-elected unopposed. Ill health meant that in March 1867, writing from Bournemouth, he

10 Cumbria Archives, Kendal, WDX 413/1.

11 *Westmorland Gazette*, 18 Oct. 1851.

12 *Lancaster Gazette*, 7 and 14 Feb. and 14 and 28 Mar. and *Preston Guardian*, 14 Mar. 1857.

13 Cumbria Archives, OWD/PW/20/4.

14 *Westmorland Gazette*, 30 Apr. 1859.

explained to his constituents that his medical adviser would not yet allow him to go back to London but to avoid the loss of his vote he had paired with another member. In July 1868 Glyn announced his decision not to stand for re-election, but this had been in his mind for some time.[15] In 1866 he was writing to one of his sons, 'I expect there will be a sharp contest at Kendal when I go – they would be wise to get a leading politician to come forward.'[16]

He was mistaken in this view. Although George Grenfell Glyn, by then Chief Whip of the Liberal Party, suggested that Gladstone might succeed him and so secure a safe seat, he preferred to contest South Lancashire and then Greenwich. When the general election came no outsider was brought in and there was not even a contest.[17] In November 1868 John Whitwell, again the mayor, issued his election poster before the dissolution was announced. He was returned, unopposed, determined 'to follow in the footsteps of Mr Glyn and to support Mr Gladstone'. Glyn in his retiring address, said that the accomplishment of religious equality in Ireland remained for legislation and he devolved the duty of contending for it to his successor.[18]

In both 1874 and 1880 Whitwell defeated Conservative opponents by two votes to one in what after 1868 was a much enlarged electorate. Whitwell died later in 1880 and James Cropper, whose uncle had been such a close colleague of Glyn's on the boards of the LBR and LNWR, retained the seat for the Liberals, with a three to two majority.[19] In June 1883 at her home in Lancaster Gate Marianne Glyn presented to the Corporation of Kendal a portrait of her husband by Stephen Pearse 'Lord Wolverton MP for Kendal 1847–68.' Cropper, the Mayor (Alderman Somervell) and Councillor Hargreaves were present, as were three of her sons: George Grenfell, Henry and Sidney. Marianne was described as being very active for her age and she looked back with pleasure to her associations with Kendal.[20]

Glyn was a member of four royal commissions, the first two of which were on bankruptcy, in 1839–40 and in 1853–54. Following the Crimean War he was a member of the commission appointed to examine the practice of the purchase of commissions in the army. He was also a member of the Royal Commission on railways appointed in 1865.

15 Ibid, 9 Mar. 1867.

16 RBS Archives, GM/1381/11, letter of 26 Jun. 1866.

17 A.F. Thompson, Gladstone's Whips and the General Election of 1868, *English Historical Review*, 63, 1948, 196.

18 Cumbria Archives, WDX 413/1.

19 *Lancaster Gazette*, 12 Mar. and 30 Apr. 1859; *Preston Guardian*, 8 Jul. 1865; *Lancaster Gazette*, 21 Nov. 1868.

20 *Kendal Mercury*, 22 and 29 Jun. 1883.

Bankruptcy law in England had a long history going back to 1543. It was complex and, particularly in the nineteenth century, subject to frequent changes and often put under scrutiny, in part because of differing views as to the role of the state in the system. By 1861, when yet another Bankruptcy Bill was under consideration, Lord Overstone was moved to say 'I doubt whether the subject is really understood by anybody'.[21] Although the 1824–25 Bankruptcy Consolidation Act reorganised the law in a more rational way, it did not reform the system. This was achieved by one of Lord Brougham's major reforms, the Bankruptcy Act of 1831. The new Bankruptcy Court took over functions previously administered by the Court of Chancery. Official assignees appointed by the Lord Chancellor took over responsibility for the day-to-day management of bankrupt estates from creditors who had acted as voluntary assignees but who could be negligent or fraudulent. At first the system only applied to London.

However this major reform did not prove to be lasting. Horsley Palmer and Glyn (or rather Glyn, Hallifax, Mills) were among the City bankers merchants, and traders who signed a petition claiming that the modes of liquidation now so frequently adopted under deeds of trust were unsatisfactory. It would be very advantageous to the mercantile community that in all cases of commercial insolvency any mode of liquidation which should be approved by a proper majority (they thought three-quarters) of creditors shall be binding upon the rest.'[22] There were other grounds for dissatisfaction: the number of bankruptcy officials, the exclusion of the provinces from the 1831 Act and the need to combine bankruptcy and insolvency law.

Consequently a royal commission was appointed in 1839 to inquire into the state and administration of the laws and particularly whether the various courts concerned might be united or rearranged. Glyn was a member together with several leading City figures, including Palmer and Benjamin Hawes, MP for Lambeth, the London businessman most closely associated with bankruptcy reform, though five of the commissioners were connected with the legal system as bankruptcy or insolvency commissioners or judges. They produced two reports in 1840 and 1841. Their most far reaching recommendation was to abolish the difference between bankruptcy and insolvency law and to extend liability to bankruptcy law to 'all persons engaged in trade or business requiring capital and credit.' Other recommendations were to reduce from £100 to £50 the amount of debt to one creditor

[21] D.P. O'Brien, ed. *The Correspondence of Lord Overstone*, 1971, 2, 146 (letter to G.W. Norman, 11 Jun. 1861).

[22] V. Markham Lester, *Victorian Insolvency, Bankruptcy, Imprisonment for Debt, and Company Winding-up in Nineteenth Century England,* 1995, 218.

needed for that creditor to be allowed to file a bankruptcy petition and that the granting of a certificate of discharge should be a purely judicial act from which creditors should be excluded.[23]

The last two recommendations were included in the Bankruptcy Law Amendment Act of 1842. It added a number of types of trader to the list of those subject to bankruptcy law, but did not take up the all-embracing definition recommended. The law was extended from London to the rest of the country, a measure which London merchants generally favoured though those in the rest of the country had more doubts. It was however not until 1861 that the distinction between bankruptcy and insolvency law was abolished.

The 1842 Act had not been the subject of extensive debate in Parliament and there was still dissatisfaction among merchants, bankers and solicitors. A London Committee of Merchants produced a bill which was introduced by Hawes in both 1845 and again in 1846, but it never became law. The provisions were generally directed towards speeding up the bankruptcy procedures and reducing costs. Brougham himself, though not a minister after 1834, introduced the Bankruptcy Consolidation Act of 1849, which despite its title included several reforms. It brought in a ranking system of certificates of conformity classed according to the actions of the debtor: 'virtuous', 'unfortunate' and 'spendthrift, 'speculating or fraudulent'. Brougham proclaimed that the simple principle behind almost all his amendments was 'prima facie the creditor was in the right and the debtor was in the wrong', but in classifying debtors he was reflecting the prevailing moral attitude to bankrupts. Churches even disciplined bankrupt members.[24]

In the 1840s and early 1850s discussion of the bankruptcy, limited liability and partnership laws were interwoven. Gladstone's Joint Stock Companies, Registration and Regulation Act provided for the registration of companies but it did not confer limited liability for companies or partnerships. In 1851 a Select Committee was established on the Law of Partnership. Glyn was a member as were Labouchere and Cobden. Their final report was cautious and the most important recommendation was for a Royal Commission to consider changes in the law of partnership, but when that body reported in 1854 it rejected change, the majority of Commissioners being unwilling to interfere with principles which had proved beneficial to the general industry of the country. This attitude was not acceptable to many MPs at a time

[23] Second Report from the Select Committee on Banks of Issue, PP, 1841, xii.

[24] Samuel Morton Peto the founding figure and most prominent member of Bloomsbury Central Baptist Chapel had to face a committee of enquiry set up by the chapel into his bankruptcy, John G. Cox, *Peto*, 70.

when some English companies were placing themselves under French law by means of a fictitious domicile in France, and the Commons passed a resolution urging the modification of the laws of partnership, which resulted in the changes made in 1855.

Glyn's described his attitude to the work of the 1851 committee in a later speech. He had for some time considered the whole scheme of commercial jurisprudence in the country to be in a most anomalous and unsatisfactory condition. He had attended the 1851 committee with an eager desire to find some remedy for the system, but he had seen nothing in the evidence, nor in the report, which led him to believe that, however desirable certain changes were, they were in a position to decide how those changes should be effected. In particular the committee had failed to deal with the question of fraud which under a system of limited liability would inevitably occur. In France where the principle of partnerships in commandite′ had been carried to the greatest extent it had been found necessary to give the bankruptcy laws an extremely penal character. Change had to come before limited liability could be introduced. The law should take account of the system of credit which was unlike that of any other country as a large portion of business in the manufacturing district was conducted by means of bills of exchange, circulating from hand to hand with endorsements bearing an unlimited liability.[25]

The Government put forward a partnership Bill in 1855, when Glyn reiterated his views, and warned against taking France or America as analogous cases. This Bill lapsed at the end of the Session but the parallel Bill on Limited Liability succeeded. Companies which went through the process of registration could claim limited liability if 15 per cent of their capital was paid up and with a quarter of the capital subscribed had at least twenty five shareholders. As Alex Rosser has pointed out it was government ministers not business men who pushed reform of limited liability.[26] Glyn was not against the principle of the bill but very doubtful about the way the principle was to be applied. Initially he wanted the bill referred to a committee to ascertain how it bore on the law of bankruptcy.[27] He did not entirely accept the view of Robert Lowe, that the case for limited liability was founded upon the general principle of freedom of contract. He particularly objected to Lowe's view that there was no distinction to be made between large and small concerns and saw no reason why an advantage

[25] PD, 134, 789–91, 27 Jun. 1854.

[26] Alex S. Rosser, Businessmen in the Parliaments of 1852–57, *Parliamentary History*, 32, 2013, 477–505.

[27] PD, 139, 1382–3, 26 Jul. 1855.

should be conferred on a joint stock company which was not given to a grocer's shop.[28] Glyn objected strongly to the Government's reduction the lower amount of capital needed from £25 to £10, as he foresaw that shopkeepers in small towns would be injuriously affected by the change. He was unable to discover what security had been provided to prevent petty joint stock companies from being started in small towns for the purpose of running down the petty traders. He spoke even more strongly after the Bill had been amended so that a company could start without capital. The amount of the shares had been reduced and the machinery for winding up had been removed from the Bill. The changes proposed were of importance to the commercial world. They would be likely to produce such pernicious effects that he trusted the question would have full attention in the Lords.[29] However the Lords were given little time and much of their debate consisted of complaints about the Bill being tabled so late in the session. The Bill received its second reading by 38 to 14.

In 1856 Glyn attacked the Government's Partnership Amendment Bill because Lowe proposed to leave the bankruptcy laws unchanged whereas in all countries where there was a similar measure there were very stringent bankruptcy laws.[30] However both the Goverment's partnership bills introduced in 1856 came to nothing, Robert Lowe saying that the Joint-stock Companies Act was only the Partnership Act under another name.[31]

Glyn took little part in Parliamentary debates in the 1860s and did not speak on the Limited Liability Bill of 1862 which was largely a consolidating measure. When the Select Committee on Limited Liability was appointed in 1867 his son G.G. Glyn was a member, one of several from the City. Probably influenced by Newmarch who argued that 'under the 1862 Act they had had five years litigation and the meaning and bearing of that Act was in course of being very rigidly settled', only minor changes were made to the law following the report.[32]

Meanwhile in the period immediately following the passage of the 1842 Bill the bankruptcy systems seemed to be working well, but fewer cases led to Government concern about the decline in court fees on which the court system depended for income which was the main reason for the setting up of another royal commission in August 1853.

28 Expressed on the second reading of the Partnership Law Amendment Bill, PD, 139, 353, 29 Jun. 1855.

29 PD, 139, 1450, 27 Jul., 1521, 30 Jul. and 1712, 1 Aug. 1855.

30 PD, 143, 341, 4 Jul. 1856.

31 PD, 143, 1477, 25 Jul. 1856.

32 Quoted in P.L. Cottrell, *Industrial Finance, 1830–1914*, 1976, 61.

Glyn, now freed from his duties as chairman of the LNWR, agreed to serve as a member. He had shown a desire for better administrative systems in a debate on the South Sea Annuities Bill when he criticised the Government for the way they proposed to secure payment of sums held by the Accountants General. He knew of no class of persons who were in a more hopeless or helpless position than those unfortunates whose funds were in the Court of Chancery.[33]

The commission was again dominated by bankruptcy lawyers, but the chairman was Spencer Walpole, who had been Home Secretary in the Derby administration of 1852, and was currently serving as chairman of the GWR. The commission concluded that reduced fees were directly related to 'the general prosperity of trade and commerce which has recently prevailed and a better and more prudent system of trading among the smaller traders.' They regarded the objective of the lower limit introduced in 1849 as 'entirely fanciful' as it was supposed to induce people to come to court early, but it had no influence as at that stage people would not believe they were hopelessly insolvent. To encourage use of the court system they suggested the limit of 5s in the pound in assets should be replaced by a total of £150 in assets. A large reduction in bankruptcy officials was recommended: the staff were too numerous and too highly paid.[34]

The report itself did not directly result in any changes to the law but provided an opportunity for chambers of commerce and other local bodies to register their general want of confidence in the law and its institutions. They particularly stressed the need for means of liquidation to be approved by a majority of creditors whose decisions should be binding on the rest. This dissatisfaction led to a movement on behalf of creditors to reform the system of bankruptcy administration and to bring it within their control. Glyn continued to take an interest in the bankruptcy laws and in April 1858 asked the Attorney General when he would be bringing in a bill on the subject and was assured it was in a very advanced state.[35] The lead was increasingly taken by the National Association for the Promotion of Social Science, founded in 1857, whose first president was Brougham. They drew up a bill which Lord John Russell, then in opposition, presented to Parliament in June 1858. Meanwhile the Attorney General in Derby's administration, Sir Fitzroy Kelly, had asked for a government bill to be prepared.

Lord Chelmsford, the Lord Chancellor, presented the Government's bill in July, but neither it nor Russell's Bill succeeded, nor did another

33 PD, 129, 1005, 29 Jul. 1853.

34 Royal Commission on Court of Bankruptcy, PP, 1854, xxiii.

35 PD, 149, 1353–4, 20 Apr. 1858.

bill introduced by Russell in 1859 However the chambers of commerce representatives met Palmerston soon after his return to office in 1859 and the outcome was that the new Attorney General, Sir Richard Bethell, introduced a lengthy bill in 1860 which met with the general approval of the chambers of commerce and the Association, but which had to be withdrawn for lack of parliamentary time. On Palmerston's visit to Leeds in October 1860, the Chamber of Commerce successfully pressed him to commit himself to reintroduce the bill.[36] A shorter version became law in 1861. In the debates on the 1860 Bill Glyn played only a minor part by pressing the case of the mercantile community. In 1860 when the clause providing for the duties of the official assignee to cease when the creditors' assignee had been appointed was considered, Glyn said he was sorry to see any objection to this: the mercantile community was anxious that a bigger role be given to the trade assignees. He was adamant that the mercantile community did not want the official assignee introduced into trust deed cases.[37]

In 1861 Glyn supported the proposal to abolish the office of accountant, but particularly in the face of the Attorney General's argument that they were bound by statute to pay the full salary and his quotation of the Duke of Wellington's dictum in 1834 when it was proposed to abolish the office of Patentee of Bankrupts 'he was as much entitled to retain his office as any one of their lordships was to retain their seat' did not press the point, while explaining that he was in favour of the principle that they were bound to give the full salary to retiring officials.[38] In the end the chambers of commerce did not entirely get their way as the Lords substantially amended parts of the Bill, in particular removing the chief judge of bankruptcy and the provision to remove the ability to transfer insolvent estates from the chancery courts to the bankruptcy courts. The power of the creditors to regulate and control the administration of the debtor's property was retained.[39]

The 1861 Act was not the end of the story. The debate on the bill had exposed considerable tension between the business community and the legal profession – the latter arguing powerfully and successfully for the retention of the role of the chancery courts. By 1864 the Attorney General, now Sir Roundell Palmer, was admitting that the 1861 Act had not been as satisfactory as desired. By 1869 there was yet another Act which largely adopted the Scottish system to end the use of commissioners and official

36 G.R. Searle, *Entrepreneurial Politics in Mid-Victorian Britain*, 1993, 135–136.

37 PD, 161, 884, 25 Feb., PD, 161, 2159, 18 Mar. 1861.

38 PD, 159, 1764, 12 Jul. 1860.

39 Markham Lester, 144.

receivers, a victory for commercial interests. In 1883 however Parliament reimposed a form of officialism because small creditors suffered under the 1869 Act.[40]

The next royal commission to which Glyn was appointed considered the long standing practice of the purchase of commissions in the army. This had its origins in the medieval companies raised by individuals or groups which offered their services for a particular campaign. They had the necessary capital to raise arms and equip a body of soldiers and commanding officers and others could sell out provided they could find a buyer. It seems to have been a feature of national armies in other countries and in England sufficiently common for it to be forbidden in the New Model Army. It became widespread under the Restoration embracing all regimental commissions from colonel to cornet and ensign. In 1684 a royal warrant recognised the system partly in an attempt by government to secure some control over what had been treated as legal by the courts. By 1719 regulations were made under which the rates at which various commissions were officially permitted to be sold were published. The practice continued in the eighteenth and early nineteenth centuries, though the artillery and the engineers always formed an exception.[41] In 1833 the Duke of Wellington wrote that it was promotion by purchase which brought into the service men of fortune and education who had some connection with the interests and fortunes of the country. Service in the British army could only be carried out by 'one educated as an English gentleman.'[42] One effect was the predominance of officers from aristocratic families in 'those higher stations of command where their sentiments, feelings and opinions influence and direct the men who are below them, and give them tone and character', as Lord Palmerston put it in 1827.[43] Modern research however suggests the possession of wealth rather than blue blood was a more important factor as it enabled both initial purchase and the subsequent provision of a private income. Bernal Osborne pointed out that in 1859 the vast majority of officers in the heavy dragoons were the sons of capitalists and gentlemen who had made their way fairly and honestly in their different occupations. The system attracted relatively little criticism in the first half of the nineteenth century. In 1840 a Royal Commission undertook a general enquiry into promotion in the army and navy – there

[40] Markham Lester, especially, 147, 155 and 208–209.

[41] Anthony Bruce, *The Purchase System in the British Army, 1660–1871*, 1980.

[42] Hew Strachan, *Wellington's Legacy: The Reform of the British Army, 1830–54*, 1984, 110.

[43] Duke of Wellington, Memorandum on Military Government, 183 (PP, 1833, vii, 276); Lord Palmerston's Memorandum for the Cabinet, quoted in Bruce, 68.

was no purchase in the navy – because of the stagnation of promotion. In so far as purchase came up witnesses expressed their belief in the great advantages gained from the system.

The system survived in part because there had been no major conflict since the Napoleonic wars to test the army. Thus the searchlight of rational Benthamite enquiry and other pressures which led to administrative reform elsewhere was missing. The Crimean War quickly tested the system and the management of both civil and military services was found wanting. In the case of the army there was a widespread popular attribution of its failings to the aristocratic senior officers which led to major criticisms of the methods of selection and promotion. W.H. Russell's dispatches in *The Times* gave enormous publicity to what Dickens called 'a confused heap of mismanagement and disorder under which the nation's bravery lies crushed and withered.'[44] Immediately Paxton and Peto were sent out to build huts, roads and railways. Both the widespread promotion of non-commissioned officers to officer to meet wartime needs and comparisons with the more efficient French army fighting alongside the British raised questions about the purchase system. The Army Reform Association was set up which published a journal and held public meetings. Its main emphasis was on ending the sale of commissions. Samuel Laing, now a radical Liberal MP – and chairman of the London Brighton and South Coast Railway, said:

> If a merchant possessing a large establishment were to attempt the purchase system in the appointment of his clerks, how long would it be before his name appeared in the Gazette? If a railway company adopted the same system in the appointment of servants to take charge of the express train, what length of time would elapse before a verdict of manslaughter were returned against them? The mainstream of all the business affairs of life is a rigid system of promotion by merit.[45]

A group of MPs led by Viscount Goderich, including radicals and professional soldiers, met regularly to consider the subject. Goderich's motion on the defects in the system of promotion and the need for the abolition of purchase was defeated by 158 to 114. But the impetus for change was growing. Palmerston, the Prime Minister, went so far as to say that if purchase did not exist no one in government would contemplate its introduction.[46] General Sir George de Lacy Evans spoke out against

44 *Household Words*, Charles Dickens, Miscellaneous Papers (1914), 496.

45 PD, 137, 1220, 27 Mar. 1855.

46 Bruce, 103.

purchase. Evans was a prominent and successful commander in the Crimea, 'the wounded hero of Alma' who had served in the Peninsular War and at Waterloo. He was also a radical MP representing Westminster from 1832–41 and 1846–65 who had long advocated reform of the army. Several MPs pointed to the experience of other countries where the aristocracy predominated but purchase was not found to be necessary. Parliamentary pressure mounted and in March 1856 de Lacy Evans supported by Goderich and Lord Edward Stanley introduced a motion against purchase. He pointed to the higher levels of efficiency in the 'Scientific Corps', the artillery and the engineers in which purchase played no part than in the cavalry and infantry. Abolition of purchase would open a path to merit and promote a greater spirit of professionalism in the army.[47] Palmerston bowed to parliamentary opinion and offered a royal commission though Lord Panmure, the Secretary of State for War, explained privately to the Queen that it was proposed rather in deference to the opinions of the House of Commons than from any expectation that any change could or ought to be made. 'Members of the Commission were to be men in whom the House of Commons has confidence and in whose hands the system of purchase is safe'.

Four of the members were ministers or former ministers. The Duke of Somerset who was in the chair had held various junior posts and as Lord Seymour had been in the Cabinet in 1851–52 as first commissioner of works; Sidney Herbert had been secretary for War in Aberdeen's administration during the Crimean War; and Edward Ellice had been Secretary at War from 1833 to 1834. Lord Edward Stanley had been under secretary at the Foreign Office in the Derby administration in 1851–52, but Panmure explained that he had been selected because he was thought to hold opinions somewhat adverse to the present system. De Lacy Evans was one of four military members but the only one known to be critical of the system. Panmure thought that his omission would do much harm and his inclusion do none. Glyn was the only member who had no ministerial or military experience. Panmure had to explain to the Queen why Glyn had been appointed. It seemed necessary that on a commission so important to the interests of the commercial portion of her subjects, a member of that body should represent it. 'By no means a small proportion of the officers of Your Majesty's army came from that class and their only hope of entering into and promotion in the Army rested upon the maintenance of the present system.' Glyn, he stated, represented this class and was a well known banker

[47] PD, 140, 1791–4, 4 Mar. 1856.

and for many years chairman of the LNWR. Panmure added that Glyn saw the vitality of the question to this class, and great reliance would be felt in his opinion.[48] Panmure as a former director of the LNWR knew Glyn well. The fact that three of Glyn's sons served in the Crimean War may also have been a factor, but was not mentioned.

Despite Panmure's belief that he had ensured a continuation of the status quo the critics' hand was reinforced by the evidence of several senior serving officers and by attacks in the *Times* by a radical journalist, M.J. Higgins, though, as the Commission itself noted that the investigation into the purchase system was rendered difficult by the fact that long established usage had so far accustomed officers to the practice that few of the military witnesses had contemplated any other system of entry or promotion.[49] The officers had no alternative plan to replace purchase and therefore the Commission asked Sir Charles Trevelyan to provide one. Trevelyan not only had responsibility in the Treasury for military questions and so had been responsible in part for the much criticised commissariat in the Crimean War, but, at Gladstone's request, he had recently produced with Northcote a report advocating entry to the highest class of the civil service by competitive examination through a central board. His submission was highly critical of the army's system and advocated a competitive entry examination. Up to captain seniority was to be given two-thirds of the weight and merit one-third. Thereafter all promotions were to be through selection. Trevelyan also maintained that a reduction in public expenditure, an effective increase in officers' pay and the saving of the price of the purchase could all be achieved by the abolition of purchase. He desired access for the sons of farmers and of those who received a liberal education, the clergy, the medical profession and upwards. Glyn does not seem to have been hostile to change but asked Trevelyan a number of questions, designed to push him into giving more detail about how he would effect the transition to a new system. Glyn himself pointed to some of the difficulties: the inspecting generals would know little about officers of lower rank; recommendations from commanding officers did not then go into merit or qualifications, and until Trevelyan fixed in his own mind a scale of retirement for general officers he could hardly form any calculation of cost at all. He drew Trevelyan out on the proposed military college designed to be self-supporting. Trevelyan thought there was an abundant class of

48 Lord Panmure to The Queen, 20 Apr. 1856, *The Panmure Papers*, ed. Sir George Douglas and Sir George Dalhousie Ramsay, 1908, II, 198–201.

49 Report of Royal Commission on Purchase and Sale of Commissions in the Army, PP, 1857 (2), xxviii, 19.

people who could afford to give their sons a first rate education. Glyn also pointed out that many would lose the price of their commission if the state did not buy it back. Trevelyan simply commented that otherwise the army must always remain as it was.

The commission in its report did not go so far as Trevelyan proposed. In the absence of alternative proposals from critical senior officers, they set out substantial arguments against the system but found that the prevalent opinion among military men was favourable to the system, or a least to its maintenance until a scheme had been devised which produced the beneficial results attributed to purchase. It therefore recommended changes which could gradually be introduced. The rank of lieutenant-colonel should be no longer be purchasable but be attainable by selection on merit and the term of the post limited to eight or ten years. They rejected immediate total abolition of purchase because of the inherent defects they considered existed in the alternatives of selection and promotion. Abolition of purchase of the lowest commissioned rank might discourage retirement as officers leaving the service would lose all the money invested in their first commissions. Inspection of the new system was recommended and the age of retirement should be fixed by reference to age or length of service. More attention should be paid to professional training and to examinations. High standards were not necessarily incompatible with the continued system of purchase. De Lacy Evans subscribed to the report but added a note to say he did not think it went far enough. Two other military members and Edward Ellice submitted minority reports.[50]

When the main report came out Trevelyan's evidence and scheme of reform were subject to severe criticism particularly because of his estimates of the cost, the difficulties of which Glyn had indicated. Indeed this evidence was examined in detail by a War Office committee,[51] which made progress on the issue more difficult. The main changes introduced in the years immediately following were the establishment of the Staff College in 1858, and reform of the education offered at both Sandhurst and Woolwich. Indeed, as Edward Spiers put it, Panmure and Jonathan Peel, his successor at the War Office, used educational reform to demonstrate their interest in raising the professional status of the officer corps, while conveniently forgetting the work of the Purchase Commission.[52] The commission did not achieve substantial change but made the question of the abolition of

[50] System of Purchase in the Army, PP, 1857–8, xix, 233.

[51] Report by a War Office Committee on the evidence given by C. Trevelyan, PP, 1857–8, xxxvii, 409.

[52] Edward M. Spiers, *Radical General, Sir George de Lacy Evans*, 1787–1870, 1983, 185.

purchase an issue which had to be faced by governments and the army and which could no longer be sidelined as easily as ministers had hoped when the commission was set up. Indeed in the twelve years after the Crimean War there were 17 Royal Commissions, 18 Select Committees and 19 internal War Office Committees which investigated various aspects of military administration.[53] The opposition of the Commander-in-Chief, the Duke of Cambridge was an important factor. Stanley commented in 1862 that Cambridge would prefer to keep things as they are. He was afraid of the officers on the one side and of the newspapers on the other, and Cornewall Lewis thought his excessive timidity arose from a fear of newspaper criticism of his domestic arrangements 'which were not such as this moral age approves having made public though they are known to all the world'.[54] Changes, even in the limited manner advocated by the royal commission, had to await Cardwell's reforms a decade later, prompted by the Franco-Prussian War.

Until the end of the 1840s Glyn's only residence was in Belgravia. He moved from 11 Eaton Place in about 1840 to 1 Upper Eccleston Street which was to remain his London home until his death. This too was on the Grosvenor estate: the houses on the north side of the street were built in about 1835 by Seth Smith. Glyn seems to have spent holidays in English resorts such as Hastings and Ramsgate as well as his eldest brother's home at Gaunts in Dorset, which Richard Plumptre had inherited on the death of their father in 1838, though when his father was still alive he told Langton that he intended to stay there a short time with him and then 'vagabondage a little'.[55] There is no record of his having ventured abroad, subsequent to his European tour with his brother Robert when he was 19.

In 1849 however Glyn made a radical change with the purchase of Stanmore Park, then in a very rural part of outer Middlesex. In 1719 James Brydges, earl of Caernarvon, became the owner of the manors of both Great and Little Stanmore. In 1725 Brydges, by then duke of Chandos, had opened an account at the Charing Cross bank of Andrew Drummond who from 1729 purchased land from Chandos and built up an extensive estate in the area. He employed John Vardy to build Stanmore Park a Palladian mansion built and which was completed after Vardy's death in 1765 by Sir William Chambers. George Drummond who died in 1789 left the estate heavily encumbered

[53] John Sweetman, *War and Administration: The Significance of the Crimean War for the British Army*, 1984, 132.

[54] *Disraeli, Derby and the Conservative Party, Journals and Memoirs of Edward Henry, Lord Stanley, 1849–1869,* ed. John Vincent, 1978, 188.

[55] Barclays Archives, 25/265, Langton Papers (LP) 321, 28 Jul. 1837.

with debt, and his son George Harley Drummond was a gambler who had to leave the bank and retired to Scotland. Stanmore Park was briefly let to Lady Aylesford and then Lord Castlereagh, and was mortgaged. It was sold in 1839 to the Marquess of Abercorn[56] whose own seat was at nearby Bentley Priory. Abercorn let Stanmore Park to the Earl of Wicklow, his son-in-law, but in August 1848 put his Middlesex estates on the market when he had debts of £400,000 to Coutts Bank.[57] He was also proposing to purchase a large estate in Sussex: Dale Park, Madehurst, from John Abel Smith the banker who was a partner in Smith, Payne, Smiths. Although Abercorn went ahead with the purchase of Dale Park in 1848 by spending nearly £100,000 which he did not possess as the Stanmore estates were heavily mortgaged, by 1860 the Marquess had sold his new acquisition in Sussex.[58]

A sale of the Bentley Priory and Stanmore Park estates and adjacent properties in a number of lots was advertised to be held on 1 November 1848. Coincidentally the auction was to have taken place at Garraways, the coffee house next to Glyn's Bank which they were to purchase in the 1860s. The sale was only partially successful. Glyn bought Stanmore Park, probably by subsequent private treaty rather than at the auction, as a note to Glyn from Abercorn survives in which the latter requested a payment of £8,000 from Glyn, the sum referred to in an agreement dated 3 July 1849 relating to the sale and purchase of an estate at Stanmore.[59] It was 1852 before the Marquess could sell the Priory when Sir John Kelk the railway contractor bought it.

Thus the Stanmore Park returned to the ownership of a banker. It was a substantial country house set in parkland with ornamental pleasure grounds, luxurious plantations, a large sheet of water, walks of great variety, conservatories and vineries, gardener's cottage and stone lodge entrance and a domain of upwards of 1,400 acres. It had an enclosed garden laid out in French style in parterres.[60]

In the late 1850s Glyn purchased a second property outside London, this time in the developing resort of Bournemouth which he liked for its climate and its proximity to his family's homes in Dorset. He bought

[56] James Hamilton (1811–85), 2nd Marquis of Hamilton, created Duke in 1868 after having served in the Disraeli administration as Lord Lieutenant of Ireland.

[57] *VCH, Middlesex*, V, 98; Eileen M. Bowlt, *Stanmore Past*, 1998, 86–87 and 93–97.

[58] Public Record Office of Northern Ireland, D623, Note on the Duke's English Estate Papers.

[59] RBS Archives, GM/369/27. Glyn was certainly in residence at Stanmore Park by the end of 1849. He wrote to Gladstone from there on 17 Dec. 1849 (BL, Add Ms 44368).

[60] *Morning Post*, 21 Aug. 1848.

Fontmell Lodge, on the East Cliff on the Meyrick Estate, then on the outskirts of Bournemouth.[61] The resort was still a small place. In 1861 the population was only 1,707 though it had more than doubled in the previous ten years. The 1840s to the early 1870s were the period when estates of large detached villas in generous plots were developed around the valley of the Bourne and on the East Cliff and the West Cliff, in secluded areas in which no commercial or lower class housing development was permitted by the landlords.[62] Fontmell Lodge was a large detached house with its main entrance from Grove Road, which ran parallel with East Cliff Road from which there was also access so that the substantial grounds overlooked the sea. In 1859 Glyn told Chandos he thought Bournemouth had a charming climate. In October 1860 he told Gladstone that they were enjoying themselves at this very quiet dry clear place. It was very fine sea air and would do you and Mrs Gladstone great good, though it seems that the Gladstones did not visit the Glyns there.[63]

Meanwhile he had increased his holdings of land in Dorset, particularly in Fontmell Magna where his father had given him land in 1824 and in nearby Melbury Abbas, much in partnership with his brother Richard, who was lord of the manor at Fontmell. The latter in the period preceding his death at the end of 1863 contributed £4,000 to the substantial rebuilding of the church of St Andrew's at Fontmell by George Evans of Wimborne. His generosity is commemorated by a memorial window erected by his brother, George.[64]

Although George Grenfell went into the bank as a partner in 1845, the limitation on the number of partners meant others had to await a vacancy or, as did four of the eight sons who grew to adulthood, turn to other professions. How far G.G.'s heart was in banking is debatable. His friend Algernon West, the civil servant who was private secretary to Gladstone when George was chief whip, said that while at Oxford George had set his heart on three things; to marry a beautiful wife, to be Whip to the Liberal Party and to be a master of hounds.[65] West said he fulfilled all three ambitions and although

[61] Listed in Harrod & Co.s, *Directory of Hampshire and the Isle of Wight*, 1865, 82.

[62] Richard Roberts, Leasehold Estates and municipal enterprise; landowners, local government and the development of Bournemouth, in David Cannadine, ed., *Patricians, Power and Politics in Nineteenth Century Towns*, 1982, 179.

[63] RBS Archives, GM/237, Glyn to Chandos, 19 Nov. 1859 and BL, Add Ms 44394, Glyn to Gladstone, 10 Oct. 1860.

[64] Fulford, 178, John Newman and Nikolaus Pevsner, *The Buildings of England, Dorset*, 1972, 207–208.

[65] Sir Algernon West, *Recollections, 1832–1886*, 1897, 1, 349.

he did not list banking as one of his ambitions, he was an active partner until he became chief whip in 1866 when he succeeded Henry Brand.

He married in 1848 Georgiana Maria, daughter of the Revd George Frederick Tufnell of Uffington, Berkshire, and West thought her beauty and reposeful yet enthusiastic temperament compensated for many of George's faults. He had remarkable drive and energy, though perhaps not possessing his father's judgment and balance, his faults were perhaps more evident in politics than in banking. West viewed him as a strange character being possessed in almost equal proportions the qualities a whip should and should not have. He had energy and fidelity indeed blind admiration and devotion to his master Gladstone, entire absorption in his work and sharpness and ability. But his devotion made him obstinate and he was overbearing to those who even ventured to differ from anything which Mr Gladstone thought right.[66] West's view was shared by others. Harcourt who saw much of Henry Fawcett in Cambridge in 1874 said Fawcett had become such an out and out Gladstonian 'that I call him Georgius Glynnus Secundus'.[67]

He and several of his brothers moved in circles into which George Carr Glyn had scarcely ventured. For a time he was a member of the Alfred Club, then the club that young men would frequent before they were elected to one of the superior ones. There he associated with Chichester Fortescue, Charles and Henry Grenfell, Thomas Baring, later the second Baron Northbrook and Henry Seymour.[68] Later many of them became members of Brooks's – George Grenfell was elected in 1854, and they were regarded as being in the same group as West who was described as tall, handsome and a favourite in society.[69] In 1850 when the Curries arrived in fashionable Bad Homburg, the place was excessively full and the young George Glyns were already there. George was elected Liberal MP for Shaftesbury in 1857. He was unopposed then and in the three subsequent general elections. He had an obscure career as a backbencher, never speaking, but serving on a few committees, including that on limited liability in 1867. He was therefore something of a surprising choice for the position of Liberal Chief Whip in 1866, particularly as he was a member of Brooks's and not of the Reform. He held the post jointly with Henry Brand until 1868. He resigned on his elevation to the Lords on the death of his father in 1873.

66 Ibid.

67 Harcourt to Dilke, 4 Nov. 1874, quoted in A.G. Gardiner, *The Life of Sir William Harcourt*, 1923, 1, 281.

68 Wolff 1.86; Memorials of Brooks's, 171.

69 West, 1, 246–247: *ODNB*, West.

His appointment in 1866 had raised acutely the Bank's relationship with politics. When his father had been approached in 1863 to support a political candidate in the City he said after discussing it with his partners that he could not help because this would mean a breach of 'our rule of avoiding interference in elections, parliamentary or civic in the City of London.' He presumably regarded such involvement in the City as quite different from his serving as MP for Kendal where Glyn's had no financial interest. When Gladstone approached G.G. Glyn about becoming Chief Whip he demurred and his father begged Gladstone not to press him for an answer. G.G.'s main difficulty was not the possible conflict of interest which might arise particularly when the Liberals were in Government but that he did not wish to accept unless he could remain a partner, though not an inactive one. Despite the doubts of some senior members of the party G.G. persisted in his view and retained his partnership.[70]

Glyn's second son, St Leger Richard was elected a director of the Union Bank of Australia in 1852 and was involved with the ANZ bank. He was a member of the militia, first in the Royal West Middlesex Regiment where he was promoted captain in 1852,[71] and then in the 2nd (Edmonton) Royal Middlesex Rifles. The latter regiment included figures such as Viscount Enfield, the colonel, Viscount Bury, the Hon George Byng, Charles Grant, and Francis Russell, all MPs, as well as Henry Riverdsale Grenfell and Jervoise Smith. Soon after the Crimean War West recalled spending a month with his militia at Barnet. He said that nearly all the officers belonged to Brooks's and were in the same society.[72] In 1855 St Leger married Florence Elizabeth, daughter of James Wilmot Williams of Herringston in Dorset, by whom he had six daughters. They lived at Bramble Hill Lodge, Bramshaw near Lyndhurst. He was a partner in Glyn's for some years from the mid-1850s, but suffered from poor health and had to retire from the bank in 1863.[73] He died in 1873 aged 47, three months before his father.

St Leger's retirement enabled George Carr Glyn's sixth son, Pascoe Charles to become a partner. Educated at Harrow and University College, Oxford, he became a partner in Bensons in 1852 and moved to Glyn's as a partner in 1864. He was a director of the Economic Life Assurance Company, and as was seen in Chapter 15 he played a leading part in some

[70] Fulford, 160–161.

[71] *Daily News*, 20 Oct. 1852.

[72] West, 1, 246–247; Memorials of Brooks's, 162. St Leger was elected in 1850.

[73] On 11 Sept. 1862 W.D. Denison of the Yorkshire Bank hoped he was in a less unfavourable condition than we lately heard he was (RBS Archives, GM/429/30).

of the overseas ventures in which Glyn's Bank was to take part or be closely associated with.

He married in 1858 Horatia Louisa, daughter of Rev St John Mildmay, rector of Chelmsford, but she died within six weeks of the wedding. In 1861 he married Caroline Henrietta, daughter of the late Captain W. Amherst Hale and had five children.

Pascoe's older brothers, Henry and Richard chose naval and military careers. Henry joined the navy on leaving Rugby. Richard went into the army. This meant both Henry and Richard were on active service at the outbreak of the Crimean War which consequently was a time of anxiety for Glyn made the greater when Sidney after Harrow and Trinity College, Cambridge, became an ensign in the Rifle Brigade in April 1855 and by the end of August was promoted lieutenant. Thus three of his sons as well as several of his nephews served in the war. Henry who was serving as a lieutenant on the outbreak of war was awarded the gold medal for distinguished service under Omar Pasha in 1854 when he rode to Routschouk to man Turkish gunboats with a party of fifty handpicked sailors from ships in the British fleet led by him and Midshipman Prince Ernest of Leiningen, half brother of Queen Victoria. The sailors served aboard Turkish gunboats before helping to build the pontoon bridge over the Danube 'much to the astonishment of the natives', and then took the boats down to Varna where they rejoined their ships.[74] He was then promoted Commander and was in the naval brigade at the bombardment of Sebastopol, being attached to the Britannia, Admiral Dundas's flagship.

Glyn told Gladstone on 4 November 1854 that he was in such painful anxiety having two sons in the Black Sea and the Crimea, one in the HMS Berkshire and one in the 8th Hussars. He said that should they be released from this anxiety they would be pleased to see Gladstone, adding apologetically that the express from North Wales did not stop at their station, Harrow, but Stanmore was accessible from London.[75] Ten days later he told Chandos that to have a son (Richard) and a nephew (Richard George, Royal Dragoons), engaged in such a murderous affair as that of the 25th, the battle of Balaclava, without hurt was indeed a cause of very great thankfulness,[76] shared apparently by the servants at Stanmore Park who contributed

[74] West, 1, 148. West was sent out to the Crimea by the Submarine Telegraph Company to establish communication to the area of war by means of a submarine cable, which was laid between Balaclava and Varna, Peter Ducker, *The Crimean War at Sea*, 2011, 54.

[75] BL, Add Ms 44382, 4 Nov. 1854.

[76] RBS Archives, GM/237, Glyn to Chandos, 16 Nov. 1854.

£1.10s to the Patriotic Fund.[77] Richard was one of the youngest officers in the 8th Hussars, who before Balaclava, had served in the eastern campaign, including the expedition into the Dobruscha in the Danube delta. He knew Mrs Fanny Duberley who accompanied her husband Henry, an officer in the 8th Hussars, to the Crimea. She told her sister that when on the march to Varna she was concerned about embarking for Sebastopol, she thought she could get on board very well and if the worst comes to the worst 'I can borrow little Glyn's frock coat and be as right as possible.'[78] He was promoted lieutenant the following day, fought at Inkerman, and was promoted captain in the Rifle Brigade in August 1855, as Mrs Duberley noted in her diary, when listing the reduced number of her friends before the assault on Sebastopol on 9 September.[79] St Leger was also involved in the Crimea, but not in a fighting role. He and Jervoise Smith, both in the same regiment of the militia, went out to the Crimea to carry out a preliminary mission of enquiry for the Crimea Army Fund set up in December 1854 which sent comforts including tobacco for the troops. They decided that the Fund had to avoid making additional calls on army transport and labour and so took out to the Crimea 24 transport animals, 20 porters and 10 muleteers. Glyn's brother in law, Sydney Osborne, also went to the Crimea acting as an unofficial chaplain at Scutari but found himself assisting in operations, working with Florence Nightingale.

Richard later went to India and served in Nepal in 1858–59. In November 1859 it was announced he was to be promoted major[80] but he died off Aden in December 1859 on the way back to England. The press accounts said that he went on foot with his men all through the Oude, up to the Terai through the summer and winter campaigns and through the subsequent searches until the dispersion of the rebels brought to him and his brigade a short rest, but the reports are not clear whether he died of disease caught during the marches or of wounds sustained during battle.[81] He was 28.

Ashley Carr after Harrow graduated from University College Oxford in 1862. He was called to the bar in 1864 and was a member of the Inner Temple. In 1867 his translation of Frederic Ozanan's *History of Civilisation in the Fifth Century* was published, but he too was involved in banking. He was on the board of the Union Bank and of the Australia and New Zealand

77 *Morning Chronicle*, 4 Nov. 1854.

78 *Mrs Duberley's War, Journal and Letters from the Crimea*, edited Christine Kelly, 2007, 50.

79 Ibid, 235.

80 *Daily News*, 16 Nov. 1859.

81 *Morning Post*, 2 Jan. *Morning Chronicle*, and *Daily News*, 3 Jan. 1860.

Bank. He was also a director of the Trust and Loan Company of Upper Canada. He was only 36 when he died in 1875.

Georgina, the elder of Glyn's two daughters did not marry. She died in 1926, aged 92. Alice married Rev Francis Godolphin Pelham the second son of the 3rd Earl of Chichester in 1870. He was a lifelong clergyman and succeeded his childless elder brother as earl in 1902 while he was vicar of Great Yarmouth. Edward, Glyn's youngest child, on leaving Harrow entered University College, Oxford, where he graduated in 1866. He was ordained in 1868, and his career in the church was to lead him to a bishopric. He too married into the aristocracy; while serving as chaplain to the Queen he married Lady Mary Emma Campbell, daughter of the 8th duke of Argyll.

CHAPTER SEVENTEEN

The London and North Western Railway's Elder Statesman

GLYN was 55 when he resigned the chairmanship of the LNWR in 1852 on grounds of ill health, but the stress of the job and the fact that he had served as chairman for fifteen consecutive years, first as head of the LBR and then the newly amalgamated LNWR were probably significant contributory factors. Thereafter his health did not prevent him from continuing to be an active director for another decade, and he only retired from the board in 1870. Moreover he was very active on other fronts until the mid-1860s especially in the family bank, as an MP and in the Grand Trunk Railway of Canada. He had periods of bad health and in 1862–63 had problems with his eyes. He was described by his son St Leger as suffering from blindness through cataract which necessitated a successful operation in October 1863.[1] However he missed few LNWR board meetings as a consequence.

Within a year of his resignation he had an important part to play when Anson retired in September 1853 having been appointed to command a division in Bengal. The possibility of an early military assignment, particularly a posting abroad, does not seem to have been taken into account by Anson himself or his colleagues on the board, and given Glyn's complaints to Panmure about the difficulties on the board one might imagine that Anson deliberately escaped to India, though there is no evidence for that. Benson who had become deputy chairman on Smith's resignation informed the board of Anson's resignation and gave notice on behalf of Glyn that at the next board meeting it was proposed to elect the Marquis of Chandos as director and chairman. There was less time for speculation in

[1] *Kendal Mercury*, 4 Oct. 1862 and 3 and 31 Oct. 1863. St Leger was deputising for his father at the annual dinner of the Kendal Agricultural Society.

the railway press than when Glyn resigned, but some consternation at the appointment of Chandos. It was alleged that Chandos had applied to the GWR for a seat on their board and undertaken to make himself useful in Parliamentary work (he was MP for Buckingham) and had been informed that on qualifying himself for a seat on the board his request would be favourably considered. Glyn heard of this and saw Chandos, flattered him that he was no tyro and that the chairmanship of the LNWR awaited his acceptance. 'How can he face the proprietors? If a shred of self respect remains among the shareholders, the whole board, and executive and all is doomed' concluded the *Railway Times*. Chandos took the chair for the first time at the November meeting.

Glyn served under two very different chairman for substantial periods. He seems to have acted as something of a mentor to the Marquess of Chandos who was only 30 when appointed with no experience as an ordinary member of the board though he had been thrown into major responsibilities following the bankruptcy of his father, the 2nd duke of Buckingham, in 1848. Glyn's relationship with Richard Moon, Chandos's successor as chairman, was rather different. Before he was elected chairman Moon had nine years service as a director, briefly served as deputy chairman and had built up a reputation as a tough and principled chairman of the Stores Committee with a much expanded remit.[2] Both the other chairman while Glyn was member of the board served only for a single year. Anson already had a little experience as a director, but Moorsom was a contemporary of Glyn's having initially been joint secretary to the LBR. Although Glyn's emphasis at times was different he does not seem to have had major difficulties with his successors and overall his judgment and experience were invaluable to the company. His own letters to Chandos suggest that Moon's advice to Chandos in the crisis of 1858 'Do not be afraid of Mr Glyn' were unnecessary.[3]

Glyn played a much less active part in the company than he had during his six years as chairman, but particularly during the years when Chandos held the chair, he was a highly influential member of the board, especially internally in discussions about structure and management and externally in relations with other companies. In addition Glyn's position in the City and as an influential backbencher with contacts with leading politicians meant that he was particularly involved in matters where the Government had some responsibility.

[2] Peter Braine, *The Railway Moon*, 2010, 58–92, for Moon's work as a member of LNWR committees and particularly the Stores Committee.

[3] Moon to Chandos 5 Sept. 1858 (Braine, 147).

However he did not play much part in the LNWR's standing committees which met fortnightly. He was never a member of the new Executive Committee, formed in 1855 and although he was a member of the Special Affairs Committee, when in 1858 this and the Executive Committee were replaced by the Special Committee membership was restricted to the Chairman, Deputy Chairman and the chairmen of the five committees (Finance, Traffic, Permanent Way, Audit and stores). Consequently Glyn was not a member of this forum which met weekly in which more and more of the company's business was conducted, nor was he a member of any of the five main committees. He served in the mid-1850s on the Parliamentary Committee – in 1855 with five other MPs who were then directors of the company and Benson, Smith and Pierrepont. He also served at times on local committees – in 1855 on the Market Harborough; St Albans; and Hampstead Committees, and was on the boards of subsidiaries such as the Hampstead Junction and the Buckinghamshire Railways. In 1859 a more systematic system of appointing board members to committees was adopted. Glyn with Moon, Cropper, Thompson[4] and Tootal, was asked to recommend the appointments to the various committees, but Glyn himself was only on the Buckinghamshire Committee and he resigned from that in the following year. Thereafter does not seem to have served on a local board. For many years he was usually a member of the small group of directors appointed to draw up the board's twice yearly report to shareholders.

He remained active in the Railway Clearing House serving as chairman until his death. The clearing system continued to grow as the railway network expanded. By 1861 when Morison died in office there were nearly 500 clerks in the clearing house. His successor P.W. Dawson, one of the original six clerks, reorganised the office to deal with the growing goods and parcels traffic. In 1864 there were 873 clerks, with 1.6 million settlements, valued at £8.9 million. A year after Glyn s death there were 1,325 clerks with a turnover with 4.9 million settlements, £16.1 million in value. The RCH covered railways operating over 90 per cent of the total route mileage in Great Britain. The RCH in Glyn's time served the railways well. Whether it adapted to the needs of the railways later in the nineteenth century is another question. Glyn however was careful to limit the role of the RCH and in 1854 a separate committee was formed of representatives of 23 companies, a predecessor to the first Railway Companies Association. He took the chair

[4] Samuel Henry Thompson of Thingwall, near Liverpool. Moon thought of him as a possible chairman of the Finance Committee, though regarded him as unsuccessful as a banker in the management of Hayward's firm. (Moon to Chandos, 1 Mar. 1858, quoted in Braine, 129).

when the Railway Benevolent Institution was formed and the first general meeting decided to invest £1,800 of the assets of nearly £2,000 in LNWR bonds.[5]

In 1855 he described his own role in the company's financial management when commenting on the report of a committee of investigation.[6] He remarked that he had never interfered in financial operations wishing while chairman to abstain from any interference with them and to avoid the implication of working them for individual benefit. 'The consequence has been that I have never sat in the Finance Committee and that, with the exception of the operations in debentures through the Bank of England which have been organised by me, I have had nothing to do with the management of the debt, but I have had the opportunity of observing the proceedings of Mr Stewart and do not think they warrant the comments of the Investigation Committee upon them.' He believed that the loans in debentures requested by the LNWR were on as favourable terms as those obtained by any other company, indeed generally more so.

He had one criticism of Stewart. In his desire to secure the best terms he appeared sometimes to run the risk of overstating his market, but considering Stewart had no commercial experience Glyn thought he had aptitude and dexterity in these affairs. The proposed appointment of financial secretary was therefore an unnecessary and expensive addition to the staff. He told Chandos that as he was no longer chairman he was willing to give more attention to this part of the company's affairs if it were wished, but would rather suggest that his son (George Grenfell) should undertake the duty with Mr Stewart and fill the office of Treasurer, avoiding the cost of a salaried officer, though this idea was not taken up. With regard to the banking arrangements he told Chandos that the balance had been fixed as requisite for the London business when Rotheram was chairman of the Finance Committee and the amount was well considered – a fair and liberal sum not more than the operations of the company's London account required. He could not speak for the country accounts, opened for the sake of convenience, but Glyn's were ready to undertake any work which could properly be done by them.[7]

When Goalen, the audit officer and Caitchen, an audit official in Liverpool, were found guilty of embezzlement in April 1854,[8] Glyn attended the meeting of the Audit Committee and suggested changes including an

5 *Illustrated London News*, 21 May 1859.

6 RAIL 1008/104, Glyn to Chandos, 16 Aug. 1855.

7 Ibid.

8 Goalen was sentenced to 14 years transportation and Caitchen to 4 years penal servitude.

improved method of remitting monies to Euston. The offices of accounts and audit were to be separated, though under the control of Stewart.

His long experience of attempts to decide how best to deal with the depreciation of the locomotive stock and the track led to his chairing the committee which in 1853 considered the reports from Huish and the engineers on the permanent way and to determine whether the required reinstatement and strengthening of the road should be defrayed out of revenue or by way of annuity in whole or in part, particularly because of the heavier locomotives by then in use. The outcome was a more sophisticated approach. Glyn and his committee insisted that positive additions to the capabilities of the track as opposed to making good wear and tear should be charged to capital rather than revenue. As a result the amount to be set aside from revenue over the next six years was reduced by a third.[9]

He continued to put forward views on management structure and the relationship between the board and officers. In 1853, when Anson announced his resignation Glyn suggested that an Executive Committee was needed as the increasing duties devolving on the chairman meant there was an absolute necessity for him to devote his time to their discharge and to remunerate his services by an annual allowance.[10] This was not immediately taken up, but in 1855 as the Special Affairs Committee had not proved to be an entirely effective, an Executive Committee was set up which took on the responsibilities of both the Road and Traffic, and Locomotive Committees, meeting twice a month alternately in London and Birmingham and supervising the six divisional traffic and locomotive committees. This reduced the control of the main board. At the same time the Works Committee was amalgamated with the Permanent Way Committee. Glyn had however warned Chandos that an Executive committee with 13 members, while preventing discord would be unwieldy, and the following year a separate Goods Committee of seven had to be created which formally reported to the Board but whose reports were in practice transmitted through the Executive.[11] Parallel with the Executive Committee a meeting of departmental heads was set up under Huish. It seems however that in Glyn's view this was a second best to a Council chaired by Chandos, as he wrote to Chandos:

> have I understood that you as Chairman will call into account the acts of the several heads of departments by pressing them into a sort of Executive Council to meet and work under your control. One great

[9] RAIL 410/22, 11 Jun. and 410/54, 7 Jul. 1853.

[10] RAIL 410/22, 11 Jun. 1853.

[11] RAIL 410/23, 15 Mar. 1856.

> advantage arising from this course will be that under your supervision the several heads of departments will be kept together and made to follow out a more cooperative and harmonious plan of proceeding. Any important changes in one department will be previously considered in this Council and objections from practical men fairly brought forward and discussed, and this without interference form the Committee. I am inclined to attach great importance to such an Executive Council. By it you, as Chairman, and through you the whole Board, would be put in possession of the practical knowledge and experience on whose proceedings in fact the whole efficiency of our system depends.[12]

A sign that Glyn thought that the company was not controlling its projects sufficiently closely had come in February 1854 when he brought up the question of the use of the powers obtained by legislation in the summer of 1852. The board therefore resolved that the several committees be instructed to take steps for proceeding with the various works authorised by the statutes then passed so that they were finished by the time prescribed.[13] Glyn could be highly critical of inefficiency. In October 1854 he told Smith, chairman of the Locomotive Committee, 'I am afraid something is very radically wrong in our Locomotive Department. Nothing can be worse than the working of trains in the Southern Division. The many recent accidents you will doubtless have heard of. I fear you will have to make extensive reforms in some way.' A fortnight later he was telling Moorsom:

> I received the enclosed this morning and I am afraid something is wrong beyond what has been shown to us. Would it not be well for us to meet at Wolverton on Tuesday and go on to Rugby if necessary to look about us. We should have Blake with us.[14] Perhaps you would cast your eye over the engines at Birmingham and look at their outward condition in comparison with the Grand Junction's and see if there are any that want repair and have been put aside for weeks.[15]

Whether the Committee system was the major problem affecting the management of the company, or the relationship of directors to officials

[12] RBS Archives, GM/237, Glyn to Chandos, nd, 1855.

[13] RAIL 410/22, 21 Feb. 1854.

[14] Woolaston Blake, LNWR board member, founder member of the Institution of Mechanical Engineers, Fellow of the Royal Society and also member of the Court of the Bank of England.

[15] RBS Archives, GM/237, Glyn to Smith, 20 Oct.; Glyn to Moorsom, 1 Nov. 1854.

or between the officials is not an easy question to answer. Glyn was quite clear that the efficiency of the company was dependent upon the practical knowledge and experience of the executive officers and the relationship between them: in the context of the locomotive department he told Chandos that the discussion he proposed would work if he could get the two heads, McConnell and Trevithick, to pull harmoniously together upon general principles. Otherwise he feared constant clashing.[16] He was concerned about the load placed on Huish. Early in 1856 he told Chandos that there was then an opportunity for making some arrangement which might be advantageous to the system of working. The extent of the business through the manager's office was so large and multifarious that not only did Huish require assistance but it was of great importance that someone under him should be capable of carrying on the business and its details in the event of his retirement or anything happening to him. He asked Chandos to consider the possibility of finding an efficient young man who would be placed under Huish control, but resident in Liverpool.[17] He also criticised Huish to Chandos, telling him that he seemed to be taking the lead in a very bold banking operation – the combining of banking with executive transactions. He had found the former just enough to manage with success.

By 1858 criticism of Huish was mounting. Samuel Ashton, one of the Lancashire directors, told Chandos that several shareholders were becoming uneasy about the unfortunate competition the LNWR was carrying on. He thought Huish's treatment of Watkin, now the general manager of the MSLR, was the first and continuous cause of this reckless proceeding. Watkin, deservedly or not, had the confidence of his party and it would be wise if Huish would bottle up his virtuous indignation and not say in writing all he might feel about Watkin.[18] Glyn too now voiced doubts about Huish's ability to get on with other companies. From his position as chairman of the RCH, Glyn was perhaps uniquely placed to judge Huish's relationships with other companies as Huish was the LNWR representative on the committee and had to debate matters with his peers in other companies. Glyn told Chandos:

> I have felt for some time past the isolated position in which the L&NW has been and is placed … I have been particularly struck by the position

[16] Ibid, GM/237, Glyn to Chandos, 15 Feb. 1855. A sub-committee advised by Joseph Whitworth, the Manchester machine tool maker investigated with the result that Trevithick left. John Pennie, *A Victorian Engineering Giant,* 2008, 19–20.

[17] Ibid, Glyn to Chandos, 14 Jan. 1856.

[18] TNA, RAIL 1008/110, Ashton to Chandos, 17 Feb. 1858.

> in which the manager of the LNWR is left at the Railway Clearing House meetings. No one supports or co-operates with him and even those companies connected with the LNWR leave the individual unsupported. I have wondered that he did not feel this and tender his resignation for he cannot shut his eyes to the detriment which such state of things causes the LNWR. I am quite disposed to admit great talent and painstaking on the part of Captain Huish and believe he has the interests of the company at heart, but he has drawbacks which have interfered with his good qualities ... Cawkwell[19] whom I have observed at the Clearing House, always appeared to me to be a plain small man and generally respected with a thorough knowledge of our northern business.[20]

Moon took a similar line. He thought everything was done in the company by weight of money and not by skilful management. 'Do not be content with Huish,' he told Chandos. He warned that there was no via media. Either Chandos worked this out to a successful conclusion or let his character as a public man and leader rank with Lord John Russell. As to future management the only mode was a small committee of directors constantly sitting and consulting each other, acting in unity in one defined plan. The concern was too big for anything less.[21]

Huish went and William Cawkwell, 'the small plain man', was appointed in his place, despite Ashton rather going back on his earlier views. The latter now said the board was making a scapegoat of Huish.[22] Moorsom complained that the salaries paid to the new men were absurdly excessive for their duties and qualifications. They were lifted out of their sphere and soon learned to think themselves necessities.[23] Glyn opposed appointing Huish to the board, as had happened with Moorsom and Creed.

Glyn was not involved in the investigation and consideration in 1859 by the Stores and Locomotive Committee of the various proposals for numbers and types of locomotives needed and the facilities for their construction, particularly the need for two locomotive works if Crewe were reorganised and expanded and the geographical boundaries between the divisions headed by Ramsbottom and McConnell revised. The episode resulted in

[19] William Cawkwell, traffic manager (there was not a general manager) of the LYR since 1853, and regarded by some directors as a possible successor to Huish.

[20] TNA, RAIL 1008/304, Glyn to Chandos, 5 Sept. 1858.

[21] TNA, RAIL 1008/101, Moon to Chandos, 6 Sept. 1858.

[22] TNA, RAIL 1008/110, Ashton to Smith, 14 Sept. 1858.

[23] TNA, RAIL 1008/ 97, Moorsom to Chandos, 14 Sept. 1858.

Moon's short-lived resignation as chairman of the Stores and Locomotive Committee when the majority on the committee led by Moorsom failed to back him. Moon remained concerned about the policy of developing two centres for locomotive building, and inquiries into the costs of McConnell's division were undertaken. In 1861 McConnell was asked to explain the discrepancy between his original estimate of £21,000 and the actual spend of £78,100. The Stores Committee voted by 8 votes to 2 to censure McConnell. The latter who seems not to have taken the original charges seriously then produced a more detailed memorandum which reduced the discrepancy to only £2,368, but made a number of other rather tactless points given his situation. The committee referred the matter to the board, which held a special meeting. Glyn seconded Benson's motion to refer the matter back as more information was needed before the board could arrive at a just conclusion. This was defeated by 14 votes to 11 and the report adopted by the same margin. McConnell then resigned and left; it was quickly decided that the two divisions should be combined under Ramsbottom with his headquarters at Crewe.

On a number of other occasions Glyn was not persuaded of the need for a change in policy, or wished to proceed more cautiously than his colleagues. The lawyers who advised railway companies from the outset were all self-employed professionals who provided a broad range of services from their own offices. In the pioneering years they guided the sometimes amateurish directors and managers drawn from many different backgrounds through the pitfalls of company promotion, raising capital and securing incorporation through an Act of Parliament, often with no regard to the cost. In the Railway Mania some solicitors partnerships served only clients from the railway world. The highly speculative ventures in the Mania and the failure of so many in which lawyers were closely involved caused the surviving companies to be much more critical of the activities of their legal advisers and of their bills. It was alleged that lawyers routinely charged their railway clients 'ten to twenty times more than they would have thought of charging a private client.'[24] In 1848 the LNWR board instructed their solicitors not to give retainers to, or employ, more than three counsel in any one case in Parliament.[25] Peter Macpherson produced *The Law Expenditure of Railway Companies, Considered with a view to its Speedy and Effective Reduction*, which described the 'present vicious law systems of railway companies'. The attack was the more powerful in that Macpherson was a practising lawyer, not an outside journalist. The LNWR

[24] *Railway Express*, 9 Jan. 1846, quoted in R.W. Kostal, *Law and English Capitalism 1825–75*, 1994, 334.

[25] TNA, RAIL 410/20, 13 May 1848.

Finance Committee recommended that major changes should be made and that the work should be in the hands of one law firm instead of six with an office at Euston station. There were six because the arrangements of the constituent companies were generally carried into the amalgamated concern. The board did not act on this report, but following further adverse publicity about railway lawyers in 1855 they set up a Law Committee to confer with the company's solicitors on future arrangements for legal expenditure. Their investigations established how much was being spent, most of it by Swift & Co. and Carter & Co. and by disbursements in counsels' and parliamentary fees. However no steps which might engender hostile feelings were thought desirable. Expenditure had increased largely because of a real increase in work caused by disputes with other companies, but the Law Committee considered that the company's remittances were an abundant source of profit to the solicitors. In 1861 the Law Committee, now under the chairmanship of Richard Dean, a director and barrister, expressed their decided view that the law expenditures were entirely disproportionate to the net earnings of the company. The only effective remedy was to secure the exclusive services of one able and experienced lawyer to work full-time for the company at Euston. When the report came to the Board Glyn moved its deferral until the next meeting. This was probably a tactical move to give time to try to persuade the solicitors of the rightness of the course proposed, but he was probably more anxious than most to want to avoid offending those with whom he had worked closely for so long – thirty years in Carter's case. He was outvoted by 17 votes to 4 and the report referred to the chairman, deputy chairman and the chairman of the Law Committee to bring it into effect.

At the next meeting it was reported that Carter and Swift had said that parts in the report were calculated to give rise to erroneous impressions respecting their professional charges and in certain respects much less than justice had been done to them. They had however been reassured that no incompetence or deceit had been implied and that the lawyers' charges had been moderate. The purpose was to have a solicitor at Euston whose attention might be given uninterruptedly to the company. There was no hope of attaining the company's aim of employing Swift or Carter personally, but Swift offered the company one of his junior partners, James Blenkinsop. He therefore became the first solicitor to be employed by a railway company or indeed any industrial company in Britain. Swift and Carter were thanked for the handsome manner in which they had offered to meet the wishes of the board and were given gold passes for the LNWR for life.

Glyn had an eye to the public reputation of the company. In December 1854 he told Chandos that they were in bad odour for their refusal to convey clothing and lint for Scutari. He pointed out that other companies carried it free and asked whether it was worth grating against public feeling over such a small matter.[26]

For some years Glyn played a particularly active role in the affairs of the CHR, not so much of the railway itself but in questions related to Anglo-Irish steamship services and the trains which served them, an area where the Government could and did lay down strict standards of performance. In 1853 public complaints about the steamer services led to a Commons Select Committee on Communications with Ireland to which Huish gave evidence. The Committee found that in a period when many advances had been made in the science of steam navigation, such as by Cunard on the New York route and by the P&O lines to the East, the service to Ireland had deteriorated. A new committee on the conveyance of mails by railway recommended a country-wide speed-up of mails. In November 1853 Chandos and Glyn were appointed by their colleagues to join the members of the CHR board to investigate and report on the question of improved communication between Holyhead and Dublin.[27]

In September 1854 Glyn was in touch with Sir James Graham, now the first Lord of the Admiralty in Aberdeen's coalition government, about the arrangements for the conveyance of mails from Ireland. The opening of the extension of the railway to Admiralty pier and of the new Holyhead station in 1851 had left untouched the contract under which the mails were conveyed to Ireland by the Dublin Steam Packet Company. However by 1854 the Admiralty was considering a new harbour. Graham sent for Glyn after he had visited Holyhead, and told him that the present mail contract was to be given up and if the LNWR could arrange it another contract would be made with the railway companies. The railway was to be extended from the present station across the old harbour by the Hibernian Inn to the inner harbour. A floating stage was to be provided by the Admiralty so that other steamers could come alongside. Large steamers should be provided capable of carrying a full number of passengers conveniently. Glyn added that no particular speed was alluded to but 'I think he is in earnest'. He advised Chandos that their first step must be, after making arrangements with the DSPC, to prepare a plan and estimate of the proposed junction from the station to the new harbour, and then to consider the amount of outlay for that and the new boats.[28] A fortnight later Glyn reported that Graham was still very determined on reform. Graham had asked to see the plans for the railway and harbour and promised to meet James Meadows

26 RBS Archives, GM/237, Glyn to Chandos, 20 Nov. 1854.

27 TNA, RAIL 410/22, 12 Nov. 1853; 12 Jul. 1854.

28 RBS Archives, GM/237, Glyn to Chandos, 15 Sept. 1854.

Rendell, the engineer advising the Admiralty. Glyn wrote and asked if the CHR directors were as serious about the matter as Graham.[29] In November he had a satisfactory interview with the City of Dublin people who were willing to go with him to see Graham.

In December he was telling Chandos that Stewart did a good day's work in Dublin, 'if the Irishman would only continue straight!' Later that month he went to Holyhead himself. He told Chandos that he had got the better of Owen Stanley and William Jackson[30] who had attacked him sharply. On his return to Euston he learned that Stewart had received a letter from Binger, the CHR general manager, full of complaints and that Peto was also agitated. 'However we must be firm.'

In 1856 with Chandos and Stewart he saw Wilson at the Treasury who told them of the proposed conditions for the accelerated communication with Ireland – Euston to Dublin, 11 hours each way, two trips a day, and the companies were to bear all risks of every description. A penalty of a 1460th part (four journeys a day for 365 days) of the whole annual payment by the government would be levied on the company for every journey not performed within the specified time from any cause whatsoever. Chandos, Glyn and Blake were asked to carry forward the negotiations, though Glyn was not on the committee appointed for the working and management of the CHR and the steam boats. When Moorsom tried to extend the journey time to not less than 11 hours 15 minutes the board voted against his proposal.[31]

The LNWR was careful to maintain its control over the CHR going to the length of holding a meeting of their representatives so that when the CHR board met they could defeat a motion from Stanley which they regarded as designed to wreck the negotiations.[32] In September 1855 the board refused to defer the payment of interest on their loan to the CHR.[33] In July 1856 the LNWR board objected to Peto's proposal that the permanent way should be under CHR control.[34]

In December 1857 the LNWR board was divided on how to carry forward the Irish service. Glyn wanted to continue the existing arrangements including a renewal of the mail contract with the Post Office, despite the

[29] Ibid, 28 Sept. 1854.

[30] Directors of the CHR. Stanley lived at Penrhos, Holyhead, and was MP for Beaumaris; Jackson was a railway contractor and was MP for Newcastle-under-Lyne.

[31] TNA, RAIL 410/23, 10 May 1856 and 27 May 1857.

[32] RBS Archives, GM/237, 13 Jun. 1857.

[33] TNA, RAIL 410/23, 15 Sept. 1855.

[34] Ibid. 12 Jul. 1856.

government's initial refusal of the LNWR's offer. Smith and others thought that the offer should not be renewed and the company should not enter upon the risks and disadvantages inseparable from any such contract, but his amendment was defeated by 14 to 11. It was agreed that negotiations should go ahead with the other companies involved on a different basis of costing and that cost reflected in the offer.[35]

The LNWR had no involvement with the construction of Brunel's Great Eastern, which had been launched at Millwall with great difficulty on 31 January 1858. It was proposed that it should tour several British ports before its maiden voyage to the USA, but although its completion was celebrated at Millwall on 8 August 1859, and the vessel was then open to the public, disputes between the Great Ship Company, and the builders about unsatisfactory work, led to a delay. It was 8 September before it left the Nore for Portland. The LNWR, particularly Chandos, wished to celebrate the ship's arrival in Holyhead. Glyn, who was in touch with the chairman of the Great Ship Company, J J R Campbell, warned Chandos on 21 August that it was difficult to do anything at Holyhead because of uncertainty about the Great Ship's movements. He later advised that the ship would be at Holyhead until the 29 September and that if Chandos still wanted a demonstration it would be better on 26 or 27. He suggested that Baring, as chairman of the Grand Trunk Railway of Canada, should be invited and also Cobden. The explosion in the forward funnel of the Great Eastern on 9 September, when five of the crew were killed, further delayed the voyage, an event which was made even more poignant by the death of Brunel on 15 September and it was 10 October before the ship reached Holyhead. However the railway managed to celebrate in style. Prince Albert visited the vessel on 16 October when Chandos, Cawkwell, Binger and other local officers, received him at Bangor and travelled on the royal train to Holyhead. There was also a separate LNWR celebration on 19 October in a special pavilion in the grounds of the Royal Hotel at Bangor, preceded by a visit to the Great Eastern by Chandos and the directors in a LNWR steamer. Glyn had invited Gladstone, then Chancellor of the Exchequer, as the directors of the LNWR remembered the many obligations the company owed to him.[36] At the dinner Chandos referred in glowing terms to the achievement of the railway in reaching Holyhead. Pakenham remarked that one could not come to Holyhead without recollecting that the harbour had arisen because of the grants voted by the House of Commons. This caused speakers to put

35 TNA, RAIL 410/23, 13 Dec. 1856.

36 BL, Add Ms 44391, letters of 8 and 12 Sept. 1859. The second letter explained the proceedings had been deferred in consequence of the disaster to the Great Eastern.

in pleas for further expenditure at Holyhead. The Great Eastern returned to Southampton for the winter and was only ready to sail for New York on 17 June 1860.[37]

Glyn's position as MP for Kendal meant that he knew well a number of those closely involved with the Kendal and Windermere and the Lancaster and Carlisle Railways, which in the 1850s were still independent companies though both had been worked by the LNWR. The Kendal company had taken the working of the line into their own hands, and in 1856 the LCR agreed to provide its own locomotives and rolling stock, so releasing about 60 engines and 110,000 train miles a year, calling into question the need to have a separate northern and north eastern locomotive departments. At the next meeting the board agree to the amalgamation, despite opposition from Hardman Earle and others who wished either to avoid Trevithick's dismissal or to appoint him in place of Ramsbottom to the combined post.[38] The attempt by the entirely separate 'little' North Western Railway (NWR) to build a line from Ingleton to link with the LNWR at Tebay and gain running powers over the LCR and the Midland Railway so providing an alternative route to Scotland disturbed the LNWR. The NWR's ambitious plans in 1846 for lines from Skipton to Kendal had only partially succeeded. In 1857 the NWR's bill did not succeed, despite the support of the GNR but the LCR itself secured approval for a line from Tebay to Ingleton, so giving the LCR the possibility of an alternative route southwards to Skipton and the Midland system. The LNWR saw its interests further threatened when the Midland agreed in 1858 to lease the NWR. The LNWR response was rapid. By August 1859 it had leased the LCR at a price, guaranteeing 4½ per cent more than its own dividend with a minimum of 8 per cent. By then a new trans-pennine route, the South Durham and Lancashire Railway had been projected. It was heavily backed by Henry Pease and other Stockton and Darlington directors, as well as by Kendal banking interests, including John Wakefield and John Whitwell. This was to run from the Stockton and Darlington, not yet part of the North Eastern, near Bishop Auckland to Tebay, so linking the iron and coal industries of the Northeast with iron mining areas of North Lancashire and Cumberland and much shortening the distances involved. The LCR was authorised to contribute, though it was the SDR which had power to lease or to amalgamate with the line. Opened in 1861 the route soon largely superseded the NER's route, via Newcastle

[37] RBS Archives, GM/237, Glyn to Chandos, 21, 27 and 29 Aug. and 3 Sept. 1859. *The Times*, 9 and 27 Aug., 9 and 12 Sept. and 11, 16 and 21 Oct. For the explosion see *The Times of* 12 Sept. and L.T.C. Rolt, *Brunel,* 1958, 295–302.

[38] TNA, RAIL 410/23, 9 Apr. and 9 May 1857.

and Carlisle, for the conveyance of hematite ore from Cumbria to Teeside and of coal from the Durham coalfield to North Lancashire. A year later the Eden Valley Railway, again promoted by SDR interests, opened from the SDLR at Kirkby Stephen to Clifton near Penrith, substantially shortening the route from the Whitehaven area to Durham and Teeside.

Glyn was not concerned with the details of the negotiations, but about the effect of these developments on the people concerned and the likely reactions of local interests. He told Chandos before the crucial meeting with the LCR that Colonel Gandy[39] was the KWR representative on the LCR board. It would be as well for Chandos to enquire whether the KWR people were assenting to their inclusion in the merger. Henry Howard, deputy chairman of the LCR, would probably know. It was desirable to avoid any new development at the meeting.[40]

He congratulated Chandos on securing a preliminary agreement with the KWR and that with the LCR, but asked whether it was prudent to dispense altogether with the LCR board. It was a popular and influential body in that country and its management was good. At the beginning of September Glyn told Chandos he hoped he would settle with the KWR people immediately. The KWR considered themselves to have been very hardly treated in their arrangement with the LCR – it was a question of money, and he sent Chandos a note of that company's views though complaining that he did not like the position of the buffer at all.[41] In October he hoped Chandos would keep the LCR board together and they would hold that country against competition.[42]

The following month Glyn called Chandos's attention to the matter of re-electing James Cropper of Ellerdale, Kendal to the LCR board. Glyn was at a loss to know the reason for not doing so. He was one of the most useful directors on that board, very attentive and intelligent and had very considerable local connections. The full efficiency of the LCR board should be maintained. The other directors would feel very considerable disgust if the re-election did not take place forthwith. Cropper remained on the board. Glyn also stressed the need to settle with the Hasell, the chairman of the LCR, and David Hodgson. He believed Chandos could do this without much difficulty, but if rival interests got ahead in that district Hodgson would be raising his frictions and seek other allies who would only be too glad to get him. He suspected there would be a great fight in that district,

39 Col. Gandy of Milnthorpe.

40 RBS Archives, GM/237, Glyn to Chandos, 21 and 29 Aug. and 3 Sept. 1859.

41 Ibid, 26, 27 and 29 Aug.; 3, 5 and 6 Sept. 1859.

42 Ibid, 10 Oct. 1859.

but perhaps Chandos was settling with the Midland.[43] He told Chandos that the LNWR board had recommended C. Howard for the LCR board. Howard,[44] he said, intended to retire but Stewart and he thought it safer not to leave him out.

At the end of November he wrote again about a proposed line from Consett Iron works to near Newcastle on the Newcastle and Carlisle which would shorten the distance from the LCR to South Durham but the NER was opposed, as it would enable the LNWR to have access to Newcastle on rails outside the NER's control. Glyn hoped that Chandos would consider the proposal. No doubt a good deal of traffic would take the line from Tebay by this route, and there was a need to protect the LNWR interests, but at the same time they could not afford to make the NER very angry though he told Chandos he knew the art of steering between these channels.[45] A Joint Committee had been proposed and the LNWR invited to be a member. This scheme failed as did a second project, the Newcastle, Derwent and Weardale, which would have had access to a quay on the Tyne, and was backed by the North British as well as the LNWR. The SDR withheld its support, essential for using the route to Tebay, and the scheme collapsed. This proved to be the catalyst which resulted in the merger between the NER and SDR.[46]

The desire to avoid being dependent on the NER led not only to the LNWR supporting the South Durham line, but to an interest in the West Hartlepool Harbour and Railway Company promoted to compete with the Stockton and Darlington. Bills were prepared to enable the LNWR to subscribe a quarter of the capital and purchase a quay and warehouse at one of the West Hartlepool Docks. This met with hostility from LNWR shareholders who accused the board of threatening aggression against the NER, and wastefully investing capital in the railway and docks facilities. At the next board Glyn told his colleagues that they needed to avoid any considerable outlay of capital in that district.[47] Nevertheless the LNWR went ahead and purchased the warehouse and quay though there was no parliamentary authority. The problem was solved shortly as the West Hartlepool

43 Ibid, 5 Nov. 1859.

44 The Hon. C.W.G. Howard of Naworth Castle, Cumberland was an LNWR nominee on the LCR board. Henry Howard of Greystoke Castle, Penrith was deputy chairman. David Hodgson was also an LNWR nominee.

45 Ibid, 19 and 29 Nov. 1859.

46 Maurice W. Kirby, *The Origins of Railway Enterprise: The Stockton and Darlington Railway, 1821–1863*, 1993, 167.

47 TNA, RAIL 410/24, 9 Mar. 1861.

company got into financial difficulties and had to sell out to the NER. The latter, no doubt to nip in the bud further LNWR ambitions concluded an agreement which gave the LNWR full facilities for the interchange and working of traffic. in 1861 Glyn was concerned about the LNWR's relations with other companies in the north east and asked the Special Committee to look into it with a view to avoiding any considerable outlay of capital.[48]

Glyn continued to liaise with other companies. Partly to counteract the alliance of the GWR with the Shrewsbury companies the LNWR embarked on a series of schemes. Peto, now chairman of the OWWR as well as the CHR, arranged that the OWWR, on the construction of which little progress had been made, should be completed on the standard gauge and worked by the Midland and LNWR. Moreover the LNWR had not abandoned its interest in securing entry to South Wales. In August 1851 Glyn, still chairman, told shareholders that he had ordered surveys to be made for a continuation of the Buckinghamshire railway to Worcester and Cheltenham and that a line from Worcester to Hereford was being actively promoted. A line on the narrow gauge had already been sanctioned from Hereford to Abergavenny, but not proceeded with. Local support for the Worcester line was weak and in October Glyn suggested limiting the line for the time being to one from Worcester to Malvern. It was lost in the Lords in 1852, despite the support of Sir George Cornewall Lewis, Bt, Liberal MP for Herefordshire and a junior minister in Lord John Russell's government who moved the second reading in the Commons, believing that railways had more to offer the farmers of his constituency than the phantom of Protection.[49] This line was authorised to be constructed jointly by the LNWR and Midland. The LNWR drive to South Wales was frustrated by the delay in the completion of the Newport, Abergavenny and Hereford line originally authorised in 1846 with an extension from Pontypool to Quaker's Yard to link with the Taff Vale Railway.

In October 1852 the board resolved it was of the utmost importance to the LNWR's interests to promote a narrow gauge railway communicating with South Wales in conjunction with their ally, the Midland.[50] With the independent Shrewsbury and Hereford line and the proposed LNWR line from Shrewsbury to Crewe, this would give the LNWR a through standard gauge line from the northwest to the South Wales coalfield. The LNWR had to resist an attempt by the Ebbw Vale Iron company which was closely

[48] TNA, RAIL 410/24, 9 Mar. 1861.

[49] R.W.D. Fenn, *The Life and Times of Sir George Cornewall Lewis, Bart, a Radnorshire Gentleman*, 2005, 97.

[50] TNA, RAIL 410/22, 7 Oct. 1852.

associated with the SCR and SBR companies to take a controlling interest in the line by taking up shares themselves, and appointing directors. Glyn himself took 100 shares. W.P Price of the Midland was also a director.[51] Opened between Pontypool and Hereford at the beginning of 1854, it was worked by the LNWR for a short time. The LNWR ran into difficulties when they were unable to purchase the line because they refused to direct traffic over the SBR or the SCR, but they arranged for Brassey, who was already working the Shrewsbury to Hereford, to work the line. In this atmosphere contacts with the local parties were all important. In July Glyn told Chandos that he had seen Joseph Robinson, a director He had the largest works in that county (Ebbw Vale) and was well disposed to the LNWR. He did not complain of the local manager but of the sea traffic and the Midland. Robinson was not satisfied with the present state of the matter but accepted that the traffic was only waiting for the completion of the LNWR arrangements.[52]

Glyn himself was involved in developments in the Shrewsbury area. He saw Lord Combermere about the construction of the Shrewsbury and Crewe's entry to Shrewsbury and was given authority with Benson and Smith to negotiate with Lord Powys with the Shrewsbury, Welshpool and Oswestry.[53]

Despite having to admit defeat in its battle to keep the GWR – and the broad gauge – out of Birmingham, in 1853 a connection between the Buckinghamshire Railway and the OWWR at Yarnton was authorised and so for some years in the 1850s the LNWR was able to maintain a hold on some of the traffic to Birmingham over the OWWR's rails via Bletchley and the Bucks line. The LNWR even ran a through train from Euston to Worcester and there were other through coaches detached from the Euston trains at Bletchley. The OWWR was in a poor state financially and saw agreement with the LNWR and Midland as its salvation, but those companies were only prepared to work the line if they controlled the working.[54]

Towards the end of the decade relations between the LNWR and GWR improved. Glyn saw the agreement of 1858 by which the LNWR would do the work of the GWR in Manchester as a remarkable point in railway working, after all the fighting and opposition. He said it was likely to stand because it was founded upon the pressure on both companies from another and a new quarter. If the Midland became more intimate with the Great

[51] For the LNWR intervention in 1851 see Hodgkins, 108–109.

[52] RBS Archives, GM/237, Glyn to Chandos, 17 Jul. 1854.

[53] Ibid, 21 Apr. 1856.

[54] TNA, RAIL 410/ 23, 14 Aug. 1855.

Northern again, he told Chandos, 'the GWR will be thrown more to us'. He believed Ponsonby (the chairman of the GWR) was quite to be trusted and if he could move alone everything would go smoothly. He had no faith in any present binding agreement with the GNR. He wished the 'Midland would be quiet without allowing feeling to carry them further away from us. Their permanent interests cannot be opposed to ours.'[55]

However in the West Midlands a new board, with a new general manager, A C Sheriff recruited from the NER brought about the amalgamation of the NAHR and the OWWR and the purchase of the WHR. The new company authorised in 1860 was known as the West Midland. Although the West Midland had through booking facilities with both the GWR and the LNWR, most of the London traffic went by the latter, though the GWR were laying mixed gauge tracks on their line to Paddington which would in any case have changed the traffic flow from its completion in April 1861.

The new West Midland then attempted to negotiate with the LNWR for a new route via Banbury to London: the LNWR's Banbury branch would be extended to meet the WMR from Honeybourne. The LNWR however found itself outflanked by another development in the same area which upset their now amicable relationship with the GWR: the London, Buckinghamshire and West Midland Junction Railway from Yarnton to London, which may have had some backing from West Midland board members. This scheme, known as the Mid-Western, was proceeding through Parliament when the amalgamation of the Great Western and the West Midland was suddenly announced.

Glyn immediately complained that under existing circumstances the GWR should have asked the LNWR to be partners to the arrangement with the OWWR. He asked Moorsom what real loss, if any, would it entail upon the LNWR – would it not make it necessary for them to make the Shrewsbury and Hereford quite safe without delay. Moorsom replied next day to say that he had just returned from a meeting with the SHR. The LNWR had offered to lease at the line at 6 per cent or about £500,000 jointly with GWR or alone but giving the GWR power to use the line. He added

> When I met Ponsonby at the dinner at the Lord Lieutenants we talked over the West Midland and agreed that with the Mid Western being thrown out it was our policy to make a joint offer to the WMR. Sheriff and Fowler seem to have got up this alliance at a heat and within a few

[55] TNA, RAIL 1008/104, 12 Jan. 1858, Glyn to Chandos.

> days of the Mid-Western case coming on and Price had been active in it. I have met Price since who had a disconcerted air but spoke sensibly and fairly as to the future.[56]

Glyn's interest in railways in the London area continued when in 1860 the question came up of an extension from Euston to Charing Cross and Southwark to join the Charing Cross Railway, the SER's extension from London Bridge to Charing Cross which was then being built. In May the board approved the principle of an extension to Charing Cross and the following month Glyn was appointed a member of a group to deal with this.[57] Although there were talks between the engineers, little came of this immediately but in 1864 the North Western and Charing Cross Railway Act was passed for a line from Hampstead Road to Charing Cross, only to fall victim to the financial crisis of 1866.

Glyn took no part in the events leading to Chandos's surprise resignation in January 1861, which arose from the proposed lease of the MSLR by the LNWR and GNR, agreed by the three general managers. The underlying policy was to counter the growing influence of the Midland which was now allying with the LYR. Chandos disagreed and persuaded Denison, the GNR chairman, not to back it.

While the breach between Chandos and the board on the policy towards the MSLR was the reason for his resignation there were probably other factors at work. Chandos spent much of his time on LNWR business to the neglect of other matters. His solicitor had complained that Chandos's reputation for regularity and punctuality would suffer from his devotion to railways' and later complained that that he was on the way to Euston 'in the hope that you will spare time to attend a little to your own affairs'.[58] Although he gave up his seat at Buckingham in 1857 to spend more time with his family, he may well have found that the LNWR took too much of his time. He was still thought of as a future minister and when J.W. Henley resigned from the Board of Trade in February 1859, Glyn told him he was delighted to find that the charm of office and the persuasive arguments of Downing Street would not induce him to lean in for the Board of Trade.[59] In June 1859 Chandos did stand unsuccessfully for Oxford University against Gladstone, and he was away for many months in 1860 accompanying the Prince of Wales to Canada. He may well have wanted to devote himself more to politics.

[56] RSB, GM/237, Glyn to Moorsom 2 May; Moorsom to Glyn, 3 May 1861.

[57] TNA, RAIL 410/24, 12 May and 22 Jun. 1860.

[58] John Beckett, *The Rise and Fall of the Grenvilles*, 1994, 265.

[59] RBS Archives, GM/237, Glyn to Chandos, 3 Mar. 1859.

It was imperative to find a new chairman at the next board meeting only a week later. Precisely who was considered is obscure. Earle and Tootal, given a little more time, might have gone for Westhead, now Brown-Westhead following the will of his uncle, J. Brown, but he was not yet back on the board though Earle and Tootal successfully proposed him in February. Senior directors may have been considered but the board, on Glyn's proposition, seconded by Tootal and supported by Earle, Cropper, Rathbone, Thompson and generally, took the easy path and elevated Moorsom, the deputy chairman, despite his failings in the chair of the general meeting when deputising for Chandos. On two occasions Glyn had to help him out. Hardman Earle, after discussion, proposed Moon as deputy chairman and Glyn seconded him.

When Moorsom took over as chairman Richard Dean called for a review of the general system of management which Glyn supported. On this occasion however Earle, supported by Moon, successfully urged the continuation of the existing system for the present, and Moon when he became chairman seems to have agreed with that view, as no such review took place.[60] Moorsom's tenure was very brief as he died in May 1862, aged 68. In June Glyn, seconded by Earle, proposed Moon as chairman. The board unanimously agreed to this appointment and to that of Brown-Westhead as deputy chairman.

Glyn had played a major part in the appointment of Moon who was to lead the company for thirty years. He presumably did not wish to see another chairman of his own and Moorsom's generation – a number of the long serving members of the board had resigned including Smith, Grant and Barrow –and Moon had by this time established a reputation as a tough chairman of committees, if often abrasive. How far Glyn was involved in the initial appointment of Moon to the LNWR board is not clear. Although Moon explained to Stewart that he was prepared to approach Glyn about a seat on the board, it is not certain that he did, as in the event he was one of a number elected when the board was expanded to 30 in 1851, and as a former Liverpool merchant he would have had substantial support from the powerful Liverpool party on the LNWR board. He had however left Liverpool for Worcestershire in 1846 and seems to have wanted to join the LNWR board to protect his and his family's substantial investments.[61] He had been an active director making his reputation as the chairman of the Stores Committee who would not tolerate waste.

60 TNA, RAIL 410/24, 9 Mar. 1861; Braine, 229.

61 Peter Braine argues that this was his main motive and this is confirmed in a short memoir by James Cropper, the nephew of Edward and LNWR representative on the LCR board. James Cropper, *Notes and Memories*, 1900, 176.

One of Moon's first actions was to appoint Glyn to the Finance and Capital Expenditure Committee. It was a time of some financial difficulty for the company. Their additional borrowing powers were not available until the new shares authorised had been created and 50 per cent paid up so that wherever practicable new works had to be postponed.[62] Glyn was a fairly regular attender, first under the chairmanship of his fellow banker Robert Benson and subsequently under Brown-Westhead, the deputy chairman. Moreover Glyn attended board meetings regularly, though not invariably, until the late 1860s. For a number of years he was a member of the Southern Division Committee, but he does not seem to have attended. However in 1869 he was not reappointed to any of the committees.

The Special Committee's fortnightly meetings were the forum where the key business of the company was done. It was a tightly knit group. Originally it was composed of the main committee chairman: Smith (Finance), Moorsom, (Traffic), Lyon (Permanent Way), Ledsam (audit and rating), Moon (stores and locomotive expenditure). However the Special Committte became something of a closed shop, largely because the chairmanship of a committee became a semi-permanent appointment. In 1863 J.P. Melville, only elected a director two years previously, and the veteran Rathbone suggested that members of the Special Committee should be re-elected at the board annually with a view to the introduction of some new members. Glyn joined the chairman and deputy chairman in opposing this as it would not be 'expedient' to make such frequent changes either in the chairmanship of the committees or in the Special Committee. Later the Committee was not entirely restricted to the chairmen and not all chairmen were on it. Earle and Tootal were early additions, and by 1865 Ledsam and Smith had gone, so it consisted of Moon, Brown Westhead, Bancroft, J.T. Chance, Earle, Lyon, Mangles and Tootal. Chance, appointed to the board in 1863, was the son of William Chance one of the founding directors of the LBR and head of Chance Bros of Spon Lane and Oldbury, a firm specialising in improving the illumination of lighthouses. He was then chairman of the Locomotive Committee. In Glyn's time there were two more surprising appointments to the Special Committee. In 1865 Sir James Fergusson was appointed and in 1867 the Duke of Sutherland, neither of whom chaired any committees, though Fergusson was first elected an MP aged 22 when serving in the Crimean War and prior to joining the LNWR board had been a director of the Caledonian for seven years. Richard Dean, who did chair committees, was also appointed. In Moon's first ten years as chairman

[62] TNA, RAIL 410/335, 18 Jul. 1861.

the committee grew from nine to thirteen, so that nearly half the board of thirty were members.

In 1861 Glyn seconded Dean's motion that the special committee should report upon the general system of management with its advantages and defects and whether any and what improvements could in their opinion be made. However when the chairman, secretary and manager reported, Hardman Earle and Rathbone's resolution that the existing system of committees be continued was accepted without a vote.[63]

To obtain a seat on the board of the largest railway company in the country was something of a prize. Over the years the board struggled from time to time with the question of how such appointments should be made. In general the board was inclined to cling to the system adopted in 1851 when it was agreed that two should be balloted out each year with the possibility of their being re-elected by the general meeting but not being proposed by the board. A minor improvement was made in 1861 when Dean successfully requested that eight days notice should be given of nominations to the board.[64] In 1866 Moon expressed dissatisfaction with the system. While in the past he had been mainly concerned to see that the main trading areas and interests of the company were represented he was now anxious about the calibre and experience of candidates as he thought their suitability was not properly considered by shareholders. 'They acted as if they were giving a ticket to an infirmary or a vote at a general election', he wrote. Glyn was included in a committee to consider the rotation of directors and they consulted some leading shareholders, but Moon had to report that they could not see a way to improve the system.[65]

In the late 1860s Glyn was still able to offer advice. He wrote to Moon in 1869 about general railway issues and the possibility of the LNWR linking with the London underground. He thought that from what John Bright, whom Gladstone appointed President of the Board of Trade in 1868, had said in the House he was more likely to give fair consideration to the interests of the railway companies than any minister at the Board of Trade since the days of Dalhousie. He thought there might be a favourable moment for obtaining some amendment of Lord Campbell's Act tackling the question of compensation for accidents. Too much must not be attempted but it might be profitable to remove the assessment of the amount of damages from the judge to some instrument of a more impartial character eg the Board of Trade or some such body as at present damages were sometimes determined by almost vindictive

63 TNA, RAIL 410/24, 9 Mar. 1861.

64 Ibid.

65 TNA, RAIL 410/25, 21 Apr., 19 May, 21 Jul. 1866; Braine, 251–252.

feelings He did not think the railways would get very far in Parliament on this issue, but this might be tried as he had heard that the judges shared this view. He also asked Moon whether he had been able to work out any plan for a connecting link with the Metropolitan District. He concluded 'It seems very desirable, if not too costly for us. The present board of that company requires more practical strength which you could give it. We must manage to get the London & North Western to Charing Cross or nearest.'[66]

Moon must have responded because on 2 September Glyn suggested that he should come down to Stanmore and sleep, though he feared nothing could be suggested likely to meet the question Moon had raised: 'How are these gigantic undertakings to be hereafter managed'. Glyn thought that the possibility of continuing the old system had passed making preferable the alternative of a small group of men with a chairman constituted more like the Government's permanent boards composed of men who should do nothing else, be sufficiently well paid and attend every day to their duties. Many men if the remuneration were sufficient would give up other callings for such a work but this essential must not be interfered with by meetings of proprietors.[67]

Glyn was again involved in debates about the nature of the British railway system following the publication in 1864 of William Galt's book *Railway Reform: its importance and practicability as affecting the nation, the shareholders and the government.*[68] Galt had been a protagonist of greater state control of railways in the 1840s and his book appeared as the twenty five year period provided in the Gladstone's Act of 1844 was nearing its close and questions were arising as to what action the government should take. Galt claimed that railways had become the highways of the country, as necessary to people as the air they breathed, and which should therefore belong to the state. They had a monopoly of traffic and could raise and lower their rates and charges at pleasure. The cost of the present system was injurious to the mercantile interest and he instanced the coal traffic to London. Lower charges would lead to a greater revenue. Railways, he argued, were obliged to raise capital by issuing too many preference shares and debentures. They then wasted it by resisting invasions by rival companies and in defending territory. They could not afford to modernise and were forced to raise charges.

Galt's book created interest in political and railway circles. Galt's cause was taken up by John Roebuck, the radical MP for Sheffield. He

[66] RBS Archives, GM/1381/13, Glyn to Moon, 15 Mar. 1869.

[67] Ibid, 2 Sept. 1869.

[68] Galt published an enlarged edition in 1865 in which he commented on some of the criticisms made on the first edition.

wrote to both Glyn and Gladstone in September to say he intended to call for a Commons committee on the subject and advocating a cross party approach. Glyn had been very ill – he had not been at the LNWR board since April – and told Gladstone that he had only glanced at Galt's book. However he doubted whether Galt had considered all the difficulties which had increased materially since Gladstone had propounded the question in 1844. He doubted whether any government could decide so complicated a question for itself. A commission might be a safe means of dealing with the preliminary proceedings. He confessed that he had not lately been mixed up with railway people, but thought that the existence and the powers of the Act had been nearly forgotten. He added that very many of those mixed up in the discussions had passed away.[69]

Gladstone told Roebuck that he agreed that consideration by a committee would not exclude a commission later. He was confident that the cabinet would be governed by practical considerations, though as will be seen from his response to Glyn it is doubtful whether practicality was his own guide.[70] He told Glyn that Roebuck 'was too confident. He has no conception of the difficulty and intricacy of the bulk at which he is gallantly prepared to tilt.' It was plain that no great measure could be passed without the unanimous or at least very general consent of the railway interest; that the railways must in no circumstances be managed by the Executive government; that the general abolition of taxes on locomotion (he had in mind the Passenger Duty tax) would be a grand thing for the country. But there remained almost an infinity of questions.

Gladstone thought a committee might enquire into the actual cost and price of locomotion both for passengers and goods by railways and whether, if the railways were owned but not managed by the state, it would be possible to reduce rates greatly and secure a greater approach to uniformity without the risk of loss or unduly burdening the revenues. Such an enquiry could not be undertaken without the concurrence or acquiescence of the railway companies and a conviction by government that there was no insurmountable financial objection.

Gladstone wrote at some length about the possible scope of a measure. The present perpetuity might be converted into a lease. General taxes on locomotion would at the same time be nearly or altogether abolished. There might be provisions for keeping alive the preferential charges and this concession might be made directly applicable to all railways. A term

69 BL, Add Ms 44403, Glyn to Gladstone, 21 Sept. 1864.

70 Ibid, Gladstone to Roebuck, 21 Sept. (from Penmaenmawr, so he could not have seen Glyn's letter from Stanmore Park). Gladstone replied to Glyn on 23 Sept.1864.

would be fixed at which the state would become universal proprietor. The old companies disburdened of their onerous proprietary interest and body might become lessees of the lines under criteria and conditions as to changes of management, and free of a huge dead weight might be better and more efficient commercial bodies than they were. Extensions and improvements of stations etc might be arranged with the companies perhaps in a manner like that which landlords follow with agricultural tenants.

The maximum of price to be given would be laid down in the Act: each bargain might be made subject to a Parliamentary veto before final ratification. The terms would come under or flow from the maximum of years purchase in proportion as the undertakings were imperfectly or fully developed. To make these important covenants it might be necessary to furnish the Executive Government with some special and independent assistance. On the pure finance of the case; Gladstone did not see any insurmountable difficulty.

Gladstone called this a very rude outline of a rude scheme. It assumed that economy could be effected which had to be a matter for inquiry. It was, he wrote, a large, bewildering, and a seductive prospect, but he had no ideé fixe about it. He looked to Glyn to see what it looked like. The best favour would be to criticise it mercilessly, and 'there are few men to whose eye I should like thus to expose it: for not many are really competent to give an opinion.'[71]

Glyn told Gladstone that there would be no difficulty in a committee enquiring into the costs and price of locomotion and this would probably branch out into very useful details upon which some important interests would give the Committee full information. The future management of railways and the mode of ascertaining and dealing with the value and the consideration to be paid for them should be excluded from the committee's first enquiry. He thought Galt was mistaken to think reforms of the Post Office and the railway systems were likely to arrive at the same results. Moreover he could not see his way to the larger reduction proposed in the scale of charges for passengers and goods. There might be some advantage in uniformity of rates and of course there would be to the public in the reduction of charges but the increase of population and of wealth would increase receipts. He did not think reduction of charges would certainly do so. He added that traffic was of two classes: pleasure and compulsion. The rate on pleasure traffic was set as low it could be on excursion trains, tourist tickets etc. Reduced rates would not tend to increase receipts much on other

[71] BL, Add Ms 44403, Gladstone to Glyn, 23 Sept. 1864.

traffic. No man in the land travelled unless compelled. From the experience of the great contest between the LNWR and GNR he believed if the very low fares charged from Manchester appeared in some degree to make up for the reduction by increased traffic that arose very much from the level of fares at Manchester and to attracting traffic from other railways which had not reduced their fares. On goods no reduction in charges could be sufficient to lower prices. Demand alone will regulate the quantity required. He therefore hesitated to admit the theory propounded by Galt on reduction and the possibility of carrying out his reforms with any immediate chance of remuneration to the Chancellor of the Exchequer for the price to be paid for their supposed advantages.

He did not think Gladstone would find railway proprietors unwilling to sell on equitable terms. The original stock and debenture holders might be easily dealt with, but he doubted whether the preference and guaranteed stockholders would be willing to submit to a reduction of their reward, and this description of stock was now a considerable proportion of the total stock. He concluded that the subject must be thoroughly examined. No one could safely jump to conclusions. The wisdom and experience of working practical men must materially elucidate and forward the enquiry.[72]

Following his correspondence with Glyn Gladstone told Palmerston that he thought the proposals in Galt's book contained materials for a very great and fruitful measure. He had for some time been considering whether a good arrangement might be made with respect to the taxes, including the railway taxes, which might secure a reversion of the railways to the state. Palmerston in a short and terse reply said it was a large question and asked how it was to be done. He added 'Suppose all existing railways could be acquired by the public, how would you deal with railways to be henceforth made; for we may be pretty certain we have not yet come to the *ne plus ultra* in the construction of railways.'[73] Gladstone than revealed to Palmerston that he had sent a rough outline of a scheme to Glyn. 'I think Mr Glyn with his long head thinks well of the subject generally.' He sent Palmerston a copy of his scheme which the Prime Minister regarded on first blush as a wild and more than doubtful project. Palmerston reminded Gladstone that the cost of buying out would be 200 to 300 million. He asked if the railways were let on short term leases would the companies incur the expense of creating the requisite plant for a railway for which they only had a 5 or 7 year lease. Gladstone told him that rolling stock could be hired even now and that the question whether the

[72] Ibid, Glyn to Gladstone, dated only Sept. 1864.

[73] Gladstone to Palmerston, 3 Oct., Palmerston's reply, 28 Oct. 1864 in P. Guedalla, ed., *Gladstone and Palmerston,* 1928, 291–292, 308.

present system would admit of a great reduction with a comparatively small loss and if so under what circumstances was one which has great claims to examination on account of the vast benefits such a railway would offer to the community.[74]

There was some support for radical change. Edward Watkin, who in 1864 had become chairman of the MSLR and MP for Stockport advocated the setting up of a Royal Commission. He suggested John Stuart Mill, Newmarch and Galt with Swift, Clarke and Allport from the railways should be members.[75] They might consider whether four or five systems bound to interchange with each other might be better than 50 or 60 smaller ones, and whether rates might be equalised and in some cases lowered.[76] Comparisons, taken up by the *Economist*, were made with the Post Office before Rowland Hill's reforms. The *Economist* believed it was easy to show that the transfer of railways to the state would be very beneficial if only it could be effected. It would increase their utility and cost to the public, reduce their expenses, and diminish the danger inseparable from travelling.[77] Nevertheless by the end of 1864 Gladstone was noting that management of railways by the state was out of the question. No plan could be adopted which would aggravate the current difficulties of making new railways. Although railway companies existing by Parliamentary and coercive powers, and founded upon exploitation, were not entitled to object to expropriation in principle – and for the great majority of railways this principle was established by the 1844 Act – no plan affecting the proprietary status of railway companies could be carried except with the general approval or good will of the shareholders; nor could any such plan be carried except with the support of a general and impartial public opinion.[78] Indeed he told Lord Stanley that purchase by the state would be impossible. The railways had too much influence. They were becoming a power in the state and the waste of means by delay and diversion of traffic was jntolerable. Control by Parliament or the Board of Trade could be made more stringent with the companies getting tax relief in return.[79]

[74] Gladstone to Palmerston, 19 and 24 Dec., Palmerston's reply 23 Dec. 1864 in Guedalla, 308, 318–319.

[75] Seymour Clarke was general manager of the Great Northern.

[76] TNA, RAIL 1105/305, 25 Jan. 1865.

[77] *Economist*, 7 Jan. 1865, reproduced in *Bagehot's Collected Works*, X, 447–453.

[78] BL, Add Ms 44753, f.187, marked D.64, reproduced in *The Gladstone Diaries*, VI, 1861–68, 320, entry for 19 Dec. 1864.

[79] John Vincent, ed., *Disraeli, Derby and the Conservative Party: journals and memoirs of Edward Henry, Lord Stanley, 1849–1869*, 1978, 229 (entry in Stanley's diary, 18 Mar. 1865).

The impartial opinion was provided by a Royal Commission which was established under the Duke of Devonshire. Glyn was a member, as were Roebuck and Rowland Hill who had been chairman of the South Eastern as well as head of the Post Office, but the criticism that the railway interest managed to pack it is hard to sustain, as other members included Lord Stanley, the Hon E F Leveson Gower, and Robert Lowe, the former Chancellor. The railway witnesses were chief officers rather than chairman and so perhaps even less likely to espouse radical causes. The Commission not surprisingly came out decisively against state purchase. The main arguments were the cost, and the 1844 Act itself which made no provision for railways constructed before 1844 and those subsequently constructed could only be acquired 25 years after their construction so making a very piecemeal approach necessary. Moreover the maximum rate of 10 per cent had become irrelevant as by 1865 railway shares were yielding 4 per cent on average, and the absence of uniform means of accounting meant that the information necessary to make the choice under the Act of 1844 between nationalisation or revision of rates could not equitably be made. Herbert Spencer and others argued that the railways had indulged in reckless branch building and but for these unprofitable extensions with consequent over-capitalisation the railways would still have been able to pay high dividends as many had before the Railway Mania. However while over-expansion certainly led to smaller dividends, railways did not seem to have consciously used this as way of avoiding being caught by the 1844 Act. Rather it was a result of competitive building largely unrestrained by Parliament or Government. When Chadwick defended the principle that the state could and should undertake all the functions on which it could possibly get its hands Stanley commented that more and more people were inclined to take the Continental view of Government, the ultimate result of which was socialism.[80] The Commission's report was something of a damp squib. It went so far as to say it did not consider it expedient, even if practicable, to adopt any legislation which would abolish the freedom which the railways enjoyed of charging what sum they regarded as expedient within the maximum rates. Gladstone seemed to have lost his enthusiasm to make any significant changes and there was not even a debate in Parliament.

This was Glyn's last contribution to the making of public policy. The 1844 Act was a matter where both then and subsequently he had been much more willing than most of his contemporaries in the railway world to contemplate the unorthodox and particularly a bigger role for the state. Some

[80] Ibid, 252, entry for 10 May 1866.

of this was self-interest in that his company had been first in the field and ways of keeping out competitors to consolidate the LNWR's position were to be welcomed. But it went deeper than that in that he did not see the status quo as fixed and was prepared to consider alternatives as his correspondence with Gladstone shows.

Glyn's last formal association with the railway world was with the RCH where he continued as chairman until his death, taking an active interest in its proceedings. He atttended his last committee in September 1872. In the mid-1860s the RCH was losing senior clerks to better paid posts in banks and the junior clerks were granted a rise. When they requested another in 1867 Glyn told Dawson, Morison's successor, that he had 'always thought the pay of the Railway Clearing House low' but he saw little likelihood of the committee agreeing to further increases as they 'now had a most sufficient supply of candidates' following the commercial collapse.[81] In 1872 when the cost of living was rising rapidly the clerks again requested a substantial rise in their salaries. Glyn told Dawson 'the low scale at which they stand demands some immediate increase for all.' Dawson put the case to the companies pointing out that clerks were leaving to enter more lucrative appointments in banks, the civil service and merchants' offices. The result was an improvement in salaries ranging from £5 a year for eighteen to twenty year olds to £100 a year for the four heads of departments.[82]

[81] Glyn to Dawson, 16 Mar. 1867, quoted in Bagwell, 155.
[82] Glyn to Dawson, 8 Sept. 1872, quoted in Bagwell, 156.

CHAPTER EIGHTEEN

Glyn's in the 1860s

THE 1860s WERE A PERIOD of great change in Glyn's Bank. When the decade started George, his elder brother, Sir Richard Plumptre and Charles Mills were all in their sixties and planning the succession was made more difficult by the illnesses of younger members of the two families.

The first change however was an innovation which did not directly affect the partnership, and may have been at least as much a consequence of the merger of the Globe Insurance Company with the Liverpool and London as a spontaneous move by Glyn to strengthen the management of the Bank, though in line with Bagehot's view expressed a decade later that the partners in the great private banks would have to appoint some species of general manager to arrange the detail for them. The want of a good organisation might cause the failure of one or more such banks and cause or intensify a failure.[1] In 1862 William Newmarch, secretary of the Globe since 1851, was brought in as general manager and in Glyn's mind his introduction may have been with a view to his eventually becoming a partner, though not since Henry Parry's death in 1807 had anyone from the staff been promoted to that status. Newmarch was then in his early forties, He was well known to Glyn. He had already established a reputation as a writer on statistical and banking matters and his value to the Globe had been marked by an increase in salary from £700 to £1,000.[2] He started his working life as a clerk in his native Yorkshire. He became second cashier in the bank of Leathem, Tew and Co. at Wakefield. In 1846 when he was 26 he moved to the Agra Bank in London and also started to write on economic questions in the

[1] Walter Bagehot, *Lombard Street*, 1873, 188. George Robins, chief clerk at Coutts from 1860 was made a partner in 1869.

[2] R.A. Ashbee, William Newmarch and Glyn's, *Three Banks Review*, 122, 1979, 49; LMA, CLC B/192/MS 11658/5, 15 Dec. 1853 and 19 Jan. 1854.

Morning Chronicle. In the following year he joined the Statistical Society of London where he had contacts with the leading statisticians and economic commentators. The first paper he read to the Society in 1850 showed that Lord Overstone had offered an opinion on bills of exchange in a paper to a parliamentary bank charter committee that was at variance with the facts. He collaborated with Tooke on volumes 5 and 6 of his History of Prices, covering the economic events of the most recent years. Indeed Tooke made it clear that the bulk of the wide-ranging work was attributable to his zealous and industrious collaborator.

In the 1850s however the Globe was in long term difficulties. There had been a few changes in policy. In 1844 an Act was obtained which enabled the company to transact re-insurance business and to reduce the paid up capital to £50 a share by returning capital to the proprietors, but the latter power was never acted upon.[3] By 1840 more than fifty of the 70 proprietary British life offices were returning at least a third of their profits to policy holders, and the Globe's Chichester agent commented that owing to the assured not participating in the profits he was able to do little business.[4] It was 1850 before the Globe belatedly allowed life policy holders to participate in profits and even then strict instructions were issued to keep such business totally distinct and separate.[5] In 1850 it was found that Walter Watts, employed in the accountants office, had abstracted £70,000 from August 1844 to February 1850, by falsifying the company's pass book on which the accounts relied instead of on the documents relating to the payments. This was not discovered by the auditors and only fully exposed in an investigation by J.E. Coleman, who was asked to look into the nature of the system which had permitted the frauds and to suggest a proper mode of protecting the Office in future. Glyn, still a director of the Globe, attended two meetings of the special committee. The passbook used was of course one of Glyn's, who insisted that it was a true copy of 'our ledgers which we cannot admit to be incorrect'[6] It was following this episode that John Denham the long-serving secretary of the Globe retired and Newmarch was appointed. In 1852 the chairman, J.W. Freshfield, had to address the whole of the establishment on the want of cordiality in the office in view of unfriendly feeling, disputes and differences between the clerks. Six years later the company was challenged by two

[3] Globe Insurance Company Act, 1844.

[4] Alborn, *Regulated Lives*, 177.

[5] Liverpool Record Office, Variation of deed of settlement, 24 Oct.1850, Orders by Directors and the Executive, 1851–55, 28 January 1852.

[6] Ibid, 31, minutes of Special Committee, Glyn's to secretary of Globe Insurance Company, 18 Mar. 1850.

stockholders who in a pamphlet raised four main points – the Watts frauds; the system of audit; the stagnation of business; and the alleged losses on large loans of £97,000 and £54,000 granted respectively to the Harvieston and Cheltenham estates. Newmarch answered these charges but his arguments did not completely undermine the points made against the company. While the Globe's UK fire business had increased from 1851 to 1856, there had been heavy losses in Canada and though there were net profits from the fire, life and reversionary businesses which enabled 5½ per cent to be paid to proprietors, despite Newmarch's assurances of a fair return on the estates, the critics thought the true picture would mean that the Globe's reserve would be consumed and the company left with its original one million capital. In 1858 there were rumours that the Globe would unite with another company, but the negotiations fell through as did an attempt to obtain a bill which would give the company the necessary powers. At this point the company concluded that it was too highly capitalised. If the capital had been about £100,000 or so, comparable to the amount of capital in similar companies, on £15,000 realised profit they could pay £15 per cent which with earnings from capital would make 20 per cent. Consequently the Globe in 1862 accepted overtures from the Liverpool and London. Founded in Liverpool in 1836 it was one of the provincial firms which extended their business across the country, and had established a London branch in 1846. This rapidly growing business was founded upon a very small paid-up capital – only £189,202. Globe shareholders obtained £20 of stock of the joint concern for each £100 share. Investments of £1,000,000 were transferred to five trustees and designated 'The Globe Six per cent Perpetual Annuity Fund'.[7] The new company did however borrow from this source. The proposals, described as far advanced, were put to a meeting of stockholders on 23 October 1862 and finally agreed on 12 December. Parliamentary sanction was obtained in 1864. The board foresaw a great saving in working expenses though all existing arrangements with agents would be carefully maintained.[8] The new company took over the Globe's site at 1 Cornhill, said to be the most valuable plot of land per square foot in existence. Eleven members of the Globe board joined the new company – the London and Liverpool and Globe, as did the Globe's actuary, Augustus Hendriks.[9] It was said that Newmarch was instrumental in organising the amalgamation.[10]

7 Cornelius Walford, *The Insurance Cyclopedia*, 1878, V, 428–431.

8 *Morning Post*, 24 Oct. 1862.

9 J. Simpson Dyer, *Our Centenary Year, The Liverpool & London & Globe Insurance Company Limited*, 1936, 43–44.

10 Ashbee, 51.

Newmarch's move from Cornhill to Lombard Street was a complete break with tradition for Glyn's as until then the clerks had reported directly to the partners, the senior clerk acting in a managerial capacity. However management did not turn out to be Newmarch's forte. Bertram Currie who became a partner in 1864 with the amalgamation of his family bank with Glyn's said in spite of his remarkable abilities he was not fitted for a managerial role. He did however bring his talents to bear in introducing a proper and scientific system of accounts in place of the obsolete and rule of thumb methods which he found in Lombard Street and he also to an extent reformed the discipline and management of the staff. In these ways he was of great service to Glyn's.[11] His reputation however rests on his achievements outside the bank. He founded the Adam Smith Club and was an active member of the Political Economy Club. He wrote for the *Economist.* With David Chadwick, who had been an agent for Globe Insurance, and W.R.Drake, a solicitor with Burchills, he was active in pressing for reforms in company law and gave evidence to the Select Committee on the Limited Liability Acts in 1867. These connections brought some business to Glyn's. When Palmer's Shipbuilding and Iron was converted to a joint stock company by Chadwick, a significant number of shareholders seem to have come into the company through Glyn's. Newmarch, who was one of the three initial purchasers, himself took 100 shares, as did Charles Mills, and Bertram and Raikes Currie. L.M. Rate, a stockbroker often associated with Glyn's, became chairman.[12]

Unusually for one who worked in the City Newmarch was a Fellow of the Royal Society, and secretary of the Statistical Society serving a term as President in succession to Gladstone in 1869–71. He provoked controversy with his published work, particularly as he shared Tooke's view that the emphasis on currency, as opposed to credit, was totally misguided and that the level of currency in circulation was determined by the level of prices and incomes, rather than vice versa. But he never became a partner in Glyn's, and the important letters did not go out under his signature. He remained an office and personnel manager rather than a general manager, though he was not popular with the staff and it seems that some of the junior staff regarded him as something of a figure of fun. Unkind stories about him circulated in the bank long after he was dead.[13] He continued as manager of the bank until he had a stroke in 1881 and died the following year.

[11] Bertram Wodehouse Currie, *Recollections, Letters and Journals*, 1901, I, 96–97.

[12] P.L. Cottrell, *Industrial Finance, 1830–1914, the Finance and Organisation of English Manufacturing Industry,* 1980, 127; TNA, BT 31/31744/2298. Rate was later a director of the Imperial Ottoman and Romanian Banks.

[13] Ashbee, 57–58.

Several of the major changes in the Bank in the 1860s related to the Glyn family. First Sir Richard Plumptre Glyn, George's older brother and senior partner since the death of Thomas Hallifax senior in 1850, died in 1863. A bachelor, he was perhaps more a Georgian, than a Victorian figure. Indeed he had been one of the Gentlemen of the Chamber to George III and had appeared at George IV's coronation in Elizabethan costume. He was a member of the Athenaeum, United University and Carlton clubs. He spent much of his time at Gaunts, where St Kenelm's at Hinton Parva was completely rebuilt at his expense in 1860. He took down the old church and replaced it with what is considered to be a fairly typical estate church. Built of stone in the neo-Romanesque style, it retains the Norman chancel arch and consists of chancel, nave, transepts, south porch supporting a spire and a tower. Richard preferred to travel to Gaunts by carriage rather than by rail which would have taken him in greater comfort and speed to Wimborne. Whether this was because, like Lady Suffield, who always drove from Blakeney to London, he preferred it to rubbing shoulders with people in trains is not clear.[14] The two earlier historians of Glyn's are agreed on his limited contribution to the affairs of the family bank. Browne claims that he took little or no part in the management of the bank though an attender in Lombard Street with considerable regularity. Fulford stated that in the archives of the bank little trace of him survives, and outside the bank he had little impact on the business life of the City, except that he was a director of the almost defunct South Sea company. He made many charitable donations, including large ones to the City of London Church Extension Scheme and to the Society for the Propagation of the Gospel. He left effects originally sworn at under £500,000 but resworn in 1865 at under £400,000.[15]

By the time of Richard Plumptre's death both St Leger Glyn and Edward Mills were in ill health. In 1862 Mills suffered from an attack, probably a heart attack. Tom Baring told G.G. Glyn that he was grieved to have his account of Edward Mills and asked whether there was any prospect of his moving southwards and W.D. Denison of the Leeds Old Bank hoped that St Leger was 'in a less unfavourable condition than we lately heard he was'.[16]

Clearly they could not be expected to play major roles in the bank in future and that may have been one factor in the next development at

[14] F.M.L. Thompson, *English Landed Society in the Nineteenth Century*, 1963, 259–260.

[15] Eric Gore Browne, *The History of Glyn Mills and Co.*, 1935, 17; Fulford, 175–178, for a list of his charitable donations in a sample year, 1861.

[16] RBS Archives, GM/99, letter of 20 Sept. and GM/429/30, letter of 11 Sept. 1862.

Glyn's. Although Glyn's had taken over Ladbroke and Co, in 1841, despite its increased business and high reputation, there had been no other attempt to enlarge the firm by amalgamation. In 1864 an opportunity presented itself and was rapidly seized when Curries, a long-established private bank in Cornhill were looking for a partner. Curries dated from 1773, and had been largely run by Isaac Currie, son of the founder for over half a century until his death in the 1840s. Succeeded by his son, Raikes Currie, who was a radical member of Parliament (MP for Northampton, 1837–57, though he failed to secure the City of London in 1857) and as his son, Bertram Wodehouse Currie put it 'had quickness, vivacity, and a considerable command of rhetoric, but these were not the qualities which made the ideal banker.'[17] Bertram did have the requisite qualities and soon became the effective power at the family bank. He urged with success upon his partners the policy of saving money and of creating a reserve, but considered that the joint stock banks were growing while Curries stood still and that the race went, if not always, at least generally, to the strong. They spoke to a number of banks – Fuller & Co., Prescott Grote & Co., Jones Loyd, Cunliffes & Co.and Robarts, Lubbock.[18] In the winter of 1862–63 Raikes Currie had approached W.D Prescott about a merger but it seems that the proposal lapsed due to difficulties over premises and a reluctance on Prescott's part to press his partners from whom he feared he might receive 'unremovable personal objections'.[19] In April 1864 Jones Loyd went not to Curries but was bought by the London and Westminster largely because of the reluctance of the younger members of the Loyd family to carry on as bankers. The sale was thought by the *Daily Telegraph* to be a big confession that the era of private firms had passed.[20] Support for this view was strengthened by other mergers between private banks in the early 1860s: Sir John William Lubbock, Forster & Co. with Robarts Curtis & Co in 1860 and Barclay, Bevan, Tritton & Co with Spooner Attwoods & Co in 1863 and then in 1864 Hanbury, Taylor and Lloyd with Barnett, Hoare as the latter needed larger premises. The diminishing share of the private banks can be seen from Collins' estimate that there was a much lower growth in private bank liabilities at 2.2 per cent per annum from 1844 to 1880 compared with 5.9 per cent in those of joint stock banks, despite an increase from £56 million to £111 million on the part of the private banks.

[17] Currie, *Recollections*, 1, 19.

[18] Ibid, 1, 52.

[19] RBS Archives, GM/1116, particularly the letter from W.G. Prescott to Raikes Currie, 28 Nov. 1862.

[20] Quoted in Gregory, 1936, 1, 283.

Glyn's growth rate from 1844 to George Carr Glyn's death was nearly 8 per cent per annum.[21]

In May 1864 talks began between Bertram Currie and Sir John Lubbock, of Robarts, Lubbock and Co. Currie went to Lubbock' s country house and thought they had come to an understanding but the younger members of the firm, who had not been consulted, protested and so the talks were broken off.[22] Charles Mills heard of the breakdown and an approach was made to Currie. Agreement in principle was rapidly reached. This was embodied in a partnership agreement dated 17 June 1864 between Carr Glyn, Charles Mills and Raikes and Bertram Currie. It became effective on 1 July 1864 when the firm's title became Glyn, Mills, Currie & Co.[23] The public announcement issued by Curries on 21 June simply stated that 'it was a pleasure to announce that we have made arrangements for uniting our business with that of our friends and neighbours, Glyn, Mills & Co.'[24]

This was virtually a take-over by the Glyn's and Mills families though such a view ignores the leading role played by Bertrtam Currie in the future despite his family having only a minority share. Henry and George Currie, the other two partners in Currie & Co. agreed to retire, as did E.W. Mills and St Leger Glyn. Mills also retired from his directorship of the GWR and died in 1865.[25] St Leger died in 1873, a few months before his father, aged only 37. All Currie's staff including Lawford, the head clerk, were transferred to the combined business.

Following Robert R Benson's death in 1846, the capital he inherited enabled Robert Benson junior to extricate himself from his Manchester cotton interests and, while retaining interests in Liverpool, to start in 1852 a London bank, Robert Benson & Co. He knew Glyn particularly through Moorsom whose daughter, Eleanor, he had married. As Glyn wanted his son Pascoe to acquire banking experience. Pascoe joined Bensons as the junior partner.[26] When St Leger resigned Pascoe became a partner in Glyn's. He told his father:

[21] Michael Collins, Long-term Growth of the English Banking Sector and Money Stock, 1844–80, *EcHR*, 36, 1983, 381. Collins points out that his estimates, particularly for private banks are speculative. The figures can only be taken as a rough guide to trends.

[22] Currie, *Recollections*, 1, 52.

[23] RBS Archives, GM/978.

[24] Ibid, GM/881/2.

[25] Mills left a daughter but no sons to follow him into the bank. He left personalty sworn at less than £250,000. (*The Times*, 16 Dec. 1865.)

[26] Wake, 61 and 91.

> I cannot sufficiently thank you for having brought about what is to me the *summum bonum* of my mercantile life. I am very sorry to leave Benson, ... but to be associated with you and George in such a position ... is the summit of my ambition. I only hope I shall prove worthy of my place, and by degrees become a really useful working member of the firm, and a good helpmate for George.[27]

George Grenfell, MP for Shaftesbury since 1857 was spending more time in politics, though up to 1866 he gave fairly regular attention to the business. Currie thought that he had the greatest respect for his father and it was to please him that he remained so long a worker in Lombard Street. Currie thought him lively, quick and intelligent and able to inspire personal regard, a valuable attribute for a banker but too fond of change and excitement to be content with the daily round and common task of City life. It was George who took the lead in Glyn's ventures in Europe described in Chapter 15.

Each of the two new partners from Curries brought £75,000 in consols for the use of the partnership as occasion might require. The books were not to be balanced at the end of June – Glyn's practice of end-year balance was to be to be followed, but Curries were paid £12,000 in lieu. Raikes Currie and Bertram became partners but the tradition of the family bank was preserved in the new partnership agreement. The Curries had a fifth share in the business, with the Glyns and Mills retaining two-fifths each. It was made clear that these portions belonged to the families and each of them could divide their portion in any way they wished. The heads of each family were not compelled to attend to the business beyond what might be suitable to their own convenience – in effect a form of pension arrangement for George Carr Glyn (67), Sir Charles Mills (72) and Raikes Currie (64). Whoever might first have begun the process which led to the amalgamation, the Glyns wished to strengthen the business for the future by taking in Bertram Currie. Currie however, according to Mills had some objection to the partnership deed not on his own account but thought that Mills had the best of it as to his son's succession. Mills did not see that Currie was affected by the arrangements between 'our two families.' He could never consent to rearrange on the death of any or every partner. Glyn told him that in principle the plan was good. He had one object – to avoid the chance of creating jealousy or differences between the younger men when they were gone. Mills replied that would certainly resist any attempt to diminish 'in my

[27] Quoted in Fulford, 178.

time or my sons the 4/10 share in the business to which we are indefinitely entitled'. If his son wanted to give anything to a banking partner it should be done in the shape of a money payment, not by relinquishing shares. He then went on, rather strangely more than a year after the promulgation of the partnership, to say he was surprised and hurt that Glyn had conferred with Currie on partnership matters without saying a word to him or his son. It would be a relief for him to know 'whether before our junction with Curries Glyn had a conversation with a partner in Huth's House as to disposing or jointstocking our concern.' Tom Dent (Dent, Palmer & Co.) had alluded to it. He ended 'implicit confidence between partners is most desirable in our great and prosperous concern. Excuse anything in the strong expression of feelings at my age.' Glyn's reply must have satisfied him because Mills wrote again the following day to say the division into families had worked well. 'We have during our lives never had any dispute or jealousy. I feel I derive benefit from your increasing wealth and the more you have the better.' This amicable exchange did not end the correspondence, because Glyn told him in December that the discussions were very annoying and he would be glad to receive from him any proposal which was likely to bring them to a close, but to let him have it in writing.[28]

However, Glyn, Mills and Currie remained a private bank, and despite the purchase of Jones Loyd, the London private banks, of which there were still 44 in 1873, retained their predominance as deposit holders over the joint stock banks until the boom of the early 1870s in contrast to the position with the country banks.[29] However their two worlds were closer. In 1863 after applications for membership from individual joint stock banks, the London Clearing House agreed that joint stock banks should be admitted. The following year the Bank of England became a member.[30]

The major financial crisis in the City in the 1860s was the failure of Overend, Gurney & Co. in 1866. John Overend and Thomas Richardson had joined forces and embarked on a new type of bill-broking whereby instead of charging commission to the provider of the capital they charged it to the party whose bill was discounted. Overend had strong connections with Gurney's bank in Norwich, and Samuel Gurney from the Norwich bank became a partner in what was then designated as Overend, Gurney & Co, with premises next door to Glyn's. The business was very successful

28 RBS Archives, GM/263, letters of 8 and 9 Sept. and 18 Dec. 1865.

29 Philip L. Cottrell, London's First 'Big Bang'? Institutional Change on the City, in *The World of Private Banking*, ed. Youssef Cassis, Philip Cottrell, Monika P. Fraser and Iain L. Fraser, 2009, 84.

30 LMA, CLC B/192/MS 32006/002, 24 Aug. 1863, 14 and 30 Mar. 1864.

in attracting funds particularly from country bankers. There was nothing unusual in this. It was normal banking practice to put surplus funds out to bill-brokers, either at call, short notice or a fixed date. A number of the country banks for whom Glyn's acted as country agents gave a general instruction to transfer funds surplus balances to Overends. In the case of the Union Bank of Scotland the limit was £100,000.[31] In 1853 Glyn's placed £50,000 from the Grand Trunk with Overends at 7 days notice at 2½ per cent.[32] In the late 1850s Overend Gurney's reputation as a top class firm was under a question mark. Samuel Gurney died in 1856. Much of the firm's reputation had been founded on his personal judgment of the bills discounted. Without him the firm made badly advised investments and tied up its assets too rapidly in the paper issued by the new contracting companies. Hammond & Co. were telling Glyn's, who had introduced them to Overends, as early as 1855 that as trustees of public money they thought that their friends Overend, Gurney & Co. had of late figured before the world

> in a different character from what we had been led to expect by mixing themselves up with speculative transactions, and which in other minds as well as ours where parties have deposited money with them must lead to disquiet. They were particularly concerned that they had no collateral security in the shape of bills – as was the case when their early connection was formed.

They asked Glyn's whether at some fitting opportunity they should request a return to the old system. Glyn's seem to advised them to make such a request or turn to another house because Hammond & Co thanked them and said they had successfully asked Overends on the basis that Overends would place securities in their account at Glyn's.[33] In 1857 when bill brokers experienced a severe drain on their resources, Glyn advised the Union Bank of Scotland,

> I cannot but help stating to you confidentially that I do not think you should employ these funds as you appear to think of doing. It is impossible at this time to say what course the Bank of England may take with regard to the operations of the bill brokers, and this source being

[31] Glyn's and the Overend Gurney Crisis, *Three Banks Review*, 72, 1966, 48, letter from Union Bank to Glyn's, 20 Jul. 1855.

[32] RBS Archives, GM/4/2, letter to William Chapman, 17 May 1853.

[33] Ibid, 48–50, Hammonds to Glyn's, 23 Jun. and 3 Jul. 1855.

closed to them, the repayment of such large sums becomes a matter of consideration.

He went on to offer to do his best for them to place the money. Glyn's could get a very sufficient rate for them in quarters in which no doubt of immediate repayment would arise.[34]

In March 1858 the York Union Bank asked Glyn's in confidence their opinion of Overend Gurney: 'Are they still after Mr Chapman has gone out considered as undoubted?'[35] In the same month the Bank of England made it clear that it would no longer offer discount facilities to bill brokers, in part because they were competing with the Bank. Overends tried to get this ruling changed, but failed. Overends with some allies then withdrew a large number of notes from the Bank with a view to reducing the Bank's reserve to the lowest possible amount. The Governor was told that if the rule excluding the discount houses were modified the notes withdrawn would be returned that night. The Bank refused to give in and two days later the notes were returned, but Overends made few friends over this episode and one important enemy – the Bank of England.

In 1861 there were false rumours that Overends had stopped payment. The Governor of the Bank, Dobree, wrote that the house had suffered heavy losses during the last 18 months. It was rather a reckless business but the profits were commensurate, and the capital was ample enough to meet any contingency.[36]

Glyn's did not abandon the practice of placing money with bill-brokers under their guarantee but only did so to a limited extent. By 1862 Glyn's had adopted the principle of opening interest paying deposit accounts, up to then a practice largely confined to joint-stock banks in London, though no publicity was given to it. W.B. Denison of the Leeds Old Bank, when he requested a transfer to their deposit account of £20,000, said they supposed that the interest allowed on the account would be 1 per cent under the bank rate.[37] In other respects there seems to have been little change in banking practices from earlier in the century. Gilbart in his *History and Principles of Banking* published in 1866 said that a country banker paid his London agent by a balance, by a commission or an annual fixed amount. The balance was an agreed sum on which no interest was paid. If he kept less than the stipulated amount he was charged interest for the deficiency; if more he was

[34] Glyn's and the Overend Gurney Crisis, 50–1, 5 Nov. 1857.

[35] RBS Archives, GM/429/67, 5 Jan. 1858.

[36] Quoted in Kynaston, 238.

[37] Ibid, GM/429/30, 2 Jan. 1862.

usually allowed interest. Examples from Glyn's in the 1860s fit this pattern. Glyn's continued to pay interest on cash balances on various formulae – the Birmingham Banking Company was given 1 per cent under bank rate for a balance of over £6,000, and Gillett Brothers of Banbury had to maintain the same balance to attract interest. Bower and Co. of Beverley and Malton paid a commission of £400 but had a cash balance of only £3,000.[38] This did not prevent changes though it might be hard to effect them as the correspondence with the Leeds Old Bank shows. Glyn's seem to have wanted to charge a higher annual fee as the traffic through their account had greatly increased. Denison was incensed and wrote to 'My Dear Glyn' arguing that the arrangement which Glyn's had suggested had worked for many years with mutual satisfaction He was particularly anxious that there should be no disturbance of it as long as his uncle continued to take an interest. He pointed out that they always kept a cash balance of £20,000 with Glyn's but the daily average over the last three years had been £30,000. In the following year Beckett raised the matter again when he was in London. Glyn suggested a fixed payment of £1.250, an increase of £250, instead of their maintaining a minimum balance, but Denison decided the change was not worthwhile. In March they had opened a loan account with Glyn's, asking that £40,000 be transferred from it to their general account next day. They would probably require the money for about a fortnight.[39]

An indication of the size of the daily transactions can also be gained from the correspondence with the manager of Bank of Liverpool, who asked for £40,000 to be transferred to his bank for the payment of LNWR dividends and six days later wrote to Glyn personally to say that he saw he would be 'over with you tomorrow £45,000, of which £20,000 will be absorbed on Friday and I shall again be over on Saturday some £40 to 50,000, the greater part of which I shall require in London on Monday.' Later that year he opened an interest account for £5,000.[40]

In 1863, perhaps on account of the impact of the American Civil War, Glyn's made a number of enquiries as to the soundness of Liverpool firms. While Finlay and Lance were deemed to be respectable cotton brokers and likely to be worth what they put their names to, other brokers were thought 'speculative'. Messrs Edward Lawrence was a more complex case. The bank of Liverpool had the personal assurance of Mr Edward Lawrence that the firm was now well off and the general opinion was that the firm had made

[38] Pressnell, 415.

[39] RBS Archives, GM/429/30, 8 Jan. 1862, 27 Mar., 11 Aug., 4 and 8 Oct. 1863.

[40] Ibid, GM/429/31, 20 and 26 Feb., 3 and 5 May 1862.

money, but in the bank's experience they were always inclined to be on a large scale and too fond of a little extra risk.[41]

By late 1865 Bertram Currie was similarly cautious about Overends on the ground that he heard that Rocca brothers, an Italian client of his, had been offered a banking commission by Overends if he would consent to accept the bills of their nominees. He thought this could only mean that all Overend's resources were locked up. At about the same time Edward Gurney wanted to borrow money from Glyn's at a special rate on securities which seemed to Currie to be of doubtful value. Currie remembered Gurney's indignation when he threw some doubt upon them. Gurney said 'Do you presume to question the credit of Overend Gurney & Co.?'[42] Currie said that some months before the event he predicted the catastrophe to Charles Mills who admitted that heavy losses had been incurred and that the management of the business was defective but put his faith on the great wealth of J.H. Gurney and the other partners in the Norwich Bank, all of whom were liable to the full extent of their fortunes.[43]

In August 1865 however Overends became a limited liability company. The general public rushed to buy shares but the City saw the move as designed to make a fresh start and salvage the sounder part of the business. The *Economist* commented that at last the public would learn the proportion which the firm's extra business bore to its legitimate bill dealing business. At first the new company seemed to be prospering. The shares went to a premium of 10 in October 1865, but by the following May the firm had failed. Its over-ambition and extension into new types of activities became enmeshed in a more general financial crisis, a bonfire which Overends themselves had helped to light.

The main stimulus to the boom which culminated in this crash was domestic rather than overseas, the principal dynamic being provided by railway construction, which rose from £8.25 million in 1859 to £212.23 million in 1865, or 29 per cent of domestic capital formation. Another factor in the boom was the growth of new banks, corporate discount houses and finance companies. The 1856 and 1862 acts which provided for limited liability included model articles of association, and provisions for proper accounts, balance sheets and annual general meetings, but this code was not compulsory. The boom in company promotions revealed many defects in the new legislation. In the autumn of 1865, Smith Knight & Co, railway contractors, failed. Such contractors depended on bill finance which came

41 Ibid, 29 Jul. and 5 Dec. 1863.

42 Currie, I, 61.

43 Currie, I, 60.

mainly from the finance companies and some of the new banks. The new sources dried up in late 1865 and early 1866 as lenders were unable or unwilling to maintain liquidity. From October 1865 the Bank did little discounting itself and restored its reserves, so squeezing credit facilities generally. In the first four months of 1866 there were several failures, including Watson and Overend which had no connection with Overend and Gurney but the coincidence of name was sufficient to add to the pressure on the latter. Pinto, Perez & Co. Spanish merchants to which Overends were heavily committed also failed. There was a run on Overend's shares. The Bank, when appealed to, refused assistance on the ground that they could not help a particular business at a time of general difficulty, but the goodwill Overends had lost in 1861 must have been a factor. George Grenfell Glyn, rather than his father was called in with R.C.L. Bevan, of Barclays and J. Kirkman Hodgson, now of Barings, but they could not suggest any means of shoring up the business.[44] At 3.30 pm on Thursday 10 May Overend & Gurney stopped payment, with liabilities of £24,000,000 against a nominal capital of £5,000,000. This had an immediate and wide impact, not least on the railway world as Overends held a considerable book of contractors bills and railway securities. Peto and Betts and two financial firms which had been financing Peto also failed. Peto was an old friend and client of Glyn's but his transactions with the London, Chatham and Dover Railway led to his downfall in 1866. The LCDR could not meet its obligations when three blocks of debentures fell for repayment. The railway's difficulties led to losses by Glyn's. In 1868 their holding of various LCDR securities was written down from £215,200 to £46,000. Credit Financiere of England held £820,975 in illiquid assets of the LCDR.[45]

Brassey too was stretched for money and on Black Friday, accompanied by Edward Blount, he called on Glyn's. He asked them to advance him a certain sum, and after much consideration they gave him £30,000 'but old Mr Glyn said he must have "some stuff" in exchange'. They returned to Brassey's office in Great George Street and filled a box with securities which they took back to Glyn. He would not even open it but told a clerk to put it in the safe. Glyn wanted Brassey to promise he would not give all his money away to his friends. Brassey demurred and on leaving Glyn's office asked Blount whether he wanted any money. He said he did not but on the steps they met a 'gentleman whom we knew well who was in a less happy condition, and in spite of my protest Mr Brassey presented him with £10,000.'[46]

[44] Fulford, 190.

[45] RBS Archives, GM/1361, Cottrell, *Investment Banking in England, II,* 447.

[46] *Memoirs of Sir Edward Blount,* ed. Stuart J. Reid, 1902, 96–97. It is not clear why Brassey

Glyn wrote to the Bank of Liverpool

> The Great Crack, the failure of Overend, Gurney and Company, will cause an immense amount of excitement and confusion which has never yet been seen. Others must soon follow, and I fear that some of the new London Banks will be shaken. ... The day has been one of the wildest excitement. There has been a run on several of the banks. The crowd outside in the streets was most extraordinary.[47]

The banks on the whole met customers who called for balances or deposits quickly. The Bank's reserves were run down from £5½ to about £3 million and Gladstone sent a letter enabling the Bank to disregard, if necessary, the limitations of the Bank Charter Act. Bank Rate was raised to 10 per cent. Overend's creditors were paid in full – the shareholders lost heavily.

Money was so tight that the London & Westminster insisted that the SER repay £80,000 due the following day and threatened to sell the stock held on security. Watkin, the chairman, was told by Cazenoves that they could not raise any money for a railway company on any terms whatsoever. Sir David Salomons, chairman of the LWB, whom Watkin met in the House of Commons, supported his staff. George Carr Glyn was unavailable but Watkin saw George Grenfell and told him 'I think you owe me something for the Grand Trunk affair'. Glyn sent a clerk to the London and Westminster and repaid the loan on the basis that Glyn's would have half the South Eastern railways business. The Great Western was another over-extended company, largely as a result of its purchases of other companies, including the West Midland, earlier in the decade. In 1865 its dividend was only 2 per cent. In September 1866 there were rumours that the company would not be able to meet its extensive debenture obligations and early in 1867 the GWR applied unsuccessfully for a loan from the Bank of England.[48]

One other effect of the collapse of Overend Gurney was the complete breakdown of negotiations for a merger with a number of Scottish banks. By the 1860s the Scottish banks considered that the extensive business of Scottish trade and industry necessitated that they opened offices in London,

borrowed £30,000 or gave £10,000 away so quickly even given his well known generosity which Blount emphasises. Brassey was one of the promoters of the Paris bank, Edward Blount & Co. RBS Archives, GM/139, records an agreement to lend Brassey £24,313 on the certificates of £4,000 Cannock Mineral shares on 14 June 1866.

47 Quoted in Chandler, I, 290.

48 Hodgkins, 286–287.

particularly because of the importance of Empire trade and bills on London. In 1863 the general managers of the Scottish banks decided that in future their banks would automatically follow the Bank of England's minimum discount rate. Scottish businessmen were keen that their banks should have facilities in London. In general the Scottish banks were inhibited by legal uncertainties as to the possibility of their operating in London, but the National Bank did open a London office in 1864, having received favourable legal advice. In 1866 a group of four Scottish banks – the Union Bank of Scotland, the Clydesdale, the Bank of Scotland and the British Linen Bank approached Glyn's with a view to owning jointly a new London bank, initially called the London and Scottish Banking Association. The Associated Scotch Bank of London, as it was later called, would operate the new bank under the Companies Act of 1862. It is not clear why they chose Glyn's as a partner. It has been suggested that Glyn's help to the Union Bank of Scotland in the 1857 crisis when they proved valuable intermediaries with the Bank of England and provided £200,000 from their own resources was a factor.[49] The subscribed capital was agreed at not less than £2,500,000 with £500,000 paid up, and stock was to be held in equal shares and held for a minimum period of five years. The Scots main aim was to have a presence in the City which would obviate having to rely on agency arrangements.[50]

Charles Mills whatever he may have thought about the arrangement with Curries took a more fundamental stance when it came to the possibility of merging with several Scottish banks to form a joint-stock bank which would include Glyn's. He told Glyn that he differed from him on private banking. 'Our business is better than ever – it is admirably managed. We have got rid of nearly all our anxieties, have paid for our experience, and shall now reap the benefits.' He could not be a party to any negotiation to joint stock. Glyn told him that the discussions were forced on them by the state of the times, and the new aspects of banking in particular. His considered that, although their position might be retained for a time, eventually private banking must give way, and therefore it was not wise for them as a matter of feeling to disregard an offer from such quarter. They would make an arrangement in London somewhere. He had feelings tending towards those of Mills, but also felt that for the advantage of all such an offer should be considered. The next day Charles Mills wrote to his son to say that although he could not consent to joint stock, if the parties and partners were willing to buy him out for a large sum he might be prepared to go. He fancied the business

[49] Richard Saville, *Bank of Scotland: A History, 1695–1995*, 1996, 413 and 501.

[50] Ibid, 366 and 412–413.

would be worth a million. He would be prepared to take £200,000, half the Mills share.[51]

Negotiations reached the stage where the Mills family were prepared to sell their share for £400,000 with 1st July agreed as the effective date. Charles Gairdner, Joint General Manager of the Union Bank, and Bertram Currie were to be the joint general managers. The Scottish banks however, who were in any case wary of unlimited liability, beat a hasty retreat following the collapse of Overend Gurney on 10 May. A. Dennison of the Bank of Scotland wrote to Bertram Currie on 14 May to say that when they parted the previous Wednesday there were no expectations of so rapid a convulsion in the money market. He therefore concluded that it would be necessary to suspend the proceedings for some time to come. He did not doubt that it would be Currie's opinion too. He added that 'limited liability was now utterly out of the question and if the other principle could not be adopted it would be advisable to abandon or indefinitely postpone the whole scheme'.[52]

Currie was clearly annoyed and replied next day to say that it required consideration and he would wait a few days until Dennison had had time to reflect on its contents before expressing any opinion. He added that if by convulsions of the money market he meant the stoppage of Overend Gurney, this was not a surprise for him. He had thought it could not be delayed beyond the present year. He was not prepared 'for the terror which it occasioned among the unreasoning multitude but he could see nothing in that event or in the collapse of other unsound companies to affect well managed banks.'[53] Although Glyn's had been pressed hard by their 'country friends' they had not felt any inconvenience or applied to the Bank of England or even taken in money on their Consols which they held in reserve for an emergency like this. He added 'of high priced "finance" paper we have always had a salutary dread.'[54] However cogent this appeal, time did not heal and the Scottish banks did not overcome their caution. The plan was abandoned and the Bank of Scotland set up its own office in London in 1867, but because of legal difficulties the Royal Bank only succeeded in 1874.

51 RBS Archives, GM/263, letters of 22 and 23 Feb. 1866, reproduced at Fulford, 195 and 196.

52 Currie, 1, 52 and Glyn's and the Overend Gurney Crisis, 57–58.

53 The *Economist* made a similar point. 'It has been signally shown how much an old name, which all really instructed people knew had lost its virtue, still retains its magical potency over the multitude', 12 May 1866.

54 Glyn's and the Overend Gurney Crisis, 57–58.

Currie wrote later that a powerful combination would no doubt have been created which might in time have absorbed both Glyn's and Curries, 'but my excellent partners, C. and A. Mills, have no cause for regrets that they still preserve their inheritance, and I will rejoice that my son is able to follow the path which has been trod by five successive generations of his family.'[55] Charles Mills, the spectre of limited liability having disappeared, continued as a partner until his death in 1872, and his son Charles Henry, who became Lord Hillingdon in 1886 was a partner until his death in 1898.

Glyn's did however benefit from the fall of Overend Gurney in one major aspect. Following the merger with Curries, 19 Cornhill, Curries' office for many years was sold for £40,000 in 1865.[56] In the following year before the expected merger with the Scottish banks and in the expectation of a growth of business they acquired Garroways Coffee House in Change Alley which ran behind Lombard Street. This longstanding city institution, famous as a sandwich and drinking spot, with wine in the day and coffee or punch at night, where bargains were concluded with champagne, with a sale room upstairs, was the first coffee house to open in the morning and the last to close at night.[57] This proved a short-term move as Overend's premises were next to Glyn's building at 67, Lombard Street fronting onto Birchin Lane but including the Corner House on Lombard Street. They came on the market and Glyn's were able to purchase for £29,000 both the Corner House and the adjoining premises in Birchin Lane.[58]

Carr Glyn had to resolve a major problem in the finances of the family and the bank following the death of his elder brother, Richard Plumptre. A reserve fund had been set up at the end of 1862 to cover not only losses arising from the Grand Trunk, but also from the Chicago & Detroit Railway and the Wolverhampton Bank. The reserve then stood at £263,485 but as there was some doubt whether this would cover contingencies the partners agreed that for any deficiency that might ultimately arise, their estates were severally liable in the proportions of their present shares in the partnership.[59] The agreement was quickly tested as Sir Richard died on 20 December 1863. By December 1864 a further sum of £130,000 was needed for the reserve. The partnership with Curries meant that it had to be cleared. To avoid dividing

[55] Currie, 1, 62. Charles and Algernon were the sons of Charles Henry Mills, the first Lord Hillingdon.

[56] *Westmorland Gazette*, 13 May 1865.

[57] D.M. Evans, *City Men and City Manners, or The Physiology of London Business*, 1852, 145–146, 167.

[58] Glyn's and the Overend Gurney Crisis, 59.

[59] RBS Archives, GM/1365, Memorandum signed by the seven partners, 7 Apr. 1863.

his brother's estate to meet the liability Glyn took the whole of the liability of the Glyn family, amounting to £172,620 upon himself. He met this by pledging £140,000 in Consols to the family bank and paying the balance in cash. In return he received Canadian Railway securities with a nominal value of £182,250.[60] He proceeded to discharge this debt in instalments, two in 1867 amounting to £50,000, four in 1868 totalling £65,000 and two in January and February 1869 amounting to £35,000.[61] A member of the Glyn family wrote to Charles Mills to thank the administrators of the estate for their liberality. Mills wrote back to say that he had to thank them for nothing as it was George Carr Glyn's act and for his part he thought it as very needless piece of feeling on Glyn's part. But as Glyn explained to Currie he took it upon himself to free the property for distribution. He did not expect the blow to fall so soon upon him. He had just contracted to buy more land in Dorset, so he got rid of that contract and Lord Normanton stepped into his place. He told Currie that it was a great relief to have discharged the liability and only fair to do so as soon as he could.[62]

By 1873 Glyn was in the process of purchasing two estates at Stour in Dorset, close to Fontmell Magna, where his brother had been lord of the manor and Glyn was now patron of the living, but this time his own death intervened. Glyn never became one of the bankers with a very considerable estate like Thomas Baring with 8,000 acres in Hampshire yielding £6,449 income a year, or Osgood Hanbury whose estates in Essex and Suffolk brought in £5,118 annually, but in the year of his death he was recorded as holding 353 acres in Dorset with an estimated rental of £622, and in Middlesex 356 acres with a rental of £1,506. In comparison his nephew Richard George who had succeeded the bachelor Richard Plumptre at Gaunts had 8,868 acres in Dorset and a rental of £12,403.[63]

Glyn's assets and liabilities which averaged £5.4 million from 1857 to 1861 rose sharply in consecutive years in 1862 and 1863. In 1862 town balances increased by a third and in 1863 deposits increased threefold to

60 Anon, Glyn's and the Grand Trunk Railway, *The Three Banks Review*, 52, 1961, 39; RBS Archives, GM/1380/4 and 881/2.

61 RBS Archives, GM/881/2, Acknowledgement by George Carr Glyn that £140,000 Consols standing in his name were the property of the bank. The repayments were subsequently noted and dated on the document.

62 Ibid, letter of 11 Feb. 1869. James Agar, 3rd Earl of Normanton, resided at Somerly, Hants. In 1873 he had 20,000 acres in Wilts, Hants and Dorset.

63 W.D. Rubenstein, Businessmen into Landowner: the question revisited, in *Land and Society in Britain, 1700–1914, Essays in Honour of F.M.L. Thompson*, ed. Negley Harte and Roland Quinault, 1996, 110; TNA, IR 26/5442 f 447; John Bateman, *The Great Landowners of England and Wales*, 1879, 471.

£1,744,000. On the other side investments rose to nearly £1,000,000 and bills discounted to £4,012,000. The total therefore reached £7,638,000 in the last year before the merger with Curries,

The number of country banks for whom Glyn's acted was unchanged at 55 in 1860.[64] Curries brought in three banks but more generally the merger with Curries had led to a large but not enormous rise in business. In 1865, the first full year led to a 12 per cent increase, but this was unsurprisingly not sustained in 1866. 1867 and 1868 were back to the 1865 level and in 1869 assets and liabilities increased from £8,876,000 to £10,460,000. By 1871 it was £13,780,000 and only slightly lower the following year. The ratio of cash to liabilities which had averaged 12.3 in the decade 1850–59 dropped to 8.0 from 1860–69 and by 1869 was only 5.5. Deposit accounts increased considerably in the 1860s, but over the decade only amounted to 17 per cent of deposits compared with 36 per cent in the Collins sample.[65] There was a steep rise in railway current accounts from £530,000 in 1866 to £4,060,000 in 1872. This was in a period when exceptionally the net working receipts of all British railways rose by over a third from £18,500,000 to £25,800,000. Town balances reached £5,500,000. The railways were also overdrawn to the extent of £2,460,000 in 1871 and £3,260,000 in 1872, though this was a short-lived phenomenon as the total was down to £240,000 in 1873.

In 1868 the bank's investments totalled £1,159,000. £100,000 was accounted for by premises with a further £30,000 for the Change Alley freehold. However much of the rest, though calculated at current values, hardly had the makings of a strong portfolio, but had the flavour of securities which were hard to sell and were held by default. £149,539 was in Grand Trunk securities of various kinds, with a nominal value of £507,940. There was about £100,000 in other North American Railways including the Atlantic and St Lawrence, with substantial investments in the Metropolitan, Metropolitan District and the London Chatham and Dover stock. The only domestic industrial firm was Palmers shipbuilding and iron with which as we have seen Glyn's had close conections. Overseas investments included the Anglo-Austrian and Imperial Ottoman banks and the Chilean 4½ per cent and the Danubian Loan.[66]

From 1864 figures for yearly turnover survive. In that year it amounted to £1,560 millions received and paid through cashbooks in the town, country

64 According to the list in Fulford, Appendix 3, 246–255.
65 Collins, The Business of Banking, 46.
66 TNA, BT 31, 3744/2298; RBS Archives, GM/682/5; Cottrell, 127.

and railway offices and discount and loans granted. By 1870 it was £2,008 million and £2,950 in 1872.[67]

The bank was prospering in this period. The first surviving run of profit figures starts in 1868 when profits were £84,683. £24.338 was carried forward from the reserve. The seven partners divided £100,000 leaving £9,021 in the reserve: £20,000 each to Charles Mills and to his son Charles Henry, and George Carr Glyn; £10,000 each to Raikes and Bertram Currie; and £20,000 between George Carr's two sons split 2:1 in favour of George Grenfell, so preserving the 4:4:2 relationship between the three families. These sums increased over the next few years. In 1870 £170,000 was divided in the same proportions so Wolverton (Carr Glyn) and the two Mills each received £30,000. In December 1872 the partners were rewarded with £240,000. Both Wolverton and C.H Mills, who had inherited the baronetcy when Charles Mills died in October 1872, had £66,000, Bertram Currie £42,000 and Raikes Currie £24,000. The two younger Glyn's split £42,000 on a 4:3 basis. Sir Charles Mills' executors were paid £25,000, not included in the £240,000. On 31 December 1872 the partners' capital stood at £1,256,550, of which £452,000 was attributed to Wolverton. The return on the partners' capital was therefore 19 per cent. In the same year Barclays distributed £99,000 to their partners, but as the bank's capital only amounted to £240,000 the return was 41 per cent.[68] However Coutts profits were greater, averaging £100,000 for the 23 years ending in 1861. Schroeders' averaged £63,000 from 1864–69, a return of 14.5 per cent on a capital of £779,000.[69]

On 31 March 1873 new articles of partnership were agreed for five years from 1 January 1873. While the underlying family interests remained on the basis agreed in 1864: Glyns, two-fifths, Mills two-fifths and Currie one-fifth, with the death of Sir Charles Mills, there was only one Mills in the partnership, C.H. Mills who had succeeded to the baronetcy. Therefore it was agree that he and Lord Wolverton should have 27½ per cent, each with Raikes Currie, 16 and Bertram Currie, 17½ per cent. George Grenfell Glyn and Pascoe were assigned 10 per cent and 7½ per cent respectively. However Lord Wolverton died four months later.[70]

One of Newmarch's legacies is a description of the organisation and staff of the bank in George Carr Glyn's last years which is found in his

67 £3 million was reached in 1874.

68 Margaret Ackrill and Leslie Hannah, *Barclays: The Business of Banking 1690–1996*, 2001, 414.

69 R. Roberts, *Schroders, Merchants and Bankers*, 1992, 74.

70 TNA, IR 926/5442 f 447.

submission in 1873 to the Civil Service Inquiry Commission which was collecting information about employment in occupations comparable to the Civil Service.[71] Glyn's then employed about 200 clerks. Recruits were taken on after recommendation by customers, but earlier most seem to have been taken on recommendation by the partners. Only those most likely were accepted for interview and the bank was not bound to take them in order of application. They were seen both initially and then when there was a vacancy. They were given a paper of questions, which Newmarch said was not history or geography but devised more to their common usefulness. Those most expert in passing the literary part of the preliminary examination did not generally correspond with actual practice. There was also a medical examination. Recruits were not older than 17 or 18, were paid £75 a year to start with and were on probation for two or three months. There was no engagement on superior terms. A good many were gentlemen's sons, often sons of army officers or clergymen. Middle class schools were more effective at arithmetic.

There were three main divisions within the office – the country office, the town office and the railway office. Recruits generally started in the county or town office. Salary increases were by merit. Reports from heads of divisions could result in an allowance of £5 to £10 for the fairly efficient. Newmarch agreed that in 20 to 25 years salaries could rise to £400. There were 10 or 20 posts where the salaries were much more considerable. Newmarch, asked to compare Glyn's terms with other City employers, admitted that there not many places in the City where a lad of 18 could get £75 a year. In the provinces it would be £40 to £50. In Glyn's they could progress to £100 in three years, and to £300 by 35 or 40 if a man of particular capacity. The guarantee scheme set up in 1842 was replaced in 1854 by a new Guarantee and Widows Fund in which a Mutual Guarantee Fund was established, any excess being available for widows and orphans of the contributors. Except in occasional special cases no pension was paid. Some of Glyn's clerks moved to positions in country banks. In 1863 the York Union Bank told Glyn's they were wanting an agent in their branch at Driffield, a small pleasant market town. The salary would be £200 to £250 with a capital house and a large garden. Glyn's were asked if they happened to know of a likely person who should be between 30 and 40 years of age.[72]

The bank was open from 9 to 4, when it was closed to the public. 50 of the clerks would be out by 5 pm, 100 more by 5.30 or 6 pm at the latest, while 50 or so an hour later. Those who had been with the bank for a certain time

[71] First Report of the Civil Service Inquiry Commission, PP, 1873, xxiii, 218.

[72] RBS Archives, GM/429/67, 11 and 15 Nov. 1863.

had a month's holiday. Others had three weeks and a great number had a fortnight. The Bank insisted on their taking it. There was a dinner interval of ¾ hour or an hour. Saturday had been a normal working day during the first half of the nineteenth century, but the City Half Holiday movement started in 1857 with clerks at Glyn's being the largest subscribers. In February 1859 Glyn, then chairman of the London Clearing House, said they could not agree to 2.00 pm closing until the general course of business in the City became materially altered, but the following month a deputation from the joint stock banks led by David Salomons of the London and Westminster was received and they agreed to closing at 3.00 pm.[73] From 19th May 1860 the banks closed at 3 pm on Saturdays. Many of the clerks wished to close at 2.00 pm, but as Reynolds, the chief clerk at Glyn's, reminded the meeting of senior clerks, their original aim had been to see if they could without inconvenience close at 3.00 pm and it was better to accept that hour first and hope to obtain 2.00 pm thereafter.[74] Until 1883 junior clerks, though no longer living 'over the shop' came in on a rota on Sundays.

[73] LMA, MS 320006/001, 8 Feb. 1859.

[74] *Bankers Magazine*, 20, 1860, 214, report of meeting on 28 Feb.

CHAPTER NINETEEN

Final Years

In 1866 Glyn wrote to one of his sons, 'I have been in public life some time but never had the slightest recognition by word or deed from my political friends and never expect to have'. He added that he 'would not object to end my days in the calm retreat of the Lords, but have as much idea of such a thing as of having a pair of wings applied to me.'[1]

Glyn did not stand at the general election in 1868 and in November 1869 Gladstone formally offered Glyn a peerage, but the proposal must have been made informally much earlier. In August Glyn wrote to Bertram Currie to ask for his advice on an offer which had taken him very much by surprise and which was unasked for by him or George. He had heard it had been suggested not by Gladstone but by Lord Granville on the ground of his fidelity to the Liberal Party. He thought it one of those opportunities which for the sake of one's family should be availed of, if practicable and compatible with other matters. What he wanted to know from Currie was whether the acceptance of a peerage would compel a man to give up his partnership; if so, he must decline the offer for no consideration would induce me to sever his property from that banking house. There were cases of peers continuing in business but their circumstances might differ from his. He added that at his time of life it could make little difference to him but he must not overlook his family and the possible benefits thereafter to its members. He warned Currie to keep it to himself as even Pascoe did not know of it, (presumably George did, but Pascoe was also a partner at the bank). He wanted Currie's advice as a partner and a man of the world.

Currie told him that he had always thought that when the present Government made any peers his name would be amongst the first as his public services and position in the world most fairly entitled him to be. There

1 RBS Archives, GM/1381/11, letter to my dear Pucky (probably St Leger), 26 Jun. 1866.

could be no earthly reason why a peer should not be a partner in a house of business and as his partner he was pleased to hear that he would stipulate that he should. Currie remembered the case of Lord Overstone and that Lord John Russell had told him he had no cause to leave his bank. Since then it must have become evident to sensible peers that it would be better that other interests than those of the land should be represented in the House of Lords.[2] Glyn told Moon immediately before the announcement that Gladstone was desirous of including one or two commercial men. He had misgivings at his time of life and in his state of health, but Gladstone had talked him over. He added that at present 'kept pretty well with care.'[3]

When he accepted the formal offer he simply said that 'at my time of life ambition has pretty well passed away, but the offer of this distinction is an expression of opinion on the part of those whose testimony I highly value and I accept with gratitude and grateful feelings the intended honour.' It was announced on November. He then informed Moon in a letter doubtless intended also for the board that after consideration he had decided upon the title of 'Wolverton' to mark his long association with and interest in the affairs of the LNWR company. The board offered their hearty congratulations upon his accession to so well merited a distinction and expressed their gratification at his selection of a title identifying him with the undertaking over which he presided so ably and honourably for so many years.[4]

The *Economist* commented that his elevation would meet with the general approval of the City. The high place which he so worthily occupied marked him out as in every way deserving of the honour. The daily service of gentlemen in his position had in them much of a public character but in his case he had done a great deal of direct service to the public in connection with the financial and economical progress of the country.[5] Glyn was the only person from what he would call the mercantile world to be ennobled at that time. Gladstone's other creations in 1869 were almost all Liberal MPs who, like Glyn, had retired at the 1868 general election, one of whom, Edward Howard, was one of the first two Roman Catholics to be created peers since the 1680s, the other being Sir John Acton. Glyn was introduced to the House of Lords on 28 April 1870 accompanied by Lord Clandeboye and Thomas George Baring, now Lord Northbrook, who had succeeded his father in 1866.[6]

[2] Ibid, GM/1063 and 1064. Glyn to Currie and Currie's reply both dated 17 Aug. 1869.

[3] RBS Archives, GM/1381/3, Glyn to Moon, 10 Nov. 1869.

[4] BL, Add Ms 44423, Glyn to Gladstone, 9 Nov. 1869; TNA, RAIL 410/26, 20 Nov. 1869.

[5] *The Economist*, 27 Nov. 1869.

[6] Lords Journals, CII, 1870, 182. Baron Clandeboye was then Chancellor of the Duchy

Glyn's health in the latter part of the decade was a matter of some concern. Bournemouth became more important to him. He told Charles Mills in February 1867 'the climate of this place agrees with me and has certainly rescued me from the state into which I had fallen in October.' He added 'they won't let me leave yet'. He had been able to get to the LNWR board in November 1866 but was not to attend again until May 1867. In February 1869 Bertram Currie congratulated him on recovering his capacity in so short a time. The following month he told Moon from Bournemouth that he was benefiting from this fresh air and in November that he was in his winter quarters.[7]

By then he had ceased to attend LNWR board meetings and in the following August he wrote to Moon to tell him the time had arrived when Moon should act upon the resignation which he had from time to time tendered and replace him at the board by one who could devote his time and influence to the company. 'I appreciate most highly the kindness which has kept me so long as a member of the board, but it must not be abused by me. Of course in writing to you on this subject old feelings and recollections crowd upon my mind, but they are all of the same character and bear testimony to the uniform kindness which I have received from everyone connected with the service of the company.' He closed his letter by requesting Moon 'to convey to his old and kind friends his sincere thanks and earnest wishes for their prosperity and that of the great undertaking administered by you and them. I am the only survivor of the original direction, though my old friend Sir Hardman Earle, comes very near me.'[8]

At the meeting in October 1870 Moon and Tootal proposed Lord Richard Grosvenor to succeed Wolverton on the board.[9] His elder brother

of Lancaster in Gladstone's government. Later Governor General of Canada and Viceroy of India. Created Marquess of Dufferin and Ava, 1888. Thomas George Baring was then under-secretary at the War Office. Unlike his uncle Thomas he was a Liberal. Gladstone preferred him to Clandeboye as Viceroy in 1872. Northbrook had married Elizabeth Harriet the daughter of Henry Charles Sturt of Crichel Down and may well have known Glyn in Dorset.

7 RBS Archives, GM/263, Glyn to Charles Mills, 16 Feb. 1867; GM/881/2, Currie to Glyn, 9 Feb. 1869; GM/1381/13, Glyn to Moon, 15 Mar. 1869; GM/1381/3, Glyn to Moon, 10 Nov. 1869.

8 TNA, RAIL 410/26, letter of 3 Aug., minutes of 20 Aug. 1870. Earle, though not on the original LBR board had been on the GJR board from its inception. Tootal, Lyon and Benson were also survivors from the original LNWR board of 1846. In 1870 all four continued to be active directors and sat on the central body – the Special Committee. Tootal died in harness in 1873, Benson in 1875, Earle aged 85 in 1877, while Lyon died in 1883.

9 TNA, RAIL 410/26, 24 Sept. 1870.

was the future duke of Westminster. Still a young man he had been elected Liberal MP for Flint in 1861 when only 24. The constituency was adjacent to the family seat at Eaton Hall, and contained Hawarden, the home of Gladstone who backed his nomination. He was already chairman of the British side of the Channel Tunnel Company, an interest perhaps sparked by the fact that William Low, the engineer, was a constituent. He followed in the footsteps of George Grenfell Glyn in that he became Gladstone's Chief Whip in 1880. He was created Lord Stalbridge in 1884 for his services in that office, succeeded Moon as chairman of the LNWR in 1891 and led the company for 20 years.

Glyn entertained Gladstone at Stanmore Park in both 1870 and 1871. The Gladstones arrived on Saturday and departed on Monday morning. On both occasions Gladstone went to the parish church morning and evening commenting in 1870 'This is a very Christian family' and in 1871 'Much good rests with these good people'.[10]

In October 1872 Charles Mills, who had been a partner in the bank for even longer than Glyn, died. He left personal property of less than £700,000. Glyn outlived him by less than a year. Early in July 1873 Glyn was well enough to visit Lombard Street but about a fortnight later he was taken seriously ill and was moved from his country home to Upper Ecclestone Street. He was attended by Sir William Gull but by 21 July his condition was described as exceedingly weak. Though he improved slightly he was not out of danger and the rally did not last. He died just after 6 am on 24 July at his London home. His son told Gladstone that day that he passed away quite suddenly and without suffering.[11] On 29 July his body was moved to Dorset for interment in the family vault in St Kenelm's Church, Stanbridge, or Hinton Parva, and the funeral took place the following day.[12] A special train brought the mourners including the principal officials from both Glyn's and the LNWR. The funeral according to the *Sherborne Journal* was a plain one. Apart from George Grenfell and his wife, his other four surviving sons, two daughters in law and the hon Miss Glyn (Georgina Mary) attended and with many clergy

[10] *The Gladstone Diaries,1968–1994*, VII, ed. H.C.G. Matthews, 24, 25 and 26 Sept. 1870 (367, 378 and 370) and VIII, 5 and 6 Aug. 1871 (17 and 18).

[11] G.G. Glyn to Gladstone, 24 Jul. 1873, BL, Add Ms 43438.

[12] *Daily Telegraph*, 21 Jul., *Pall Mall Gazette*, 22, 23 and 24 Jul., and *Daily News*, 30 Jul. 1873, The small church on the road near the entrance to Gaunt's House is now disused but contains plaques dedicated to the memory, not only of George Carr Glyn but also Marianne, his brother Richard Plumptre, and sons, Richard Riversdale, St Leger, Ashley, Edward and his daughter.

and gentry formed a procession of 50 persons. Glyn's brother-in-law Revd Lord Sydney Osborne read the service.

The local papers were already giving more attention to the by-election at Shaftesbury caused by George Grenfell succeeding his father as Lord Wolverton. Indeed Sir Richard Glyn was the first speaker at an election meeting at Shaftesbury Town Hall on the evening of the funeral.[13]

Glyn's was the subject of obituaries in the *Economist* as well as *The Times* and other papers. Lord Overstone and G W Norman privately struck a different note regarding the *Economist* article, written by Newmarch, as a fulsome panegyric. Norman told Overstone that 'you and your brother directors at the Bank of England well knew in your day that in dealing with George Glyn every man must take good care of himself.'[14] Sir Edward Watkin who was on his way to the half-yearly meeting of the SER when he heard the news, put it very differently:

> When the history of railways comes to be written the name of Lord Wolverton will stand out as conspicuously on the page as, or more so, than that of Stephenson or any of the other pioneers of our noble industry. Lord Wolverton brought to bear upon its initiation and progress that which Stephenson never could have accomplished. Faith in his character and in his judgment led the English capitalist to embark on what at first was looked upon as a doubtful if not a chimerical enterprise, so doubtful that the rejection of the third reading of the Liverpool and Manchester Railway Bill was moved by the late Lord Derby. If therefore so distinguished a man, so prescient and so wise, should have doubts enough to justify moving the rejection of that Bill we must see how much the public at large, and mankind in general owe to Lord Wolverton for bringing the people of this country to risk their savings in the prosecution of railways.[15]

John Bright wrote to his son 'I had a great regard for your father – there was a gentleness with his wisdom which to me was always striking and attractive.'[16]

Glyn's will was proved on 14 August by three of his sons who were his executors – George, Henry and Pascoe. His personalty was sworn at under £1,000,000 (£967,788) and stamp duty of £13,500 was paid. He left

13 *Sherborne, Dorchester and Taunton Journal*, 31 Jul. 1873.
14 Overstone, III, 1251–2, Overstone to G.W. Norman, 5 Aug. 1873.
15 TNA, RAIL 635/11, 24 Jul. 1873.
16 Fulford, 132.

Marianne £4,000 a year for life, which included her marriage settlement, with an immediate legacy of £1,000, with the furniture, plate and personal effects at Stanmore Park and the use of Stanmore Park for life. He left substantial legacies to his younger children, the precise amounts depending on the marriage settlements which several of them had received, amounting to £267,000, £500 to his nephew General Sir Edward Greathed[17] and an annuity of £100 to his housekeeper, Elizabeth Allwright. The whole residue of the personalty and the realty was left to George Grenfell Glyn[18] For the purpose of supporting the family interest in Glyn, Mills, Currie, & Co. he left £60,000 in 3 per cent government stock to such of his sons as should be members of the firm at his death (George and Pascoe), following the precedent of his father and brother, and he expressed a wish that his sons should continue the practice. £5,000 was left for building, and £1,000 for endowing, a church in Bournemouth or elsewhere, as a memorial to his son Richard Riversdale. In fact the bequest was used to build a new church, St Nicholas, at Beverley in the East Riding of Yorkshire, a town with which the family became closely associated as Edward was vicar of St Mary's, the principal parish church from 1872 until 1875, and was followed by his brother-in-law Francis Pelham (Alice's husband) from 1876 until 1881. Marianne laid the foundation stone in June 1877 and Edward preached at the opening in August 1880. His mother gave £1,000, the cost of the tower.[19] Meanwhile George Grenfell had erected the west window at St Andrew's Fontmell Magna in memory of his father.

Marianne who was only five years younger than George survived him until March 1892 when she was in her ninetieth year. She lived in Lancaster Gate. Her funeral service was held at St Mary Abbott's Kensington, where her son Edward was vicar. Her other surviving sons, Pascoe, and Sidney and her two daughters were present, as was her brother-in-law, Froude, aged 86. The following day her remains were interred in the family vault at Stanbridge where her brother-in-law, Revd John Carr Glyn, now 92 had been rector since 1830, reputedly Britain's longest ever serving parish priest.

By then the family had disposed of Stanmore Park. The house itself with gardens and 19 acres of grassland was advertised to be let or leased in 1880 and the whole estate of 381 acres, including the house was advertised for

17 The son of George Carr Glyn's sister, Mary Elizabeth.

18 TNA, IR 26/2815 f 665, and 5442 f 447; *Hampshire Advertiser,* 23 Aug., *The Observer*, 31 Aug. and *Huddersfield Daily Chronicle,* 25 Aug. 1873.

19 *Pall Mall Gazette,* 30 Jun. 1877; *York Herald,* 5 and 8 Aug. 1880.

sale by auction in 1883.[20] In 1887 it was sold to Frederick Gordon, the hotel proprietor, who in 1881 had purchased the Bentley Priory estate from Sir John Kelk, the contractor, who had owned it since 1863. In the late 1880s the house became a boys' preparatory school run by Herbert Kemball-Cook, who moved his school from Brighton. By 1894 the park had been partly cut up for villa residences, but mostly given up to Stanmore Golf Club.[21] The school remained in the house until it was moved to Hertford in 1937, and the house was then acquired by the Royal Air Force and without any consultation with the local council it was pulled down in 1938 to make way for No.3 Balloon Centre of the Royal Auxiliary Air Force. After World War II was used by Strike Command. Nothing now remains of Glyn's Stanmore Park except the lake north of Gordon Avenue and gate posts both in that Avenue, to one of which a plaque has been fixed commemorating Glyn and the mansion, and in Uxbridge Road. Stanmore Golf Club still uses part of the Park.[22]

After succeeding his father George Grenfell, remained active in politics, and was particularly close to Gladstone being part of the inner circle who advised him especially in times of crisis. Gladstone stayed several times at Glyn's house, Coombe Wood near Kingston-upon-Thames, and in 1882 Gladstone was a guest on his 450 ton yacht. The following year the Gladstones stayed for a month at Glyn's villa in Cannes – Chateau Scott. When Gladstone returned to power in 1880 Glyn became Paymaster General, though not in the Cabinet, so that he might be formally associated with the Government. Eddie Hamilton, Gladstone's private secretary, commented that his loyalty to Mr Gladstone deserved recognition, but a less judicious advisor it was impossible to conceive.[23] When Gladstone's short-lived third ministry in 1885–86 was formed he was considered for the post of Lord Lieutenant of Ireland by Gladstone and Granville, but Harcourt threatened to resign if he was appointed, so he became Postmaster General. West commented that this post suited him better.[24] He gave his salary as postmaster to secure beds in

[20] *Morning Post*, 29 Nov. 1880; *The Standard*, 27 Jun. 1883, though a buyer was probably not found as the property was advertised again in 1884.

[21] *Kelly's Directory of Essex, Hertfordshire and Middlesex*, 1894, 293; *VCH, Middlesex*, V, 98–99.

[22] Eileen M. Bowlt, *Stanmore Past*, 1998, 97 and 130. The gate piers in Uxbridge Road are a listed Grade II building.

[23] *The Diary of Sir Edward Walter Hamilton 1880–1885*, ed. Dudley W.R. Bahlmann 1, 1972, 6 (entry for 1 May 1880).

[24] A.B. Cooke and John Vincent, *The Governing Passion: Cabinet Government and Party Politics in Britain, 1885–86*, 1974, 365. They comment that West's impression (West, *Recollections*, 2, 263) that Wolverton was actually offered the post looks unfounded.

a convalescent home for sick London postmen. He was a firm supporter of Gladstone's Home Rule policy, giving it financial support and holding several large meetings in Dorset, including a large anti-coercion demonstration at Templecombe a month before he died. He owned race horses and was a master of hounds in Dorset where he built Iwerne Minster in 1878 designed by Alfred Waterhouse, the most ambitious Victorian mansion in Dorset. He often rode with his cousin, Richard George, the third baronet who was Master of the Blackmoor Vale Hounds, and lived at Gaunt's. He kept on Fontmell Lodge at least for a time.[25] By the 1880s the Glyns were considerable landowners in Dorset. George Grenfell had added considerably to his estate and in 1883 his cousin, Sir Richard George's, Dorset estates had increased to 9,620 acres with a gross annual value of £12,676.[26] In 1899 Gaunts was enlarged, refaced and extensively altered, and little remains visible of the mansion of 1809. Sir Richard George and his successors occupied Gaunts until World War II when it was occupied by the army and by evacuees. The Fontmell estate was sold in 1926. After the war a boy's preparatory school, Dumpton, moved to Gaunts from Kent, but the house was returned to the Glyn estate in 1988 and since 1989 the Richard Glyn Foundation, created by the present baronet, Sir Richard Lindsay Glyn, has used it for residential and one day conferences and private retreats. The Foundation is an educational charity embracing creativity, culture, education and spirituality. St Kenelm's church served as a chapel to Dumpton school but is now a redundant church, though still containing plaques in memory of George Carr, Marianne and most of his children, who were also buried there.

The second Lord Wolverton died suddenly on 6 November 1887 in the Bedford Hotel, Brighton after visiting the races at Plumtree and Brighton, and was buried at Ham, but in the following August his body was reburied at Iwerne Minster, Dorset, near Iwerne House. He left £1,817,725. His widow died in 1894. They had no children so the title passed to his nephew Henry Richard, son of Vice-Admiral Henry Carr Glyn, who like his brother St Leger, had died before their elder brother. By what was probably a technical error in George Grenfell Glyn's will the reversion of some £1,500,000 passed owing to the death of St Leger Richard, the expected heir at the time the will was drawn up, to St Leger's five daughters. However they generously released their claim to the money in favour of the third baron. He, Henry Richard, died in July 1888 from a protracted tubercular illness

[25] Newman and Pevsner, The Buildings of England, Dorset, 1972, 239. Wolverton was recorded as living at Fontmell Lodge in 1875. *Post Office Directory of Hampshire, Wilts and Dorset*, 1875, 43.

[26] *The Complete Peerage*, XII (ii), 1959, 827–828.

at the early age of 26. He had not married and his heir was his only brother Frederic, then aged 23. He lived until 1932, having become senior partner in the Bank. He was then succeeded by his second and oldest surviving son, Nigel Reginald Victor.

Two of George Carr Glyn's younger sons also briefly represented Dorset constituencies. Sidney was Liberal MP for Shaftesbury from 1880–85, the constituency George had represented until 1873. He lived until 1916. Pascoe was defeated in 1881 in an attempt to gain the seat of East Dorset, but succeeded in 1885, only to lose it in the following year, standing as a Gladstonian Liberal after the split with the Unionists. Edward had been ordained in 1868. He was curate of Doncaster under Dr Vaughan, and then domestic chaplain to the Archbishop of York. He was then successively vicar of St Mary Beverley, Doncaster and Kensington and then Bishop of Peterborough from 1897 to 1916. Appointed chaplain to the Queen in 1881 he married in 1882 Lady Mary Campbell, daughter of the eighth duke of Argyll. He died in 1928, His unmarried sister, Georgina had died in December 1926, aged 92.

From the late 1860s Bertram Currie was the major force in the bank. He became to be regarded as the City's most eminent financial authority, and his opinion was sought by Chancellors of the Exchequer. By 1891 Glyn's had by far the largest capital and the greatest deposits of any private bank in London and their deposits were only exceeded by two joint stock banks, the London and Westminster and, marginally, by the Union Bank of London.[27] The partners in the bank left fortunes on a different scale to the overwhelming majority of private bankers and joint stock bank directors. While George Grenfell Glyn left the largest fortune, Charles Henry Mills left £1,479,000, Bertram Currie, £696,000 and Pascoe Glyn, £636,000.[28]

Charles Henry Mills was the senior partner. He bought Wildernesse, at Seal near Sevenoaks, in 1884 and substantially enlarged it. He was created Lord Hillingdon in 1886. Despite having favoured the merger with the Scottish banks, Currie and his partners resisted becoming a joint stock bank until 1885, when they became a private joint stock bank though continued to refer to themselves as partners. They abandoned some of the secrecy that had surrounded the operations of private banks by starting to publish a six-monthly balance sheet, but decided against joining other private banks or country banks, and there was no change in the bank's structure. According to Eddie Hamilton, Lord Wolverton was sanguine that he had made a coup

[27] Youssef Cassis, *City Bankers, 1890–1914*, 1994 (Table 1), 20. The comparison excludes those joint stock banks with branch networks.

[28] Ibid, 200.

by this step and other banking institutions would probably have to follow, though Hamilton also records Gladstone as saying he was 'a Tory and old fashioned enough not to wish to see the entire break up of the private bank system'.[29] It helped the bank as the size of its business had generally been underestimated, and its assets rose by 50 per cent from 1885 to 1889. In 1891 Glyn's had by far the highest level of deposits of the London private banks: £14.02 million compared with Barclays £7.98 million and Coutts £6.37 million. It had a large range of industrial customers and remained engaged in international finance. In 1890 there were still ten private banks but by 1910 as concentration grew there were only two banks in the City (Glyn's and Robarts Lubbock) that were properly private banks – deposit banks, not merchant banks, though Glyn's had some of the features of the latter.[30] As Algernon Mills, one of Charles Henry's sons, later put it 'I believe that we shall do best by preserving a characteristic which we alone of the large and serious banks possess alone of all the large and serious banks possess, namely of having only one front door.'[31] A possible merger with Coutts in the late 1870s and wider groupings in 1893 and again in 1900 which could have included West End banks and also Becketts of Leeds and Lambtons of Newcastle came to nothing, which would have paralleled on a smaller scale the bringing together of the 20 banks which formed Barclay & Co in 1896.[32] In 1914 Glyn's was one of only five London banks which had been founded before 1793.[33]

Charles Henry Mills' son Charles William, the second Lord Hillingdon, had become a partner in 1879. Like his father he married a peer's daughter: Alice Marion Hubbard, daughter of Lord Suffield and they lived in some style at Camelford House and at Wildernesse. He retired from the bank in 1907 owing to ill health. Algernon, his brother was also a partner who played a major role at the bank in World War I. Pascoe Glyn continued as a partner, though he was not very active at the bank for some years before his death in 1904. His son Maurice followed in the family interest, as did the fourth Lord Wolverton. Both were partners until after World War I. The Mills succession was interrupted when Charles William's son, Charles Thomas, a partner from 1910 of whom much was expected, was killed on the western front in 1915. However in 1919 General Sir Herbert Alexander Lawrence, who had married a daughter of the first Lord Hillingdon, joined the bank and steered

29 Bahlmain, 2, 774, entry for 16 Jan. 1885.

30 Youseff Cassis and Philip L. Cottrell, 2015, 166.

31 Fulford, 226–227.

32 Cassis and Cottrell, 169.

33 Ibid, 39.

the merger with Holt & Co., bankers and army agents in 1922, which had much expanded in the war, and in 1923 with Child & Co., the Fleet Street bank, following the early death of the Earl of Jersey, the owner. General Lawrence proved to be the dominant force between the wars. In 1939 the partners were mostly young men and there was a risk that some of them would be killed in the approaching war. This could have meant substantial death duties on their family holdings in the bank. Consequently the Bank was sold to the Royal Bank of Scotland in 1939 for £3,700,000, which meant the end of the last traditional private bank in the City. Glyn Mills continued to trade separately, managed by its own board of directors and offering its own range of services. It acquired the banking businesses of both the British Overseas Bank and the Anglo-International Bank in 1944, and an accepting house, A. Ruffer & Sons, established in 1872, in 1946. In 1970 the Royal Bank of Scotland rationalised its subsidiaries by merging Glyn Mills, Williams Deacon's and part of the National Bank to form Williams & Glyn's Bank, but in 1985 Williams & Glyn's was fully merged in the Royal Bank of Scotland. The RBS acquired the National Westminster in 2000, but later was required divest some 300 branches under the European Union's state aid requirements. Initially RBS planned to sell off the branches as a separate business under the title Williams & Glyn, but in 2016 decided to sell the branches to another bank. As they did not succeed, RBS and the UK Government have proposed to the European Commission that more choice in banking services in the United Kingdom should be provided by different measures. Consequently the name of Glyn will not again adorn the title of a bank.

Appendix
Glyn's Liabilities and Assets

Glyn's Liabilities and Assets at decennial intervals 1820–1860, 1865, 1868 (with profit and loss account) and 1872

1820

Liabilities (£000s)			Assets (£000s)		
Current Accs			Bank of England*		
Town	679		Cash in hand		181
Country	347		Debit balances		
Railway			Town	37	
		1026	Country	114	
Deposit Accs**		...	Railway		
					151
			Investments		8
			Bill Discounted		686
		1026			1026

* The balance at the Bank of England was £130.

** First opened in 1856.

1830

Liabilities (*£000s*)			*Assets* (*£000s*)		
Current Accs			Bank of England		14
Town	1406		Cash in hand		239
Country	327		Debit balances		
Railway	15		Town	107	
			Country	170	
Deposit Accs**			Railway		
		1748			277
		...	Investments		28
			Bill Discounted		1190
		1748			1748

** First opened in 1856.

1840

Liabilities (*£000s*)			*Assets* (*£000s*)		
Current Accs			Bank of England		86
Town	1897		Cash in hand		195
Country	398		Debit balances		
Railway	142		Town	93	
		2437	Country	149	
Deposit Accs **		....	Railway	....	
					242
			Investments		49
			Bill Discounted		1865
		2437			2437

** First opened in 1856.

1850

Liabilities (*£000s*)			*Assets* (*£000s*)		
Current Accs			Bank of England		69
Town	2414		Cash in hand		298
Country	819		Debit balances		
Railway	376		Town	163	
		3609	Country	268	
Deposit Accs **		...	Railway	15	
					446
			Investments		364
			Bill Discounted		2432
		3609			3609

** First opened in 1856.

1860

Liabilities (*£000s*)			*Assets* (*£000s*)		
Current Accs			Bank of England		464
Town	2991		Cash in hand		154
Country	969		Debit balances		
Railway	463		Town	124	
		4423	Country	836	
Deposit Accs		609	Railway	22	
					982
			Investments		531
			Bill Discounted		2901
		5032			5032

1865

Liabilities (£000s)			*Assets (£000s)*		
Current Accs			Bank of England		600
Town	4157		Cash in hand		263
Country	1420		Debit balances		
Railway	800		Town	59	
		6377	Country	1046	
Deposit Accs		2222	Railway	143	
					1248
			Investments		818
			Bill Discounted		5670
		8599			8599

1868

Liabilities (£000s)			*Assets (£000s)*		
Current Accs			Bank of England		307
Town	4629		Cash in hand		246
Country	1840		Debit balances		
Railway	1250		Town	183	
		7719	Country	340	
Deposit Accs		1157	Railway	416	
					939
			Investments		1157
			Bill Discounted		6226
		8876			8876

1868
Profit and Loss Account from GM/695/1

Debtors			*Creditors*		*Actual figures*
Bad debts	7191		Reserve	51530	
Met Dis R	20000	27191	Int net (Town & Cy)	112250	
Rent, Rates *	9460		Commission	53524	
Salaries	35197		Brokerage, net	2585	
IT, Pensions etc**	5067				219889
Trade Expenses	7878	57602	Int on Investment		49781
Special Outlays		12903			
LCDR		46000			
Bad debts reserve		16950			
Bad debts reserve	24338				
Profits	84683	109021			
		269670			269670

* Includes sinking fund.
** Includes Income Tax (2692), pensions (1,239), housekeeping (444) and charities (690).

1872

	Liabilities (£000s)		*Assets (£000s)*		
Current Accs			Bank of England		382
Town	5440		Cash in hand		330
Country	1760		Debit balances		
Railway	4060		Town	158	
		11260	Country	340	
Deposit Accs		1990	Railway	3260	
					3758
			Investments		1040
			Bill Discounted		7740
		13250			13250

Sources: RBS Archives GM/718/1 and, for profit and loss account, GM/695/1.

Bibliography

Archives

Barclays Archives
The Baring Archive
British Library (BL)
Centre for Buckinghamshire Studies
Cumbria Archives, Kendal
Dorset Record Office
Durham University Library
Hull History Centre
Institution of Mechanical Engineers Archives
Leicestershire Record Office
Library and Archives Canada (LAC)
Liverpool Record Office
Liverpool Maritime Museum
London Metropolitan Archives (LMA)
Museum of Docklands Archives
Nottingham University Library, Department of Manuscripts and Special Collections
Royal Bank of Scotland (RBS) Archives
Royal Statistical Society
Scottish Record Office
Suffolk Record Office
The National Archives (TNA)
University of London Library

Parliamentary papers

Committee of Secrecy on Bank of England Charter, PP, 1831–2, vi
Duke of Wellington, Memorandum on Military Government, PP, 1833, vii
Reports of Select Committee on State of Communication by Railway, PP, 1839, x; and PP, 1840, xiii

Report of Committee on London and Birmingham Railway Bill, PP, 1839, xiii
Report of Select Committee on Banks of Issue, Second Report, PP, 1841, v
Report of Select Committee on Laws Regulating the Interest on Money, PP, 1841, xii
Report of the Select Committee on Railways, PP, 1844, xi
Copies of any Memorial to Sir Robert Peel by certain directors and others connected with Railway Companies, against the Railway Bill now before this House and of any correspondence thereupon between the Board of Trade and the aforesaid Memorialists, PP, 1844, xli
Return of Alphabetical List of Names of Persons subscribing to Railway Subscription Contracts, PP, 1845, xli
Report of Select Committee on Railway Acts, PP, 1846, xiv
Report of the Royal Commission on Metropolitan Termini, PP, 1846, xvii
Return of Alphabetical List of Names of Persons subscribing to Railway Subscription Contracts, PP, 1846, xxxviii
Report of Select Committee on Commercial Distress, PP, 1847–8, viii
Report of Select Committee of the House of Lords on Commercial Distress, PP, 1847–8, viii
Further correspondence relative to the projected railway from Halifax to Quebec, PP, 1852, xlviii
Report of the Select Committee on the Principle of Amalgamation applied to Railway or Railway and Canal Bills, PP, 1852–3, xxxviii
Report of Royal Commission on Court of Bankruptcy, PP, 1854, xxiii
Report of Select Committee on the Bank Acts, PP, 1857, x
Report of Royal Commission on Purchase and Sale of Commissions in the Army, PP, 1857 (2), xxviii
System of Purchase in the Army, PP, 1857–8, xix
Report by a War Office Committee on the evidence given by C. Trevelyan, PP, 1857–8, xxxvii
Report of Royal Commission on Railways in Great Britain and Ireland, PP, 1872–3, xxxxviii
First Report of the Commission to enquire into the method of selecting civil servants, PP, 1875, xxiii

Books

Margaret Ackrill and Leslie Hannah, *Barclays: the business of banking, 1690–1996*, 2001
John P. Addis, *The Crawshay Dynasty, 1765–1867*, 1957
George Thomas, Earl of Albemarle, *Fifty Years of My Life*, 1876
Timothy Alborn, *Regulated Lives, Life Insurance and British Society, 1800–1914*, 2009
Jonathon Andrews, *The History of Bethlem*, 1997
Anon, *Glyn and Gaunts, a brief history*, privately printed, n.d. (4pp)
A.J. Arnold and S. McCartney, *George Hudson, The Rise and Fall of the Railway King*, 2004

Charles H. Babbage, *A comparative view of the various institutions for the assurance of lives*, reproduced in D.T. Jenkins and T. Yoneyama, *The History of Insurance*, 2000, IV
The Collected Works of Walter Bagehot, ed. Norman St John Stevens, X, Economic Essays, 1978
Philip Bagwell, *The Railwaymen: The History of the National Union of Railwaymen*, 1963
—, *The Railway Clearing House in the British Economy, 1842–1922*, 1968
M. Baker and M. Collins, Crisis Management, English Financial Markets in the 1830s, in *Monetary and Banking History, Essays in Honour of Forrest Capie*, 2011
Michael R. Bailey, ed., *Robert Stephenson, the Eminent Engineer*, 2003
Journals and Correspondence from 1808 to 1852 of Sir Francis Thornhill Baring, edited by his son the Earl of Northbrook, 1905
G.F. Russell Barker and Alan H. Stenning, *The Westminster School Register from 1764 to 1883*, 1892
T.C. Barker and Michael Robbins, *A History of London Transport*, 1963
E.G. Barnes, *The Rise of the Midland Railway, 1844–74*, 1966
Peter Baskerville, ed., *The Bank of Upper Canada, A Collection of Documents*, The Champlain Society, 1987, cxviii
A.S.J. Baster, *The Imperial Banks*, 1929
John Beckett, *The Rise and Fall of the Grenvilles*, 1994
James Bettley and Nikolaus Pevsner, *Buildings of England, Suffolk, West*, 2015
Frederick Blayney, *Life Assurance Societies considered as to their Comparative Merits*, 1848, reproduced in Jenkins and Yoneyama, 2000, V
Memoirs of Sir Edward Blount, ed. Stuart J. Reid, 1902
G. Body, *Great Railway Battles*, 1994, 62
H.M. Boot, *The Commercial Crisis of 1847*, 1984
Henry Booth, *Henry Booth*, 1980
Eileen M. Bowlt, *Stanmore Past*, 1998
Peter Braine, *The Railway Moon*, 2010
Sir Joseph G. Broadbank, *History of the Port of London*, 1921
S.A. Broadbridge, *Studies in Railway Expansion and the Capital Markets in England, 1825–1873*, 1970
Memorials of Brooks's: from the foundation of the club 1764 to the close of the nineteenth century: compiled from the records of the club, ed. J.F. Webb-Prosser, 1907
Samuel Brown, *Defects in the Practice of Life Assurance and Suggestions for their Remedy*, 1848, reproduced in D.T. Jenkins and T. Yoneyama, 2000, VI
Eric Gore Browne, *The History of Glyn Mills and Co.*, 1935
Anthony Bruce, *The Purchase System in the British Army, 1660–1871*, 1980
Private Diary of Richard, Duke of Buckingham and Chandos, KG, 1862
Algernon Burkett, *The History of White's from 1743 to 1848*, 1894
S.J. Butlin, *The Australia and New Zealand Bank: The Bank of Australasia and the Union Bank of Australia, 1829–1951*, 1961
A.M. Carlos and F. Lewis, The Profitability of Early Canadian Railroads: Evidence from the Grand Trunk and Great Western Railway Companies in C. Golin and H. Rockoff, ed., *Strategic Factors in Nineteenth-century American Economic History*, 1992

Robert E. Carlson, *The Liverpool and Manchester Railway Project*, 1969
Youssef Cassis, *City Bankers*, 1994
Mark Casson, *The World's First Railway System, Enterprise, Competition, and Regulation on the Railway Network in Victorian Britain*, 2009
David Cecil, *Lord M.*, 1954
George Chandler, *Four Centuries of Banking, as illustrated by the bankers, customers, and staff associated with the constituent banks of Martins Bank Limited*, 1964
Geoffrey Channon, *Railways in Britain and the United States, 1830–1940*, 2001
S.D. Chapman, *The Rise of Merchant Banking*, 1984
S.G. Checkland, *The Gladstones, A Family Biography, 1764–1851*, 1971
—, *Scottish Banking, A History, 1695–1973*, 1975
Susan Chitty, *The Beast and the Monk, a Life of Charles Kingsley*, 1975
Sir John Clapham, *The Bank of England, A History*, 1944
Edith Clay, *William Gell in Italy, 1831–35*, 1976
The American Diaries of Richard Cobden, ed. Elizabeth Hoon Cawley, 1952
Michael Collins, *Money and Banking in the UK: A History*, 1988
A.B. Cooke and John Vincent, *The Governing Passion: Cabinet Government and Party Politics in Britain, 1885–86*, 1974
P.L. Cottrell, La Cooperation financiere, Franco-Anglaise, 1850–1880, in *La position internationale de la France: aspects économiques et financiers XIXe-XXe siècles*, ed Maurice Lévy-Leboyer, 1977
—, *Industrial Finance, 1830–1914, the Finance and Organisation of English Manufacturing Industry*, 1980
—, *Investment Banking in England, A Case Study of the International Financial Society*, 1985
—, London's First 'Big Bang'? Institutional Change on the City, in *The World of Private Banking*, ed. Youssef Cassis, Philip Cottrell, Monika P. Fraser and Iain L. Fraser, 2009
P.L. Cottrell and Lucy Newton, Banking in England and Wales in *Banking Liberalisation*, ed. R. Sylla, R. Tilly and G. Tortelli, 1999.
John G. Cox, Samuel Morton Peto, 1809–1889, *The Achievements and Failings of a Great Railway Developer*, 2008
James Cropper, *Notes and Memories*, 1900
A.W. Currie, *The History of the Grand Trunk Railway of Canada*, 1957
Bertram W. Currie, *Recollections, Letters and Journals*, ed. C.C. Currie, 1905
Martin Daunton, *State and Market in Victorian Britain: War, Welfare and Capitalism*, 2008
Charles Dickens, Household Words, *Miscellaneous Papers*, 1914
Benjamin Disraeli, *Coningsby*, 1841
—, *Endymion*, 1881
Frank Dobbin, *Forging Industrial Policy, The United States Britain and France in the Railway Age*, 1994
George Dow, *Great Central*, 1, 1959
Lord Durham's Report on the Affairs of British North America, ed. C.P. Lucas, 1912
Mrs Duberley's War, Journal and Letters from the Crimea, ed. Christine Kelly, 2007
Peter Ducker, *The Crimean War at Sea*, 2011
Bryan Dunleavy, *The Lost Streets of Wolverton*, 2012

J. Simpson Dyer, *Our Centenary Year, The Liverpool & London & Globe Insurance Company Limited*, 1936
Edhem Eldem, *A History of the Ottoman Bank*, 1999
The Elgin-Grey Papers, 1847–1852, ed. Sir Arthur Doughty, 1937
Henry English, *A Complete View of the Joint Stock Companies formed during the years 1824 and 1825*, 1827
D.M. Evans, *City Men and City Manners or the Physiology of London Business*, 1852
Stirling Everard, *The History of the Gas Light and Coke Company, 1812–1849*, 1949
Joseph Farington, *The Farington Diary*, ed. James Greig, 1922–28
Mrs Fawcett, *The Life of the Rt Hon Sir William Molesworth*, 1901
C.R. Fay, *Huskisson and His Age*, 1951
R.W.D. Fenn, *The Life and Times of Sir George Cornewall Lewis, Bart, a Radnorshire Gentleman*, 2005
Niall Ferguson, *The World's Banker, The History of the House of Rothschild*, 1998
D.R. Fisher, ed. *History of Parliament, The House of Commons, 1820–1832*, V, 2009
Sir William Forbes, *Memoirs of a Banking-House*, 1860
E.M. Forster, *Marianne Thornton, A Domestic Biography*, 1956
C.D. Foster, *Privatisation, Public Ownership and Natural Monopoly*, 1992
R. Fulford, *Glyn's, 1753–1853: Six Generations in Lombard Street*, 1953
John Francis, *History of the English Railway*, 1851
John S. Galbraith, *The Hudson's Bay Company as an Imperial Factor, 1821–1869*, 1957
William Galt, *Railway Reform: its importance and practicability as affecting the nation, the shareholders and the government*, 1864
A.G. Gardiner, *The Life of Sir William Harcourt*, 1923
Norman Gash, *Sir Robert Peel: The Life of Sir Robert Peel after 1830*, 1972
The Letters of Mrs Gaskell, ed. J.A.V. Chapple and Arthur Pollard, 1966
Richard Gatty, *Portrait of a Merchant Prince, James Morrison, 1789–1857*, 1977
A.D. Gayer, W.W. Rostow and A.J. Schwartz, *The Growth and Fluctuations of the British Economy, 1790–1850*, 1953
The Birth of the Great Western Railway, Extracts from the Diary and Correspondence of George Henry Gibbs, ed. Jack Simmons, 1971
The Gladstone's Diaries, 1968–1994, III, ed. M.R.D. Foot and H.C.G. Matthews and VII, ed. H.C.G. Matthews
Robert Glyn's *Diary of Tour in France, Switzerland, etc* 1816, manuscript in the possession of Sir Richard Glyn, Bt
T.R. Gourvish, *Mark Huish and the London & North Western Railway, A Study in Management*, 1972
Adrian Gray, *South Eastern Railway*, 1990
Greville Diaries, ed. P.W. Wilson, 1927, 1
The Greville Memoirs, ed. Lytton Strachey and Roger Fulford, 1938, V
Charles H. Grinling, *The History of the Great Northern Railway*, 1903 edition
P. Guedalla, ed., *Gladstone and Palmerston: The Correspondence of Lord Palmerston with Mr. Gladstone, 1851–1865*, 1928
Lady Charlotte Guest, Extracts from Her Journal, 1833–1852, ed., the Earl of Bessborough, 1950
Ivor Guest, *Dr John Radcliffe and his Trust*, 1991

Montague Guest and W.B. Bolton, *Memorials of the Royal Yacht Club, 1815–1900*, 1903
The Diary of Sir Edward Walter Hamilton 1880–1885, ed. Dudley W.R. Bahlmann 1, 1972
Daniel Hardcastle, *Banks and Bankers*, 1842
Sir Francis Bond Head, *Stokers and Pokers, or the London and North Western Railway*, 1849
Edna Healey, *Coutts & Co., 1692–1992, The Portrait of a Private Bank*, 1992
A. Helps, *Life and Labours of Mr Brassey*, 1878
Elizabeth Hennessy, The Governors, Directors and Management, in *The Bank of England, Money, Power and Influence*, ed. Richard Roberts and David Kynaston, 1995
R. Hidy, *The House of Baring in American Trade and Finance*, 1949
Francis Hincks, *Canada: Its Financial Position and Resources*, 1849
Allen B. Hinds, *A History of Northumberland*, III, 1896
David Hodgkins, *The Second Railway King, The Life and Times of Sir Edward Watkin, 1819–1901*, 2002
Bernard Holland, *The Life of Spencer Compton, Eighth Duke of Devonshire*, 1911
Robert Martin Holland, *The London Bankers Clearing House*, in The National Monetary Commission's report on The English Banking System, Washington DC, 1910
John Hutchins, *History and Antiquities of the County of Dorset*, 1868
Albert M. Hyamson, *David Salamons*, 1939
Imperial Continental Gas Association, 1824–1974, 1974
L.H. Jenks, *The Migration of British capital to 1875*, 1927
David Jenkins and Takau Yoneyama, eds, *History of Insurance*, 2000
David Jenkins, The practice of Insurance against fire, 1750–1840, in Oliver Westall, ed., *The Historian and the Business of Insurance*,1984
D.M. Joslin, *A Century of Banking in South America*, 1963
W.T.C. King, *History of the London Discount Market*, 1936
Maurice W. Kirby, *The Origins of Railway Enterprise: The Stockton and Darlington Railway, 1821–1863*, 1993
R.W. Kostal, *Law and English Railway Capitalism,1825–1875*, 1994
David Kynaston, *Cazenove & Co.: A History*, 1991
—, *The City of London, 1, A World of its Own, 1815–1890*, 1994
—, The Bank and the Government in *The Bank of England, Money, Power and Influence, 1694–1914*, ed. Richard Roberts and David Kynaston, 1995
Richard S. Lambert, *The Railway King, 1800–71*, 1934
David S. Landes, *International Finance and Economic Imperialism in Egypt*, 1958
Peter Lecount, *The History of the Railway between London and Birmingham*, 1839
—, *A Practical Treatise on Railways*, 1839
Brendan Lehane, *Dorset's Best Churches*, 2006
Robin Leleux, *East Midlands, Regional History of the Railways of Great Britain*, 9, 1976
Lord William Pitt Lennox, *Fifty Years Biographical Reminiscences*, 1863
H.G. Lewin, *Early British Railways*, 1925
—, *The Railway Mania and its Aftermath, 1845–1852*, 1936

G. Lipscomb, History and Antiquities of Buckingham, 1847
V. Markham Lester, *Victorian Insolvency, Bankruptcy, Imprisonment for Debt, and Company Winding-up in Nineteenth Century England*, 1995
R.S. Longley, *Sir Francis Hincks, A Study of Canadian Politics, Railways and Finance in the Nineteenth Century*, 1943
E.T. MacDermott, *History of the Great Western Railway*, 1927
Miles MacNair, *William James (1771–1837)*, 2007
Peter Mathias, *The First Industrial Nation*, 1983 edition
R C O Matthews, *A Study in Trade Cycle History*, 1954
L.G. Mitchell, *Lord Melbourne, 1779–1848*, 1997
Christopher Monkhouse, Railway Hotels in *Railway Architecture*, ed. Marcus Binney and David Pearce, 1979
K. Morison, *Origins and Results of the Clearing System*, 1846
James Morrison, *Defects of the English System of Railway Legislation*, 1846
John Newman and Nikolaus Pevsner, *The Buildings of England, Dorset*, 1972
Micheline Nilsen, *Railways and the Western European Capitals: Studies of implantation in London, Paris, Berlin and Brussels*, 2008
D.P. O'Brien, ed., *The Correspondence of Lord Overstone*, 1971
Osborne's London and Birmingham Railway Guide, 1840
A.A. den Otter, *The Philosophy of Railways: The Transcontinental Railway Idea in British North America*, 1997
The Panmure Papers, ed. Sir George Douglas and Sir George Dalhousie Ramsay, 1908
Henry Parris, *Government and Railways in the Nineteenth Century*, 1965
A.J. Peacock, *George Hudson, 1800–71, The Railway King*, 1989
Robin Pearson, *Insuring the Industrial Revolution: Fire Insurance in Great Britain, 1700–1850*, 2004
Recollections of Lady Georgiana Peel compiled by her daughter Ethel Peel, 1920
John Pennie, *A Victorian Engineering Giant*, 2008
Nikolaus Pevsner and Elizabeth Williamson, *Buildings of England, Buckinghamshire*, 1994
D.C.M. Platt, *Foreign Finance in Continental Europe, and the United States, 1815–1870*, 1984,
Una Pope-Hennessy, *Canon Charles Kingsley, A Biography*, 1948
L.S. Pressnell, *Country Banking in the Industrial Revolution*, 1956
J.B. Radford, *Introduction to The Nottingham and Derby Railway Companion* 1839, 1979 reprint
Eric Richards, *The Leviathan of Wealth*, 1972
M.C. Reed, *Railways and the Growth of the Capital Market in the Victorian Economy*, ed. M.C. Reed, 1969
—, ed., I*nvestment in Railways in Britain, 1820–1844*, 1975
—, *The London & North Western Railway*, 1996
R. Roberts, *Schroders, Merchants and Bankers*, 1992
Richard Roberts, Leasehold Estates and municipal enterprise; landowners, local government and the development of Bournemouth, in David Cannadine, ed., *Patricians, Power and Politics in Nineteenth Century Towns*, 1982

L.T.C. Rolt, *Thomas Telford*, 1958
—, *Isambard Kingdom Brune*l, 1957
W.D. Rubenstein, Businessmen into Landowner: the question revisited, in *Land and Society in Britain, 1700–1914, Essays in Honour of F.M.L. Thompson*, ed. Negley Harte and Roland Quinault, 1996
K. Salt, *Facts and Figures, principally relating to Railways and Commerce*, 1848
Richard Salvucci, *Politics, Markets and Mexico's 'London Debt' 1823–1887*, 2009
R.S. Sayers, *Lloyds Bank in the History of English Banking*, 1957
G.R. Searle, *Entrepreneurial Politics in Mid-Victorian Britain*, 1993
Richard Saville, *Bank of Scotland: A History 1695–1995*, 1996
J.J. Sheehan, *History and Topography of Buckinghamshire*, 1862
W. Shipp and J.C. Hudson, *The History and Antiquities of the County of Dorse*t, 1868
W. Teignmouth Shore, *D'Orsay or the Complete Dandy*, 1911
Jack Simmons, *The Railway in England and Wales, 1830–1914, 1, The System and its Working*, 1978
—, Railways and Hotels in Britain, 1839–1914, in *the Express Train*, 1994
W.O. Skeat, *George Stephenson – the Engineer and His Letters*, 1973
A.W. Skempton, *Civil Engineers and Engineering in Britain, 1600–1830*, 1996
—, ed. *Biographical Dictionary of Civil Engineers, in Great Britain and Ireland, 1500–1830*, 2001
Adam Smith, *Inquiry into the Nature and Causes of the Wealth of Nations*, ed. W.B. Todd, 1976
Andrew Smith, *British Businessmen and Canadian Confederation: constitution making in an era of Anglo-globalisation*, 2008
—, *Bubble of the Age, or the Fallacies of Railway Investments, Railway Accounts, and Railway Dividends, 1848*
G. Royde Smith, *Old Euston*, 1938
Selected Letters of Sidney Smith, ed Nowell C. Smith, 1953
Henry Solly, *These Eighty Years or the Story of an Unfinished Life*, 1893
Edward M. Spiers, *Radical General, Sir George de Lacey Evans*, 1787–1870, 1983
Disraeli, Derby and the Conservative Party, Journals and Memoirs of Edward Henry, Lord Stanley, 1849–1869, ed. John Vincent, 1978
Wilfred L. Steel, *The History of the London & North Western Railway*, 1914
E. Cleveland Stevens, *English Railways and Their Relationship to the State*, 1915
George Griffin Stonestreet, *The Portentious Globe: An enquiry*, 1800
Hew Strachan, *Wellington's Legacy: The Reform of the British Army, 1830–54*, 1984
Clement E Stretton, The History of the Midland Railway 1901
Barry Supple, *The Royal Exchange Assurance, A History of British Insurance, 1720–1970*, 1970
—, Insurance in British History in Oliver M. Westall, ed., *The Historian and the Business of Insurance*, 1984
John Sweetman, *War and Administration: The Significance of the Crimean War for the British Army*, 1984
Millington Henry Synge, *Great Britain One Empire, On the union of the Dominions of Great Britain by intercommunication with the Pacific and the East via British North America with suggestions for the profitable colonisation of that wealthy territory*, 1862

Lawrence E. Tanner, *Westminster School, A History*, 1934
F.M.L. Thompson, *English Landed Society in the Nineteenth Century*, 1963
M.F. Thorp, *Charles Kingsley*, 1937
The History of The Times, 1, The Thunderer in the Making, 1785–1841, 1935
Thomas Tooke, *History of Prices and the State of the Circulation*, 1855–56
Gerard L. Turnbull, *Traffic and Transport, An Economic History of Pickfords*, 1979
Michael Tutton, *Paddington Station, 1833–1854,* 1999
Kenneth H. Vickers, *A History of Northumberland*, XI, 1922
Jehanne Wake, *Kleinwort Benson: the History of Two Families in Banking,* 1997
Cornelius Walford, *The Insurance Cyclopedia*, 1878, V
C. Walker, *Thomas Brassey, Railway Builder,* 1969
Yale Edition of *Horace Walpole's Correspondence with George Montagu*, ed W.S. Lewis and R.S. Brown, 9, 1937
J.G.H. Warren, *A Century of Locomotive Building by Robert Stephenson & Co., 1823–1923*, 1923
E.W. Watkin, *Canada and the States, Recollections, 1851–1887,* 1887
Anthony Webster, *The Twilight of the East India Company, The evolution of Anglo-Asian Commerce and Politics, 1790–1860*, 2009
Norman W. Webster, *Britain's First Trunk Line, The Grand Junction Railway*, 1972
Sir Algernon West, *Recollections, 1832–1886*, 1897
Francis Whishaw, *The Railways of Great Britain and Ireland*, 1842
J. Whitehead, *Railway Management, A Letter to George Carr Glyn Esq., Chairman of the London and North Western Railway,* 1848
Frederick S. Williams, *The Midland Railway: Its Rise and Progress*, 1886 edition
H. Drummond Wolff, *Rambling Recollections*, 1908
Dieter Ziegler, *Central Bank, Peripheral Industry: The Bank of England and the Provinces, 1826–1913*, 1990
Philip Ziegler, *The Sixth Great Power, Barings, 1762–1929,* 1988

Directories etc

Oxford Dictionary of National Biography
Burke's Peerage and Baronetage, 7th edition, 2003
Dictionary of Canadian Biography
An Inventory of the Historical Monuments of the County of Dorset, Royal Commission on Historical Monuments, 1975
Kelly's Directory of Essex, Hertfordshire and Middlesex, 1894
Directory of Hampshire and the Isle of Wight, 1865
The Survey of London, 21, the Parish of St Pancras, 1949
Victoria County History of Middlesex, IV, ed. F.T. Baker, J.S. Cockburn and R.B. Pugh, 1971

Periodicals

Anon, The Nineteenth-Century Bankers Clerk, *Three Banks Review*, 36, Dec. 1957, 37–50
Anon, Glyns and the Bank of England, *Three Banks Review*, 40, Dec. 1958, 21–32

Anon, The Canadian Financial Agency, *The Three Banks Review*, 49, Mar. 1961, 29–39

Anon, Glyn's and the Grand Trunk Railway, *Three Banks Review*, 52, Dec. 1961, 28–40

Anon, Glyn's and the Bank of Upper Canada, *Three Banks Review*, 55, Sep. 1962, 40–52

Anon, The Esdaile Crisis, *Three Banks Review*, 70, June 1966, 39–47

Anon, Glyn's and the Overend Gurney Crisis *Three Banks Review*, 72, Dec. 1966, 47–59

R.A. Ashbee, William Newmarch and Glyn's, *Three Banks Review*, 122, June 1979, 49–61

—, George Carr Glyn and St Katharine's Dock, *Three Banks Review*, 129, Mar. 1981, 49–54

Iain S. Black, The London Agency System in English Banking, 1780–1825, *London Journal*, 21, 1996, 29–59

P. Butterfield, Grouping, Pooling and Competition: the Passenger Policy of the London & North Eastern Railway, *Journal of Transport History*, 7, 1985, 21–47

P.J. Cain, Railway Combination and Government, 1900–1914, *Economic History Review*, 25, 1972, 623–641

Ann M. Carlos and Frank D. Lewis, The Creative Financing of an Unprofitable Enterprise: The Grand Trunk Railway of Canada, 1853–1881, *Explorations in Economic History*, 32, 1995, 273–301

Rex Christiansen, The Growing Pains of a Railway, *JRCHS*, xxvi, 1980, 34–46

Michael Collins, The Business of Banking: English Bank Balance Sheets, 1840–1880, *Business History* XXVI, 1984, 43–58

—, Long-term Growth of the English Banking Sector and Money Stock, 1844–80, *EcHR*, 36, 1983, 374–394

P.L. Cottrell, The Coalescence of a Cluster of Corporate International Banks, 1855–75, *Business History*, 33, 1991, 31–52

—, The Anglo-Austrian Bank, *Business History*, 11, 1969, 106–119

R. Draper, The City of London and Slavery: evidence from the first dock companies, 1795–1800, *EcHR*, 61, 2008, 432–466

Wyndham Harding, Facts bearing on the Progress of the Railway System, *Journal of the Statistical Society of London*, XI, 1848, 322–343

V.A. Hatley, Northampton hoodwinked? How a main line of railway missed the town a second time, *Journal of Transport History*, 7, 1965–66, 160–72

F.B. Heath, The Grenvilles in the nineteenth century: the emergence of commercial affiliations, *Huntingdon Library Quarterly*, XXV, 1961–62, 29–49

Charles R. Hickson, John D. Turner and Qing Ye, The Rate of Return on Equity across industrial sectors on the British Stock Market, *EcHR*, 64, 2011, 1218–41

David Hodgkins, The GWR comes to London – Why Paddington? *Journal of the Railway and Canal Historical Society*, 36, 2010, 40–50

—, Railway Rhymes, *JRCHS*, 38, 2015, 227–234

J.K. Horsefield, The Opinions of Horsley Palmer, Governor of the Bank of England, 1830–33, *Economica*, 16, 1949, 143–158

Anthony Howe, Free Trade and the City of London, c 1820–1870, *History*, 77, 1992, 380–411

—, From 'Old Corruption' to 'New Probity': The Bank of England and its Directors in the Age of Reform, *Financial History Review*, 1, 1994, 23–41

John Ireland, John Dunn and the Bankers, *Ontario History*, LXII, 1970, 83–100.

Adrian Jarvis, James Cropper, Liverpool Docks and the Liverpool and Manchester Railway, *Journal of Transport History*, 19, 1998, 18–32

D.M. Joslin, London Private Bankers, 1720–85, *EcHR*, 7, 1954, 167–186

John Liffen, Introduction of the electric telegraph in Britain, *Journal for the History of Engineering and Technology*, 80, 2010, 268–299

K. McCartney and A.J. Arnold, Financial reporting in the context of crisis: reconsidering the impact of the 'mania' on early railway accounting, *The European Accounting Review*, 11, 2002, 401–417

Iain Mclean and Christopher Foster, The Political Economy of Regulation, Interests, Ideology and Voters and the UK Regulation of Railways Act, 1844, *Public Administration*, 70, 1992. 313–331

F.C. Mather, The Railways, the Electric Telegraph, and Public Order during the Chartist Period, *History*, xxxviii, 47, 40–53

R.C. Michie, Income, expenditure and investment of a Victorian millionaire: Lord Overstone, 1823–83, *Bulletin of the Institute of Historical Research*, 58, 1985, 59–77

Michael J. Piva, Financing the Union: The Upper Canadian Debt and Financial Administration in the Canadas, 1837–45, *Journal of Canadian Studies*, 25, 1990–91, 209–227

—, Community and Crisis: Francis Hincks and Canadian Economic Policy, *Canadian Historical Review*, 66, 1985, 185–210

D.C.M. Platt and Jeremy Adelman, London Merchant Bankers in the First Phase of Heavy Borrowing: The Grand Trunk Railway of Canada, *The Journal of Imperial and Commonwealth History*, 18, 1990, 208–227

Harold Pollins, A Note on Railway Construction Costs, 1825–1850, *Economica*, 19, 1952, 395–407

—, Aspects of Railway Accounting before 1868, *Studies in the history of Accounting*, ed. A.C. Littleton and B.S. Yamey, 1956, 333–355

M.C. Reed, George Stephenson and W.T. Salvin: the Early Capital Market at Work, *Transport History*, 1, 1968, 10–20

M. Robbins, The North Midland Railway and its Enginemen, *Journal of Transport History*, 4, 1960, 180–186

—, ed, From R.B. Dockray's Diary, *Journal of Transport History*, vii, 1965, 1–13, 109–119, 149–159

Nicholas Rogers, Money, land and leverage: the big bourgoisie of Hanoverian London, *Social History*, 4, 1979, 437–454

Alex S. Rosser, Businessmen in the Parliaments of 1852–57, *Parliamentary History*, 32, 2013, 477–505

Walter M. Stern, The First London Dock Boom and the Growth of the West India Docks, *Economica*, 19, 1952, 59–77

D. Swann, The Pace and Progress of Port Investment in England, *Yorkshire Bulletin of Economic and Social Research*, 12, 1960, 32–44

James Taylor, Business in Pictures: Representations of Railway Enterprise in the Satirical Press in Britain, 1845–1870, *Past and Present*, 189, 2005
A.F. Thompson, Gladstone's Whips and the General Election of 1868, *English Historical Review*, 63, 1948, 189–200
Sean Thomas, The Origins of the Factors Acts, 1823 and 1825, *Journal of Legal History*, 32, 2011, 151–188
Penny Watts-Russell, Travelling Steam: Pascoe Grenfell MP and the London Northern Railroad, *JCHR*S, 210, 201, 34–46
—, Travelling Steam: Pascoe Grenfell and the Great Western Railway, *JCRHS*, 217, 2013, 10–20

Newspapers etc

Aris Birmingham Gazette
Bankers Magazine
Bradshaw's Shareholders' Guide
Circular to Bankers
Daily News
Daily Telegraph
Derby Mercury
Durham County Advertiser
The Economist
Frasers Magazine
Hampshire Advertiser
Herapath's Railway Journal
Huddersfield Daily Chronicle
Illustrated London News
*Ipswich Journa*l
Kendal Mercury
Lancaster Gazette
Leeds Mercury
Liverpool Mercury
Mechanics Magazine
The Observer
Preston Guardian
Morning Chronicle
Morning Post
Quarterly Review
Pall Mall Gazette
Railway Express
Railway Times
Sherborne, Dorchester and Taunton Journal
The Globe
The Standard
The Times
Westmorland Gazette

Index

(Banks including acceptance houses etc; insurance companies; and railways are listed under those headings. Married women appear under their maiden names.)